GREEN
HARVEST
AN INTRODUCTION TO BIOLOGY

Kendall Hunt
publishing company

MICHAEL JAY FARABEE, Ph.D.

www.kendallhunt.com
Send all inquiries to:
4050 Westmark Drive
Dubuque, IA 52004-1840

For my father, Gary, who taught me more than biology,
my mother Ann who taught me grace
and
my wife Anne for her belief, love and support.

Brief Contents

Contents

Preface

This book represents more than two decades writing, editing, and maintaining the *Online Biology Book* (*OLBB*), used by several million users over the years. If you are familiar with that work, you will notice several similarities, but also a number of differences. This project is enabling me to see many ideas to fruition, to take the old and tired textbook to the next level. In 1995, I was part of a focus group with several prominent biology textbook authors. The *OLBB* at the time was in its infancy, but was still the first of its kind, an e-book, although I did not coin that term for it. I made one announcement that stunned the assembled authors: the textbook is dead. As you might imagine this produces quite a bit of an uproar, although one particular author (since deceased) got what I meant. Since that time the textbook has indeed changed. Textbook Companion Websites are no longer a collection of links; e-books are common; animations have allowed static textbook images to acquire a new level of importance in lectures.

When representatives from this publisher dropped by to visit me in my office, they asked me a profound question: where do you see the textbook going next? While it may be "dead" as I termed it in 1995, we still use textbooks as a vehicle to impart information to our students that we cannot impart in person (there is not enough class time as we all know). This book and project represent my vision of where and how we can deliver information to our students wherever and whenever they are working on their class.

Features

Chapter Opener Images: These should serve as an engagement vehicle to spur reader interest, hopefully something you will want to deploy when introducing the topic. Biology is a very visual science.

Animations: I was amazed many years ago by my intro biology students' inability to visualize how one image in a textbook illustrating a sequential process could lead to the next image. To me it was a series of still shots of a process of a cell dividing; to my students it was unrelated pictures. Narrated animations have the power to connect these still images and reveal the dynamic process we tell them that is going on. While every book now uses numerous animations, this book includes assessments specifically written to measure student comprehension and learning of the concept covered in that animation. These can be given in a class after showing the animation or assigned in the companion Learning Management System (LMS), with grades being automatically recorded for each student.

Interactive Glossary: The great thing about an e-book is that terms we normally boldface in the printed text can now hyperlink to the definition. More than that we can include the pronunciation of the term (how often do students hesitate to ask a question not because they have no questions but because they have a long polysyllabic technical term they cannot pronounce?). The interactive glossary in the e-book version of this text also includes links to illustrations of the term, and in a few cases short videos or animations.

Flash Cards: Biology can be a term-heavy course. To facilitate student learning the LMS has flash cards both in a printable form as well as online interactive. The terms on the cards are the end of chapter key terms, with explanation as to the significance of each term in that chapter/topic.

Learning Objectives: Assessment is the big buzz on campus these days. Use these objectives, keyed to specific areas of the text, as well as questions in the test bank to jump-start or expand your assessment efforts. Look for the objective call outs in the margin of the pertinent part of the text.

Videos with Assessments: The LMS includes several preloaded, streaming videos covering select choke points to student learning. Some of these will be a short mini-lecture by the author covering areas that 30+ years of higher education teaching have shown where students need a little extra instructional boost. Think of these as mini tutorials on topics, such as energy in living things, life cycles, and so on.

List of Videos

Practice Tests: These practice tests are available as a word file as well as interactively in the LMS. Best practices repeatedly show that student learning improves when they take practice tests.

Prelecture Quizzes: These five point five question quizzes are available as word files so you can print one out to give to your class to test their comprehension of the material BEFORE you conduct your initial lecture on the material. Prelecture quizzes are also available for assignment in the LMS. How do we know our students are coming to class prepared? This is one tool we offer.

Testbanks: Each chapter has a variety of questions available in word as well as question banks in the LMS. Questions are of different types, ranging from True/False to multiple-choice, to short answer/essay. The test banks in the LMS are customizable so you can add, delete, and edit all questions for your use on your own campus.

Unit 1

Science, Chemistry, and Cells

CHAPTER 1

The Nature of Biology and Science

Images © Shutterstock Inc

Chapter Opener

The cover of our book was constructed to demonstrate the diversity of life on our planet. Images of the animals and plants that occur on our cover hint at the marvelously diverse forms of life on our little blue rock. The book title reflects the significance of plants and photosynthetic organisms in transforming our planet over several billion years.

Objectives

- Name the special hereditary molecule that sets living things apart from the nonliving world and be able to explain why this molecule is important.
- Be able to distinguish between single-celled organisms and multicellular organisms.
- Arrange in order, from smallest to largest, the levels of organization that occur in nature and to write a brief description of each.
- Define the term metabolism and explain what it means to the cell and the organism.
- Organisms use a molecule known as ATP to transfer chemical energy from one molecule to another. Explain why is this molecule essential for living things to exist.
- Homeostasis is defined as a state in which the conditions of an organism's internal environment are maintained within tolerable limits. What mechanisms in your body are involved with homeostasis?
- Reproduction is the means by which each new organism arises. Be able to explain why this is an essential characteristic of life.
- Describe how DNA and cellular reproduction are linked together in the process of inheritance.
- A trait that assists an organism in survival and reproduction in a certain environment is said to be adaptive. Describe one adaptive trait you have, including how this may or may not aid your survival and reproduction.
- List the major domains and kingdoms of life that are currently recognized by most scientists; tell generally what kinds of organisms are classified in each kingdom.
- Be able to arrange in order, from the fewer to the greater numbers of organisms included, the following categories of classification: class, family, genus, domain, kingdom, order, phylum, and species.
- Explain what the term biological diversity means to you, and speculate about what caused the great diversity of life on Earth.
- Define natural selection and briefly describe what is occurring when a population is said to evolve.
- Outline a set of steps that might be used in the scientific method of investigating a problem.
- Explain why a control group is used in an experiment.
- Define what is meant by a theory; cite an actual example that is significant to biology.
- Contrast the general functions of the processes known as photosynthesis and aerobic respiration.

(continued)

- Be able to define and discuss an example of homeostasis.
- Explain the origin of trait variations that function in inheritance.
- Explain the use of genus and species names by considering your scientific name, *Homo sapiens*.
- Explain what is meant by the term biological diversity and speculate about what caused the great diversity of life forms on Earth.
- Define what is meant by the term theory as used by scientists. Cite a biological example and one from another discipline of science.

Introduction

Biology literally means "the study of life." This is such a broad field, covering the minute workings of the chemical machines inside our cells, to broad scale concepts of ecosystems and global climate change. Biologists study intimate details and functioning of the human brain, the structure, composition, and function of our genes, and even the functioning of our reproductive system that allows us to pass those genes on to the next generation. Scientists have deciphered the human genome, the sequence of deoxyribonucleic acid (DNA) bases that determines much of our innate capabilities and predispositions to certain forms of behavior and illnesses. DNA sequences have played major roles in criminal cases (the reversal of death penalties for wrongfully convicted individuals, elimination of suspects, indictment and conviction of others). We are bombarded with headlines about possible health risks from favorite foods and beverages as well as the potential benefits of eating other foods. Many Americans are turning to herbal remedies to ease arthritis pain, improve memory, as well as to improve their mood. Once illegal drugs such as *Cannabis* may actually play important roles in medicine.

Can a biology book give you the answers to these questions? No, but it will enable you learn how to sift through the biases of investigators, the press, and others in a quest to critically evaluate a given question. To be honest, 5 years after you are through with your Biology class it is doubtful you would remember all the details of cellular metabolism. However, you will know where to look and maybe a little about the process of science that will allow you to make an informed decision. Will you be a scientist? Yes, in a way. You may not be formally trained as a science major, but you can think critically, solve problems, and have some idea about what science can and cannot do.

1.1   Science and the Scientific Method

Science may be defined as an objective, logical, repeatable attempt to understand the principles and forces operating in the Universe. The term science derives from the Latin word, *scientia*, which translates as "to know." Science literally is "a way of knowing." Good science is an ongoing process of testing, evaluating, retesting, and reevaluating ideas. One of the hoped-for benefits of this course is that you will become familiar with the process of science: how scientists view, study, and solve a problem.

Humans seem innately interested in why the world we live in is the way it is. Science is a means to answer some of those whys. When you shop for groceries, you are conducting a kind of scientific experiment. When you shop for clothes you are experimenting. Going on a date? Yep, another experiment!

To conduct science, we must learn the rules of the game. The scientific method is the method by which scientific ideas are evaluated. Steps in the scientific method are shown in Figure 1.1.

After a hypothesis has been repeatedly tested, a hierarchy of scientific thought develops. Hypothesis is the most common, with the lowest level of certainty. A theory is a hypothesis repeatedly tested with little modification, for example, the Theory of Evolution. A scientific law explains a major organizing principle in the Universe, for example, the Laws of Thermodynamics. To a scientist, theory means something very different than it does to a nonscientist.

Scientific experiments must isolate variables. A good science experiment does not simultaneously test multiple variables, but rather a single one that can be evaluated against a control. Controlled experiments have all factors the same between two test subjects, except for the single experimental variable.

Consider a commonly conducted science fair experiment. Sandy wants to test the effect of rap music on pea plant growth. She plays rap music 24 hours a day to a series of pea plants grown

Step	Description of Step	Example
1	**Observation**: defining the problem you wish to explain.	Otherwise healthy young men with a variety of extremely rare diseases are going to doctors. What is making them sick?
2	**Hypothesis**: one or more falsifiable explanations to explain the observation.	A. Something common to their environment, work, living, recreational space. B. An infectious agent such as a virus, bacteria, or fungus common to all of the patients.
3	**Experimentation**: Controlled attempts to test one or more hypotheses.	A. Doctors examined the living quarters, work spaces, etc., of all patients looking for a common factor. B. Examination of blood and tissue samples to try and isolate a common infectious agent.
4	**Conclusion**: did the experimental data support the hypothesis or not?	A. No common environmental factor was found, hypothesis rejected. B. A previously unknown virus was discovered and found to occur in all patients; hypothesis is not rejected.
5	After this step the hypothesis is either modified or rejected, and the process begins testing a different or modified hypothesis.	Hypothesis B is modified, tested, and evaluated again. Ultimately, a virus is identified as the cause of the disease. Next step: how is the virus transmitted?.

FIGURE 1.1 Steps in the scientific method.

© Kendall Hunt Publishing

under light, and watered every day. At the end of her experiment, she concludes rap music is conducive to plant growth. Her teacher grades her project very low, citing the lack of a control group for the experiment. Sandy returns to her experiment, but this time she has a separate group of plants under the same conditions as the rapping plants, but with soothing Mozart songs playing. She comes to the same conclusion as before, but now has a basis for comparison. Her teacher gives her project a better grade.

1.2   Organizing Theories of Modern Biology

Modern biology is based on several great ideas, or theories (Table 1.1). Each of these began as a hypothesis and underwent countless tests and revisions.

1.2.1   Cell Theory

Englishman Robert Hooke (1635–1703) examined pond water, cork, and scrapings from his teeth with a microscope. He referred to the cavities he saw in cork as "cells." In 1838, German botanist Mattias Schleiden (1804–1881) stated that all plants consisted of cells. In 1839, German physiologist Theodore Schwann (1810–1882) came to a similar conclusion for animals. German doctor Rudolf Virchow (1821–1902) combined the two ideas, formulating the Cell Theory. All your body's cells develop by the division of preexisting cells. You are a result of the fusion of your parents' egg and sperm cells. All life on our planet is composed of one or more cells. The cell theory states that all organisms are composed of one or more cells, and that those cells have arisen from preexisting cells. Examples of cells are shown in Figure 1.2.

TABLE 1.1 Organizing Theories in Biology

Theory	Summary of Theory
Cell Theory	All living things are made of cells; cells arise from existing cells.
Gene Theory	Heredity depends on genes composed of DNA that are inherited on chromosomes.
Homeostasis	Cells/Organisms maintain a dynamic internal equilibrium within which they best function.
Thermodynamics and Energy	Cells acquire and use adenosine triphosphate (ATP) by converting sunlight energy to chemical energy, and finally to energy locked inside the ATP molecule.
Evolution by Natural Selection	All life shares common ancestry and adapts to environmental changes, so the best-adapted individuals pass their genes onto the next generation.

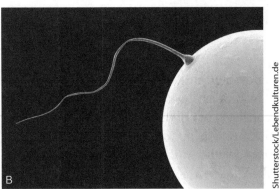

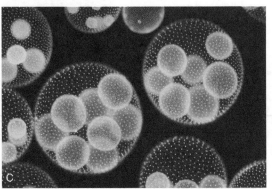

FIGURE 1.2 A. Plant epidermal cells; B. Sperm cell penetrating the egg; C. *Volvox aureus*, a colonial green alga with daughter colonies inside the parent colony.

1.2.2   Gene Theory

Gene theory involves two significant ideas: 1) the discovery in 1865 of the rules of heredity by Austrian monk Gregor Mendel (1822–1884); and 2) the deciphering of the structure of the DNA in 1953 by American biologist James D. Watson (b. 1928) and English biologist Francis Crick (1916–2004). Mendel's work explained the existence of discrete packets of inheritance, what we now call genes, and their segregation and assortment into sex cells known as gametes.

In a landmark paper published in 1865, Mendel outlined his statistically based analysis of inheritance of traits in the common garden pea. Without knowing the mechanism of chromosome separation (meiosis), Mendel figured out how the pea plant's traits assorted during gamete formation. Unfortunately his work would be ignored for several decades until its rediscovery in the early 20th century.

In 1953, James Watson and Francis Crick developed the double helix model for deoxyribonucleic acid (DNA), a chemical that other scientists had determined to be the physical carrier of inheritance. Figure 1.3 illustrates this model. Crick also figured out the mechanism for DNA replication. Other scientists linked DNA to proteins, referred to as Crick's central dogma, with information being transferred from DNA to RNA (ribonucleic acid) and then to proteins.

1.2.3   Homeostasis

Homeostasis, first described in 1865 by French physiologist Claude Bernard (1813–1878), states that living things maintain a dynamic range of conditions within which they function best. In 1932, American physiologist Walter Bradford Cannon (1871–1945) coined the modern term homeostasis. Temperature, blood gas levels, pH, and energy are major aspects of this concept. For example, when your blood levels of carbon dioxide increase due to exertion, sensors in the brain send signals to the muscles that control your breathing rate. When you breathe faster, the flow of oxygen-rich (and carbon dioxide poor) air into your lungs increases. The carbon dioxide passes from the blood vessels into the air sacs of the lungs (Figure 1.4) and is expelled from your body when you exhale.

1.2.4   Thermodynamics

Theromodynamics covers the laws governing energy transfer, and thus the basis for life on eEE-arth. Energy is the ability to do work. It exists in several forms. Living things must convert energy into a particular form in order to utilize it: the molecule adenosine triphosphate (ATP) (Figure 1.5A). This molecule is important to the cell: an adult doing normal activity requires the energy of 3–5 pounds of ATP, but all the ATPs in the human body weigh less than 1/5 ounce. Ultimately this energy comes from the Sun via plants, bacteria, and algae, which convert sunlight energy into the chemical energy of sugar (Figure 1.5B).

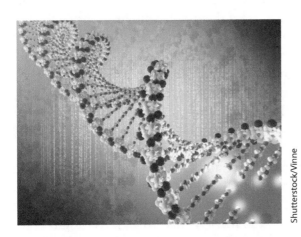

FIGURE 1.3 Structure of the DNA double helix, after the work of Watson and Crick.

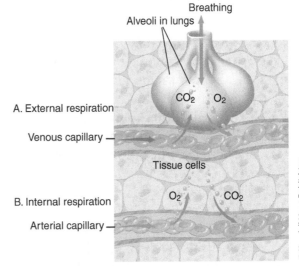

FIGURE 1.4 Gas exchanges in the lungs are an important homeostatic mechanism.

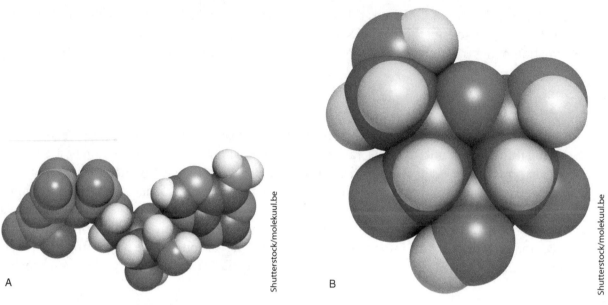

A

B

FIGURE 1.5 Adenosine triphosphate (ATP), the molecule that is also known as the energy currency of the cell. A. Molecular representation of the ATP molecule. B. Glucose sugar molecule. Atoms are represented as spheres with conventional color-coding: hydrogen (white), carbon (gray), oxygen (red).

1.2.5   Evolution by Natural Selection

Evolution. The other theories that serve as the foundations of modern biology are nowhere near as controversial as evolution. Over 150 years after the concept of evolution was first proposed, evolution is still plagued by a misunderstanding of what it is, and more importantly, what it is not. British naturalist Charles Darwin (1809–1882) secured a position on the British exploratory vessel, the H.M.S. Beagle. This voyage provided Darwin a unique opportunity to study adaptation and gather a great deal of proof he would later incorporate into his theory of evolution. Darwin began to secretly ponder the seeming "fit" of organisms to their mode of existence. Concerned about the scandal implicit in his idea, Darwin shared his private thoughts with few others. In 1858, this all changed when he received a letter from British naturalist Alfred Russel Wallace (1823–1913). Wallace worked independently and came to the same conclusions as the secret work of Mr. Darwin! Darwin and Wallace settled on four main points of the theory (Table 1.2).

While both Darwin and Wallace developed the theory, Darwin's Darwin's book, *On the Origin of Species by Means of Natural Selection*, published in 1859, became an instant (and controversial) best seller. Public debates were held on the topic, not just for audiences of scientists, but also for the interested public. Within a few decades of its publication, most biologists were won over to Darwin's meticulously documented arguments and the amassed evidence he and supporters presented. While there have been some changes to the theory since 1859, most notably the incorporation of genetics and DNA into what is termed the Modern Synthesis during the 1940s, most scientists today accept evolution as the guiding theory on which modern biology is based.

Darwin viewed evolution as a branching process, much like a tree. In fact his preserved notes reveal a repeated theme of tree patterns. We use this idea in the construction of phylogenies, evolutionary hypotheses summarizing the relationships of groups of organisms (Figure 1.6).

TABLE 1.2 Main Points of Evolution by Natural Selection

Adaptation	Organisms adapt to their environments.
Variation	Organisms exhibit variation in their traits.
Over-reproduction	Organisms tend to reproduce beyond their environment's capacity to support them.
Differential survival and reproduction	Since not all organisms are equally well adapted to their environment, some will survive and reproduce better than others.
Natural selection	Sometimes referred to as "survival of the fittest"; the reproductive success of the organisms.

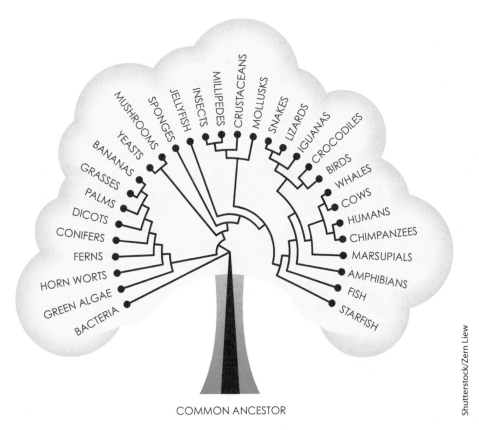

COMMON ANCESTOR

FIGURE 1.6 The evolutionary tree of life showing diversification and branching.

1.3   The Diversity of Life

What seemed to open up Darwin to the possibility of descent with modification (what we call evolution) was the immense variety of living things he observed while on the Beagle voyage. This diversity has an inherent rhyme and reason that Darwin eventually deduced, and it is in this diversity that we find much of the great wonder and amazement as well as evidence to answer the question of how did life get this way.

The Swedish botanist Carolus Linnaeus (1707–1778) attempted to pigeonhole life in his classification scheme that we still employ today. When fossils and new discoveries are added, the pigeonholes are modified. Despite Linnaeus' development of his classification scheme in the days before evolutionary theory, we still use it. The major modification of the categories is the addition of the domain level during the 1990s. Table 1.3 illustrates the classification of cats and dogs.

Linnaean classification relies on a series of categories nested within progressively larger units. For example, one or more species make up a genus (Table 1.3). One or more genera comprise a family. Families are grouped into orders, which in turn are grouped into classes. A phylum contains one or more classes. Linnaeus considered the kingdom to be the largest grouping. In 1977, American microbiologist Carl Woese (1928–2012) recognized a level above the kingdom, later called the domain.

All living things share a great many common features (discussed later in this chapter). A simple phylogenetic representation of three domains is shown in Figure 1.7. The branching points are the common ancestors of the successive branches.

Domain Bacteria (Figure 1.8; Table 1.4), contains living organisms remarkably similar to ancient fossils. Organisms in this group lack the structures found in our cells (nucleus, mitochondria) and are known as prokaryotes. Heterotrophic bacteria and photosynthetic cyanobacteria are the major forms of life in this domain. Heterotrophic bacteria have numerous impacts on humans, most notably the wide range of diseases they cause. Cyanobacteria include forms strongly similar to ancient fossils dated to more than 3 billion years old. Early cyanobacteria made major contributions to the Earth's atmosphere, including the production of dioxygen (O_2), the form of oxygen we need to breathe.

The Archaea (Table 1.4) are mainly restricted to habitats such as hot springs, salt flats, and areas with high acidity (Figure 1.9). Scientists long considered archaeans to be bacteria. Investigations revealed the two groups are as unlike each other as they are each unlike the eukaryotes. The

TABLE 1.3 Classification of Some Members of the Canidae and Felidae

Category				
Domain	Eukarya			
Kingdom	Animalia			
Phylum	Chordata			
Class	Mammalia			
Order	Carnivora			
Family	Canidae	Canidae	Canidae	Felidae
Genus	*Canis*	*Canis*	*Canis*	*Felis*
Species	*familiaris*	*lupus*	*latrans*	*catus*
Common name	Domesticated dog, Siberian husky ©Shutterstock/ Paisit Teraphatsakool	Gray wolf ©Shutterstock/ Holly Kuchera	Coyote ©Shutterstock/Marc Bruxelle	House cat ©Shutterstock/Seiji

TABLE 1.4 The Diversity of Life.

Domain/Kingdom	Nutrition	Organization	Significance	Examples
Bacteria	Photosynthesis, chemo-synthesis, decomposer, parasitic	Single-celled, filament, or colony of cells; all prokaryotic	Food webs, oxygen production, organic nitrogen, some vitamins, some antibiotics	Bacteria cyanobacteria
Archaea	Heterotrophic	Unicellular	Make methane as a waste gas	Halophiles, methanogens, thermacidophiles
Protista (Eukarya)	Autotrophs, Heterotrophs	Single-celled, filamentous, colonial, and multicelled; all eukaryotic	Food webs, phyto-plankton, algae, red tides, some diseases	Kelp, diatoms, dinoflagellates, Protozoa, coralline algae
Fungi (Eukarya)	All heterotrophs	Unicellular, filamentous, to multicelled	Decomposers, para-sites, antibiotics, bak-ing, and brewing; crop parasites	Mushrooms, molds, mildews, rusts and smuts, yeasts
Viridiplantae (Eukarya)	Autotrophic	Unicellular to multicellular	Food source, medi-cines, drugs, dyes, building material, fuel and biofuels	Angiosperms, gymno-sperms, ferns, moss, liverworts, horsetails, green algae
Animalia (Eukarya)	All heterotrophs	Multicellular, capable of movement at some stage during their life history	Consumers in food chains; food sources, transportation, recreation, and companionship	Sponges, worms, shellfish, insects, star-fish, fish, birds, rep-tiles, mammals, etc.

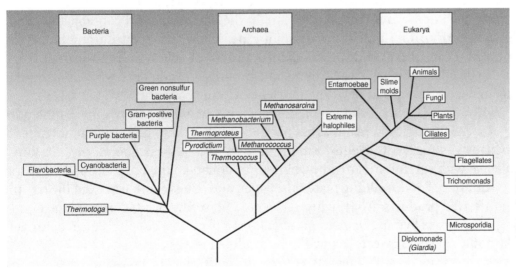

FIGURE 1.7 The three domains of life.

FIGURE 1.8 Petri dishes showing bacterial colonies growing on nutrient agar.

FIGURE 1.9 A geothermal pool located in Yellowstone National Park. Pools like these often are inhabited by archaeans, due to the harsh environmental conditions too extreme for most other forms of life to tolerate.

archaeans thus make up a separate branch on the tree of life (Figure 1.7). Archaeans cause no human disease and lack economic significance.

Protista (Figure 1.10) is a term applied collectively to the more primitive members of the eukaryotic domain Eukarya. Recent studies have allowed us to begin classifying this group into more natural kingdoms. Unfortunately, the number of kingdoms is not universally accepted. For this section of our initial chapter, I shall refer to the group as protista, or protists. These eukaryotic organisms have membrane-bound structures in their cells that allow for dedication of areas of the cell to specific functions. Economic uses of protistans include food additives (carageenan, an algal extract added to commercial ice creams), food (the Japanese snack food *Nori* is dried seaweed), and as a major component in agar used in microbiology applications.

Organisms in the kingdom Fungi (Figure 1.11) are almost entirely multicellular **heterotrophs**. Fungi and bacteria decompose and recycle nutrients in the environment. Economically, fungi provide us with food and antibiotics. The first antibiotic, penicillin, was isolated from the fungus *Penicillium*. Some fungi are also crop parasites damaging several billion dollars worth of crops per year. Fungi can be edible (Figure 1.11A). Some mushrooms grow on dead wood, illustrating the role of fungi in decomposing and recycling nutrients within ecosystems (Figure 1.11B).

Kingdom Viridiplantae (Figure 1.12) includes organisms that are all autotrophic by the process of photosynthesis. Ecologically, plants act as producers, along with photosynthetic bacteria and protists. In many environments, plants form the base of food webs. Economically, this kingdom is unparalleled, with agriculture providing billions of dollars to the economy as well as the foundation of civilization. Food, building materials, paper, and drugs (both legal and illegal) are among the plant-derived products. *Iris*, (Figure 1.12A) is a flowering plant, currently the dominant plant group. The Venus flytrap (*Dionaea muscipula*) is a plant that supplements its nitrogen supply from the bodies of small insects trapped in its modified leaves (Figure 1.12B).

Kingdom Animalia (Figure 1.13) consists entirely of multicellular, ingestive heterotrophs capable of mobility at some point during their life history. Animals act as consumers, which can

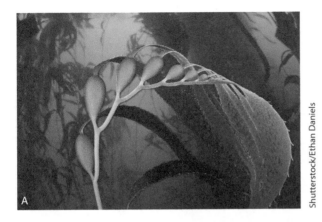

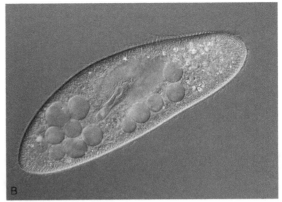

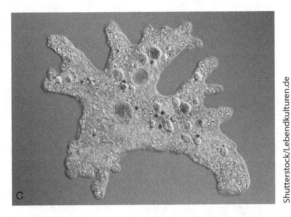

FIGURE 1.10 Representative protistans. A. Giant kelp forest (*Macrocystis pyrifera*) grows along the coast of northern California, near Monterey Bay. This area is rich in marine life and is a popular scuba diving area; B. *Paramecium caudatum*, a single-celled protistan commonly examined in biology labs; C. *Amoeba proteus*, a protozoan protistan.

FIGURE 1.11 Representative fungi. A. Close-up of an assortment of edible mushrooms; B. Colorful inedible mushrooms growing on pine stump in the autumn forest.

FIGURE 1.12 Representative plants. A. Flower bed with many irises at the Nikitskiy botanic garden in Yalta, Ukraine; B. Venus flytrap (*Dionaea muscipula*), carnivorous plant.

FIGURE 1.13 Representative animals. A. Opalescent nudibranch (*Hermissenda crassicornis*); B. Red-eyed tree frog (*Agalychnis callydrias*) in Costa Rican jungle; C. Leafy sea dragon.

be subdivided into herbivores and carnivores. Humans are omnivores that can eat both plants and animals. Some animals lack skeletons and most organ systems, such as the nudibranch (Figure 1.13A), while others display bright colors and adaptations to life on land (Figure 1.13B) and still others illustrate camouflage (Figure 1.13C).

1.4   Levels of Organization

We can study biology at many different levels of organization (Figure 1.14), from collections of organisms (communities) to the inner workings of a cell (organelle), or even at the level of the atoms that are the smallest level of organization. Biology is a complex science that can be examined in smaller, more manageable pieces.

Biosphere: All living things taken in conjunction with their environment. Life occurs from the upper atmosphere to the bottoms of the oceans. We divide the Earth into atmosphere (air), lithosphere (rock and soil), hydrosphere (water), and biosphere (life).

Ecosystem: The relationships of smaller groups of organisms with each other and their environment. Scientists often speak of the interrelatedness of living things. We can discuss the flow of energy through an ecosystem from photosynthetic autotrophs to herbivores to carnivores.

Community: The relationships between groups of different species. For example, the desert communities consist of rabbits, coyotes, snakes, birds, mice, and plants. Fire, landslides, lava flows, and the effects of population pressure may disturb the structure and biological richness of a community.

Species: Groups of similar individuals who tend to mate and produce viable, fertile offspring comprise a species.

Populations: Groups of similar individuals that tend to mate with each other within a limited geographic area. This can be as simple as a field of flowers, which is separated from another field by a hill or other area where none of these flowers occur.

Organism: One or more cells characterized by a unique arrangement of DNA "information." Individual organisms may be unicellular or multicellular. The multicellular individual exhibits specialization of cell types and division of labor into tissues, organs, and organ systems.

Organ System: A group of cells, tissues, and organs performing specific major functions for the multicellular organism. For example: the cardiovascular system functions in circulation of blood, transport of oxygen, carbon dioxide, food, chemicals, heat, and metabolic wastes.

Organ: A collection of cells and/or tissues performing an overall function. For example, the heart is an organ that pumps blood within the cardiovascular system.

Tissue: A group of cells performing a specific function. For example, heart muscle tissue is found in the heart and its unique contraction properties aid the heart's functioning as a pump.

Cell: The fundamental unit of living things. Each cell has hereditary material (DNA), energy acquiring chemicals, structures, etc. Living things, by definition, must have the

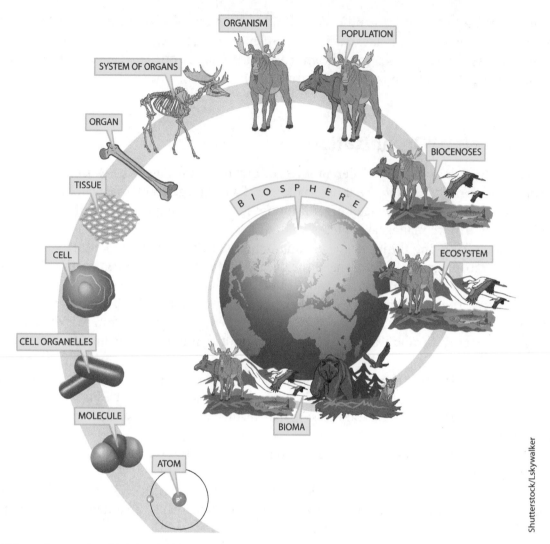

FIGURE 1.14 Levels of biological organization.

metabolic chemicals plus a nucleic acid hereditary information molecule and the ability to make proteins.

Organelle: A subunit of a cell, an organelle is involved in a specific subcellular function, for example, the ribosome or mitochondrion.

Molecules, atoms, and subatomic particles: The fundamental functional levels of biochemistry.

1.5   Characteristics of Life

Before we can begin studying life we need to consider what characteristics occur among all living things (Table 1.5, Figure 1.15). In essence we need to define life. Living things have a variety of common characteristics.

TABLE 1.5 Characteristics of Life

Characteristic	Description	Example
Homeostasis	Maintaining a dynamic equilibrium	Water balance; acidity of blood, blood sugar levels, body temperature
Adaptation	Living things are fitted to their mode of existence by specialized features	Binocular vision, the human wrist, feathers and hair, leaves
Reproduction	The production of new individuals by sexual or asexual methods	Salmon spawning once during their lives, sea turtles laying eggs on land, birth
Heredity	DNA controls the form and function of a cell and is passed to the next generation by gametes	Genes that control hair color, eye color, hair texture, ear shape, etc.
Growth and Development	Multicellular creatures begin as zygotes and pass through a series of developmental stages.	Oak tree growing from an oak seed; babies developing into college students, butterfly metamorphosis
Energy acquisition and release	The sum of all energy related chemical reactions in an organism; the production of ATP molecules.	Aerobic respiration requires the presence of oxygen. Anaerobic respiration can occur without oxygen Fermentation.
Detection and Response to stimulus	Organisms respond to stimulus n a variety of ways.	Fight or flight response Phototropism Animal navigation
Interaction	Three types of symbiosis, or organismal interactions occur.	Mutualism Commensalism Parasitism Predation
Communication	Communication occurs between cells as well as between organisms, by a variety of methods.	Nerve cell synapse Verbal and nonverbal communication Pheromones

Homeostasis is the maintenance of a more or less constant (yet also dynamic) internal environment of an organism in terms of temperature, levels of acidity, water concentrations, etc. Much of our own metabolic energy goes toward keeping our bodies within their homeostatic limits.

Adaptation. Living things are suited to their mode of existence. Charles Darwin began the recognition of the marvelous adaptations all life has that allow those organisms to exist in their environment.

Reproduction and Heredity. Since all cells are produced by already existing cells, they must have some way of reproducing. There are two types of reproduction: 1) asexual where there is no recombination of genetic material, in essence one parent producing a clone of themselves in

Shutterstock/Theodore Mattas

Shutterstock/Tanya Puntti

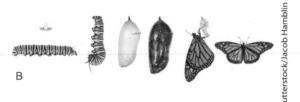

Shutterstock/Jacob Hamblin

CORAL ANATOMY

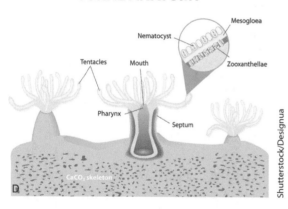

Shutterstock/Designua

Shutterstock/aquapix

FIGURE 1.15 Illustrating some of the characteristics of life. A. Reproduction: Lions mating; B. Stages in growth and development of the Monarch Caterpillar; C. Response to stimulus: Mandrill with mouth open showing sharp teeth, possibly in aggression; D. Interaction: Coral polyps tend to live in colonies and form the building blocks of the reef. Note the layer of zooxanthellae inside the coral animal's body; E. Communication: Common cuttlefish (*Sepia officinalis*) illustrating the color-changing nature of its skin.

their offspring; or 2) sexual where there is a recombination of genetic material with two parents contributing equally to the production of the offspring. All living things use the chemical deoxyribonucleic acid (DNA) as the physical carrier of inheritance, the molecule storing genetic information.

Growth and development. Even single-celled organisms grow. When first formed by cell division, they are small, and must grow and develop into mature cells. Multicellular organisms pass through a more complicated process of differentiation and growth because they have so many more cells to develop.

Energy acquisition and release. Energy is the ability to do work. However, not just any energy will do for living things. The majority of life on eEarth acquires energy (from sunlight, inorganic chemicals, or another organism), and releases it in the process of forming ATP (adenosine triphosphate) shown in Figure 1.5. The term metabolism applies to all the chemical reactions involved in this process.

Detection and response to stimuli (both internal and external). Living things respond to various stimuli, such as touch, vibration, and chemicals. You respond to stimuli. When you hear an unusual sound, like at night when you are asleep, your body still detects and responds. The response may be to be suddenly wide-awake, with your heart racing, pupils dilating, breathing a little faster than normal. You are experiencing a fight or flight response: your body is preparing to fight whatever caused that unusual sound, or to run away. While we call this fight or flight it really could be flight or fight, as flight is often the option animals take in such cases. What also happened during fight or flight is that blood flow to your brain decreases, sometimes causing you to make the wrong choice. Sometimes we experience this reaction in a classroom, say before (or during!) a big exam. If we can master our response and relax we always perform better on the exam!

Interactions. Living things interact with their environment as well as with each other. Organisms obtain raw materials and energy from their environment or from another organism. The various types of symbioses, organismal interactions with each other, are examples of this. When two organisms interact and both benefit from the relationship, we call that mutualism. An example of mutualism is the small dinoflagellate algae known as zooxanthellae that inhabit the bodies of many corals. As long as the corals are close enough to the ocean surface, the zooxanthellae receive enough light that they produce both food and oxygen for the coral. In return, the algae get a safe place to live.

Commensalism is the term applied to a relationship where one of the two organisms benefits but the other suffers no harm. Parasitism is the type of symbiosis where one organism, the parasite, causes harm to its host.

Communication. While speech is essentially a human trait, organisms display a variety of communication styles. Color can serve as a communication, whether it is the mesmerizing color patterns displayed by cuttlefish, or warning coloration of poisonous frogs and snakes.

Terms

adaptation
adenosine triphosphate (ATP)
animalia
antibiotics
archaea
avexvel
asexual reproduction
atmosphere
atoms
autotrophic
bacteria
binomial nomenclature
biochemistry
biosphere
cardiovascular system
carnivores
cell division
cell theory
cells
central dogma
classes
commensalism
community
communities
consumers
control
cyanobacteria
deoxyribonucleic acid (DNA)
dinoflagellate
DNA replication
division
domain

ecosystem
energy
eukaryotic
family
food webs
fungi
gametes
genes
genus
heart
heart muscle tissue
herbivores
heredity
heterotrophic
homeostasis
hydrosphere
hypothesis
kingdom
law
lithosphere
matter
metabolic energy
meiosis
metabolism
modern syntnesis
mitochondrion
multicellular
multinucleate
mutualism
natural selection
orders
organ
organ system

organelles
organisms
parasites
parasitism
photosynthesis
phylogenies
phylum
phosphate
populations
producers
prokaryotes
proteins
protista
protozoa
retroviruses
ribonucleic acid (RNA)
ribosome
scientific method
sexual
sexual reproduction
species
symbiosis
taxonomy
theory
theromodynasics
tissue
unicellular
uniformitarianism
uninucleate
viridiplantae
viruses
zooxanthellae

Review Questions

1. Which of these scientific terms has the greatest degree of certainty?
   a. hypothesis;
   b. theory;
   c. law;
   d. guess.

2. The purpose of a control in a scientific experiment is to ___.
   a. provide a basis of comparison between experimental and nonexperimental;
   b. indicate the dependent variable;

    c. indicate the independent variable;

    d. provide a baseline from which to graph the data.

3. Which of these theories is not a basis for modern biology?
    a. evolution;
    b. creationism;
    c. cell theory;
    d. gene theory.

4. The molecule that is the physical carrier of inheritance is known as ____.
    a. ATP; b. RNA; c. DNA; d. NADH

5. Cyanobacteria belong to the taxonomic domain _____.
    a. Viridiplantae;
    b. Archaea;
    c. Animalia;
    d. Eukarya;
    e. Bacteria.

6. Mushrooms belong to which of these taxonomic kingdoms?
    a. Viridiplantae;
    b. Protista;
    c. Animalia;
    d. Fungi;
    e. Bacteria.

7. *Papaver somniferum*, the opium poppy, belongs to which of these taxonomic kingdoms?
    a. Viridiplantae;
    b. Protista;
    c. Animalia;
    d. Fungi;
    e. Bacteria.

8. The sum of all energy transfers within a cell is known as _____.
    a. photosynthesis;
    b. cellular respiration;
    c. metabolism;
    d. replication;
    e. conjugation.

9. The molecule that is the energy coin of the cell is ____.
    a. ATP; b. RNA; c. DNA; d. NADH

10. Which of these is NOT a living organism?
    a. cactus;
    b. cat;
    c. algae;
    d. virus;
    e. yeast.

11. Which of the following is the least inclusive (smallest) unit of classification?
    a. kingdom;
    b. species;
    c. genus;
    d. class;
    e. phylum.

12. The scientist(s) credited with developing the theory of evolution by natural selection were _____.
    a. James Watson and Francis Crick;
    b. Aristotle and Lucretius;
    c. Charles Darwin and Alfred Wallace;
    d. Robert Hooke and Rudolph Virchow;
    e. James Watson and Charles Darwin.

13. When an organism consists of a single cell, the organism is referred to as ___.
    a. uninucleate;
    b. uniport;
    c. unisexual;
    d. unicellular.

14. According to science, the Eearth is ___ years old.
    a. 4.5 billion;
    b. 4.5 million;
    c. 10 billion;
    d. 10,000;
    e. 450 million.

15. Which of these is not an economic use of bacteria?
    a. food;
    b. biotechnology;
    c. mushrooms;
    d. food spoilage.

Links

Discovery, Chance and the Scientific Method: Site by: Fran Slowiczek, Ed.D and Pamela M. Peters, Ph.D. Read a case study of how to apply the scientific method and the work of many scientists contributed to Alexander Fleming's "chance" discovery of penicillin. This page was developed for the Access Excellence site Classic Collection. (link is http://www.accessexcellence.org/AE/AEC/CC/chance.php)

Darwin's Darwin's Origin of Species: Available to cure all insomnia! Read the online text of what many scientists consider the most important book ever written. Darwin's style was common for his time, and many readers consider the book a sure fire cure insomnia, but if you want more information on Darwin's ideas you need to go to the source. Other vital books are available online from the Classics at the Online Literature Library site (http://www.literature.org/authors/). (link is http://www.literature.org/authors/darwin-charles/the-origin-of-species-6th-edition/index.html)

Welcome to Evolution 101!: University of California Museum of Paleontology (UCMP), Berkeley. Explore evolution, with excellent articles on the history of evolutionary thought as well as basics of evolutionary theory. (link is http://evolution.berkeley.edu/evolibrary/article/evo_01)

The Bad Bug Book (Second Edition): U.S. Food and Drug Administration information on bacterially caused diseases related to food, such as typhoid and botulism. You can download a pdf file of this free government publication, released in 2012. (link is http://www.fda.gov/food/foodborneillnesscontaminants/causesofillnessbadbugbook/default.htm)

Introduction to the Bacteria: UCMP site that covers the types of bacteria, their classification, ecology, and history. (link is http://www.ucmp.berkeley.edu/bacteria/bacteria.html)

Introduction to the Dinoflagellata: UCMP site that explores dinoflagellates, an important group of marine and freshwater algae that have been used in oil exploration, linked to red tides, and fish kills. Learn about this group here. (link is http://www.ucmp.berkeley.edu/protista/dinoflagellata.html)

Dinoflagellates: This British website provides a great many images of fossil dinoflagellates, as well as information about the group. (link is http://www.ucl.ac.uk/GeolSci/micropal/dinoflagellate.html)

Nathan's Nathan's Fungi Thumbnails: Plenty of small pictures of fungi. Click on any image and learn more about the photograph as well as the organism. (link is http://www.collective-source.com/fungi/thumbnails.html)

Introduction to the Fungi: UCMP site that offers information about the ecology, systematics, fossil history, and morphology of fungi. (link is http://www.ucmp.berkeley.edu/fungi/fungi.html)

Introduction to the Plantae: UCMP site to learn about the systematics, fossil record, morphology, and ecology of the representatives of the plant kingdom. (link is http://www.ucmp.berkeley.edu/plants/plantae.html)

Non-Flowering Plant Family: Access page sorted by family on the nonflowering plants. Thumbnail photos are linked to larger versions. This site is a great educational resource maintained by Gerald D. Carr, although not updated since 2002. (link is http://www.botany.hawaii.edu/faculty/carr/nfpfamilies.htm)

Kingdom Animalia Introduction to the Metazoa: Animals, Animals, Animals!: UCMP site offers excellent information about the evolution and diversity of various animal groups. (link is http://www.ucmp.berkeley.edu/phyla/phyla.html)

A Structure for Deoxyribose Nucleic Acid: An annotated copy of Watson and Crick's landmark paper. (link is http://www.exploratorium.edu/origins/coldspring/printit.html)

Mendelweb: Site maintained by Roger B. Blumberg (as of 2010). View Mendel's paper in German or English, as well as an annotated version of the paper. (link is http://www.mendelweb.org)

Darwin Online: Edited by John van Wyhe. Not to be outdone, Darwin also has a great resource site. (link is http://darwin-online.org.uk)

Wallace Online: Edited by John van Wyhe. Wallace is the co-discoverer of evolution, so it is perhaps fitting he has a similar site to the Darwin one listed above. (link is http://wallace-online.org)

References

Darwin, C. 1859. On the Origin of Species by Means of Natural Selection, or the Preservation of Favoured Races in the Struggle for Life. London, John Murray.

Mendel, G. 1865. Versuche über Pflanzen-Hybriden. *Vorgelegt in den Sitzungen vom 8. Februar und 8. März 1865* (Experiments in Plant Hybridization. *Read at the meetings of February 8th, and March 8th, 1865*) (available at mendelweb.org).

Watson, J. D., and Crick, F. H. 1953. A Structure for Deoxyribose Nucleic Acid. *Nature*, volume 171:737–738.

CHAPTER 2
Chemistry and Life

Chapter Opener

Water is one of the more common molecular substances in our planet. You might very well ask why open this chapter with water. As we understand it now, life depends on water, it is in fact one reason there is such an abundance of life on Earth. Learn more about this amazing substance in this chapter.

Objectives

- List the six major elements in living things.
- Describe how protons, electrons, and neutrons form atoms.
- Define the terms atomic number and atomic mass and describe their significance.
- Atoms with the same atomic number but a different mass number are isotopes. List the isotopes of hydrogen and of carbon.
- Describe radioisotopes and list three ways they can be used in biology.
- List and describe the three types of chemical bonds occurring in biological molecules.
- Describe the distribution of electrons in the space around the nucleus of an atom.
- An atom tends to react with other atoms when its outermost shell is only partly filled with electrons. Explain why this happens.
- Define the two types of ions and discuss how ionic bonds form between positive and negative ions.
- In a covalent bond, atoms share electrons. List several elements that tend to form covalent bonds.
- Distinguish between a nonpolar covalent bond and a polar covalent bond and give an example of each.
- Define hydrogen bond and give an example of a substance where these binds are important.
- Explain how the polarity of water molecules allows them to interact with one another.
- Describe several solutions that you use everyday in terms of what is the solvent and what is the solute.
- Define acid and base and be able to cite a common example of each.
- List the four main groups of organic macromolecules and their functions in living things.
- Describe how a condensation reaction links monomers to form polymers.
- Describe what occurs during a hydrolysis reaction.
- Describe the structure of carbohydrates and list their functions.
- List examples of common polysaccharides and describe their functions.
- Describe the structure and function of lipids.
- Distinguish between a saturated fat and an unsaturated fat. Be able to discuss why such a distinction is a potential life and death matter for many people.
- Describe the importance of phospholipids to all living things.
- Define steroids and describe their chemical structure. Be able to discuss the importance of the steroids known as cholesterol and at least one steroid hormone.

(continued)

- Describe proteins and list their functions.
- Diagram and describe the three parts occurring in every amino acid.
- Describe and define the primary, secondary, tertiary, and quaternary structures of proteins.
- Describe the three parts of a nucleotide.
- Describe the functions of deoxyribonucleic acid (DNA) and ribonucleic acid (RNA) molecules in living things.

Introduction

The study of biology can encompass the many levels of organization listed in Chapter 1: ecology, populations, individual organisms, or how atoms and molecules are arranged to drive the biochemical reactions fundamental to life itself. Students often complain that this topic seems more like chemistry than like biology. They are correct. Chemistry is an essential tool to understand the myriad of wonders of biology. However, we need only a little chemistry, not an entire course worth! So, let us begin at the basic level—the atom.

2.1   Atoms

Most of the Universe consists of matter and energy. Energy is the capacity to do work. Matter has mass and occupies space. All matter is composed of basic chemical elements that cannot be broken down to substances with different chemical or physical properties. Elements are substances consisting of one type of atom, for example, carbon atoms makeup the mineral diamond (Figure 2.1), and also graphite. Pure (24-karat) gold (Figure 2.1) is composed of only one type of atom—gold atoms. Atoms are the smallest particle into which an element can be divided. The ancient Greeks thought all matter was composed of some combination of five elements: earth, air, water, fire, and ether. Smoke was considered a mixture of air and fire, mud was a mixture of earth and water, and so on. We now recognize 89 naturally occurring elements (with dozens more formed in nuclear reactors).

The ancient Greek philosophers developed the concept of the atom, although they considered it the fundamental particle that could not be broken down. Italian physicist Enrico Fermi (1901–1954) and his colleagues split the atom in the 1930s. The atom is composed of smaller units called sub-atomic particles. These subatomic particles (see Table 2.1) were discovered during the 1800s.

FIGURE 2.1 Gold bars and diamonds, aka bling! Two objects each composed of collections of the same type of element.

Shutterstock/Foto-Ruhrgebiet

TABLE 2.1 Subatomic particles

Particle Name	Location in Atom	Electrostatic Charge	Mass (in Atomic Mass Units)
Proton	In the nucleus	+1	1
Neutron	In the nucleus	0	*1+
Electron	Orbitals surrounding the nucleus	−1	1/1800

*The mass of the neutron is a little less than the mass of a proton plus the mass of an electron.

The **proton** is located in the center (or **nucleus**) of the atom. Each atom has at least one proton. Protons have an electrostatic charge of +1, and a mass of approximately 1 atomic mass unit (amu). An atomic mass unit is usually defined as the mass of the particle relative to the mass of carbon-12. Since this is a pretty small number (something like 10^{-27} kg, or 0.000000000000000000000000001 kg), chemists have defined the atomic mass unit to allow discussion in whole numbers. Elements differ from each other in the number of protons they have. Hydrogen has one proton, while helium has two, and uranium has 92.

The **neutron** also is located in the atomic nucleus (except in hydrogen, which often lacks a neutron). The neutron has no charge, and a mass of slightly over 1 amu. Some scientists propose the neutron is made up of a proton and electron-like particle.

The **electron** is a very small particle located outside the nucleus. Because their movement has been recorded at near the speed of light (about 186,000 miles/second), the precise location of electrons is hard to pin down. Electrons occupy orbitals, areas where they have a high probability of being found. The charge of an electron is −1, the exact opposite of the proton's charge. The electron's mass is negligible (approximately 1800 electrons equal the mass of one proton). **Orbitals** are grouped into electron shells around the nucleus of the atom. Each orbital can hold a maximum of only two electrons. Older renderings of electrons in orbit around the nucleus showed the electron in a fixed location.

The **atomic number** is the number of protons an atom has. It is characteristic and unique for each element. For example, your social security number is a unique number that specifies you and only you. The atomic number specifies only atoms with that many protons characteristic for that element. Add or subtract protons and you now have changed the element! The atomic number is typically written as a subscript ahead of the elemental symbol, for example, Carbon has an atomic number of six, and its elemental symbol is C, so we can write carbon as ^{6}C.

CARBON ATOM

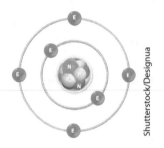

Shutterstock/Designua

FIGURE 2.2 Atomic structure of a carbon atom.

The atomic mass of an atom is the number of protons plus neutrons. We write the atomic mass as a superscript before the elemental symbol. The most common form of carbon has an atomic mass that rounds to 12, so we can refer to this as Carbon-12 or as ^{12}C.

Atoms of an element that have differing numbers of neutrons (but the same atomic number) are isotopes. The isotopes of hydrogen are shown in Figure 2.3. Isotopes are simply atoms of an element with different numbers of neutrons. Hydrogen-1 (Figure 2.3A) has one proton, and a mass of 1. Hydrogen-2 (Figure 2.3B) has one proton *plus* one neutron, for a mass of 2. Note that each atom of hydrogen has only one proton, but their atomic mass differs.

Isotopes can be used to determine the diet of ancient peoples by determining proportions of isotopes in mummified or fossilized human tissues. Biochemical pathways have been studied using isotopes. The age of fossils and artifacts can be determined (Figure 2.4C) by using radioactive isotopes, either directly on the fossil or on the rocks that surround it. Isotopes also generate the radiation used in medical diagnostic and treatment procedures (Figure 2.4A, B).

Some isotopes are radioisotopes, which spontaneously decay and release radioactivity, while other isotopes are stable. Examples of unstable radioisotopes are Carbon-14 (^{14}C) and deuterium (^{2}H). Stable isotopes of these elements are ^{12}C and ^{1}H.

The periodic table of the elements (Figure 2.5) provides a great deal of information about the various natural and human-made elements. Russian chemist Dmitri Mendeleev (1834–1907) developed the Periodic Table during the 1850s. Each element had a one or two letter symbol (representative elements are summarized in Table 2.2). We use these symbols as a quick way of referring to the element. Instead on saying uranium, we will often write U, and all chemically literate folks know that U stands for uranium (not the U that stands for you while U R texting). Mendeleev grouped elements that behaved in similar chemical ways into columns. We now know this similarity of chemical behavior results from the numbers of electrons in the outer electron shell of the atom. For example, sodium (Na) and potassium (K) are both placed in column 1 of

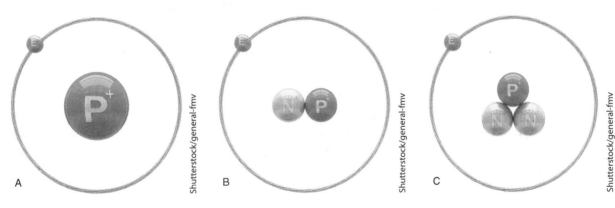

Shutterstock/general-fmv

FIGURE 2.3 The first three isotopes of hydrogen. Note that each of these hydrogen isotopes has only one proton, a characteristic of all atomic forms of the element. Isotopes differ from each other in the number of neutrons, not in the number of protons. A. Hydrogen-1 (also known as hydrogen, or ^{1}H); B. Hydrogen-2 (deuterium, or ^{2}H); C. Hydrogen-3 (tritium, or ^{3}H). Note: the isotopes usually do not have special names like the example shown here, but are referred to by element and mass, like Uranium-235 (^{235}U).

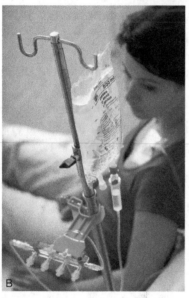

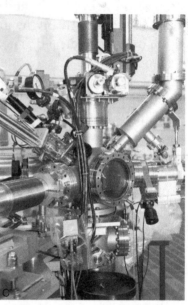

FIGURE 2.4 Uses of radioisotopes. A. Radiologist with an elderly patient looking at CT scan results; B. Chemotherapy patient. C. View of important electronic and mechanical parts of a mass spectrometer, a scientific tool used for dating rocks and certain fossils.

the table since they tend to lose one electron in the process of forming an ion. However, sodium has a mass less than that of potassium. Mendeleev further placed the lighter elements on top, and heavier ones below. We now know that potassium has one more shell of electrons outside its nucleus than sodium has.

Each Roman numeral column on the table indicates how many electrons are in the outer shell of the atom (for the first two columns and the last six; the middle of the table is more complicated, but fortunately we do not need that in biology). Each numbered row on the table tells us how many electron shells an atom has. For example, carbon is in Group IVa, row 2, so that tells us it has four electrons in its outer shell, and that it has a total of two shells. Furthermore, we know it cannot have a second shell until is inner (first) shell is filled, so carbon has a total of six electrons (which match the six protons in its nucleus).

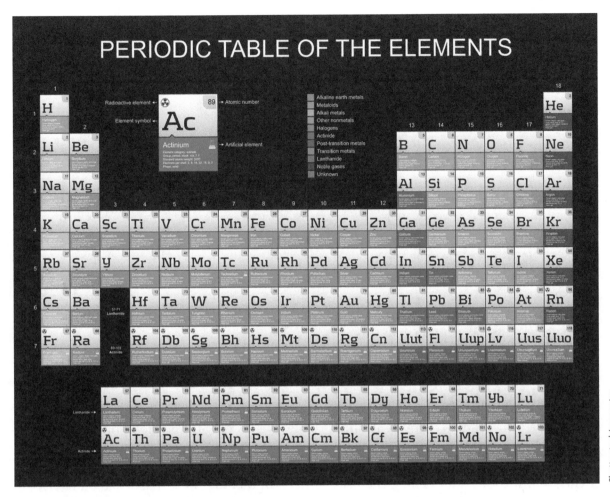

FIGURE 2.5 The periodic table of the elements.

TABLE 2.2 Select Biologically Important Elements and Their Symbols

Element Name	Element Symbol	Element Name	Element Symbol
Hydrogen	H	Phosphorous	P
Carbon	C	Sodium	Na
Oxygen	O	Chlorine	Cl
Nitrogen	N	Calcium	Ca
Potassium	K		

2.2   Molecules

When atoms are bonded together in a specific ratio, we refer to this as a **molecule**. Table salt has molecules consisting of one sodium atom and one chlorine atom. We use a shorthand designation of the molecule sodium chloride as NaCl (not Na_1Cl_1). When we have more than one of a particular atom, we indicate that as a subscript behind the elemental symbol. Water has two hydrogen atoms for every oxygen atom, so we indicate the molecular formula of water as H_2O. One molecule of the sugar glucose (Figure 2.6) has six carbon atoms, twelve hydrogen atoms, and six oxygen atoms. We summarize this with the formula $C_6H_{12}O_6$.

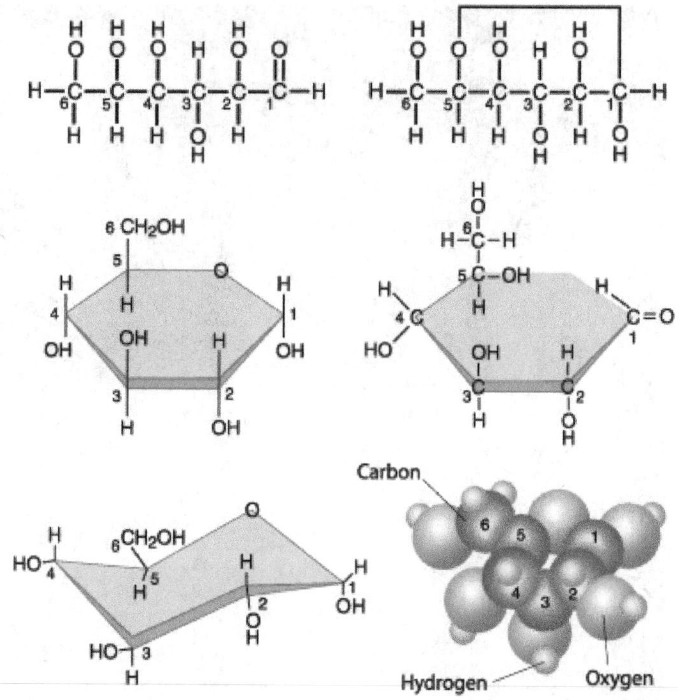

FIGURE 2.6 Representations of glucose molecules.

2.3   Chemical Bonding

During the 19th Century, chemists arranged elements according to chemical bonding, recognizing that one group (the furthermost right column on the Periodic Table, referred to as the Noble Gases) tended to occur in elemental form (in other words, not in a molecule with other elements). During the 20th Century, chemists figured out that the Noble Gases had outer electron shells containing two (as in the case of helium) or eight electrons (as in the case of all the other elements in the group: neon, xenon, radon, krypton, etc.). The numbers 2 and 8 will be important in our examination of chemical bonding.

As a general rule, the atoms likely to occur in biological systems tend to gain or lose their outer electrons to achieve a Noble Gas outer electron shell configuration of two or eight electrons. The number of electrons that are gained or lost from this outer shell is characteristic for each element. These electrons ultimately determine the number and types of chemical bond atoms of that element forms.

The Octet Rule

1. Atoms tend to fill or empty their outer electron shells so those shells will have *two* or *eight* electrons.
2. The first shell can have two electrons maximum.
3. The second and subsequent shells can have up to eight electrons maximum.
4. Inner shells are filled (for our purposes in biology) before electrons occupy outer shells.

Ionic bonds form when atoms become ions as they gain or lose electrons to fill or empty their outer electron shell so it resembles a Noble Gas configuration. Ions are charged atoms with an imbalance of positive and negative charges.

Chlorine is in a group of elements with seven electrons in their outer shells (Figure 2.7A). The atomic number of chlorine is 17, meaning that an atom of chlorine has 17 protons (positive charges) in its nucleus, with 17 electrons (negative charges) in electron shells around that nucleus. Atoms are electrically neutral, where the number of positive proton charges equals the number of negative electron charges. Members of this group tend to gain one electron, acquiring a charge of −1. Sodium is in another group with elements having one electron in their outer shells (Figure 2.7A). Members of this group tend to lose their outer electron, acquiring a charge of +1. Oppositely charged ions are attracted to each other, thus Cl^- (the symbolic representation of chlorine) and Na^+ (the symbol for sodium, using the Greek word *natrium*) form an ionic bond, becoming the molecule sodium chloride (Figure 2.7).

Covalent bonds (Figure 2.8) form when atoms share electrons. Since electrons move very fast they can be shared, effectively filling or emptying the outer shells of the atoms involved in the covalent bond. Such bonds are referred to as electron-sharing bonds. An analogy can be made to child custody: The children are like electrons, and tend to spend some time with one parent and the rest of their time with the other parent. In a covalent bond, the electron clouds surrounding the atomic nuclei overlap.

Carbon (C) is in Group IVa, meaning it has four electrons in its outer shell (Figure 2.5). Thus to become a "happy atom," Carbon can either gain or lose four electrons, alternately filling and emptying its outer shell. Hydrogen is in Group Ia, and has a single electron in its outer shell (Figure 2.5). Hydrogen and carbon will share their outer shell electrons, forming single covalent bonds between each of the hydrogen atoms and the centrally located carbon atom (Figure 2.8C).

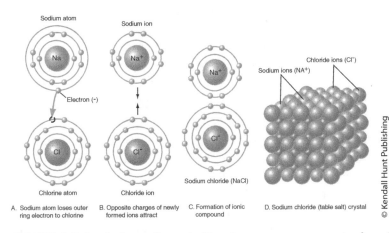

A. Sodium atom loses outer ring electron to chlorine
B. Opposite charges of newly formed ions attract
C. Formation of ionic compound
D. Sodium chloride (table salt) crystal

© Kendall Hunt Publishing

Shutterstock/pzAxe

FIGURE 2.7 Ionic bonding. A. Electron arrangement of sodium (top) and chlorine (bottom). B. The transfer of electrons produces charge imbalances in each ion. The opposite charges attract each other. C. The attraction forms the ionic bond. D. Since each charged ion occupies three-dimensional space, the positively charged sodium ions are surrounded by up to six negatively charged chloride ions. The resulting molecule is known as sodium chloride. E. Salt crystals; note the cubic shape of the crystals, which is due to the atomic arrangement shown in figure D.

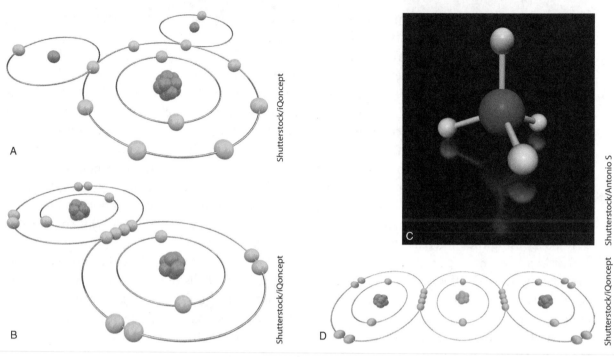

FIGURE 2.8 Covalent bonding. A. Covalent bonding in water; B. Double covalent bond (four shared electrons) bonds dioxygen (O_2); C. Molecular model of methane showing the four covalent bonds as sticks connecting the atoms; D. Carbon dioxide atomic diagram.

Elemental carbon is a solid substance, while elemental hydrogen is a gas. When these atoms bond together a new compound forms, methane, also known as natural gas.

The molecule methane (chemical formula CH_4) has four covalent bonds, one between the central carbon atom and each of the four hydrogen atoms. Carbon contributes an electron, and hydrogen contributes an electron to the formation of the covalent bind. The sharing of a single electron pair is termed a single covalent bond. A double covalent bond forms when two pairs of electrons are shared (Figure 2.8B, D). Carbon can share two of its outer shell electrons with an atom of oxygen, making a double bond. When this is repeated, carbon dioxide (CO_2) forms (Figure 2.8D). Triple bonds are known, wherein three pairs (six electrons total) are shared as in acetylene gas (CH_2, a common gas used in welding) or nitrogen gas (N_2, the major gas in our atmosphere). We represent a pair of shared electrons (a single covalent bond) with a single line (or bar $-$, $C - C$), and a double covalent bond as a double line (or double bar $=$, $C = C$).

Sometimes electrons tend to spend more time with one atom than with another. In such cases, a polar covalent bond develops. Oxygen and a few other atoms, such as nitrogen, tend to hog the electrons in a covalent bond. Water (H_2O; Figure 2.9) is an example of a polar covalently bonded molecule. Since the electrons spend so much time with the oxygen (oxygen having a greater electronegativity or electron affinity) that end of the molecule acquires a slightly negative charge.

Conversely, the loss of the electrons from the hydrogen end leaves a slightly positive charge. The water molecule is polar as it has a positive and a negative side. One problem we encounter in an introductory biology course is figuring out if a covalent bond is polar or nonpolar. The bonds between carbon atoms are nonpolar, as are the bonds between carbon and hydrogen atoms. Any bond involving oxygen, nitrogen, or phosphorous is likely to be polar covalent bonds.

Hydrogen bonds result from the weak electrical attraction between the positive end of one molecule and the negative end of another. Water molecules are bonded to each other with these individually very weak bonds. However, taken in a large enough quantity, the result is strong enough to hold molecules together (the strands of the DNA molecule are held together by hydrogen bonds) or in a three-dimensional shape (as we will see with proteins later in this chapter). These bonds also account for the surface tension of water (Figure 2.10A). The water molecules have hydrogen bonds between water molecules, but do not make such bonds with air at the water's surface. This allows us to float paperclips on water (Figure 2.10A) or have water striders walk on the water (Figure 2.10B).

FIGURE 2.9 Representation of water molecules. These space-filling models show the slightly positive side where the white hydrogen atoms are and the slightly negative side where the red oxygen atom is. In water, the molecules naturally line up positive side of one molecule to negative sides of others.

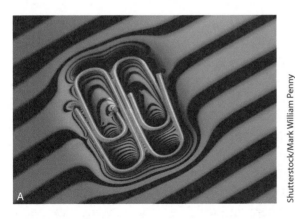

FIGURE 2.10 Results of hydrogen bonding. A. Photograph of two red paperclips resting on the water surface. The projected blue lines are refracted due to the change in surface tension of water caused by hydrogen bonding of water molecules that allows the paperclips to float on the surface; B. Water strider; note the distortion of the water surface where the bug's foot makes contact.

2.4   Chemical Reactions

Chemical reactions occur naturally as atoms and molecules interact. During a reaction, chemicals known as reactants interact to make products. We see generally two types of reactions, combination and disassociation. In combination reactions, two reactants combine to result in a single product. During a disassociation reaction, the reactant is broken down, resulting on two products. We employ chemical equations to represent how chemical reactions occur. Combination reactions occur when two separate reactants are bonded together, such as A + B → AB. We would say, "Reactant A plus Reactant B react to produce Product AB." The arrow indicates the phrase *react to produce*. Disassociation reactions occur when a compound is broken into two products, such as AB → A + B.

2.5   The Significance of Water

Earth is the water planet. Four-fifths of our planet's surface is covered in water. Our planet is the only known planet in our solar system where water exists as a liquid. Biologists have concluded that life began in water, and only recently (in geological terms) made the transition to land. Water is the universal solvent: given enough time, water will erode the tallest mountains. Water causes floods that kill thousands of people annually, yet is the essential liquid for life. We will examine the physical properties of water that allow it to hold such a preeminent place among inorganic chemicals. However, water is not the entire story. Living things make many chemicals for use in their cells. These chemicals and their structure are important to the biochemical functioning of life.

2.5.1   Structure of Water

It can be correctly argued that life exists on Earth because of the abundant liquid water. The chemical nature of water is thus one we must examine as it permeates living systems. Water is a universal solvent, and can be too much of a good thing for some cells to deal with.

Matter can exist in three classic states: solid, liquid, and gas. On Earth, water exists as liquid water, ice (solid water), and water vapor (gaseous water). Water also occurs on the other inner planets, Mars and Venus. While Mars shows a great deal evidence of running water in its (presumed) distant past, scientists suspect that today Mars is a waterless planet, with water only existing as small amounts of atmospheric water vapor or as ice. Venus, the second planet from the Sun, is a greenhouse planet due to its high temperatures that allow water only to exist in its gaseous state. Planetary scientists have determined that the temperature at the poles of Venus exceeds 400°C; four times what it takes to boil water here on Earth! Why is there such abundant life on Earth? Water is a major part of that answer.

Water has polar covalent bonds within the molecule. Covalent bonds are electron-sharing bonds. Unequal sharing of the electrons between atoms in a covalent bond results in molecules with a slightly positive side and a slightly negative side. Water is the classic example of a polar covalently bonded molecule (Figure 2.9). Other covalently bonded molecules, such as methane, are nonpolar, having neither a positive nor a negative side.

Water molecules link up by forming very weak hydrogen bonds between the positive side of one molecule and the negative side of another molecule. Due to the large number of these very weak bonds between individual water molecules, water has a great interconnectivity of individual molecules. When taken in such large numbers, these bonds allow water to support the weight of a water strider, as well as to flow as a cohesive unit from a pitcher, or to bead up on a freshly waxed automobile hood. These hydrogen bonds are responsible for the cohesion of water molecules to each other and the adhesion of water molecules to certain polar substances.

Water has been referred to as the universal solvent. How does water dissolve something? Water in effect surrounds materials that are added to it (or with which it comes in contact). Consider salt added to a glass of water. Salt consists of molecules of the ironically bonded sodium chloride (NaCl). Ionic bonds are weak bonds, when dry. Once in water the collective effect of the attractions between the polar sides of the water molecules and the sodium (Na^+) and chloride (Cl^-) ions breaks the ionic bonds, dissolving the salt. The oppositely charged end of numerous water molecules surrounds each ion of sodium or chloride. Living things are composed of atoms and molecules within aqueous solutions (solutions that have materials dissolved in water), so the ability of water to dissolve materials is very important to life's chemical processes.

The solubility, or capacity to dissolve in a solvent, of many molecules is controlled by their molecular structure. You are probably familiar with the phrase "mixing like oil and water." The biochemical basis for this phrase is that the organic macromolecules known as lipids have areas that lack polar covalent bonds. The polar covalently bonded water molecules act to exclude nonpolar molecules, causing the fats to clump together. The structure of many molecules can greatly influence their solubility. Sugars like glucose have many hydroxyl groups (OH) that increase the solubility of the molecule by providing charged areas of the sugar molecule where water can bond. In the hydroxyl, the oxygen causes the H ion to be slightly positive, while the unequal sharing of the electrons between the O and H produce a slightly negative charge on the O.

2.5.2   Acid and Base

Water tends to dissociate into H^+ and OH^- ions. In this disassociation, the oxygen retains the electrons and one of the two hydrogen atoms, becoming a negatively charged ion known as hydroxide. Pure water has the same number (or concentration) of H^+ as OH^- ions. Acidic solutions have more H^+ ions than OH^- ions. Basic solutions have the opposite. An acid causes an increase in the numbers of H^+ ions and a base causes an increase in the numbers of OH^- ions.

Chemists have devised the pH scale (Figure 2.11) to indicate the relative acidity in a solution. The pH scale is a logarithmic scale representing the concentration of H^+ ions in a solution. If we have a solution where 1 in every 10 molecules is H^+, we refer to the concentration of H^+ ions as 1/10. You may recall from an algebra class (ugh) that we can write a fraction as a negative exponent, thus 1/10 becomes 10^{-1}. Conversely 1/100 becomes 10^{-2}, 1/1000 becomes 10^{-3}, and so on. Logarithms (log) are exponents to which a number (usually 10) has been raised. For example, log 10 (pronounced "the log of 10") = 1 since 10 may be written as 10^1. The log 1/10 (or 10^{-1}) = −1. The pH is a measure of the concentration of H^+ ions. We define it as the negative log of the H^+ ion concentration (or $-\log[H^+]$). For example, if the pH of a glass of water is 7, we know the concentration of H^+ ions is 10^{-7}, or 1/10,000,000. In the case of strong acids, such as hydrochloric acid (HCl, an acid secreted by the lining of your stomach), $[H^+]$ (the concentration of H^+ ions, written in a chemical shorthand) is 10^{-1}; therefore the pH is 1.

Most of the chemicals with extremely high or low pH numbers are definitely on the list of "do not drink these"! Recall from Chapter 1 the concept of homeostasis. One of the major homeostatic jobs living things must accomplish is to protect the cell/organism from rapid swings in pH. Multicellular organisms (like ourselves) accomplish this by special solutions known as buffers. Blood and saliva are two of our solutions that act as buffers.

2.6   Organic Molecules

Organic molecules are essentially based on chains of covalently bonded carbon atoms. The simplest of these is methane (CH_4) that we examined earlier in this chapter. If we link a series of methane molecules together we form a chain consisting of only hydrogen and carbon atoms. Such chains are termed hydrocarbons. Substitution of the hydrogen atoms in a hydrocarbon occurs, with various units termed functional groups.

Polar molecules (which can have either positive or negative charges) attract water molecules. Molecules that attract water are said to be hydrophilic. Nonpolar molecules are repelled by water and do not dissolve in water. Since these molecules do not associate (or bond) with water, they are said to be hydrophobic. Hydrocarbons are hydrophobic except when they have an attached ionized functional group such as carboxyl, which makes the molecule hydrophilic. Since cells are between 70% and 90% water, the degree to which organic molecules interact with water affects their function. One of the most common groups is the −OH (hydroxyl) group. Its presence will enable a molecule to be water soluble.

Isomers are molecules with identical molecular formulas but which differ in arrangement of their atoms (e.g., glucose, fructose, and galactose; Figure 2.12). The sugars glucose, fructose,

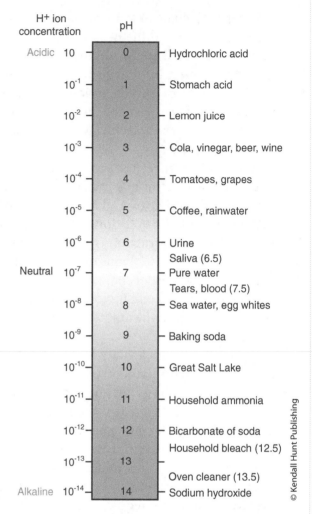

FIGURE 2.11 The pH scale showing the pH of some common substances.

and galactose all have the same chemical formula ($C_6H_{12}O_6$), but behave with different chemical properties resulting from their functional groups: glucose is a type of chemical known as an aldehyde, while fructose is a ketone. Each of these sugars has a different taste and reacts in chemical tests differently. In a word, structure matters.

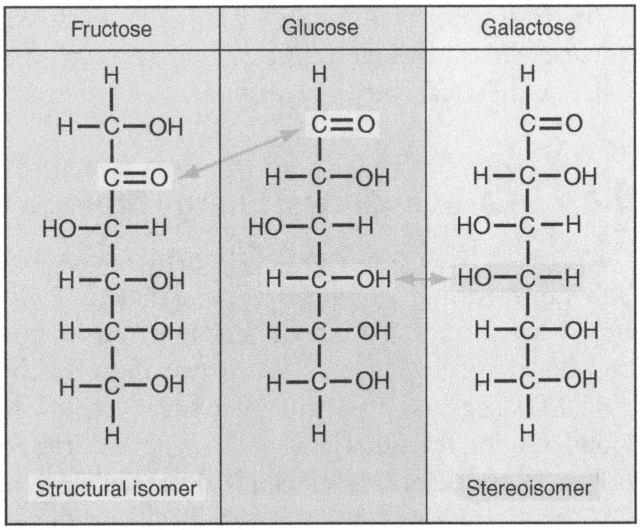

Chemical bonds store energy. We measure this energy and express it as kilocalories per mole. A mole is a convenient way to refer to a quantity of atoms. In a similar way, you might know the quantity meant by the terms *dozen* (12) or *gross* (a dozen dozen, or 144). By definition a mole is a very large number of atoms: 6.02×10^{22} atoms, or 6,020,000,000,000,000,000,000 atoms. This number is referred to as Avogadro's

Fructose	Glucose	Galactose

FIGURE 2.12 Isomers of three sugar molecules. All three sugars, glucose, fructose, and galactose have the same chemical formula, but differ in how those atoms are arranged in the molecule.

© Kendall Hunt Publishing

number, named in honor of Italian scientist Amedeo Avogadro (1776–1858). Unlike the terms dozen or gross, a mole was specifically chosen to relate to a gram equivalent: thus one mole of hydrogen weighs 1 g, one mole of carbon weighs 12 g, and so on. A kilocalorie is 1000 calories, or enough energy to raise 1 g of water 1000°C. Energy exists in one of two forms: kinetic (or energy in use/motion), or potential (or energy at rest or in storage).

The single covalent bond between carbon atoms in a hydrocarbon has 83.1 kcal/mole (kilocalories), while the double covalent bond between two carbon atoms has 147 kcal/mole. Ionic and hydrogen bonds store a great deal less energy. Chemical bonds store potential energy until they are broken, releasing, and converting that stored energy into kinetic energy (according to the laws of thermodynamics). Energy can thus be stored in chemical bonds. Life utilizes this energy.

Each organic molecule group has small molecules (monomers) that are linked to form a larger organic molecule (macromolecule). Monomers can be joined together to form polymers that are large macromolecules made of from three to millions of individual monomer subunits.

Macromolecules are polymers of smaller units known as monomers. The formation of covalent bonds between monomers is also referred to as polymerization. To form polymers, a type of chemical reaction known as a chemical **condensation reaction** happens. The atoms to make a water molecule are removed from functional groups on both of the involved monomers. Cellular enzymes, the chemical machines of the cell, carry out this condensation by removing a hydroxyl group (OH^-) from one monomer, and a hydrogen ion (H^+) from the other monomer. This allows a covalent bond to form between the monomers, and the removed ions to form a molecule of water. Usually, different enzymes perform the reversal of the condensation reaction, the hydrolysis of polymers.

There are four major groups of organic macromolecules: carbohydrates, lipids, proteins, and nucleic acids. Molecules, such as glucose, starch, and adenosine triphosphate (ATP), belonging to these chemical classes perform a variety of functions in cells.

2.6.1   Carbohydrates: Energy Storage and Structure

Carbohydrates are perhaps the group of macromolecules you have heard about. Functions of carbohydrates include energy storage and structure. Monomers of carbohydrates are simple sugars or monosaccharides. Commonly encountered monosaccharides include glucose, fructose, ribose, and deoxyribose (Figure 2.13). If two monosaccharides bond together they form a disaccharide. Milk sugar (lactose) and table sugar (sucrose) are common disaccharides (Figure 2.13F, G). Condensation reactions link single sugars to form polymers known as polysaccharides. Common polysaccharides include starch glycogen, cellulose, and chitin.

Glucose is a common monosaccharide produced in great abundance by plants, as well as the form of sugar in your bloodstream. The products of photosynthesis in plants, algae, and certain bacteria are assembled to make a glucose molecule. Fructose is a common sugar also referred to as fruit sugar. Taste tests suggest human beings consider fructose a sweeter sugar than glucose. Fructose occurs in sweet fruits, such as the grapes and berries. Sugars form when sunlight energy is converted into the carbon–carbon covalent bond energy locked in glucose. This energy is released in living organisms in such a way as to not generate enough heat to incinerate the organism.

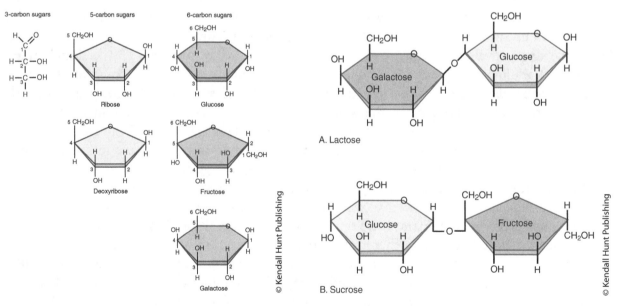

FIGURE 2.13 Monosaccharides and disaccharides. A. Ribose; B. Deoxyribose; C. Glucose; D. Fructose; E. Galactose; F. Lactose; G. Sucrose. Note: these sugars are shown in the ring form.

Disaccharides form when two monosaccharides chemically bond together. Sucrose is a common plant disaccharide made from of glucose and fructose. We collect and modify this sucrose as sugar cane (used to sweeten soft drinks many decades ago, also in rum production) and maple syrup. Lactose (the sugar in milk) is a disaccharide composed of the monosaccharides glucose and the galactose (Figure 2.13F).

Polysaccharides are large molecules (polymers) comprised of individual monosaccharide units. The plant polysaccharide starch is made from many glucose molecules linked together. Two forms of polysaccharide, amylose and amylopectin (Figure 2.14), makeup what we commonly call starch. Glycogen is an animal storage product that accumulates in the vertebrate liver and muscle cells.

When we eat a starchy food, like a potato, our bodies break the starch down into glucose molecules. These glucose molecules are distributed to all of the cells making up our bodies though our bloodstream. Once the glucose molecules get into our cells, we either use the glucose for energy or store it for later as glycogen. When our blood glucose level falls, chemical messages go out to certain of our cells (muscle and liver) to break the glycogen back down into glucose and release it into our bloodstream. The hormone insulin regulates intake of glucose into our cells. The release of stored glucose from glycogen in our cells is controlled by the hormone glucagon.

Cellulose is a polysaccharide found in plant cell walls, forming the fibrous part of the plant. Cellulose is indigestible, and thus forms an important, easily obtained part of dietary fiber. Compared to starch and glycogen, which are each made up of mixtures of different forms of glucose molecules, cellulose (and the animal structural polysaccharide chitin) consist of only one form of the glucose molecule. We eat starch and our bodies can break itch down into glucose molecules. When we eat cellulose, our bodies cannot breakdown the cellulose, so it forms dietary fiber. Both starch and cellulose play important roles in human health.

2.6.2 Lipids: Long-Term Energy Storage, Structure, and Control

You have most likely heard of the term "sweet tooth." It can be argued that all of us are alive because our remote ancestors had a "fat tooth." Early humans

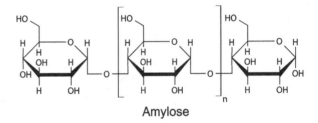

FIGURE 2.14 Polysaccharides. A. Amylose; note that the glucose molecules can be repeated many times, as shown by the **n** outside the brackets; B. Amylopectin.

Amylose

Amylopectin

Shutterstock/chromatos

encountered sugar only in fruits, never in a refined state. Fats, on the other hand, were a bountiful source of energy that was lightweight and quite energy rich. Bone marrow is a wonderful source of such fats. When our ancestors could get this rich energy source it provided enough calories to keep them going at least a day or two. However, a fat tooth in a society that provides ample and diverse fats for consumption is not such a good thing! Most of us can get our fat tooth "scratched" with milk, cheese, ice cream, nuts, as well as fatty meats. High fat diets have been linked to increased risks of cancer, obesity, diabetes, and heart disease. Our once essential "fat tooth" clearly needs to be pulled, or at least capped!

Lipids function as long-term energy storage. Generally, they do not dissolve in polar substances, such as water. Secondary functions of lipids are as structural components (as in the case of phospholipids that are the major building block in cell membranes) and as "messengers" (hormones) that play roles in communications within and between cells. Lipids typically consist of three fatty acids (usually) covalently bonded to a 3-carbon glycerol. The fatty acids are composed of CH_2 units, and are hydrophobic (not water soluble).

Fatty acids can be saturated (Figure 2.15A), meaning they have as many hydrogen atoms bonded to their carbon atoms as possible, or unsaturated (Figure 2.15B) with one or more double covalent bonds connecting their carbon atoms, which results in there being fewer hydrogen atoms.

Fats and oils are used for energy storage. Fats are solid at room temperature, while oils are liquid. The fatty acids in oils are mostly unsaturated, while those in fats are mostly saturated.

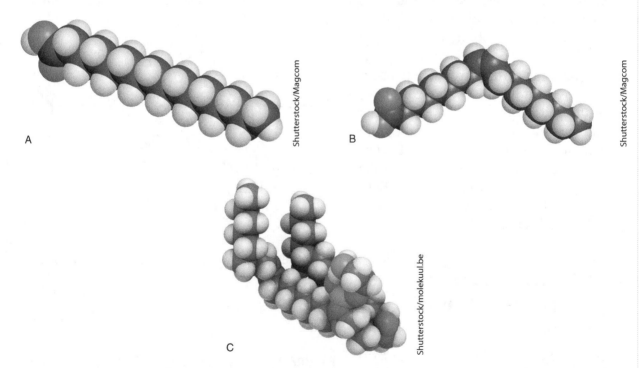

A
Shutterstock/Magcom

B
Shutterstock/Magcom

C
Shutterstock/molekuul.be

FIGURE 2.15 Fatty acids. A. Palmitic acid, palm oil, a saturated fatty acid; B. Oleic acid, olive oil, an unsaturated fatty acid; C. Phospholipids. Note the substitution of a phosphate group (yellow) in place of the third fatty acid.

Animals convert excess sugars (beyond their glycogen storage limits) into fats. Most plants store excess sugars as starch, although some seeds and fruits have energy stored as oils (such as corn, canola, and sunflower oils). Fats yield more than three times as much energy carbohydrates do.

Diets are attempts to reduce the amount of fats present in specialized cells known as adipose cells that accumulate in certain areas of the human body. By restricting the intakes of carbohydrates and fats, the body is forced to draw on its own stored fats to makeup the difference. The body responds to this by lowering its metabolic rate, often resulting in a drop of "energy level." Successful diets usually involve three things: decreasing the amounts of carbohydrates and fats; exercise; and behavior modification.

Another use of fats is as insulators and cushions. The human body naturally accumulates some fats in the "posterior" area. Subdermal ("under the skin") fat plays a role in insulation.

Phospholipids (Figure 2.15C) and glycolipids are important structural components of cell membranes. Phospholipids are modified so that a phosphate group (PO_4^-) is added to one of the fatty acids. The addition of this group makes a polar "head" and two nonpolar "tails."

Steroids (Figure 2.16) are a very distinctive group of lipids. All steroids have a common ring structure with side chains of other molecules. Several steroids are important hormones: testosterone, estrogen, and progesterone (Figure 2.16). Testosterone (Figure 2.16B) is the male sex

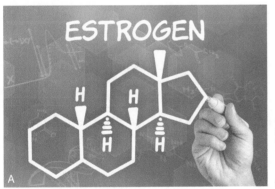
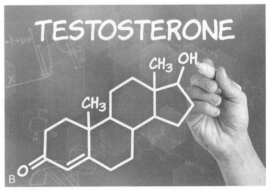

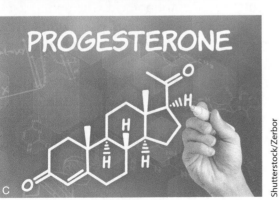
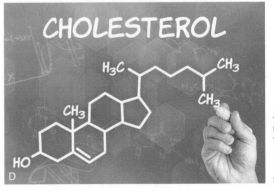

FIGURE 2.16 Structure of four steroid molecules. A. Estrogen; B. Testosterone; C. Progesterone; D. Cholesterol.

hormone produced in the male testes that targets a number of cells throughout the male body. Among changes resulting during male puberty as a result of increasing testosterone are a deepening of the voice, change in musculature, and development of the sex drive and sex organ function. Testosterone is the male hormone that you see all the time on television ads. As men age their testosterone levels naturally decline. Supplements of testosterone can augment the aging male's own natural supply, although studies also point to potential harmful side effects. Estrogen and progesterone (Figure 2.16A, C) are the female sex hormones. Both are produced in a woman's ovaries. Changes in the female body during puberty include change in the shape of the body, growth and development of the breasts, ovulation, and maintaining the female secondary sex characteristics. As women enter menopause many use estrogen supplements to maintain a more youthful look.

Cholesterol (Figure 2.16D) has many biological uses, such as its presence in cell membranes, and its role in forming the sheath of some nerve cells. Excess cholesterol in the blood has been linked to atherosclerosis, hardening of the arteries, and increased risk of heart attack and stroke.

Most mention of steroids in the news is usually negative. Athletes seeking an extra edge over their competitors have employed anabolic steroids as performance enhancing drugs. The American cyclist and 7-time Tour de France winner Lance Armstrong finally admitted to his use of performance enhancing drugs in 2013. Numerous athletes have either admitted or been suspected of using steroids.

2.6.3   Proteins: Structure and Control

Proteins are very important in biological systems as control molecules and structural components of cells. Enzymes and protein hormones perform the control functions of proteins. Enzymes are proteins that act as organic catalysts to promote but are not be changed by chemical reactions. Structural proteins function in the cell membranes, as major parts of muscle tissue, and as components of cilia and flagella.

The monomers of proteins are the amino acids (Figure 2.17). Each amino acid has three major areas: 1) an amino end (NH_2); 2) a carboxyl end (COOH); and 3) an R-group. The R indicates the variable component (R-group; Rest of the molecule) of each amino acid. The amino acids Alanine and Valine are both nonpolar, but they differ, as do all amino acids, by the composition of their R-groups (Figure 2.17). Some of the amino acids have polar R-groups, while others have sulfur-containing R-groups.

All living things, you, your pet, lions, tigers, bears (oh my), pine trees, cacti, bacteria, fungi, and even viruses (when they are inside their hosts) use various combinations of the same "toolkit" of 20 amino acids to make their proteins. All living things use the same 20 amino acids to build their proteins. This is very powerful evidence for the shared ancestry of all living things.

Amino acid monomers link together to form proteins during protein synthesis. Joining the amino end of one amino acid to the carboxyl end of another, while removing a hydroxyl (OH^-) from one amino acid and a hydrogen ion (H^+) form the other, allows the formation of a type of covalent bond known as a peptide bond.

Amino acids are linked together into a polypeptide, producing the primary structure (Figure 2.18A) of a protein. The primary structure of a protein is the sequence of amino acids,

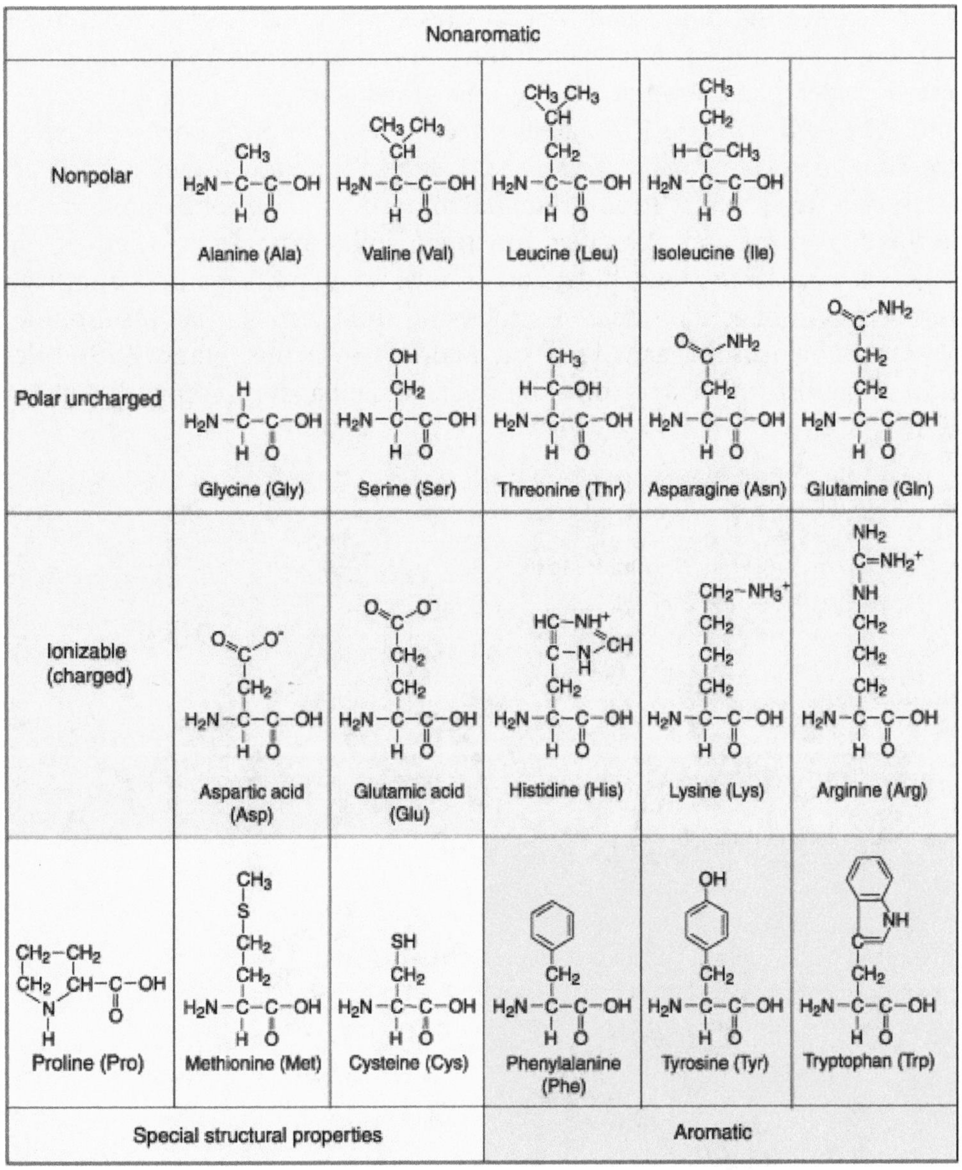

FIGURE 2.17 Amino acids. Each amino acid differs in its R-group.

which is directly related to the sequence of information in the RNA molecule, and is in turn, is a copy of a small segment of the information stored in the DNA molecule. Changes in the primary structure can alter the proper functioning of the protein. Protein function is usually tied to their three-dimensional structure. The primary structure is the sequence of amino acids in a polypeptide.

The secondary structure (Figure 2.18B) is the tendency of the polypeptide to coil or pleat due to hydrogen bonding between R-groups. Since the arrangement of amino acids in a primary structure is almost infinite, the shapes assumed in secondary structure can vary greatly.

Interaction between the amino acid R-groups results in a three-dimensional folding known as the tertiary structure (Figure 2.18C) of a protein. Like the secondary structure, these interactions ultimately depend on the amino acid (primary) sequence.

Many proteins, such as hemoglobin are formed from one or more polypeptides. Such structure is termed quaternary structure (Figure 2.18D). Structural proteins, such as collagen, have regularly repeated primary structures. Like the structural carbohydrates, the components determine the final shape and ultimately function. Collagens have a variety of functions in living things, such as the tendons, hide, and corneas of a cow. Keratin is another structural protein that occurs in fingernails, feathers, hair, and rhinoceros horns. Insulin, the hormone regulating uptake of glucose sugar, is a protein made of two chains (Figure 2.19). Microtubules, important in cell division and structures of flagella and cilia, are composed of globular structural proteins.

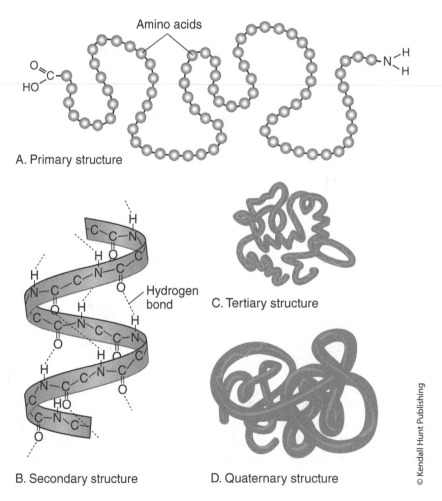

© Kendall Hunt Publishing

FIGURE 2.18 Levels of protein structure. A. Primary structure; B. Secondary structure; C. Tertiary structure; D. Quaternary structure. Note that not all proteins have a quaternary structure.

2.6.4 Nucleic Acids: Information, Protein Synthesis, and Energy Transfers

Probably, the most well known organic molecule these days is deoxyribonucleic acid (DNA). It has been a key component in criminal trials and television dramas (is CSI still on TV?). Evidence based on DNA has been used in criminal cases to free wrongfully convicted individuals as well as to pinpoint guilt and remove reasonable doubt for a jury. During the summer of 2000, Celera Genomics and the Human Genome Project jointly announced the for all intents and purposes complete sequencing of the human genetic makeup. News accounts are flooded with discoveries of new genes for obesity, diabetes, alcoholism, intelligence, and so on. Our genes have acted as a musical score used by our cells to assemble a human being: what goes where and in what sequence as well as what innate capabilities and flaws will this individual have.

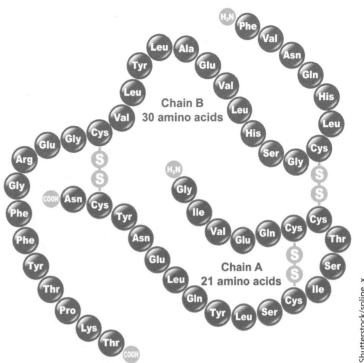

Human Insulin

FIGURE 2.19 Stylized chemical structure of human insulin. Note the amino acids in each chain with each amino acid indicated by its three-letter abbreviation.

DNA cannot operate alone. Ribonucleic acid (RNA) is a vital molecule that transfers the DNA information into the amino acid sequence of a protein. The primary structure of a protein determines the functionality and shape of that protein. If the DNA that made the RNA had errors, the protein might not function at all.

Protein synthesis is among the processes that requires cellular energy in the form of adenosine triphosphate (ATP), the energy coin of the cell. Just think, the structure of DNA and all this information was not definitively known until the 1950s!

Nucleic acids are polymers of monomer units known as nucleotides. Nucleic acids functions are listed in Table 2.3. Nucleotides consist of a 5-carbon sugar (either ribose or deoxyribose), one of five nitrogen-containing bases also known as nitrogenous bases (Figure 2.20B), and a phosphate group (Figure 2.20A). There are five types of nitrogenous bases: double-ringed purines (Adenine and Guanine) and single-ringed pyrimidines (Cytosine, Thymine, and Uracil) (Figure 2.20B).

DNA is the physical carrier of inheritance. The bases in DNA are Cytosine (C), Guanine (G), Adenine (A), and Thymine (T). DNA is life's information storage molecule (Figure 2.20C). The sequence of bases along the DNA molecule is the genetic code. Storing information in sequences

TABLE 2.3 Organic Macromolecule Groups.

Macromolecule Group	Monomer	Function	Examples
Carbohydrates	Monosaccharides	Energy storage	Glucose, fructose, deoxy-ribose, ribose, starch, glycogen
Lipids	Glycerol and fatty acids	Long-term energy storage Structure Control	Fats, oils, waxes Phospholipids, steroids Hormones
Proteins	Amino acids	Structure Control	Membrane proteins Enzymes, hormones
Nucleic acids	Nucleotides	Information storage Protein synthesis Control Energy transfer	DNA RNA Ribozymes ATP, NADH

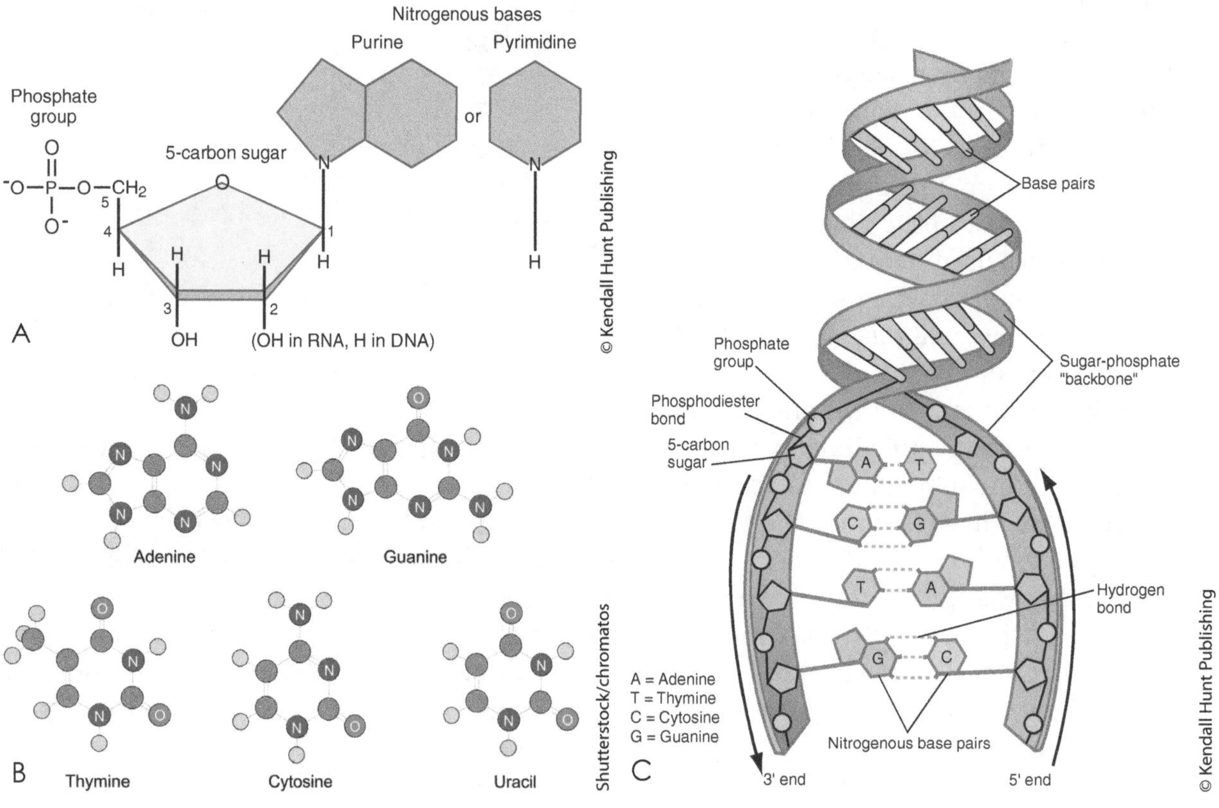

FIGURE 2.20 Nucleic acids. A. Structure of a nucleotide; B. Structural chemical formulas of purine and pyrimidine nitrogenous bases; C. Structure of DNA.

is something we all have some familiarity with. The English alphabet has 26 letters that combine to form over 50,000 words. The DNA base sequence stores codes for the 20 words (the 20 amino acids) that can make an infinite variety of sentences (translated from DNA language into proteins). In the English language, changes in the arrangement of the letters can alter the meaning of a sentence. It is the same with DNA.

Changes in DNA information may be translated into changes in the primary structure of a polypeptide, and then to changes in the secondary and tertiary structures of a protein. Often a single base change is enough to cause serious changes in the protein produced. A mutation is any change in the DNA base sequence. Most mutations are harmful.

RNA (Figure 2.21) was discovered after DNA was. DNA, with the exception of the chloroplasts and mitochondria, is restricted to the nucleus (in eukaryotes, the nucleoid region in prokaryotes). RNA occurs in the nucleus as well as in the cytoplasm (also remember that it occurs as part of the ribosomes that line the rough endoplasmic reticulum).

Adenosine triphosphate, better known as ATP (Figure 2.22), the energy currency or coin of the cell, transfers energy from chemical bonds to energy absorbing reactions within the cell. Structurally, ATP consists of the adenine nucleotide (ribose sugar, adenine base, and phosphate group, PO_4^{-2}) plus two other phosphate groups.

Energy is stored in the covalent bonds between phosphates, with the greatest amount of energy in the bond between the second and third phosphate groups. This covalent bond is known as a pyrophosphate bond.

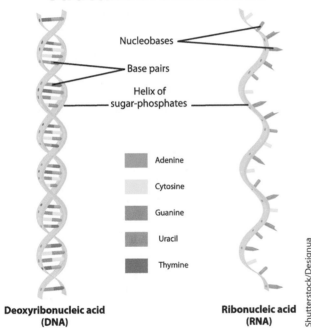

Structure of DNA & RNA

Nucleobases

Base pairs

Helix of
sugar-phosphates

Adenine

Cytosine

Guanine

Uracil

Thymine

**Deoxyribonucleic acid
(DNA)**

**Ribonucleic acid
(RNA)**

Shutterstock/Designua

FIGURE 2.21 Comparison of RNA and DNA structure. The difference between the nitrogenous bases of DNA and that of RNA is that thymine (T) in DNA is replaced by uracil (U) in RNA. The sugars in nucleotides also differ.

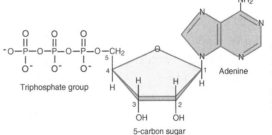

Triphosphate group

5-carbon sugar

Adenine

© Kendall Hunt Publishing

FIGURE 2.22 Structure of adenosine triphosphate (ATP).

Summary

Our study of biology involves the concepts of energy and atoms. Atoms can bond together to form molecules. Certain of these molecules are quite large and perform a number of vital functions in living things. Carbohydrates are involved in energy storage and structure in cells. Lipids function in cells has structural components, long-term energy storage, and control of certain processes. Proteins are carryout structure and control jobs in living things. The nucleic acids serve as hereditary molecules, play important roles in protein synthesis, and act as energy carriers. As a chemist once said, "all life is chemistry."

Terms

acid
acidic
adenosine triphosphate
  (ATP)
adhesion
adipose
amino acid
atom
atomic mass
atomic number
base
basic
biochemical pathways
buffers
carbohydrates
cell walls
cellulose
cholesterol
cilia
cohesion
condensation reaction
covalent bonds
deoxyribonucleic acid (DNA)
disaccharides
dissociate
DNA
electron
elements
energy
enzymes
fats
flagella

fossils
functional groups
genetic code
glucagon
glucose
hydrocarbons
hydrophilic
hydrophobic
hemoglobin
hormones
hormone insulin
hydrogen bonds
ions
ionic bonds
isomers
isotopes
kilocalorie
kinetic
laws of thermodynamics
lipids
macromolecules
matter
mole
molecules
monomer
monosaccharides
mutation
neutron
nucleic acids
nucleoid
nucleotide
nucleus

oils
orbitals
ovaries
peptide bond
phosphate group
phospholipids
photosynthesis
polar covalent bond
polymers
polysaccharides
potential energy
primary structure
proteins
proton
purines
pyrimidines
pyrophosphate bond
quaternary structure
radioactivity
radioisotopes
rough endoplasmic reticulum
ribonucleic acid (RNA)
ribosomes
saturated fat
secondary structure
solvent
steroids
subatomic particles
testes
tertiary structure
thermodynamics
unsaturated fat

Review Questions

1. Which of these is not a subatomic particle?
    a. proton;
    b. ion;
    c. neutron;
    d. electron

2. The outermost electron shell of every Noble Gas element (except Helium) has ____ electrons.
    a. 1;
    b. 2;
    c. 4;
    d. 6;
    e. 8

3. An organic molecule is likely to contain all of these elements except ____.
    a. C;
    b. H;
    c. O;
    d. Ne;
    e. N

4. The chemical bond between water molecules is a ____ bond.
    a. ionic;
    b. polar covalent;
    c. nonpolar covalent;
    d. hydrogen

5. A solution with a pH of 7 has ____ times more H ions than a solution of pH 9.
    a. 2;
    b. 100;
    c. 1000;
    d. 9;
    e. 90

6. The type of chemical bond formed when electrons are shared between atoms is a ____bond.
    a. ionic;
    b. covalent;
    c. hydrogen

7. The type of chemical bond formed when oppositely charged particles are attracted to each other is a ____ bond.
    a. ionic;
    b. covalent;
    c. hydrogen

8. Electrons occupy volumes of space known as ____.
    a. nuclei;
    b. periods;
    c. wavelengths;
    d. orbitals

9. Carbon has an atomic number of 6. This means it has ____.
    a. six protons;
    b. six neutrons;
    c. six protons and six neutrons;
    d. six neutrons and six electrons

10. Each of the isotopes of hydrogen has ____ proton(s).
    a. 3;
    b. 1;
    c. 2;
    d. 92;
    e. 1/2

11. A molecule is ___.
    a. a mixture of various components that can vary;
    b. a combination of many atoms that will have different ratios;
    c. a combination of one or more atoms that will have a fixed ratio of its components;
    d. more important in a chemistry class than in a biology class

12. The chemical reaction where water is removed during the formation of a covalent bond linking two monomers is known as ___.
    a. dehydration;
    b. hydrolysis;
    c. photosynthesis;
    d. protein synthesis

13. The monomer that makes up polysaccharides is ____.
    a. amino acids;
    b. glucose;
    c. fatty acids;
    d. nucleotides;
    e. glycerol

14. Proteins are composed of which of these monomers?
    a. amino acids;
    b. glucose;
    c. fatty acids;
    d. nucleotides;
    e. glycerol

15. Which of these is not a function of lipids?
    a. long-term energy storage;
    b. structures in cells;
    c. hormones;
    d. enzymes;

16. All living things use the same ___ amino acids.
    a. 4;
    b. 20;
    c. 100;
    d. 64

17. The sequence of ___ bases determines the ___ structure of a protein.
    a. RNA, secondary;
    b. DNA, quaternary;
    c. DNA, primary;
    d. RNA, primary

18. Which of these is not a nucleotide base found in DNA?
    a. uracil;
    b. adenine;
    c. guanine;
    d. thymine;
    e. cytosine

19. Which of these carbohydrates constitutes the bulk of dietary fiber?
    a. starch;
    b. cellulose;
    c. glucose;
    d. fructose;
    e. chitin

20. A diet high in _____ is considered unhealthy, since this type of material is largely found in animal tissues.
    a. saturated fats;
    b. testosterone;
    c. unsaturated fats;
    d. plant oils

21. The form of RNA that delivers information from DNA to be used in making a protein is
    _____.
    a. messenger RNA;
    b. ribosomal RNA;
    c. transfer RNA;
    d. heterogeneous nuclear RNA

22. The energy locked inside an organic molecule is most readily accessible in a ___ molecule.
    a. fat;
    b. DNA;
    c. glucose;
    d. chitin;
    e. enzyme

23. Phospholipids are important components in _____.
    a. cell walls;
    b. cytoplasm;
    c. DNA;
    d. cell membranes;
    e. cholesterol

Links

Chemicool: A colorful and easy to use Periodic Table. More information about elements than most of us would want. [http://www.chemicool.com]

WebElements Scholar Edition: This is intended for college-level chemistry use. This site offers details about the history, discovery, used, and physical data for each element. [http://www.webelements.com/webelements/scholar/index.html]

Diamond: Images of diamond and graphite crystal structure. [http://www.bris.ac.uk/Depts/Chemistry/MOTM/diamond/diamond.htm]

The Structure of the DNA Molecule: (Access Excellence) From the Access Excellence Classic Collection, an activity about DNA structure. [http://www.accessexcellence.org/AE/AEC/CC/DNA_structure.php]

The RNA World: (IMB Jena, Germany) Links to WWW RNA sites and resources. Lots of very cool images. [http://www.rna.uni-jena.de/rna.php]

CHAPTER 3
Cells and Cellular Organization

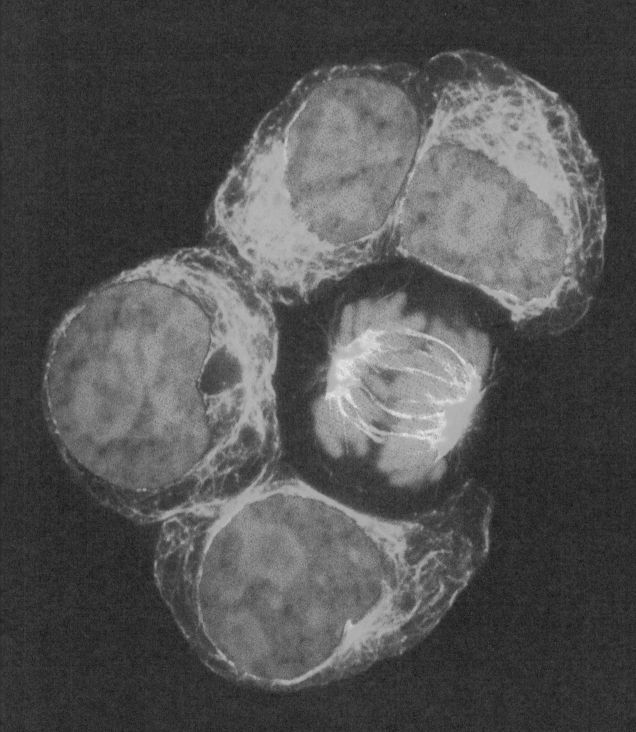

Chapter Opener

Leukosis cell line labeled with fluorescent dyes. One cell in division illustrates an aspect of the Cell Theory: all cells arise from existing cells. The other part of the cell theory states that all living things are composed of cells. Your own body consists of over 60 trillion (60,000,000,000,000) cells.

Objectives

- List the basic physical and biological requirements for life.
- Discuss the main parts of the Cell Theory.
- Describe cellular features and their functions: plasma membrane, cytoplasm, nucleus, nucleoid, chloroplast, mitochondrion, and cytoskeleton.
- Be able to use and convert between units we employ to measure cells and cellular structures: micrometer, nanometer, and Ångstrom.
- Describe the structure of heterotrophic and autotrophic prokaryotic cells.
- Describe the types of microscopes and information scientists obtain using each one.

Introduction

Life, as we have seen, is a biochemical mélange: some DNA, a little RNA, 3 cups of glucose, 5 teaspoons of ATP, and some lipids. Life exists on Earth because water and the chemistry of life is here, and has been for well over three *billion* years. One of biology's major unifying theories, the Cell Theory, states that all cells arise from pre-existing cells. Every cell in your body formed by cell division from cells derived from that first cell formed from your parent's sperm and egg. What you can produce, how you live, reproduce, and carry on the characteristics of life discussed in Chapter 1 all depend on your cells!

3.1   Types of Cells: Prokaryote vs. Eukaryote

One of the characteristics of life is the acquisition and use of energy. There are several methods by which living things do this. Humans (and other animals) obtain their nutrition from another organism. If an organism obtains its energy/food from another it is a heterotroph. All animals, all fungi, many bacteria, and many protistans are heterotrophs. There are different types of heterotrophy (shown in Figure 3.1): carnivores, like a cheetah, shark, or lion, eat only other animals; herbivores, like a gazelle, panda, or deer, eat only plants, while omnivores, like a human, bear, or rat, eat both plants and animals.

An autotroph is an organism that makes its own food by converting energy from an inorganic source into energy in the form of an organic molecule such as **glucose**. Photosynthesis is the conversion of sunlight energy into the carbon-to-carbon covalent bonds of a carbohydrate, the

FIGURE 3.1 Modes of nutrition. A. Carnivore, Great white shark (*Carcharodon carcharias*) breaching in an attack on a seal, South Africa; B. Herbivore, young panda with bamboo leaves in mouth; C. Omnivore, bear eating a leaping salmon at Katmai National Park, Alaska.

process by which the vast majority of autotrophs obtain their energy. Most organisms obtain their energy either directly or indirectly from photosynthetic autotrophs such as plants, algae, or cyanobacteria. Chemosynthesis is the capture of energy released by certain inorganic chemical reactions. At mid-ocean ridges, scientists have discovered black smokers, vents on the ocean floor that release chemicals into the water. These chemical reactions could have powered early ecosystems prior to the development of an ozone layer that would have permitted life to occupy the shallower parts of the ocean.

3.2 Cell Size and Shape: A Question of Scale

The size and shape of different cell types varies. The neurons that comprise the human nervous system are much longer (some stretching more than one meter in length) than they are wide. Parenchyma, a common type of plant cell, and erythrocytes, red blood cells in our bodies, are equidimensional. Some cells are encased in a rigid wall, which constrains their shape, while others have a flexible cell membrane (and no rigid cell wall).

The size of cells is also related to their functions. Eggs can be very large and are often the largest cells (in terms of volume) that an organism produces (Figure 3.2). There is a relationship between the volume of a cell and its surface area. The larger the volume of the cell, the less surface area exists for exchange of materials. This is known as the surface to volume problem. Actively metabolizing cells must constantly exchange materials across their cell membrane. If a cell is too large, its surface area for these exchanges is limited relative to the cell's volume. Soon after fertilization, the large single-celled zygote undergoes a series of cell divisions to produce a ball of cells that still has the same volume, but which is made of cells that are smaller and that have a better ratio of surface to volume.

Some parts of biology can be viewed with the unaided eye, such as a pigeon, chicken egg, or great tree (Figure 3.2). Microscopes of various types must be used to view the smaller structures inside that bird or tree. The unaided human eye can distinguish objects down to 0.5 mm. Most cells are smaller than the unaided eye can resolve.

Scientists employ the metric system to measure the size and volume of specimens. The basic unit of length is the meter (slightly over 1 yard). Prefixes are added to the "meter" to indicate multiple meters (kilometer) or fractional meters (millimeter). Units we use to measure cells and cellular structures are shown in Table 3.1.

3.3   Microscopes

You have probably seen microscopes in movies: they show that we are in a science lab. Microscopes are important tools for studying cellular structures. Pictures taken with a microscope are referred to as micrographs. There are many different types of microscopes. These include the light microscopes (dissecting, compound), and electron microscopes (transmission and scanning) shown in Figure 3.3. The various types of light microscopes differ in the way they treat the light passing through the microscope. Fluorescence microscopy relies on various dyes added to the specimen, which will fluoresce and emit color when subjected to light of specific wavelengths.

3.3.1   The Light Microscope

Light microscope focus light through glass (or plastic) lenses. The quality of the lenses plays a very large role in the images seen through a light microscope. The compound microscope (Figure 3.3A) has a rotating objective containing a number of lenses that can be moved into place. The specimen must be thin enough to allow light to pass through it. Live material, or preserved and stained specimens, may be viewed with the light microscope. The other type of light microscope is the dissecting microscope. In this case light can be bounced off the specimen, or in some cases, passed through the specimen.

Magnification and resolution are terms used frequently in the study of cell biology. Magnification is a ratio of the enlargement (or reduction) of an image, usually expressed as X1, X1/2, X430, X1000, and so on. Another way to show magnification is the use of a scale bar, if a scale bar indicates that length of the bar is 10 μm and that bar on the picture is 10 mm long, we

Item	Size
Giant Redwood (*Sequoia*)  Shutterstock/Rob van Esch	99 m
Humpback Whale  Shutterstock/idreamphoto	16 m
Person  Shutterstock/Halfpoint	1.5 m
Pigeon  Shutterstock/panbazil	44.5 cm
Chicken and the Egg  Shutterstock/Tsekhmister	57 mm

Item	Size
Frog Eggs 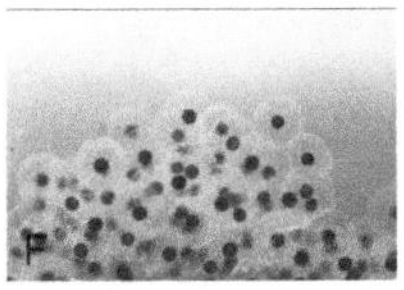 Shutterstock/BMJ	3 mm
Eukaryotic Sperm and Egg 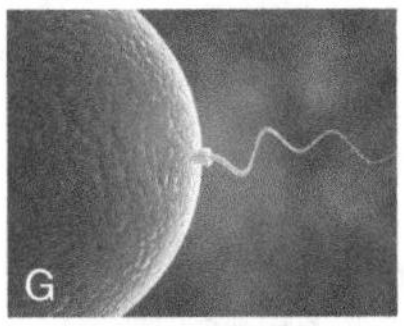 Shutterstock/Jezper	Egg: 100 μm Sperm: head 5 × 3 μm, tail 50 μm
E. coli Bacterial Cells 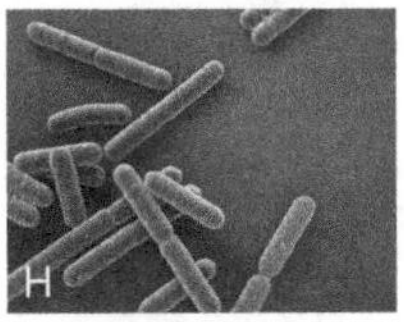 Shutterstock/dreamerb	1 μm
Ebola Virus 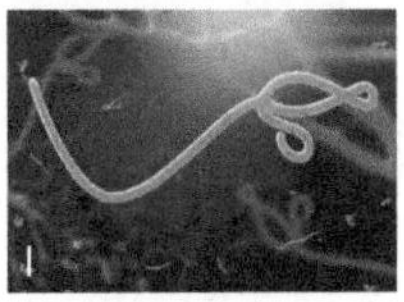 Shutterstock/jaddingt	80 nm
Hemoglobin Macromolecule 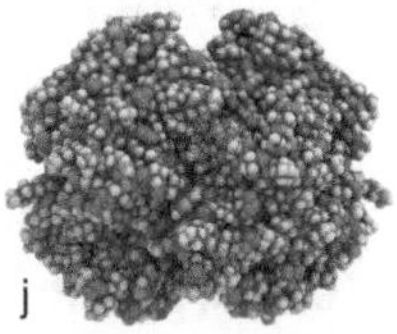 Shutterstock/molekuul.be	10 nm
Oxygen Atom 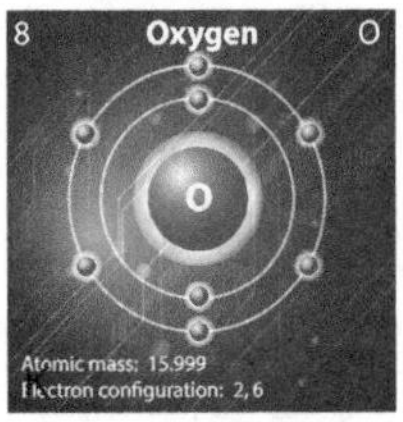 Shutterstock/BlueRingMedia	Less than 1 nm

FIGURE 3.2 Sizes of viruses, cells, and organisms.

TABLE 3.1 Units of measure in biology

Unit	Normal notation	Scientific notation
Meter (m)	1 m = 100 cm 1 m = 1,000 mm 1 m = 1,000,000 μm 1 m = 1,000,000,000 nm	1 m = 10^0 m 1 m = 10^2 cm 1 m = 10^3 mm 1 m = 10^6 μm 1 m = 10^9 nm
Centimeter (cm)	1 cm = 1/100 m 1 cm = 10 mm 1 cm = 10,000 μm 1 cm = 10,000,000 nm	1 cm = 10^{-2} m 1 cm = 10^1 mm 1 cm = 10^3 μm 1 cm = 10^6 nm
Millimeter (mm)	1 mm = 1/1000 m 1 mm = 1/10 cm 1 mm = 1000 μm 1 mm = 1,000,000 nm	1 mm = 10^{-3} m 1 mm = 10^{-1} cm 1 mm = 10^3 μm 1 mm = 10^6 nm
Micrometer (μm)	1 μm = 1/1,000,000 m 1 μm = 1/10,000 cm 1 μm = 1/1000 mm 1 μm = 1000 nm	1 μm = 10^{-6} m 1 μm = 10^{-4} cm 1 μm = 10^{-3} mm 1 μm = 10^3 nm
Nanometer (nm)	1 nm = 1/1,000,000,000 m 1 nm = 1/10,000,000 cm 1 nm = 1/1,000,000 mm 1 nm = 1/1000 μm	1 nm = 10^{-9} m 1 nm = 10^{-7} cm 1 nm = 10^{-7} mm 1 nm = 10^{-3} μm

can calculate the magnification of the image as 1000×. If the light passes through two lenses (an objective lens and an ocular lens), we multiply the 10× ocular value by the value of the objective lens (say it is 4X): 10 × 4 = 40, or 40X magnification.

Resolution is the capability to distinguish between two points. Generally, resolution increases with magnification, although there does come a point of diminishing returns where as you increase magnification you gain no added resolution. What microscopes do is to bring small objects "closer" to the observer by increasing the magnification of the sample. Objects such as a human hair appear (and feel) smooth when viewed with the unaided eye. However, put a hair under a microscope and it takes on quite a different look due to the increased resolution of the microscope.

Light microscopes remain the most commonly used microscopes today. The best resolution obtainable by a light microscope is 0.2 μm. Magnification of light microscopes is generally limited by the properties of the glass used to make lenses and the physical properties of the light sources. The generally accepted maximum magnifications in biological uses are between 1000X and 1250X.

3.3.2   Electron Microscopes

Electron microscopes are more rarely encountered by beginning biology students. There are two basic types of electron microscope: the transmission electron microscope (TEM, Figure 3.3C), and the scanning electron microscope (SEM, Figure 3.3B). Rather than using

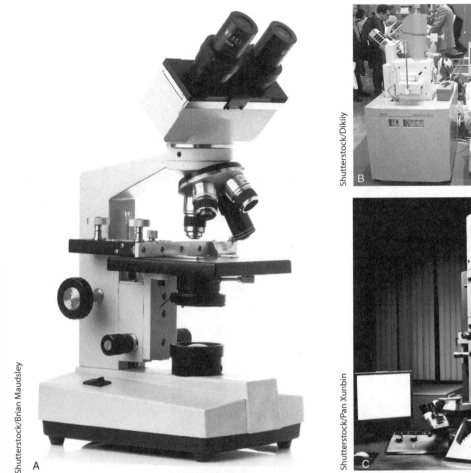

Shutterstock/Brian Maudsley

Shutterstock/Dikiiy

Shutterstock/Pan Xunbin

FIGURE 3.3 Microscopes. A. Light microscope; B. Scanning electron microscope; C. Transmission electron microscope.

light as an imaging source, a high-energy beam of electrons is focused through electromagnetic lenses (instead of glass in the light microscope). The increased resolution of electron microscopes results from the shorter wavelength of the electron beam. The TEM has a theoretical resolution limit of 0.2 nm. The magnifications achieved by TEMs are commonly over 100,000×X, depending on the nature of the sample and the operating condition of the TEM. Specimens for use with most TEMs are sliced to thicknesses of a few hundred nanometers, placed inside the specimen chamber of the microscope, and bombarded with the electron beam. This produces images of the inside of cells and other specimens. The SEM uses different methods of electron capture and displays images on high-resolution video monitors. The resolution and magnification of the SEM are less than that of the TEM, although still a great deal better than the light microscope. Figure 3.4 illustrates red blood cells as seen in each of the three types of microscope.

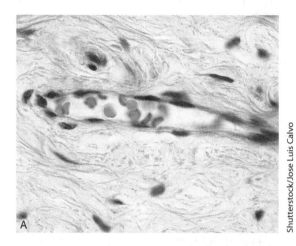

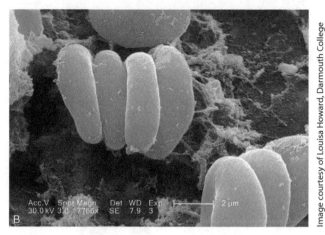

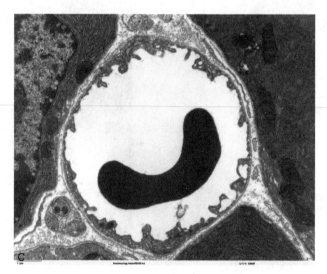

FIGURE 3.4 Red blood cells as seen through various microscopes. A. Light micrograph of a capillary showing red blood cells; B. Red blood cells seen in a colorized scanning electron micrograph, image from CDC/Janice Haney Carr; C. Red blood cell in a tiny capillary in a pancreas. Image courtesy of Louisa Howard, Dartmouth College.

3.4   The Cell

The **cell theory** proposed by Virchow during the 1800s is one of the foundations of modern biology discussed in Chapter 1. Its major tenets include that: 1) all living things are composed of one or more cells; 2) the chemical reactions of living cells take place within cells; 3) all cells originate from pre-existing cells; and 4) that cells contain hereditary information that is passed from one generation to another.

There are two major types of cellular life: prokaryotic and eukaryotic. The domain system of classification recognizes this major split, with two domains of prokaryotic cells, the Archaea and Bacteria, and one domain for eukaryotic cells, the Eukarya. **Prokaryotes** are among the most ancient and primitive forms of life on Earth. Prokaryotic organisms lack membrane-bound organelles, although some photosynthetic bacteria exhibit internal membrane lamellae associated with the photosynthesis.

Eukaryotic cells (Figures 3.5C, and 3.6; Table 3.2) contain membrane-bound organelles such as a nucleus, mitochondria, and chloroplasts. These organelles act as compartments within which specialized chemical reactions can be carried out. Eukaryotic cells are normally much larger than prokaryote cells, and have many linear chromosomes as opposed to the single circular chromosome that all prokaryotes possess (Table 3.2). Eukaryotic cells are much less ancient than prokaryotes. Most fossil and biochemical studies suggest the origin of eukaryotic cells about no older than 2 billion years ago.

Despite their great differences (Table 3.2), all cells have certain common structures. The first of these is the cell membrane (also known as the plasma membrane). The structure of the membrane was deciphered by Singer and Nicholson (1972). The membrane not only separates the inner parts of the cell from the outer environment, but it acts also as a selectively permeable barrier to allow certain chemicals, such as water, oxygen, and carbon dioxide, to pass and others to not pass. In multicellular organisms with immune systems, such as humans and cats, certain chemicals on the membrane surface act as identification markers to facilitate the immune system's role in the recognition of self. These recognition chemicals (trademarks, or labels if you wish) identify cells belonging to the individual to the immune system cells. These labels are also known as antigens. Antibodies are chemicals (Y-shaped proteins) produced by an animal's immune system in response to a specific antigen. This is the basis of immunity and vaccination.

Hereditary material (both DNA and RNA) is needed for a cell to be able to replicate and/or reproduce. Cells use DNA as the molecule to store the instructions to make a new cell. Viruses and viroids sometimes employ RNA as their hereditary material. Retroviruses include human immunodeficiency virus (HIV, the cause of AIDS) and feline leukemia virus (the only retrovirus for which a successful vaccine has been developed).

Viroids are naked pieces of RNA that lack cytoplasm, membranes, and so forth. They are parasites of some plants. Prokaryotic DNA is organized as a circular chromosome contained in an area known as a nucleoid. Eukaryotic DNA is organized in linear structures, the eukaryotic chromosomes, which are associations of DNA and histone proteins confined by a nuclear envelope, an area known as the cell nucleus.

Organelles are formed bodies within the cytoplasm that perform certain functions (Table 3.3). Protein synthesis occurs at ribosomes. Ribosomes are not membrane-bound organelles occurring in all cells, although there are differences between the size of a ribosome's subunits. Membrane-bound organelles occur only in eukaryotic cells. They will be discussed in detail later in this chapter. Eukaryotic cells are generally larger than prokaryotic cells. Internal complexity is greater in eukaryotes, with their compartmentalized membrane-bound organelles, than in prokaryotes. Some prokaryotes, such as *Anabaena azollae*, and *Prochloron*, have internal membranes associated with photosynthetic pigments.

The cell wall is a structure surrounding the cell membrane. Prokaryote and eukaryote cell walls differ in their structure and chemical composition. Plant cells have cellulose in their cell walls. Bacterial cell walls contain peptidoglycan. Cell walls of archaeans have a chemical similar, but not identical, to peptidoglycan.

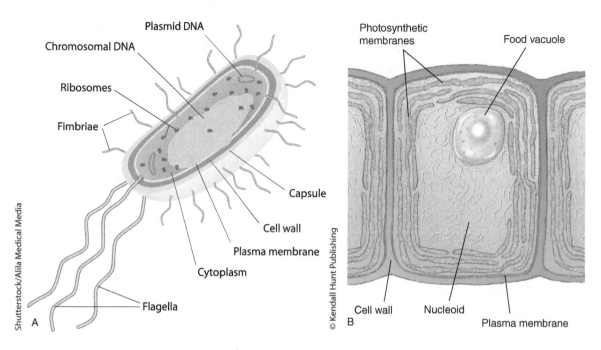

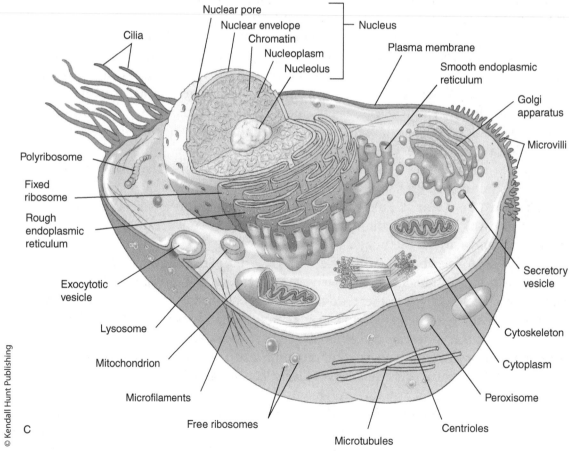

FIGURE 3.5 (Continued)

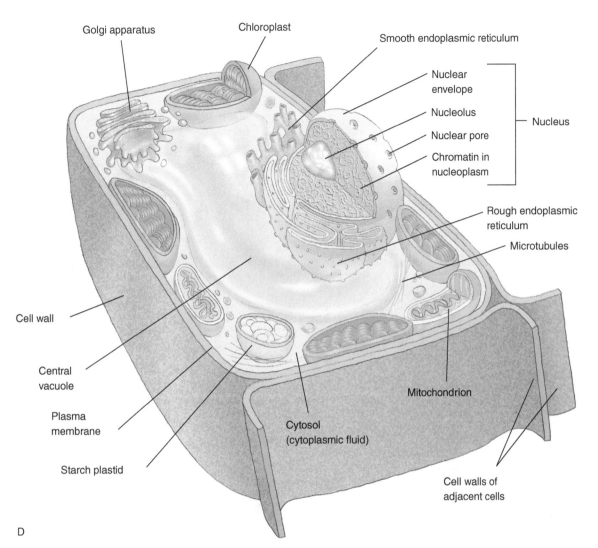

Golgi apparatus   Chloroplast   Smooth endoplasmic reticulum

Nuclear envelope
Nucleolus
Nuclear pore
Chromatin in nucleoplasm
Nucleus

Rough endoplasmic reticulum

Microtubules

Cell wall

Central vacuole

Plasma membrane

Starch plastid

Mitochondrion

Cytosol (cytoplasmic fluid)

Cell walls of adjacent cells

D

© Kendall Hunt Publishing

FIGURE 3.5 Cells. A. Generalized bacterial cell; B. Cyanobacteria cell diagram; C. Generalized animal cell; D. Generalized plant cell.

The plasma membrane (Figure 3.6F) forms a selectively permeable barrier surrounding every cell. The membrane allows some molecules to cross while confining most organically produced chemicals inside the cell. Electron microscopic examinations of cell membranes during the early 1970s led to the development of the fluid mosaic model. The most common molecule in the cell membrane is the phospholipid, which has a polar (hydrophilic) head and two nonpolar (hydrophobic) tails. These phospholipids are aligned tail to tail so the nonpolar areas form a hydrophobic region between the hydrophilic heads on the inner and outer surfaces of the membrane. The phospholipids of members of the Archaea differ slightly from those in Bacteria and Eukarya. Proteins, carbohydrates and lipids also occur in the membrane. Chapter 4 explores the structure of the membrane in greater detail.

TABLE 3.2 Comparison of prokaryotic and eukaryotic cells

Feature	Bacteria	Archaea	Eukaryotic Cells
Size range in micrometers (μm)	1–10	1–2	10 to over 100
Membrane-bound organelles	No	No	Yes
Chromosome(s)	A single, circular chromosome	A single, circular chromosome	Between 4 and 212 linear chromosomes
Age of oldest fossils	Over 3.5 billion years from cellular fossils	Chemical fossils suggest Archaea from 3.8 billion years	2 billion years
Cell division	Binary fission	Binary Fission	Mitosis (asexual) and/or meiosis (sexual); Binary fission in primitive eukaryotes
Mode of nutrition	Heterotrophic, Photosynthetic, or Chemosynthetic	Heterotrophic	Heterotrophic or Photosynthetic
Cell wall structure*	Peptidoglycan	Do not use peptidoglycan, some use a similar chemical, no cellulose or chitin	Cellulose (plants, algae), Chitin (fungi)
Shape	Bacillus (rod) Coccus (sphere) Spirillum (spiral)	Bacterial shapes plus others	Variable from spheres to rectangles and squares
*Not all eukaryotes have a cell wall.			

The contents of the cell make up the protoplasm, and are further subdivided into cytoplasm (all of the protoplasm inside the cell membrane except the contents of the nucleus) and nucleoplasm (all of the material, plasma, and DNA within the cell's nucleus).

Some cells have a cell wall outside their cell membrane. The cell wall provides strength and support to the cells. Bacteria, Archaea, plants, fungi, and some protists (such as the algae) have cell walls. Animals and some other eukaryotes lack cell walls. Cells in those groups have only a plasma membrane to uphold the structural integrity of the cell. Plant cells do have cell walls (Figure 3.7), and often have a variety of chemicals incorporated into those walls. Cellulose is the most common chemical in the plant primary cell wall. Some plant cells also have lignin and other chemicals embedded in a secondary wall. Fungi, bacteria, and many protists have cell walls although those walls do not contain cellulose, but instead have other chemicals, such as peptidoglycan (bacteria) or chitin (fungi).

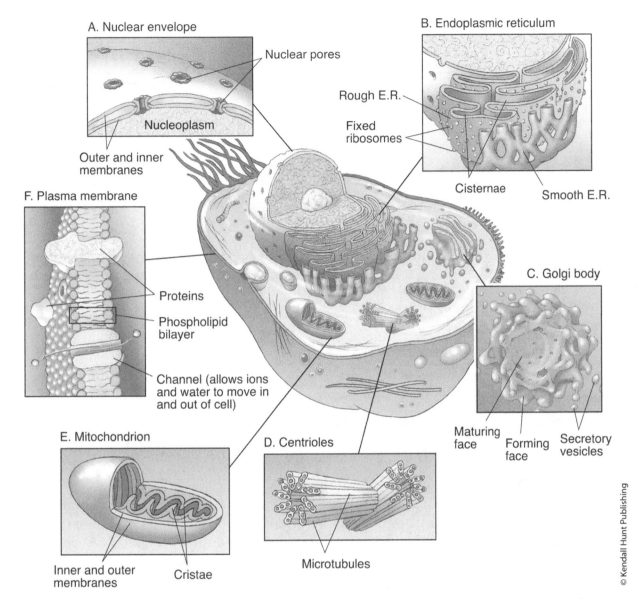

A. Nuclear envelope

Nuclear pores

Nucleoplasm

Outer and inner membranes

B. Endoplasmic reticulum

Rough E.R.

Fixed ribosomes

Cisternae

Smooth E.R.

F. Plasma membrane

Proteins

Phospholipid bilayer

Channel (allows ions and water to move in and out of cell)

C. Golgi body

Maturing face

Forming face

Secretory vesicles

E. Mitochondrion

Inner and outer membranes

Cristae

D. Centrioles

Microtubules

FIGURE 3.6 Exploded view of an animal cell. A. Nuclear envelope; B. Endoplasmic reticulum; C. Golgi body; D. Centrioles; E. Mitochondrion; F. Plasma membrane.

3.4.1 The Nucleus: Control Center of the Cell

The nucleus (Figures 3.6A and 3.8) occurs only in eukaryotic cells. Most of the eukaryotic cell's DNA occupies the nucleus. The German scientist Joachim Hämmerling (1901–1980) experimented with the green alga *Acetabularia* and showed the cell nucleus controlled the shape and features of the cell. A cell's nucleus acts as the library or control center of the cell. Deoxyribonucleic acid (DNA) is the physical carrier of inheritance. Most of the cell's DNA occurs inside the nucleus. Plastids such as mitochondria and chloroplasts also contain a small amount of DNA. The nucleolus is an area of the nucleus where ribosome components form. Ribosomes consist

TABLE 3.3 Cell components and their functions

Organelle	Function(s)	Prokaryote	Eukaryote
Plasma membrane	Cell integrity, selectively permeable barrier	X	X
Cell Wall	Cell integrity	X	X (some)
Nucleoid	Location of DNA in cytoplasm	X	0
Nucleus	Location of DNA, ribosome synthesis, surrounded by membrane with nuclear pores	0	X
Mitochondrion	Powerhouse of the cell, ATP generation	0	X
Chloroplast	Photosynthesis and carbohydrate synthesis	0	X
Ribosome	Protein synthesis	X	X
Golgi Apparatus	Packaging	0	X
Endoplasmic reticulum (ER)	Protein synthesis (Rough ER) Lipid synthesis (Smooth ER)	0	X
Vacuoles/Vesicles	Storage	0	X
Flagella	Cell movement	X	X
Cilia	Cell movement	0	X
Pseudopodia	Cell movement	0	X
Cytoskeleton	Organization of cytoplasmic structures	0	X
Presence indicated by an X, absence by a 0.			

of RNA and proteins. The ribosomal components move to the cytoplasm where the ribosome aids in the assembly of proteins. The nuclear envelope is a double-membrane structure separating the nuclear contents from the cytoplasm. Numerous nuclear pores (Figure 3.6A) perforate the nuclear envelope. These pores allow RNA and other chemicals to pass into and out of the nucleus. However, the nuclear pores allow DNA to only enter the nucleus, not to leave.

3.4.2 Cytoplasm: The "Stuff" of the Cell

The cytoplasm was defined earlier as the material between the cell membrane and the nuclear envelope. Fibrous proteins that occur in the cytoplasm, referred to as the cytoskeleton, maintain the shape of the cell as well as anchoring organelles, moving the cell, and controlling internal movement of structures. Microtubules function in cell division and serve as a "temporary scaffolding" for other organelles. Actin filaments are thin threads that function in cell division and cell motility. Intermediate filaments are between the size of the microtubules and the actin filaments. The cytoskeleton can be seen in Figures 3.6D, 3.8A, and 3.9.

Cells are capable of a variety of movement in response to environmental stimulus. Cell movement is both internal (referred to as cytoplasmic streaming commonly observed in *Elodea* cells during labs) and external (referred to as motility, commonly observed in labs observing *Paramecium*

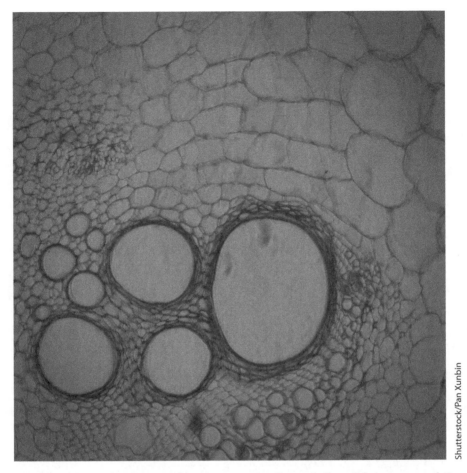

Shutterstock/Pan Xunbin

FIGURE 3.7 Cell walls in cells of pumpkin stem, note the relative thicknesses of these cells.

and *Amoeba*). The internal organization and movements of organelles are controlled by the cell's cytoskeleton (Figure 3.9). The cytoskeleton also helps anchor organelles like mitochondria and the endoplasmic reticulum in place (Figure 3.9), as well as providing the shape for the cell. Cells that have cell walls have the wall to define their shape. The cytoskeleton must do this for cells lacking cell walls. Cell motility is accomplished by special organelles for locomotion (Figure 3.10).

Cilia and flagella are two of the more common organelles used for cell motility. They have a similar structure, except for their length, with cilia being much shorter, and occurring in greater numbers on a cell. Both organelles in eukaryotic cells have a characteristic 9 + 2 arrangement of microtubules (Figure 3.10D).

Flagella (Figure 3.10) work as whips pulling (as in the alga *Chlamydomonas* or *Halosphaera*) or pushing (as in dinoflagellates, a group of single-celled algae) the organism through the water. Cilia work like oars on a Viking long ship. Pseudopodia are features used by many animal and protozoan cells, such as *Amoeba, Chaos (Pelomyxa)*, and human leukocytes (white blood cells) for movement. Pseudopodia can also function in the feeding of these cells by allowing them to engulf their prey. Pseudopodia are not structures as such but rather are associated with actin filaments that constantly being deposited and then removed as needed near the moving edge of the cell.

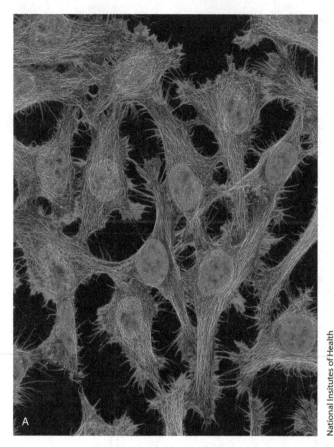
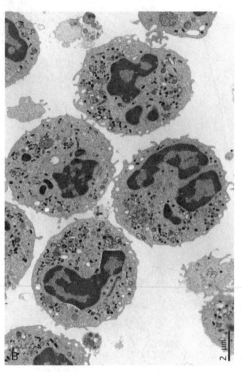

National Insitutes of Health

Shutterstock/Dlumen

2 µm

FIGURE 3.8 Nucleus. A. Picture of HeLa-II cells stained to show the nucleus, image courtesy of the National Institutes of Health (NIH); B. Transmission electron micrograph of a group of human neutrophils, showing the dark stained lobes of each cell's nucleus.

3.4.3   Vacuoles and Vesicles: Storage Structures

Vacuoles are single-membrane organelles that are essentially part of the outside that is located within the cell. Many organisms use vacuoles as storage areas for water, starch, fats, and other molecules. Vesicles are much smaller than vacuoles and function in the transport of molecules within the cell as well as transport of these molecules to the outside of the cell.

While many plant cells have large vacuoles (Figure 3.5D), only a few animal cells have these. Chief among these is the adipose, or fat cells (Figure 3.11A, B). Lipids and fats are stored in the vacuole, which can enlarge as more material is stored. When a person loses weight, the vacuoles shrink but do not disappear. This explains the unfortunate situation where people who lose weight often gain it back on much faster than they lost it.

Contractile vacuoles (Figure 3.11C) occur in many freshwater protists like *Amoeba* and *Paramecium*. In Chapter 4, we will examine the details of these structures and their function. For now, we recognize one or more of these vacuoles that act as a pump to expel excess water from the cell.

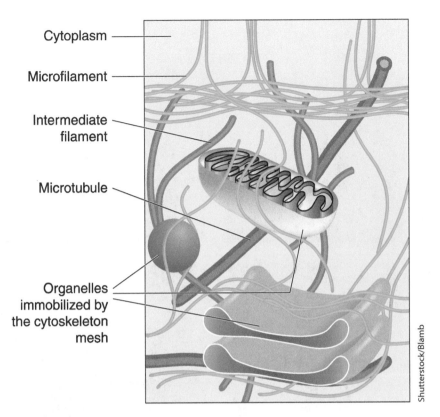

Cytoplasm

Microfilament

Intermediate filament

Microtubule

Organelles immobilized by the cytoskeleton mesh

Shutterstock/Blamb

FIGURE 3.9 The cytoskeleton.

3.4.4 Ribosomes: The Sites of Protein Synthesis

Ribosomes are the cellular structures where protein synthesis occurs. They are not membrane-bound and thus occur in both prokaryotes and eukaryotes. Eukaryotic ribosomes are slightly larger than prokaryotic ones. Structurally, the ribosome consists of a small and larger subunit. Biochemically, the ribosome consists of ribosomal RNA (rRNA) and 50 structural proteins. Often ribosomes cluster on the endoplasmic reticulum, in which case they resemble a series of factories adjoining a railroad line or highway.

3.4.5 Endoplasmic Reticulum: Protein and Lipid Synthesis

The endoplasmic reticulum (Figures 3.6B and 3.12) is a mesh of interconnected in-folded membranes that function in protein synthesis, lipid synthesis, and transport. The infolding of membrane material increases the surface area without a corresponding increase in volume. Rough endoplasmic reticulum (Figure 3.12A, B) exhibits a rough appearance when seen with the TEM. This results from the presence of numerous ribosomes that occur its edges. Rough endoplasmic reticulum connects to the nuclear envelope through which the messenger RNA (mRNA) that acts as the blueprint for proteins travels to the ribosomes. Smooth endoplasmic

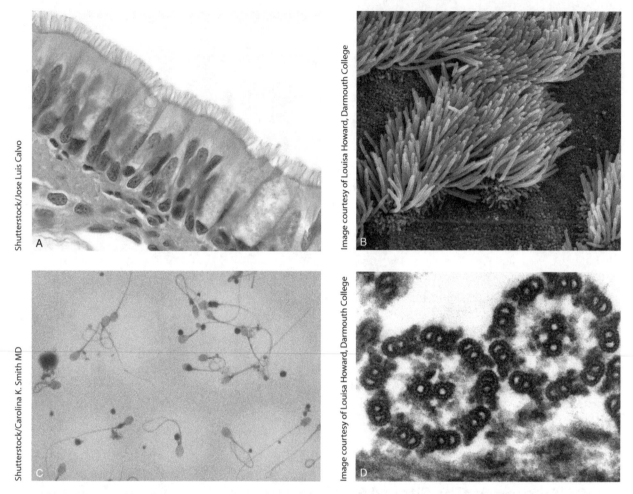

FIGURE 3.10 Cilia, flagella, and pseudopodia. A. Ciliated pseudostratified columnar epithelium of the trachea. Light microscope micrograph. These cilia trap dust, pollen, and bacteria and prevent contamination deeper in the lungs; B. Scanning electron micrograph of lung trachea epithelium. There are both ciliated and on-ciliated cells in this epithelium. Note the difference in size between the cilia and the microvilli (on nonciliated cell surface); image courtesy of Louisa Howard, Dartmouth College; C. Light micrograph of a prepared slide of human sperm illustrating flagellum; D. Microtubules as seen in a transmission electron micrograph.

reticulum (Figure 3.12C) lacks the ribosomes characteristic of Rough ER and is thought to be involved in transport and a variety of other functions, including lipid synthesis and detoxification of poisons.

3.4.6   Golgi Complexes and Lysosomes: Packaging and Packages

Golgi complexes (Figures 3.6C and 3.13) are flattened stacks of membrane sacs. Italian researcher Camillo Golgi (1843–1926) used the light microscope to discover these structures in

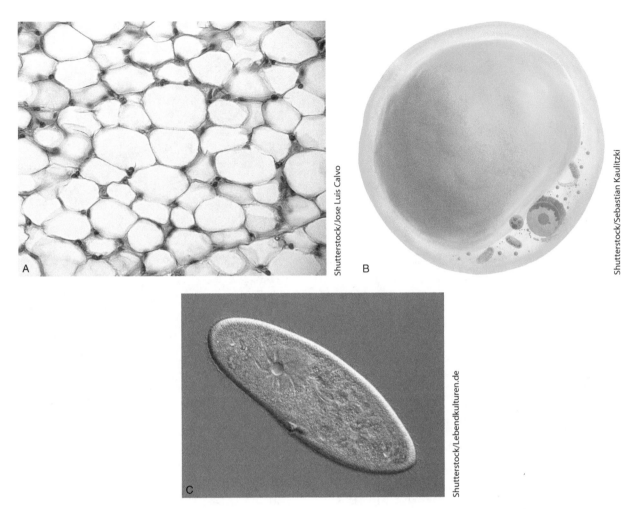

FIGURE 3.11 Vacuoles. A. Light micrograph of white adipose tissue stained with hematoxylin and eosin. Adipocytes (fat cells) contain a large lipid droplet; B. Rendering of a fat cell illustrating the large central vacuole in the fat cell; C. *Paramecium caudatum* differential interference contrast, focus to contractile vacuole, cilia, food vacuoles, crystals.

1897, although their precise function was not deciphered until the mid-20th century. The Golgi complexes function as a packaging plant, modifying vesicles produced by the rough endoplasmic reticulum for export or for use within the cell. New plasma membrane material is assembled in various membrane stacks of the Golgi. Golgi complexes occur in all eukaryotic cells; however, they are larger in plant cells and were named dictyosomes.

In a way the Golgi complex is like the rack of plastic bags at the grocery store checkout. Something gets placed into a vesicle that pinches off of the forming face (Trans in Figure 3.13B) of the Golgi complex. You place bread, milk, and PBR into a plastic bag at the grocery store. The analogy is somewhat imperfect as chemical changes can occur within the Golgi complex. Fortunately, your milk and PBR do not react (UGH!) in the bag as you leave the store!

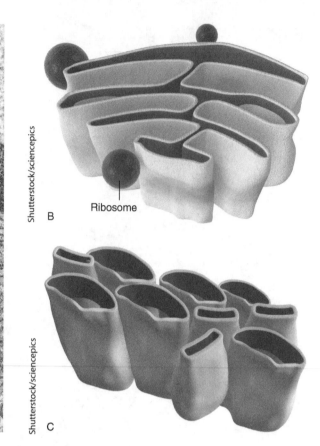

Image courtesy of Louisa Howard, Darmouth College

Shutterstock/sciencepics

Ribosome

B

Shutterstock/sciencepics

C

FIGURE 3.12 Endoplasmic reticulum. A. Transmission electron micrograph of rough endo-plasmic reticulum (with ribosomes) and mitochondria in pancreatic cells from a mouse; image courtesy Louisa Howard, Dartmouth College; B. Diagram of rough endoplasmic reticulum (ribosomes removed) showing a three-dimensional perspective of the folded membranes; C. Diagram of the smooth endoplasmic reticulum showing the tubular look of this type of reticulum.

Lysosomes are relatively large vesicles formed by the Golgi complex. They may contain enzymes that could destroy the cell if they were not confined within a lysosome. The lysosomes, Golgi, and endoplasmic reticulum comprise the endomembrane system that functions in pro-duction of cell materials for export (Figure 3.13B).

3.4.7   Mitochondria: The Cell's Power Station

Mitochondria (Figure 3.14) are small, membrane-bounded organelles in eukaryotic cells that act as the powerhouse of the cell by converting the energy locked in sugar molecules into energy temporarily stored in ATP. Mitochondria are surrounded by two membranes, contain their own DNA (termed mtDNA, and possess small, prokaryotic-type ribosomes. They are unlike any other eukaryotic organelle except the chloroplast in having their own

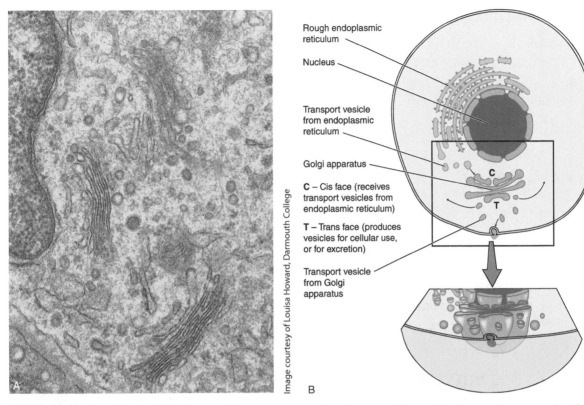

Image courtesy of Louisa Howard, Darmouth College

Rough endoplasmic reticulum

Nucleus

Transport vesicle from endoplasmic reticulum

Golgi apparatus

C – Cis face (receives transport vesicles from endoplasmic reticulum)

T – Trans face (produces vesicles for cellular use, or for excretion)

Transport vesicle from Golgi apparatus

Shutterstock/Blamb

FIGURE 3.13 Golgi. A. Golgi complexes as seen in a transmission electron micrograph of mouse pancreas cell; B. Functional and spatial relationships between the endoplasmic reticulum, Golgi, and vesicles.

DNA. The endosymbiosis hypothesis of Lynn Margulis proposes modern mitochondria descended from bacteria incorporated into primitive eukaryotic cells more than 700 million years ago (perhaps even as far back as 1.5 billion). The outer membrane of the mitochondrion derives from the original host, while the inner mitochondrial membrane derives from the cell membrane of the original symbiont. The inner membrane infolding produces the cristae, greatly increasing the surface area of the cristae for the chemicals that produce ATP.

Mitochondria function as the sites of energy release (after sugar has begun its breakdown by the process of glycolysis in the cytoplasm) and ATP formation. The inner mitochondrial membrane infolds to produce a number of cristae that are the surfaces on which the ATP generating molecules reside. Cristae extend into a fluid material known as the matrix. Mitochondrial DNA and mitochondrial ribosomes are located within the matrix.

A 1987 study claimed to trace the mitochondrial decent of all living humans to a woman who probably lived in eastern Africa between 99,000 and 180,000 years ago. This assertion remains controversial due to some of the assumptions and methods the scientists used in their work. However, this does agree with fossil evidence that points to Africa as the cradle of humanity.

3.4.8   Plastids: Photosynthesis and Storage

Plastids are membrane-bound organelles that only occur in plants and other photosynthetic eukaryotes. There are a variety of plastids, all of which are involved in some way with pigments or the storage of sugar. Leukoplasts usually store excess sugar produced by the plant as the polysaccharide starch. Occasionally protein or oils will also be stored in a leukoplast. Chromoplasts are plastids that store pigments that cause the bright colors of flowers and fruits. Red peppers are red because their outer covering has cells packed with red pigment-containing chromoplasts, while a yellow sunflower is yellow because its petals are likewise crammed with yellow pigment-containing chromoplasts.

Chloroplasts (Figure 3.15) are the membrane bound organelles in which photosynthesis occurs. Chlorophyll, the green pigment essential for photosynthesis, and associated accessory pigments (such as carotenes) are arranged into collections of pigment molecules known as photosystems. These photosystems are embedded in membranous sacs, thylakoids (collectively a stack of thylakoids are a granum [plural = grana]) floating in a fluid termed the stroma. Chloroplasts, like mitochondria, contain a small amount of DNA, which is located in their stroma. Chloroplasts also contain many different types of accessory pigments, depending on the taxonomic group of the organism being observed.

3.5   Endosymbiosis: The Origins of Eukaryote Cells

Prokaryotes never did develop a multicellular organization, but instead are either single celled or arranged in filaments (or strings) of cells. The earliest eukaryotic cells were unicellular, although later evolving forms exhibited filaments, colonies, and finally multicellularity. The evolution of multicellular organization allowed eukaryotes to develop specialized areas of their bodies, a

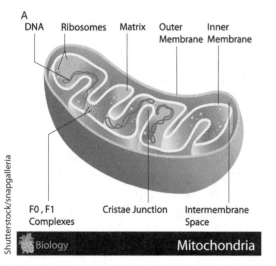
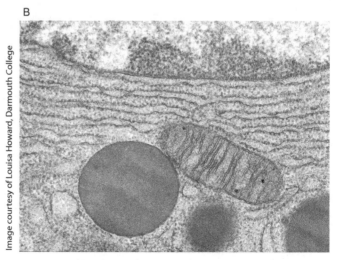

FIGURE 3.14 Mitochondrion. A. Diagram representing a mitochondrion and its structure; B. Transmission electron micrograph of a mouse pancreas cell showing numerous cristae inside, and the double membrane surrounding, a mitochondrion; image courtesy of Louisa Howard, Dartmouth College.

Chloroplast Anatomy

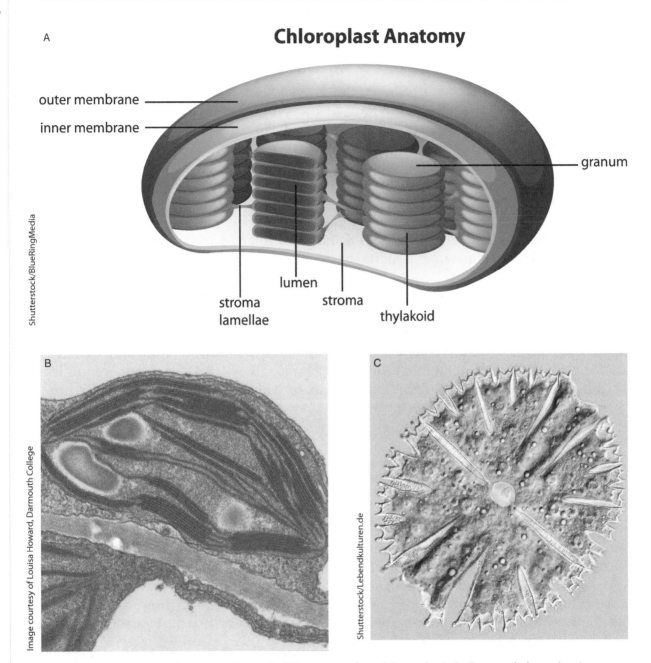

FIGURE 3.15 Chloroplast structure. A. Diagram of a chloroplast; B. Transmission electron micrograph of a chloroplast from a *Coleus* plant; image courtesy of Louisa Howard, Dartmouth College; C. Light micrograph of the chloroplasts in the green alga *Micrasterias*.

division of labor, allowing specialization of cells to carry out certain functions. Animals eventually evolved muscle fibers specialized to contract the body, and neurons, cells that transmit nerve messages. The oldest prokaryote cellular fossils occur in rocks approximately 3.5 billion years old. Eukaryotic unicellular fossils occur in rocks dated to approximately 1.8 billion years old. Certain chemical fossils suggest a possibly even earlier origin, but that data is not conclusive.

Multicellular fossils, purportedly of animals, have been recovered from 750 million year old rocks in various parts of the world.

American biologist Lynn Margulis (1938–2011) proposed the theory of endosymbiosis during the 1980s to explain the origin of eukaryotic mitochondria and chloroplasts from permanent resident prokaryotes. According to this idea, a larger prokaryote (or perhaps early eukaryote) engulfed or surrounded a smaller prokaryote some 1.5 billion to 700 million years ago.

Instead of digesting the smaller organisms, the large one and the smaller one entered into a type of symbiosis known as mutualism, where both creatures benefit and neither is harmed. In the case of the two separate endosymbiosis events that produced mitochondria and chloroplasts, the larger organism gained excess ATP provided by the "protomitochondrion" and excess sugar provided by the "protochloroplast," while providing a stable environment and the raw materials the endosymbionts required. This relationship has been going on so long that now eukaryotic cells cannot survive without mitochondria (likewise photosynthetic eukaryotes cannot survive without chloroplasts), and the endosymbionts cannot survive outside their hosts. Nearly all eukaryotes have mitochondria. Mitochondrial and chloroplast division is remarkably similar to the prokaryotic methods that will be studied in a later chapter.

Like mitochondria, chloroplasts have their own DNA, termed cpDNA. Chloroplasts of Green Algae and plants are thought to have originated by endosymbiosis of a prokaryotic bacterium similar to living *Prochloron* (Prochlorobacteria). Chloroplasts of Red Algae are very similar biochemically to cyanobacteria. It seems likely that more than one endosymbiotic event occurred to produce eukaryotes.

Summary

All living things are composed of one or more cells. The types of cells a multicellular creature has dictate what that creature can do. For example, trees do not get up and walk, except the Ents in the late Professor Tolkien's <u>Lord of the Rings</u>, because they lack muscle cells for mobility. We cannot make our own food by photosynthesis since we lack cells containing chloroplasts. Cells carry out specific functions, reflected in the cell structure. Yet all cells have certain common features like DNA, ribosomes, a cell membrane, and so forth. You began your genetic existence as a single cell when your parents' egg and sperm fused. That one cell has grown and developed into the sixty trillion cells that make a human being. We have just scratched the surface of cells and their significance.

Terms

actin	carbohydrate	chemosynthesis
amino acids	carnivores	chitin
antibodies	carotenes	chlorophyll
antigens	cell theory	chloroplasts
archaea	cellulose	chromoplasts
autotroph	cell wall	chromosome

cristae
cyanobacteria
cytoplasm
cytoplasmic streaming
cytoskeleton
dinoflagellates
ecosystems
endoplasmic reticulum
endosymbiosis
erythrocytes
eukaryotic
fluid-mosaic model
fossil
glycolysis
golgi complexes
grana
green algae
herbivores
heterotroph
histone protein
human immunodeficiency
   virus (HIV)
hydrophilic
hydrophobic
immune systems
leukocytes

leukoplasts
lignin
lysosomes
macromolecules
magnification
matrix
messenger RNA (mRNA)
microtubules
mitochondria
multicellularity
muscle fibers
mutualism
nervous system
nuclear envelope
nuclear pores
neuron
nucleic acids
nucleoid
nucleolus
nucleus
organelles
ozone layer
parasites parenchyma
parenchyma
peptidoglycan
phospholipid

photosynthesis
photosystems
plasmodesmata
plastid
polysaccharide
prokaryotes
proteinoid
proteins
protistans
pseudopodia
red algae
resolution
retroviruses
rough endoplasmic reticulum
ribosomal RNA (rRNA)
ribosomes
ribozymes
smooth endoplasmic
   reticulum
stroma
symbiosis
thylakoids
vacuoles
viroids
viruses
zygote

Review Questions

1. Which of these is not a type of cell?
   a. bacterium;
   b. amoeba;
   c. sperm;
   d. virus

2. The Earth's early atmosphere apparently lacked ___.
   a. oxygen;
   b. carbon dioxide;
   c. water vapor;
   d. ammonia

3. The oldest fossil forms of life are most similar to _____.
   a. animals;
   b. bacteria;
   c. plants;
   d. fungi

4. A prokaryotic cell would lack which of these structures?
    a. ribosome;   c. cell membrane;
    b. nucleus;   d. cell wall

5. Heterotrophic organisms obtain their food _____.
    a. from another creature;
    b. by photosynthesis;
    c. by chemical synthesis;
    d. by AMP synthesis.

6. Ribosomes are cellular structures involved in _____.
    a. photosynthesis;
    b. chemosynthesis;
    c. protein synthesis;
    d. carbohydrate synthesis

7. The earliest microscopes used _____ to image the specimens.
    a. high-energy electron beams;
    b. interatomic forces;
    c. low-energy electron beams;
    d. light

8. There are _____ micrometers (µm) in one millimeter (mm).
    a. 1;   d. 1000;
    b. 10;   e. 1/1000
    c. 100;

9. Human cells have a size range between ___ and ___ micrometers (µm).
    a. 10–100;   c. 100–1000;
    b. 1–10;   d. 1/10–1/1000

10. Chloroplasts and cyanobacteria are ___ in size.
    a. similar;
    b. at different ends of the size range;
    c. exactly the same;
    d. none of these.

11. The cell membrane does all of these in a eukaryote except _____.
    a. contain the hereditary material;
    b. acts as a boundary or border for the cytoplasm;
    c. regulates passage of material in and out of the cell;
    d. functions in the recognition of self

12. Which of these materials is not a major component of the plasma membrane?
    a. phospholipids;
    b. glycoproteins;
    c. proteins;
    d. DNA

13. Cell walls occur in members of these kingdoms, except for ___, which all lack cell walls.
    a. plants;
    b. animals;
    c. bacteria;
    d. fungi

14. The polysaccharide ___ is a major component of plant cell walls.
    a. chitin;
    b. peptidoglycan;
    c. cellulose;
    d. mannitol;
    e. cholesterol

15. Plant cells have ___ and ___, which are not present in animal cells.
    a. mitochondria, chloroplasts;
    b. cell membranes, cell walls;
    c. chloroplasts, nucleus;
    d. chloroplasts, cell walls

16. The ___ is the membrane-enclosed structure in eukaryotic cells that contains the DNA of the cell.
    a. mitochondrion;
    b. chloroplast;
    c. nucleolus;
    d. nucleus

17. Ribosomes are constructed in the ___ of a eukaryotic cell.
    a. endoplasmic reticulum;
    b. nucleoid;
    c. nucleolus;
    d. nuclear pore

18. Rough endoplasmic reticulum is the area in a cell where ___ are synthesized.
    a. polysaccharides;
    b. proteins;
    c. lipids;
    d. DNA

19. The smooth endoplasmic reticulum is the area in a cell where ___ are synthesized.
    a. polysaccharides;
    b. proteins;
    c. lipids;
    d. DNA

20. The mitochondrion functions in ____.
    a. lipid storage;
    b. protein synthesis;
    c. photosynthesis;
    d. DNA replication;
    e. ATP synthesis

21. The thin extensions of the inner mitochondrial membrane are known as _____.
    a. cristae;
    b. matrix;
    c. thylakoids;
    d. stroma

22. The chloroplast functions in ____.
    a. lipid storage;
    b. protein synthesis;
    c. photosynthesis;
    d. DNA replication;
    e. ATP synthesis

23. Which of these cellular organelles have their own DNA?
    a. chloroplast;
    b. nucleus;
    c. mitochondrion;
    d. all of these

24. The theory of ___ was proposed to explain the possible origin of chloroplasts and mitochondria.
    a. evolution;
    b. endosymbiosis;
    c. endocytosis;
    d. cells

25. Long, whip-like microfibrils that facilitate movement by cells are known as ___.
    a. cilia;
    b. flagella;
    c. leather;
    d. pseudopodia

Links

- **Cells Alive!** Very interesting site with new features each month. [http://www.cellsalive.com]
- **Cyanobacteria Morphology** [http://www.ucmp.berkeley.edu/bacteria/cyanomm.html] and **Introduction to the Archaea Life's Life's extremists......** [http://www.ucmp.berkeley.edu/archaea/archaea.html] These University of California Berkeley sites from their Museum of Paleontology (UCMP) offer some pertinent information about a group of organisms that resemble some of the earliest known fossils.
- **Tracing Ancestry with MtDNA, by Rick Groleau:** This PBS site explores the science tracing our maternal ancestry back to the woman known as mitochiondrial Eve. [http://www.pbs.org/wgbh/nova/neanderthals/mtdna.html]
- **Virtual Plant Cell**: Zoom in on a virtual plant cell. An excellent first step. [http://www.life.uiuc.edu/plantbio/cell/]
- **Hammerling's** *Acetabularia:* An excellent illustrated summary of Hammerling's classic experiment to determine the role of the nucleus. Site by Access Excellence. [http://www.access-sexcellence.com/AB/GG/hammerling_s.html]

Reference

Singer SJ, and Nicolson GL. The fluid mosaic model of the structure of cell membranes. *Science.* 1972 Feb 18;175(4023):720–31.

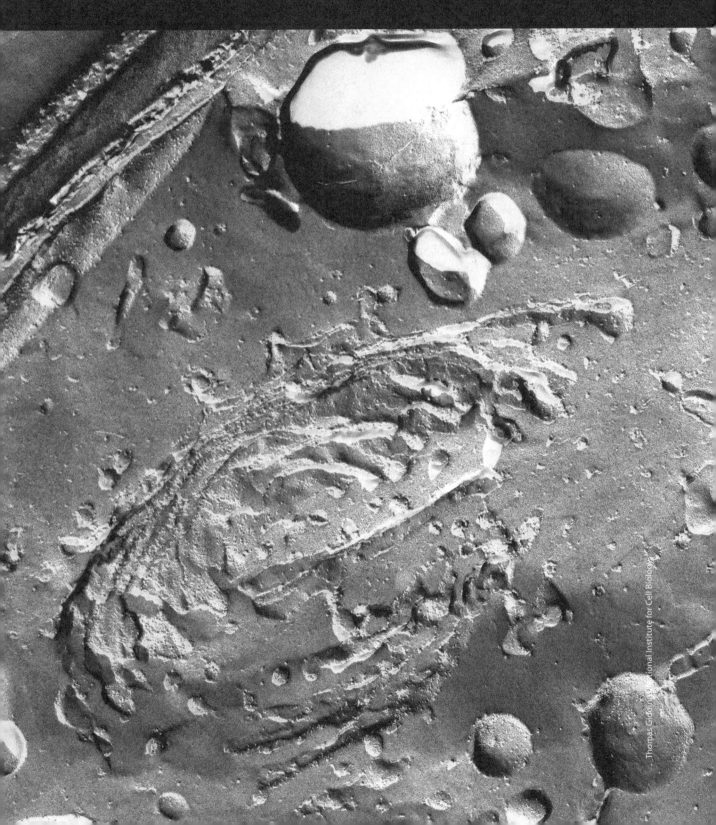

CHAPTER 4

Transport In and Out of Cells

Chapter Opener

Freeze-fracture micrograph illustrating the Golgi apparatus and rough endoplasmic reticulum (RER) of a cell of the green alga *Micrasterias*. This technique was employed to study the structure of the cell membrane. Image courtesy of Thomas Giddings.

Objectives

- Describe the general structure of a phospholipid molecule and what makes it suitable as a major component of cell membranes.
- Explain the behavior of a great number of phospholipid molecules in water.
- Describe the most recent version of the fluid mosaic model of membrane structure.
- Distinguish between solute and solvent.
- Explain osmosis in terms of a differentially permeable membrane.
- Define tonicity and be able to apply the terms isotonic, hypertonic, and hypotonic.
- When water moves into a plant cell by osmosis, the internal turgor pressure developed pushes on the wall. Explain what this does to your understanding of a neglected houseplant.
- Be able to provide examples and compare and contrast active and passive transports.

Introduction

The cell membrane acts as the boundary of the cell. It is at this border that the cell interacts with its environment by importing food and oxygen molecules, exporting cellular products such as hormones, proteins, and waste molecules like carbon dioxide. The cell's boundary has labels displayed on its surface (like a highway sign reading "Welcome to the Cell") that may cause the body's immune system to react. These cell labels determine if a donor organ is a suitable match for a transplant recipient, or whether the cell is susceptible to attack by a virus. The cell membrane also has component molecules that play vital roles in the functioning of the cell.

4.1   Cell Membrane Structure

The cell membrane functions as life's boundary, allowing certain molecules to cross it while fencing the majority of organically produced chemicals inside the cell. Electron microscopic examinations of cell membranes have led to the development of the fluid-mosaic model (Figure 4.1) by Singer and Nicholson in 1972. The most common molecule in the model is the phospholipid (Figure 4.2), which has a polar (hydrophilic) head and two nonpolar (hydrophobic) tails. Membrane phospholipids align tail-to-tail so the nonpolar areas form a hydrophobic region between the hydrophilic heads on the inner and outer surfaces of the membrane. This layering forms a bilayer.

Plasma Membrane Structure

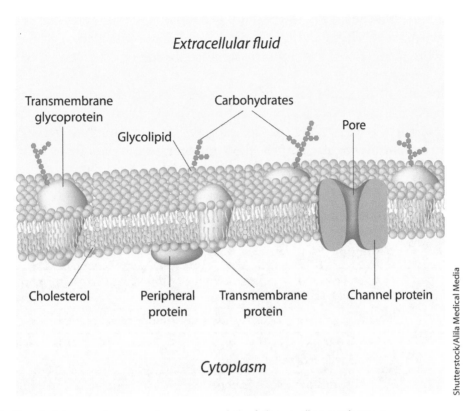

FIGURE 4.1 The fluid mosaic membrane model of the cell membrane.

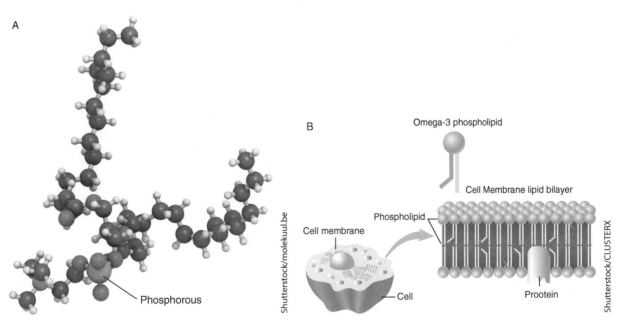

FIGURE 4.2 Phospholipids. A. Molecular structure of a phospholipid; B. Phospholipids in a bilayer.

Phospholipids and glycolipids are important structural components of cell membranes (Figure 4.2; Table 4.1). Phospholipids are modified so one phosphate group (PO_4^-) replaces one of the three fatty acids normally found in a lipid. The addition of this group makes a polar "head" and two nonpolar "tails." Glycolipids are carbohydrate chains attached to a lipid. Cholesterol is another important component of cell membranes embedded in the hydrophobic areas of the inner (tail-tail) region.

Proteins floating in the sea of phospholipids have a variety of functions (Table 4.1). They may serve as gateway proteins, enzymes controlling chemical reactions inside the cell, cellular recognition molecules, or as binding sites for substances to be brought into the cell. Still other proteins in membranes serve as channels allowing materials to pass freely into or out of the cell. Finally, some proteins act as gates that open and close to facilitate active transport of large molecules.

TABLE 4.1 Components of the Cell Membrane and their Functions

Molecule	Function
Phospholipid	Major molecule of the membrane. Phospholipids have hydrophobic as well as hydrophilic regions.
Cholesterol*	Allows membrane flexibility, especially important in animal cells.
Glycolipids	Carbohydrate chains attached to a lipid. Function in cell recognition and the recognition of self.
Glycoproteins	Carbohydrate chains attached to a protein. Function in cell recognition and the recognition of self.
Carrier Proteins	Allow ions and certain molecules to pass through the membrane, when the channel protein is activated or primed. Example: the GLUT proteins that function in the uptake and release of glucose sugar.
Receptor Proteins	Proteins that are shaped so that hormones or other signal molecules can fit into the protein and trigger a change in the cell. Example, human growth hormone in the pygmy people.
Protein Pumps	When primed by energy from ATP (often by attaching a phosphate to the protein) the protein will act to transport materials across the membrane against the concentration gradient of those materials. Example: The Sodium-Potassium (Na^+-K^+) pump involved in nerve message transmission; cytochrome proteins in the electron transport system.
Enzymatic Proteins	Enzymes embedded on typically an interior surface of the membrane. These enzymatic proteins are often located close together and arranged in pathways to promote efficient production of the pathway product.
Cell Recognition Proteins	Function in the recognition of self, an important concept in organ transplants. Example: The major histocompatibility complex (MHC) labels that influence the suitability of an organ for transplant.
Integral Membrane Proteins	Substrate specific transport proteins that pass all the way through the membrane. Example, aquaporins that allow water to pass across the membrane.

*Note: not all membranes have cholesterol, these functions pertain to those where cholesterol is present.

Channel proteins (Figure 4.3) play important roles in living systems. Charged molecules such as ions cannot cross the cell membrane. Channel proteins allow these ions to cross, providing the channel is open. The best example of this involves a human disease, cystic fibrosis. People suffering from cystic fibrosis produce faulty chloride ion channels on their cell membranes. The resulting buildup of chloride ions leads to production of a thick mucus that clogs pancreatic ducts as well as the surface of the cell. This mucus inhibits the passage of molecules such as dioxygen (O_2) across the membrane. The mucus is also an excellent place for bacterial growth, resulting in lung infections. Treatments for cystic fibrosis involve ultra-low sodium diets as well as manipulation of the lungs (pounding or patting on the back). There is no cure, only treatment of the symptoms. We will examine the inheritance of cystic fibrosis in a later chapter.

Enzymatic proteins typically occur on the inner side of the membrane. The reactants fit into the enzymatic protein and a chemical reaction happens. The products of the reaction leave the enzymatic protein, and in the case of enzymatic pathways, pass next to the next enzymatic protein in the pathway. Think of these pathways like they were an assembly line in a factory. The enzymatic pathways are like the workers. The product from one worker is passed to the next

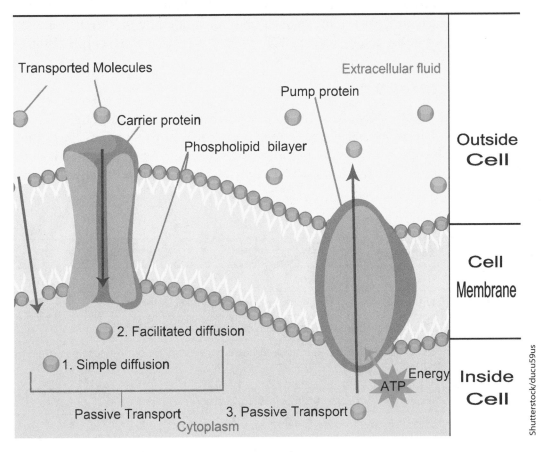

FIGURE 4.3 Types of transport across membranes.

worker who carries out their job before passing the product along the line. In similar fashion, the product from one enzymatic protein becomes the reactant for the next enzymatic protein.

Receptor proteins usually occur on the outside of the membrane. A signal molecule attaches to the receptor protein, triggering a message or response within the cell. An example of this is the growth hormone in the pygmy people of Africa. These people are genetically isolated from most other populations and have developed a mutation in the growth hormone receptor. The pygmy males are less than 4 feet 11 inches tall. One hypothesis suggests this is not due to their underproduction of growth hormone but rather to the alteration (and reduced effectiveness) of the receptor.

Cell recognition proteins act as cell identifiers. Every cell in your body is labeled with these identifying labels: I belong to YOU! They in a way shout to your body's immune system. Immune system cells check the cell identifiers to determine if the cell belongs to that organism. If the proteins are a close enough match no further immune action occurs. If, however, the proteins are not a match, the immune system mobilizes against that now-identified-as-foreign cell and destroys it. The labels that are most often checked in this identification-of-self are the major histocompatibility complex (MHC). Matching these proteins is essential for successful organ transplants.

Protein pumps (Figure 4.3) use cell energy (in the form of adenosine triphosphate [ATP]) to move materials from low to high concentrations. One of the biggest energy uses in our bodies while we sleep is the Sodium-Potassium pump. Every time a nerve cell transmits a message the nerve cell must spend a great deal of energy resetting the Sodium and Potassium ions along the cell membrane before another nerve message can be transmitted by that nerve cell. Scientists estimate that one-third of the energy you need while sleeping is used to reset this pump.

4.2   Passive Transport

When the cell uses the free energy of the environment to move materials around we refer to this as passive transport. Diffusion and osmosis are two examples of passive transport (Table 4.2). When a cell has to spend its own energy to move materials, we refer to this as active transport (Table 4.2). Protein pumps and endocytosis and exocytosis are examples of active transport.

TABLE 4.2 Types of Cellular Transport

Transport Type	Summary
Passive	
Diffusion	Net movement of materials from high to low concentration
Osmosis	Diffusion of H_2O across a selectively permeable membrane
Facilitated Diffusion	Diffusion of molecules across a membrane through a membrane protein carrier
Active	
Protein Pumps	Movements across membranes against a gradient
Endocytosis	Importation of macromolecules by forming vesicles
Exocytosis	Exporting macromolecules by forming vesicles

4.2.1   Diffusion

Water, carbon dioxide, and oxygen (Figure 4.4) are among the few simple molecules that can cross the cell membrane by diffusion (or a special type of diffusion known as osmosis). Lipid-soluble molecules also diffuse across membranes. Diffusion is one principle method for movement of substances into and out of cells.

Diffusion is the net movement of a substance from an area of higher concentration to one of lower concentration. Many small molecules, like dioxygen (O_2) and carbon dioxide (CO_2) cross the cell membrane by diffusion (Figure 4.4). Diffusion operates with every breath in your lungs (Figure 4.5) to exchange carbon dioxide (a waste gas produced from cellular metabolism in every cell of your body) for dioxygen (a vital gas essential for cellular metabolism). Carbon dioxide diffuses into the thin walled capillaries that occur throughout your body. Capillaries carry the waste carbon dioxide gas to veins and eventually to the lungs. In the lungs, the veins connect to capillaries wrapped around an alveolus, blind sacs connected to the network of air tubes in the lungs (Figure 4.5). Since there is more carbon dioxide in the capillaries than in the alveolus, the carbon dioxide diffuses into the alveolus (4.5B). At the same time, the dioxygen in the alveolus is greater in concentration than in the capillaries. This causes the dioxygen to diffuse from the alveolus into the capillary (Figure 4.5B). The good news for you is that this process happens even if you do not know about diffusion.

Examples of diffusion occur all around us. If you have ever been in a crowded classroom (and who hasn't), you have noticed someone sitting near you who put on too much body spray or perfume. At first only those near the source notice the smell, but soon enough it the entire class smells it. Ripe apples emit a sweet smelling gas, ethylene. When you take an apple out of a sack, the smell of the apple is quite nice. After a few minutes the gas has diffused into the room air and the apple does not smell as sweet anymore.

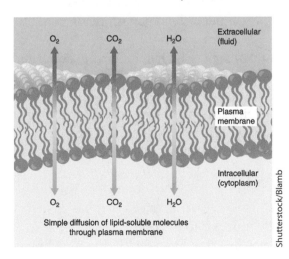

FIGURE 4.4 Simple diffusion through a plasma membrane.

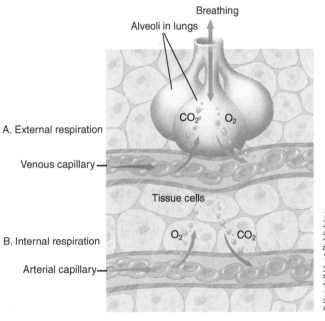

FIGURE 4.5 Diffusion in lungs. A. Structure of an alveolus and associated capillaries; B. Enlarged view of the interface between the alveolus and capillary carrying red blood cells.

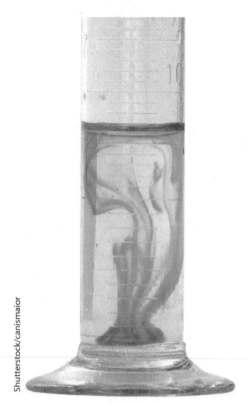

Shutterstock/canismaior

FIGURE 4.6 Diffusion of dye molecules placed in a beaker of water. Eventually random molecular motion will move the dye into a state of equilibrium within the beaker.

Molecules of any substance (solid, liquid, or gas) are in random motion when that substance is above absolute zero (0 degrees Kelvin or −273°C). The energy powering these movements is referred to as the free energy of the system. It is a property of matter that molecules will move *en masse* from a higher concentration area to an area of lower concentration. The majority of the molecules will move from higher to lower concentration, although there will be some that move from low to high due to the total randomness of molecular movements. The overall (or net) movement is thus from a high to low concentration (shown by dye in Figure 4.6). Eventually, if no additional energy is input into the system, the molecules will reach a state of equilibrium where they will be distributed equally throughout the system. If this is Kool-Aid in a pitcher of water, we do not want to wait for this, so we stir the liquid. This adds energy, hastening the solution reaching equilibrium.

4.2.2   Osmosis

Water balance is a critical function of life in which the cell membrane plays a pivotal role. Too much water and the cell will swell and burst. Too little water and the cell will shrivel up. The plasma membrane acts as a barrier to most, but not all, molecules. Water is a molecule that can freely pass through the membrane. The development of a plasma membrane that could allow some materials to pass while constraining the movement of other molecules was a major step in the evolution of the cell. Plasma membranes are selectively permeable barriers separating the inner cellular environment from the outer external environment.

Water potential is the tendency of water to move from an area of higher water concentration to one of lower water concentration. Water molecules move according to differences in water potential. The energy to power this movement comes from the environment.

Osmosis is the diffusion of water across a selectively permeable membrane. The plasma membrane, (as well as dialysis tubing and cellulose acetate sausage casing) acts as a selectively permeable membrane that not all molecules can cross. To understand osmosis, we need to know that the presence of a solute decreases the amount of water in a given volume of a solution. There is more water per unit of volume in a glass of freshwater than there is in an equivalent volume of seawater. Freshwater has much less salt (the solute) than the seawater. In a cell that has so many organelles and other large molecules, the water generally moves into the cell.

Many experiments demonstrate the process of osmosis (such as Figure 4.7). The membrane placed into the beaker is selectively permeable since not all substances can move across it. The larger solute molecules cannot cross the membrane but smaller water molecules can. We often list the percentage of solute in a solution, say 10% NaCl, or 15% glucose. The larger the amount of solute, the less water there is in the solution. For example, a 10% NaCl solution has 90% water, while a 5% NaCl solution has 95% water. If we placed the 10% NaCl solution on the right side of a membrane and the 5% NaCl on the left side of the membrane, water will cross the membrane. This will be seen as the water on the right side of the membrane rises.

Hypertonic solutions (Figure 4.8) are those in which more solute (and hence lower water potential) is present. Hypotonic solutions are those with less solute (again read as higher water potential). Isotonic solutions have equal (iso-) concentrations of substances. Water potentials are thus equal, although equal amounts of water move in and out of the cell, so the net flow is zero. For example, if a blood cell is placed in a solution of pure distilled water, water will flow into the cell causing it to lyse (or burst). Plant cells (Figure 4.8) have a cell wall that prevents bursting in such a situation. The plant equivalent of lysis is said to be a turgid cell exhibiting turgor pressure. The opposite situation also occurs where a cell loses water to the outside environment. If a plant cell is placed in a 10% NaCl solution, the plant cell will lose water since plant cells are 99% water. Plant cells have their cytoplasm pull away from the cell wall, the plant cells are said to be plasmolysed (Figure 4.8B). An animal cell in a similar situation shrivels up as it loses water, assuming a spiked appearance as the cell experiences crenation.

One of the major functions of blood in animals is to maintain an isotonic internal environment. This eliminates the problems associated with water loss or excess water movement into or out of cells. Again we return to homeostasis. Cells function best when in an isotonic solution.

Paramecium and other single-celled freshwater organisms have difficulty since they are usually hypertonic relative to the outside environment. Thus, water will tend to flow across the cell membrane, swelling the cell and eventually bursting it. Not good for any cell! The contractile vacuole (Figure 4.9) is the *Paramecium's* answer to this problem. Water collects in the canals of the contractile vacuole. Eventually this water is expelled from the cell. The pumping of water out of the cell by this method requires the cell to spend its own ATP energy rather than relying on the free energy of its

High concentration of H_2O molecules

Low concentration of solute (NaCl) molecules

Membrane is permeable to water, but not to solutes

Higher concentration of solute (NaCl) molecules results in fewer H_2O molecules on right side of membrane

A.

H_2O molecules move through membrane to create equilibrium of solute concentrations, resulting in higher volume on right side

B.

© Kendall Hunt Publishing

FIGURE 4.7 Osmosis. A. Initial setup of experiment, with less water on the right side of the membrane. B. Ions of Na and Cl cannot cross the membrane, only water can do that. This causes the rise we see in B.

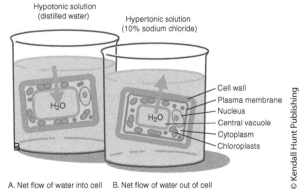

Hypotonic solution (distilled water)

Hypertonic solution (10% sodium chloride)

Cell wall
Plasma membrane
Nucleus
Central vacuole
Cytoplasm
Chloroplasts

H_2O

H_2O

A. Net flow of water into cell   B. Net flow of water out of cell

© Kendall Hunt Publishing

FIGURE 4.8 Explanation of plasmolysis.

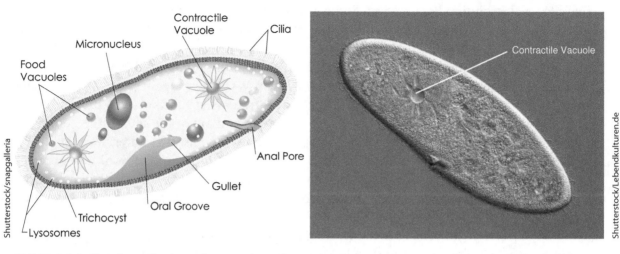

FIGURE 4.9 The functioning of a contractile vacuole in *Paramecium*. A. Diagram of structure of a *Paramecium*; B. *Paramecium* live cell illustrating the contractile vacuole.

environment. Energy is needed since the water is moving against the concentration gradient. Under a microscope *Paramecium* appears to have a "heart" beating at either end of the cell. Not a heart, but a water pump keeping the cell homeostatic and functioning. Many times in a laboratory setting, we add a solution to microscope slides of *Paramecium* to slow down the organisms so we can better observe their structures. Unfortunately, this slows down the contractile vacuole, causing the cells to swell as they lose their battle to pump out the incoming water.

In your body, the kidneys and excretory system maintain water balance. When you eat salty food, say popcorn loaded with salts and flavoring at the movies, you might notice your rings fit snugger the next day. The influx of salt changes your osmotic balance so that you body's cells release water. You also might be thirsty, so you drink more water. The kidneys eventually restore the osmotic balance in your body. However, what happens if your kidneys are not properly functioning? Excess water and wastes build up. Dialysis is a process of filtering wastes from the blood for people whose kidneys no longer function. During dialysis, the blood is withdrawn from the patient's body and flows into a machine where filtration occurs. Patients are weighed after dialysis and often lose several pounds of water. Dialysis is a short-term solution to kidney failure for some lucky individuals who receive a kidney transplant from a tissue-matched donor.

4.2.3   Facilitated Diffusion

Facilitated diffusion occurs when the cell maintains a protein channel through the membrane. As long as the channel remains open, certain large molecules can diffuse through the membrane channel protein along a concentration gradient from high to low concentration. While the cell does spend energy to build the channel protein, the use of the protein costs the cell no energy. Like all passive transport, this method relies on the free energy of the environment. Figure 4.10 illustrates the role of facilitated diffusion in glucose uptake into a cell. The carrier protein must be primed or opened by a signal, in this case the hormone insulin. Insulin binds to its receptor, which ultimately causes the GLUT-4 proteins to move to the cell membrane. Once the GLUT-4 receptors reach the cell membrane surface, the glucose diffuses into the cell (as long as there is more glucose outside the cell than inside it). Once inside the cell, the cell's enzymes add a phosphate group, preventing the glucose from diffusing back out of the cell. The GLUT-4 carriers are active only on adipose cells and striated muscle cells.

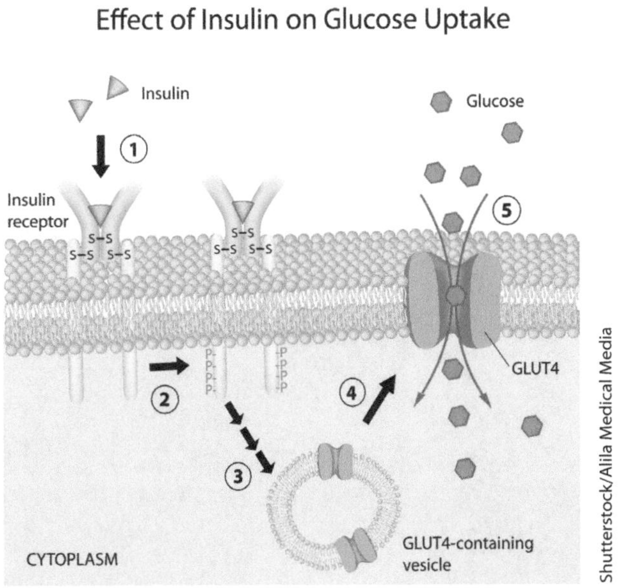

4.3   Active Transport

Energy is required to any type of movement. In some cases, this energy can come from the free energy of the environment, a situation that is termed passive transport (Figure 4.4) since it requires no energy from the cell. Passive transport moves materials along a concentration gradient from high to low concentrations.

Effect of Insulin on Glucose Uptake

FIGURE 4.10 Effect of the hormone insulin on glucose uptake.

However nice such free transport might be, cells must sometimes pump or move materials across the cell membrane *against* the concentration gradient. Such cases are termed active transport (Figure 4.11) since the cell has to spend its own energy to move molecules. Active transport requires the cell to spend energy, usually in the form of ATP. Examples of active transport include transport of large molecules that are not lipid soluble, the sodium-potassium pump that is needed so nerve cells can transmit a nerve message, and the pumping of H^+ ions into the thylakoid space and inner mitochondrial compartments for the chemiosmotic synthesis of ATP. Active transport requires the expenditure of cellular ATP energy to transport molecules against a concentration gradient. Think of moving a large round rock. Would you rather roll it downhill, expending none of your own energy, or uphill, spending a great deal of energy? Sometimes you just need to spend that energy to accomplish some task. Like active transport.

4.3.1   Protein Pumps

Proteins embedded in the cell membrane may play various roles in transport of materials that cannot diffuse through the membrane. These integrated transport proteins are often highly selective about the chemicals they allow to cross. Some of these proteins can move materials across the membrane only when assisted by the concentration gradient, a type of carrier-assisted passive transport (Figure 4.10) known as facilitated diffusion. Both diffusion and facilitated diffusion are driven by a concentration gradient. Glucose enters most cells by facilitated diffusion. There seems to be a limited number of glucose-transporting proteins. The rapid breakdown of glucose in the cell (a process known as glycolysis) maintains the concentration gradient. When the external concentration of glucose increases, however, the glucose transport does not exceed a certain rate, suggesting the limitation on transport.

Ionic Basis of the Resting Membrane Potential

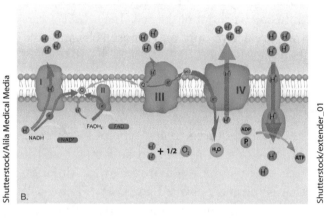

FIGURE 4.11 Types of active transport in cells. A. Sodium-Potassium pump resets the ions along a nerve cell membrane so that another message can be sent along that nerve cell; B. Chemiosmosis. The passage of electrons through the proton pumps allows H^+ ions to be pumped across the membrane against a concentration gradient.

In the case of active transport (Figure 4.11A), the protein pump moves material *against* the concentration gradient. The sodium-potassium pump (Figure 4.11A) operates only in nerve cells. Sodium (Na^+) is maintained at low concentrations inside the cell and potassium (K^+) is at a higher concentration. The ion concentrations are reversed on the outside of the cell, with the sodium concentration being higher than that of potassium. Nerve messages move along the outside of the nerve cell by the passage of these ions across the membrane. After the message has passed that area of the nerve cell, the ions must be actively transported back to their "starting positions" across the membrane. This is analogous to setting up 100 dominoes and then tipping over the first one. To reset them you must pick each one up, again at an energy cost. Up to one-third of the ATP used by a resting animal is used to reset the Na-K pump.

Later in this course, we will examine the production of ATP by chemiosmosis (Figure 4.11B). For right now, we will just focus on the role of proton pumps that use energy from the passage of electrons to pump H^+ ions (protons) against the concentration gradient. The passage of the H^+ ions eventually yields the energy converted to make Adenosine Diphosphate (ADP) into ATP.

4.3.2   Exocytosis

Vesicles and small vacuoles that fuse with the cell membrane may be utilized to release or transport chemicals out of the cell or to allow them to enter a cell. Exocytosis, sometimes called secretion, is the term applied when such transport is out of the cell. Transmission of a nerve message between nerve cells (Figure 4.12A) is accomplished by exocytosis. Neurotransmitter chemicals produced in one nerve cell are dumped into the synaptic cleft between two nerve cells. These neurotransmitters diffuse across the synaptic cleft and bind to chemical receptors on the surface of the other cell, causing the nerve message to be transmitted in that cell.

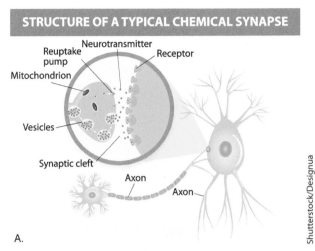

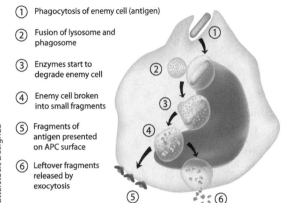

FIGURE 4.12 Exocytosis and Endocytosis. A. The role of exocytosis in transmission of nerve messages from cell to cell by neurotransmitter chemicals; B. Action of antigen presenting cell in human immune response illustrates the role of endocytosis (1; phagocytosis) taking in the cell, and exocytosis (6) discharging the remnants.

Endocytosis (Figure 4.12B) is the case when a molecule causes the cell membrane to bulge inward, forming a vesicle. Phagocytosis (Figure 4.12B) is the type of endocytosis where an entire cell is engulfed. Pinocytosis is when the external fluid is engulfed in vesicles that are then inside the cell. Receptor-mediated endocytosis occurs when the material to be transported binds to certain specific molecules in the membrane. Examples include the transport of insulin and cholesterol into animal cells.

Endocytosis also plays a role in the endomembrane system. Vesicles containing enzymes produced at the rough endoplasmic reticulum contain enzymes and then move to the Golgi Complex for further processing, once released from the Golgi Complex, the lysosomes remain in the cytoplasm. When a bacterium is brought into the cell by phagocytosis, the lysosome fuses with the incoming vesicle, digesting its contents.

Pinocytosis occurs when the cell forms vesicles at the cell membrane. Inside these vesicles is some amount of the extracellular fluid and its solutes. Pinocytosis is also known as cell drinking.

Receptor-mediated endocytosis involves specific substances binding to a specific receptor to promote the formation of the vesicle. In humans, this is how LDL cholesterol enters the cell. Iron also enters the cell in this manner.

Summary

The cell membrane is very aptly termed "life's boundary." The membrane controls and constrains transport across itself. Components of the membrane perform a number of tasks significant to our lives, like immunity, allergies, and metabolism. Osmoregulation is also an important process for the cell, and water balance is an important aspect of homeostasis.

Terms

active transport
adenosine triphosphate (ATP)
adenosine diphosphate (ADP)
alveolus
capillaries
cellular metabolism
cholesterol
chemiosmosis
contractile vacuole
crenation
cystic fibrosis
diffusion
dialysis
endocytosis
enzymes
equilibrium
exocytosis

fluid-mosaic model
facilitated diffusion
glycolipids
golgi complex
homeostasis
hydrophilic
hydrophobic
hypertonic
hypotonic
immune system
insulin
ions
isotonic
kidneys
lungs
lyse
lysosomes
mitochondrial
neurotransmitter

osmosis
passive transport
phagocytosis
pinocytosis
plasma membrane
phosphate group
phospholipid
plasmolysed
receptor-mediated endocytosis
rough endoplasmic reticulum
sodium-potassium pump
solute
synaptic cleft
turgor pressure
thylakoid
vacuoles
vesicles
veins

Review Questions

1. If the inside of a cell is 99% water, what term is applied to that cell when it is placed in a solution of 99% water?
   a. isotonic;
   b. hypertonic;
   c. hypotonic;
   d. hair tonic

2. The term applied when water passes through a selectively permeable membrane from an area of high to low concentration is ___.
   a. diffusion;
   b. tonicity;
   c. active transport;
   d. osmosis

3. Potatoes, like most cells, are composed of approximately 99% water. When freshly peeled potatoes are placed into a bowl of pure water, what will happen to the potatoes?
   a. they will shrink due to water leaving the potato;
   b. they will have no change since the amounts of water entering the potatoes will balance the amounts of water leaving the potatoes;
   c. the potatoes will absorb some of the water and become firmer;
   d. the potato cells will absorb a great deal of water and burst

4. Which of these is not a component of the cell membrane?
   a. phospholipids;
   b. RNA;
   c. cholesterol;
   d. proteins

5. An example of vesicle-mediated transport would be ___.
   a. diffusion of oxygen;
   b. diffusion of lipid-soluble molecules across the membrane;
   c. the actions of the sodium-potassium pump;
   d. cell secretion by exocytosis

6. Which of these transport processes is operating in the transmission of a nerve message from the fingertips to the brain?
   a. sodium-potassium pump;
   b. diffusion;
   c. exocytosis;
   d. all of these are involved in the transmission of a nerve message

7. The energy to power passive transport comes from ___.
   a. ATP;
   b. lysosomes;
   c. the sodium-potassium pump;
   d. the free energy of the system

8. The energy to conduct active transport comes from ___.
   a. ATP;
   b. lysosomes;
   c. the sodium-potassium pump;
   d. the free energy of the system

9. Which of these transport mechanisms accomplishes passage of glucose from the blood into a cell?
   a. active transport;
   b. diffusion;
   c. facilitated diffusion;
   d. osmosis

10. Glycolipids and glycoproteins function as _____ in the cell membrane.
    a. enzymes;
    b. cell recognition components;
    c. pumps involved with active transport;
    d. exit points for water passing out of the cell by osmosis

11. When a red blood cell is placed in a hypotonic environment, the cell will ____.
    a. crenate;
    b. become turgid;
    c. lyse;
    d. plasmolyse

Reference

Singer SJ, Nicolson GL. The fluid mosaic model of the structure of cell membranes. *Science.* 1972 Feb 18;175(4023):720–31.

Unit 2

Energy and Metabolism

CHAPTER 5

Energy and Enzymes

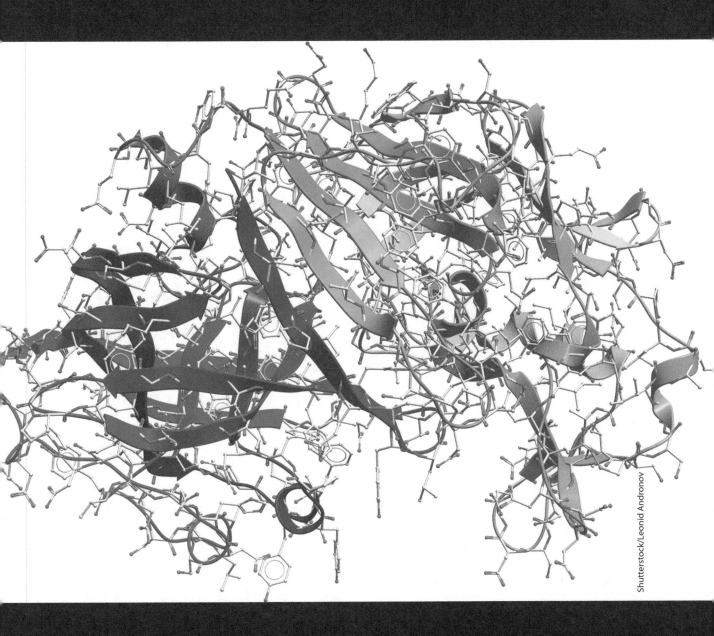

Chapter Opener

3D model of the enzyme pepsin that digests food proteins into peptides.

Objectives

- Define energy, and state the first and second laws of thermodynamics.
- Entropy is a measure of the degree of randomness or disorder of systems. Be able to explain this concept in terms of a cell phone.
- Explain how life maintains a high degree of organization.
- Reactions that show a net loss in energy are said to be exergonic; reactions that show a net gain in energy are said to be endergonic. Describe an example of each type of chemical reaction.
- Describe a reversible reaction and explain its significance to a cell.
- Explain the function of metabolic pathways in the chemistry of a cell and explain their significance.
- Detail the structure and importance of enzymes.
- Explain what happens when enzymes react with substrates.
- List factors that influence enzyme activity.
- Describe the structure of adenosine diphosphate (ADP) and adenosine triphosphate (ATP).
- Explain the functioning of the ATP/ADP cycle.
- Describe the components, organization, and functions of an electron transport system.
- Adding a phosphate to a molecule is called phosphorylation. List and describe the two methods cells use to phosphorylate ADP into ATP.

Introduction

$E = mc^2$. Over 100 years ago, the German physicist Albert Einstein (1879–1955) developed what is probably the most famous physics equation in the world. From this equation we have the atomic bomb as well as nuclear power plants. What, you may rightly ask, does this have to do with biology? **Everything!** Just as we had to learn a little chemistry to understand the chemical aspects of life, we now need to learn a little physics to understand the energy transformations happening in your cells and all other cells. Energy and metabolism are one of the basic properties of life. Energy transformations give you the power to make new cells, to grow, to copy your DNA, to repair your DNA when it has become damaged. You use energy to fight off infections and to produce antibodies against deadly viruses. How your body acquires and deals with this energy and what rules govern energy transformations make up this and the next two chapters.

5.1   Energy

Energy is the ability to bring about change or to do work. It exists in many forms, such as heat, light, chemical energy, and electrical energy (Figure 5.1). You have no doubt experienced the energy locked in pieces of wood as it is released by a fire, or used the energy in natural gas to heat a pot of water. Most of us are somewhat familiar with the use of electrical energy to cool or warm our homes, to light our streets, and to power computers. Some of us have been revived after heart stoppage by the power of electrical energy. We might be familiar with the concept that the food we eat is energy (Figure 5.1). What rules govern energy and its uses?

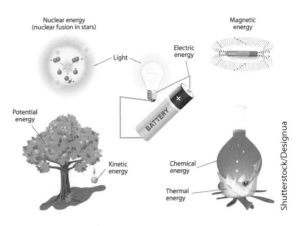

Potential energy, as the name implies, is energy that has not yet been used. Kinetic energy is energy that is currently in use (or motion). A tank of gasoline has a certain potential energy that is converted into kinetic energy by your car's engine. When the potential energy in the gasoline has all been converted into kinetic energy, you're outta gas! Batteries, when new or recharged, have a certain potential energy. We have all experienced the modern frustration of low battery on our cell phone (Figure 5.2)! When freshly recharged, there is a certain amount of talk/text/use time on the battery. However, as we use the device, the potential energy stored in its battery gets converted into kinetic energy. When the battery's potential energy is all used up, our phone is dead. In the case of rechargeable batteries, recharging can restore their potential energy. Now we can text again! LOL! ROTFLMFAO! Whatever that means.

FIGURE 5.1 Forms of energy.

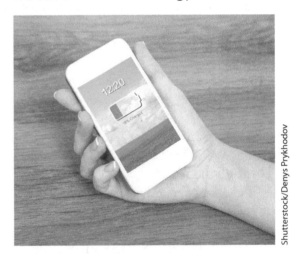

FIGURE 5.2 Woman holding a smart phone with low battery.

Potential energy is in food. One 12-ounce can of cola has 157 Calories. A Calorie is a measure of energy. When you drink that soda, the sugars in the cola are absorbed into your bloodstream and dispersed to cells around your body. Once inside your cells, those sugars may be broken down and converted into kinetic energy to power your cells.

5.2   Laws of Thermodynamics

Thermodynamics is the field of science dealing with the study of energy. The First Law of Thermodynamics states that energy can be changed from one form to another, but it cannot be created or destroyed. The total amount of energy and matter in the Universe remains constant, merely changing from one form to another. The First Law of Thermodynamics states that energy is always conserved, and that it cannot be created or destroyed. In essence, energy can be converted from one form into another.

Think back to the example of the cell phone earlier in this chapter. The fully charged cell phone battery has energy for a certain amount of talk time. The battery does not create the energy, according to the first law. It does, however, *convert* the potential energy in its battery into kinetic energy needed to talk, text, surf the Web, etc. Once the potential energy has been all converted to kinetic energy, your phone is dead. You cannot use the device until you connect it to a power source and recharge the battery.

The Second Law of Thermodynamics states that in all energy exchanges, if no energy enters or leaves the system, the potential energy of a system will always be less what it was initially. This is also commonly referred to as entropy. A spring-driven watch will run until the potential energy in the spring is converted, and not again until energy is reapplied to the spring to rewind it. That is an application of the First Law. A car that has run out of gas will not run again until you walk 10 miles to a gas station and refuel the car. That is also an application of the First Law.

In the process of energy transfer, some energy will be lost as heat. When you drive to school and observe the temperature gauge on your car progress from cold to between cold and hot. That heat is a consequence of the Second Law: energy conversions are not 100% efficient, some energy is lost as heat. Your cell phone battery seems to not last as long the more times you charge and use it. Again, a consequence of the Second Law. When you charge your phone, have you ever noted that phone was warm to the touch? Care to guess which Law this is a manifestation of? Correct, the Second Law explains this. When you exercise your body rids itself of excess heat by sweating. Where does this heat come from? The metabolism of sugars in your muscles produces ATP, but also a great deal of heat. Again, this is a consequence of the Second Law of Thermodynamics.

Entropy is a measure of disorder: Cells are not disordered and so have a low entropy. The flow of energy into living things allows them to maintain order and life. Entropy wins when organisms cease to take in energy and die.

When we look at any natural environment we can break down the complex organization into a series of trophic levels along a food chain. At the base of any food chain are the primary producers, typically photosynthetic organisms like cyanobacteria, algae (Figure 5.3), or plants. In marine ecosystems, we refer to these creatures as phytoplankton. The organisms that eat the producers are the primary consumers. Typically small protists or animals occupy this level in marine environments. Primary consumers are eaten in turn by secondary consumers, larger animals and so up the food chain to the top consumer, in the case of our illustration, the quaternary consumer (fourth trophic level). With each change in trophic level, the amount of energy available decreases. This is a direct result of the actions of the Second Law of Thermodynamics.

Almost all life on Earth depends directly or indirectly on the Sun. Photosynthetic producers convert unusable sunlight energy into the stored energy in sugar molecules such as glucose. The Sun produces an incredible amount of energy. Only about 2% of this energy is used during photosynthesis. That's 98% waste energy! When the energy stored in the carbon-carbon covalent bonds of glucose is released, about 39% of this energy is trapped in the pyrophosphate bond of ATP. The remaining 61% of the energy is wasted as heat. With each successive trophic level the amount of available energy decreases. It takes quite a few organisms to support the trophic level above. When we look at the top carnivores in any environment their number is quite small compared to the number of producers at the base of the food chain.

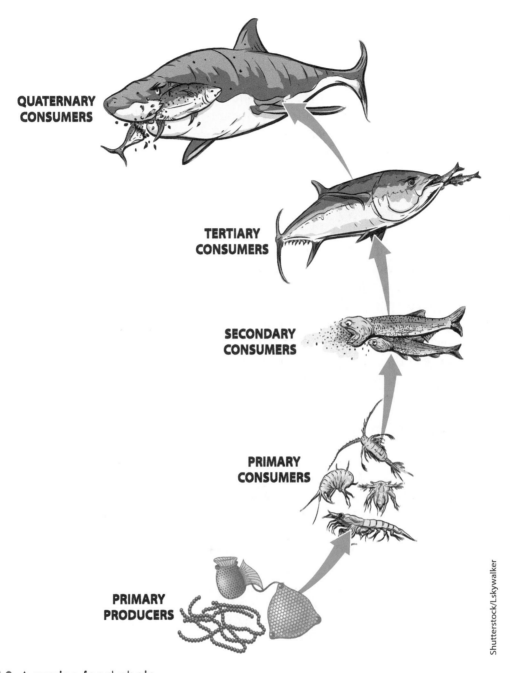

QUATERNARY
CONSUMERS

TERTIARY
CONSUMERS

SECONDARY
CONSUMERS

PRIMARY
CONSUMERS

PRIMARY
PRODUCERS

Shutterstock/Lskywalker

FIGURE 5.3 A marine food chain.

Chemicals can be considered as potential or kinetic energy. For example, one pound of sugar has a certain potential energy: if that pound of sugar is burned, the energy is released all at once as kinetic energy (heat). So much is released that organisms would burn up if all that sugar energy was released at once. Organisms must release the energy a little bit at a time. Cells convert potential energy, usually in the form of C–C covalent bonds or ATP molecules, into kinetic energy to accomplish cell division, growth, biosynthesis, and active transport, among other things.

5.3   Chemical Reactions

Living things need energy. Thermodynamics is the study of how this energy is conserved and transferred. One view of living systems is that they are an amazing series of biochemical reactions almost all of which are controlled by specialized protein machines known as enzymes. These machines allow energy to be released as well as captured in a manner that will not be harmful to the cell. These enzyme-mediated chemical reactions have a few general characteristics that are worth a quick study before addressing the nature and functioning of enzymes.

5.3.1   Endergonic and Exergonic Reactions

Energy releasing reactions are termed exergonic reactions. Burning wood in a fire, releasing the energy locked in gasoline in your automobile, and running a flashlight using batteries are all examples of exergonic reactions. Reactions that require energy input and which tend to produce products with greater energy than the beginning products are known as endergonic reactions. Storing energy in a car battery is an example of an endergonic reaction. All natural processes tend to proceed in such a direction that the disorder or randomness of the Universe increases (the consequence of the Second Law of Thermodynamics). However, if energy is input, the second law can in a way be bypassed, for a while at least.

5.3.2   Oxidation and Reduction Reactions

Biochemical reactions in living organisms are essentially energy transfers. Often these energy-transferring reactions occur together, "linked" in what are referred to as oxidation/reduction reactions (Figure 5.4). Reduction is the gain of an electron. Sometimes we also have H⁺ ions along for the ride, so reduction can also become the gain of H⁺ ions. Oxidation is the loss of an electron (or hydrogen).

In oxidation/reduction reactions (Figure 5.4), one chemical is oxidized, and its electrons are passed to another chemical that then becomes reduced. Reactions like this are referred to as coupled reactions. The metabolic processes glycolysis, the Citric Acid cycle, and electron transport chain involve the transfer of electrons (at varying energy states) by these oxidation and reduction reactions.

5.3.3   Catabolism and Anabolism

Anabolism is the term applied to the total series of chemical reactions involved in synthesis of organic compounds. Catabolism is the term applied to the series of chemical reactions which breakdown larger molecules into smaller ones. Energy is released from catabolic breakdown. Some of this

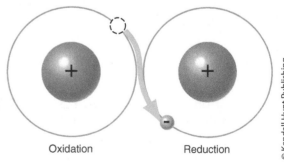

Oxidation   Reduction

© Kendall Hunt Publishing

FIGURE 5.4 Oxidation and reduction involve the transfer of electrons.

energy is utilized for anabolism. Anabolic processes may reassemble the products of catabolism into new anabolic molecules.

Autotrophs must manufacture, or synthesize, all of the organic compounds they need. They do this most commonly by the process of photosynthesis using sunlight energy to produce carbohydrates. The other autotrophs use chemosynthesis in which the energy of the Earth's internal heat drives the production of carbohydrates. Heterotrophs can obtain some of their compounds in their diet (along with their energy). You may recall discussions of these concepts earlier. Humans and other animals are heterotrophs, while plants, algae, and cyanobacteria are autotrophs. For example, humans can synthesize 12 of the 20 amino acids that we need to make all of our proteins. We must obtain the other 8 amino acids in our diet. To form the 12 amino acids, our bodies go through a series of anabolic processes. Those 8 amino acids we cannot make ourselves must be obtained from our food, by catabolic processes to break animal and plant proteins down into amino acids that our cells can then use in the anabolic processes of building human proteins.

5.4 Enzymes: Organic Catalysts

Many chemical reactions occur spontaneously when the reactants "bump" into each other to form the products of the reaction. Often these types of chemical reactions may need a greater energy (in their environment) than living cells can withstand. If a reaction is to occur in a living system, the energy needed to make the reaction proceed must be at a level that cells can tolerate. Numerous cellular chemical machines, better known as enzymes, facilitate such chemical interactions. Much like a fight promoter, who brings together two fighters, but who is normally not involved in the fight, enzymes bring together substrate molecules and promote a chemical change. Enzymes allow many chemical reactions to occur within the homeostasis limits of a living system. Without enzymes, almost every chemical reaction we need to function would **not** occur. Almost all enzymes are proteins, composed of amino acids assembled by cells according to directions stored in the cell's DNA. Like machines in an assembly line, enzymes work only on one chemical reaction. Enzymes function as organic catalysts. A catalyst is a chemical involved in, but not changed by, a chemical reaction. Since enzymes are not changed by the reaction they are involved in, they are then available for further reactions. Many enzymes function by lowering the activation energy (Figure 5.5) of chemical reactions. By bringing the reactants closer together, chemical bonds may be weakened and reactions will proceed faster (and at a lower energy level) than without the catalyst.

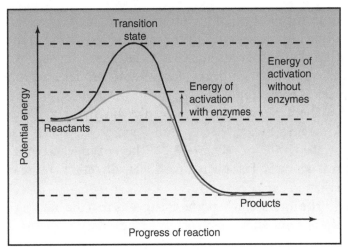

FIGURE 5.5 Activation energy.

© Kendall Hunt Publishing

When enzymes work correctly, we do not even know they are there. However, enzyme defects can sometimes have fatal consequences. Tay–Sachs disease is an inherited genetic condition that usually results in the deaths of sufferers by the age of three or four. Tay–Sachs results from a defective enzyme known as hexosaminidase A (or Hex A). The properly functioning form of Hex A helps break down chemicals known as GM2 gangliosides inside lysosomes within cells, mostly in the brain. Sufferers from Tay–Sachs have their nerve cells choked with innumerable lysosomes that contain GM2 gangliosides and nonfunctioning Hex A so that the cells no longer function. Tay–Sachs is an inherited disease, with each parent contributing an altered Hex A-coding gene to his or her child.

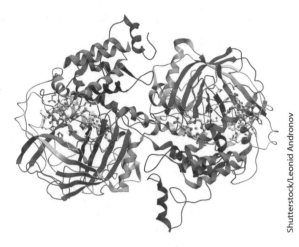

FIGURE 5.6 Structure of the enzyme catalase.

Enzymes can act rapidly, as in the case of carbonic anhydrase (enzymes typically end in the -ase suffix), which causes the chemicals to react 107 times faster than without the enzyme present. Carbonic anhydrase speeds up the transfer of carbon dioxide from cells to the blood. There are over 2000 known enzymes, each of which is involved with one specific chemical reaction. Enzymes are substrate specific. The enzyme peptidase (which breaks peptide bonds in proteins) will not work on starch (which is broken down by human-produced amylase in the mouth).

Almost all enzymes are proteins (Figure 5.6). The enzyme catalase, for example, is a complex protein with ribbons and helixes of amino acids. How an enzyme functions is determined by the shape of the protein, which is in turn controlled by the amino acid sequence of the protein, otherwise known as the protein's primary structure. This sequence is ultimately determined by the information stored in the DNA molecules (usually) in the cell's nucleus. In the case of Tay–Sachs disease discussed above, the patient lacks the DNA to produce a properly functioning Hex A enzyme.

The arrangement of molecules on the enzyme produces an area known as the active site within which the specific substrate (or substrates) will "fit" (Figure 5.7). The enzyme recognizes, confines, and orients the substrate in a particular direction so the enzyme-mediated reaction can occur.

The induced fit hypothesis suggests that the binding of the substrate to the enzyme alters the structure of the enzyme, placing some strain on the substrate and further facilitating the reaction. Cofactors are inorganic molecules that are not proteins but are essential for enzyme activity. Ions

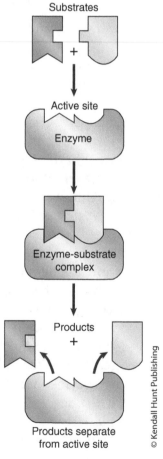

FIGURE 5.7 Enzyme-substrate interaction.

such as K^+ and Ca^{+2} are cofactors. Coenzymes are nonprotein organic molecules bound to enzymes near the active site.

5.4.1 Metabolic Pathways

Metabolic pathways (Figure 5.8) result from a series of enzyme-dependent chemical reactions. In the example illustrated in Figure 5.8, the end product, the amino acid isoleucine, depends on the successful completion of five reactions, each mediated by a different specific enzyme. The enzymes in a series can be located adjacent to each other in an organelle or in the membrane of an organelle, thus speeding the reaction process. Also, intermediate products tend not to accumulate, making the process more efficient. By removing intermediates (and by inference end products) from the reactive pathway, equilibrium effects are minimized, since equilibrium is not attained, and so the reactions will proceed in the "preferred" direction. Some reactions have a tendency to reverse when concentrations of the products build up to a certain level. In the pathway shown in Figure 5.8, the end product deactivates the first enzyme in the pathway, thus shutting down the pathway.

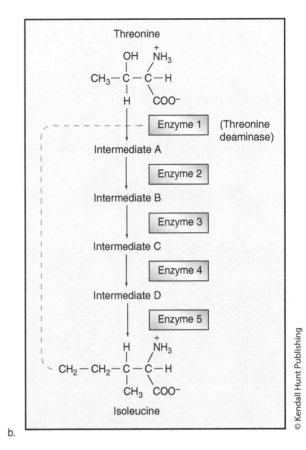

b.

FIGURE 5.8 Metabolic pathway for the synthesis of the amino acid isoleucine from the amino acid threonine. The process cannot be accomplished in a single reaction. Note also that the production of isoleucine serves as a feedback mechanism to turn off the entire metabolic pathway.

© Kendall Hunt Publishing

5.4.2 Control of Enzyme Activity

Cells do not normally leave their enzyme machines permanently turned on. Some level of control over the action of enzymes occurs. There are many factors that influence or control enzyme action.

Increases in temperature (Figure 5.9) will speed up the rate of reactions not mediated by enzymes. Likewise, temperature increase will speed up enzyme-mediated reactions, but only to a point. When heated too much, enzymes (since they are proteins whose function depends on their shape) lose that shape. When the temperature drops, the enzyme may regain its shape, and thus its function. Likewise, if an enzyme is chilled, it will lose some of its shape and hence its functionality. When warmed to its optimum temperature, the enzyme will resume its normal activity level. Thermolabile enzymes cause the color distribution on different body areas of Siamese cats (Figure 5.9) and seasonal color camouflage of the Arctic hare. These enzymes work better

Shutterstock/Matt Gore

FIGURE 5.9 Thermolabile enzyme activity in a Siamese cat. The cooler temperatures on the cat's extremities cause the change in coat color.

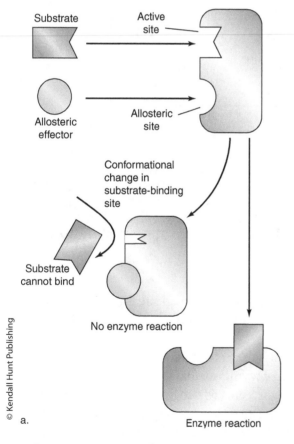

© Kendall Hunt Publishing

FIGURE 5.10 Allosteric interaction controls the shape of the active site as a negative control on the action of an enzyme.

(or work at all) at lower temperatures. The dark areas on a Siamese cat are on the extremities of the body: tail, paws, ears, and snout.

The concentration of substrate and product also will control the rate of reaction, providing a biofeedback mechanism. If we have one machine working at a given speed, logic tells us we can produce more products with more machines. This is correct as long as the supply of raw materials does not become a limit on the functioning of the machines. In a similar fashion, the more copies of an enzyme functioning in a cell, the more products of that enzyme-mediated reaction can be made. If too much of the product builds up, enzyme activity will be reduced.

Some enzymes need to be activated in a separate chemical reaction before they will begin to function. Chymotrypsin is an enzyme in the stomach that must be activated by the high acidity in the stomach. The need for such activation protects a cell from the hazards or damage the enzyme might cause, until it is needed.

Changes in pH denature the enzyme by changing its shape. Enzymes may also be adapted to operate at a specific pH or within a range of pH values.

Allosteric interactions (Figure 5.10) allow an enzyme to be temporarily inactivated. Binding of an allosteric molecule to the allosteric site on the enzyme changes the shape of the enzyme's active site, inactivating it while the allosteric molecule is still bound. Such a mechanism is commonly employed in feedback inhibition, a type of negative feedback control that shuts off the production of the product. Often one of the products, either an end or near-end product, acts as an allosteric effector by blocking or shunting the pathway that produced it in the first place. In the isoleucine synthesis pathway illustrated in Figure 5.8, when enough isoleucine end product of the pathway forms, some of the isoleucine binds as an allosteric effector molecule to the first enzyme in the pathway, effectively shutting down production. Once enough isoleucine has been used, the bound isoleucine diffuses away from the first enzyme in the pathway, allowing that enzyme to now begin again production of more isoleucine.

Competitive inhibition works by the competition of an inhibitor molecule and substrate for the binding site. If enough molecules of the inhibitor bind to enough enzymes, the pathway is shut down or at least slowed down. Para-aminobenzoic acid (PABA) is a chemical essential to bacteria that infect animals. Sulfanilamide drugs are similar enough in shape that they compete with PABA, shutting down an essential bacterial (but not animal) pathway.

Noncompetitive inhibition occurs when the inhibitory chemical, which does not have to resemble the substrate, binds to the enzyme other than at the active site. For example, the element Lead (Pb) binds to a certain functional group on many organic molecules by this mechanism. Irreversible inhibition occurs when the chemical either permanently binds to or massively denatures the enzyme so that the tertiary structure (shape) of the enzyme cannot be restored. Nerve gas permanently blocks pathways involved in the transmission of a nerve message, resulting in death. Penicillin, the first of the "wonder drug" antibiotics, permanently blocks the pathways certain bacteria use to assemble their cell wall components.

5.5   ATP: The Energy Currency of the Cell

Living things need energy. Thermodynamics tells us the rules that govern energy exchanges. Enzymes are life's chemical machines that facilitate chemical reactions that either use or liberate energy. So just how is this energy made available for the numerous uses, such as cell division, protein synthesis, and so on, that life has for it? What form of energy is the energy currency of the cell, the most readily usable form of energy for life's purposes? As you might guess there is a chemical involved, ATP. Your body needs the energy stored in between three and five pounds of ATP every day, yet we only have about 1/5 of an ounce of ATP. What is ATP and what does it mean to me?

Adenosine triphosphate (ATP) is the energy currency of the cell. Life needs a molecule that can temporarily store some energy, an energy shuttle if you would. This role is accomplished in every form of life by ATP, which transfers energy released from chemical bonds of organic molecules like glucose to endergonic (energy absorbing) reactions within the cell. All cells have a small amount of ATP. Cells are also capable of making more ATP when the need (for example cell division) arises. Perhaps the most amazing aspect of ATP is that all living things use it as their energy currency. The manner in which it is made is remarkably consistent from bacteria to animals.

Structurally, ATP consists of the adenine nucleotide. Nucleotides are composed of a sugar, a nitrogen-containing base, and a phosphate group. ATP has the sugar ribose, the base adenine, and three phosphate groups (Figure 5.11). ATP stores energy in the covalent bonds between phosphates. By far the greatest amount of energy (approximately 7 kcal/mole) is stored in the covalent bond between the second and third phosphate groups. This covalent bond is known as a pyrophosphate (or high energy) bond. When ATP loses this third phosphate, it becomes a lower energy molecule, adenosine diphosphate (ADP).

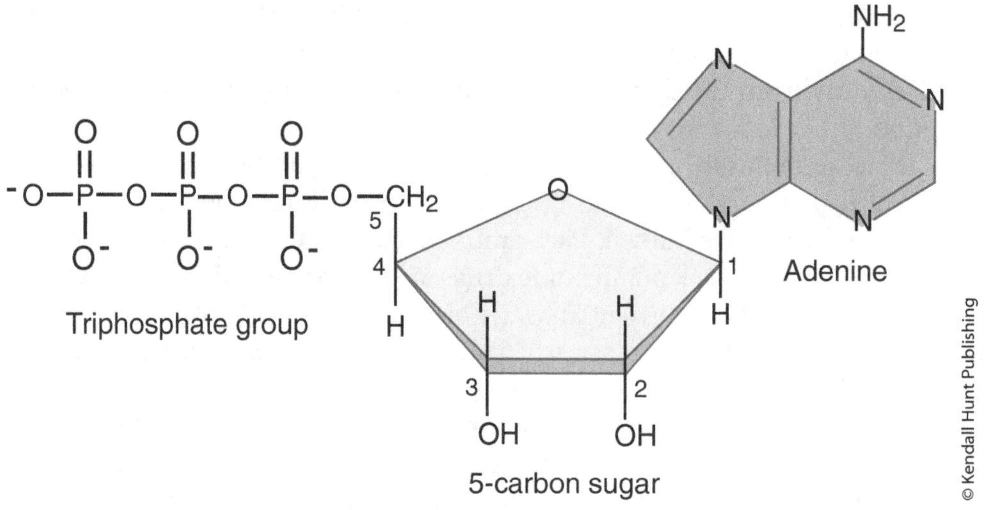

FIGURE 5.11 Structure of Adenosine Triphosphate (ATP).

An analogy between ATP and rechargeable batteries is appropriate. The batteries are used, giving up their potential energy until it has all been converted into kinetic energy and heat/unusable energy. Used batteries can be **only** used after the input of additional energy. Thus, ATP is the higher energy form (the recharged battery) while ADP is the lower energy form (the used battery). When the last (or third) phosphate is cut loose, ATP becomes ADP (Adenosine Diphosphate ADP; di = two), and the stored energy is released for use in a biological process. The input of additional energy (plus a phosphate group) "recharges" ADP into ATP (as in the analogy of the spent batteries that are recharged by the input of additional electrical energy). Our next chapter will explore ATP synthesis in detail.

Summary

Energy is the ability to do work. The form of energy living things use is stored in the carbon–carbon covalent bonds of carbohydrates, fats, and proteins. Breaking these bonds allows the low-energy molecule ADP to add a phosphate group and become ATP, the energy currency of the cell.

Terms

activation energy
active site
adenine
adenosine diphosphate
 (ADP)
adenosine triphosphate
 (ATP)

anabolism
autotrophs
catabolism
chemiosmosis
chemosynthesis
chloroplast
Citric Acid cycle

coenzymes
covalent bonds
cytoplasm
electron transport chain
endergonic
endergonic reactions
energy

entropy
enzyme
exersonic
exergonic reactions
food chain
glycolysis
heterotrophs
homeostasis
kinetic energy
mitochondrion
negative feedback

nucleotide
oxidation
phosphorylation
photosynthesis
phytoplankton
potential energy
primary consumer
primary producers
primary structure
reduction
ribose

Second Law of
  Thermodynamics
secondary consumers
substrate-level
  phosphorylation
First Law of
  Thermodynamics
thermodynamics
trophic levels

Review Questions

1. Which of these does not represent potential energy?
   a. a full tank of gasoline;
   b. electricity in the wiring of a building;
   c. water falling though a dam and spinning a turbine;
   d. a candy bar

2. The conversion of potential energy is coal into the kinetic energy that heats steam is an expression of _____.
   a. the first law of thermodynamics;
   b. the second law of thermodynamics;
   c. both laws;
   d. neither law

3. If we consider a gallon of gas as having 100 units of energy, and 25 of those units are used to move the car, what law of thermodynamics accounts for the other 75 units of energy?
   a. the first law;   b. the second law

4. If a sandwich has 100 units of energy, and the cell uses 40, what accounts for the other 60 units of energy?
   a. the first law of thermodynamics;
   b. the second law of thermodynamics law

5. Which of these is not a component of a molecule of adenosine triphosphate (ATP)?
   a. adenosine;   c. deoxyribose sugar;
   b. phosphate;   d. ribose sugar

6. Which of these would not be a process in cells that would likely use ATP energy?
   a. active transport;   c. diffusion;
   b. cell division;   d. protein synthesis

7. Most enzymes end in the suffix ___.
   a. –opsin;   c. –ose;
   b. –ase;   d. none of these, there is no such rule

8. When a gasoline engine burn gasoline, what type of chemical reaction is occurring?
   a. endergonic;
   b. enzymatic;
   c. exergonic;
   d. existential

9. Exergonic reactions produce products with a ___ energy level than they started out with.
   a. lower;
   b. higher;
   c. the same

10. The contraction of muscles is an example of a ___ reaction.
    a. coupled;
    b. exergonic;
    c. endergonic;
    d. reversible

11. When chemical X is reduced, which of these expressions would be an accurate representation of its reduced state?
    a. XO;
    b. XH;
    c. X

12. Which of these is most likely to happen when we place an enzyme in a strongly acidic pH?
    a. the reaction will happen much faster at the extreme acidity;
    b. no reaction will happen;
    c. reaction will occur as if the enzyme were at neutral pH

13. If an enzyme is the subject of allosteric interaction, which of these have happened?
    a. the allosteric inhibitor has bound to the active site of the enzyme;
    b. the allosteric inhibitor has competed with the regular substrate;
    c. the allosteric inhibitor has bound to the allosteric site on the enzyme;
    d. none of these

14. The chemical bond that attaches the phosphates to ATP is a type of ___ bond.
    a. ionic;
    b. covalent;
    c. metallic;
    d. hydrogen

Links

- **Interactive Cytochrome Oxidase:** You will need to download the Chime plug-in (available from this site), but it will be well worth it. View either of the subunits of cytochrome oxidase as well as related molecules. You can check buttons on the left frame to display selected portions of the molecule, zoom in, and zoom out. [http://www-bioc.rice.edu/~graham/CcO.Chime.html]

- **National Tay–Sachs and Allied Disease Association**: Learn more about Tay–Sachs disease, a fatal enzyme-based illness. [http://www.ntsad.org/]

- **The Bioluminescence Web Page**: This site clearly illuminates the phenomenon of bioluminescence, the generation of light by living things. This is often done using the enzyme luciferase through an enzymatic reaction. Learn about the variations and organisms that carry out bioluminescence. [http://lifesci.ucsb.edu/~biolum/]

CHAPTER 6
Cellular Metabolism: How Cells Produce Adenosine Triphosphate (ATP)

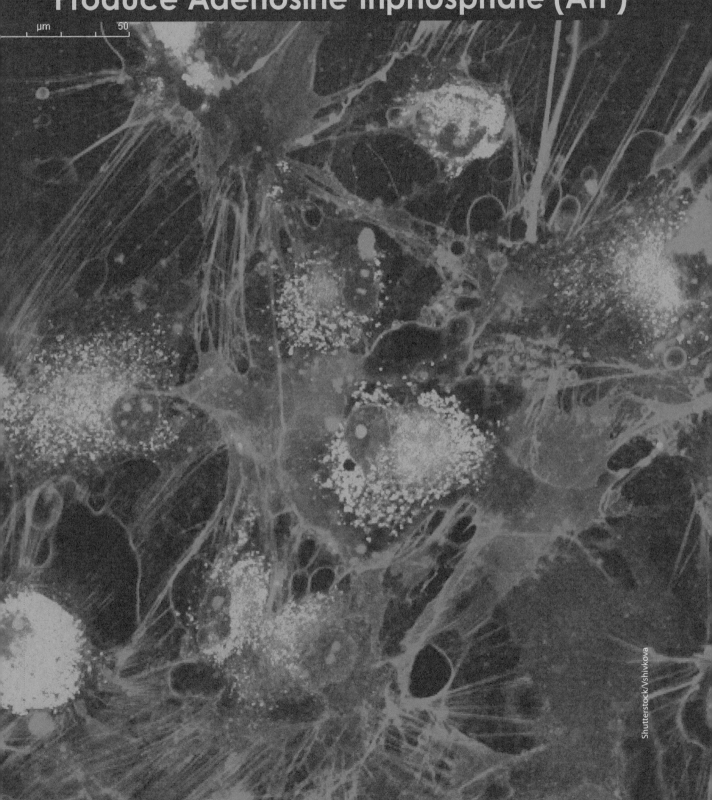

Chapter Opener

Skin cells labeled with fluorescent dyes. Mitochondria show as red, membrane shows as blue. This image illustrates the small size of mitochondria and their large numbers in cells. Why does a cell need so many mitochondria? Read on.

Objectives

- Describe the production of adenosine triphosphate (ATP) by the processes in cellular respiration.
- List and explain the main anaerobic pathways and the types of organisms that use them.
- Write the overall equation for aerobic respiration and indicate what forms of energy occur in this equation.
- List the beginning and end products of glycolysis. How much energy does this process produce? Where in a cell does glycolysis occur?
- Discuss the role of oxygen in aerobic respiration.
- Summarize the energy yield when a cell is under anaerobic conditions and what types of products are produced.
- List and describe the process of how and how many ATP molecules are produced during glycolysis, the Citric Acid cycle, and the electron transport system (ETS).
- Discuss the significance of fermentation.
- Explain what cells do with simple sugars, amino acids, fatty acids, and glycerol that exceed what the cells need for synthesizing their own assortments of more complex molecules.

Introduction

One day you remember that New Year's resolution to quit being a couch potato and start exercising (actually it was several new years ago, but *that's* not that significant now). Digging in your closet you locate a very old pair of running shoes and gear up for a run around your neighborhood. You feel good! As you begin running your muscles place a call to your body for more oxygen and sugar. For a short time (since your major form of exercise has been working the television remote control) your body responds to that call. Soon, however, your heart and lungs cannot supply the oxygen you need. Deprived of oxygen, your muscles still obey your will (to run, run, run!). Lacking the oxygen that allows the cells in your body to produce the most ATP from sugar, your cells begin fermentation. Ahhh, fermentation makes alcohol. You're going to get a buzz from this exercise thing. Unfortunately, humans do not convert sugar into alcohol, but rather into lactate that causes muscle cramps. All too soon your cells cannot meet the ATP energy demands of running, and you stop. Not bad, you made it past your neighbor's house! Slowly, oh so slowly, you limp home.

Next day you feel good. The day after your muscles begin making their presence known, with aches and pains of muscle stiffness. This is a result of the lactate, or as it is also known, lactic acid, fermented by your muscles while you were exercising. Over the next few days, however, the lactate is transferred from muscles to your liver. There, the lactate is broken down and metabolized. The breakdown of sugar into lactate is one aspect of how life harvests the energy locked in foods such as sugar. If you continue your exercise program you will improve your body's cardiovascular fitness and be able to exercise longer and longer periods of time before you begin fermenting lactate.

Life needs an energy source. For animals and most organisms on Earth that energy source is the Sun. Photosynthesis captures solar energy and converts it into chemical energy stored in the carbon–carbon covalent bonds of glucose. Glucose is the energy source animals and other heterotrophs need to stay alive, to make new organic chemicals, to grow, and to reproduce. This chapter will look at how the energy stored by photosynthesis in glucose is harvested and converted into ATP.

6.1   Overview: Four Processes of Cellular Respiration

Cellular respiration involves four processes: 1) Glycolysis; 2) Preparatory Reaction; 3) Citric Acid Cycle (also known as Krebs' Cycle); and 4) Electron Transport. The occurrence and sequence of these is summarized in Figure 6.1. These four processes occur when dioxygen (O_2) is present, what we refer to as aerobic conditions. The absence of O_2 is referred to as anaerobic conditions.

All living organisms begin the breakdown of their food by glycolysis. Usually this food is in the form of monosaccharide sugars, but other organic molecules, such as proteins and fats, can also serve as food. Glycolysis is a process consisting of nine sequential chemical reactions (or steps), each of which is catalyzed by a different reaction-specific enzyme. Whether or not oxygen is present, all organisms carryout glycolysis in their cytoplasm. Since glycolysis occurs in all organisms, we conclude it is a very ancient process that formed at or near the time of the very first cells. Glucose enters the glycolysis process, and two molecules of pyruvate exit the process, along with some ATP and other energy carriers.

The pyruvate molecules next enter the Preparatory Reaction where they are converted into a molecule known as acetyl Co-A. In breaking off one molecule of carbon dioxide (CO_2), some energy is trapped in an energy carrier molecule.

The acetyl Co-A molecule formed in the Preparatory Reaction next enters the Citric Acid Cycle, where the final release of carbon dioxide occurs. A great many energy carriers plus some ATP also form.

The energy carriers are cashed in by the ETS, producing the greatest amount of ATP. Dioxygen is required at the end of the ETS. Chemiosmosis converts the energy into the ATP molecules.

We can summarize the overall process of the release of energy stored in glucose as a chemical equation:

$$C_6H_{12}O_6 + 6O_2 \rightarrow 6CO_2 + 6H_2O + \textbf{energy (ATP and heat)}$$

Glucose + 6 molecules of dioxygen produces 6 molecules of carbon dioxide plus 6 molecules of water plus energy in the forms of ATP and heat.

During these reactions:

Glucose is **oxidized** to produce Carbon Dioxide

Oxygen is **reduced** to form water

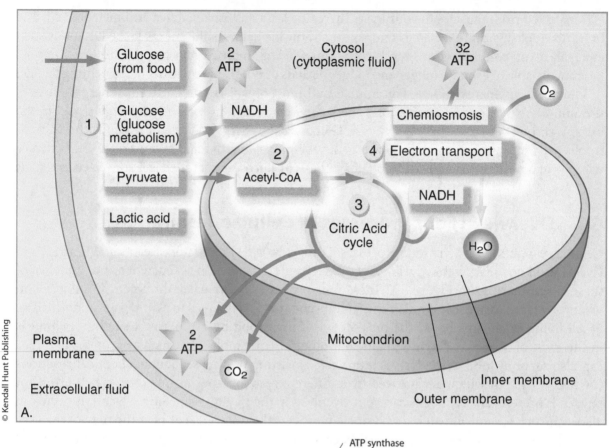

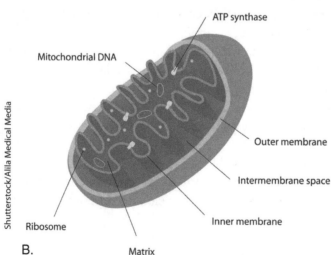

FIGURE 6.1 Cellular Respiration. A. Overview of the cellular respiration process; B. Diagram of a mitochondrion.

If O_2 is absent, **fermentation** works on the pyruvates formed by glycolysis. Animals and bacteria ferment pyruvate into lactate. Yeast ferments pyruvate into ethanol alcohol. There is energy yield from either form of fermentation other than the small amount of ATP that is actually produced by glycolysis.

6.2   Glycolysis: The Universal Process

Glycolysis (Figure 6.2) is a series of chemical reactions, each moderated by a specific enzyme. The process can be broken down into three separate steps: 1) Loan of energy; 2) Repayment of energy loan; and 3) harvest of ATP energy. The products of glycolysis are ATP, and energy carrier molecule nicotinamide adenine dinucleotide (NADH), and pyruvate. The phosphates from ATP are attached (phosphorylated) onto the glucose, transferring some of the energy from ATP to the glucose, leaving the lower energy adenosine diphosphate (ADP). This

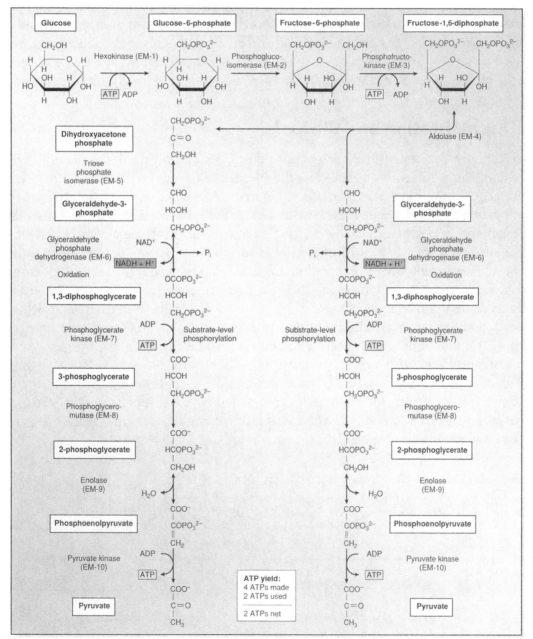

FIGURE 6.2 Detailed steps in the glycolysis process.

phosphorylation occurs at steps 1 and 3 (Figure 6.2). This energy is recovered at steps 6 and 9 when ADP is converted into the higher energy ATP by substrate-level phosphorylation. At step 5, NAD$^+$ is converted into NADH + H$^+$, an energy carrier molecule that shuttles some of the energy from glycolysis and other processes to make ATP by chemiosmosis with an electron transport chain later on.

Glycolysis works on glucose, a six-carbon (6-C) monosaccharide, converting it into several other 6-C molecules (Figure 6.2) until step 4 splits the 6-C into two 3-C molecules, glyceraldehyde phosphate (G3P) and dihydroxyacetone phosphate (DHAP). G3P is the more readily used of the two, although dihydroxyacetone phosphate can be converted into G3P by the enzyme isomerase. At certain steps in the process, ADP is chemically reduced to form ATP, and NAD is reduced to form NADH. The end result (Figure 6.2) for glycolysis is the production of two pyruvate (3-C) molecules, and a net gain of two ATP and two NADH for every glucose molecule that enters the glycolysis process (Table 6.1). Dioxygen is not required for glycolysis to occur.

6.3   Fermentation and Biofuels

The metabolic processes pyruvate enters after glycolysis depend on the availability of oxygen (Figure 6.3). Under anaerobic conditions (the absence of oxygen), pyruvate can next enter one of the three pathways: alcohol fermentation (Figure 6.3A), lactate fermentation (Figure 6.3B), or cellular (anaerobic) respiration. These biochemical pathways, with their reactions each catalyzed by reaction-specific enzymes (all under genetic control), are extremely complex. We will only skim the surface in this chapter. Most anaerobic metabolic processes do not produce an abundance of ATP, especially when compared to the yield from aerobic respiration of glucose.

Alcohol fermentation (Figure 6.3A, B) is the formation of alcohol from sugar. Yeast (most commonly some strain of *Saccharomyces cerevisiae*) is a unicellular fungus. Its cells, when under anaerobic conditions, convert glucose to pyruvate by glycolysis, and then convert pyruvate into ethanol, a C-2 compound. Alcohol fermentation also produces carbon dioxide gas.

Many organisms will also ferment pyruvate into other chemicals, such as lactate. Animals ferment lactate in their muscles where oxygen becomes depleted, resulting in localized anaerobic conditions. This lactate causes the muscle stiffness felt by couch potatoes after starting a new exercise program. The bacterium *Lactobacillus* ferments milk sugars into lactate as part of the process of making yogurt (Figure 6.3C).

TABLE 6.1 Summary of glycolysis. Location: Cytoplasm

Input	Output
1 Glucose (6-C)	2 Pyruvate (3-C)
2 NAD; 2 H$^+$	2 NADH
2 ATP	2 ADP + 2P
4 ADP + 4P	4 ATP (net gain of 2 ATP per glucose)

Biofuel production has become increasingly important to farm state economies. The crop, such as corn, is fermented to produce alcohol that can be used as a fuel or mixed with traditional gasoline. Cellulosic biofuel is becoming increasingly sought for as we are diverting the non-food part of the plant to make biofuel, not the food part of the plant, such as corn.

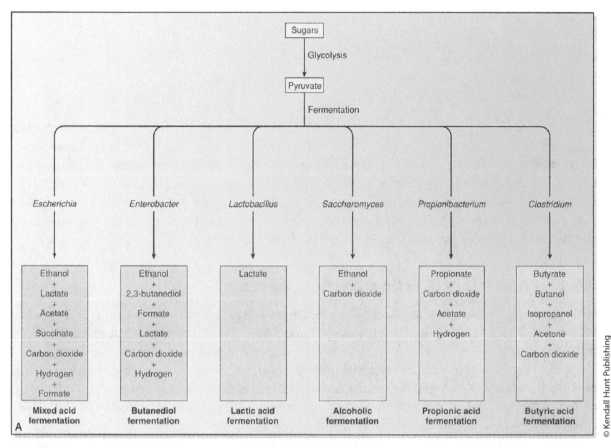

| Sugars |
| Glycolysis |
| Pyruvate |
| Fermentation |

Escherichia	*Enterobacter*	*Lactobacillus*	*Saccharomyces*	*Propionibacterium*	*Clostridium*
Ethanol + Lactate + Acetate + Succinate + Carbon dioxide + Hydrogen + Formate	Ethanol + 2,3-butanediol + Formate + Lactate + Carbon dioxide + Hydrogen	Lactate	Ethanol + Carbon dioxide	Propionate + Carbon dioxide + Acetate + Hydrogen	Butyrate + Butanol + Isopropanol + Acetone + Carbon dioxide
Mixed acid fermentation	**Butanediol fermentation**	**Lactic acid fermentation**	**Alcoholic fermentation**	**Propionic acid fermentation**	**Butyric acid fermentation**

A

© Kendall Hunt Publishing

B

Shutterstock/Martin M303

C

Shutterstock/Maurizio Milanesio

FIGURE 6.3 Fermentation. A. Alcohol and lactate fermentation; B. Detail of inside mash tun while making whisky; C. Production of yogurt by *Lactobacillus* bacteria.

TABLE 6.2 Fermentation and its results. Location: Cytoplasm

Input from Glycolysis	Output from Fermentation	Products We Make or Use by This Process
Pyruvate (3-C) and NADH	Alcohol, CO_2, and NAD	Alcoholic beverages, rising of bread, alcohol-based biofuels, animal feed
Pyruvate (3-C) and NADH	Lactate and NAD	Yogurt, Kim chi, sour beer, soy sauce

6.4   Aerobic Respiration

The presence of oxygen is required for aerobic respiration to occur. This set of three processes (Figure 6.1) generates a tremendous amount of energy trapped in ATP molecules. Most organisms will undergo three processes after completing glycolysis: more steps (Figure 6.1) to produce their ATP; the Preliminary Reaction; the Citric Acid Cycle, and Electron Transport (ETS). Only the ETS requires oxygen, which acts as the final acceptor for electrons that have been passed along from protein to protein. In eukaryotes, the aerobic processes occur inside the mitochondria. Prokaryotes perform aerobic respiration in their cytoplasm.

6.4.1   Preparatory Reaction: Getting Seated

Glycolysis again is our starting point, with a 6-C glucose molecule broken into two 3-C pyruvate molecules. Since dioxygen is present, each pyruvate will not be fermented, but rather it will be transported into the matrix of the mitochondrion. Pyruvate is first altered in the Preparatory Reaction (Figure 6.4) by removal of a carbon and two oxygens that will combine to form carbon dioxide, a metabolic waste gas. When the carbon dioxide is removed, energy is released from the carbon–carbon covalent bond of the pyruvate. Some of this energy is collected by NAD^+, which is reduced into the higher energy form NADH. A molecule of Coenzyme A, already present in the matrix, binds to the remaining 2-C (acetyl) unit, forming the molecule acetyl Co-A. Acetyl-CoA can then enter into the Citric Acid Cycle (Figure 6.4).

Think of the Preparatory Reaction and Citric Acid Cycle as if the two processes were a fancy restaurant. You do not just walk in and sit down at a table in such an establishment. You must first speak to a greeter. This person passes you to a seater, who takes you to your seat. Another person comes to bring you water, and yet another person takes your order, etc. In this analogy, the greeter and seater are like the Preparatory Reaction. The Preparatory Reaction prepares the pyruvate to enter the Citric Acid Cycle in a way like the greeter and seater prepare you for your fine dining experience.

6.4.2   Citric Acid Cycle: Energy Carriers and Carbon Dioxide

The British physician and physiologist Sir Hans Krebs (1900–1981) described the Citric Acid Cycle in 1937 after his emigration from Nazi Germany, where anti-Semitic laws forbade him practicing medicine. His work resulted in a Nobel Prize in 1953. Sometimes this cycle is called

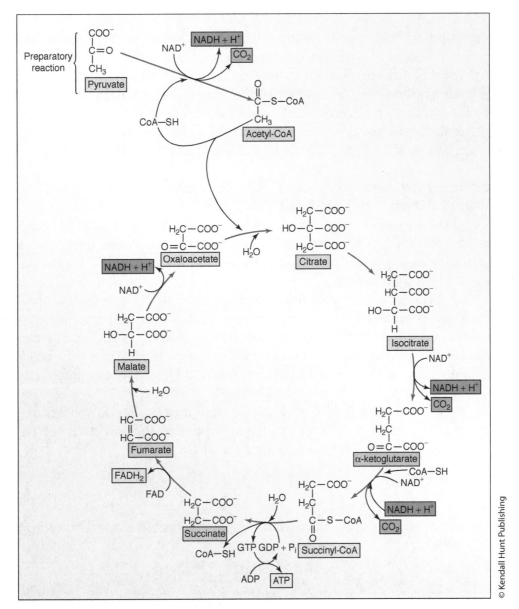

FIGURE 6.4 Preparatory Reaction prepares pyruvate to enter the Citric Acid Cycle.

Krebs' Cycle in his honor. These enzyme-mediated reactions completely oxidize the pyruvate into carbon dioxide. Energy carrying molecules, such as NADH, produced by the cycle (as well as some produced by Glycolysis and the Preparatory Reaction) pass their electrons (and energy) into the ETS (a series of proteins located in the cristae membranes of the mitochondrion, Figure 6.1). As the electrons pass along the electron transport chain, chemiosmotic synthesis of ATP occurs. Much more energy locked in the glucose sugar is released to form ATP by the reactions of aerobic respiration than was produced solely by glycolysis.

Acetyl Co-A (the 2-C molecule from the Preparatory Reaction) reacts with a 4-C chemical (oxaloacetate) in the mitochondrial matrix (Figure 6.4). Coenzyme A is released to react with another pyruvate. The 2-C acetyl and 4-C oxaloacetate form a 6-C molecule, citrate (another name for citric acid). The remaining reactions in the Citric Acid Cycle involve the removal of carbons (releasing carbon dioxide), and atomic rearrangements to glean the rest of the energy from the molecules. Every molecule of acetyl-CoA that enters the Citric Acid Cycle produces: 1) two ATP molecules by substrate-level phosphorylation; 2) six NADH; and 3) two $FADH_2$ energy-carrying molecules. By the end of the cycle, oxaloacetate has reformed, allowing the cycle to run again.

The reaction converting isocitrate (6-C) into α-ketoglutarate (5-C) releases carbon dioxide and energy that NAD^+ traps as it is reduced to form NADH. Between α-ketoglutarate (5-C) and succinate (4-C) the release of carbon dioxide and reduction of NAD^+ into NADH happens again. Guanine triphosphate (GTP), which transfers its energy to ATP, is also formed at this step by attaching a phosphate to guanine diphosphate (GDP). A molecule of ATP is eventually formed by substrate-level phosphorylation.

The remaining energy carrier-generating steps in Citric Acid Cycle involve the shifting of atomic arrangements within the 4-C molecules. Between succinate and fumarate, the molecular shifting does not release enough energy to make ATP or NADH. A new energy carrier, flavin adenine dinucleotide (FAD), captures this energy. The molecule of FAD is reduced by the addition of two hydrogen ions to become $FADH_2$. However, $FADH_2$ is not as rich an energy carrier as NADH, yielding less ATP.

The last step of the Citric Acid Cycle is the reaction of malate to reform oxaloacetate, which completes the cycle. Energy is given off and trapped by the reduction of NAD^+ to form NADH. The cycle can begin again with another acetyl-Co A.

TABLE 6.3 Summary of the preparatory reaction and citric acid cycle. Location: Matrix of the mitochondrion

Inputs	Outputs
Pyruvate (3-C)	Acetyl-CoA (2-C)
Coenzyme A (CoA)	CO_2
NAD + H	NADH
Inputs	Outputs
Acetyl-CoA (2-C)	2 CO_2 and CoA
FAD and 2 H^+	$FADH_2$
ADP and P	ATP
3 NAD and 3 H^+	3 NADH

6.4.3   Electron Transport System

At this point, all the carbon atoms in the glucose that started out in our glycolysis process have been oxidized to form carbon dioxide. Very few ATP molecules formed by substrate-level phosphorylation: 2 in Glycolysis and 2 in the Citric Acid Cycle. The NADH and FADH$_2$ energy carriers produced by Glycolysis, the Preparatory Reaction, and the Citric Acid Cycle still contain a great deal of energy. However, this energy is not in the form of ATP, the energy form most accessible to cells. The last process in aerobic respiration, the ETS converts this energy from the electron carrying molecules into energy stored in ATP.

The reactions of the Citric Acid Cycle and the Preparatory Reaction occur in the mitochondrial matrix. The last process of aerobic respiration, the (ETS, Figure 6.5), is a series of proteins embedded in the cristae membranes of the mitochondrion. The Citric Acid Cycle completely oxidized the carbons in the pyruvates, producing a small amount of ATP, and reducing NAD

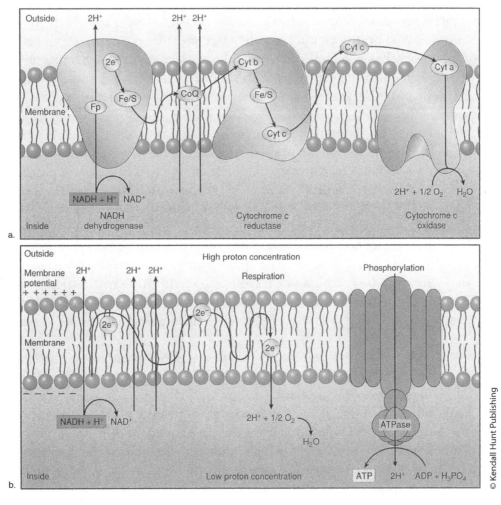

FIGURE 6.5 Chemiosmosis and the generation of ATP.

TABLE 6.4 Summary of the Electron Transport System. Location: Cristae membranes of the mitochondrion

Input	Output
Dioxygen (O_2)	Water (H_2O)
NADH	NAD and H
$FADH_2$	FAD and 2 H
ADP (GDP) and P	ATP (GTP)

and FAD into higher energy forms (NADH and $FADH_2$, respectively). In the ETS, those higher energy forms are "cashed in," producing a great harvest of ATP (Table 6.4).

Chemiosmosis (Figure 6.5) involves more than the single enzyme of substrate-level phosphorylation to make ATP. Enzymes in chemiosmosis occur in an electron transport chain embedded in a membrane. In eukaryotes chemiosmosis occurs in chloroplasts and mitochondria. Prokaryotes carryout chemiosmosis, but since they lack membrane bound organelles, they have their electron transport chains in their cell membrane. According to the chemiosmosis hypothesis proposed in 1961 by British chemist Peter Mitchell (1920–1992), a special ATP-synthesizing enzyme is also located in the membranes. Mitchell would win the Nobel Prize for Chemistry in 1978 for his work.

During chemiosmosis in eukaryotes (Figure 6.5), certain membrane proteins pump H^+ ions across an organelle membrane into a confined space (bounded by membranes in eukaryotic organelles) containing numerous hydrogen ions. The energy for the electron pumping comes from the coupled oxidation-reduction reactions in the electron transport chain. Electrons are passed from one membrane-bound enzyme to another, losing some energy with each transfer (as per the Second Law of Thermodynamics). This "lost" energy allows for the pumping of hydrogen ions *against* the concentration gradient (there are fewer hydrogen ions outside the confined space than there are inside the confined space). The confined hydrogen ions cannot diffuse back through the membrane except through the ATP synthesizing enzyme that is located in the confining membrane. As the hydrogen passes through the ATP synthesizing enzyme, energy from the enzyme is used to attach a third phosphate to ADP, converting it into ATP.

Cytochromes (Figure 6.5) are the molecules that pass the "hot potatoes" (electrons) along the ETS chain. Energy released by the "downhill" passage of electrons is captured as ATP by ADP molecules. The ADP is reduced by the gain of electrons. ATP formed in this way is made by the process of chemiosmosis (Figure 6.5). As electrons pass between the cytochromes, some of this energy is used to transport hydrogen ions from the matrix, where they are in low concentration, into the inner membrane space, where the H^+ ions are in much greater concentration. This establishes a gradient of H^+ ions across the inner mitochondrial membrane. These ions cannot pass through the membrane except through a special ATP synthesizing enzyme that facilitates the transfer of energy onto ADP, reducing it to form ATP. NADH passes its electrons into the

ETS chain at the beginning, yielding 3 ATP per NADH. $FADH_2$ enters at Co-Q (a cytochrome further along the chain), producing only 2 ATP per $FADH_2$.

At the end of the ETS, the electrons attach to oxygen. The resulting oxygen ion (O^{2-}) has a charge of -2, so it attracts two positively charged hydrogen ions (H^+) to form water. If oxygen is not present, neither the Citric Acid Cycle nor the ETS functions.

6.5   Energy Yield From Glucose

The breakdown of one glucose molecule results in a maximum production of either 36 or 38 ATP molecules. This represents about 39% of the potential energy of the C–C covalent bonds within the glucose molecule. The difference in energy content of reactants (glucose and oxygen) and products (carbon dioxide and water) is 686 kcal. One ATP pyrophosphate bond has 7.3 kcal of energy. Since one glucose molecule yields 36 ATP produced in aerobic respiration, $36 \times 7.3 = 263$ kcal. We can calculate the efficiency of the energy captured as ATP by dividing 263 kcal by 686 kcal, which produces a 39% efficiency of energy capture. The rest of the energy is lost as heat.

6.6   Tearing Down and Building Up Organic Molecules

The majority of the glucose molecules a cell imports it breaks down by the cellular respiration processes discussed above. If more sugar enters the cell than are needed for ATP-generating purposes, the cell assembles those sugars into polysaccharides such as starch or glycogen. Cells, however, have other organic molecules they must either synthesize or obtain from outside the cell. At various places in cellular respiration the building blocks of amino acids can be diverted from cellular respiration, as can the components to make lipids.

TABLE 6.5 Breakdown of ATP yield per glucose molecule

Process	Energy Yield	Total ATP Production in Eukaryotes (in prokaryotes*)
Glycolysis	2 ATP 2 NADH	2 ATP 4 ATP (6 ATP)
Preparatory Reaction	2 NADH	6 ATP
Citric Acid Cycle	6 NADH 2 $FADH_2$ 2 ATP (from GTP)	18 ATP 4 ATP 2 ATP
Electron Transport	All NADH and $FADH_2$ run through this process to produce ATP	36 ATP (38 ATP)

* Difference between prokaryotic and eukaryotic yield is due to the active transport of pyruvate into the mitochondrion.

Not all food we eat is sugar. A balanced diet also includes protein and fats. These are also possible energy sources that can be broken down and enter the cellular respiration process at various points. Proteins consist of linked amino acids, so the 2-Carbon amino acid backbone can enter into the respiration process after glycolysis. Certain of the R-Groups of the amino acids can also enter the catabolic breakdown process at certain points. Likewise Fats, which you recall from Chapter 2 consist of a 3-C glycerol plus three hydrocarbon fatty acid chains. Ingested fats are broken down and converted into energy by the aerobic respiration processes.

If these foods can be broken down, it is also possible to synthesize macromolecules by diverting breakdown products at certain stages of the process. For example 2-C acetyl units can be diverted to synthesize either amino acids or fatty acids. Three-Carbon molecules can be diverted to form carbohydrates and polysaccharides, glycerol, or R-groups. So aerobic respiration is not *just* for energy molecule (ATP) production.

Summary

Living things require energy to carry out a variety of tasks: reproduction, protein synthesis, response to stimulus, etc. This just cannot be any old energy, but rather in the form stored in the pyrophosphate bond of the ATP molecule. Sugars like glucose store energy. However, until that energy is converted into ATP energy living things cannot use that energy. All living things begin the breakdown of glucose by the process of Glycolysis to produce pyruvate in the cytoplasm of their cells. Fermentation occurs when anaerobic conditions occur in the cell. Aerobic conditions yield a greater amount of ATP energy using the Preparatory reaction, Citric Acid Cycle, and Electron Transport. One glucose molecule can yield energy to form up to 38 ATP molecules. Glucose is not the only fuel living things can burn to produce ATP. The process of photosynthesis covered in our next chapter produces glucose.

Terms

acetyi Co-A
aerobic conditions
anaerobic conditions
chemiosmosis
chloroplasts
Citric Acid Cycle
coenzyme A
covalent bonds
cristae

cytochromes
cytoplasm
electron transport chain
electron Transport System
enzyme
FAD and FADH$_2$
fermentation
glucose
glycolysis

matrix
mitochondria
monosaccharide
nicotinamide adenine
    dinucleotide (NADH)
phosphorylation
photosynthesis
preparatory reaction
pyrophosphate bond

Review Questions

1. Which of these cellular metabolic processes occurs in all living things?
   a. glycolysis;
   b. Citric Acid Cycle;
   c. Electron Transport System;
   d. photosynthesis

2. Which of these molecules is not produced by glycolysis?
   a. ATP;
   b. NADH;
   c. pyruvate;
   d. $FADH_2$

3. Where in a eukaryotic cell do the reactions of glycolysis occur?
   a. cytoplasm;
   b. mitochondrion matrix;
   c. mitochondrion cristae;
   d. chloroplast thylakoid

4. Where in a prokaryotic cell do the reactions of glycolysis occur?
   a. cytoplasm;
   b. nucleoid;
   c. ribosome;
   d. cytoplasmic thylakoid

5. The absence of oxygen is referred to as ___.
   a. aerobic conditions;
   b. anaerobic conditions;
   c. oxidizing environment;
   d. none of these

6. Which of these processes will occur in a human cell under low oxygen conditions?
   a. fermentation of alcohol;
   b. glycolysis;
   c. fermentation of lactate;
   d. a and b;
   e. a and c

7. Which of these cell organelles would you expect to find in abundance inside a eukaryotic cell that needs to produce a large amount of ATP?
   a. endoplasmic reticulum;
   b. mitochondria;
   c. chloroplasts;
   d. ribosomes

8. Which of these processes is used to make the ATP produced by glycolysis?
   a. chemiosmosis;
   b. substrate-level phosphorylation;
   c. enzyme-mediated hydrolysis;
   d. none of these are the correct process

9. Citric Acid Cycle produces all of the following chemicals except ___.
   a. NADH;
   b. ATP;
   c. oxygen;
   d. $FADH_2$

10. Citric Acid Cycle occurs in the ___ of a eukaryotic cell.
    a. matrix of the mitochondrion;
    b. cristae membranes of the mitochondrion;
    c. nucleus;
    d. cytoplasm

11. Which of the following is a not a chemical produced during Citric Acid Cycle?
    a. citrate;
    b. succinate;
    c. oxaloacetate;
    d. chlorophyll

12. The pumping of hydrogen ions (protons) across membranes during chemiosmosis is an example of which type of cellular transport?
    a. active;
    b. facilitated diffusion;
    c. osmosis;
    d. endocytosis

13. The energy used in the pumping of hydrogen ions during chemiosmosis comes from ___.
    a. the energy in the environment;
    b. the energy "wasted" as electrons are passed along the electron transport chain;
    c. the release of ATP energy;
    d. none of these

14. The first release of carbon dioxide during aerobic respiration happens during the ____.
    a. Citric Acid Cycle;
    b. Electron Transport System;
    c. Preparatory Reaction;
    d. chemiosmotic synthesis of ATP

15. The NADH that enters the Electron Transport System is produced by all of the following processes except ___.
    a. Glycolysis;
    b. Preparatory Reaction;
    c. Fermentation;
    d. Citric Acid Cycle

16. Where in the cell does the Electron Transport System operate?
    a. cytoplasm;
    b. matrix of the mitochondrion;
    c. cristae of the mitochondrion;
    d. endoplasmic reticulum

17. When NADH passes its electrons into the Electron Transport System, NADH is chemically ___.
    a. oxidized;
    b. enzymized;
    c. hydrolyzed;
    d. reduced

18. Which of these molecules is not formed by the activity of the Electron Transport System?
    a. NAD^+;
    b. oxygen;
    c. FAD;
    d. water

19. The yield to ATP from the complete aerobic oxidation of one glucose molecules is ___ ATP.
    a. 23;
    b. 36;
    c. 56;
    d. 72

Links

- **10 Steps of Glycolysis:** This About.com site reviews the steps in the initial breakdown of glucose. [http://biology.about.com/od/cellularprocesses/a/aa082704a.htm]

- **Virtual Cell Animations:** This National Science Foundation funded site offers a wealth of animations of biological concepts relating to this as well as other chapters. Of note here are the Glycolysis, Citric Acid, and Electron Transport Chain ones. [http://vcell.ndsu.nodak.edu/animations/citricacid_overview/index.htm]

- **Khan Academy Carbohydrate Metabolism:** The Khan Academy has produced a wonderful set of video lectures on many topics. Check out the ones on glucose metabolism. [https://www.khanacademy.org/test-prep/mcat/biomolecules/carbohydrate-metabolism/v/glycolysis]

- **How Beer Works by Karim Nice:** This site explains an application of fermentation that many people (of age at least) are familiar with. [http://science.howstuffworks.com/innovation/edible-innovations/beer4.htm]

CHAPTER 7

Photosynthesis: The Green Harvest

Chapter Opener

Giant redwood forests exist in California where they thrive in the moist, humid, foggy coastal climate. California redwoods can grow over 350 feet tall and live more than 2000 years. The leaves of these plants remove carbon dioxide from the atmosphere. Much of this carbon forms the cells of the tree trunks.

Objectives

- Study the general equation for photosynthesis and be able to indicate in which process each reactant is used and each product is produced.
- List the two major processes of photosynthesis and state what occurs in those sets of reactions.
- Distinguish between organisms known as autotrophs and those known as heterotrophs as pertains to their modes of nutrition.
- Describe the nature of light and how it is associated with the release of electrons from a photosystem.
- Describe how the pigments found on thylakoid membranes are organized into photo-systems and how they relate to photon light energy.
- Describe the role that chlorophylls and the other pigments found in chloroplasts play to initiate the Light-Dependent Reactions.
- Describe the function of electron transport systems in the thylakoid membrane.
- Explain the role of the two energy-carrying molecules produced in the Light-Dependent Reactions [adenosine triphosphate (ATP) and nicotinamide adenine dinucleotide phosphate hydrogen (NADPH)] in the Light-Independent Reactions.
- Describe the Calvin cycle in terms of its reactants and products.
- Explain how C-4 photosynthesis provides an advantage for plants in certain environments.
- Describe the phenomenon of acid precipitation, and how photosynthesis relates to acid precipitation and the carbon cycle.
- Discuss how photosynthesis might be employed to address issues such as climate change and energy requirements so vital to modern society.

Introduction

Earth is often considered the water planet. Biologists would consider the Earth as a photosynthetic planet. Photosynthesis powers most of the life on Earth. You either eat the direct products of photosynthesis or some organism that eats those direct products. Last chapter we learned the vital role of oxygen in getting the energy from sugars. Photosynthesis produced both the oxygen and the sugars! The process of photosynthesis has affected the most dramatic change in the chemistry of the oceans and atmosphere, changing the Earth from a reducing to an oxidizing planet by the production of dioxygen (O_2). Photosynthesis also limits the amounts of carbon dioxide in the atmosphere. Our nearest neighbors in space, Mars, and Venus, have carbon dioxide levels in their atmospheres well above 90%, Earth's atmosphere does not. Photosynthesis has been suggested as a way to mitigate the rate of climate change. This book is titled *Green Harvest* in recognition of the vital role photosynthesis plays in the life and atmosphere of our planet. So, what is this important process, and how does it impact each of us?

7.1   Overview of Photosynthesis

Photosynthesis is the process by which plants, some bacteria, and some algae (Figure 7.1) use the energy from sunlight to produce sugar, which cellular respiration converts into adenosine triphosphate (ATP), the "fuel" used by all living things. The conversion of unusable sunlight energy into usable chemical energy, is associated with the actions of the green pigment chlorophyll. Most of the time, the photosynthetic process uses water and releases the oxygen that we absolutely must have to stay alive. Oh yes, we need the food as well!

FIGURE 7.1 Photosynthetic creatures. A. Stromatolites of cyanobacteria on the Shark Bay beach in Western Australia; B. Giant kelp (*Macrocystis pyrifera*) grows in extensive forests off the coast of northern California; C. Forest waterfall and rocks covered with moss, plants that carry out photosynthesis.

We can write the overall reaction of this process as:

$$6CO_2 + 6H_2O \rightarrow C_6H_{12}O_6 + 6O_2$$
carbon dioxide + Water → glucose sugar + dioxygen

Water is *oxidized* to form dioxygen while carbon dioxide is *reduced* to form sugar in the presence of light and chlorophyll

Since most of us don't speak chemicalese, the above chemical equation translates as: six molecules of water plus six molecules of carbon dioxide produce one molecule of sugar plus six molecules of oxygen. This reaction will not happen without two important things: chlorophyll and sunlight.

7.2   Leaves and Leaf Structure

Plants are the only photosynthetic organisms to have leaves (and not all plants have leaves). A leaf (Figure 7.2) may be viewed as a solar collector crammed full of photosynthetic cells. The raw materials of photosynthesis, water and carbon dioxide, enter the cells of the leaf, and the products of photosynthesis, sugar and oxygen, diffuse out of the leaf (Figure 7.2).

Water enters the root and is transported up to the leaves through specialized plant cells known as xylem (pronounced zigh-lem). Xylem acts very much like a straw, when liquid is withdrawn at the top of the straw fluid is drawn up the straw. Land plants must guard against drying out (desiccation) and so have developed specialized structures known as stomata to allow gas to enter and leave the leaf (Figure 7.2A–C). Carbon dioxide cannot diffuse through the protective waxy layer covering the leaf (the cuticle), but it can enter the leaf by passing through an opening (the stoma; plural = stomata; Greek for hole) in the leaf. Each stoma is flanked by two guard cells. Likewise, oxygen produced during photosynthesis can only diffuse out of the leaf through the open stomata. Unfortunately for the plant, while these gases are moving between the inside and outside of the leaf, a great deal water is also lost. Mature cottonwood trees on a 100-degree day, will lose 100 gallons of water per hour. By contrast, a farmer resting in the shade of that tree loses about 1 quart of water during the same amount of time. Carbon dioxide enters single-celled and aquatic autotrophs through no specialized structures as they lack the cuticle covering.

The gases diffuse across the membranes of the interior leaf cells. Inside certain cells of the leaf are numerous chloroplasts (Figures 7.2), the cellular organelles that carryout photosynthesis. Photosynthesis basically breaks down into two processes (Figure 7.3): the Light-Dependent Reactions, and the Light-Independent Reactions. Each of these occurs in a different part of the chloroplast.

7.2.1   Chloroplast Structure

Chloroplasts (Figure 7.2D) are the sites of photosynthesis in eukaryotic cells. Chlorophyll, the green pigment essential for photosynthesis to occur, and associated accessory pigments (such as carotenoids) are arranged into collections of pigment molecules known as photosystems. These photosystems are embedded in membranous sacs, thylakoids. Thylakoids are stacked like pancakes in stacks known collectively as grana. The areas between grana are referred to as stroma.

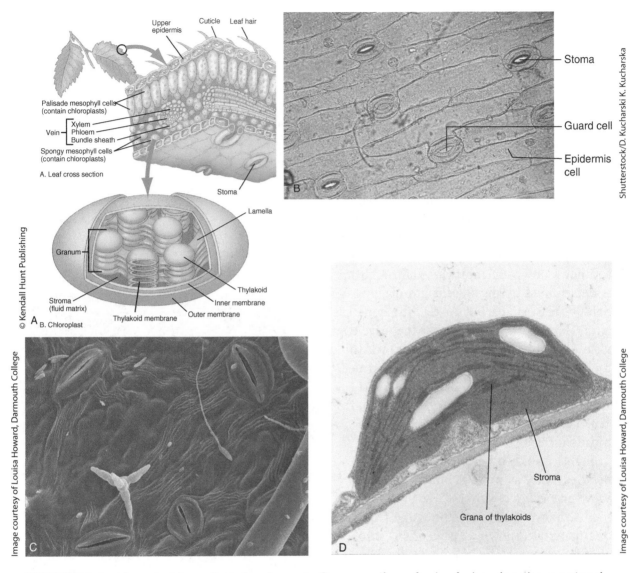

FIGURE 7.2 Leaf and chloroplast structure. A. Cross section of a leaf, showing the anatomical features important to the study of photosynthesis: stoma, guard cell, mesophyll cells, and vein; B. Light micrograph of a stomata apparatus showing guard cells and stoma; C. Scanning electron micrograph of the lower leaf surface of apple. Also present are bacteria and fungi; image courtesy of Louisa Howard, Dartmouth College; D. Transmission electron micrograph of a chloroplast from a cell of *Arabidopsis thaliana* showing thylakoids in stroma, with large starch grains; image courtesy of Louisa Howard, Dartmouth College.

While the mitochondrion has two membranes surrounding it, the chloroplast has three, forming three compartments.

The thylakoid is the structural unit of photosynthesis. Both photosynthetic prokaryotes and eukaryotes have these flattened membrane sacs that contain photosynthetic chemicals. Cyanobacteria and other photosynthetic prokaryotes have their thylakoids in the cytoplasm. Eukaryotes have chloroplasts with a surrounding membrane embedded in their cytoplasm.

7.3   The Nature of Light and Energy

We live in a world of color: red lights, green lights, color television sets, color computer monitors, purple orchids, etc. When white light passes through a prism (Figure 7.4A), the light is separated into the different colors (or wavelengths): red, orange, yellow, green, blue, indigo, and violet. Light is a form of electromagnetic energy and has some aspects that behave like a wave in water. Wavelength (Figure 7.4B), one of these wave properties of light, is the distance from peak to peak (or trough to trough). Energy of a wave is inversely proportional to the wavelength: the longer wavelengths have less energy than shorter ones.

The order of colors if visible light in a spectrum, such as a rainbow or when light is passed through a prism) is determined by the wavelength of light. Visible light is one small part of the electromagnetic spectrum (Figure 7.4B). The longer the wavelength of visible light, the more red is the color, and the lower the energy of the light. Likewise the shorter wavelengths are towards the violet side of the spectrum, which also has a higher energy. Wavelengths longer than red are referred to as infrared (IR), while those shorter than violet are ultraviolet (UV).

Light, unlike other forms of energy, behaves both as a wave and a particle. Wave properties of light include the bending of the wave path when passing from one material (known as a medium) into another. Examples of this include when light passes through a prism, droplets of water in the atmosphere splitting white light to form rainbows, and a pencil in a glass-of-water that appears bent or broken. The particle properties are demonstrated by the photoelectric effect. This property was in fact the discovery that won Albert Einstein his Nobel Prize. When a metal is exposed to ultraviolet UV light, the metal becomes positively charged because light energy forces electrons from the metal. These electrons can create an electrical current. The metals sodium, potassium, and selenium, all have critical wavelengths in the visible light

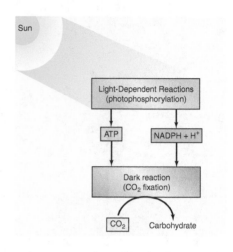

© Kendall Hunt Publishing

FIGURE 7.3 Overview of photosynthesis.

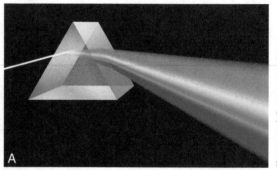

Shutterstock/Peter Hermes Furian

FIGURE 7.4 Light. A. The splitting of white light into its component colors by a prism; B. Electromagnetic spectrum.

range. The critical wavelength is the maximum wavelength of light (visible or invisible) that creates a photoelectric effect. This physical phenomenon (using IR energy as opposed to visible light) is responsible for remote control garage door openers, television remote controls, remotely armed car alarms, and Bluetooth technology, among other products. It is also the basis for photosynthesis. Electrons are emitted from organic molecules, and pick up some of the energy of visible light, transferring it into the synthesis of sugar.

7.4   Chlorophyll and Accessory Pigments

A pigment is any substance that absorbs light (Figure 7.5). The color that we see a pigment as comes from the wavelengths of light reflected by that pigment. Scientists use specialized devices known as spectrophotometers (Figure 7.5B) to measure the percentage of absorption of specific wavelengths of light. Light passes through a specimen to a detector that measures the percent of absorption *for the specified wavelength*. Data gathered can be displayed on a graph like the one shown in Figure 7.5A. The lower levels of absorption are those that are reflected back (in other words, not absorbed). These tend to be in the green wavelength area of the visible light spectrum. Chlorophyll (Figure 7.6C), the green pigment common to all photosynthesizers, absorbs all wavelengths of visible light except green, which it reflects to be detected by our eyes. White pigments reflect all or almost all of the energy striking them. Pigments have their own characteristic absorption spectra, the absorption pattern of a given pigment.

Chlorophyll (Figure 7.6, Table 7.1) is a complex molecule. One part of the chlorophyll is a long chain of hydrocarbons, much like the handle on a tennis racquet (Figure 7.6C). The other part of the chlorophyll is a flattened area with a large magnesium ion, much like the head on the tennis racquet (the ion would be the "sweet spot" that transfers the greatest amount of energy from racquet to ball in this analogy). When light of the critical wavelength strikes this "head," an electron is emitted from the magnesium. Several slight chemical modifications of chlorophyll occur among plants and other photosynthetic organisms (Table 7.1). All photosynthetic organisms (plants, algae, and cyanobacteria) have chlorophyll *a*. Other pigment molecules, including various forms of chlorophyll, occur in photosynthetic organisms (Table 7.1). These pigments are

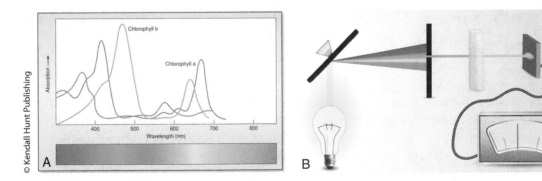

FIGURE 7.5 Absorption spectra. A. Absorption of the different wavelengths of light by chlorophyll *a* and chlorophyll *b*; B. Spectrophotometry technique simplified mechanism scheme.

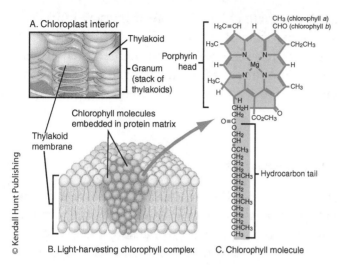

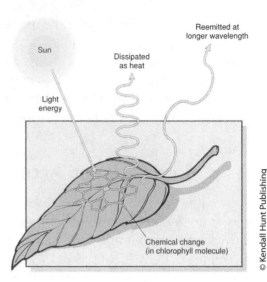

FIGURE 7.6 Chlorophyll. A. Chloroplast interior; B. Photosystem containing chlorophyll and accessory pigments embedded in the thylakoid membrane; C. Structure of the molecules chlorophyll *a* and chlorophyll *b*.

FIGURE 7.7 What happens to light striking a leaf.

TABLE 7.1. Photosynthetic pigments occurring in bacteria, algae, and plants.

Taxonomic Group	Photosynthetic Pigments
Cyanobacteria (such as *Oscillatoria, Anabaena*)	chlorophyll *a*, chlorophyll *c*, phycocyanin, phycoerythrin
Chloroxybacteria (such as *Prochloron*)	chlorophyll *a*, chlorophyll *b*
Green Algae (Chlorophyta such as *Volvox, Spirogyra*)	chlorophyll *a*, chlorophyll *b*, carotenoids
Red Algae (Rhodophyta such as *Mastocarpus*)	chlorophyll *a*, phycocyanin, phycoerythrin, phycobilins
Brown Algae (Phaeophyta such as *Fucus, Laminaria*)	chlorophyll *a*, chlorophyll *c*, fucoxanthin and other carotenoids
Dinoflagellates (Pyrrophyta such as *Pfiesteria, Peridinium*)	chlorophyll *a*, chlorophyll *c*, peridinin and other carotenoids
Plants	chlorophyll *a*, chlorophyll *b*, carotenoids

known as accessory pigments. Accessory pigments absorb energy not absorbed by chlorophyll *a*. These pigments include chlorophyll *b*, also chlorophyll *c*, anthocyanin, and carotenoids.

Chlorophyll *a* (Figure 7.6C) absorbs energy from the violet-blue and reddish orange-red wavelengths, and very little from the intermediate (green-yellow-orange) wavelengths. Carotenoids (such as carotene) and chlorophyll *b* absorb some of this energy in the green wavelengths that chlorophyll *a* does not (Figure 7.5A). Both chlorophylls also absorb in the orange-red end of the spectrum, where the light has longer wavelengths and lower energy.

The action spectrum of photosynthesis (Figure 7.5A) is the relative effectiveness of different wavelengths of light at generating electrons from either individual pigments or from an array of pigments. When a pigment absorbs light energy (Figure 7.7), one of three events will occur: 1) energy is dissipated as heat; 2) energy may be emitted immediately as a longer wavelength, a phenomenon known as fluorescence; or 3) energy may also trigger a chemical reaction as occurs in photosynthesis. Chlorophyll only triggers a chemical reaction when it is associated with proteins embedded in a membrane as in a chloroplast or the thylakoids found in photosynthetic prokaryotes. We can extract photosynthetic pigments from leaves by using a blender in which we have added a solvent such as acetone. These pigments can then be studied in detail.

7.5   Stages of Photosynthesis

Photosynthesis (Figure 7.3) is a two-stage process. The first stage, the Light-Dependent Reactions (formerly known as the Light Reactions), uses the energy of light to energize electron energy carrier molecules ATP and NADPH that are subsequently used to synthesize carbohydrates. During this first stage, in the most common form of photosynthesis, water is split, generating electrons that pass into the photosystem and give off O_2 as a waste product. These electron carriers transfer energy (and electrons) to the next stage, the Light-Independent Process (formerly known as the Dark Reactions). The Light-Independent Process occurs when the electron energy carrying molecules produced during the first stage of photosynthesis are used to the form C–C covalent bonds of a carbohydrate. The carbon to make these carbohydrates comes from carbon dioxide in the environment. The Light-Independent Process can usually occur in the dark if the energy carriers produced by the Light-Dependent Process are Present. Studies suggest that a major enzyme of the Light-Independent Process is indirectly stimulated by light, thus the term Dark Reaction is somewhat misleading. The chemical reactions of the Light-Dependent Process occur in the grana and the reactions of the Light-Independent Process take place in the stroma of the chloroplasts.

7.5.1   Light-Dependent Process: Converting the Energy of Light into Chemical Energy

In the Light-Dependent Reactions (Figure 7.8), light of the critical wavelength strikes a molecule of chlorophyll *a* and excites electrons to a higher energy level. These electrons then pass into a series of oxidation/reduction reactions, where their energy is converted (by an electron transport chain) to chemically reduce adenosine diphosphate (ADP) plus a phosphate into ATP. At the end of the chain, the electrons are passed to another photosystem. Light reenergizes this second photosystem and once again excites the electrons into a short-electron transport chain that ends with an enzyme that reduces Nicotinamide Adenine Dinucleotide Phosphate (NADP) into NADPH. Since the electron does not cycle back to the first photosystem, the system will eventually need more electrons. It gets them by splitting water (H_2O). Water is split in the process, releasing dioxygen (O_2) as a by-product of the reaction. The electrons and passing the electrons into the photosystem where they replace the electrons that have passed through the process and are now part of the NADPH molecule. The energy temporarily locked in the ATP and NADPH molecules is later used to make the C–C covalent bonds of a carbohydrate during the Light-Independent Reactions.

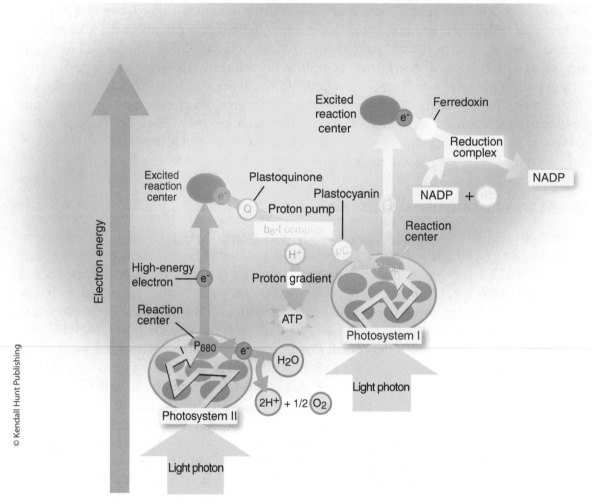

© Kendall Hunt Publishing

FIGURE 7.8 The Light-Dependent Reactions.

Photosystems are arrays of chlorophyll and accessory pigments packed into the thylakoid membranes. There are two different photosystems, numbered Photosystem I and Photosystem II. Some prokaryotes have only one photosystem that recycles its electrons. Eukaryotes and cyanobacteria use both photosystems and shuttle the electrons into the Light-Independent Process. To replace the lost electrons, organisms that use both photosystems draw electrons from the splitting of water, generating oxygen as a waste byproduct. The chlorophyll *a* in Photosystem I, referred to as P700 (because it emits light at the 700 nm wavelength). Photosystem II uses a form of chlorophyll *a* known as P680 (with a corresponding 680 nm critical wavelength). Electrons emitted from activated P700 or P680 forms of chlorophyll *a* will then pass to an electron acceptor and into an electron transport chain.

Photophosphorylation (Figure 7.8) is the process of converting energy from a light-excited electron into the pyrophosphate bond of an ADP molecule, making ATP. This occurs when the electrons from water are excited by light when in the presence of the P680 form of chlorophyll a. The electrons pass through a series of membrane bound cytochromes that carryout chemiosmotic electron transport to generate ATP, similar to what occurred in the mitochondria. Light energy causes the removal of electrons from a molecule of P680 that is part of Photosystem II. The P680 molecule replaces the "lost" electrons by breaking water into hydrogen and oxygen ions. The oxygen ions combine to form the dioxygen (O_2) that is released. Electrons are excited (or "boosted") to a higher energy level and attached to a primary electron acceptor that begins a series of oxidation-reduction reactions, passing the electron through a series of electron carriers and eventually attaching it to a molecule in Photosystem I. During these reactions, energy is stored in the pyrophosphate bond when ADP is reduced to form ATP.

Light excites a molecule of P700

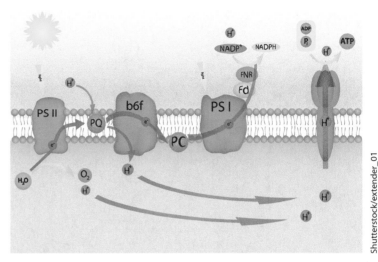

FIGURE 7.9 Chemiosmosis and ATP production in the chloroplast.

in Photosystem I, causing electrons to be "boosted" to a still higher potential. The electrons are attached to a different primary electron acceptor (that is a different molecule from the one associated with Photosystem II). The electrons are again passed through a short series of redox reactions, eventually being reduced onto $NADP^+$ and H^+ to form NADPH, an energy carrier needed in the Light-Independent Reaction. Electrons from Photosystem II replace the excited electrons lost by the P700 molecule. There is thus a continuous flow of electrons from water to NADPH. These electrons (and energy) are used during the construction of a carbohydrate during the Light-Independent Process.

Cyclic electron flow occurs in anaerobic photosynthetic bacteria and, occasionally, some eukaryotes. No NADPH is produced by this form of the Light-Dependent reactions only ATP. Since the electrons are cycled back to their original photosystem, water is not split and no oxygen is produced. Certain photosynthetic bacteria perform this type of photosynthesis. Since they live in extremely acidic environments, hydrogen for use in a carbohydrate comes from the environment, not from NADPH. Among eukaryotes, cyclic electron flow occurs when cells may require additional ATP, or when there is no $NADP^+$ to reduce to NADPH.

The generation of ATP occurs by chemiosmosis. As electrons are passed along the electron transport chain adjacent to Photosystem II (Figure 7.8), the transport to H ions into the thylakoid space and the conversion of ADP + P into ATP is driven by electron gradients established in the thylakoid membrane (Figure 7.9).

7.5.2   The Light-Independent Process: Let's Make a Carbohydrate!

In the Light-Independent Process, carbon dioxide from the atmosphere (or water for aquatic/marine organisms) is captured and chemically reduced by the addition of hydrogen to form carbohydrates. Recall from Chapter 2 that the general formula for carbohydrates is $[CH_2O]_n$; where n is the number of units in the carbohydrate molecule. The incorporation of carbon dioxide into organic compounds is known as carbon fixation. The energy to power this process comes from the first stage of the photosynthetic process, the Light-Dependent Reactions. Living

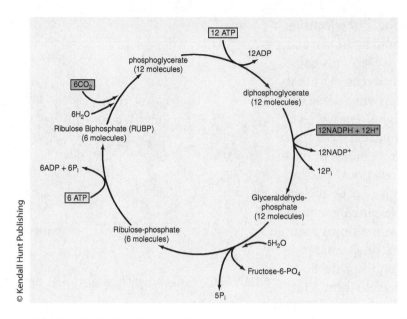

FIGURE 7.10 The Calvin Cycle.

systems cannot directly utilize light energy, but can, through a complicated series of reactions, convert some of that light energy into C–C bond energy that can be released by glycolysis and other metabolic processes studied in Chapter 6. Carbon-fixing reactions take carbon dioxide and chemically reduce it to form carbohydrates.

The Calvin Cycle is a series of enzymatic reactions that will reduce carbon dioxide into a carbohydrate (Figure 7.10). This cycle occurs in the stroma of chloroplasts, as well as in the cytoplasm of prokaryotic cells. Carbon dioxide is captured (or fixed) by the chemical ribulose biphosphate (RuBP), a 5-C chemical (Figure 7.10). Six molecules of carbon dioxide enter the Calvin Cycle, eventually producing one molecule of glucose.

We often refer to the Light-Independent process as the Calvin cycle in honor of American biochemist Melvin Calvin (1911–1997) who conduced his research with Andrew Benson (b. 1917) and James Breeson (1922–2012) using radioactive ^{14}C to trace carbon dioxide fixation.

The first stable product of the Calvin Cycle is phosphoglycerate (PGA), a 3-C chemical (Figure 7.12). The energy from ATP and NADPH energy carriers generated by the photosystems is used to attach phosphates to (phosphorylate) the PGA (Figure 7.12). Eventually, there are 12 molecules of glyceraldehyde phosphate (also known as phosphoglyceraldehyde or PGAL, a 3-C molecule), two of these are removed from the cycle to make one molecule of glucose. The remaining PGAL molecules are converted by ATP energy to reform six RuBP molecules, and thus start the cycle again. A different reaction-specific enzyme catalyzes each reaction in the Calvin Cycle.

7.5.3   The C-4 Pathway: Separation of Carbon Fixation and Carbohydrate Synthesis in Space

In order to improve efficiency of carbon fixation, as well as combat this problem of photorespiration, some plants have developed several versions of a precursor step to the Calvin Cycle (which

FIGURE 7.11 Examples of C-4 and CAM plants. A. Sugar cane field; B. Cornfield; C. Saguaro cactus; D. Agave.

is also referred to as a C-3 pathway). This step is known as C-4. While most carbon fixation begins with RuBP, the C-4 process starts with a new molecule, phosphoenolpyruvate (PEP), which is a 3-carbon chemical. The PEP molecule becomes oxaloacetate (OAA, a 4-C chemical) when a carbon dioxide is added to it. The OAA is converted to malate (another C-4 chemical) and then transported from the mesophyll cell into the bundle-sheath cell, where OAA is broken down into PEP plus carbon dioxide. The carbon dioxide then enters the standard Calvin Cycle with PEP returning to the mesophyll cell. The resulting sugars are now adjacent to the leaf veins and can readily be transported throughout the plant.

The fixation of carbon dioxide by PEP in a C-4 plant is mediated by the enzyme PEP carboxylase, which has a stronger affinity for carbon dioxide than does RuBP carboxylase. When carbon dioxide levels decline below the threshold for RuBP carboxylase, RuBP is catalyzed with oxygen instead of carbon dioxide. The product of that reaction forms glycolic acid, a chemical that can be broken down by photorespiration, producing neither NADH nor ATP—in effect, dismantling the Calvin Cycle.

C-4 plants often grow close together. Over time, their ancestors adjusted to decreased levels of carbon dioxide by raising the carbon dioxide concentration in certain leaf cells to prevent photorespiration. Most C-4 plants evolved in the tropics and are better adapted to higher temperatures than are the C-3 plants found at higher latitudes. This is due to PEP carboxylase working better at higher temperatures than does RuBP carboxylase. Common C-4 plants include crabgrass, corn, and sugar cane (Figure 7.11A, B). All C-4 plants separate carbon fixation from carbohydrate synthesis in space.

7.5.4   Crassulacean Acid Metabolism (CAM): Separation of C-Fixation and Carbohydrate Synthesis in Time

The CAM pathway often occurs among succulent plants that grow in deserts, including plants in the cactus family (Figure 7.11C), and agaves (Figure 7.11D). CAM plants partition carbon fixation from carbohydrate synthesis by time. During the night, CAM plants fix CO_2 forming C-4 molecules. The C-4 molecules are stored in large vacuoles. During daylight, these C-4 molecules release CO_2 to the Calvin Cycle (C-3 pathway). CAM plants separate C fixation from carbohydrate synthesis in time.

7.6   The Global Carbon Cycle

There is a relationship between photosynthesis and cellular respiration. Cellular respiration releases carbon dioxide, some of which is used in photosynthesis. Photosynthesis in turn releases oxygen used in cellular respiration. Animals and other heterotrophs depend on photosynthetic organisms for food, energy, and oxygen. In the global carbon cycle (Figure 7.12), organisms exchange carbon dioxide with the atmosphere and oceans. On land, plants take up carbon dioxide by the photosynthesis process and incorporate it into the organic chemicals used by themselves and heterotrophs. When living things carryout aerobic respiration, some of this carbon returns to the atmosphere in the molecules of carbon dioxide. In aquatic ecosystems, carbon dioxide from air combines with water to produce carbonic acid, which breaks down to bicarbonate ions. Bicarbonate ions are a source of carbon for algae. When aquatic organisms respire, they release carbon dioxide that becomes bicarbonate (HCO_3). The amount of bicarbonate in water is in equilibrium with amount of carbon dioxide in air.

The global carbon cycle (Figure 7.12) is used to trace the movement into sinks and out of sources for carbon. Sources for carbon include the burning of wood and fossil fuels, as well as the cellular respiration of living things. Plants and other photosynthetic organisms are carbon sinks, removing carbon dioxide from the atmosphere and oceans by fixing it into organic chemicals. Fossil fuels, such as coal and natural gas, are formed by alternation of the organic remains of once living creatures. The other major carbon sink is the mineral calcite

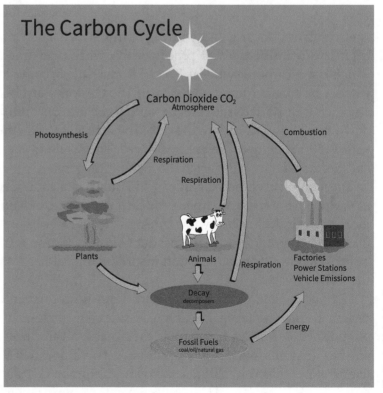

FIGURE 7.12 The global carbon cycle.

(calcium carbonate, $CaCO_3$), which is inorganically formed in warm shallow water to make the sedimentary rock limestone. Plants also produce some carbon dioxide by their cellular respiration, but this is quickly reused by photosynthesis. Animals are carbon dioxide producers that derive their energy from carbohydrates and other chemicals produced by plants through the process of photosynthesis.

The balance between plant carbon dioxide removal and animal carbon dioxide generation is equalized also by the formation of carbonate minerals (such as calcite) in the oceans removing excess carbon dioxide from the air and water (both of which are in equilibrium with regard to carbon dioxide).

FIGURE 7.13 The Okefenokee Swamp in Georgia and Florida is a modern environment very much like an ancient coal swamp.

Fossil fuels, such as petroleum, natural gas, and coal, as well as more recently formed fuels, such as peat and wood, generate carbon dioxide when burned. Fossil fuels are formed ultimately by organic processes, and also represent a tremendous carbon sink.

Living and dead organisms are reservoirs of carbon in carbon cycle. More than 800 billion tons of organic carbon occurs in the cells and tissues of the world's biota. The vast majority of this carbon is mainly in cells of trees. An additional 1,000–3,000 billion tons are in the plant and animal remains occurring in soil. Fossil fuels formed during various times of the geologic past when exceptional amount of organic matter were rapidly buried in an environment that locally lacked biologic activity, such as a coal swamp or depositional basin (Figure 7.13). Inorganic calcium carbonate ($CaCO_3$) accumulates in limestone and the calcite of shells of marine and freshwater animals.

Human burning of fossil fuels and wood has increased the amount of carbon dioxide released in the atmosphere to consistently over 400 parts per million (ppm) as measured at the Mauna Loa observatory in Hawaii. Between 1958 and 2014 the level rose from 300 ppm to over 400 ppm. While not all of that is human-related, the trend demands attention *and* action.

Increased carbon dioxide levels contribute to the greenhouse effect (Figure 7.14A), where gases such as carbon dioxide and methane trap incoming solar energy as heat. Instead of radiating from the Earth back into space, this heat is trapped by the gases, contributing to global warming. We know from studies of glacial ice cores that increased atmospheric carbon dioxide correlates with warming of our planet. The greenhouse effect is a warming of our lower atmosphere caused by increasing amounts of certain greenhouse gases (notably carbon dioxide and methane) that allow rays of the Sun to pass through, but then reflect or reradiate heat to the Earth. In this way, heat is trapped on Earth much the same way heat is trapped behind the glass panels of a greenhouse (Figure 7.14B).

The increase in carbon dioxide and other pollutants in the air has also led to acid rain, where water falls through polluted air and chemically combines with carbon dioxide, nitrous oxides, and sulfur oxides, producing weak acids that lower the pH of rainfall to as low as 4. The result is fish kills and changes to the soil pH, which can alter the natural vegetation and uses of the land.

The global climate appears to have risen about 0.5°C since the beginning of the Industrial Revolution. Reports in 2014 indicated that twelve of the previous 15 years had been the hottest on record. With the Industrial Revolution of the 19th Century came an increase in the use of fossil fuels, as well as production of certain greenhouse gases that were extremely rare before industrialization.

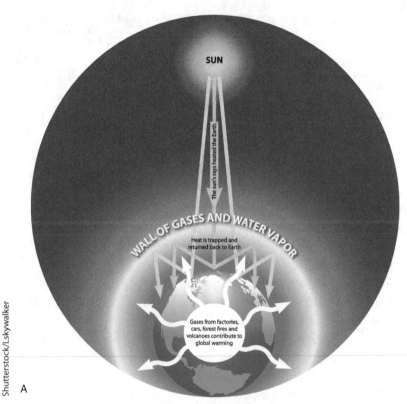

Shutterstock/Lskywalker

A

Shutterstock/Mikhail Olykainen

B

FIGURE 7.14 Greenhouse effect. A. Global warming of the Earth and the greenhouse effect; B. The University of Helsinki Botanical Garden at Kaisaniemi in winter on March 06, 2013 in Helsinki. The Palm House, built in 1889. Outside it is snowy and cold, but because of the heat trapped by the glass inside the greenhouse if warm and toasty.

Computer models predict a rise from 1.5°C to 4.5°C by the year 2060. Although a long-term rise of 2°C would seem minor, this is thought sufficient to completely melt the glacial ice caps in Antarctica and Greenland, causing sea levels to rise 100 m over a 300-year time span. This can alter climate patterns such as rainfall. Climate changes can have biological (such as migrations) as well as geopolitical and economic consequences. Federal government agency studies no longer discuss the matter of global warming as an "if" but as a "when."

The ecological effects of such a sudden rise in global temperature would be noticeable. From studies of fossils, we can estimate how long it would naturally take for such rises in temperature. The effects of human activity on the atmosphere will accelerate this rise from a span of centuries to just a few decades. As oceans warm, temperatures in the polar-regions would likely rise to a greater degree than other areas. Glaciers would melt and sea levels would rise due to melting and expansion of warm water. Water evaporation would increase with increased rainfall along coasts and dry conditions inland. Droughts would reduce agricultural productivity and trees would die off. Expansion of forests into Arctic areas would not likely offset loss of forests in temperate zones. Coastal agricultural lands and deltas in Bangladesh, India, and China would be inundated. In China, 800 million people live in low-lying coastal areas. Many of these areas will be flooded by rising sea levels. Coastal areas in Europe and other continents would be similarly affected.

Earth's climate fluctuates both short-term and long-term. There have been periods of Earth history with higher temperatures than we have today, as well as the reverse, when glaciers covered parts of the Northern and Southern hemispheres. We are currently between ice ages, the last of which ended nearly 10,000 years ago. Climate fluctuations have left evidence in the distribution of fossils, living forms and their close relatives, and locations of certain types of sedimentary rocks. Studies of fossils and the sedimentary rocks they occur in have led to estimates of temperature. Paleoecology is the branch of science that deals with such data in an attempt to reconstruct the environments of the distant (and not so distant) past.

Some scientists are concerned that global climate will warm at a rate ten times faster than in the past. Study of the carbon dioxide levels in the atmosphere provides clues about the possible impacts of climatic changes. In 1850, the atmospheric carbon dioxide level was about 280 ppm. Today, it is over 400 ppm.

One possible solution is carbon sequestration. Biological examples of carbon sequestration include reforestation, biofuel synthesis, and other activities that ultimately rely on photosynthesis to remove carbon dioxide from the atmosphere. One common method of biofuel synthesis is the distillation of corn or other fruits to produce ethanol. This can then be mixed with fossil fuel-derived gasoline. Various cyanobacteria and green algae, such as various strains of the green alga *Botryococcus braunii*, have been studied for their potential to produce biofuel precursors. Nearly 20% of the dried biomass of this alga is usable as a biofuel precursor. Nonbiological methods involve the physical sequestration of atmospheric carbon below ground. Success of these and new methods will be important to us all in the decades ahead.

Summary

This book is titled *Green Harvest*. Our reliance on plants and photosynthesis stems from the green pigment chlorophyll that drives the conversion of sunlight energy into organic chemical energy in the form of carbohydrates and other organic macromolecules. These molecules can find their way to parts of the plant we eat, wear, or repurpose. They may also find their way to animals we eat or whose products we use or wear. Photosynthetic bacteria transformed our plant's atmosphere and oceans billions of years ago, paving the way for modern life. So photosynthesis is a biochemical process whose significance cannot be overstated. Have you hugged your trees today?

Terms

acid rain
accessory pigments
autotrophs
adenosine diphosphate (ADP)
adenosine triphosphate (ATP)
bundle-sheath cell
Calvin Cycle
carbon fixation
carotenoids
chemiosmosis

chloroplasts
chlorophyll
chlorophyll *a*
chlorophyll *b*
cellular respiration
critical wavelengths
cuticle
dark reactions
equilibrium
electron transport chain

electron transport system
enzyme
fossil fuels
fluorescence
glucose
grana
guard cells
leaves
light reactions
light-dependent reactions

light-independent reactions
light-independent process
mesophyll cells
NADPH
phosphoglyceraldehyde
  (PGAL)
phosphoglycerate (PGA)

phosphorylate
photoelectric effect
photic zone
photophosphorylation
photosynthesis
photosystems
RUBP (Ribulose Biphosphate)

sinks and sources
stomata
stroma
thylakoid
xylem

Review Questions

1. The organic molecule produced directly by photosynthesis is:
   a. lipids;
   b. sugar;
   c. amino acids;
   d. DNA

2. The photosynthetic process removes ___ from the environment.
   a. water;
   b. sugar;
   c. oxygen;
   d. chlorophyll;
   e. carbon dioxide

3. The process of splitting water to release hydrogen ions and electrons occurs during the _____ process.
   a. light-dependent;
   b. light-independent;
   c. carbon fixation;
   d. carbon photophosphorylation;
   e. glycolysis

4. The process of fixing carbon dioxide into carbohydrates occurs in the____process.
   a. light-dependent;
   b. light-independent;
   c. ATP synthesis;
   d. carbon photophosphorylation;
   e. glycolysis

5. Carbon dioxide enters the leaf through_____.
   a. chloroplasts;
   b. stomata:
   c. cuticle;
   d. mesophyll cells;
   e. leaf veins

6. The cellular transport process by which carbon dioxide enters a leaf (and by which water vapor and oxygenexit) is___.
   a. osmosis;
   b. active transport;
   c. co-transport;
   d. diffusion;
   e. bulk flow

7. Which of the following creatures would not be an autotroph?
   a. cactus;
   b. cyanobacteria;
   c. fish;
   d. palm tree;
   e. phytoplankton

8. The process by which most of the world's autotrophs make their food is known as_____.
   a. glycolysis;
   b. photosynthesis;
   c. chemosynthesis;
   d. herbivory;
   e. C-4 cycle

9. The process of ____ is how ADP + P are converted into ATP during the light-dependent process.
   a. glycolysis;
   b. Calvin Cycle;
   c. chemiosmosis;
   d. substrate-levelphosphorylation;
   e. citric acid cycle

10. Once ATP is converted into ADP + P, it must be _____.
    a. disassembled into components (sugar, base, phosphates) and then reassembled;
    b. recharged by chemiosmosis;
    c. converted into NADPH;
    d. processed by the glycolysis process;
    e. converted from matter into energy.

11. Generally speaking, the longer the wavelength of light, the ____ the available energy of that light.
    a. smaller;
    b. greater;
    c. same

12. The section of the electromagnetic spectrum used for photosynthesis is ____.
    a. infrared;
    b. ultraviolet;
    c. x-ray;
    d. visiblelight;
    e. none of the above

13. The colors of light in the visible range (from longest wavelength to shortest) are ____.
    a. ROYGBIV;
    b. VIBGYOR;
    c. GRBIYV;
    d. ROYROGERS;
    e. EBGDF

14. The photosynthetic pigment that is essential for the process to occur is ____.
    a. chlorophyll a;
    b. chlorophyll b;
    c. beta carotene;
    d. anthocyanin;
    e. fucoxanthin

15. When a pigment reflects red light, _____.
    a. all colors of light are absorbed;
    b. all colors of light are reflected;
    c. green light is reflected, all others are absorbed;
    d. red light is reflected, all others are absorbed;
    e. red light is absorbed after it is reflected into the internal pigment molecules.

16. Chlorophyll *a* absorbs light energy in the _____ color range.
    a. yellow-green;
    b. red-orange;
    c. blue-violet;
    d. a and b;
    e. b and c.

17. A photosystem is ___.
    a. a collection of hydrogen-pumping proteins;
    b. a collection of photosynthetic pigments arranged in a thylakoid membrane;
    c. a series of electron-accepting proteins arranged in the thylakoid membrane;
    d. found only in prokaryotic organisms;
    e. multiple copies of chlorophyll *a* located in the stroma of the chloroplast.

18. The individual flattened stacks of membrane material inside the chloroplast are known as
    ___.
    a. grana;
    b. stroma;
    c. thylakoids;
    d. cristae;
    e. matrix

19. The fluid-filled area of the chloroplast is the ___.
    a. grana;
    b. stroma;
    c. thylakoids;
    d. cristae;
    e. matrix

20. The chloroplast contains all of these except ___.
    a. grana;
    b. stroma;
    c. DNA;
    d. membranes;
    e. endoplasmic reticulum

21. The chloroplasts of plants are most close in size to ___.
    a. unfertilized human eggs;
    b. human cheek cells;
    c. human nerve cells;
    d. cyano bacteria in a lake;
    e. viruses

22. Which of these photosynthetic organisms does not have a chloroplast?
    a. plants;
    b. red algae;
    c. cyanobacteria;
    d. diatoms;
    e. dinoflagellates

23. The photoelectric effect refers to _____.
    a. emission of electrons from a metal when energy of a critical wavelength strikes the metal;
    b. absorption of electrons from the surrounding environment when energy of a critical
       wavelength is nearby;
    c. emission of electrons from a metal when struck by any wavelength of light;
    d. emission of electrons stored in the daytime when stomata are open at night;
    e. release of NADPH and ATP energy during the Calvin Cycle when light of a specific
       wavelength strikes the cell.

24. Light of the green wavelengths is commonly absorbed by which accessory pigment?
    a. chlorophyll *a*
    b. chlorophyll *b*
    c. phycocyanin;
    d. beta carotene;
    e. none of these

25. The function of the electron transport proteins in the thylakoid membranes is ___.
    a. production of ADP by chemiosmosis;
    b. production of NADPH by substrate-level phosphorylation;
    c. pumping of hydrogen ions into the thylakoid space for later generation of ATP by chemiosmosis;
    d. pumping of hydrogen ions into the inner cristae space for later generation of ATP by chemiosmosis;
    e. preparation of water for eventual incorporation into glucose

26. ATP is known as the energy currency of the cell because _____.
    a. ATP is the most readily usable form of energy for cells;
    b. ATP passes energy along in an electron transport chain;
    c. ATP energy is passed to NADPH;
    d. ATP traps more energy than is produced in its formation;
    e. only eukaryotic cells use this energy currency.

27. Both cyclic and noncyclic photophosphorylation produces ATP. We can infer that the purpose of ATP in photosynthesis is to _____.
    a. supply hydrogen to the carbohydrate;
    b. supply carbon to the carbohydrate;
    c. supply energy that can be used to form a carbohydrate;
    d. transfer oxygen from the third phosphate group to the carbohydrate molecule;
    e. convert RuBP into PGA

28. The role of NADPH in oxygen-producing photosynthesis is to _____.
    a. supply hydrogen to the carbohydrate;
    b. supply carbon to the carbohydrate;
    c. supply energy that can be used to form a carbohydrate;
    d. transfer oxygen from the third phosphate group to the carbohydrate molecule;
    e. convert RuBP into PGA.

29. The dark reactions require all of these chemicals to proceed except ___.
    a. ATP;
    b. NADPH;
    c. carbon dioxide;
    d. RuBP;
    e. oxygen

30. The first stable chemical formed by the Calvin Cycle is _____.
    a. RuBP;
    b. RU/18;
    c. PGA;
    d. PGAL;
    e. Rubisco

31. The hydrogen in the carbohydrate produced by the Calvin Cycle comes from ___
    a. ATP;
    b. NADPH;
    c. the environment if the pH is very acidic;
    d. a and b;
    e. a and c

32. The carbon incorporated into the carbohydrate comes from ___.
    a. ATP;
    b. NADPH;
    c. carbon dioxide;
    d. glucose;
    e. organic molecules

33. C-4 photosynthesis is so named because_____.
    a. it produces a 3-carbon compound as the first stable product of photosynthesis;
    b. it produces a 4-carbon compound as the first stable product of photosynthesis;
    c. it produces four ATP and four NADPH molecules for carbon fixation.;
    d. there are only four steps in this form of carbon fixation into carbohydrate.

Links

- **ASU Photosynthesis Center:** This site continues to grow in its rich presentation of information. Check out the section on early events in photosynthesis. [http://bioenergy.asu.edu]

- **Photosynthetic Molecules Section:** This site offers 3D models of a number of important molecules in the photosynthesis process, including chlorophyll and carotene. [http://www.nyu.edu:80/pages/mathmol/library/photo]

- **Biofuels:** This National Geographic site provides information about biologically derived fuels. [http://environment.nationalgeographic.com/environment/global-warming/biofuel-profile]

- **The Science and Politics of Global Warming:** Plenty of blame to cast on both American political parties, all summarized at the PBS site. [http://www.pbs.org/wgbh/pages/frontline/hotpolitics/etc/cron.html]

Unit 3

Cell Division and Genetics

CHAPTER 8

Cell Division: Binary Fission, Mitosis, and Meiosis

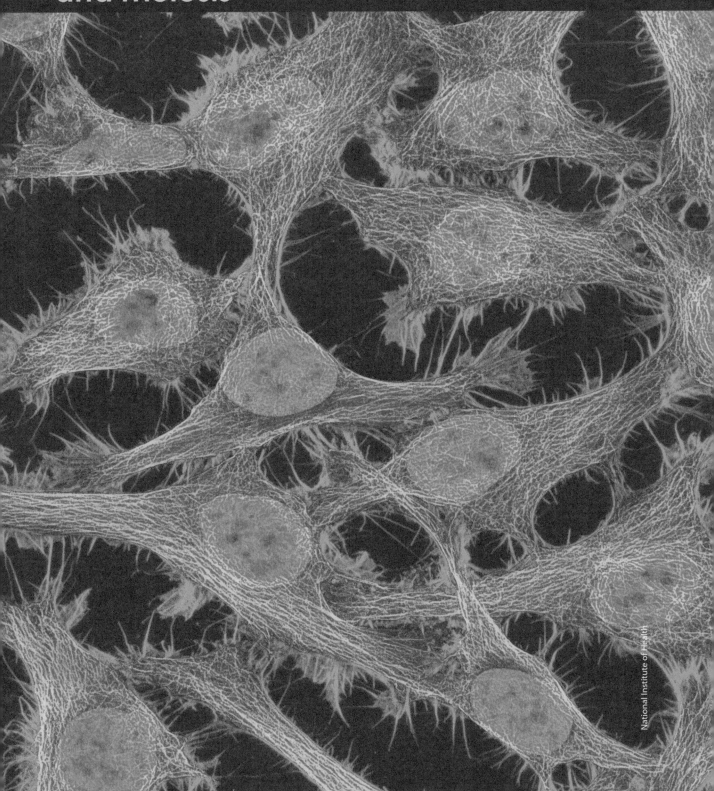

Chapter opener

Multiphoton fluorescence image of HeLa cells stained with the actin binding toxin phalloidin (red), microtubules (cyan), and cell nuclei (blue).

Objectives

- Reproduction is one of the fundamental characteristics of life. Review that section of Chapter 1 and list and define the features of the two major types of reproduction: asexual and sexual.
- Mitosis refers to the division of the cell's nucleus; division of the cell's cytoplasm is known as cytokinesis. Describe the types of cytoplasmic organelles that must be divvied up during cytokinesis.
- Be able to name and describe the events that occur in the prokaryotic cell division mechanism.
- Describe the differences between prokaryotic and eukaryotic chromosome structure.
- Discuss the major events in the Cell Cycle.
- Describe the role of the part of a chromosome known as a centromere.
- Interphase of the cell cycle consists of G_1, S, and G_2 stages. Describe the events that occur in each phase of interphase.
- Describe and/or draw how chromosomes move during the different stages of mitosis.
- Describe the events occurring in the different phases of mitosis: prophase, metaphase, anaphase, and telophase.
- Discuss the differences between cytokinesis in plant and animal cells.
- Mitosis and meiosis refer to the division of the cell's nucleus; division of the cell's cytoplasm is known as cytokinesis. Briefly describe the similarities and differences between mitosis and meiosis.
- Define asexual and sexual reproduction.
- Describe the roles of mitosis and meiosis in relation to the chromosome number of a species.
- Contrast the meaning of haploid and diploid chromosome numbers.
- Describe the mechanism a species uses to restore its diploid chromosome number after meiosis has reduced it.
- Define and discuss the relationship between the following terms: homologous chromosomes, diploid, and haploid.
- Discuss the type(s) of cell division that germ line and somatic line cells undergo.
- Describe the two different divisions of meiosis and what events occur in each of their phases.
- Describe the processes of spermatogenesis in male animals and oogenesis in female animals.
- Compare and contrast the events in the life cycles of plants and animals.

Introduction

Reproduction is one of the characteristics of life. The cell theory states that all cells form from preexisting cells. There are two major types of reproduction: asexual and sexual. Asexual reproduction produces cells that are exact genetic copies of each other. Single-celled organisms, such as *Paramecium* and bacteria, reproduce almost entirely by this method. Sexual reproduction involves the recombination of genetic information from two parents. This produces offspring with unique combinations of both parents' traits. Multicellular organisms can reproduce by this method. Plants and some other creatures have asexual methods for reproducing new organisms. Humans (and what we term the higher animals) must use sexual reproduction for the continuation of the species.

8.1   Overview of Cell Division

Three cell division processes occur. Binary Fission in prokaryotes (and some primitive eukaryotes) is a simple copying of the cell's lone chromosome and segregation of each copy to opposite sides of the cell, followed by cytoplasm division. Mitosis is a more complicated process eukaryotes employ to copy and segregate their chromosomes to opposite sides of the cell, followed by cytoplasmic division. Both mitosis and binary fission produce cells that are genetically identical to each other, and each process may therefore be involved in asexual reproduction. Meiosis is the eukaryotic cell division process where cells produce new copies that are genetically dissimilar. This process is restricted to eukaryotic organisms that reproduce sexually.

We have seen how cells are organized, and how their membranes function in exchange of materials. Every one of us started our genetic existence as a single-celled zygote that formed after our parents' sperm and egg cells fused during the process of fertilization. This single-celled you has undergone countless cell divisions to become what you are today—a multicellular organism with over 100 trillion cells. That looks more impressive if we write out the numbers: 1 zygote divides until it produces a multicellular individual consisting of more than 100,000,000,000,000 cells! Growth from a single cell is accomplished by cell division. Repair of the cuts and scrapes we all suffered is accomplished by cell division. Even today we are undergoing this process, repairing, growing, and replacing cells to maintain our bodies. Cell division is a vital process to life.

Despite differences between prokaryotic and eukaryotic cells, there are several features common to all methods of cell division. Replication (or copying) of the cell's DNA must occur (Figure 8.1). Segregation of the "original" and its "replica" are next in the sequence. Cytokinesis (splitting of the cell's cytoplasm) ends the cell division process. Whether the cell was eukaryotic or prokaryotic, these basic events must occur.

Consider what happens when you miss a class. You have missed a (hopefully) vital lecture and its information and want to borrow or copy a fellow student's notes. If they are smart, they will not give you their notes, but rather go to a copy machine and make a copy of their notes (replication), hand you the copy (segregation), and then go on their way (cytokinesis).

The events of cell division may be represented as a cycle, the Cell Cycle. Cytokinesis is the process where one cell splits off from its sister cell, usually after cell division. The Cell Cycle

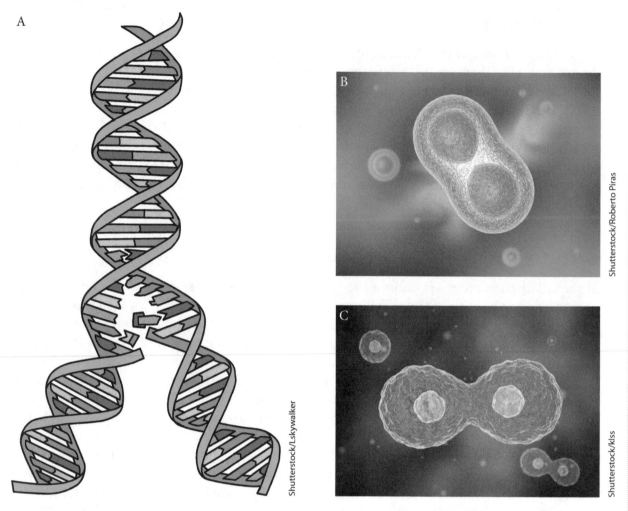

FIGURE 8.1 Three processes common to all cell division. A. Replication, copying the DNA molecule; B. Segregation, separation of the copies to opposite sides of the cell; C. Cytokinesis, separation of the cytoplasm.

(Figure 8.2) is the sequence of growth (the G_1 phase), DNA replication (the S phase), growth (the G_2 phase), and cell division (the M phase) that all cells must go through. Understanding this cycle is pivotal to our knowledge of cancer (uncontrolled cell division), the process of development (undifferentiated cells becoming functional muscle, heart, or nerve cells), and ways to regenerate cells that no longer divide (heart muscle cells and nerve cells).

Beginning after cytokinesis, the daughter cells are quite small and low on adenosine triphosphate (ATP). They produce new ATP and increase in size during the G_1 phase of Interphase. Most cells are observed in Interphase, the longest duration phase of the Cell

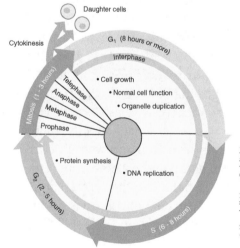

FIGURE 8.2 The Cell Cycle.

Cycle. After growing to a sufficient size and recharging their ATP supply, cells progress to the S phase where they undergo DNA synthesis. During this process the original DNA molecule is copied, producing one "new molecule" eventually destined for each new cell. This happens during the S phase. Since the formation of new DNA is an energy-intensive process, the cell undergoes a second growth and energy-acquisition stage in the G_2 phase. The energy acquired during G_2 is used in cell division. Some cells, such as heart muscle cells and nerve cells no longer divide after they form. Others, such as skin cells and stem cells in bone marrow, divide continuously.

Regulation of the cell cycle is accomplished in several ways. Some cells divide rapidly (beans, for example, take 19 hours to complete the cycle while human red blood cells take 23). Nerve and muscle cells lose their capability to divide once they reach maturity. Liver cells retain but do not normally utilize their capacity for division. Liver cells will divide if part of the liver is removed. The division continues until the liver reaches its former size. The ancient Greeks incorporated this in the myth of the Titan Prometheus. As punishment for giving fire to humans, the Greek god Zeus chained Prometheus to a rock, where an eagle ate his liver all day. At night his liver regrew and the cycle continued for all time until his release by the hero Hercules.

Cancer cells undergo a series of rapid divisions, such that the daughter cells divide before they have reached "functional maturity." Environmental factors, such as changes in temperature, pH, and declining nutrient levels, lead to declining cell division rates. When cells stop dividing, they stop usually at a point late in the G_1 phase, the R point (for restriction).

8.2   Prokaryotic Cell Division: Binary Fission

Prokaryotes display a much simpler organization than eukaryotes. There are a great many organelles in eukaryotes, as well as more chromosomes. The usual method of prokaryote cell division is termed binary fission (Figure 8.3). The prokaryotic chromosome is a single DNA molecule that first replicates, and then attaches each copy to a different part of the cell membrane. When the cell begins to pull apart (Figure 8.3), the replicate and copied chromosomes are separated. Following cell splitting (cytokinesis), there are then two cells of identical genetic composition (except for the rare chance of a spontaneous mutation). This process rapidly (in as little as 15 minutes) produces a great many cells. If we started with 100 bacterial cells, and each cell divided every 15 minutes (four times an hour),we would have 200 bacteria after 15 minutes, 400 bacteria after 30 minutes, 800 bacteria after 45 minutes, and 1600 bacteria after 60 minutes. At the end of a 24-hour day, we would have 96 cell divisions, resulting in a mass of $2^{96} \times 100$ cells (or 7,922,820,000,000,000,000,000,000,0 00cells, a very large number indeed!).

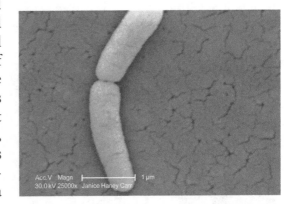

FIGURE 8.3 Colorized scanning electron micrograph of a *Salmonella typhimurium* bacterium undergoing cytokinesis after binary fission. Magnification 25,000xX; image CDC/Bette Jensen, photo by Janice Haney Carr.

Binary fission is an asexual method of reproduction since the cells produced are identical genetic copies of each other. One consequence of this method is that all organisms in a colony are genetically identical. When treating a bacterial disease, a drug that kills one bacterium of a specific type will also kill all other members of that colony it comes in contact with.

8.3   Mitosis: Cell Xeroxing

Because of their increased numbers of chromosomes, organelles, and complexity, eukaryote cell division is more complicated. Eukaryotes have a nucleus, which divides by the process of mitosis, whereas the cytoplasm is divided by cytokinesis. Despite the increased complexity, the same processes of replication, segregation, and cytokinesis still occur. Mitosis is the process of forming identical daughter cells by replicating and dividing the original chromosomes; in effect, making a cellular copy. The two processes of nuclear and cytoplasmic division are commonly confused. Mitosis deals only with the segregation of the chromosomes into daughter nuclei, while cytokinesis splits up the cell's organelles into daughter cells.

Since mitosis is the division of a cell's chromosomes, we need to understand eukaryotic chromosome structure. Eukaryotic cells divide by mitosis and have a greater number of linear chromosomes in their nucleus than do prokaryotic cells with their (usually) single, circular chromosome. The condensed replicated eukaryotic chromosome (Figure 8.4A) has several structures of interest. The kinetochore is the point where the spindle fibers attach. The spindle is a eukaryotic structure that pulls the replicated chromosomes apart, much like the cell membrane does in prokaryotic binary fission. Replicated chromosomes consist of two molecules of DNA (along with their associated histone proteins), known as chromatids. The area where the chromatids are in contact with each other is known as the centromere, and the kinetochores are on the outer sides of the centromere. Remember that chromosomes are condensed chromatin (Figure 8.4B) DNA plus histone proteins.

During mitosis, replicated chromosomes move to near the middle of the cytoplasm and then separate so that each daughter cell receives a complete set of chromosomes. For example, if you start with 46 chromosomes in the parent cell, you should end up with 46 chromosomes in each daughter cell. To do this, cells utilize arrays of microtubules referred to as the spindle apparatus to "pull" chromosomes into each side of the dividing cell. Animal cells (except for a group

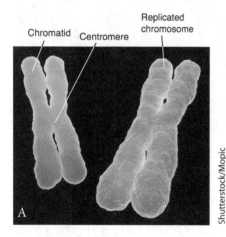

FIGURE 8.4 Structure of a eukaryotic chromosome. A. Electron micrograph of a replicated chromosome; B. Diagram illustrating condensation of the chromatin to form a replicated chromosome.

of worms known as nematodes) have a centriole. Plants and most other eukaryotic organisms lack centrioles. Centrioles are organizing centers for the microtubule array that make up the spindle. Cells that contain centrioles also have a series of smaller microtubules, the aster, that extend from the centrioles to the cell membrane. The aster is thought to serve as a brace for the functioning of the spindle fibers.

8.3.1   The Phases of Mitosis

Unlike binary fission, mitosis is a complicated process traditionally divided into phases: prophase, metaphase, anaphase, and telophase. These phases of mitosis are sometimes difficult to separate from each other (Figures 8.5–8.7). Remember that the process of mitosis is a dynamic one, not the static process displayed of necessity in a textbook.

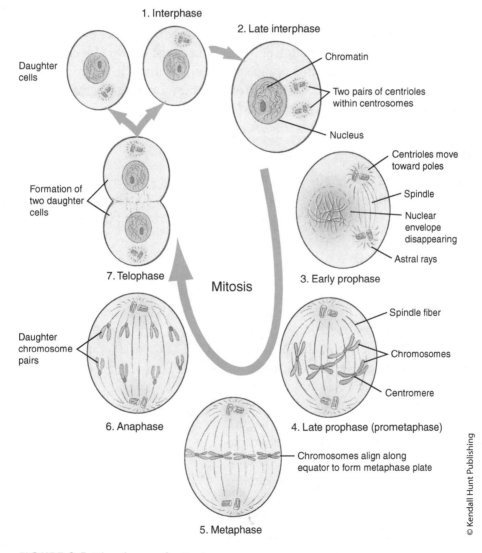

© Kendall Hunt Publishing

FIGURE 8.5 The phases of mitosis.

8.3.1.1   Prophase

Prophase (Figures 8.5, 8.6A, B) is the first stage of mitosis. It is also the most complicated phase, with a number of events. Chromatin, the uncoiled DNA in the nucleus, condenses to form replicated chromosomes consisting of two chromatids held together by a centromere. During Interphase S, the DNA in the nucleus replicates. The nucleolus, the site of ribosome assembly, dissolves. Since DNA cannot pass out through the pores in the nuclear envelope, the cell must dissolve the nuclear envelope to allow free movement of the chromosomes. Centrioles (if present) divide and migrate to opposite sides of the cell. Kinetochores and kinetochore fibers are assembled as part of the growing spindle apparatus. By the end of prophase, the cell is quite different in appearance than when it started: its nuclear membrane and nucleoli are dissolved, chromatin has condensed into chromosomes, and the spindle fibers have begun to stretch across the cell.

8.3.1.2   Metaphase

Metaphase (Figures 8.5, 8.6C), the next phase, follows immediately after prophase. During metaphase, the replicated chromosomes (which at this point consist of two chromatids held together by a centromere) migrate to the equator of the spindle apparatus. Fibers from the spindle apparatus attach to the kinetochore fibers on the chromosomes, forming a metaphase plate of chromosomes lined up at the equator of the spindle.

8.3.1.3   Anaphase

Anaphase (Figures 8.5, 8.6D) begins with the separation of the centromeres and the pulling of chromosomes (we call them chromosomes after the centromeres are separated) to opposite poles of the spindle. This pulling is accomplished by chemical breakdown of the spindle fibers at the centromere.

8.3.1.4   Telophase

Telophase (Figures 8.5, 8.6E, F) begins when the single-stranded chromosomes reach the poles of their respective spindles. Essentially, this phase is a reversal of the events in prophase. The cell reassembles the nuclear envelope. The nucleolus reforms as the chromosomes unravel and return to their chromatin form. Where there was one cell at the beginning of mitosis, there are now two smaller cells each with exactly the same number of chromosomes and genetic information contained on those chromosomes. These cells may then develop into different adult forms via the processes of development. At the end of telophase the cell splits its cytoplasm into two cells by the process of cytokinesis.

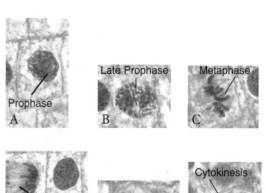

FIGURE 8.6 Mitosis stages in onion cells.
A. Prophase ; B. Late Prophase ; C. Metaphase ;
D. Anaphase ; E. Telophase ;
F. Cytokinesis in a Telophase cell.

Plants have their mitosis localized in regions known as meristems. Meristem tissue in the shoot and root tips retains its ability to divide throughout the life of the plant. This allows the plant to continue growing taller as well as deepening its roots. Lateral meristems, known as cambia (singular cambium), allow trees and woody shrubs to increase their girth.

Plant cells lack centrioles and asters, but have a centrosome and spindle and the same stages of mitosis as animals. Cytokinesis is different in plants, with the formation of anastomosing vesicle producing cell plate that grows outward to separate the newly divided cells. In laboratory classes we often examine mitosis in onion (*Allium*) root tips.

8.3.1.5 Cytokinesis

Cytokinesis is the process of splitting the daughter cells apart. Whereas mitosis is the division of the nucleus, cytokinesis is the splitting of the cytoplasm and allocation of the mitochondria, Golgi, plastids, and cytoplasm into each new cell. Animal cells form a contracting ring of microfibrils that pinches the cytoplasm as the ring contracts inward (Figure 8.7A). Plant cells, which have a cell wall, form new wall material in their Golgi complexes, assembling their new walls from the inside outward (Figure 8.7B).

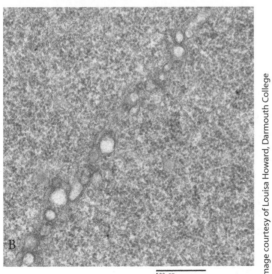

National Institute of Health

Image courtesy of Louisa Howard, Darmouth College

FIGURE 8.7 Cytokinesis. A. Animal cell cytokinesis in human HeLa-V cells; image courtesy of the National Institutes of Health; B. Plant cell cytokinesis forms a cell plate between the new lettuce root cells.

8.4 Meiosis and Sexual Reproduction

Strange as it might seem to us, not all organisms carry out sexual reproduction. Sexual reproduction makes new organisms that have *different* genetic properties from either of the two parents. Bacteria engage in a type of parasexuality where small amounts of the DNA are

Shutterstock/Michelangelus

FIGURE 8.8 Rendering of sperm approaching an egg cell.

TABLE 8.1 Major events during mitosis

Phase	Events
Prophase	Nucleolus dissolves Chromatin condenses to form chromosomes Nuclear envelope dissolves Centrioles divide and migrate to opposite sides of the cell Spindle fibers form
Late Prophase	Spindle fibers attach to opposite sides of the centromere of replicated chromosomes Spindle fibers move replicated chromosomes toward equator of the spindle apparatus
Metaphase	Replicated chromosomes align along the metaphase plate at the equator of the spindle apparatus
Anaphase	Centromeres break Chromatids, now chromosomes, are pulled toward opposite poles of the spindle apparatus Certain spindle fibers push against each other at the equator if the spindle apparatus elongating the cell
Telophase	Chromosomes reach poles of the spindle apparatus Cell plate (or cleavage furrow depending on the organism) forms, beginning process of cytokinesis Nuclear envelope reforms Chromosomes uncoil to form chromatin Nucleolus reforms Cytokinesis produces two identical cells

exchanged between cells. However, sexual reproduction results in a *complete* recombination of genetic material. Sexual reproduction occurs only in eukaryotes. During the formation of sex cells known as gametes, the number of chromosomes in a cell is reduced by half, and later returned to the full amount when two gametes fuse during fertilization. Sperm and eggs are the gametes most sexually reproducing organisms produce. Meiosis is the process that reduces the numbers of sets of chromosomes in cells in preparation for their becoming gametes. Both single-celled and multicelled eukaryotes can perform meiosis. Within a multicelled organism, meiosis occurs in specific organs, called gonads. Whereas mitosis is constantly occurring within a eukaryote, meiosis does not constantly occur: women do most of their meiosis months before being born; men wait until after puberty to begin doing their meiosis. We are all here because our parents went through the process of meiosis. The least we can do is learn more about it!

8.4.1   Genes, Chromosomes, Meiosis, and Sex

How is it that inheritance occurs? The Austrian monk Gregor Mendel determined, in 1866, the basic principles of genetics by studying inheritance in pea plants. He concluded that peas had

Apoptosis: Programmed Cell Death

Apoptosis decreases the number of cells. This happens during animal development to remove unwanted tissue, for example, the tail of tadpole and webbing between human fingers and toes (Box Figure 1). Apoptosis also plays a role in functioning of the immune system where cytotoxic T-cells send a signal to their target. That signal initiates the target cell's apoptosis process.

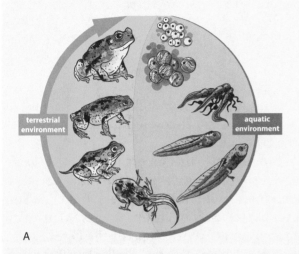
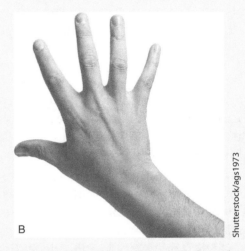

BOX FIGURE 1 Examples of apoptosis. A. Stages in development of a tadpole; B. Changes in the webbing between human fingers result from apoptosis of the cells.
Shutterstock/LSkywalker

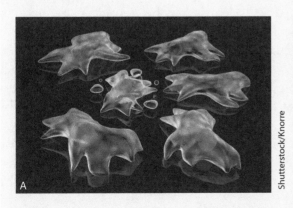
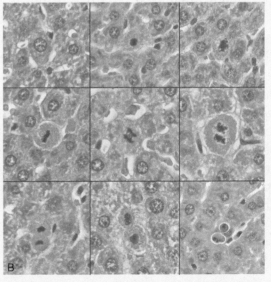

BOX FIGURE 2 Apoptosis. A. A group of eukaryotic cells. One of the cells activated its program of self-destruction—apoptosis ; B. Liver cells (hepatocytes) undergoing mitosis, cell in lower right is undergoing apoptosis.

The process begins after an initial signal, sometimes internal other times external, to the cell. Caspases are the enzymes responsible for apoptosis. Inhibitor chemicals control the activity of caspases. Cells respond to some signal to begin apoptosis. The cell undergoing apoptosis begins to shrink, losing cytoplasm, and packing organelles more closely together. Chromatin condenses near the nuclear envelope. Blebs begin to form (Box Figure 2) and the nucleus fragments. Cellular fragments are engulfed by nearby cells.

Apoptosis plays an important role in preventing cancer. Cancer may be viewed as some combination of cell proliferation and a lack of (or decrease in) apoptosis. If cancer cells proceed through apoptosis, immune system cells clean up the fragmental remains. Continuing research is exploring the potential for stimulating apoptosis in cancerous cell masses as a target method of their destruction.

two sets of traits, one set from each parent. While this may not sound like a big deal to us, his research was groundbreaking. The process of mitosis was not discovered until after Mendel's death, while the events in meiosis were deciphered even later.

The concept of ploidy, the number of sets of chromosomes that an organism has, is useful to understand genetics as well as cell division. Diploid organisms are those with two sets of chromosomes (*di*= two). Human beings, most animals, and many plants are diploid, a condition abbreviated as $2n$. Not all organisms have just two sets of chromosomes. Many plant species are polyploid, having many sets of chromosomes. Wheat, one of the cereal grains on which modern civilization depends, is a polyploid plant. Haploid cells have only one set of chromosomes, abbreviated as n. Many protozoa, protists, and some fungi are haploid organisms.

Diploid organisms have two sets of chromosomes, receiving one set from each parent at fertilization. Chromosomes are the carriers of genes, which we think of as segments of DNA. Chromosomes that carry the same genes are known as homologous chromosomes. Humans have 23 pairs of homologous chromosomes (a total of 46 chromosomes). Mom's egg carried 23 chromosomes, and Dad's sperm had 23 chromosomes.

Meiosis (Figure 8.9) is a special type of nuclear division that segregates one copy of each homologous chromosome into each newly formed cell. Meiosis may be viewed as a reduction–division process, where first the number of sets of chromosomes is reduced from $2n$ to n followed by a division of the replicated chromosomes. Mitosis maintains the cell's original ploidy level (for example, one diploid $2n$ cell producing two diploid $2n$ cells, one haploid n cell producing two haploid n cells, etc.). Meiosis, on the other hand, reduces the number of sets of chromosomes by half, so that when gametes recombine at fertilization, the ploidy of the parents will be reestablished in the offspring.

Most cells in the human body result from mitosis. These somatic line or body cells comprise the majority of the 60 trillion cells in your body. Germ line cells become gametes. The vast majority of cell divisions in the human body are mitosis, with meiosis being restricted to the gonads.

The events in meiosis are very similar to those in mitosis. In fact, we even use the same names for the phases: Prophase, Metaphase, Anaphase, and Telophase. Meiosis has two tasks

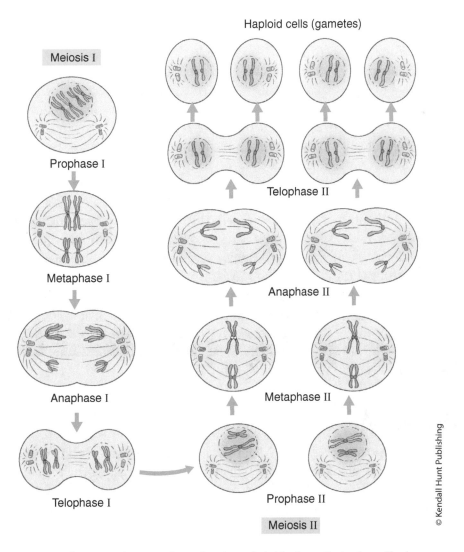

FIGURE 8.9 Overview of meiosis showing the reduction of ploidy from 2*n* in the cells that start meiosis, to *n* in each cell that completes the process.

to accomplish: reduce the number of sets of chromosomes from two to one, and to divide the replicated chromosomes so that each cell at the end of the process has only one set of single-stranded chromosomes. Two successive nuclear divisions occur: Meiosis I (reduction) and Meiosis II (division). Meiosis produces up to four haploid cells for every diploid cell that begins the process. Mitosis produces two cells for every cell that begins that process. Older biology textbooks refer to meiosis as reduction/division, a very apt description of what happens in this two-step cell division process. Meiosis I reduces the ploidy level from 2*n* to *n* (reduction) while Meiosis II divides the remaining set of chromosomes in a mitosis-like process (division). Most of the differences between the processes of mitosis and meiosis occur during Meiosis I.

8.4.2   Prophase I

The basic events of Prophase I (Figure 8.9) resemble those in Prophase of mitosis: the chromosomes condense, nucleolus dissolves, spindle forms, and nuclear envelope dissolves. However, Prophase I differs from prophase of mitosis by a unique event—the pairing of homologous chromosomes. Homologous chromosomes do not pair during mitosis, only during Prophase I of Meiosis I. Synapsis is the process of linking of the replicated homologous chromosomes. The resulting chromosome formation is termed a tetrad, being composed of two chromatids from each replicated chromosome, forming a thick (4-strand) structure. Crossing-over (Figure 8.10) may occur at this point. During crossing over chromatids break and may be reattached to a different chromatid of the homologous chromosome tetrad. This greatly increases the variation in the genetic composition of the gametes produced. Without crossing over, the number of different gamete gene combinations is 2^n, where n is the haploid chromosome number for a given species. If we consider a human cell, which has $n = 23$, this value becomes 2^{23}, or 8,388,610. Even one crossing-over per chromosome results in a much larger number of different possible combinations.

Thus, instead of producing only two types of chromosomes in each daughter cell, four different types of chromosomes are produced. One single crossing-over event doubles the variability of gametes. The occurrence of a crossing-over event is indicated by a special structure, a chiasma (plural chiasmata). Near the end of Prophase I, the homologous chromosomes begin to separate slightly, although they remain attached at chiasmata.

8.4.3   Metaphase I

Metaphase I (Figure 8.9) also resembles Metaphase of mitosis (when chromosomes line up at the equator of the spindle). During Metaphase I, the tetrads line-up along the equator of the spindle, not the individual replicated chromosomes. Spindle fibers attach to the centromere region of each homologous chromosome pair rather than to opposite sides of the same chromosome as they do in mitosis.

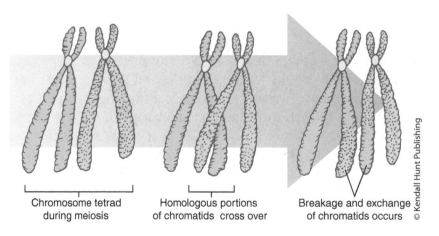

Chromosome tetrad   Homologous portions   Breakage and exchange
during meiosis   of chromatids cross over   of chromatids occurs

© Kendall Hunt Publishing

FIGURE 8.10 Crossing-over.

8.4.4   Anaphase I

During Anaphase I (Figure 8.9), the tetrads separate and homologous chromosome pairs are drawn to opposite sides of the cell by the spindle fibers. The centromeres in Anaphase I remain intact, unlike the centromeres in Anaphase of mitosis. At this stage in the process each chromosome consists of two sister chromatids.

8.4.5   Telophase I

Events in Telophase I (Figure 8.9) resemble those in Telophase of mitosis, except that only *one* set of replicated chromosomes is in each "cell." Chromosomes still consist of two sister chromatids (replicated chromosomes). Depending on the species, new nuclear envelopes may or may not form. Some animal cells may have division of the centrioles during this phase. Cytokinesis separates the cytoplasm into two cells after Telophase I.

8.4.6   Prophase II

During Prophase II of Meiosis (Figure 8.9), nuclear envelopes (if they reformed during Telophase I) dissolve, and spindle fibers reform. All other events in Prophase II resemble those of Prophase of mitosis. Indeed, Meiosis II is very similar to mitosis. Chromosomes consist of two sister chromatids, although only one *set* of chromosomes is present in each cell.

8.4.7   Metaphase II

Metaphase II (Figure 8.9) recalls the events of Metaphase of mitosis. Spindles move the replicated chromosomes into the equatorial area of the spindle apparatus and attaching to the opposite sides of the centromeres in the kinetochore region. Remember that in Metaphase I the spindle fibers are attached to *either* of the replicated homologous chromosomes not to *opposite* sides of the replicated chromosome as they do in Prophase II and Metaphase II.

8.4.8   Anaphase II

During Anaphase II (Figure 8.9), the centromeres split and spindle fibers pull the former chromatids (now chromosomes) to opposite sides of the cell. This step very much resembles Anaphase of mitosis.

8.4.9   Telophase II

Events in Telophase II (Figure 8.9) recall those in Telophase of mitosis. The nucleolus reforms in each cell, the chromosomes uncoil into chromatin, and the nuclear envelope reforms. Cytokinesis separates the cells.

TABLE 8.2 Major events during meiosis

Phase	Events
Prophase I	Nucleolus dissolves Chromatin condenses to form chromosomes Homologous chromosomes line up during synapsis forming tetrads Crossing over may occur, exchanging material between chromosomes in the tetrad Nuclear envelope dissolves Centrioles divide and migrate to opposite sides of the cell Spindle fibers form
Late Propahse I	Spindle fibers attach to one side of the centromeres of each of replicated homologous chromosomes tetrads Spindle fibers move tetrads toward equator of the spindle apparatus
Metaphase I	Tetrads align along the metaphase plate at the equator of the spindle apparatus
Anaphase I	Centromeres do not break One member of each tetrad is pulled to each pole of the spindle apparatus Certain spindle fibers push against each other at the equator if the spindle apparatus elongating the cell
Telophase I	Chromosomes reach poles of the spindle apparatus Cell plate (or cleavage furrow depending on the organism) forms, beginning process of cytokinesis Nuclear envelope reforms Chromosomes uncoil to form chromatin Nucleolus reforms Cytokinesis produces two identical cells
Prophase II	Cell begins Meiosis II with half the number of chromosome sets as its parent began Meiosis I with Nucleolus dissolves (if it reformed after Meiosis I) Chromatin condenses to form chromosomes (if they uncoiled after Meiosis I) Nuclear envelope dissolves (if it reformed after Meiosis I) Centrioles divide and migrate to opposite sides of the cell Spindle fibers form
Late Propahse II	Spindle fibers attach to opposite sides of the centromere of each replicated chromosome Spindle fibers move replicated chromosomes toward equator of the spindle apparatus
Metaphase	Replicated chromosomes align along the metaphase plate at the equator of the spindle apparatus
Anaphase II	Centromeres break Chromatids, now chromosomes, are pulled toward opposite poles of the spindle apparatus Certain spindle fibers push against each other at the equator if the spindle apparatus elongating the cell

Phase	Events
Telophase II	Chromosomes reach poles of the spindle apparatus Cell plate (or cleavage furrow depending on the organism) forms, beginning process of cytokinesis Nuclear envelope reforms Chromosomes uncoil to form chromatin Nucleolus reforms Cytokinesis produces two identical cells

8.5   Comparison of Mitosis and Meiosis

The events of mitosis and meiosis may seem a blur of moving chromosomes, dissolving and then reappearing nuclei, and so on. Despite specific differences (Figure 8.11, Table 8.3) both processes involve the segregation of chromosomes. Mitosis *maintains* the ploidy level of cells, while meiosis *reduces* ploidy by one half. Mitosis produces cells for growth and repair, while meiosis produces cells that directly or indirectly become gametes that are used in sexual reproduction. Meiosis may be considered a reduction phase followed by a slightly altered mitosis division. Meiosis occurs in a relative few cells of a multicellular organism, while mitosis is more common in such a creature. Homologous chromosomes only pair up during Prophase I of meiosis. During mitosis they are present but no tetrads are formed. Mitosis produces two cells while meiosis can produce up to four cells. The products of mitosis are genetically identical (clones in a sense) to each other as well as to the original cell that underwent mitosis. Cells produced by meiosis are not genetic copies of each other and have half the number of chromosomes as the original cell that began meiosis.

8.6   Gametogenesis

Gametes result from meiosis of animal cells in the process of gametogenesis (Figure 8.12). Gametes are by definition haploid (n) cells produced by (in animals) diploid ($2n$) cells of the germ line. Animals have two sexes, male and female, with different events and timelines for production of sperm cells and egg cells. The products of meiosis in plants are spores, which will develop by mitosis and growth into the haploid gametophyte generation of the plant's life cycle. The gametophyte produces the gametes by mitosis.

Spermatogenesis (Figure 8.12A) is the process of forming sperm cells by meiosis in specialized organs known as testes, the male gonads. After division, the cells undergo differentiation and maturation to become mature sperm cells. Oogenesis (Figure 8.12C) is the process of forming an ovum (egg) by meiosis in specialized gonads known as ovaries. Whereas in spermatogenesis all four meiotic products develop into gametes, oogenesis places most of the cytoplasm into a single large egg. The other cells, the polar bodies, do not develop. Thus, almost all of the cytoplasm and organelles go into the egg. Human males produce 200,000,000 sperm cells per day, while the female produces one egg (usually) each menstrual cycle.

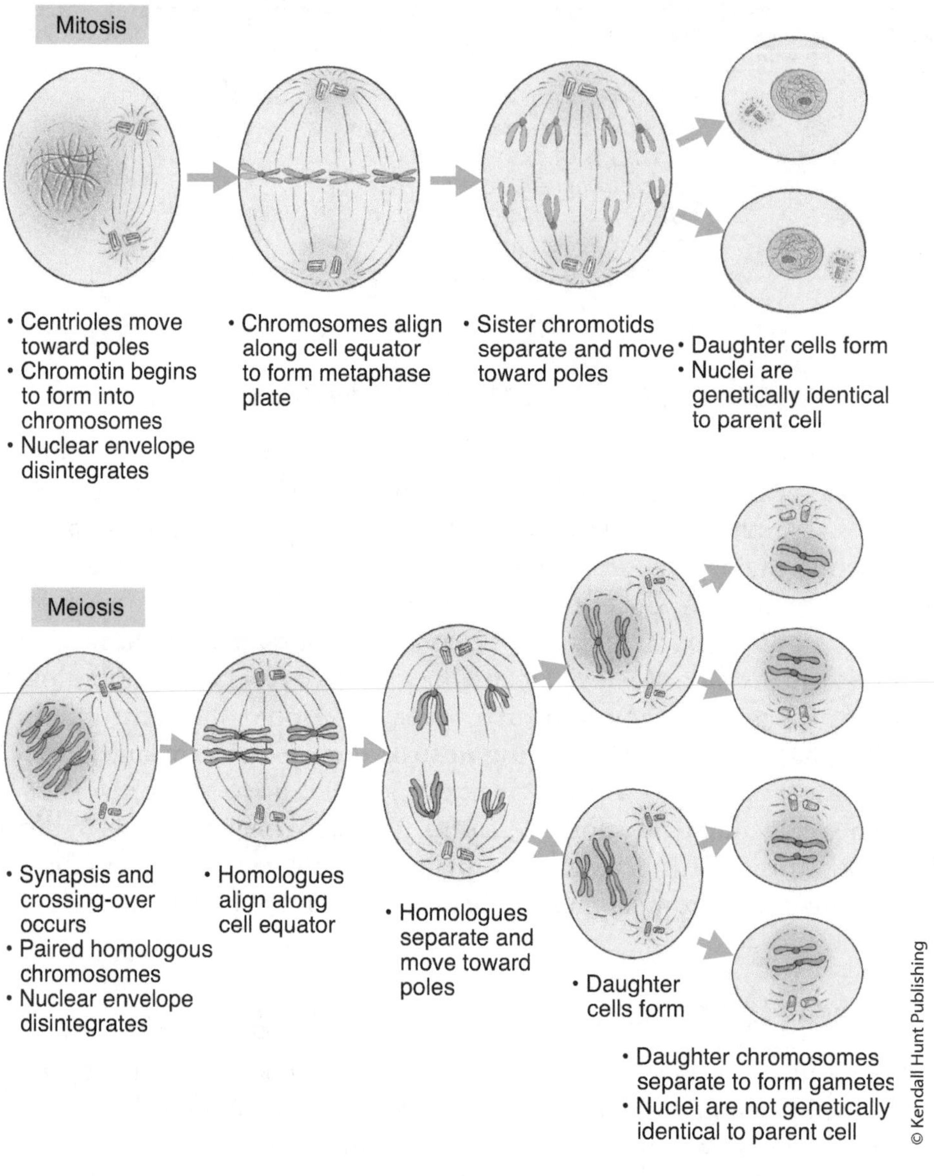

Mitosis

- Centrioles move toward poles
- Chromotin begins to form into chromosomes
- Nuclear envelope disintegrates

- Chromosomes align along cell equator to form metaphase plate

- Sister chromotids separate and move toward poles

- Daughter cells form
- Nuclei are genetically identical to parent cell

Meiosis

- Synapsis and crossing-over occurs
- Paired homologous chromosomes
- Nuclear envelope disintegrates

- Homologues align along cell equator

- Homologues separate and move toward poles

- Daughter cells form

- Daughter chromosomes separate to form gametes
- Nuclei are not genetically identical to parent cell

© Kendall Hunt Publishing

FIGURE 8.11 Comparison of mitosis and meiosis.

TABLE 8.3 Features of mitosis and meiosis

Feature	Mitosis	Meiosis
Ploidy	Maintained	Reduced
Synapsis and Crossing over	None	May occur
Cells that participate	Somatic	Germ
Genetic variation caused by the process	None	Yes by recombination and crossing over

Spermatogenesis

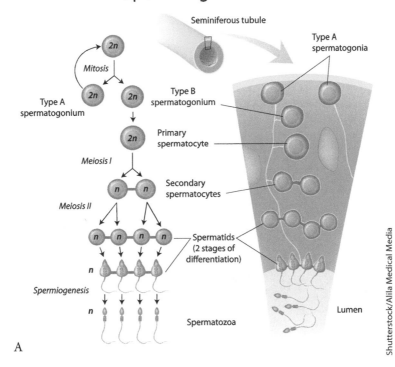

A

SPERMATOZOON

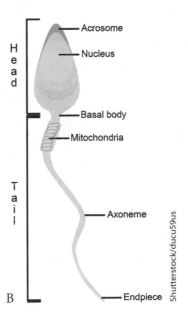

FIGURE 8.12 (*Continued*)

B

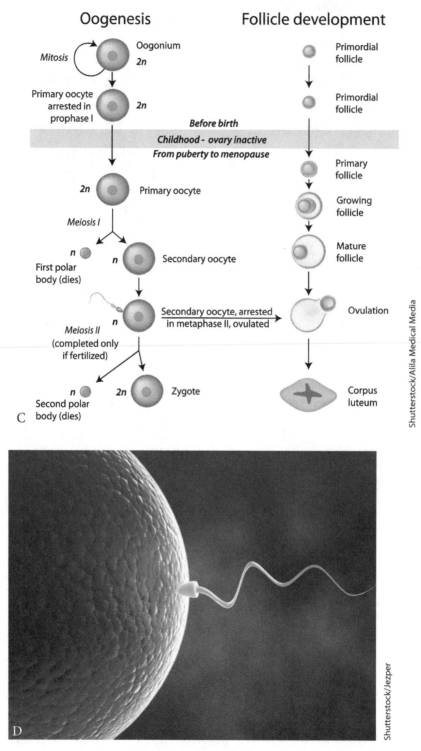

FIGURE 8.12 Gametogenesis. A. Process of spermatogenesis; B. Structure of a sperm cell; C. Process of oogenesis; D. Fertilization of an egg by a sperm.

Summary

Cell division accomplishes a number of tasks. Mitosis is essential for growth and repair of eukaryotes, producing smaller but genetically identical cells. Meiosis occurs in most eukaryotes and reduces the number of sets of chromosomes by half. The products of meiosis in animals become the sex cells, the gametes. You began your genetic existence as a single-celled zygote formed when your mother's egg and father's sperm cells fused. Mitosis next occurs as you grow and develop into the 60-trillion-celled individual, that is, you. We will next look at how the genes are passed along and how they function.

Terms

alternation of generations	gametes	ploidy
anaphase	gametophyte	polyploid
apoptosis	germ line	prokaryotes
asexual reproduction	germ line cells	prophase
aster	gonads	replication
binary fission	haploid	segregation
cambia	histone proteins	sexual reproduction
cell cycle	homologous chromosomes	somatic line
cell theory	kinetochore	spindle apparatus
centriole	life cycles	spindle fibers
centromere	meiosis	sperm
chiasma	menstrual cycle	spermatogenesis
chromatin	metaphase	sperm cells
chromatids	meristems	sporophyte
chromosomes	microtubules	synapsis
crossing-over	mitosis	telophase
cytokinesis	nucleolus	testes
diploid	nucleus	tetrad
egg	oogenesis	zygote
eukaryotes	ovaries	
fertilization	ovum	

Review Questions

1. Prokaryotic cells divide by the process of _____.
   a. mitosis;
   b. binary fission;
   c. meiosis;
   d. fertilization

2. Which of the following answers describes the correct sequence of events in the cell cycle, staring with cell division?
   a. S, G_2, G_1, M;
   b. G_1, S, M, G_2;
   c. S, G_1, G_2, M;
   d. G_1, S, G_2, M

3. The replication of DNA occurs during which of these stages of the cell cycle?
   a. M;
   b. S;
   c. G_1,
   d. G_2

4. Which of these cells is likely to not continue to divide?
   a. skin cell;
   b. nerve cell;
   c. epithelial cells lining the cheeks;
   d. all of these

5. Which of these is not the correct sequence for the phases of mitosis?
   a. prophase, interphase, metaphase, telophase;
   b. prophase, metaphase, telophase, anaphase;
   c. prophase, metaphase, anaphase, telophase;
   d. interphase, prophase; metaphase, anaphase

6. Which of these events does **not** occur during prophase?
   a. chromosomes coil and condense;
   b. centromeres separate;
   c. nuclear envelope dissolves;
   d. nucleolus dissolves

7. Which of these events occurs during metaphase?
   a. chromosomes coil and condense;
   b. centromeres separate;
   c. chromosomes migrate to equator of the spindle;
   d. nucleolus reforms

8. Which of these events occurs during anaphase?
   a. chromosomes coil and condense;
   b. centromeres separate;
   c. chromosomes migrate to equator of the spindle;
   d. nucleolus reforms

9. Cytokinesis in animal cells _____.
   a. occurs after telophase;
   b. is accomplished by a ring of contractile fibers;
   c. works from the outside inward;
   d. all of these

10. How many parents are necessary for asexual reproduction to occur?
    a. 1.;
    b. 2;
    c. 3;
    d. a whole village

11. How many parents are necessary for sexual reproduction to occur?
    a. 1.;
    b. 2;
    c. 3;
    d. a whole village

12. Meiosis _____ the ploidy of cells.
    a. reduces;
    b. maintains;
    c. increases

13. Homologous chromosomes pair up during _____.
    a. prophase of mitosis;   c. prophase II;
    b. prophase I;   d. metaphase I

14. Crossing-over events may occur during _____.
    a. prophase of mitosis;   c. prophase II;
    b. prophase I;   d. metaphase I

15. Cells produced at the end of telophase I have _____ as many _____ chromosomes as cells that started the process.
    a. half, replicated;   c. half, single stranded;
    b. twice, single stranded;   d. four times, single stranded

16. Cells produced at the end of telophase II have _____ as many _____ chromosomes as cells that started the process.
    a. half, replicated;   c. half, single stranded;
    b. _twice, single stranded;   d. four times, single stranded

17. In human males, meiosis occurs in cells of the _____.
    a. ovaries;   c. bone marrow;
    b. testes;   d. skin

18. In human females, meiosis occurs in cells of the _____.
    a. ovaries;   c. bone marrow;
    b. testes;   d. skin

19. During oogenesis, ___ cells develop by meiosis.
    a. four;   c. two;
    b. three;   d. one

20. During spermatogenesis, ___ cells develop by meiosis.
    a. four;   c. two;
    b. three;   d. one

21. Reduction of the number of sets of chromosomes occurs during ___.
    a. prophase I;   c. meiosis II;
    b. meiosis I;   d. mitosis

22. Division of replicated chromosomes occurs during _____.
    a. prophase I;
    b. meiosis I;
    c. meiosis II;
    d. mitosis

Links

- **Apoptosis and the human hand**: Smart site from University of California, Davis presents a series of electron micrographs illustrating changes in human hand development in the womb. [https://smartsite.ucdavis.edu/access/content/user/00002950/bis10v/media/ch17/apoptosis.html]
- **Videos of Cells and Embryos**: George von Dassow maintains this site with some fantastic videos and images of his research into mitosis of sea urchins. [http://gvondassow.com/Research_Site/Video_-_Mitosis_in_urchin_embryos.html]
- **Cells Alive! Meiosis:** This site from the folks at Cells Alive offers a nice animation of meiosis. [http://www.cellsalive.com/meiosis.htm]

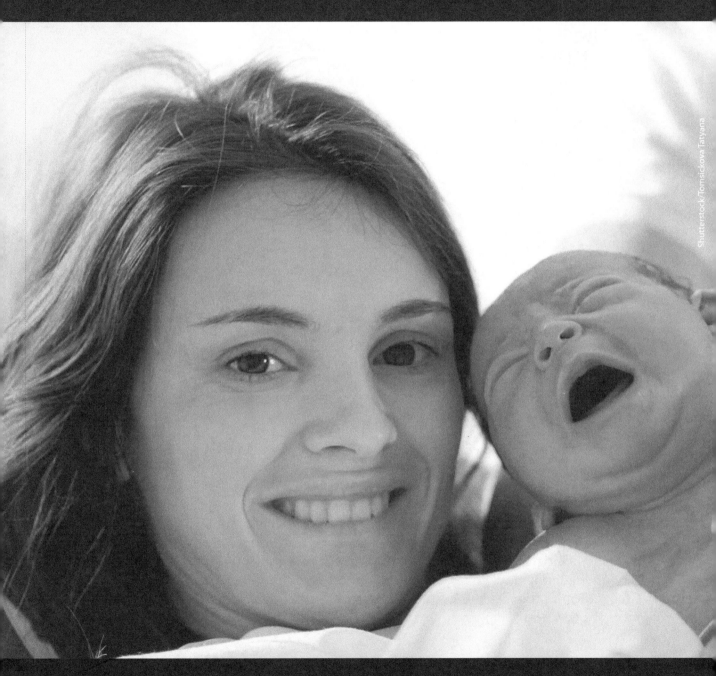

Shutterstock/Tomsickova Tatyana

"What a beautiful baby! Oh, she has your eyes!"
Sound heard when you were born.
"WHICH end of this kid do we slap?"
Sound heard when I was born.

Chapter Opener

Mother with her newborn. Genetics helps explain familial resemblances as well as our innate capabilities.

Objectives

- Discuss the various ideas that had been proposed to explain heredity before Mendel's work on the garden pea.
- Garden pea plants are naturally self-fertilizing, but Mendel took steps to cross-fertilize them for his experiments. Be able to explain why the garden pea was an excellent choice on which to perform genetic experiments.
- Define the terms allele, gene, genotype, phenotype, dominant, and recessive.
- Explain the difference between a heterozygous individual and a homozygous one.
- Describe how many different types of gametes an individual whose genotype is Tt can make compared with homozygous individuals.
- State Mendel's Principle of Segregation in terms of the role played by meiosis.
- Explain the probability of flipping heads on two successive coin tosses and how that relates to genes.
- Employ a Punnett Square to solve genetics problems.
- Describe a dihybrid cross distinguish it from a monohybrid cross.
- State the Principle of Independent Assortment formulated by Mendel in terms of the role played by meiosis.

Introduction

Genetics is the study of the patterns of inheritance: why do you have the hair color you do (or did), why are you left-handed and everyone else in your family is right-handed? We stand at the beginning of a great exploration not of outer space, but of ourselves, and what makes us human beings. Amazing cures for inherited genetic diseases and understanding of certain behavior patterns may be in the works. Genetics is the ongoing revolution in biology. The principles of inheritance were only deciphered in the 1860s; the structure and role of DNA as the physical carrier of inheritance dates from the 1940s to 1950s. The deciphering of the human genome was announced during the summer of 2000. All of this flows from the work of the Austrian monk, Gregor Mendel, who determined the fundamental rules of inheritance that led to the establishment of a new field of biology.

9.1   Historical Perspective of Heredity

For much of human history, people were unaware of the scientific details of how babies were conceived and how heredity worked. Clearly babies *were* conceived, and clearly there *was* some hereditary connection between parents and children, but the precise mechanisms of heredity were not readily apparent. The Greek philosopher Theophrastus (371–277 BCE) proposed male flowers caused female flowers to ripen. Hippocrates (460–377 BCE) speculated that "seeds" produced by various body parts were transmitted to offspring at the time of conception. Aristotle (384–322 BCE) thought that male and female semen mixed at conception. In 458 BCE, Aeschylus (525–456 BCE) proposed the male as the parent, with the female as a "nurse for the young life sown within her."

During the 1700s, the Dutch microscopist Anton van Leeuwenhoek (1632–1723) discovered "animalcules" in the semen of humans and other animals. Some scientists speculated they saw a "little man" (homunculus) inside each sperm cell. These scientists formed a school of thought known as the "spermists." They contended the only contribution of the female to the next generation was the womb in which the homunculus grew, and the resulting prenatal influences of the womb.

The ovists believed that the future human was in the egg, and that sperm merely stimulated the growth of the egg. Ovists thought women carried eggs containing boy and girl children, and that the gender of the offspring was determined well before conception.

Pangenesis (Hippocrates' old idea) proposed that males and females formed "pangenes" in every organ. These pangenes subsequently moved through the blood to the genitals and then to the baby at conception. The concept originated with the ancient Greeks and influenced biology until little over 100 years ago. The terms "blood relative," "full-blooded," and "royal blood" are relics of pangenesis. Francis Galton, Charles Darwin's cousin, experimentally tested and disproved pangenesis during the 1870s.

Blending theories of inheritance supplanted the spermists and ovists during the 19th century. The mixture of sperm and egg resulted in progeny that were a "blend" of both parents' characteristics. According to the blenders, when a black furred animal mates with white furred animal, you would expect all resulting progeny would be gray (a color intermediate between black and white). This is often not the case. Blending theories ignore characteristics that skip a generation. Charles Darwin had to deal with the implications of blending in his theory of evolution. He was forced to recognize blending as not important (or at least not the major principle of inheritance), and suggested that science of the mid-1800s had not yet got the correct answer. That answer came from an unknown contemporary, an Austrian monk named Gregor Mendel. Darwin apparently never knew of Mendel's work, or Mendel of Darwin's.

9.2   Gregor Mendel and Inheritance in Peas

Johann Gregor Mendel (1822–1884; Figure 9.1) developed the fundamental principles that would become the modern science of genetics. Mendel demonstrated that heritable properties are parceled out in discrete units, independently inherited. These eventually were termed genes.

Mendel reasoned an organism for his experiments should have a number of different traits that can be studied. He was reportedly engaged in the study of heredity when he found an abnormal pea plant growing on the grounds in his monastery. Mendel planted this abnormal pea plant next to a "normal" plant to see if Lamarck's ideas of environmental influence on heredity were correct. The presence of the abnormal pea plant had no effect on the normal plant. Mendel

Shutterstock/rook76

Shutterstock/Susan Law Cain

FIGURE 9.1 Mendel. A. Johann Gregor Mendel on an Austrian postage stamp; B. *Pisum sativum*, the garden pea Mendel used in his research.

also thought a plant should be self-fertilizing and have a flower structure that limits accidental contact. To study inheritance, Mendel also suggested that the offspring of self-fertilized plants should be fully fertile. On all these factors, the garden pea was an ideal experimental organism.

Mendel's experimental organism was a common garden pea (*Pisum sativum* Figure 9.1B), which has a flower that lends itself to self-pollination. The male parts of the flower are termed the anthers. They produce pollen, which contains the male gametes (sperm). The female parts of the flower are the stigma, style, and ovary. The egg (female gamete) is produced in the ovary. The process of pollination (the transfer of pollen from anther to stigma) occurs prior to the opening of the pea flower. The pollen grain grows a pollen tube that allows the sperm to travel through the stigma and style, eventually reaching the ovary. The ripened ovary wall becomes the fruit (in this case, the pea pod). Most flowers allow cross-pollination, which can be difficult to deal with in genetic studies if the male parent plant is not known. Since pea plants are self-pollinators, the genetics of the parent can be more easily understood. Peas are also self-compatible, allowing self-fertilized embryos to develop as readily as out-fertilized embryos. Mendel tested all 34 varieties of peas available to him through seed dealers, using nearly 28,000 pea plants. This number allowed him to statistically analyze the data. The garden peas were planted and studied for eight years, with Mendel often brushing pollen from one plant onto the stigma of another to control the breeding. Each character studied had two distinct forms (Table 9.1), such as tall or short plant height, or smooth or wrinkled seeds.

TABLE 9.1 Mendel's Traits in Pea Plants

Trait	Dominant trait	Recessive trait	F_1 generation	F_2 dominant	F_2 recessive
Plant height	Tall	Short	All tall	787	277
Seed color	Yellow	Green	All yellow	7022	2001
Seed shape	Round	Wrinkled	All round	5474	1850
Pod shape	Inflated	Constricted	All inflated	882	299
Pod color	Green	Yellow	All green	428	152
Flower color	Purple	White	All purple	705	224
Flower position	Axial	Terminal	All axial	651	207

Mendel's work demonstrated each parent contributes one factor of each trait shown in off-spring. The spermists and ovists had each contended that one gender made a major (or the only) contribution to the heredity of the offspring. Mendel's methodical approach forever dismissed their contentions. His work also showed that the two members of each pair of factors segregate from each other during gamete formation. The processes of cell division and gamete formation would not be worked out for decades at the time Mendel did his active research. The then currently favored blending theory of inheritance was discounted by each cross Mendel performed. In no instance did intermediate forms appear in the offspring of a cross between contrasting traits. The idea of the French scientist Jean-Baptiste Lamarck (1744–1829) that inherited traits were acquired by an organism and then passed on to offspring was shown to be invalid.

Mendel's contribution was unique because of his methodical approach to a definite problem, use of clear-cut variables, and application of mathematics (statistics) to the problem. Using pea plants and statistical methods, Mendel was able to demonstrate that traits were passed from each parent to their offspring through the inheritance of what we now call genes. For example, Mendel noted that if he allowed the offspring of his first cross, termed the F_1 generation (for first filial), to self-fertilize, the trait missing in the F_1 reappeared. To deal with the large numbers of offspring, Mendel divided each number by the smaller number. For example, the F_2 of flower color had 705 purple flowered plants to 224 white flowered plants. Dividing each number by 224 produced a ratio of 3.15 purple flowered plants to 1 white flowered plant. Subsequent analyses allowed Mendel to determine of the result was significantly different from the 3:1 ratio. It was not.

9.3   The Principle of Segregation

Mendel began his study of pea plant inheritance with seed shape (Table 9.1). A cross that involves only one trait is referred to as a monohybrid cross. Mendel crossed pure-breeding (also referred to as true-breeding) smooth-seeded plants with a variety that had always produced wrinkled seeds (60 fertilizations on 15 plants). All resulting seeds in the F_1 generation were smooth.

Mendel planted these seeds and allowed them to self-fertilize the following year. He recovered 7324 seeds: 5474 smooth and 1850 wrinkled to make up the F_2 generation. To help with record keeping, generations were labeled and numbered. The parental generation is denoted as the P generation. The offspring of the P generation are the F_1 generation (first filial). The self-fertilizing F_1 generation produced the F_2 generation (second filial).

Mendel applied statistics to help solve biological problems. Modern biology uses statistics and other types of mathematics in just this way. He brought the use of probability to his genetic experiments. Statisticians can study probability using a probability matrix, with the possible outcomes on the outside of the square, and possible combinations of outcomes on the inside of the square (Figure 9.3). Punnett squares are a type of probability matrix developed by the

Let R = round seeds and r = wrinkled seeds.
Crossing two pure-breeding plants, one with wrinkled seeds and one with round seeds produces an F_1 generation of all round seeds. Planting these seeds and allowing them to self-pollinate produced 5474 round and 1850 wrinkled seeds.

P Generation: RR × rr Gametes have either an R or r allele
F_1 Generation: all Rr, with the R allele from the round seeded parent and the r from the wrinkled seeded parent
F_2 Generation: 5474 round and 1850 wrinkled seeds; this works out to a ratio of approximately 3 round to 1 wrinkled seed.

Explanation: Members of the F_2 Generation made gametes with either R or r. The F_2 round seeded plants had allele makeup of RR, and Rr; the wrinkled seed has only rr.

FIGURE 9.2 Results and a possible explanation for the inheritance of seed shape in pea plants.

FIGURE 9.3 A probability matrix showing possible combinations from the simultaneous tossing of two coins. H = Heads; T = Tails. Possible outcomes of one coin flip on outside of the matrix; combination of two tosses inside the matrix.

Problem	A tall pea plant has a short parent. When crossed with a similar plant, what will be the ratio of the plants from such a mating?

TABLE 9.2 Steps in Solving a Genetics Problem

Step	Action	Example
Step 1	Definition of alleles and determination of dominance. We often use a single letter to symbolize genes in genetics problems. Dominant forms of the gene are indicated with an uppercase letter, recessive forms with a lowercase letter.	T = tall t = short We know from our problem that the tall plant had a short parent, and from Table 9.1 that tall is dominant over short.
Step 2	Determination of alleles present in all different types of gametes	Each plant in our problem has a short parent that donated a t to the plant, as well as a tall parent that donated a T. This makes the genetic makeup of each plant in the cross Tt.
Step 3	Construction of the square	Each plant in the cross produces gametes with either a T or a t. These go on the outside of the Punnett Square. By convention we list the dominant forms first.
Step 4	Recombination of alleles into each small square	The upper left part of the square has TT; the upper right has Tt; the lower left has Tt, and the lower right has tt.
Step 5	Determination of Genotype and Phenotype ratios in the next generation	Genotype ratio: 1 TT: 2 Tt: 1 tt Phenotype ratio: 3 dominant: 1 recessive
Step 6	Labeling of generations, e.g., P_1, F_1, etc.,	The plants in the mating would be F_1, their offspring would be F_2.

British geneticist Reginald Punnett (1875–1967). Instead of showing heads and tails, like a probability matrix might do, Punnett squares show the recombination of alleles in possible offspring. The results of a Punnett square deal only with the probability of a genotype showing up in the next generation. Usually if enough offspring are produced, Mendelian ratios will also be produced.

While answering genetics problems, there are certain forms and protocols that will make unintelligible problems easier to do (Table 9.2). The term "true-breeding strain" is a code word for homozygous. Dominant alleles are those that show up in the next generation in crosses between two different "true-breeding strains." The key to any genetics problem is the recessive phenotype (more properly the phenotype that represents the recessive genotype). It is that organism whose genotype can be determined by examination of the phenotype. Usually homozygous dominant and heterozygous individuals have identical phenotypes (although their genotypes are different). This becomes even more important in dihybrid crosses involving two traits.

Another way to study probability is mathematically. The chance of any event happening is that event out of the total possible outcomes.

> We can write this as: $P_{(event)}$ = the event/the total possible outcomes

For example, the chance of flipping a coin has two outcomes, heads or tails. The chance of flipping a coin and getting heads is heads/heads + tails. If we assign a "1" to each of the words in the previous expression, we get: $P_{(event)} = 1/1 + 1 = 1/2$. In other words, the chance of flipping a coin and getting heads is 1/2, or 50%. Likewise, the chance of getting tails is 1/2, or 50%. Probability also lets us deal with sequences of events. The probability of a sequence of events occurring (if they occur at random) is the product of each individual probability.

> Again, we can write this as: $P_{(sequence\ of\ two\ events)} = P_{(event\ 1)} \times P_{(event\ 2)}$

For the odds on flipping two coins and getting heads on each toss, we multiply the chance of each coin toss producing a heads result:

> $P_{(heads,\ heads)} = P_{(heads\ on\ toss\ 1)} \times P_{(heads\ on\ toss\ 2)} = 1/2 \times 1/2 = 1/4.$

Note that in Figure 9.3, the odds of this is one square out of four!

What happened to the smooth seeds in the first generation of Mendel's cross? Mendel concluded that one of the traits, in this case wrinkled seeds dominated the other (the recessive in this case smooth seeds). When the smooth seeded plants of the F_1 were allowed to self-fertilize, they produced mostly wrinkled seeds, but some smooth ones as well. So where did the wrinkled seeds come from in the F_2? Meiosis, a process unknown in Mendel's day, explains how the traits are inherited. Mendel, however, concluded that there were two traits, and the recessive trait could be hidden by a dominant trait. He proposed the principle of segregation, that there were two copies of every trait, and that during gamete formation the traits were segregated. This is precisely what happens during meiosis (Figure 9.4).

Mendel studied seven traits (Table 9.1) that appeared in two discrete forms (such as tall plants and short plants), rather than continuous characters that are often difficult to distinguish (such as weight and skin color in humans). When "true-breeding" tall plants were crossed with "true-breeding" short plants, all of the offspring were tall plants. The parents in the cross were the P generation, and the offspring represented the F_1 generation. The trait referred to as tall was considered dominant, while short trait was recessive. Mendel defined dominant traits as those that appeared in the F_1 generation in crosses between true-breeding strains. Recessive traits were those which "skipped" a generation, being expressed only when the dominant trait is absent. Mendel's plants exhibited complete dominance, in which the phenotypic (or physical) expression of alleles was either dominant or recessive, but not "in-between." This lack of "in-betweens" was **not** compatible with the blending theory of inheritance.

When members of the F_1 generation were crossed, Mendel recovered mostly tall offspring, with some short ones also occurring. Upon statistically analyzing the F_2 generation, Mendel determined the ratio of tall to short plants was approximately 3:1. Short plants skipped the F_1

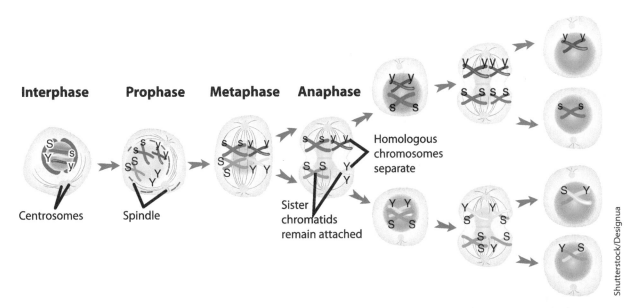

Interphase   Prophase   Metaphase   Anaphase

Centrosomes   Spindle

Homologous
chromosomes
separate

Sister
chromatids
remain attached

Shutterstock/Designua

FIGURE 9.4 Segregation of traits during gamete formation is accomplished by meiosis, a process not yet known in Mendel's day.

generation, and showed up in the F$_2$ and successive generations. Mendel concluded that the traits under study were governed by discrete (separable) factors. These factors were inherited in pairs, with each generation receiving a pair of trait factors, one from each parent. We now refer to these trait factors as alleles, alternate forms of a gene. Having traits inherited in pairs allows for the observed phenomena of traits "skipping" generations.

Mendel's results for each trait studied showed that the F$_1$ offspring showed only one of the two parental traits, and always the same trait whether or not that trait came from the male or female parent. There was no blending of parental traits in the offspring. The results of the breeding experiments were always the same for a particular trait, regardless of which male parent (domi-nant or recessive) donated the pollen. The gender of the parent was not a factor in the inheritance of a given trait. The trait not shown in the F$_1$ reappeared in the F$_2$ in about 25% of the offspring. Traits remained unchanged when passed to offspring. The traits did not blend in any offspring, but instead behaved as separate and discreet units. Reciprocal crosses showed each parent made an equal contribution to the offspring.

Mendel concluded that his results indicated that factors could be hidden or unexpressed, and that these are the recessive traits. The phenotype refers to the outward appearance of a trait, while the genotype is the genetic makeup of an organism. Male and female contributed equally to the offspring's genetic makeup, therefore the number of traits was probably two (the simplest solution).

Mendel reasoned that factors must segregate from each other during gamete formation (remember, meiosis was not yet known) to retain the two traits. The Principle of Segregation proposes the separation of paired factors during gamete formation, with each gamete receiving one or the other factor, but usually not both. Organisms carry two alleles for every trait. These traits separate during the formation of gametes.

9.4   The Principle of Independent Assortment

Mendel realized the need to conduct his experiments on more complex situations, since in Nature more than a single trait is inherited. He performed experiments tracking two seed traits: shape and color (Figure 9.5). A cross concerning two traits is known as a dihybrid cross. The resulting (F_2) generation did not have the 3:1 dominant to recessive phenotype ratio characteristic of a monohybrid cross. However, if the two traits were considered to inherit independently, the results are consistent with the principle of segregation. Instead of four possible genotypes from a monohybrid cross, dihybrid crosses have as many as 16 possible genotypes. There will also be an increase in the number of possible phenotypes.

Mendel started with true-breeding plants that had smooth, yellow seeds and crossed them with true-breeding plants having green, wrinkled seeds. All seeds in the F_1 had smooth yellow seeds. The F_2 plants self-fertilized, and produced four phenotypes: 315 smooth yellow, 108 smooth green, 101 wrinkled yellow, and 32 wrinkled green.

Again, meiosis helps us understand the behavior of alleles (Figure 9.6). The parents started out a double heterozygotes (SsYy). In a monohybrid heterozygote cross (of the F_1 generation), each gene could make gametes with either a dominant or recessive allele. When we add a second allele our number of possible gametes increases dramatically. The possible gamete combinations are SY, Sy, sY, or sy (Figure 9.5). Each gene is in a different homologous chromosome pair, so each gene behaves independently of the other, producing a greater number of different combinations after meiosis. The same is true for the other parent in the cross.

Mendel analyzed each trait for separate inheritance as if the other trait were not present. The 3:1 ratio was seen when each trait was considered separately (as a monohybrid cross) and was in accordance with the principle of segregation. In a monohybrid cross, the chance of the dominant

P Generation: SSYY x ssyy Gametes: SY and sy				
F_1 Generation: All SsYy				
F_1 Gametes: SY, Sy, sY, and sy from each parent				
F_2 offspring: 9 Smooth Yellow: 3 Smooth Green: 3 Wrinkled Yellow: 1 Wrinkled Green				
F_2 Punnett Square				

	SY	Sy	sY	sy
SY	SSYY	SSYy	SsYY	SsYy
Sy	SSYy	SSyy	SsYy	Ssyy
sY	SsYY	SsYy	ssYY	ssYy
sy	ssYy	ssyy	ssYy	ssyy

FIGURE 9.5 A dihybrid cross. In the above cross, smooth seeds (S) are dominant over wrinkled seeds (s), and yellow seed color (Y) is dominant over green (y).

phenotype showing up in one of the offspring is 3/4. If we consider the dihybrid cross (Figure 9.5) where both dominant traits show up in the offspring, we are considering a sequence, which is the product of the individual probabilities: 3/4 for yellow and 3/4 for smooth seeds. Multiplying 3/4 × 3/4 gives 9/16. For a combination of smooth (a dominant trait) and green (a recessive) we multiply the chance of the dominant trait by the chance of the recessive trait. Recall that recessive traits show up in the F_2 in one of the four boxes of the Punnett Square, or 1/4 of the offspring. Multiplying 3/4 × 1/4 gives us 3/16. Another way to view the possible outcomes is 9/16 smooth yellow, 3/16 smooth green, 3/16 wrinkled yellow, and 1/16 wrinkled green. Removing the 16s gives a predicted ratio of 9:3:3:1. This is precisely the ratio Mendel obtained in each of his dihybrid crosses!

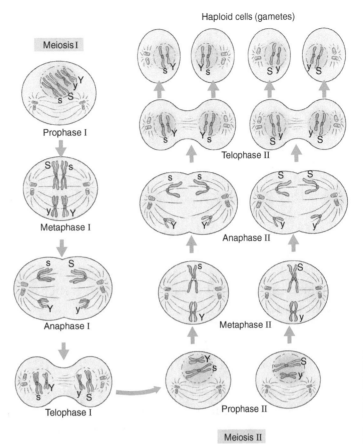

FIGURE 9.6 Dihybrid cross viewed as a result of meiosis and segregation of alleles during gamete formation.

The segregation of S and s alleles must have happened independently of the segregation of Y and y alleles (Figure 9.6). The probability of any gamete having a Y is 1/2; the chance of any one gamete having an S is 1/2. The probability of a gamete having both Y and S is the product of their individual probabilities (or 1/2 × 1/2 = 1/4). The chance of two gametes forming any given genotype is 1/4 × 1/4 (remember, the product of their individual probabilities). Thus, the Punnett Square for a cross of individuals heterozygous for both traits has 16 boxes. Since there are more possible combinations to produce a smooth yellow phenotype (SSYY, SsYy, SsYY, and SSYy), that phenotype is more common in the F_2 than are the other phenotypes.

From the results of the second experiment, Mendel formulated his Principle of Independent Assortment, stating that when gametes are formed, alleles assort independently. If traits assort independent of each other during gamete formation, the results of the dihybrid cross can make sense. Since Mendel's time, scientists have discovered chromosomes and DNA. We now interpret the Principle of Independent Assortment as alleles of genes on different homologous chromosomes are inherited independently during the formation of gametes.

Mendel published his results and the scientific world ignored them. Years after his death Mendel's results would be rediscovered in the early 20th century.

9.5   Mutations

Dutch botanist Hugo de Vries (1948–1935) was one of three early 20th century scientists who rediscovered the work of Mendel. Unaware of Mendel's earlier paper, de Vries work verified the principles Mendel discovered. German botanist Carl Correns (1864–1933) and Austrian botanist Erich Tschermak (1871–1962) were the other two scientists credited with the rediscovery of Mendel. De Vries recognized that occasional abrupt, sudden changes occurred in the patterns of inheritance in the primrose plant. He termed these sudden changes mutations. De Vries proposed that new alleles arose by mutations. Charles Darwin, in his 1859 book on evolution, *Origin of Species*, could not describe how heritable changes passed on to subsequent generations, or how new adaptations arose. Mutations provided answers to these problems. The patterns of Mendelian inheritance explained the perseverance of rare traits in organisms, which increased variation, a major part of Darwin's theory.

9.6   The Chromosome Theory of Inheritance

Mendel worked out the basic principles of genetic inheritance: the segregation and independent assortment of genes during gamete formation. His work was ignored. With the rediscovery of Mendel's experiments and conclusions, scientists began to evaluate those ideas on all sorts of organisms. Could blending be reconciled with Mendel's rules? Did human genes follow these principles? What they found was that the basic rules worked, but that there some special cases that added to Mendel's work.

German biologist Walther Flemming (1843–1905) discovered the events of mitosis in the late 1800s. Édouard van Beneden (1846–1910) discovered the process of meiosis in 1883–1884. Other scientists proposed that "qualities" were transmitted on chromosomes to daughter cells by the process of cell division. In 1903 American biologist Walter Sutton (1877–1916) and German scientist Theodor Boveri (1862–1915) independently concluded that chromosomes contain the genes. This is often referred to as the Boveri–Sutton Chromosome Theory of Inheritance and is one of the foundations of genetics as it explains the physical reality of Mendel's principles of inheritance.

During the early 1900s, American geneticist Thomas Hunt Morgan (1866–1945) and his coworkers determined genes (Mendel's factors) occur on chromosomes. Morgan's experimental organism was the fruit fly (*Drosophila melanogaster*), with which he deduced the role of chromosomes in determination of sex. Fruit flies are ideal organisms for genetics, having a small size, ease of care, susceptibility to mutations, and a short (7–9 day) generation time.

Diploid organisms have two sets of chromosomes on which they carry two copies of every gene. During Metaphase I of meiosis, homologous chromosomes, line up at the middle of the spindle apparatus to form a bivalent. A photograph showing these homologous chromosomes (Figure 9.7), known as a karyotype, can be assembled through cutting and arranging photomicrographs of these chromosomes. Studies of these chromosomes reveal that two types of chromosome pairs occur. Autosomes resemble each other in size and placement of their centromeres. Pairs of chromosome 21 are the same size, while pairs of chromosome 9 are of a different size from pair 21. Sex chromosomes, the second type of chromosome pair, may differ in their size, depending on the species of the organism they are from. In humans and the fruit fly, males have a smaller sex chromosome, termed the Y-chromosome, and a larger one, termed the X-chromosome. Males are XY and are termed heterogametic. Females are XX, and are termed homogametic.

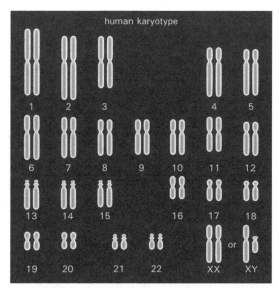

FIGURE 9.7 Human karyotype. Normal human karyotype showing the diploid pairing of the chromosomes. The first 22 are known as autosomes. The 23rd pair is the sex chromosomes: XX in females, and XY in males.

Morgan discovered a white mutant eye color in fruit flies and attempted to use this mutant as a recessive (to the dominant red allele) to duplicate Mendel's results. He failed, and instead of achieving a 3:1 red to white F_2 ratio, determined the ratio was closer to 4:1. Most mutations are recessive, so the white mutant offered a chance to test Mendel's ratios on animals. The F_1 generation also had no white-eyed females. Morgan hypothesized that the gene for eye color was only on the X-chromosome, specifically in that region of the X that had no corresponding region on the Y-chromosome. White-eyed fruit flies were also more likely to die prior to adulthood, thus explaining the altered ratios.

If the gene for eye color is on the X-chromosome, a red-eyed male will pass his red-eyed X-chromosome to only his daughters. Since the male fruit fly passes only the Y-chromosome to his sons, their eye color is determined entirely by the single X-chromosome they receive from their mother.

Morgan's experiments on fruit flies led to the concept of sex linkage, the occurrence of genes on that part of the X-chromosome that lacks a corresponding location on the Y-chromosome. Sex-linked recessive traits (such as white eyes in fruit flies, hemophilia, male pattern baldness, and color blindness in humans) occur more commonly in males, since there is no chance of the male being heterozygous and thus a carrier for the trait. Such a condition is termed hemizygous. Sons cannot inherit the trait from their fathers, since they get their father's Y-chromosome, but daughters can since they get their father's X-chromosome.

Only a few genes have been identified on the human Y-chromosome, among them the testis-determining factor (TDF) that promotes development of the male phenotype.

All mammalian females deactivate one or the other of their X-chromosomes. Since females have two X-chromosomes, the Lyon hypothesis suggests that one or the other X-chromosome is inactivated in each somatic cell during embryonic development. Cells mitotically produced from these embryonic cells likewise have the same inactivated X-chromosome.

Calico cats (Figure 9.8), sometimes called tortoiseshell cats, are almost always female since some areas of the cat's fur expressing one allele and others expressing the other color cause the calico trait. The coat color genes (with alleles for gray or yellow) reside on the X chromosome. Fertile calico cats are always female heterozygotes for the coat color genes. No two calico cats have the exact same color pattern due to deactivation of either of the X-chromosomes. Can there be a male calico cat? How would such a cat get its genes? Remember that fur color in cats is a sex-linked feature. Would the male calico be fertile or sterile?

FIGURE 9.8 Deactivation of specific X-chromosomes helps explain the color in calico cats.

Summary

The Austrian monk Gregor Mendel deciphered the rules for inheritance. Genes assort independently of each other and segregate from their copies during meiosis. These rules apply to all eukaryotic organisms. Alleles, alternate forms of a gene, form by mutations. These mutations are the raw material of variation essential to evolution by natural selection.

Terms

adaptations
albinism
alleles
anthers
autosomes
centromeres
chromosomes
chromosome theory of
   inheritance
complete dominance
dihybrid cross
dominant
evolution
flower
gametes
genes

genetics
genome
genotype
hemizygous
hemophilia
heterogametic
homogametic
homologous chromosomes
karyotype
lyon hypothesis
monohybrid
monohybrid cross
mutations
ovary
phenotype
pollen

pollen tube
pollination
principle of independent
   assortment
principle of segregation
recessive
sex chromosomes
sex linkage
somatic
sperm
spindle apparatus
stigma
style
zygote

Review Questions

1. Which of the following is a genotype?
   a. TA;
   b. ta;
   c. Tt;
   d. none of these

2. An organism with the genotype TtSs can normally make all of the following gamete combinations except ___.
   a. TS;
   b. TT;
   c. Ts;
   d. tS

3. The organism used by Mendel for his genetics experiments was the ___.
   a. fruit fly;
   b. garden pea;
   c. breadfruit plant;
   d. lab mouse

4. The spermists believed that ___.
   a. the male made the only hereditary contribution to the offspring;
   b. the male and female traits were blended in the offspring;
   c. the female made the only hereditary contribution to the offspring;
   d. both male and female made equal contributions to the next generation.

5. The ovists believed that ___.
   a. the male made the only hereditary contribution to the offspring;
   b. the male and female traits were blended in the offspring;
   c. the female made the only hereditary contribution to the offspring;
   d. both male and female made equal contributions to the next generation.

6. Which of these could not be explained by the blending idea of inheritance?
   a. traits skipping one or more generations;
   b. blending of parental traits in the offspring;
   c. inheritance of traits;
   d. all of these could be explained by the blending idea.

7. The phenotype ratio for a monohybrid cross of heterozygotes is ___.
   a. 9:3:3:1;
   b. 1:1;
   c. 3:1;
   d. 1:1:1:1

8. Which of these is a heterozygous genotype?
   a. Tt;
   b. TT;
   c. ta;
   d. tt

9. Which of these is a heterozygous genotype for a dihybrid?
   a. Tt;
   b. TtSs;
   c. TTSS;
   d. ttSs

10. The phenotype ratio for a dihybrid cross of heterozygotes is ___.
    a. 9:3:3:1;
    b. 1:1;
    c. 3:1;
    d. 1:1:1:1

11. The segregation of alleles occurs during ___.
    a. mitosis;
    b. binary fission;
    c. meiosis;
    d. none of these

12. The probability of a dihybrid cross producing an individual exhibiting both recessive traits is ___.
    a. 9/16;
    b. 1/4;
    c. 3/16;
    d. 1/16

13. The probability of a monohybrid cross producing an individual exhibiting the recessive trait is ___.
    a. 3/4;
    b. 1/4;
    c. 100%;
    d. 1/16

14. Which of the following would be an indication of incomplete dominance?
    a. production of a new phenotype not found in either of the parents;
    b. one of the phenotypes showing up in all offspring of a cross between homozygotes;
    c. the skipping of a generation by one trait that was not expressed in a cross between homozygotes;
    d. all of these

15. Thomas Hunt Morgan and his students studied the inheritance of traits in ___.
    a. garden peas;
    b. bees;
    c. fruit flies;
    d. snapdragons

16. Chromosomes that carry the gender determining genes are known as ___.
    a. hemizygotes;
    b. sex chromosomes;
    c. autosomes;
    d. centrosomes

17. A ___ is a photograph of the chromosomes found in a particular species.
    a. karyogenesis;
    b. karyotype;
    c. mutation;
    d. meiotic spindle

18. Sex-linked genes are more likely to be expressed in the ___.
    a. males;
    b. females;
    c. both males and females equally;
    d. none of these

19. Males inherit their Y-chromosome from ___.
    a. their mother;
    b. their father;
    c. their mother's father;
    d. either parent.

20. When a recessive trait is on the X-chromosome ___.
    a. males will never express it;
    b. females will always express it;
    c. males can express it more often than females will;
    d. it will only be expressed in 1/4 of the offspring

21. The presence of which chromosome determines gender in humans?
    a. the X-chromosome;
    b. chromosome 21;
    c. the Y-chromosome;
    d. both the X- and the Y-chromosome

22. What term best describes genes on the X chromosome?
    a. sex determining;
    b. sex linked;
    c. autosomal;
    d. recessive

23. One clue that trait might be sex-linked is that ___.
    a. it is more common in females than in males;
    b. it occurs in each sex equally;
    c. it is more common in males than in females;
    d. it only is seen in a homozygote

Links

Genetics Education Center: This University of Kansas website offers a numerous links to similar websites. [http://www.kumc.edu/gec]

MendelWeb: Hey, how many folks have their own Web pages over a century after their deaths? [http://www.mendelweb.org]

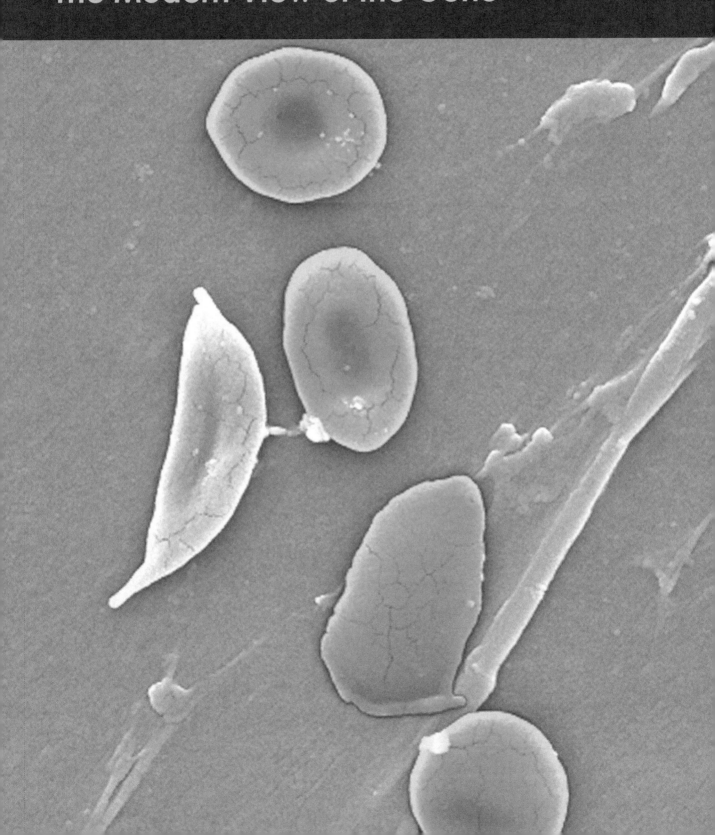

Chapter Opener

Digitally colored scanning electron micrograph showing some of the differences between normal red blood cells, and a sickle cell red blood cell (left) found in a blood specimen of an 18-year-old female suffering from sickle-cell anemia (Hb^SHb^S). People with this form of sickle-cell disease inherit two sickle-cell genes (Hb^S), one from each parent. Image courtesy of CDC/Sickle Cell Foundation of Georgia: Jackie George, Beverly Sinclair.

Objectives

- Distinguish between complete dominance, incomplete dominance, and codominance.
- Give an example of a gene that has multiple alleles.
- Define the terms epistasis and pleiotrophy, and give an example of each.
- Describe sex chromosomes and autosomes and detail the types of genes occurring on each type of chromosome.
- When gametes or cells of an affected individual end up with one extra or one less than the parental number of chromosomes, it is known as either monosomy or trisomy. List some of the disorders that fall into each category.
- Discuss meiotic difficulties a person with Down syndrome or extra sex chromosomes faces in life and in forming gametes.
- Define the term karyotype and state why it is useful and how the procedure is done.
- Describe how the karyotype of a Klinefelter individual differs from the normal karyotype.
- Describe how the karyotype of a Turner individual differs from the normal karyotype.
- Define the sex chromosomes and autosomes and generally distinguish the types of alleles that occur on each.
- Describe the characteristics of several genes that show autosomal dominant inheritance, for example Huntington disease.
- List and describe the characteristics of X-linked inheritance and summarize the characteristics of hemophilia A as an example.
- When gametes or cells of an affected individual end up with one extra or one less than the parental number of chromosomes, it is known as monosomy or trisomy. Describe what causes this and some of the syndromes or disorders that result from this.

Introduction

What Mendel referred to as traits, we now know are genes that are segments of the DNA molecule that carry the genetic code for specific proteins. The DNA is thus the molecular basis of the genotype. The proteins coded for by the genes are responsible for the production and expression of the phenotype. The basic principles of segregation and independent assortment as worked out by Mendel are applicable, even for sex-linked traits discussed above, as well as for the variations on inheritance discussed below.

10.1 Codominant Alleles

Codominant alleles occur when the heterozygotes express both homozygous phenotypes simultaneously, rather than expressing an intermediate phenotype. An example is in human ABO blood types. There are several alleles for the gene I, which are indicated as superscripts on the gene (Table 10.1). Individuals with the heterozygote AB blood type manufacture blood plasma antibodies to both A and B blood types. People with type A blood manufacture only anti-B antibodies, while blood type B people make only anti-A antibodies. Codominant alleles are both expressed. Heterozygotes for codominant alleles fully express both alleles. Blood type AB individuals produce both A and B antigens. Since neither A nor B are dominant over the other, and they are both dominant over O, they are said to be codominant.

10.2 Incomplete Dominance

Incomplete dominance is a condition when neither allele is dominant over the other. The condition is recognized by the heterozygotes expressing an intermediate phenotype relative to the parental phenotypes. If a red flowered plant (Figure 10.1) is crossed with a white flowered one, the progeny will all be pink. This would appear to support the blending ideas of inheritance that were popular during the 19th century. However, when one of the pink flowered plants is crossed with another pink flowered plant, the progeny have a phenotype (and genotype) ratio of one red, two pink, and one white.

Flower color in snapdragons is an example of incomplete dominance.

10.3 Multiple Alleles

Many genes have more than two alleles (even though any one diploid individual can only have at most two alleles for any gene), such as the ABO blood groups in humans (Table 10.1), which is an example of multiple alleles. Multiple alleles result from different mutations of the same gene. Coat color in rabbits is determined by four alleles. Human ABO blood types are determined by the alleles I^A, I^B, and I^o. The alleles I^A and I^B are codominant alleles since both dominate over I^o. The only possible genotype for a type O person is I^oI^o, or homozygous for O. Type A people have either I^AI^A or I^AI^o genotypes. Type B people have either I^BI^B or I^BI^o genotypes. People

TABLE 10.1 The Inheritance of Human Abo Blood Types

Blood Type (phenotype)	Genotype	Antigens on Red Blood Cells	Antibodies in Blood Plasma
A	I^AI^A; I^AI^o	A	Anti B
B	I^BI^B; I^BI^o	B	Anti A
AB	I^AI^B	A and B	Both Anti A and Anti B
O	I^oI^o	None	None

Shutterstock/mikeledray

Shutterstock/konzeptm   P

Shutterstock/AKI's Palette   F1

Let R = Red, R' = White P Generation RR (red) x R'R' (white) F1 Generation all RR' (pink)

	R	R'
R	**RR**	**RR'**
R'	**RR'**	**R'R'**

F2

FIGURE 10.1 Inheritance of flower color in snapdragons.

who have blood type AB have only the $I^A I^B$ genotype (heterozygous AB). The A and B alleles of gene I produce slightly different glycoproteins (antigens) that are on the surface of each cell. Homozygous A individuals have only the A antigen, homozygous B individuals have only the B antigen, homozygous O individuals produce neither antigen, while a fourth phenotype (AB) produces both A and B antigens.

Consider the case of a young man, Charles, who is accused of fathering a child with Joan. During the paternity case blood tests reveal Charles' blood is type O, while the child's blood is type AB. Joan's blood type is AB. According to blood type, can Charles be the father?

No. Charles could only give the allele I^o to his supposed child. That would mean Joan gave the allele I^A to her child. The child in that case would have had a blood type A, with genes $I^A I^o$, not the $I^A I^B$ type AB blood the child had.

10.4   Gene Interactions

Genes produce gene products that affect the phenotype of the organism. Often, genes will have their products interact and affect each other's. For example, the gene that produces a widow's peak in humans is masked by the expression of the baldness gene. Even though the man is bald he still has the genes to produce a widow's peak.

10.4.1   Epistasis

Epistasis is the term applied when one gene interferes with the expression of another (as in the baldness/widow's peak mentioned above). English geneticist William Bateson (1861–1926), who coined the term genetics and popularized the subject in Great Britain, reported a different phenotypic ratio in sweet peas than could be explained by simple Mendelian inheritance. Humans also have epistatic genes, notably albinism, a recessive gene that prevents the production of pigments for eye color, hair color, and freckles. Albino people (Figure 10.2A, B) lack eye pigments, hair pigments, and skin pigments. Albinism occurs in humans as well as other animals (Figure 10.2C, D). Albino snakes and zebras also occur.

The albinism allele interferes with metabolic pathways producing pigments. Even though a person might have the genes to make dark hair, albinism overprints that effect, producing white to pale blonde hair. The person might also have the alleles for freckles, but the albinism gene's epistatic effect blocks production of the pigments coloring a person's freckles.

10.4.2   Environment and Gene Expression

The environment can affect the expression of phenotypes. In the aquatic emergent buttercup (*Ranunculus peltatus*), leaves below water level are finely divided and look like branches, while those above water are broad, floating, photosynthetic, and leaf-like. The only difference between these leaves is their location above or below water, yet they have a dramatically different appearance. Many trees display a variety of leaf form, depending where on the tree the leaf is located.

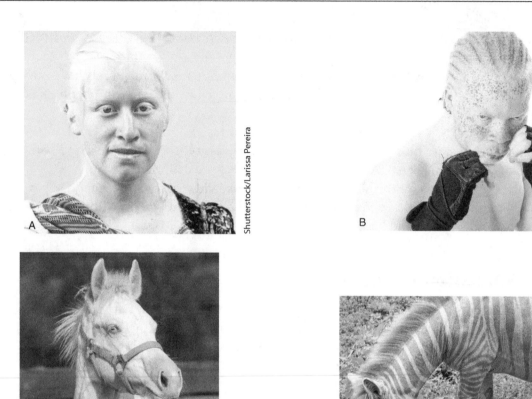

FIGURE 10.2 Albinism. A. Portrait of a traditionally dressed albino Mayan woman taken on the street while she was selling her crafts. September 16, 2013 in Antigua, Guatemala; B. Portrait of an albino African-American boxer; C. Albino horse; D. An extremely rare Albino Plains Zebra (*Equus quagga*) in Kenya, Africa. Albinism is a lack of melanin pigment, rendering the black stripes an orange or brown color.

Siamese cats are darker on their extremities (Figure 10.3A), due to temperature effects on phenotypic expression. Expression of phenotype is a result of interaction between genes and environment. Siamese cats and Himalayan rabbits (Figure 10.3) both animals have dark colored fur on their extremities. This is caused by an allele that controls and enzyme involved in pigment production being only able to function at the lower temperatures found on those extremities. Environment determines the phenotypic pattern of expression.

10.4.3 Pleiotropy

Sickle-cell anemia (Figure 10.4) is an autosomal incompletely dominant condition. Nine percent of African-Americans are heterozygous for this condition. Approximately 0.2% are homozygous for the sickle-cell allele. The sickle-cell allele (denoted with the letter combination Hb^s)

FIGURE 10.3 Environmental effects on phenotype. A. Siamese cat; B. Himalayan rabbit.

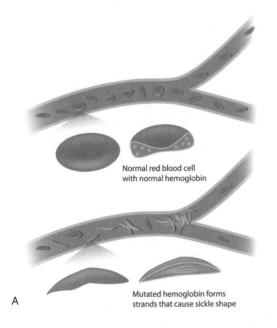

Normal red blood cell with normal hemoglobin

Mutated hemoglobin forms strands that cause sickle shape

A

Parents are heterozygous for sickle cell. $Hb^A Hb^S$ x $Hb^A Hb^S$ Punnett square:		
	Hb^A	Hb^S
Hb^A	$Hb^A Hb^A$	$Hb^A Hb^S$
Hb^S	$Hb^A Hb^S$	$Hb^S Hb^S$

Children Homozygous for Hb^A would be prone to malaria
Children Heterozygous ($Hb^A Hb^S$) would be immune to malaria
Children Homozygous for Hb^S would have sickle-cell anemia

B

FIGURE 10.4 A. Comparison of the cells produced by normal (top images) and sickle-cell individuals; B. The inheritance of the autosomal disease sickle-cell anemia.

causes a single amino acid substitution in the beta chains of hemoglobin, a protein composed of two alpha and two beta chains found on the surface of red blood cells. Normal hemoglobin beta chains are produced by the Hb^A allele. When oxygen concentration is low, a heterozygote ($Hb^A Hb^S$) that normally has round red blood cells will have the cells sickle (Figure 10.4A). Heterozygotes make enough good beta-chain hemoglobin, so they do not suffer so long as oxygen concentrations remain high, for example, at or near sea level. The sickled cells block passage of red blood cells in capillaries and smaller vessels.

Sickle-cell anemia occurs in people living in warm lowland tropical areas. These locations also have the malarial parasite that passes from its mosquito host to people through mosquito bites. Individuals heterozygous for the sickle-cell allele ($Hb^A Hb^S$) resist malaria since the malarial parasite cannot pass from the mosquito to the person. Sickle-celled individuals suffer from a number of problems, all of which are pleiotropic effects of the sickle-cell allele. These problems include circulatory difficulties, nervous system damage, organ failure, and pain.

10.5   Polygenic Inheritance

Polygenic inheritance (Figure 10.5) is a pattern responsible for many features that seem simple on the surface. The cumulative effects from several genes govern traits such as height, shape, weight, skin color, and metabolic rate. Polygenic traits are not expressed as absolute or discrete characters, as was the case with Mendel's pea plants. Instead, polygenic traits express as a gradation of small differences that form a continuous range of variation. Take height for example: if we line up everybody in a large class, we see a range of heights, not a class of tall people and a class of smaller people. The results form a bell-shaped curve, with a mean value and extremes in either direction.

Height in humans is a polygenic trait, as is outer husk color in wheat kernels. Height in humans is not discontinuous. If you line up the entire class, a continuum of variation is evident with an average height and extremes in variation (very short [vertically challenged?] and very tall [vertically enhanced]). The additive effects of two or more separate gene pairs usually control traits that show continuous variation. This is an example of polygenic inheritance. The inheritance of each gene follows Mendelian rules.
Polygenic traits are usually distinguished by

1. Traits are usually quantified by measurement rather than counting.
2. Two or more gene pairs contribute to the phenotype.
3. Phenotypic expression of polygenic traits varies over a wide range.

Human polygenic traits include height, weight, eye color, intelligence, skin color (Figure 10.5), and certain forms of behavior.

10.6   Genes and Chromosomes

Gregor Mendel discovered the basic rules of inheritance and applied them to situations of complete dominance of one trait over another. However, not all genes are completely dominant. Some are incompletely dominant, others have multiple alleles that combine to produce a common phenotype. The environment also interacts with genes, as do various genes with each other. Genes are located on chromosomes.

The phenomenon of linkage occurs when genes are on the same chromosome. Remember that sex-linked genes are on the X-chromosome, one of the sex chromosomes. Thus, all the genes on the X-chromosome comprise a collection of linked genes known as a linkage group. These genes pass into gametes (during meiosis) as a block, much like tourists on a tour bus

B

Parental genotypes: AaBbCc x AaBbCc								
Possible genotypes of their children:								
	ABC	aBC	AbC	ABc	Abc	aBc	abC	abc
ABC	AABBCC	AaBBCC	AABbCC	AABBCc	AABbCc	AaBBCc	AaBbCC	AaBbCc
aBC	AaBBCC	aaBBCC	AaBbCC	AaBBCc	AaBbCc	AaBBCc	AaBbCc	aaBbCc
AbC	AaBbCC	AaBbCC	AAbbCC	AABbCc	AAbbCc	AaBbCc	AabbCC	AabbCc
ABc	AABBCc	AaBBCc	AABbCc	AABbCc	AABbcc	AaBBcc	AaBbCc	Aabbcc
Abc	AABbCC	AaBbCC	AAbbCc	AaBbCc	AAbbcc	AaBbcc	AabbCc	AaBbcc
aBc	AaBBCc	aaBbCC	AaBbCc	AaBBcc	AaBbcc	aaBBcc	aaBbCc	aaBbcc
abC	AaBbCC	AaBbCc	AabbCC	AaBbCc	Aabbcc	aaBbCc	aabbCC	aabbCc
abc	AaBbCc	aaBbCc	aaBbCc	AABbCc	Aabbcc	aaBbcc	aabbCc	aabbcc

© Kendall Hunt Publishing

FIGURE 10.5 Polygenic traits. A. Inheritance of a polygenic trait, skin pigmentation, which is governed by three separate genes. B. A group of people illustrating the range of skin colors.

remain together for the duration of the tour. Linkage groups are invariably the same number as the pairs of homologous chromosomes an organism possesses. Recombination of these linked genes occurs when crossing-over, the breaking and reattachment of homologous chromosomes during meiosis, has broken linkage groups. This happened in the case of the genes for wing size and body color of the fruit flies that Morgan studied. The frequency of crossing-over gave early geneticists a tool with which to map the locations of genes on chromosomes.

Mutations can be induced in organisms by applying either radiation or chemicals. Morgan and his team induced the formation of new alleles by subjecting their fruit flies to mutagens. Genes are located on specific regions of a certain chromosome, termed the gene locus (plural: loci). A gene, therefore, is a specific segment of the DNA molecule.

The American geneticist Alfred Sturtevant (1891–1970), while an undergraduate student in Morgan's lab, postulated that crossing-over would be less common between genes adjacent to each other on the same chromosome. He reasoned it should be possible to plot the sequence of genes along a fruit fly chromosome by using crossing-over frequencies. Distances on gene maps are expressed in map units (one map unit = 1 recombinant per 100 fertilized eggs; or a 1% chance of recombination). Modern molecular techniques have more or less replaced the classical mapping Sturtevant developed.

10.6.1   Chromosome Abnormalities

Chromosome abnormalities include inversion, insertion, duplication, and deletion. These are types of mutations. Mutations increase the variation within a species. Most mutations are harmful to the individual, although very rarely they may be beneficial. Since DNA is information, and information typically has a beginning point, an inversion would produce an inactive or altered protein due to the amino acids being in the place in the protein's primary structure. This usually results in a protein that fails to function properly. Likewise, deletion or duplication will alter the gene product by changing the primary amino acid sequence of the protein.

An inversion involves a segment that has become separated from the chromosome and is reinserted backward at the same place. A translocation occurs when a chromosome segment moves from one chromosome to a non-homologous chromosome. Deletions occur when an end of a chromosome breaks off or when two simultaneous breaks lead to the loss of a segment. Gene duplication occurs when a chromosomal segment is copied. Some forms of cancer seem linked to duplication of oncogenes.

Cri du chat syndrome is a human genetic condition caused by a deletion of part of chromosome 5. Sufferers have a small head, some mental impairment, facial abnormalities, and an abnormal glottis and larynx resulting in a cry resembling that of a cat (hence the name, which is French for "cry of the cat").

Some mutations involve changes in the number of chromosomes. Monosomy is a condition that occurs when an individual has only one of a particular chromosome, so that a diploid individual is not $2n$, but $2n - 1$. Trisomy, the presence of three of a particular chromosome, can also happen. Individuals in this case would be $2n + 1$. Both conditions are caused by nondisjunction, the failure of chromosomes to separate during meiosis. Autosomal monosomy and trisomy are in most cases lethal. Nonlethal human monosomies and trisomies include Turner syndrome, a monosomy where the individual (female) has a single X-chromosome and Klinefelter syndrome, where the male has two X-chromosomes plus a Y-chromosome. Down syndrome is the most common human trisomy. People with Down syndrome usually have an extra copy of the 21st chromosome (Figure 10.6).

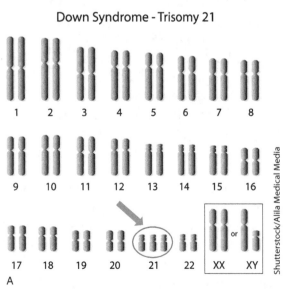

FIGURE 10.6 Down syndrome. A. Karyotype of a Down syndrome individual B. Portrait of a boy showing typical eye shape of the condition.

10.7   Human Genetics

Humans belong to the animal kingdom. Our genes are composed of DNA, as are the genes of all other living things. Although our sense of grandeur might espouse that we are something special, we must ask "are we *that* different from other creatures"? Other animals run faster than we can. Still others swim better than even our best Olympic swimming medalists. We cannot fly or dive to great depths unassisted. However, we do have our minds and the capabilities they facilitate to think differently, get outside the box, and to dream of future days. How much of this ability is genetic we do not yet know. We do know that we are biological creatures whose innate abilities are at least in part genetic.

10.7.1   The Human Karyotype: A Picture of Our Genes

There are 44 autosomes and 2 sex chromosomes in the human genome, for a total of 46 chromosomes. Autosomes are homologous chromosomes that carry the same genes (although not necessarily the same *alleles* for those genes). Size, shape, banding pattern, and position of the centromere all combine to distinguish the autosomes. Figure 10.7 shows the human chromosomes. Note that in each pair of the first 22 chromosomes, each homologous chromosome is the same size as its partner. The sex chromosomes, the 23rd pair or chromosomes, are the X- and Y-chromosomes. Males have one X-chromosome and one Y-chromosome. Females have two X-chromosomes. Scientists can take a picture of an organism's chromosomes, a karyotype. Homologous chromosomes are shown lined up together during Metaphase I of Meiosis in a traditional karyotype (Figure 10.7). The chromosome pictures are then arranged by size and pasted onto a sheet (or now, done on a computer).

However, our genes are more than bands on chromosomes. A gene is a segment of the DNA molecule that stores the genetic code to make a protein. Thus, our chromosomes are collections of these DNA base sequences. Different sequences of the DNA bases may produce different proteins. An allele is an alternate form of a gene. We now know that an allele is an alternate base sequence for a gene.

No one individual will have all the alleles and variations for their entire species. A genome is the collection of all the genes occurring in members of a species. In 1986 the U.S. government launched a massive project to sequence the genes of all the human genome. This project was essentially finished during the summer of 2000. What we do with this book of humans remains to be seen.

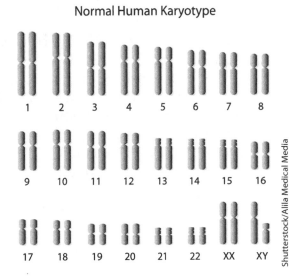

Normal Human Karyotype

Shutterstock/Alila Medical Media

FIGURE 10.7 Normal human karyotypes. Female would have XX as her 23rd pair, male would have XY as his 23rd pair.

10.7.2   Human Chromosomal Abnormalities

Human genetic defects are caused both by problems with individual chromosomes as well as individual alleles on chromosomes. The classic example of a chromosomal abnormality is Down syndrome (Figure 10.6A), where one extra chromosome (number 21) causes a number of difficulties for the afflicted individual. Down syndrome and other chromosomal problems are usually caused by nondisjunction of chromosomes during meiosis that leads to formation of gametes. Human allelic disorders include hemophilia, where one part of the gene coding for a blood clotting protein produces an abnormal protein. The result is a defective protein that causes hemophiliacs to suffer from uncontrolled bleeding. Mutations are defined as any change in the DNA base sequence. Mutations are the ultimate cause of alleles, both good and bad ones. However, evolution would not operate if not for the variation these mutated alleles produce.

A common chromosomal abnormality is caused by nondisjunction, the failure of replicated chromosomes to segregate during Anaphase I or Anaphase II. This lack of the separation of chromosomes can produce a variety of gametes that either have an extra chromosome ($n + 1$) or lack one of their chromosomes ($n - 1$).

In humans, nondisjunction is most often associated with the 21st chromosome, producing a condition known as Down syndrome (also referred to as trisomy 21; Table 10.2). Those affected by Down syndrome suffer mild to severe mental retardation, short stocky body type, large tongue leading to speech difficulties, and (in those who survive into middle-age) a propensity to develop Alzheimer's disease. Ninety-five percent of Down syndrome cases result from nondisjunction of chromosome 21. Occasional cases result from a translocation in the chromosomes of one parent. Remember that a translocation occurs when one chromosome (or a fragment) is transferred to a non-homologous chromosome. The incidence of Down syndrome increases with the age of the mother, although 25% of the cases result from an extra chromosome from the baby's father.

Sex-chromosome abnormalities (Figure 10.8) may also be caused by nondisjunction of one or more sex chromosomes. Any combination (up to XXXXY) produces maleness, as long as there is one Y-chromosome present. Males with more than one X are usually underdeveloped and sterile and suffer from Klinefelter syndrome (Figure 10.8A). XXX and XO women are known, although in most cases they are sterile. Women with only one complete X chromosome suffer from Turner syndrome (Figure 10.8B). They tend to be of short stature, thick-necked, have immature breast development, and are sterile. Jacobs syndrome occurs when males have two Y chromosomes (Figure 10.8C) and are XYY instead of the normal XY.

There are a number of conditions or syndromes associated with extra or missing syndromes shown in Table 10.2

10.7.3   Human Allelic Disorders

In 1903 William Curtis Farabee (1865–1925) detected the first Mendelian trait in humans, brachydactyly. There are now many variants of brachydactyly known. All involve some fusion or alteration of the middle bones of all the digits and a short stature. The gene is inherited as an

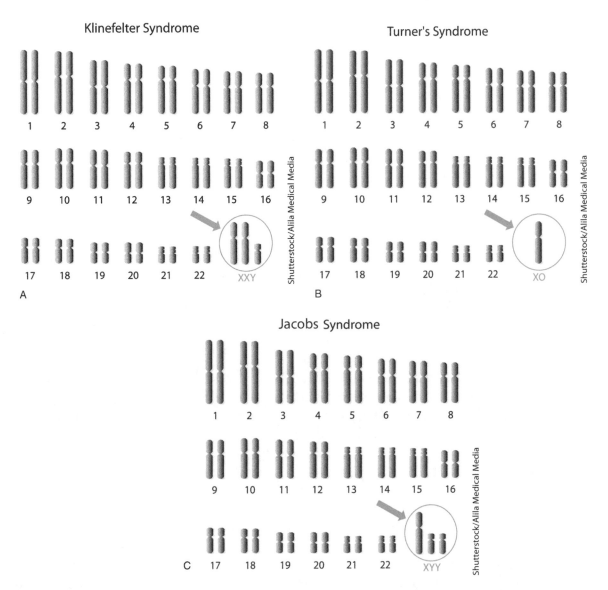

FIGURE 10.8 Human sex chromosome abnormalities. A. Karyotype for Klinefelter syndrome; B. Karyotype for Turner syndrome; C. Karyotype for Jacobs syndrome.

autosomal dominant. The family that Farabee studied passed along the gene for at least three successive generations. Not all of the human allelic disorders are dominant, some are recessive and still others are incompletely dominant and other variations. Autosomal dominants are rare, although they are (by definition) more commonly expressed. Now more than 3500 human genetic conditions are known.

Albinism (Figure 10.9; designated as a lower case "a"), the lack of pigmentation in skin, hair, and eyes, is also a Mendelian human trait. Homozygous recessive (aa) individuals make no pigments, and so have face, hair, and eyes that are white to yellow. For heterozygous parents with normal pigmentation (Aa), two different types of gametes may be produced: A or a. From a cross

TABLE 10.2 Human Chromosomal Abnormalities

Condition Name	Gender of Sufferers	Chromosomes Involved	Frequency in Live Births	Frequency in Miscarriages
Down	Either Male or Female	Extra Copy of Chromosome 21	1/40	1/700
Patau	Either Male or Female	Extra Copy of Chromosome 13	1/33	1/15,000
Edward	Either Male or Female	Extra Copy of Chromosome 18	1/200	1/6,000
Klinefelter	Male	XXY or XXXY	0	1/1,500
Jacobs	Male	XYY	unknown	1/1,000
Turner	Female	X	1/18	1/2,000 to 1/2,500
Metafemale	Female	XXX or XXXX	0	1/1,500

of individuals heterozygous for albinism, 1/4 of the children could be albinos, a standard Mendelian ratio. Albinos cannot make the brown pigment melanin, which results in their skin being white, regardless of their race or ethnicity (Figure 10.2A, B). Melanin is the pigment most people produce that protects their skin from the Sun's ultraviolet radiation. Depending on ethnicity, people will have greater or lesser amounts of this pigment.

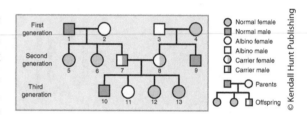

FIGURE 10.9 Pedigree chart showing the inheritance of albinism.

Mutations in several genes seem to cause albinism, from the lack of one or another enzyme along the melanin-producing pathway; to the inability of the enzyme to enter the pigment cells and convert the amino acid tyrosine into melanin.

Phenylketonuria (PKU) is a recessive disorder whose sufferers lack the ability to synthesize an enzyme (phenylalanine hydroxylase) to convert the amino acid phenylalanine into the amino acid tyrosine. Amino acids are the building blocks of proteins, one of the four major organic macromolecule groups essential to the cell's functioning. Humans can make only 12 of the 20 amino acids that all living things use to make their proteins, the other 8 are obtained in our diets. Homozygous recessive individuals for this allele have a build-up of phenylalanine and abnormal breakdown products in their urine and blood. The breakdown products can be harmful to developing nervous systems and lead to mental retardation. Early detection of PKU can lead to effective treatments involving a low phenylalanine diet. One out of every 15,000 infants suffers from this problem. Most states now routinely test for PKU. If you look closely at a product containing Nutra-sweet artificial sweetener, you will see a warning to PKU sufferers because phenylalanine is one of the amino acids in the sweetener. PKU sufferers are placed on a diet low in phenylalanine; they can have enough for metabolic needs, but not enough to cause the buildup of harmful intermediates.

Tay-Sachs Disease is an autosomal recessive condition resulting in degeneration of the nervous system. Symptoms manifest after birth. Children who are homozygous recessive for this allele rarely survive past five years of age. Sufferers lack the ability to make the enzyme N-acetylhexosaminidase, which breaks down the GM2 ganglioside lipid. This lipid accumulates in lysosomes in brain cells, eventually killing the brain cells. Although rare in the general population (1 in 300,000 births), it was (until recently) higher (1 in 3600 births) among people of Eastern Central European Jewish descent. One in 28 American Jews is thought to be a carrier, since 90% of the American Jewish population emigrated from those areas in Europe. The disease is a recessive trait, and unless there is a family history it may not be suspected. Development of a chemical test to detect the presence of the allele in heterozygous carriers and genetic counseling offered through synagogues has greatly reduced the incidence of Tay-Sachs among the U.S. Jewish population. Most Tay-Sachs baby births in the United States occur to non-Jewish parents.

Cystic fibrosis (Figure 10.10) is an autosomal recessive disease that is the most common lethal genetic disease among American Caucasians. About 1 in 20 Caucasians carries the allele for cystic fibrosis. Cystic fibrosis occurs in about 1 in 2,500 births. Homozygous recessive individuals produce of a viscous form of mucus in their lungs and pancreatic ducts. Accumulation of mucus interferes with gas exchange in the lungs. Once a fatal illness that killed before afflicted individuals reached their teens, new cystic fibrosis treatments have raised the average life expectancy to beyond 50 years. Common forms of treatment include replacement of pancreatic enzyme, oral salt supplement, pulmonary postural drainage, and antibiotic therapy. The cause of cystic fibrosis is a mutated gene on chromosome 7. Research has shown that chloride ions (Cl^-) fail to pass through plasma membrane proteins in cystic fibrosis patients. Since water normally follows Cl^-, the lack of water in the lungs causes the thick mucus.

Huntington disease (known as Woody Guthrie's disease, after the American folk singer who died from this disease in the 1960s) is an autosomal dominant resulting in progressive destruction of brain cells. If a parent has the disease, 50% of the children will have it (unless that parent was homozygous dominant, in which case all children would have the disease). The disease usually does not manifest until after age 30, although some instances of early onset phenomenon are reported among individuals in their twenties.

Polydactyly is the presence of a sixth digit. In modern times, the extra finger has been cut off at birth and individuals do not know they carry this trait. There are several different types of polydactyly, including presence of an extra thumb, or presence of an extra middle finger. Some varieties of this disease seem more prevalent among African-Americans (Polydactyly Postaxial, Type A1), and among Native Americans (Polydactyly, Preaxial I) than among Caucasians. Anne Boleyn, one of the many wives of Henry VIII of England (and mother of Queen Elizabeth I) is rumored to have had an

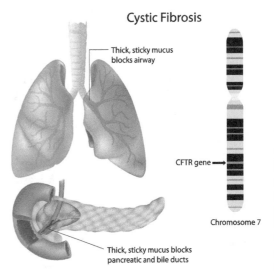

Cystic Fibrosis

Thick, sticky mucus blocks airway

CFTR gene

Chromosome 7

Thick, sticky mucus blocks pancreatic and bile ducts

Shutterstock/Alila Medical Media

FIGURE 10.10 Cystic fibrosis.

extra finger. In certain southern U.S. families the trait is more common. The extra digit is rarely functional.

10.7.4   Sex-linked Traits

Humans determine gender by the presence of a Y-chromosome, specifically the one or more genes in the Testis-Determining Factor region. Females have two copies of the X-chromosome (XX) and males have one X-chromosome and one Y-chromosome. Since the number of genes on the X-chromosome is much larger than the corresponding genes on the Y-chromosome, whatever the male gets on the X chromosome his mother gives him at conception will be expressed in his phenotype. The male cannot be heterozygous for a sex-linked trait, females can. When looking at sex-linked genes the gender of the individual must be considered along with the genotype of the particular gene.

Color blindness is associated with the X chromosome, and afflicts 8% of human males and 0.04% of females. Color perception depends on three genes, each producing chemicals sensitive to different parts of the visible light spectrum, specifically red, green, and blue. Red and green detecting genes are on the X-chromosome, whereas the blue detection gene is on an autosome.

Hemophilia is a group of diseases in which blood does not clot normally. Normal individuals produce chemicals (or factors) in their blood that are involved in clotting. Hemophilia is X-linked and inherited by males from their mother (Figure 10.11). Hemophiliacs lacking the normal Factor VIII are said to have Hemophilia A, the most common form. Normal Factor VIII can be supplied at a high dollar cost and health risk, although the development of biotechnologically engineered Factor VIII produced by bacteria lessened the health risk. During the 1980s a number of hemophiliac males contracted HIV from blood transfusions designed to provide them with the missing blood factor. England's Queen Victoria was a carrier (heterozygote) for this disease. The allele was passed to two of her daughters (both of whom were carriers) and one son (who died of hemophilia). Since royal families in Europe commonly intermarried, the allele spread to the Russian monarchy (Czar Nicholas II's son Alexei is thought to have suffered from hemophilia A inherited from his mother, Alexandra one of Victoria's granddaughters, who carried Victoria's genetic secret). The Russian monk Rasputin rose to power and influence due to his reported ability to help young Nicholas. Controversy over Rasputin and his relationship with the Russian royal family may have weakened the monarchy, although it eventually fell to the Bolshevik revolution in 1917.

Muscular dystrophy is a term encompassing a variety of muscle-wasting diseases. The most common and severe type, Duchenne Muscular Dystrophy (DMD), affects cardiac and skeletal muscle, as well as some mental functions. Over

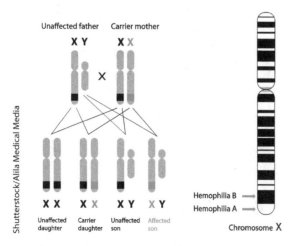

FIGURE 10.11 Hemophilia inheritance.

time, the muscles deteriorate and no longer function, eventually resulting in death. DMD is an X-linked recessive disorder occurring in one in 3500 newborns. DMD usually manifests itself before the child is 3 years old. The victim is confined to a wheelchair by age 12. Most sufferers die before their 20th birthday. In 1987, American physician Louis Kunkel isolated a protein, dystrophin, present in "normal" individuals (about 0.002% of their muscle protein) but absent in individuals with DMD. The lack of dystrophin is accompanied with a condition of muscle hardening known as fibrosis, which restricts blood supply to the muscle, causing the muscle to die. The molecular gene technologies, discussed in Chapter 12, have been employed to sequence and clone the dystrophin gene, which is the largest known human gene (some 2–3 million base pairs), with 60 exons and many large introns. Scientists are investigating gene replacement therapy in animal models. A modified virus has been used to incorporate a normal gene into mouse skeletal and cardiac muscle, although application to humans suffering from this disease is many years away.

The Y-chromosome carries only a few genes, most notably (from the male perspective at least) is the gene region that determines gender. The Y-chromosome has also been involved in the historical controversy of whether Thomas Jefferson had fathered one or more children with Sally Hemmings, one of his slaves. The evidence that has seemingly removed any question comes from the Y-chromosome shared by Thomas Jefferson and his paternal uncle, Field Jefferson. Thomas Jefferson's white descendants do not share this Y-chromosome, being descended from his daughter. Comparison of the Y-chromosome sequence of one of the Hemmings descendants with a male descendant of Jefferson's uncle show a similarity of DNA sequences on the Y-chromosome that has a probability of occurring by chance of less than one percent. Despite the DNA evidence, the claim remains controversial.

10.8   The Human Genome Project

My generation had a large science project to amaze us: sending men to the Moon and bringing them safely back to Earth. The Apollo space projects grabbed public consciousness as the space race and Cold War with the old Soviet Union led numerous scientific accomplishments and advances: Teflon, remote sensing, improved knowledge about how the human body works, and so on. The Department of Energy and the National Institutes of Health began an ambitious project in 1990, the Human Genome Project, that is your generation's Apollo project. The project's goals are the identification of all the genes in human DNA; determination of the sequences of the 3 billion chemical base pairs that make up human DNA; storage and access to this information in databases; development of tools for data analysis; dissemination of related technologies to the private sector; and discussion of the ethical, legal, and social issues certain to arise from the project.

Summary

Genes and their interactions are more than the simple complete dominance situations Mendel worked with on his pea plants. Traits such as height and skin color result from multiple genes that produce a continuous range of variation. Not all genes have just two alleles, some have three or four alleles for a gene. Mutations are changes in the sequence of DNA bases. Alleles result from mutations. Chapter 11 will explore how genes work.

Terms

amino acid	genome	mutations
antibodies	gene locus	mutagens
albinism	hemoglobin	nondisjunction
autosomes	hemophilia	phenotype
codominant alleles	homologous chromosomes	pleiotropy
complete dominance	Huntington's disease	polydactyly
crossing-over	incomplete dominance	polygenic inheritance
cystic fibrosis	insertion	recombination
deletion	inversion	sickle-cell anemia
discontinuous	karyotype	sex chromosomes
duplication	Klinefelter's syndrome	sex linkage
dystrophin	linkage	translocation
epistasis	lysosomes	trisomy
evolution	melanin	Turner's syndrome
genes	monosomy	

Review Questions

1. Which of the following would be an indication of incomplete dominance?
   a. production of a new phenotype not found in either of the parents;
   b. one of the phenotypes showing up in all offspring of a cross between homozygotes;
   c. the skipping of a generation by one trait that was not expressed in a cross between homozygotes;
   d. all of these

2. Thomas Hunt Morgan and his students studied the inheritance of traits in ___.
   a. garden peas;
   b. bees;
   c. fruit flies;
   d. snapdragons

3. Chromosomes that carry the gender determining genes are known as ___.
   a. hemizygotes;
   b. sex chromosomes;
   c. autosomes;
   d. centrosomes

4. A ___ is a photograph of the chromosomes found in a particular species.
   a. karyogenesis;
   b. karyotype;
   c. mutation;
   d. meiotic spindle

5. Sex-linked genes are more likely to be expressed in the ___.
   a. males;
   b. females;
   c. both males and females equally;
   d. none of these.

6. Males inherit their Y-chromosome from ___.
   a. their mother;
   b. their father;
   c. their mother's father;
   d. either parent.

7. When a recessive trait is on the X-chromosome ___.
   a. males will never express it;
   b. females will always express it;
   c. males can express it more often than females will;
   d. it will only be expressed in 1/4 of the offspring

8. The presence of which chromosome determines gender?
   a. the X-chromosome;
   b. chromosome 21;
   c. the Y- chromosome;
   d. both the X- and the Y-chromosome

9. What term best describes genes on the X-chromosome?
   a. sex determining;
   b. sex linked;
   c. autosomal;
   d. recessive

10. When a trait is expressed as a continuum or range or measurements that trait is most likely to be ___.
    a. completely dominant;
    b. incompletely dominant;
    c. caused by multiple alleles;
    d. caused by multiple genes

11. One clue that trait might be sex-linked is that ___.
    a. it is more common in females than in males;
    b. it occurs in each sex equally;
    c. it is more common in males than in females;
    d. it only is seen in a homozygote

12. When two extreme phenotypes are crossed and all of the progeny have an intermediate phenotype, what might be the cause?
    a. complete dominance of one trait over another;
    b. incomplete dominance;
    c. codominance;
    d. sex linkage

13. Which of these children's blood type could not be produced by parents with type A and type O blood types?
    a. Type O;
    b. Type A;
    c. Type AB;
    d. all of these are possible

14. A mutation is ___.
    a. any change in the information stored on the RNA molecule;
    b. any change in the information stored in the DNA molecule;
    c. impossible and has never been observed;
    d. of no value to the evolutionary fitness of a species

15. If a karyotype shows an extra copy of the 21st chromosome, the patient has the disease _____.
    a. Turner syndrome;   c. sickle-cell disease;
    b. cystic fibrosis;   d. Down syndrome

16. Which of these human genetic conditions cannot be diagnosed by a karyotype?
    a. Patau syndrome;   c. Klinefelter syndrome;
    b. Huntington disease;   d. Jacobs syndrome

17. Sufferers of which of these syndromes would be male?
    a. Turner syndrome;   c. metafemale;
    b. Klinefelter syndrome;   d. all of these

18. During the medical procedure known as ___, a thin needle is used to draw amniotic fluid from the placenta.
    a. amniocentesis;   c. ultrasound;
    b. chorionic villi sampling;   d. in vitro fertilization

19. The first human trait demonstrated to be inherited by Mendelian rules was ___.
    a. Huntington disease;   c. cystic fibrosis;
    b. brachydactyly;   d. alcoholism

20. The human genetic disease that results from the production of faulty chloride ion channels is ___.
    a. polydactyly;   c. albinism;
    b. cystic fibrosis;   d. hemophilia

21. _____ is the human genetic disease where no pigmentation is made.
    a. polydactyly;   c. albinism;
    b. cystic fibrosis;   d. hemophilia

22. Tay-Sachs disease is prominent among ___.,
    a. African-Americans;   c. Native Americans;
    b. Italian-Americans;   d. Jewish-Americans

23. Sickle-cell disease is prominent among ___.
    a. African-Americans;   c. Native Americans;
    b. Italian-Americans;   d. Jewish-Americans

24. Children who suffer from Tay-Sachs disease have the inability to ___.
    a. make pigments;
    b. metabolize phenylalanine;
    c. make a proper N-acetyl-hexosaminidase enzyme;
    d. make proper chloride ion channels in lung cells.

25. Which of these is not a human sex-linked disease?
    a. Huntington disease;
    b. hemophilia A;
    c. male pattern baldness;
    d. Duchenne muscular dystrophy

26. Male hemophiliacs inherit the disease from their ___.
    a. mother;
    b. father;
    c. paternal grandfather;
    d. uncle

27. When someone is said to be a carrier for a genetic disease, their genotype is ___.
    a. homozygous dominant;
    b. heterozygous;
    c. homozygous recessive;
    d. incompletely dominant

28. Duchenne muscular dystrophy is a human genetic defect caused by ___.
    a. a defective channel protein;
    b. a defective protein known as dystrophin;
    c. two copies of the allele for the disease;
    d. a defective gene on the Y-chromosome

Links

- **A Gene Map of the Human Genome:** As of mid-1999. Click on a chromosome number and view an enlarged map of that chromosome, continue clicking for details about that chromosome's genes and their sequences. [http://www.ncbi.nlm.nih.gov/genemap99/]

- **OMIM™ Online Mendelian Inheritance in Man:** This searchable database is invaluable for looking up genes and genetic conditions. Much of this is written for the scientific audience, but the basics of what the gene does and where it is can be pretty easily ascertained. [http://www.ncbi.nlm.nih.gov/omim]

- **Genetics Education Center:** This University of Kansas website offers a numerous links to similar websites. [http://www.kumc.edu/gec/]

- **An Introduction to Skin Cancer:** Learn more about skin cancer, especially the environmental and hereditary aspects of it. [http://www.south-seas.com/introto.html]

- **Sickle Cell Anemia Information Center:** Learn more about the human aspects of this genetic disease that has been extensively discussed in this chapter. [http://scinfo.org]

- **Klinefelter Syndrome:** This series of pages from MedicineNet.com provide more details about this chromosomal abnormality. [http://www.medicinenet.com/Script/Main/art.asp?li=MNI7d=271&ArticleKey=9610]

CHAPTER 11

DNA Structure, Protein Synthesis, and Gene Control

Chapter Opener

Model of the deoxyribonucleic acid (DNA) molecule showing its double helix structure.

Objectives

- Before 1952, protein molecules and amino acid molecules were suspected of housing the genetic code. Discuss the reasons DNA was not thought of as a likely candidate for the hereditary material.
- Make and label a sketch of a DNA nucleotide.
- List and discuss the significance of the pieces of information about DNA structure that Rosalind Franklin discovered through her X-ray diffraction research.
- Describe in a couple of sentences the model of DNA structure that Watson and Crick proposed.
- Explain what is meant by base pairing, and explain the mechanism that causes bases of one DNA strand to join with bases of the other strand.
- Describe how double-stranded DNA replicates.
- Describe the process of DNA replication.
- Describe the roles of the promoter, regulatory, and operator genes in an operon.
- Compare and contrast the functioning of the *lac* and *trp* operons. What is meant by the terms inducible and repressible?
- Discuss the viral infection cycle, including both the lytic and lysogenic aspects.
- Diagram Crick's Central Dogma and show where reverse transcription fits in.
- Be able to compare and contrast the organization of the prokaryotic and eukaryotic chromosomes.
- Describe how are exons spliced together to make a functional ribonucleic acid (RNA) molecule.
- Discuss how control over eukaryotic genes and the cell cycle might facilitate new and improved treatments for cancer.

Introduction

We finally come to the crux of the gene: what is it and how does it work. This is one of the great stories of science inquiry and experimentation that gradually pieced together an answer. Mendel's work showed the basic rules of inheritance of the factors that were later termed genes. Modifications of Mendel's patterns, such as incomplete dominance, multiple alleles, and sex-linked genes, were worked out during the early 1900s. However, the nature of the physical carrier of inheritance still had not been resolved. Scientists knew that genes were on chromosomes that resided in the eukaryotic nucleus. They also knew these chromosomes were composed of protein and DNA. We know, by virtue of hindsight, that DNA is the physical carrier of inheritance. The discovery of the role DNA plays in living systems is a great detective story spanning decades of scientific inquiry. Applications of this inquiry have led us to DNA "fingerprinting" of military personnel so we may no longer have "unknown soldiers" to entomb, a powerful forensic tool for investigating crimes as well as questions of ancestry. DNA evidence has been used to convict criminals, to free innocent convicts, and to relieve human suffering. The Human Genome Project revealed the sequence of DNA information with which we *could* make a person, at least in theory. Information encoded in the DNA molecule is life's blueprint, the code that gives us our innate capabilities and challenges. Will we be able to resist (or should we even think of resisting) the challenge of monkeying with our own genes to eliminate genetic defects? As with all science, the answer lies with society, not solely with the scientist.

11.1   The Search for the Physical Carrier of Inheritance

The time between the early 1900s and World War II has been considered the "golden age" of genetics. Scientists still had not determined that DNA, and not protein, was the hereditary material. However, during this time, a great many genetic discoveries were made and the link between genetics and evolution became established.

In 1869, Swiss biochemist Friedrich Miescher (1844–1895) isolated DNA from fish sperm and the pus of open wounds. Since it came from nuclei, Miescher named this new chemical nuclein. Subsequently, nuclein was changed to nucleic acid and finally to DNA. German chemist Robert Feulgen (1884–1955) discovered in 1914 that a modified fuchsin dye stained only DNA when applied to a cell. The DNA was found in the nucleus of all eukaryotic cells.

During the 1920s, Lithuanian-American biochemist Phoebus A. Levene (1869–1940) analyzed the components of the DNA and RNA molecules. He found DNA contained four nitrogenous bases: cytosine (C), thymine (T), adenine (A), and guanine (G); deoxyribose sugar; and a phosphate group. Levene concluded the basic unit, the nucleotide, (Figure 11.1) consisted of one of the four bases attached to a sugar molecule attached to a phosphate. He erroneously concluded the proportions of bases were equal and the molecular structure was a tetranucleotide forming a repeating structure of the molecule. This meant the structure of DNA was too simple in structure to act as the genetic molecule containing information. Levene's work on the nucleotide, however, remains as the fundamental unit (monomer) of the nucleic acid polymer. The tetranucleotide (to Levene and others) ruled out DNA as the molecule that carried the genetic code.

During the early 1900s, the link between Mendel's work and that of cell biologists resulted in the chromosomal theory of inheritance discussed in the previous chapter. British physician Archibald Garrod (1857–1936) proposed the link between genes and "inborn errors of metabolism," and the question was formed: what is a gene? The answer came from the study of pneumonia, a deadly infectious disease.

The great influenza epidemic of 1918 had killed between 30 and 50 million people (over 675,000 of them Americans), mostly from

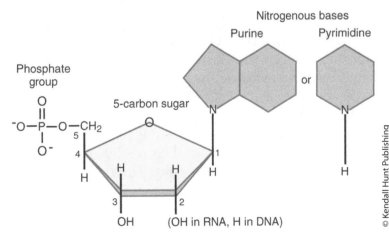

FIGURE 11.1 Structure of a nucleotide.

pneumonia contracted by the victims after the flu had weakened them. There were no antibiotics (like penicillin, discovered during the late 1920s) to treat pneumonia in 1918–1919. During the 1920s, British physician Frederick Griffith (1879–1941) studied the difference between a strain of the pneumonia causing bacteria (*Streptococcus pneumoniae*) and a strain that did not result in pneumonia. The pneumonia-causing strain (known as the S strain) was surrounded by a structure known as a capsule. The other strain (the R strain) lacked a capsule and also did not cause pneumonia. Frederick Griffith (in 1928) was able to induce a nondisease causing strain of the bacterium *S. pneumoniae* to become pathogenic. Griffith injected the different strains of bacteria into mice. The S strain killed the mice; the R strain did not. He further noted that if the heat killed S strain was injected into a mouse, it did not cause pneumonia. When he combined heat-killed S with live R and injected the mixture into a mouse (remember neither alone will kill the mouse) the mouse developed pneumonia and died. Bacteria recovered from the mouse had a capsule and killed other mice when injected! Griffith eventually concluded that live R bacteria had been transformed into live S bacteria by some "transforming factor." Griffith attributed this change to a hereditary transforming factor.

In the 1940s, the Canadian-American research team of Oswald Avery (1877–1955), Colin MacLeod (1909–1972), and Maclyn McCarty (1911–2005), working at the Rockefeller Institute in New York, demonstrated that the transforming factor was DNA by repeating Griffith's work with an added enzyme that cuts up DNA. Instead of the expected transformation that Griffith obtained, Avery's team found no such transformation, and concluded the hereditary material was more like DNA than protein. While many scientists took the Avery team's work as conclusive evidence that DNA and not protein was the hereditary material, other scientists considered the evidence strong but not totally conclusive. The then-current favorite for the hereditary material was protein; DNA was not considered by many scientists to be a strong candidate.

The breakthrough in the quest to determine the hereditary material came from the work of Max Delbrück (1906–1981) and Salvador Luria (1912–1991) during the 1940s. Delbrück was German, and Luria was Italian. Both men moved to the United States where they began their collaboration. They studied bacterial virus structure and how viruses reproduced. Bacteriophages (Figure 11.2) are a type of virus that attacks bacteria. Viruses are obligate intracellular parasites that must gain entry to a host cell to reproduce. The viruses Delbrück and Luria studied attacked *Escherichia coli*, a bacterium found in human intestines. Bacteriophages consist of a protein coat, protein tail fibers, and a core of DNA. Bacteriophages infect a cell by injecting DNA into the host cell. This viral DNA then "disappears" while taking over the bacterial machinery and beginning to make new virus instead of new bacteria. After 25 minutes the host cell bursts, releasing hundreds of new viruses. The bacteriophages consist of DNA and protein, making them ideal to resolve the nature of the hereditary material.

The American geneticists Alfred D. Hershey (1908–1997) and Martha Chase (1927–2003) conducted a series of experiments (Figure 11.3) in 1952 to determine whether protein or DNA served as the hereditary material. By labeling the DNA and protein with different radioisotopes (Figure 11.3), they determined that DNA, not protein, got into the bacteria, and that DNA served as the hereditary material. Since DNA contains phosphorous (P) but no sulfur (S), they tagged the DNA with the radioactive isotope phosphorous-32 (^{32}P). Conversely, protein lacks phosphorous but does have sulfur, thus it could be tagged with the radioactive isotope sulfur-35 (^{35}S). Hershey and Chase found that the radioactive sulfur remained outside the cell while the

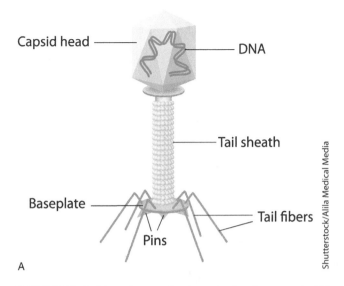

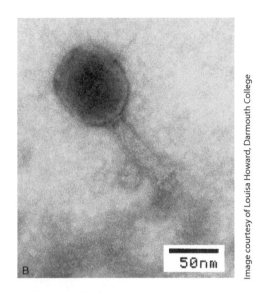

FIGURE 11.2 Structure of a bacteriophage. A. Diagram of a bacteriophage; B. Transmission electron micrograph of a bacteriophage. Photo courtesy of Louisa Howard, Dartmouth College.

radioactive phosphorous was found inside the cell, indicating that DNA was the physical carrier of heredity.

11.2 The Structure of DNA

The Hershey–Chase experiments convincingly demonstrated DNA as the genetic material. Precisely, how DNA served as genes was not yet certain during the early 1950s. DNA must carry information from parent cell to daughter cell. It must contain information for replicating itself. It must be a chemically stable molecule, relatively unchanging. However, it must be capable of mutational change. Without mutations there would be no process of evolution.

Many scientists attempted to decipher the structure of DNA, among them were English physicist Francis Crick (1916–2004) and American biologist James Watson (b. 1928) (Figure 11.4) working at the University of Cambridge in England. Watson was a young American who previously worked with Luria and had a keen interest in the structure of DNA. Crick was a Ph.D. student who shared an office with Watson. Together they built the first accurate model of DNA even though they were supposed to be working on other projects. British crystallographer Rosalind Franklin (1920–1958) and British physicist and molecular biologist Maurice Wilkins (1916–2004) both worked at King's College in London. Wilkins and Franklin each employed X-rays to study the molecular structure of organic molecules and both investigated the structure of DNA. However, a series of miscommunications prevented them from collaborating with each other. The British-born Franklin is the anomaly among the scientists who studied DNA: an educated and very talented scientist who happened to be a woman. Wilkins previously worked as a physicist on the development of the atomic bomb, the Manhattan Project, during World War II.

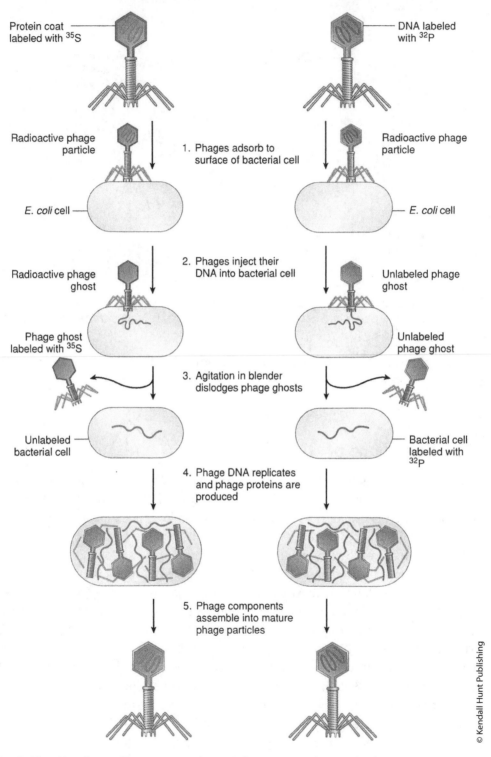

Protein coat labeled with ^{35}S

DNA labeled with ^{32}P

Radioactive phage particle

1. Phages adsorb to surface of bacterial cell

Radioactive phage particle

E. coli cell

E. coli cell

Radioactive phage ghost

2. Phages inject their DNA into bacterial cell

Unlabeled phage ghost

Phage ghost labeled with ^{35}S

Unlabeled phage ghost

3. Agitation in blender dislodges phage ghosts

Unlabeled bacterial cell

Bacterial cell labeled with ^{32}P

4. Phage DNA replicates and phage proteins are produced

5. Phage components assemble into mature phage particles

FIGURE 11.3 The Hershey–Chase experiment that proved conclusively that DNA and not protein is the hereditary material.

Watson and Crick gathered all available data in an attempt to develop a model of DNA structure (Figure 11.4). Franklin took X-ray diffraction photographs of DNA crystals, the key to the puzzle. The data known at the time was that DNA was a long molecule. The Hershey–Chase experiment had shown that DNA must be capable of storing information, so Levene's tetranucleotide hypothesis had been wrong. Proteins were known to be helically coiled molecules. Franklin, along with her research assistant Raymond Gosling (b. 1926), took many photographs of DNA, including the famous Photo 51. This photograph, when Wilkens showed it to Watson, confirmed Watson's belief that DNA was a double helix structure. He then arranged with Crick to build their model.

Erwin Chargaff (1905–2002), an Austrian-born American biochemist, analyzed the DNA bases in many different creatures and concluded that the amount of purines did not always equal the amount of pyrimidines as Levene proposed in the 1920s. Chargaff concluded that the amount of A equaled the amount of T and the amount of C equaled the amount of G for any given species (Table 11.1).

The Watson and Crick model shows DNA as a double helix (Figure 11.4), with the nitrogenous bases to the center (like steps on a ladder) and sugar-phosphate units along the sides of

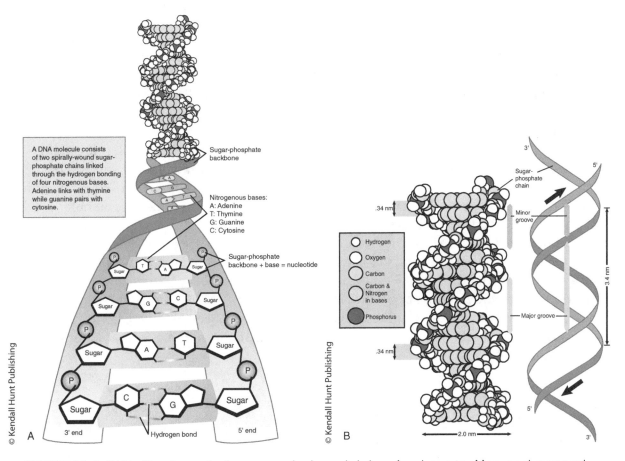

FIGURE 11.4 DNA structure. A. An expanded model showing base pairing and general structure. B. Models of the DNA molecule.

TABLE 11.1 Select data from Chargaff's studies

Organism	% Adenine	% Thymine	% Cytosine	% Guanine
Escherichia coli	26.0	23.9	24.9	25.2
Yeast	31.3	32.9	18.7	17.1
Sea Urchin	32.8	32.1	17.7	18.4
Rat	28.6	28.4	21.4	21.5
Human	30.3	30.3	19.5	19.9

Source: Data modified from Chargaff E. and Davidson J. eds. (1955). *The Nucleic Acids.* Academic Press.

the helix (like the sides of a twisted ladder). Spiral staircases are a form of a helix you might be familiar with. The strands of the DNA molecule are complementary (deduced by Watson and Crick from Chargaff's data). Adenine (A) pairs with thymine (T) and cytosine (C) pairs with guanine (G) are shown in Figure 11.4A. The base pairs are held together by hydrogen bonds (Figure 11.4A). Notice that a double-ringed purine is always bonded to a single-ring pyrimidine (Figure 11.4A). Purines are adenine and guanine. We have encountered adenosine triphosphate (ATP) before, although in that case the sugar was ribose, whereas in DNA it is deoxyribose. The pyrimidine bases are cytosine and thymine. According to the Watson and Crick model, the bases are complementary, with A on one side of the molecule you only get T on the other side, similarly with G and C. If we know the base sequence of one strand, then we know the base sequence on its complement (Figure 11.4A).

One of Watson and Crick's great insights was that DNA was a double helix molecule composed of two molecules oriented in opposite directions, a term known as antiparallel. This is shown in Figure 11.4A. The sugars are oriented in opposing directions. There can be no hydrogen bonding between the bases if one of the strands is not "upside down." In organic molecules we number the carbon atoms. Carbons in the bases are given normal numbers. To distinguish between carbon atoms in the bases and the sugars of the nucleotides, we designate carbon atoms in the sugar as 1' (pronounced as 1 prime), 2', and so on. As you look at the DNA in Figure 11.4A, the left-hand strand is the 3'–5' strand, while the right hand (as you see it) is the 5'–3' strand.

Watson, Crick, and Wilkins shared the Nobel Prize in 1962 for their work on DNA. Rosalind Franklin had died several years earlier, and the rules of the Nobel Committee do not allow for the award posthumously. Yet, it was her contribution, the famous Photo 51 that unlocked the secret structure of DNA.

11.3   DNA Replication: Copying the Code

The Hershey and Chase experiment proved DNA was the hereditary material. The model built by Watson and Crick deciphered DNAs structure. The logical next step was how DNA copied its information and how that was expressed in the phenotype. Watson and Crick suggested that one method for DNA replication would be for each strand to serve as a template for the making of the new strands, a method known as semiconservative replication. Two American biologists, Matthew Meselson (b. 1930) and Franklin W. Stahl (b. 1929), designed an experiment to that validated Watson and Crick's hypothesis of a semiconservative method of DNA replication.

Semiconservative replication (Figure 11.5) produces two DNA molecules, each of which had one strand of the parental DNA along with an entirely new complementary strand. In other words, the new DNA would consist of one new and one old strand of DNA. The existing strands would serve as complementary templates for the new strand.

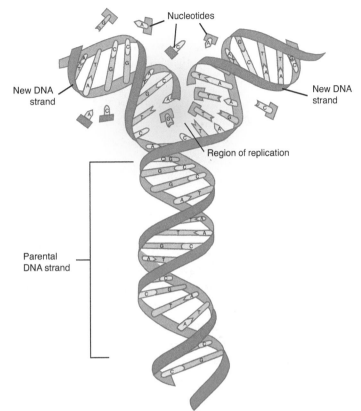

FIGURE 11.5 Replication of DNA.

DNA replication involves a great many building blocks, enzymes, and a great deal of ATP energy (remember that after the S phase of the cell cycle, cells have the G_2 phase to regenerate energy and synthesize material needed for cell division). Replication of DNA in humans occurs at a rate of 50 nucleotides/second. Prokaryote replication occurs at a rate of 500 nucleotides/second. Nucleotides have to be assembled and available, along with ATP energy to make bonds between nucleotides.

DNA polymerase and other enzymes unzip the helix (Figure 11.5) by breaking the hydrogen bonds between bases on each strand. Once the polymerases have opened the molecule, an area known as the replication bubble forms. Along the DNA molecule, many replication bubbles form simultaneously. New nucleotides move to the fork of the bubble and link to the corresponding parental nucleotide already there following the complementary base pairing rule of A with T, C with G. Each new strand forms as the complement of the parental/original strand. Prokaryotes open a single replication bubble, while eukaryotes have multiple bubbles. The entire length of the DNA molecule is replicated as the bubbles meet.

Since the DNA strands are antiparallel, and replication proceeds in the 5'–3' direction on *each* strand replication of the two strands is not the same. One of the strands will form a continuous copy, while the other will form a series of short fragments known as Okazaki fragments. These fragments are eventually connected together by a DNA-splicing enzyme.

11.4   Protein Synthesis

During the 1930s, despite great advances, geneticists had several frustrating questions yet to answer: What exactly are genes? How do they work? What produces the unique phenotype associated with a specific allele?

Answers from physics, chemistry, and the study of infectious disease gave rise to the field of molecular biology. Biochemical reactions are controlled by enzymes, and often are organized into chains of reactions known as metabolic pathways. Loss of activity of a single enzyme can inactivate an entire pathway.

British physician Archibald Garrod (1857–1936), in 1902, first proposed the relationship through his study of alkaptonuria and its association with large quantities "alkapton." He reasoned unaffected individuals metabolized "alkapton" (now called homogentistic acid) to other products so it would not buildup in their urine. Garrod suspected a blockage of the pathway to break this chemical down, and proposed that condition as "an inborn error of metabolism." He also discovered alkaptonuria was inherited as a recessive Mendelian trait.

The research team of American geneticists George Beadle (1903–1989) and Edward Tatum (1909–1975) during the late 1930s and early 1940s established the connection Garrod suspected between genes and metabolism. They used X-rays to cause mutations in strains of the mold *Neurospora crassa*. These mutations affected single genes and single enzymes in specific metabolic pathways. Beadle and Tatum proposed the "one gene one enzyme hypothesis" for which they won the Nobel Prize in 1958.

Since the chemical reactions occurring in the body are controlled by enzymes, and since enzymes are proteins and thus heritable traits, there must be a relationship between the gene and proteins. George Beadle, during the 1940s, proposed that mutant eye colors in *Drosophila* were caused by a change in one protein in a biosynthetic pathway.

In 1941, Beadle and coworker Edward Tatum decided to examine step by step the chemical reactions in a pathway. They used the red bread mold *Neurospora crassa* as an experimental organism. *Neurospora* had a short life cycle and was easily grown. Since it is haploid for much of its life cycle, mutations would be immediately expressed. The meiotic products could be easily inspected. Chromosome mapping studies on the organism facilitated their work. *Neurospora* can be grown on a minimal medium (one lacking all 20 of the amino acids needed to assemble proteins), and its nutrition could be studied by its ability to metabolize sugars and other chemicals the scientist could add or delete from the mixture of the medium. The mold could normally synthesize all of the amino acids and other chemicals needed for it to grow, thus mutants in synthetic pathways would easily show up. X-rays produced mutations in *Neurospora*, and the mutated spores were placed on growth media enriched with all essential amino acids. Crossing the mutated fungi with non-mutated forms produced spores that were then grown on media supplying only one of the 20 essential amino acids. If a spore lacked the ability to synthesize a particular amino acid, such as Pro (proline), it would only grow with Proline present in the growth medium. Biosynthesis of amino acids (the building blocks of proteins) is a complex process with many chemical reactions mediated by enzymes, which if mutated would shut down the pathway, resulting in no-growth. Beadle and Tatum proposed the **"one gene one enzyme"** hypothesis. According to their hypothesis, one gene codes for the production of one protein. "One gene one enzyme" has since been modified to "one gene one polypeptide" since many proteins (e.g., hemoglobin) consist of more than one polypeptide.

11.5   Ribonucleic Acid

Ribonucleic acid (RNA) was discovered some years after Miescher's discovery of DNA in 1869. The DNA that makes up the genes is confined to the eukaryotic nucleus. Proteins are synthesized at the ribosomes out in the cytoplasm. The RNA can occur in the both nucleus and cytoplasm.

Scientists suspected a link between DNA and proteins. Cells of developing embryos contain high levels of RNA. Rapidly growing *E. coli* has half its mass as ribosomes. Ribosomes are 2/3 RNA [a type of RNA known as ribosomal RNA (rRNA)] and 1/3 protein. When viruses infect cells, RNA is synthesized from viral DNA before protein synthesis begins. Some viruses, for example, tobacco mosaic virus (TMV) have RNA in place of DNA. If RNA extracted from a virus was injected into a host cell the cell began to make new viruses. Clearly RNA was involved in protein synthesis.

11.5.1   Crick's Central Dogma

Information flow (Figure 11.6), with the exception of reverse transcription, is from DNA to RNA via the process of transcription, and then to protein via translation. Transcription is the making of an RNA molecule off a DNA template. Translation is the construction of an amino acid sequence (polypeptide) from an RNA molecule. Although originally called dogma, this idea has been tested repeatedly with almost no exceptions to the rule being found (save retroviruses). Francis Crick proposed this idea in 1956.

11.5.2   Types of RNA

Several classes of RNA molecules exist in cells. Messenger RNA (mRNA) serves as the blueprint for construction of a protein. Ribosomal RNA (rRNA) is the major component of ribosome, the construction site where the protein is assembled. Transfer RNA tRNA) is the truck delivering the correct amino acid to the ribosome as called for the mRNA molecule. In 1982, a new class of RNA was discovered: ribozymes. Ribozymes are RNA molecules that have enzymatic properties.

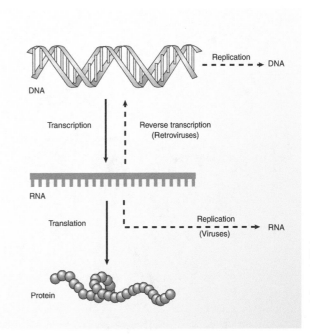

© Kendall Hunt Publishing

FIGURE 11.6 The central dogma of information flow from DNA to protein.

The RNA nucleotide has ribose sugar instead of the deoxyribose sugar occurring in DNA (Figure 11.7). Ribose has one more oxygen atom than does deoxyribose, although both have five carbon atoms. The base uracil (U) replaces the base thymine (T) in RNA molecules. When uracil bonds to either a complementary DNA or RNA nucleotide it bonds to adenine (A). Most RNA is single stranded (Figure 11.7), although tRNA will form a "cloverleaf" structure (Figure 11.8) due to complementary base pairing.

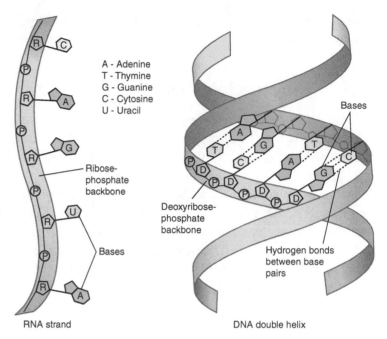

A - Adenine
T - Thymine
G - Guanine
C - Cytosine
U - Uracil

FIGURE 11.7 Comparison of DNA and RNA.

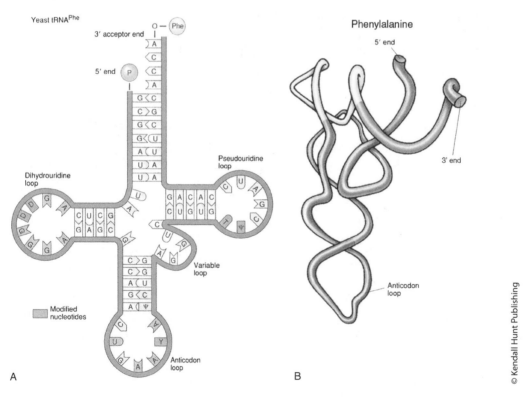

FIGURE 11.8 Structure of a tRNA molecule. A. Molecular diagram showing bases along the molecule. Note that complementary base pairing causes the molecule to assume the cloverleaf shape; B. Molecular model illustrating the three-dimensional shape of the molecule.

© Kendall Hunt Publishing

11.5.3   Transcription: Making an RNA Copy of a DNA Sequence

The DNA molecule in the eukaryotic nucleus may be though of as a noncirculating book in your campus library. It cannot leave the library that is the nucleus. During cell division, the nuclear envelope breaks down to allow the chromosomes to move about the cell. If you need information in a noncirculating library book you must go and make a copy of that part of the book you need. Our DNA operates very much this way as well. There are many genes used during embryonic development that are never used by that organism again. Other genes must be frequently copied as their products are almost always needed by the cell. The process of transcription is the way DNA information in the nucleus transfers to an RNA copy. The RNA molecule *can* pass through the nuclear pores out to the cytoplasm to the ribosome where protein synthesis occurs.

The enzyme RNA polymerase opens the part of the DNA to be transcribed (Figure 11.9). Only one strand of DNA (the template strand) gets transcribed. The RNA nucleotides link together similar to the DNA process.

11.5.4   Translation: Making an Amino Acid Sequence

After RNA has been transcribed from the template strand of the DNA gene, it moves to the ribosome for translation (Figure 11.10), the process of assembling amino acids in a specified sequence. Directions for this assembly come ultimately from the DNA base sequence, the gene.

Prokaryotic gene regulation differs from eukaryotic gene regulation, but since prokaryotes are much easier to work with, we focus on prokaryotes at this point. Promoters are sequences of DNA that

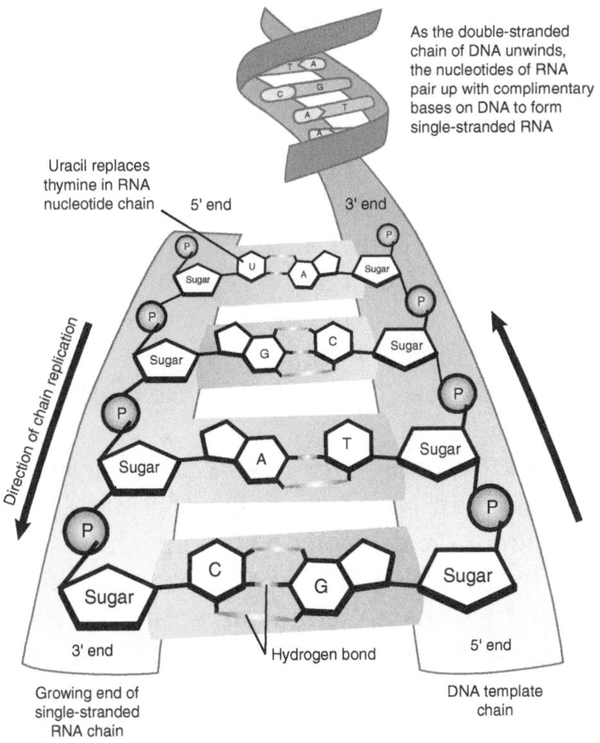

As the double-stranded chain of DNA unwinds, the nucleotides of RNA pair up with complimentary bases on DNA to form single-stranded RNA

Uracil replaces thymine in RNA nucleotide chain

5' end

3' end

Direction of chain replication

Sugar   U   A   Sugar

Sugar   G   C   Sugar

Sugar   A   T   Sugar

Sugar   C   G   Sugar

3' end

Hydrogen bond

5' end

Growing end of single-stranded RNA chain

DNA template chain

© Kendall Hunt Publishing

FIGURE 11.9 Transcription of an RNA sequence.

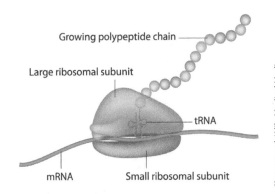

Growing polypeptide chain

Large ribosomal subunit

tRNA

mRNA

Small ribosomal subunit

Shutterstock/Alila Medical Media

FIGURE 11.10 Overview of protein synthesis and the role of the ribosome and mRNA.

are the start signals for the transcription of an mRNA molecule. Terminators are the signals that stop transcription. Most mRNA molecules are long (500–10,000 nucleotides).

Ribosomes are the structure in all cells where proteins synthesis occurs. In the intestinal bacterium *E. coli* ribosomes consist of small (30S) and large (50S) subunits. The 30S unit has 16S rRNA and 21 different proteins. The 50S subunit consists of 5S and 23S rRNA and 34 different proteins. The smaller subunit has a binding site for the mRNA. The larger subunit has two binding sites for tRNA. The structure of the eukaryotic ribosome (Figure 11.11) is larger (80S total, with a smaller 40S and larger 60S subunits) than the prokaryotic 70S ribosome.

FIGURE 11.11 Subunits of a ribosome.

The tRNA is basically a cloverleaf-shaped molecule. Each tRNA carries the proper amino acid to the ribosome when the codons on the mRNA call for them. At the top of the large loop of the tRNA are three bases, the anticodon, which is the complement of the codon on the mRNA. There are 61 different tRNA molecules, each having a different binding site for the amino acid and a different anticodon. For the codon UUU, the complementary anticodon is AAA. The tRNA having the AAA anticodon only binds to the amino acid phenylalanine. Enzymes control the linkage of the correct amino acid to the correct tRNA.

Translation is the process of converting the mRNA codon sequence into an amino acid sequence. The initiator codon AUG codes for the tRNA carries the amino acid N-formylmethionine (f-Met, methionine). No transcription occurs without the AUG codon. The amino acid f-Met always occurs first in a polypeptide chain, although it is often removed after translation. The initiator tRNA/mRNA/small ribosomal unit is called the initiation complex. The larger subunit attaches to the initiation complex. After the initiation phase (Figure 11.12), the polypeptide grows longer during the elongation phase.

The tRNA molecule specified by the next three-base codon on the mRNA molecule brings its amino acid to the open binding site on the ribosome/mRNA complex. Energy from ATP in the cell is used to form a peptide bond between the amino acids. The complex then shifts along the mRNA to the next triplet, opening the A site. A new tRNA carrying the codon-specified amino acid, enters at the A site. When the codon in the A site is a termination codon, a releasing factor binds to the site, stopping translation, and releasing the ribosomal complex and mRNA.

Often in prokaryotes, many ribosomes will sequentially read the same message, a structure known as a polysome forms. In this way, a cell may rapidly (almost simultaneously) make multiple copies proteins. Each mammalian cell contain an estimated 10,000,000 ribosomes.

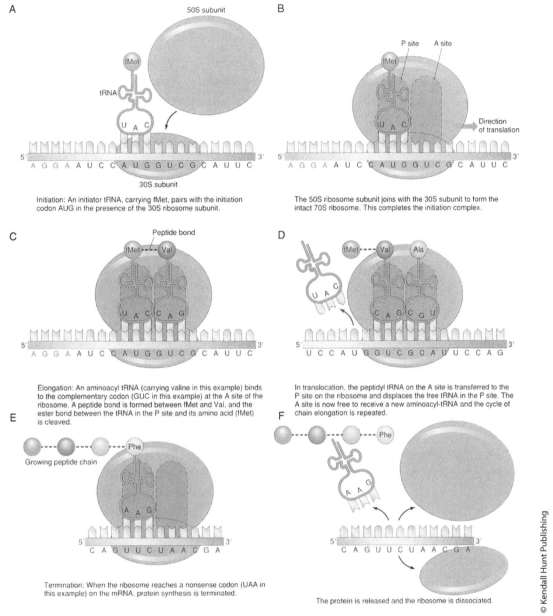

A

50S subunit

fMet

tRNA

U A C

30S subunit

5' A G G A A U C C A U G G U C G C A U U C 3'

Initiation: An initiator tRNA, carrying fMet, pairs with the initiation codon AUG in the presence of the 30S ribosome subunit.

B

P site   A site

fMet

U A C

Direction of translation

5' A G G A A U C C A U G G U C G C A U U C 3'

The 50S ribosome subunit joins with the 30S subunit to form the intact 70S ribosome. This completes the initiation complex.

C

Peptide bond

fMet ---- Val

U A C C A G

5' A G G A A U C C A U G G U C G C A U U C 3'

Elongation: An aminoacyl tRNA (carrying valine in this example) binds to the complementary codon (GUC in this example) at the A site of the ribosome. A peptide bond is formed between fMet and Val, and the ester bond between the tRNA in the P site and its amino acid (fMet) is cleaved.

D

fMet ---- Val   Ala

U A G   C A G C G U

5' U C C A U G G U C G C A U U C C A G 3'

In translocation, the peptidyl tRNA on the A site is transferred to the P site on the ribosome and displaces the free tRNA in the P site. The A site is now free to receive a new aminoacyl-tRNA and the cycle of chain elongation is repeated.

E

Phe

Growing peptide chain

A A G

5' C A G U U C U A A C G A 3'

Termination: When the ribosome reaches a nonsense codon (UAA in this example) on the mRNA, protein synthesis is terminated.

F

Phe

A A G

5' C A G U U C U A A C G A 3'

The protein is released and the ribosome is dissociated.

© Kendall Hunt Publishing

FIGURE 11.12 Steps in translation.

11.6   The Genetic Code

We now know that DNA stores information in the sequence of its bases. Changes in those base sequences are mutations that sometimes result in changed proteins *and* the results of those protein action or inaction. So what is this code of life that all living things use to construct their proteins?

The **genetic code** consists of at least three bases, according to Russian-born astronomer George Gamow (1904–1966). To code for the 20 amino acids, all proteins are made from a genetic code must consist of at least a 3-base set (triplet) of the 4 bases. If we consider the possibilities of arranging 4 things 3 at a time (4 × 4 × 4), we get 64 possible code words, or codons, a 3-base sequence on the mRNA that codes for either a specific amino acid or a control word.

The genetic code was broken by American biochemist Marshall Nirenberg (1927–2010) and German biochemist Heinrich Matthaei (b. 1929), a decade after Watson and Crick's work. Nirenberg discovered that RNA, regardless of its source organism, could initiate protein synthesis when combined with contents of broken *E. coli* cells. By adding a molecule of RNA consisting solely of Uracil, poly-U, to each of 20 test tubes (each tube having a different "tagged" amino acid) Nirenberg and Matthaei were able to determine that the codon UUU (the only one in poly-U) coded for the amino acid phenylalanine.

Likewise, an artificial mRNA consisting of alternating A and C bases would code for alternating amino acids histidine and threonine. Gradually, a complete listing of the genetic code codons was developed.

The genetic code (Figure 11.13) consists of 61 amino acid coding codons and three termination codons, which stop the process of translation. The genetic code is thus redundant (degenerate in the sense of having multiple states amounting to the same thing), with, for example, glycine coded for by GGU, GGC, GGA, and GGG codons. If a codon is mutated, say from GGU to CGU, is the same amino acid specified? Looking at Figure 11.13, we break down the codon sequence of the first codon (GGU) by tracing the first letter G across the bottom of the figure. The possible amino acids coded for with a codon having the first letter G are: valine, alanine, aspartate, glutamate, and glycine. The second letter (G) defines the amino acid in this case to be glycine. If we consider the second codon (CGU), the amino acids coded for by the first letter (C) are: leucine, proline, histidine, glutamine, and arginine. In the second letter (G), we see this codon is one of four that codes for the amino acid arginine. Thus, changing the first letter of our GGU codon will definitely alter the amino acid coded for (in this case at least).

There are four control codons in the genetic code (Figure 11.13). All polypeptides initially begin with the amino acid methionine, coded for by the codon AUG. There are three stop codons: UAA, UAG, and UGA. These do not code for an amino acid, but terminate the amino acid synthesis.

11.7   Mutations: Changes in the DNA Sequence

We earlier defined mutations as any change in the DNA. We now can refine that definition: a mutation is a change in the DNA base sequence that results in a change of amino acid(s) in the polypeptide coded for by that gene. Alleles result from alternate sequences of DNA bases. At the molecular level, the products of alleles differ often by only a single amino acid, which can have a ripple effect on an organism by changing the function of enzymes. Addition, deletion, or substitution of nucleotides may alter the amino acid sequence of the polypeptide coded for by that DNA sequence. Point mutations are the result of the substitution of a single base. Frame-shift mutations occur when the reading frame of the gene is shifted by addition or deletion of one or more bases. With the exception of mitochondria, all organisms use the same genetic code; powerful evidence for the common ancestry of all living things.

11.8   Control of Gene Expression

While the period from 1900 to the Second World War has been called the "golden age of genetics," we may now be in a new golden (or platinum) age. The first golden age featured the rediscovery

Second Base

First Base	U	C	A	G	Third Base
U	UUU phenylalanine	UCU serine	UAU tyrosine	UGU cysteine	U
	UUC phenylalanine	UCC serine	UAC tyrosine	UGC cysteine	C
	UUA leucine	UCA serine	UAA stop	UGA stop	A
	UUG leucine	UCG serine	UAG stop	UGG tryptophan	G
C	CUU leucine	CCU proline	CAU histidine	CGU arginine	U
	CUC leucine	CCC proline	CAC histidine	CGC arginine	C
	CUA leucine	CCA proline	CAA glutamine	CGA arginine	A
	CUG leucine	CCG proline	CAG glutamine	CGG arginine	G
A	AUU isoleucine	ACU threonine	AAU asparagine	AGU serine	U
	AUC isoleucine	ACC threonine	AAC asparagine	AGC serine	C
	AUA isoleucine	ACA threonine	AAA lysine	AGA arginine	A
	AUG(start) methionine	ACG threonine	AAG lysine	AGG arginine	G
G	GUU valine	GCU alanine	GAU aspartate	GGU glycine	U
	GUC valine	GCC alanine	GAC aspartate	GGC glycine	C
	GUA valine	GCA alanine	GAA glutamate	GGA glycine	A
	GUG valine	GCG alanine	GAG glutamate	GGG glycine	G

FIGURE 11.13 The genetic code.

of Gregor Mendel's work, studies on the nature of DNA and protein, as well as expansion (and establishment of) genetics as a separate discipline in the biological hierarchy. Work in the field of genetics exploded after the war, with the key discoveries of Avery and the Hershey–Chase experiment showing DNA as the hereditary material, Watson and Crick's deciphering the structure of DNA, and the breaking of the genetic code. Recombinant DNA technology and other techniques now allow us to manipulate the DNA genes, the very essence as it were, of living organisms and to make conscious changes in that DNA.

Prokaryotes, with only one exception, possess only a single chromosome. Eukaryotes have a larger number of chromosomes, from four to several hundred. Since prokaryotic organisms are simpler and easier to work with, scientists were able to determine much about how bacterial genes are organized and how they work. We understand prokaryote genetic systems better than eukaryote systems. We have the genetic code and we have the gene sequences, what's next?

11.8.1   Prokaryotic Gene Control

The only chromosome of the common intestinal bacterium *E. coli* is circular and contains some 4.6 million DNA base pairs and over 4000 genes coding for proteins. If we stretched this chromosome out, it would reach nearly one millimeter (mm) long, but only 2 nanometers (nm) wide. Often small loops of extra-chromosomal DNA occur in the bacterial cytoplasm. These are plasmids.

A segment of the DNA that codes for a specific polypeptide is known as a structural gene. Structural genes often occur together on a bacterial chromosome. The location of the polypeptides, which may be enzymes involved in a biochemical pathway, for example, allows for quick, efficient transcription of the mRNAs from the DNA code of the structural genes and their translation into proteins. The bacterium *E. coli* can synthesize 1700 enzymes. Therefore, this small bacterium, less than 1 μm long, has the genes to make 1700 different mRNAs. However, it does not need all of these enzymes at once, and so must have some mechanism (or mechanisms) for controlling the expression of those genes.

French biologists François Jacob (1920–2013) and Jacques Monod (1910–1976) proposed the operon model (Figure 11.14) of prokaryotic gene regulation in 1961. Their work later resulted in a Nobel Prize. Jacob and Monod studied the series of genes involved in the breakdown of lactose, which they termed the *lac* operon. Their model proposes that groups of genes coding for related proteins are arranged in units known as operons. An operon consists of an operator, promoter, regulator, and one or more structural genes. The regulator gene produces a repressor protein (Figure 11.14) that binds to the operator, obstructing the promoter, and blocking transcription of the structural genes. The regulator does not have to be adjacent to other genes in the operon. If the repressor protein is removed, transcription may occur (Figure 11.14).

Operons can be either inducible or repressible, according to the control mechanism. More than 75 different operons controlling at least 250 structural genes have been identified for *E. coli*. Both repression and induction are examples of negative control since the repressor proteins turn off transcription.

Normally, *E. coli* uses glucose as its primary energy source. However, in the absence of glucose, one of the energy sources that *E.coli* can utilize is lactose, the disaccharide that occurs in milk. Lactose is split by the enzyme β-galactosidase (beta-galactosidase), producing glucose and galactose monosaccharide sugars. The enzyme β-galactosidase is inducible, since it occurs in

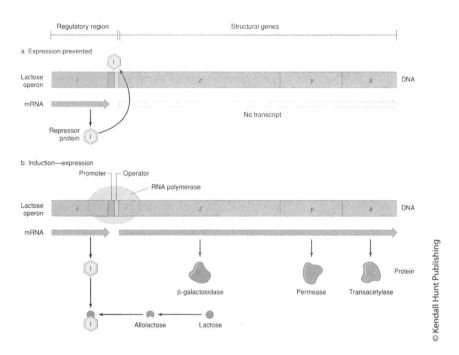

FIGURE 11.14 The operon model for prokaryotic gene control. A. The structure of an operon. B. The action of an operon.

large quantities *only* when lactose, the substrate on which it operates, is present. This induction occurs when lactose binds to the repressor, inactivating it, and allowing transcription to proceed.

Enzymes for synthesizing the amino acid tryptophan are produced continuously in growing cells unless tryptophan is present. When tryptophan is present, the production of tryptophan-synthesizing enzymes is repressed (Figure 11.15). When the amount of tryptophan in the cell decreases the repression ends and transcription and translation of the genes in the *trp* operon begins again.

11.8.2   Eukaryotic Gene Control

The eukaryotic chromosome consists of DNA and proteins that appear to play a major role in regulation of eukaryote genes. The DNA of each eukaryotic chromosome is a long, single molecule of double-stranded DNA. Eukaryotic DNA comes in two forms. Chromatin is the uncoiled form of DNA and is over 50% protein. Chromosomes are coiled DNA/protein that form during the early stages of cell division.

The proteins associated with DNA are collectively known as histones. They are relatively short polypeptides that are positively charged (basic) and thus attracted to the negatively charged (acidic) DNA. The cell synthesizes histones in quantity during the S-phase of interphase. One function of these proteins seems to be the folding and packaging of DNA into chromosome form (Figure 11.16A). The 2 m length of DNA in a human cell is packaged into 46 chromosomes with a combined length of 200 nm (a nanometer, nm, you might recall is 1/1,000,000 m). Some 90 million histone molecules occur in a single cell with the majority (30 million) being H1 histones. Five types of histone are known—H1, H2A, H2B, H3, and H4. With the exception of H1, most eukaryote histones are similar.

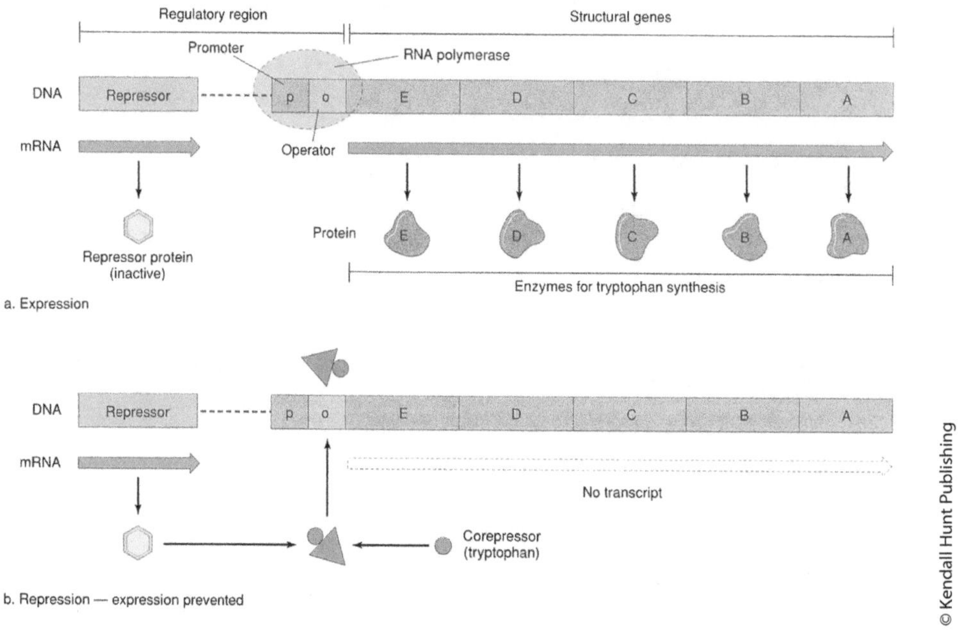

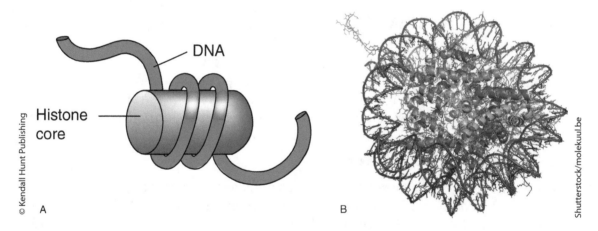

FIGURE 11.15 The *trp* operon and its interaction of the amino acid tryptophan in controlling transcription.

FIGURE 11.16 Eukaryotic genes, A. Histone proteins and eukaryotic DNA; B. The nucleosome consists of a DNA double helix wrapped around a core of histone proteins. DNA is colored gray, histone H3 red, histone H4 green, H2a blue, and H2b orange.

A **nucleosome** (Figure 11.16B) is the fundamental packing unit of eukaryotic DNA. The nucleosome core consists of two molecules each of H2A, H2B, H3, and H4, around which the DNA is wound twice. The H1 histone is outside the core. Between 150 and 200 nucleotide pairs are associated with the core and linker DNA. This level of packing is known as "beads on a string."

The next level of chromosome organization is known as the 30-nm strand, whose details of organization are not yet well known. The 30-nm strands are further condensed into 300-nm-wide looped domains. Looped domains are part of condensed sections of chromosomes (the replicated chromosome being 1400-nm wide at Metaphase I).

The unique processes that make up multicellular development complicate eukaryotic gene regulation in multicellular organisms. Each multicellular organism begins as a single-celled zygote that divides by mitosis. Cells differentiate into the different mature functional types by using some of their genes but ignoring others. For example, a muscle cell has the same DNA as a nerve cell; the muscle cell just turns on different genes to become a muscle cell than the nerve cell does. Homeotic genes establish the body plan and position of organs in response to gradients of regulatory molecules. The timing of certain gene expressions seems to follow a sequence, such as the production of different types of fetal hemoglobin molecules by mammalian red blood cells, which switch to adult hemoglobin sometime after birth. Clearly, the inactivation of certain genes occurs in every adult cell; therein lies the cure for cancer, old age, and so on.

The term genome refers to all of the alleles possessed by an organism (or by a population, species, or larger taxonomic group). While the amount of DNA for a diploid cell is more or less constant within a species, the differences can be great between species. Humans have 3.5×10^9 base pairs, the tiny fruit fly has 1.5×10^8, toads have 3.32×10^9, and salamanders have 8×10^{10} base pairs of DNA per haploid genome. Much of the DNA in each cell has either no function or has a function not yet known. While most eukaryotes have only 10% of their DNA coding for proteins, we humans may have a little as 1% of our DNA coding for proteins. Viruses and prokaryotes use a great deal more of their DNA.

Almost half the DNA in eukaryotic cells is repeated nucleotide sequences that code for no proteins. Noncoding regions of the eukaryotic chromosome break up protein-coding regions. These noncoding interruptions are known as intervening sequences or introns (Figure 11.17). Coding sequences that are expressed are exons. The cutting and splicing is accomplished by ribozymes. It is therefore possible for a gene to produce more than one mRNA sequence posttranscription.

Most, but not all, eukaryote genes are structural and contain introns. Although transcribed, these introns are excised or cut out before translation occurs. The number of introns varies with the particular gene, even occurring in tRNAs, rRNAs, and viral genes! Generally, the more complex and recently evolved the organism, the

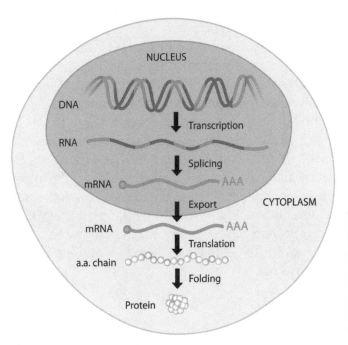

FIGURE 11.17 Organization of a eukaryotic gene shows introns and exons that must be processed to make a complete mRNA copy. Introns are shown in green and exons are shown in red on the mRNA in the nucleus.

more numerous and larger the introns. Which came first: continuous genes lacking introns or interrupted genes containing introns? Introns have been hypothesized to promote genetic recombination (by the process of crossing-over), thus speeding up the evolution of new proteins. Exons are also thought to code for different functional regions of proteins.

Gene families are made up of similar, but not identical, genes. The globin family is the most studied gene family. Hemoglobin consists, in humans, of 2 alpha-chains and 2 beta-chains clustered about a common center. Human beta-globin genes are scattered at five loci on human chromosome 11. These genes are expressed sequentially during development, and resemble each other, with same-length introns in similar positions in each gene. Some of the genes represent inactivated copies, while others function only during certain phases of development. The actin family of genes also exhibits a similar pattern.

The process of transcription in eukaryotes is similar to what occurs in prokaryotes, although there are some differences. Eukaryote genes are not grouped in operons as are prokaryote genes. Each eukaryote gene is transcribed separately, with separate transcriptional controls on each gene. Where prokaryotes have only one type of RNA polymerase to transcribe for all of their different types of RNA (mRNA, tRNA, and rRNA), eukaryotes have a different RNA polymerase producing each type of RNA. One version of the RNA polymerase enzyme works only on mRNA-coding genes that will code for structural proteins. Another form of the RNA polymerase enzyme works only on for genes that code for the larger rRNAs that comprise the ribosome. Yet, a third variant of RNA polymerase transcribes the smaller rRNAs and tRNAs. Obviously, some control over transcription of these genes might occur by control of the enzymes.

Prokaryote translation begins even before transcription has finished. Eukaryotes have the two processes separated in time and location (remember the nuclear envelope in eukaryotes separates the nucleus, where transcription occurs, from the cytoplasm, where translation happens). After eukaryotes transcribe a molecule of RNA, the RNA transcript is extensively modified before export to the cytoplasm where it will be translated into a protein (Figure 11.17). A string of adenine bases (as many as 200 nucleotides long, known as a poly-A tail) is added to the 3′ end of the mRNA after it has been transcribed. The function of a poly-A tail is not known, but it can be used to capture mRNAs for study. Introns are cut out of the message and the exons are spliced together before the mRNA leaves the nucleus. There are several examples of identical messages being processed by different methods, often turning introns into exons and vice versa. Protein molecules are attached to mRNAs that are exported, forming ribonucleoprotein particles (mRNPs) that may help in transport through the nuclear pores and also in attaching to ribosomes.

Summary

DNA is the physical carrier if inheritance. Replication of the DNA molecule occurs by a semiconservative method where each parental strand of the molecule acts as a template for the newly synthesized strand. One of the DNA strands serves as the sense or template strand for the transcription of RNA molecules. These RNA molecules move to the cytoplasm in a eukaryotic cell where translation occurs to produce a polypeptide chain of amino acids. The genetic code is the sequence of three base units known as codons. Changes in the codons are mutations.

Terms

actin	guanine	pyrimidines
adenine	haploid	regulator gene
adenosine triphosphate (ATP)	hemoglobin	retroviruses
	histones	ribonucleic acid (RNA)
alleles	homeotic genes	ribosomal RNA
amino acid sequence	hydrogen bonds	ribozymes
anticodon	hypothesis	reverse transcriptase
bacteriophages	initiation	ribose
capsid	initiator codon	RNA polymerase
capsule	introns	RNA transcript
cell cycle	lysogenic cycle	S phase
chromatin	lytic cycle	semiconservative replication
chromosomes	messenger RNA (mRNA)	structural gene
codons	metabolic pathways	template strand
complementary bases	mitosis	transcription
crossing-over	nuclear pores	transfer RNA (tRNA)
cytosine	nucleic acid	transformation
deoxyribonucleic acid (DNA)	nucleotide	translation
deoxyribose sugar	nucleotide sequences	thymine
DNA polymerases	nucleosome	transduction
elongation	nucleus	transforming factor
enzymes	one gene one polypeptide	uracil
exon	operator	viruses
gene	operon	X-ray diffraction
genetic code	promoter	zygote
genome	purines	

Review Questions

1. The period of time referred to as the "Golden Age of genetics" was ___.
   a. the 1860s;
   b. the early 1900s;
   c. the 1950s;
   d. the 1990s

2. The tetranucleotide hypothesis was developed by ___.
   a. Franklin;
   b. Watson and Crick;
   c. Levene;
   d. Chargaff

3. Griffith's experiment involved bacteria that cause ___.
   a. pneumonia;
   b. syphilis;
   c. cooties;
   d. AIDS

4. A nucleotide consists of all of the following except ___.
   a. sugar;
   b. nitrogenous base;
   c. lipid;
   d. phosphate group

5. Chargaff discovered that ____
   a. the tetranucleotide hypothesis was correct;
   b. for any organism, the amount of A was equal to the amount of T and the amount of C was equal to the amount of G;
   c. DNA was a double helix;
   d. for any organism, the amount of T was equal to the amount of C and the amount of G was equal to the amount of A

6. Assume that the two parent strands of DNA have been separated and that the base sequence on one parent strand is A–T–T–C–G–C; the DNA base sequence that will complement that parent strand is ____.
   a. G–C–C–A–T–C;   c. T–A–A–C–G–C;
   b. G–A–T–T–A–C;   d. T–A–A–G–C–G

7. The purines are ____.
   a. adenine and guanine;   c. cytosine and thymine;
   b. cytosine and guanine;   d. ribose and deoxyribose

8. The pyrimidines are ____.
   a. adenine and guanine;   c. cytosine and thymine;
   b. cytosine and guanine;   d. ribose and deoxyribose

9. The sugar found in DNA is ____.
   a. ribose;   c. deoxyribose;
   b. dextrose;   d. galactose

10. Bacteriophage viruses have which of the following macromolecules?
    a. DNA and lipid;   c. DNA and sugars;
    b. DNA and RNA;   d. DNA and protein

11. DNA lacks which of these atoms?
    a. carbon;   c. phosphorous;
    b. sulfur;   d. nitrogen

12. Proteins are composed of some combination of ____.
    a. nucleotides;   c. amino acids;
    b. sugars;   d. triglycerides

13. The Hershey–Chase experiment disproved which of these molecule groups as the physical carrier of inheritance?
    a. protein;   c. lipids;
    b. nucleic acids;   d. polysaccharides

14. DNA is described best as ____.
    a. a triple helix;
    b. a double helix;
    c. a single helix

15. Which of these following scientists did not win a Nobel Prize for their work on the structure of the DNA molecule?
   a. Franklin;
   b. Watson;
   c. Crick;
   d. Wilkins

16. The tool used to show the structure of DNA was ___.
   a. mass spectroscopy;
   b. gravity centrifugation;
   c. X-ray diffraction;
   d. electron microscopy

17. The two strands of the DNA molecule are said to be ___.
   a. complementary;
   b. polite;
   c. antiparallel;
   d. a and c;
   e. a and b

18. In the Watson and Crick model of DNA structure, the sides of a ladder are analogous to ___.
   a. the DNA bases;
   b. the phosphates and bases;
   c. the phosphates and sugars;
   d. all of these

19. DNA replicates by a ___ mechanism.
   a. semiconservative;
   b. dispersive;
   c. conservative;
   d. liberal

20. The DNA polymerase enzyme ___.
   a. unwinds the helix;
   b. adds new nucleotides to the growing strands;
   c. facilitates the making of RNA off of the DNA;
   d. none of these

21. The strand of DNA that replicates by making small fragments and joining them together is the ___ strand.
   a. template;
   b. lagging;
   c. continuous;
   d. nonsense

22. The chromosome of bacteria is ___ shaped.
   a. linear;
   b. circular;
   c. triangular;
   d. octahedral

23. ___ gene systems are arranged into operons.
   a. prokaryotic;
   b. viral;
   c. eukaryotic;
   d. human

24. Exons and introns are characteristic of ___ gene systems.
   a. prokaryotic;
   b. viral;
   c. eukaryotic;
   d. retroviral

25. Lactose, milk sugar, is composed of which of these pairs of monosaccharides?
   a. glucose and fructose;   c. galactose and glucose;
   b. galactose and fructose;   d. fructose and ribose

26. The enzyme that breaks down lactose is ___.
   a. β-galactosidase;   c. isomerase;
   b. tryptophan;   d. RNA polymerase

27. When a virus infects a cell and knits its DNA into the host DNA, the virus is said to have taken the ___ route.
   a. lytic;   c. lysogenic;
   b. lysine;   d. obligate intracellular parasitic

28. The enzyme ___ allows retroviruses to copy their RNA genes into DNA genes.
   a. reverse transcriptase;   c. DNA polymerase;
   b. RNA polymerase;   d. diastase

29. Genes can naturally move around on chromosomes via ___.
   a. plasmids;
   b. transposons;
   c. F plasmids;
   d. none of these, genes are always in the same place

30. Which of these levels of eukaryotic chromosome structure is the smallest?
   a. looped domains;   c. replicated chromosome;
   b. nucleosome;   d. single chromatid

31. Master genes in the eukaryotic chromosomes that are responsible for the assembly of the major body regions in a multicellular organism are known as ___ genes.
   a. homozygous;   c. recessive;
   b. homeotic;   d. hemizygous

Links

- **A Structure for Deoxyribose Nucleic Acid:** Text of the original paper that Watson and Crick published in the journal **Nature** in 1953. (http://www.nature.com/nature/dna50/watsoncrick.pdf)

- **Genetics in Context a Comparative Timeline:** This timeline links out to selected sites and other presentations detailing the timeline for the genetic field's development. (http://www.esp.org/timeline/)

- **Amino Acids:** Linear formulas and links to images of the 20 amino acids common to all life (at least as we know it).

- **The RNA World (IMB Jena, Germany):** Links to WWW RNA sites and resources. Lots of very cool images. (http://www.rna.uni-jena.de/rna.php)

CHAPTER 12

Biotechnology and the Genetics Revolution

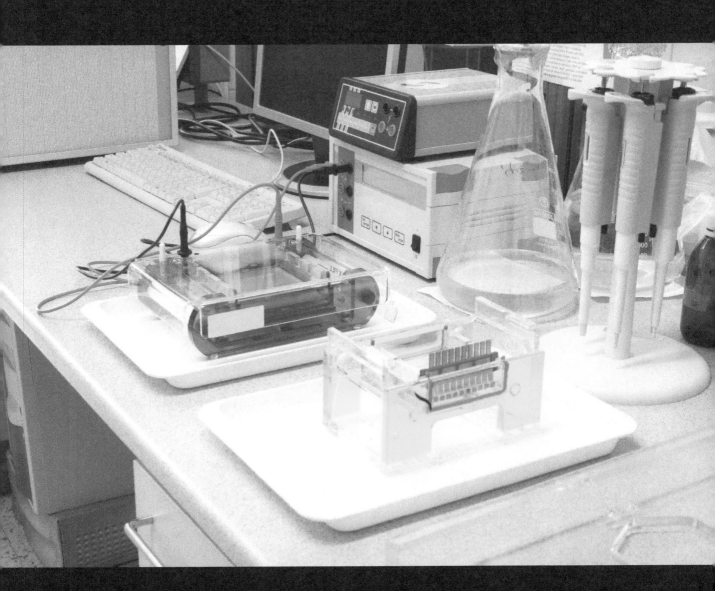

Chapter Opener

Gel electrophoresis is a technique often employed in what we call "biotech". We live now in a brave new world of genetically modified organisms, cloning, and change. Learn about some techniques affecting this change in this chapter.

Objectives

- Describe the steps involved in forming a recombinant deoxyribonucleic acid (DNA) molecule.
- Discuss how polymerase chain reaction (PCR) process is employed in biotech.
- Discuss the pros and cons of the production and uses of transgenic organisms.
- Compare and contrast the techniques and pros and cons of gene therapy.
- Discuss the significance and potential applications of the Human Genome Project.

Introduction

The 1960s movie The Graduate has a famous scene in which a young college graduate is counseled by a friend of his family about his future in the business world with the phrase "plastics, Benjamin, plastics." Were that movie to be remade today the phrase might very well be "plasmids, Maria, plasmids." This reflects the rise of a new field of biotechnology and genetic engineering. During the fall of 2000 a private biotechnology company, Celera Genomics, along with a federal agency, announced the completion of the Human Genome Project. The scientific consensus is that we are on the verge of an explosion of knowledge as well as products that can be used to cure diseases as well as provide better answers to who we are and why we work the way we do. Oh yes, some products that can be sold for profit may come from this. This chapter will look at the biotechnology frontier and examine the biology behind the biotech.

12.1   Biotechnology in Human History

Humans have been manipulating domesticated plants and animals for thousands of years. Favored individuals (with desirable traits) have been bred, producing a next generation with a preponderance of the desired traits. Over countless generations of selective breeding we developed stocks or strains of domesticated organisms with the desired characteristics. Most domesticated animals and agricultural plants have been developed through such selective breeding. All dogs (Figure 12.1) belong to the same species, *Canis familiaris*. Generations of selective breeding changed the appearance and abilities of these animals. Many selectively bred organisms developed over thousands of years; others within the past century or two. Even bacteria and fungi may be selectively bred. Wine making utilizes specific strains of fungus to produce the desired qualities of the wine.

FIGURE 12.1 Breeds of dogs.

12.2   Recombinant DNA Technology

The newest techniques for modifying the genetic makeup of a species, collectively termed bio-technology, began developing during the mid-1970s. This technology produced revolutionary change. Instead of taking countless generations of selective breeding and culling, we can now make dramatic changes literally overnight. Indeed, we no longer have to breed for the desired characteristic as long as we can isolate the responsible gene in some organism and get bacteria to incorporate the gene for that characteristic/product into their own genome.

We stand at the beginning of the biotechnology revolution, with recombinant techniques

FIGURE 12.2 A sign that says "Say No To GMOs Poison" held by a protestor during the global March Against Monsanto as they pass in front of Whole Foods grocery store on May 25, 2013 in Manhattan.

being applied to studying basic biological processes such as gene regulation. Many hope this leads to development and production of commercial products, such as disease-resistant plants, improved medicines, foods, and improved ability to diagnose and treat genetic disorders. But, this revolution is not smooth. In some instances, there has been tremendous pushback (Figure 12.2) against genetically modified organisms (GMOs).

A small group of techniques in recombinant DNA technology are used to accomplish a desired end. The biotechnology revolution began with the discovery of restriction enzymes produced by a number of different species of bacteria. These enzymes produce DNA fragments cut at specific base sequences. The next step linked these DNA fragments to vectors to create recombinant DNA molecules. A vector is a segment of DNA that can carry the desired gene or gene fragment into a host, such as a bacterium. Cutting the vector and fragment with the same enzyme produces "sticky ends" that allow the vector and fragment to join. The third step involved replication of the recombinant DNA in a host to clone the inserted segment. Retrieval of the cloned DNA for study and production of the gene product coded for by the cloned DNA made up the forth step. Sounds simple, right? As you must guess by now there are many steps and bits of evidence to consider.

Restriction enzymes attach to DNA molecules at specific sites and cut both strands of DNA at that place. A restriction enzyme is a bacterial enzyme that stops viral reproduction by cutting the viral DNA at a certain set of sequences that are not found in the bacterial chromosome. *Escherichia coli* produces a restriction enzyme known as *Eco*RI that makes palindromic sequences that read the same on either strand, as shown in Figure 12.3. Restriction enzymes are named with the first three letters of the organism name (*E. coli* becomes *Eco*), the letter R indicates that this is a restriction enzyme, and a Roman numeral (in this example I) indicates this is the first restriction enzyme found in that organism. Thus, *Eco*RI was the first restriction enzyme found in *E. coli*. Restriction enzymes have been recovered for many other bacteria.

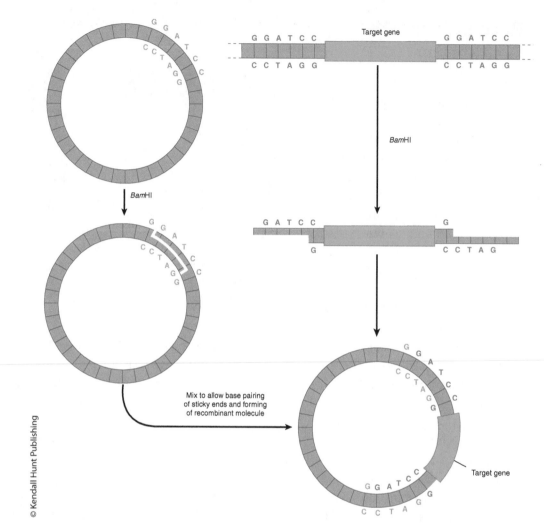

FIGURE 12.3 Restriction enzymes can cut DNA in such as way as to produce "sticky ends."

Restriction enzymes like *Eco*RI create DNA molecules with single-stranded tails that can form hydrogen bonds with other similarly cut DNA sequences (Figure 12.3). These sticky ended sequences are glued together by the enzyme DNA ligase, forming recombinant DNA molecules. DNA ligase links together Okazaki fragments these segments of DNA. The enzyme is naturally occurring and links together the fragments formed by the lagging strand during DNA replication. During production of recombinant DNA, the DNA ligase joins foreign DNA to vector DNA.

Vectors are DNA molecules that can be joined with DNA fragments that are to be cloned. Plasmids (Figure 12.4) are self-replicating DNA fragments found in bacterial cells (but not in the single circular bacterial chromosome). Plasmids are an important source of vectors. Many different restriction enzymes will cut different regions on a plasmid. These cut regions can be used for insertion of the DNA segments to be cloned.

Application of the enzyme DNA ligase to the DNA fragments and to vectors cut with the same restriction enzyme will form a recombinant DNA molecule as shown in Figure 12.3. The

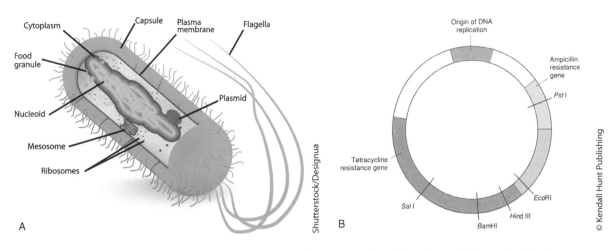

FIGURE 12.4 Plasmid. A. Diagram of a bacterium showing the plasmid located in the cytoplasm. B. The pBR322 plasmid.

recombinant DNA is composed of human DNA (if that was the source) plus plasmid DNA, (Figure 12.3). Recombinant DNA consists of DNA from more than one source that has never before existed in this new combination. The recombinant DNA inserts into a bacterial cell. Every time the bacterium divides the recombinant DNA is copied (or cloned). Cloning, as used in this context, is the production of many identical copies of a desired gene. The entire process is summarized in Figure 12.5 and Table 12.1.

One problem that scientists discovered was that not all the bacteria would pick up the plasmids. The use of a plasmid with an antibiotic resistance gene (most commonly the gene providing resistance to the antibiotic ampicillin) allows visual verification that the plasmid has been acquired. The original bacteria lack the ampicillin resistance gene. If they are transferred to a Petri dish containing ampicillin, the unmodified bacteria will be killed by the ampicillin. Only those bacteria that have acquired the plasmid with the ampicillin resistance gene can survive and grow.

Bacterial cells will acquire recombined plasmids when the cells are treated with calcium chloride ($CaCl_2$). The calcium chloride makes the cells more permeable to the recombined plasmids. Usually, an antibiotic resistance gene is in the plasmid so we can easily see if the inserted gene is replicated and expressed. When this happens scientists can recover the cloned gene or protein product.

Not all vectors are plasmids. Viruses can act as a vector to bring recombinant DNA to bacterial cells. When a virus invades a cell, the viral DNA enters the cytoplasm where it may direct reproduction of more viruses. Each virus from a viral vector contains a copy of the foreign gene. Some viruses also knit their DNA into the host cell's DNA. This also serves as a vector because when the bacterial cell replicates its DNA it will also replicate the viral plus the recombinant DNA.

12.3   PCR: Amplifying DNA

Cloning is a labor and time intensive process. A new, faster, technique was developed in 1983 by Kerry Mullis. **Polymerase chain reaction (PCR)** is a relatively simple and is a fast way of copying very small amounts of DNA, as outlined in Figure 12.6. Use of PCR allows scientists to amplify

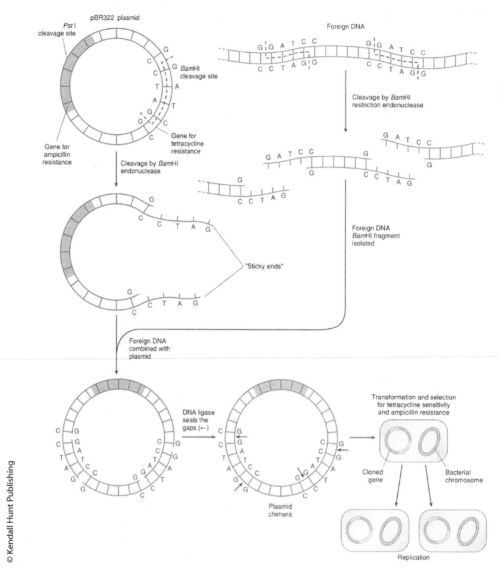

FIGURE 12.5 Summary of steps in causing the bacteria to take up modified plasmids.

TABLE 12.1 Summary of the Cloning Process.

1.	DNA to be cloned is isolated and treated with a restriction enzyme
2.	Segments cut by the enzyme are linked into a recombinant DNA molecule, possibly incorporated into a vector
3.	Vectors with the to-be-cloned-DNA are inserted into bacteria, where they replicate
4.	Cloned DNA can be recovered from the bacterial hosts and used for further experiments or in the production of gene products

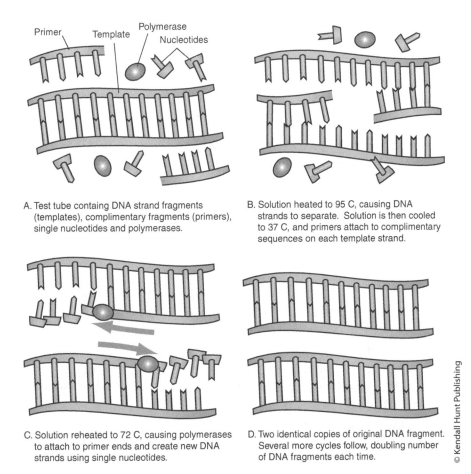

A. Test tube containg DNA strand fragments (templates), complimentary fragments (primers), single nucleotides and polymerases.

B. Solution heated to 95 C, causing DNA strands to separate. Solution is then cooled to 37 C, and primers attach to complimentary sequences on each template strand.

C. Solution reheated to 72 C, causing polymerases to attach to primer ends and create new DNA strands using single nucleotides.

D. Two identical copies of original DNA fragment. Several more cycles follow, doubling number of DNA fragments each time.

© Kendall Hunt Publishing

FIGURE 12.6 The PCR process amplifies small amounts of DNA.

the DNA contained in cells at the base of a single hair. The process has been automated and billions of copies of DNA can be easily produced with small effort.

Cells make copies of their DNA using the enzyme DNA polymerase. Biotechnology, in the PCR process, uses DNA polymerase to rapidly make multiple copies of target DNA in a test tube instead of a cell. Each DNA copy subsequently reacts with DNA polymerase, causing a chain reaction effect and mass production of DNA copies. This technique can make millions of copies of a single gene or a specific piece of DNA in a test tube.

PCR is very specific since the targeted DNA sequence can be less than one part in a million of the total DNA sample. A single gene can be amplified using PCR. This process does not replace gene cloning, since cloning produces many more copies of a gene, and is used whenever a large quantity of a gene or a protein product is needed. The advantage of PCR is its capability to make large amounts of desired DNA genes or segments rapidly.

As shown in Figure 12.6A, DNA primers must be used in the PCR process. Primers are 20-base sequences complementary to bases on either side of the DNA target. Primers are required because DNA polymerase only continues or extends the replication process; it must have a place to start, which the primers provide. After the primers bind to the DNA strand, DNA polymerase copies the target DNA.

Most modern labs that use the PCR process routinely have PCR machines (Figure 12.7). However, while the automation speeds the process, it requires temperature-insensitive DNA polymerase molecules that can function at high temperatures. The PCR process can be repeated up to 30 times, which will produce about one billion DNA copies. The upper temperature in PCR is about 95°C (recall that water boils at 100°C). However, eukaryotic enzymes become denatured and do not func-

FIGURE 12.7 Example of a PCR cycler machine.

tion at temperatures above 40°C. Some bacteria, known as extremophiles, live in conditions too extreme for most other organisms. Those bacteria that like it hot are known as thermophiles are one such group that thrive in high temperatures. The DNA polymerase typically used for PCR is from *Thermus aquaticus*, an extreme thermophile bacterium. The enzyme survives the temperature cycling involved, and therefore does not need to be replaced each time a cycle is completed.

PCR has been used for the detection of DNA sequences. Diagnosis of genetic diseases routinely employs PCR. DNA fingerprinting, the detection of bacteria or viruses (notably HIV), and research into human evolution all benefit from the PCR process. The PCR process was developed by and American scientist, Kary Mullis (b. 1944), one day while driving on a California highway. Mullis shared the Nobel Prize in Chemistry in 1993 for developing PCR. Mullis, an employee of the Cetus Company at the time, received a $10,000 bonus from his company, which later sold the patent right to PCR for US$300 million!

12.4   DNA Fingerprinting: Who Dunnit?

In May 2011, the U.S. government announced the killing of terrorist Osama bin Laden. One of multiple lines of evidence that the U.S. had killed the right man was DNA testing. Samples of DNA from the body were compared with samples from known members of the terrorist's family.

In 1998, President Bill Clinton was confronted with undeniable evidence of his indiscretion with White House intern Monica Lewinsky: DNA analysis from her stained dress pointed a glaring finger squarely at Bill Clinton alone among all the six billion people on the planet. What was this "smoking gun" that shed so much light on a married man's indiscretion?

When former NFL running back O.J. Simpson was tried (and acquitted) of murdering his second wife and another man, the DNA evidence looked staggering. Blood found at the crime scene could only have come from Mr. Simpson. What science was behind the statistics that pinned the blood to the defendant?

The 1990s murder case of a west Phoenix, AZ man arrested for killing a woman whose body was found in a grove of Palo Verde trees hinged on DNA. The body was found with the defendant's pager. The man offered an alibi that the woman had robbed him and taken his pager, but she had been alive when she left his pickup truck. He claimed never to have been to the spot where the woman was found. DNA fingerprinting of Palo Verde fruits in his truck placed him where the body was found. The man was convicted and set for release in 2015.

These and numerous other examples are applications of the DNA fingerprinting process. DNA fingerprinting can identify deceased individuals from skeletal remains, perpetrators of crimes from blood or semen samples, and help determine the genetic makeup of long-dead individuals or extinct organisms.

DNA fingerprinting uses DNA fragment lengths, which result from restriction enzyme cleavage, to identify particular individuals. Often this DNA is amplified by application of PCR. The DNA is first treated with restriction enzymes, which cut it into fragments. Each individual's DNA has different sequences of nitrogenous bases, resulting in different-sized DNA fragments. This procedure, shown in Figure 12.8, is known as restriction fragment length polymorphism (RFLP) analysis.

Gel electrophoresis (Figure 12.9) is a technique that allows the DNA fragments to separate according to length. This produces a pattern of bands, as shown in Figure 12.9B. Radioactive probes allow specific sequences to be separated from all other fragments, and the resulting pattern can be recorded on X-ray film by the process of autoradiography. Comparison of the pattern of fragments will allow determination of the question of "whose DNA was that."

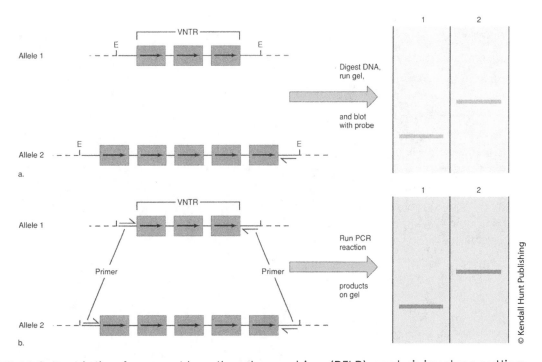

FIGURE 12.8 Restriction fragment length polymorphism (RFLP) analysis involves cutting DNA from several individuals with the same restriction enzyme, and then separating the resulting fragments using electrophoresis. The process is also known as DNA fingerprinting.

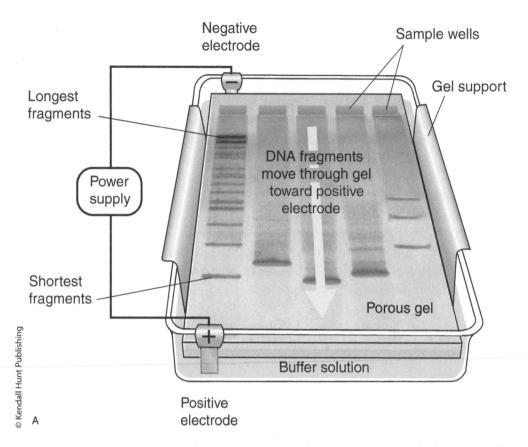

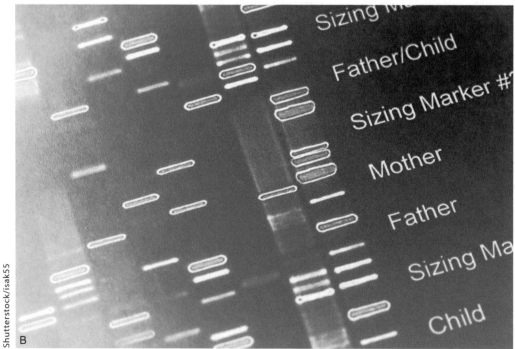

FIGURE 12.9 Electrophoresis. A. Electrophoresis apparatus diagram. B. DNA fingerprint data.

In some analyses, the DNA fragments can be recovered and analyzed further. PCR will amplify the small amount of original DNA. After performing PCR, the DNA segments will be numerous enough to be analyzed.

12.5   Genetic Engineering and Its Implications

The fields of law, medicine, agriculture, and industry have been revolutionized by recombinant DNA technology. New treatments for genetic disorders, providing evidence in a criminal trial, development of new foods and products, improved livestock and crops; all result of DNA technologies.

Traditionally, human genetic diseases have been diagnosed after the birth of the baby. In the case of Huntington's disease, this might only occur when the "baby" is over 40 years old and *after* they have had children of their own. Modern medical and molecular technology has developed a series of tests that can be administered to prospective parents or applied to fetal cells obtained by amniocentesis or chorionic villi sampling. Genes produce proteins, as well as RNA intermediates. The development of gene markers has led to our ability to now detect the presence of possibly lethal diseases such as Tay-Sachs and Huntington's before birth. The problem is what, if anything, do prospective parents do with this knowledge?

Restriction enzymes, such as *Hpa* I, were used in a study on sickle-cell disease. Restriction enzymes cut DNA into small fragments, but only at specific sequences of nucleotides. These fragments can then be mixed with a person's DNA to see where the fragments hybridize. If the hybridization occurs in an afflicted individual and not in an unafflicted individual, then we have a test that can be of use. The probe in the sickle-cell study hybridized in normal hemoglobin (denoted by Hb^A) with two fragments 7000 or 7600 nucleotides long. Sickle-cell hemoglobin (Hb^S) had hybridization with a 13,000 nucleotide single sequence. A similar result has been obtained from amniocentesis studies, providing a tool to screen fetus and adult for the presence of the sickle-cell allele. The markers where hybridization occurred are referred to as RFLPs. The longer fragment in sickle-cell individuals is interpreted as evidence of a mutation in the recognition sequence. Two nucleotide sequences close together on the same DNA molecule tend to stay together. In the sickle cell DNA, the beta-chain hemoglobin gene has become linked with another gene that somehow alters the recognition sequence at which *Hpa* I hybridizes. Heterozygotes (Hb^{A}Hb^S) will have both long and short fragments, while a single type (short or long) will occur in homozygous dominant (Hb^{A}Hb^A) and recessive (Hb^{S}Hb^S) individuals, respectively.

James F. Gusella and his research team used RFLPs to identify a marker to Huntington's disease. Testing a large library of human DNA fragments, Gusella and his coworkers found the needle in the haystack. The enzyme used was *Hind* III. Four fragments have been identified in an American family that has members suffering from the disease. The presence of fragment A has been identified in individuals who suffer from (or will eventually suffer from) Huntington's disease. Pattern A occurs in 60% of the population, as well as the Huntington's sufferers. In the area surrounding Venezuela's Lake Maracaibo, there is a family of 3000 members descended from a German sailor who had Huntington's disease. This family had a strong correlation between Fragment C and the disease. Pattern C is much less common among the general population in the United States.

Despite the existence of the test, many individuals do not wish to know if they will develop this disease. The late American folk singer and activist Woody Guthrie's children stand a 50% chance of inheriting the Huntington's gene from their father. They have chosen not to be tested.

Cystic fibrosis (CF) has also been studied with RFLP technology. This disease is the most common genetic disease among Caucasians. A blood test has been developed that would allow those who take the test to learn if they are carriers for the CF allele. A proposal to test the U.S. population to this end was made during the 1990s but ultimately rejected on cost effectiveness basis. It was estimated that to prevent the birth of one baby with CF would cost about $2 million per baby.

A great many hemophiliacs suffer from defective blood clotting factor VIII, which can be detected in fetuses 20 weeks old. A more accurate test, which can also be administered earlier during pregnancy, involves the use of a radioactive probe (a 36-nucleotide RNA fragment) that hybridizes restriction fragments. The gene for hemophilia is 186,000 base pairs, and has 26 exons (DNA pieces that code for a specific sequence of amino acids) separated by 25 introns (noncoding regions of the DNA). Mutations in the gene can be detected by RFLPs.

This technology has also been used to detect the single base-pair difference between normal and mutated beta-chains, a screen for sickle-cell anemia. A DNA probe has been developed that hybridizes with the gene for dystrophin. The previous screening for Duchenne muscular dystrophy (DMD) was a sex screen, with option to abort a male. The new technique allows differentiation between the healthy and diseased male fetus, so parents have more information with which to make an informed choice. The hybridization only occurs if the normal dystrophin gene is present, no hybridization occurs in the DMD sufferer.

12.6   The Human Genome Project and Gene Mapping

Humans were thought, prior to January 2001, to carry between 50,000 and 100,000 genes. Information released in 2001 by Celera Genomics and others suggested a total human genome of between 30,000 and 40,000 genes. Much less that previously thought. As of 2012, the number has been revised downward to fewer than 20,500 genes. That number compares to the number of genes the mouse genome has.

The Human Genome Project was an effort to locate and analyze the nucleotide sequence of more than 50,000–100,000 human genes thought to exist when the project started in 1990. A genome is the set of genes carried by an individual. The project was estimated to cost over $3 billion and to be completed around 2005. The international governmental and private science research project known as the Human Genome Project had several objectives: 1) identify the location of approximately 100,000 human genes on all chromosomes; and 2) determine the sequence of the three billion base pairs in the human genome. The project was for all intents and purposes finished ahead of schedule in January 2001.

Approximately 4000 genes cause genetic disorders. The discoveries arising from the work based on the Human Genome Project will continue to impact clinical medicine, genetic counseling, and treatment for genetic disorders. Identifying genes that cause conditions such as type II diabetes, certain forms of cancer, manic depression, schizophrenia, and high blood pressure will be payoffs for the investment of public funds in this basic research. Knowing where a gene is located and the nature and action of its product will facilitate developing new treatments for that disorder.

How will society react to this information? What legal, ethical, and moral issues will arise from our increased self-knowledge? The Human Genome Project budget actually called for a certain percent of the funds to be spent in efforts to deal with these and other "nonscientific" issues.

Several methods have been employed in attempts to map human chromosomes. One utilized mRNA molecules that had been isolated from cells. A molecule of mRNA is a transcript of a gene, and through complementary base pairing we can decipher the DNA base sequence of the gene once we know the mRNA base sequence (Figure 12.10). Once the mRNA has been

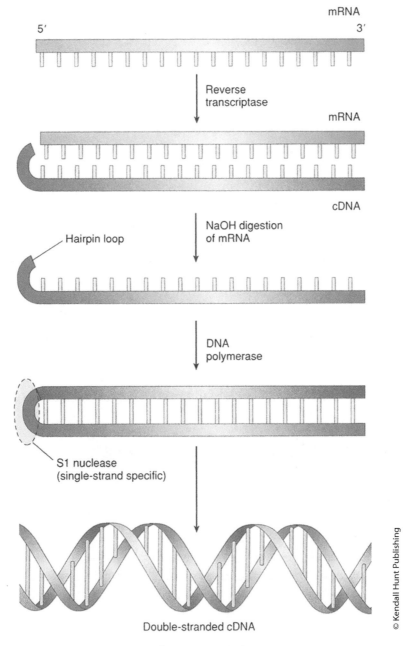

FIGURE 12.10. Steps in making a DNA from an mRNA.

recovered from a cell, the retroviral enzyme reverse transcriptase is used to produce a complementary DNA (cDNA) copy of the gene that produced that mRNA. The cDNA copy is attached to a fluorescent dye probe to determine to which chromosome it belongs. Base pairing of probe and chromosome occurs on a microscope slide. The use of a microscopy technique known as fluorescence allows us to see where the gene is located. This is known as the "clone-by-clone" method.

American biologist Craig Venter (b. 1946), the founder of Celera Genomics, devised a much quicker (and less expensive) method to sequence genes. Instead of cutting the DNA into 150,000-base segments, as had been previously done, Venter's technique, nicknamed the "whole-genome shotgun" method, cut the DNA into smaller bits, and used advanced computers to help reassemble the correct DNA base sequence.

Genes can sometimes be located on a chromosome by their relationship to genetic markers on specific chromosomes. This has allowed the development and application of genetic marker sequences linked to a specific disease-causing gene. Human genetic disorders, such as sickle cell, CFcystic fibrosis, Huntington disease, and Duchenne muscular dystrophy (DMD), are routinely detected with tests that employ genetic markers.

One of the first commercial successes of recombinant DNA technology was the production of proteins to treat diabetes, human insulin (sold as humulin), and hemophilia (genetically engineered blood clotting factors). Emphysema is a human disease of the respiratory tract that has many causes. An inheritable form is caused by a defective enzyme alpha-1-antitrypsin. Transgenic sheep have had the corrected human gene incorporated into their cells and produce milk that contains alpha-1-antitrypsin. With the deciphering of the human genome, these examples are just the tiny tip of a biotech iceberg.

Many products are produced without the chance of introducing diseases, such as clotting factors free of HIV contamination. However, some controversy surrounds the approval of recombinant DNA-derived bovine growth hormone (BGH) to boost milk production. In 1995, approximately 15% of the United States milk used this hormone. It is estimated that by 2000 this total would rise to 70%. Monsanto sold its BGH business in 2008 for over 300 million dollars. Despite governmental statements of the lack of ill effects, controversy persists.

12.7   Applications of Human Gene Science

Now that we have the human genome "figured out," what will we do with it? Prenatal detection of inherited diseases, screening of prospective parents who might be carriers of diseases; production of disease-resistant strains of wheat, rice, and corn; alteration of human genes to permanently remove harmful alleles all are among the beneficial outcomes of this new technology and our increased awareness of who and what we are. There are potential negatives to this as well: production of antibiotic resistant "superbugs" by terrorist nations; development of a new set of "germ warfare" agents; laws dictating who may and may not have children; fuel for misapplications of science in support of ethnic cleansing; and escape of genetically engineered organisms with unforeseen capabilities. Some of these "science fiction" ideas may become science facts.

12.7.1   Detection

Cystic fibrosis (CF) is a recessive allele occurring in 1/2000 births among Caucasians. Mapping the CF gene took several steps: Large families with CF were examined to find a marker. An exclusion map of chromosomes where the gene was NOT linked was produced. Discovery of CF gene linked to a marker for chromosome 7.

Since genes produce a protein product, and CF is an autosomal recessive, the product it produces must be defective. The CF gene produces a defective protein called cystic fibrosis transmembrane conductance regulator (CFTCR) that controls the passage of chloride ions into and out of the cell, most notably cells lining the lungs. The discovery of the CF gene took five years. Studies on the function of the CFTCR protein will lead to new treatments. Heterozygotes (4% of the Caucasian population) can be detected and those at risk of having a CF child can be identified and counseled. This underscores the value of recombinant DNA in gene mapping. However, during the late 1990s, the Federal Government decided the costs of preventing CF births were too high, some $2 million dollars per CF birth. Planned population-wide genetic screening was canceled.

Prenatal testing can detect a genetic disorder in an embryo or fetus, usually by amniocentesis or chorionic villi sampling. The recovered cells are then analyzed using PCR and other techniques to detect gene markers for harmful alleles. If the markers are found, the parents have a little more information with which to make choices and/or plans.

Unlike CF, sickle cell disease cannot be diagnosed prenatally using conventional methods. The mutation that causes sickle cell anemia destroys a restriction enzyme cutting site, changing the length and number of DNA fragments.

Presymptomatic screening allows the diagnosis of a genetic disorder that becomes expressed later in life, such as polycystic kidney disease (PKD). Presymptomatic screening raises social and ethical questions: should children in families with disorders be tested? Should children be told their condition? The answers to these questions are for everyone to decide, not scientists alone.

12.7.2   Treatment

Production of clotting factors or insulin is a treatment of symptom not cause. Gene transfer therapy for the first time allows us to envision a cure that supplies the corrected gene. To incorporate desired genes, a vector is used.

Viruses are natural vectors to deliver DNA into a host cell. Viruses reproduce inside their host cell. The viral DNA either incorporates into the host DNA or takes over the cell and begins producing new viruses. A human gene can be inserted into the viral genome. The ability of the virus to cause disease is also deactivated, and then the patient is infected by the altered virus.

In 1990, a human gene was inserted into a virus that was subsequently allowed to infect the white blood cells of a girl suffering from severe combined immunodeficiency (SCID). She now leads a normal life with a functioning immune system. However, in 2000, a young man died as a result of gene therapy. His family sued the university that conducted the research, and won a large judgment.

A different approach to the infection of the patient with a modified virus is the infection of cells from the patient that have been removed from the patient's body. These cells are infected and then returned to the patient.

12.8   Transgenic Organisms

Transgenic bacteria protect and improve the health of plants. Frost-minus bacteria protect the vegetative parts of plants from frost damage, allowing cultivation outside the natural environmental and physiological climate range of the plants. Plants in the pea family, referred to commonly as legumes, normally contain symbiotic bacteria in nodules on their roots. The bacteria take inorganic atmospheric nitrogen and convert it to forms of nitrogen that the plants can use. However, nonlegumes do not or cannot harbor these bacteria and so gain the nitrogen they produce. Infecting nonlegumes with engineered nitrogen-fixing bacteria might reduce fertilizer needs and thus water pollution from agricultural fields.

Bacteria able to breakdown petroleum can be improved by genetic engineering. These organisms can be deployed in the case of oil tanker spills (or as in the Gulf War of the early 1990s in case of deliberate release of petroleum into the environment). The bacteria can be engineered to use only petroleum as a source of carbon, and when the petroleum spill is cleaned up, the bacteria will die. These bacteria were available during the 1989 Exxon Valdez spill in Alaska (Figure 12.11), but were not used. During the 2010, Deepwater Horizon spill in the Gulf of Mexico, these bacteria were used and studies suggest they mitigated the damage caused by the spill to a degree. The effectiveness and safety of this approach remain unclear.

Bacteria can act as biofilters to prevent airborne chemical pollutants from being released into the air. These organisms can also remove sulfur from coal before it is burned and help clean up toxic dumps. With the power crises of early 2001 fresh in their minds, the George W. Bush administration proposed increased reliance on burning of fossil fuels to meet power demands. Coal is by far our most abundant fossil energy source. However, most domestic coal has high sulfur content. When burned to make electrical power, this sulfur becomes a dangerous atmospheric pollutant that contributes both to acid rain and global warming associated with the greenhouse effect.

Bacteria can also be used in the large-scale production of chemicals and other chemicals. The amino acid phenylalanine is used in the dietary sweetener aspartame (trade name NutraSweet˚). The production of this aspartame involves engineered bacteria.

Transgenic bacteria can also process minerals. Many major mining companies already use bacteria to obtain various metals. Genetically

FIGURE 12.11 Oil pooled on the beach rocks after the Exxon Valdez oil spill in 1989. Genetically, engineered bacteria were available but not utilized to clean this oil spill.

engineered "bioleaching" bacteria extract copper, uranium, and gold from low-grade ore. Bioleaching has been used to extract sulfide ores, gold bearing pyrites, and arsenopyrites.

There are a wide variety of transgenic plants that have been developed over the past two decades. About 50 types of genetically engineered plants have entered field trials. Major crops that have been improved with this technology include soybean, cotton, alfalfa, rice, potato, and corn. Corn has been genetically engineered by blasting desired genes into corn cells. Herbicide resistance has been incorporated into corn, and is being tested. Field tests for genetically altered tomatoes, potatoes, and cotton are also underway. Eventually, transgenic plants will be heat-, cold-, drought-, and/or salt-tolerant. They will be more nutritious and can be stored and transported without fear of damage. It is hoped that transgenic plants will require less fertilizer or will produce chemicals and drugs that are of value to humans.

Since animal cells will not take up bacterial plasmids, scientists had to develop other methods insert genes into the eggs of animals. A common method uses silicon-carbide needles that make tiny holes in the animal cell nucleus, through which the DNA can enter. Many types of animal eggs have been injected with bovine growth hormone (bGH) to produce larger creatures.

We can now transfer genes into human cells to cure inherited diseases. Can we not also alter the evolution of our species by modifying the genetic makeup of individuals? Most gene therapy is in somatic line cells. Is germ line therapy ethical? Can short children be treated to increase their height? How about making tall children taller for success in basketball? Should genetically engineered food be labeled (it is not required to be so labeled in many U.S. states)?

Summary

Biotechnology grows out of Watson and Crick's work deciphering the structure and function of the DNA molecule. These technologies allow us to create recombinant DNA molecules to insert a desired gene into an organism. Testing parents for rare recessive diseases could lead to decline of these illnesses. These techniques are not without controversy, however.

Terms

amniocentesis
biotechnology
chorionic villi
  sampling
cystic fibrosis (CF)
DNA ligase
DNA polymerase
EcoRI
exons
gel electrophoresis

genetically modified
  organisms (GMOs)
genome
Human Genome Project
introns
Okazaki fragments
palindromic sequences
plasmids
polymerase chain reaction
  (PCR)

recombinant DNA molecules
recombinant DNA
  technology
restriction enzymes
restriction fragment length
  polymorphism (RFLP)
sickle cell disease
sticky ends
thermophiles
vector

Review Questions

1. The DNA polymerase used in the PCR process comes from which of these groups of organisms?
   a. Archaeans;
   b. Bacteria;
   c. Plants;
   d. Animals

2. The Human Genome Project announced its completion in _____.
   a. 1989;
   b. 2001;
   c. 2013;
   d. the project has not yet been completed

3. Cystic fibrosis is _____.
   a. an autosomal recessive;
   b. characterized by buildup of mucus;
   c. caused by production of a defective protein known as CFTCR;
   d. all of these are true

4. *Eco*RI is _____.
   a. a restriction enzyme isolated from *Nostoc*;
   b. a DNA replicating enzyme;
   c. a restriction enzyme isolated from *E. coli*;
   d. a plasmid produced by the restriction enzyme *Hind*III.

5. Which of these procedures would not be used in prenatal testing for a suspected genetic defect?
   a. PCR;
   b. amniocentesis;
   c. phrenology;
   d. chorionic villi sampling

6. Gene pharming involves the use of farm animals to produce pharmaceuticals. True or False

7. The Federal Government played no role in the Human Genome Project. True or False

8. The number of human genes as of 2014 is _____.
   a. 100,000;
   b. 20,500;
   c. 4000;
   d. 23,500

9. Members of the _____ family have symbiotic bacteria living in their root nodules.
   a. cactus;
   b. pea;
   c. hemp;
   d. grass

10. Which of these would not be a vector for genetic modifications?
    a. bacterial chromosome;
    b. plasmid;
    c. virus;
    d. all of these

11. The retroviral enzyme that assembles a cDNA copy is _____.
    a. RNA polymerase;
    b. DNA polymerase;
    c. reverse transcriptase;
    d. isomerase

Links

From Corned Beef to Cloning: This memoir, taken from Access Excellence, recounts the work of Stanley Cogen and others in the potential applications of bacterial plasmids to change an organism's genome. (http://www.accessexcellence.org/AB/WYW/cohen/index.html)

Polymerase Chain Reaction—Xeroxing DNA: This short page from Access Excellence clearly outlines the basics of the PCR technique. (http://www.accessexcellence.org/RC/AB/IE/PCR_Xeroxing_DNA.php)

Polymerase Chain Reaction: This page, written by Mark V. Bloom and hosted on the Access Excellence site, gives a succinct description of PCR and related techniques in biotechnology. (http://www.accessexcellence.org/RC/CT/polymerase_chain_reaction.php)

DNA Fingerprinting in Human Health and Society: This short page from Access Excellence gives the basics of DNA fingerprinting and its applications in diagnosis of inherited diseases, personal identification, as well as issues of paternity. (http://www.accessexcellence.org/RC/AB/IWT/DNA_Fingerprinting_Basics.php)

Critters, Critters Everywhere: This short, but nicely illustrated, page from the Why Files site gives background and other facts about thermophilic archaeans, highlighting their uses in biotechnology (PCR) as well as the soda pop industry. (http://whyfiles.org/2011/biology-critters-that-should-not-exist)

Killer's Trail: This NOVA website accompanied a 1999 season program examining the infamous Sam Sheppard (not to be confused with the actor and playwright) murder case that inspired the television show and movie *The Fugitive.* Examine DNA and other modern evidence and see what your verdict would have been in the case. (http://www.pbs.org/wgbh/nova/sheppard)

DNA Fingerprinting: You Be the Judge! This 1992 entry to the Access Excellence Activities Exchange give a printable example of the application of DNA fingerprinting in a criminal case. This page was developed by Carolyn Napier Martin. (http://www.accessexcellence.com/AE/AEPC/WWC/1992/DNA_printing.php)

Free at Last! This series of pages from the Why Files website offers some history, science, and legal aspects of the DNA fingerprinting. (Link is at http://whyfiles.org/126dna_forensic)

The Human Genome Project: The website detaining the federally funded part of the hu8man genome initiative. Learn about the history and progress made with this revolutionary project. (http://www.genome.gov/HGP)

Celera Genomics: This site is the commercial side of the human genome project. Of note is the section dealing with education, as well as news releases. (http://www.celera.com/)

Human Genome Project Information: This page, part of the U.S. Department of Energy's human genome effort, offers another perspective on the American and international efforts on solving and then applying the information learned about our genes. (http://web.ornl.gov/sci/techresources/Human_Genome)

Unit 4

Evolution and Biodiversity

CHAPTER 13

The Theory of Evolution

Shutterstock/Chantal de Bruijne

Chapter Opener

Close up of a zebra in a herd. While all zebras are striped, there is variation.

Objectives

- Be able to define evolution.
- Describe and discuss the evidence for evolution.
- Elaborate on how the Modern Synthesis combined genetics and evolutionary biology.
- List the five conditions necessary to maintain a Hardy–Weinberg equilibrium and be able to answer simple questions about allele frequency changes over time.
- Be able to compare and contrast the three types of natural selection and discuss examples of each type.
- Define a species and provide examples illustrating the process of speciation.
- Discuss how adaptive radiation can lead to speciation.
- Compare and contrast gradualism and punctuated equilibrium.
- Discuss how systematics may be employed to classify organisms.
- Compare and contrast traditional and cladistic classifications.
- Be able to discuss similarities and differences between a five-kingdom and a three-domain system.
- Be able to discuss the classification of human beings, providing examples of animals in each taxonomic category beside us.

Introduction

In 1859, a revolution shook biology. Mendel's revolution was still decades in the future, and Watson and Crick's work nearly a century distant. This revolution was not confined to biology but affected society in general. The revolutionaries were an unlikely pair of scientists: Charles Darwin and Alfred Russell Wallace. The two men worked independently of each other in different parts of the world, yet each arrived at a remarkable series of ideas that explain the unity and diversity of living things and how life had changed over time: evolution by natural selection.

13.1   Development of Evolutionary Theory

The ancient Greek philosopher Anaximander (611–547 BCE) and the Roman philosopher Lucretius (99–55 BCE) developed the concept that all living things were related and had changed over time. Another ancient Greek philosopher, Aristotle (384–322 BCE) developed his *Scala Naturae*, or *Ladder of Life*, to explain his concept of the advancement of living things from inanimate matter to plants, then animals and finally people. This concept of man as the top of the ladder still plagues modern evolutionary biologists. American biologist Stephen Jay Gould (1941–2002) in his 1989 book *Wonderful Life* provides a more detailed discussion of this idea.

Post-Aristotelian ideas about the origin of life were constrained by the prevailing thought patterns of the Middle Ages—the inerrancy of the biblical book of Genesis and the special creation of the world in a literal six days of the 24-hour variety. In the mid-1600s, Archbishop of Armagh (Church of Ireland) James Ussher (1581–1656) calculated the age of the Earth based on the biblical book of Genesis. Working backward from the crucifixion, Ussher calculated the Earth formed on October 22, 4004 BCE. These calculations were part of Ussher's book *Annals of the Old Testament, deduced from the first origins of the world, the chronicle of Asiatic and Egyptian matters together produced from the beginning of historical time up to the beginnings of Maccabees.* The chronology he developed was taken as factual, even being printed in the front pages of many *Bibles* into the 21st century. Ussher's ideas were readily accepted since they posed no threat to the social order of the times.

Geologists doubted the accuracy of a 5,000-year-old Earth. The Italian scientist and artist Leonardo da Vinci (1452–1519) calculated the sedimentation rates in the Po River of Italy, and concluded it took 200,000 years to form some nearby rock deposits. The Italian scientist Galileo (1564–1642), convicted heretic for his contention that the Earth was not the center of the Universe, studied fossils and concluded that they were real and not inanimate artifacts.

James Hutton (1726–1797), the Scottish farmer regarded as the father of modern geology, developed the Theory of Uniformitarianism in 1795. According to Hutton's work, certain geological processes operated in the past in much the same fashion as they do today. Many geological structures and processes cannot be scientifically explained if the Earth is only 6,000 years old. British geologist Charles Lyell (1797–1875) refined Hutton's ideas during the 1800s to include slow change over long periods of time. His book *Principles of Geology* had profound effects on young Charles Darwin and Alfred Wallace.

13.2   Evolutionary Thought During the 1700s

Swedish botanist Carl Linne, more commonly known by his Latinized name Linnaeus (1707–1778), attempted to classify all known species of his time (1753) into immutable categories. We still utilize many of these categories are biological classification. Modern biologists base classification on evolution and not immutability of species as Linnaeus did. Linnaean hierarchical classification was based on the premise that the species was the smallest unit, and that each group (or taxon) belonged to a higher category.

The French nobleman-scientist Georges-Louis Leclerc, Comte de Buffon (pronounced Bu-fone; 1707–1788) in the middle to late 1700s proposed that species could change. He published a 44-volume natural history of all then known plants and animals. This was a major break from earlier concepts that species were created by a perfect creator and therefore could not change. Buffon also provided evidence of descent with modification and speculated on various causative mechanisms for the change of living things. Buffon wrote of several factors that could influence change: influences of the environment, migration, geographical isolation, overcrowding, and the struggle for existence. However, Buffon vacillated as to whether or not he believed in the change in living things, and professed to believe in special creation and the fixity of species in response to political influence in France.

Erasmus Darwin (1731–1802; grandfather of Charles) was a British physician and poet in the late 1700s. He proposed and provided some evidence that life had changed over time. His writings on both botany and zoology contained many comments that suggested the possibility of common descent based on changes undergone by animals during development, artificial

The Age of the Earth

Radiometric age assignments based on the rates of decay of radioactive isotopes, not discovered until the late 19th century, suggest the Earth is over 4.5 billion years old. Based on radiometric dates of meteorites, Earth is thought to be older than 4.5 billion years, with the oldest known rocks being 3.96 billion years old. Geologic time divides into eons, eras, and smaller units (Figure Box 1).

Geologists divide time into two categories: relative time and absolute time. Relative time was developed first historically and places events in a relative sequence from oldest to youngest. Absolute time places a numerical date on an event. For example, when we say that dinosaurs died out 65 million years ago we are using absolute time, but if we say dinosaurs characterized rocks of the Mesozoic era we are employing a relative time concept.

French physicist Antoine Henri Becquerel (1852–1908) discovered radioactivity in 1896. Later recognition of isotopic decay sequences is now used as a way to place numerical dates on rock samples. In 1903, New Zealand physicist Ernest Rutherford (1871–1937) proposed the use of radioactivity in determining the age of a rock sample. Rutherford also worked out the concept of half-life.

Radioactive decay is the process where unstable nuclei spontaneously transform into another element. A half-life is the amount of time needed for one-half of a radioisotope to decay into its stable end product (or daughter). By measuring the various isotopes in a sample, geologists can calculate the age of the specimen. Long-lived radioactive isotope pairs have half-lives in millions or billions of years (Figure Box 2). The U-Pb series isotopes are used to date ancient igneous intrusive rocks such as granite. Likewise, Rb-Sr isotope ratios can be applied to ancient rocks and meteorites. Fine-grained volcanic rocks, such as bentonite and basalt, are dated by the ratios of K-Ar.

The isotope pairs mentioned above allow us to date only the rock surrounding the fossil, not the fossil itself. Carbon-14 dating based on the ratio of ^{14}C–^{12}C in an organic sample originated from work done by 1960 Nobel laureate in chemistry Willard Frank Libby (1908–1980). This technique allows us to date the fossil itself. However, the technique is valid only for samples less than 70,000 years old. Living things take in both isotopes of carbon (carbon-12 and carbon-14). Carbon-14 is radioactive, and decays into nitrogen-14. As long as the organism was alive, the ratio of carbon-12 to carbon-14 was in equilibrium with its environment. When the organism dies, the "clock" starts as the carbon-14 decays, changing the ratio. The longer the time since death, the more the isotopic ratio will have changed.

There are some sources for uncertainty with radiometric dates. Addition or subtraction of radioactive or daughter material after the formation of the sample could affect the date. Metamorphism and recrystallization may also affect the date accuracy.

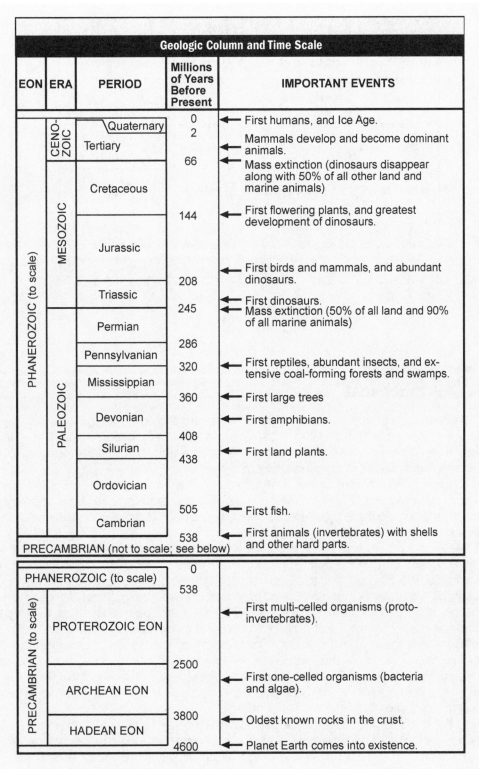

FIGURE BOX 1 Geologic time chart.

Isotope		Half-life of parent (years)	Useful range (years)
Parent	Daughter		
Carbon 14	Nitrogen 14	5,730	100 – 70,000
Potassium 40	Argon 40	1.3 billion	100,000 – 4.5 billion
Rbubidium 87	Strontium 87	47 billion	10 million – 4.5 billion
Uranium 238	Lead 206	4.5 billion – 710 million	10 million – 4.6 billion
Uranium 235	Lead 207		

FIGURE BOX 2 Some common isotope pairs and their half-lives.

The Geologic Time Scale

The modern geologic time scale is a hybrid with a relative sequence of units measured against a framework of radiometric (absolute) dates. The time scale was first assembled using fossils and relative dating techniques decades before the development of radiometric dating techniques during the early 20th century.

The longest duration units of the time scale are the eons. Each eon is subdivided into eras, which are in turn split into periods. Geologists use even smaller time units known as epochs, most commonly in the more recent parts of geologic time. Scientists recognize three eons: the Archean, the Proterozoic, and the Phanerozoic.

The Archean Eon encompasses the time from the formation of the Earth until 2.5 billion years ago. Rocks that formed during this eon are the most ancient rocks known, up to 3.96 billion years old. The nature of this rock indicates that even older rocks might still exist. Perhaps the most significant development during the Archean was the origin of life. Fossil evidence supports the origin of life on Earth earlier than 3.5 billion years ago. Life appears to have begun soon after the cooling of the Earth and formation of its atmosphere and oceans.

These ancient fossils occur in marine rocks, such as limestones and sandstones, which formed in ancient oceans. The organisms living today that are most similar to ancient life forms are the bacteria. Recent discoveries of bacteria at mid-ocean ridges add yet another possible origin for life: at these mid-ocean ridges where heat and molten rock rise to the Earth's surface.

The Proterozoic Eon covers the time span from 2.5 billion to 540 million years ago. Simple, prokaryotic cells still dominated the world's environments until the evolution of simple eukaryotes approximately 2 billion years ago. With the appearance of eukaryotes comes the development of sexual reproduction, which greatly increased the variation that natural selection could operate on. A major environmental change, initiated by living things, was the development of oxygenic photosynthesis. This led to increasing oxygen levels during later Proterozoic. Geologists refer to the "great iron crisis" when the rising levels of oxygen in the world's oceans caused the formation or iron oxide (Fe_2O_3), often preserved as the banded iron formation (an important commercial source of iron). During the Proterozoic Earth experienced at least one episode of planetary freezing known as a Snowball Earth. Around this same time, we see the first appearance of multicellular organisms.

The Phanerozoic Eon represents the past 540 million years of geologic time. The term "Phanerozoic" literally translates as "time of visible life." During this eon animals, which had evolved during the late Proterozoic, developed hard parts that led to an increase in fossilization. Major events of the Phanerozoic Eon include the evolution of plants and vertebrate animals, movement of multicellular organisms onto land, development of complex social behaviors in animals, and the evolution of humans. The Phanerozoic Eon can be subdivided into three eras: Paleozoic, Mesozoic, and Cenozoic.

selection by humans, and the presence of vestigial organs. However, this Darwin offered no mechanism to explain the change of living things over time. Often his ideas were written in verse.

British geologist William "Strata" Smith (1769–1839), employed by the English coal mining industry, developed the first accurate geologic map of England. From his extensive travels, he also developed the Principle of Biological Succession. This idea states that each period of Earth history has its own unique assemblages of fossils. In essence Smith fathered the science of stratigraphy, the correlation of rock layers based on (among other things) their fossil contents.

German geologist Abraham Gottlob Werner (1749–1817) and French naturalist Baron Georges Cuvier (1769–1832) were among the foremost proponents of catastrophism, the theory that the Earth and geological events had formed suddenly, as a result of some great catastrophe (such as Noah's flood). This view was a comfortable one for the times and thus was widely accepted. Cuvier eventually proposed that there had been several creations that occurred after catastrophes. Swiss geologist Louis Agassiz (1807–1873) proposed between fifty and eighty of these catastrophes and creation events.

French nobleman-scientist Jean Baptiste de Lamarck (1744–1829) developed one of the first theories on how species changed. In 1809 Lamarck concluded organisms of higher complexity evolved from preexisting, less complex organisms. He proposed the inheritance of acquired characteristics to explain, among other things, the length of the giraffe neck. Lamarckian viewed modern giraffe's long necks resulting from their short-necked ancestors progressively gaining longer necks from stretching to reach food higher in trees (Figure 13.1). According to

FIGURE 13.1 Five million year old fossil jawbone of an extinct short-necked giraffe (Sivathere), West Coast Fossil Park, South Africa.

Shutterstock/EcoPrint

the 19th century medical concept of use and disuse, the stretching of necks resulted in their development, which was somehow passed on to their progeny. Today we realize that only bacteria are able to incorporate non-genetic (aka non-heritable) traits. Lamarck's work clearly stated that life had changed over time and provided a mechanism to explain this change. Unfortunately this mechanism does not work.

13.3   Evolution by Natural Selection

The idea that species could change over time was not immediately acceptable to many: the lack of a mechanism hampered the acceptance of this idea, as did its implications regarding the biblical views of creation. Charles Darwin and Alfred Wallace both worked independently of each other, traveled extensively, and eventually developed similar ideas about the change in life over time as well as a mechanism for that change: natural selection.

Charles Darwin (1809–1882, Figure 13.2A), a divinity student and former medical student (he simultaneously took three bachelor's degrees: natural science, geology, and theology), secured an unpaid position on the British naval ship H.M.S. Beagle. The voyage would provide Darwin a unique opportunity to study adaptation and gather a great deal of the evidence he would later incorporate into his theory of evolution by natural selection. The Beagle visited many Spanish and Portuguese cities in South America. Prone to seasickness, young Mr. Darwin often happily traveled overland to meet the ship at its next port of call.

Darwin spent much time ashore collecting plant, animal and fossil specimens, as well as making extensive geological observations. Several noteworthy events occurred that colored his later thinking about evolution. While travelling through Argentina with the *gauchos* (cowboys) Darwin encountered two species of large, flightless birds: the greater Rhea in the north (Figure 13.2C), and a smaller bird, the lesser Rhea (Figure 13.2D), in the south. Examination of the stomach contents revealed each bird ate the same food. Darwin wondered in his journal why there should be two birds where one would seem to do. On the west coast of South America, Darwin observed the aftermath of an earthquake that raised the sea floor several meters above sea level. Travelling higher up in the Andes Darwin noted several other raised shorelines with their associated seashells, sometimes hundreds of meters above sea level. Darwin also excavated the fossil remains of a number of extinct large mammal fossils, including the glyptodont and ground sloth. The glyptodont in particular intrigued him, as it very closely resembled the smaller armadillos he observed scurrying through the landscape.

Perhaps his most famous stop on the voyage was the Galápagos Islands off the coast of Ecuador. These volcanic islands are now known to be less than five million years old. All of the life on these islands came from somewhere else. Darwin marveled about the sheer numbers of unique creatures on these islands (Figure 13.3). The island from which the tortoises (Figure 13.4) originated could be identified by the crest of their shell: low crested shells indicated a well-watered island; high peaked shells indicated a drier island. The Spanish brought the ancestors of these animals to the islands. On each island, Darwin eventually surmised, they had changed and adapted.

Upon his return to England in 1836, Darwin began to collaborate with numerous specialists to catalog his collections. On his own, he began to consider the seeming "fit" of organisms to

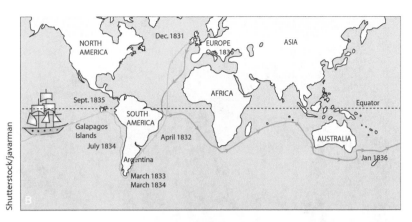

FIGURE 13.2 Charles Darwin and the voyage of HMS Beagle. A. Drawing of Darwin later in life; B. Map illustrating the Beagle's voyage. C. Portrait of a Greater Rhea (*Rhea americana*) a flightless bird from Argentina; D. Darwin's rhea (*Rhea pennata*) walking in the field.

their mode of existence. He married his cousin Emma Wedgewood and began to raise a family. Seeming quite ordinary to the outside, he worked in secret on a radical idea. He eventually settled on four main points of the theory.

1. Adaptation: all organisms adapt to their environments.
2. Variation: all organisms are variable in their traits. This variation is passed on by a hereditary mechanism.
3. Over-reproduction: all organisms tend to reproduce beyond their environment's capacity to support them (this is based on the work of Thomas Malthus, who studied how populations of organisms tended to grow geometrically until they encountered a limit on their population size).
4. Since not all organisms are equally well adapted to their environment, some will survive and reproduce better than others—this is known as natural selection. Sometimes this is called "survival of the fittest." In reality this merely deals with the reproductive success of the organisms, not solely their relative strength or speed.

FIGURE 13.3 Various organisms from the Galápagos Islands. A. Close up of blue-footed booby at Galápagos island of North Seymour Island; B. Large turtle (*Megalochelys gigantea*) at the sea edge on background of a tropical landscape; C. Marine Iguana tanning on rock; D. Frigate Bird courting display; E. Flightless cormorant.

Unlike Darwin, British naturalist Alfred Russel Wallace (1823–1913) came from a different social class. Wallace spent many years in South America, publishing salvaged notes in *Travels on the Amazon and Rio Negro* in 1853. In 1854, Wallace left England to study the natural history of Indonesia, where he contracted the mosquito-borne disease malaria. He

Shutterstock/Roman Zherdytskyi

Shutterstock/Pablo Hidalgo-Fotos593

FIGURE 13.4 Galápagos tortoises. A. Giant tortoise. Note the low crest to the shell; B. A giant Galápagos turtle, Galápagos Islands, Ecuador, note the higher peaked shell on this variety.

also explored and collected extensively on the numerous islands of the area. He began to formulate ideas about the role selection and adaptation played in fitting organisms to their environment.

In 1858, Darwin received a letter from Wallace in which Darwin's as-yet-unpublished theory of evolution and adaptation was precisely detailed. Darwin and his colleagues arranged for Wallace's paper to be read at the July 1, 1858 meeting of the Linnaean Society, along with a letter on the same subject by Darwin. Wallace's paper, published in 1858, defined the role of natural selection in species formation. Darwin rushed to finish his major book offering copious evidence supporting his idea. His book *On the Origin of Species by Means of Natural Selection* remains one of the most influential books ever written. To be correct, we need to mention that both Darwin and Wallace developed the theory, although Darwin's major work was not published until 1859. While there have been some changes to the theory since 1859, most notably the incorporation of genetics and DNA into what is termed the "Modern Synthesis" during the 1940s, most scientists today accept evolution as the guiding theory on which modern biology is based.

Careful field observations of organisms and their environment led both Darwin and Wallace to the role of natural selection in formation of species. They also utilized the works of British geologist Charles Lyell and English clergyman Thomas Malthus (1766–1834). Malthus' ideas were first published in 1798, and noted that the human population was capable of doubling every 25 years. Population would soon outstrip the food supply, leading to starvation, famine and war, which would reduce the human population. Wallace and Darwin adapted Malthus' ideas about how scarce resources could affect populations of any type of organism.

The Wallace-Darwin Theory

1. Individuals in a population have variable levels of agility, size, ability to obtain food, and different successes in reproducing.
2. Left unchecked, populations tend to expand exponentially, leading to a scarcity of resources.
3. In the struggle for existence, some individuals are more successful than others, allowing them to survive and reproduce.
4. Those organisms best able to survive and reproduce will leave more offspring than those unsuccessful individuals.
5. Over time, there will be heritable changes in phenotype (and genotype) of a species, resulting in a transformation of the original species into a new species similar to, but distinct from, its parent species.

13.4   Evidence for Evolution

Evolution, which started out as a hypothesis, rests now on copious amounts of evidence from many fields of science. Remember that in science we need evidence that supports our hypotheses and theories. The compelling mass of evidence from many fields of science has if effect won the debate: evolution happens, ignore it at your own peril!

13.4.1   Fossils: Evidence of Past Life

The fossil record is the history of life recorded by remains from the past. Fossils (Figure 13.5) include skeletons, footprints, shells, seeds, insects trapped in amber, dung, DNA and other chemicals, imprints of leaves, and tracks of organisms that lived in the distant past. Most fossils are at least 10,000 years old.

There are two basic types of fossils: direct and indirect. Direct fossils are parts of the body (in extremely rare cases the complete body) of an organism. Pollen, spores, leaves, seeds, fruits, teeth, bones, shells, DNA and other chemicals, and feathers are examples of direct fossils. Indirect fossils, sometimes known as trace fossils, indicate the activity of the organism. Footprints, feeding traces, tail drags, fossilized feces, worm burrows, and fossilized trails are examples of indirect fossils.

Fossilized feces are known as coprolites. Analysis of coprolites allows us to infer much about the diet of now extinct animals. Examination of fossil track ways allows us to infer the behavior of the animals making the tracks, as well as their stride length, size, and possibly weight. That is a lot of information from a few footprints! Worms usually leave a poor fossil record because of their soft bodies. Many marine worms, however, will secrete material stabilizing their burrows in the ocean floor. These burrows can become fossilized (Figure 13.5G).

The fossil record traces history of life and allows us to study history of particular organisms. Fossil evidence supports the common descent hypothesis as fossils can be linked over time due to a similarity in form. Transitional fossils reveal links between groups. The early bird fossil *Archaeopteryx* (Figure 13.6A, B) indicates the evolutionary connection between reptiles/dinosaurs and birds. *Eusthenopteron* is an amphibious fossil fish (Figure 13.6C), while *Seymouria* is a reptile-like amphibian. The extinct animal group the therapsids were mammal-like reptiles possessing some mammalian as well as ancestral reptilian featured.

FIGURE 13.5 Examples of fossils. A. Fossil of a dragonfly; B. Fossilized fern leaf fossil; C. Ammonite fossils; D. Partial skeleton of an ichthyosaur fossil; E. Impression of a dinosaur footprint; F. Fossilized pollen. G. Fossilized worm tubes.

Shutterstock/Redchanka

A

Shutterstock/Linda Bucklin

B

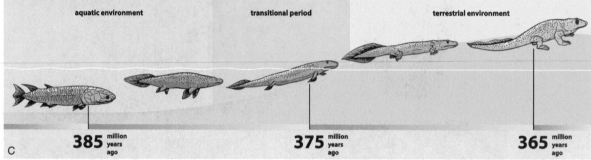

Shutterstock/Lskywalker

aquatic environment   transitional period   terrestrial environment

385 million years ago   **375** million years ago   **365** million years ago

C

FIGURE 13.6 Transitional fossils. A. *Archaeopteryx*, a transitional fossil linking birds and dinosaurs; B. Reconstruction of *Archaeopteryx*; C. Evolution of lobe-finned fish to amphibians.

Darwin wrote extensively of evolution working much like a tree branches. There will be common points before a branch forms. We refer to these common points as a common ancestor. Fossils leading up to and slightly after the common ancestor may be considered transitional forms.

An example of transitional forms comes from the fossils that record the evolution of mammals. All living mammas have jaws composed of a single bone, the dentary. Reptiles, the group most closely related to mammals, have a jaw composed of three bones, the dentary, quadrate, and articular. Mammals belong to a group known as the synapsids. Reptiles belong to a group known as diapsids. There are many extinct forms in each group. Along the synapsid lineage, the dentary becomes larger and more prominent. Numerous transition fossils illustrate the shrinking and migration of the quadrate and articular bones to become part of the mammalian inner ear hearing mechanism.

The fossil record allows us to trace the history of the modern-day horse *Equus*. The earliest fossil in this lineage is *Eohippus* (Figure 13.7), which is often described as the size of a small dog, with cusped low-crowned molars, four toes on each front foot, three on each hind foot—all adaptations for forest living. The name *Eohippus* translates as "horse of the dawn." The animal lived in forests of North America during the Eocene epoch of the Tertiary period. Grasslands replaced forests as the

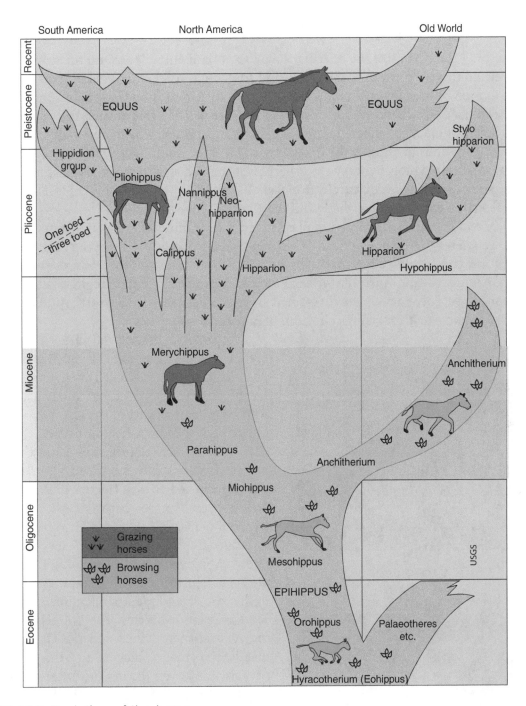

FIGURE 13.7 Evolution of the horse.

climate changed. Many plants in the grass family extract silica from the soil and form phytoliths inside their cells. This causes the teeth of grazing animals to wear down faster. Natural selection for durable grinding teeth, speed, with an increase in size and decrease in toes occurred. The descendants of *Eohippus* got bigger, faster, and ate tougher grasses. Living organisms resemble most recent fossils in the line of descent; underlying similarities allow us to trace a line of descent over time.

13.4.2   Biogeography: Separation and Divergence

Biogeography is the study of the distribution of plants and animals around the world. The process of related forms evolving in one locale and spreading to other accessible areas can explain the distribution of organisms. Darwin observed South America had no rabbits; he concluded rabbits originated elsewhere. Wallace also did extensive work in this area; in fact some consider him the father of modern biogeography. Biogeography explains why many finch species are on the Galápagos Islands but not on the mainland. In his book on human evolution, *The Descent of Man*, Darwin utilized biogeography along with the occurrence of the animals closest in anatomy to us, the apes, live today in Africa. He proposed that humans originated in Africa. Fossils verifying this assertion were not unearthed until the 1960s.

Physical factors, such as the location of continents, determine where a population can spread. Cacti are restricted to North American deserts and euphorbias grow in African deserts, yet some euphorbs are commonly called cacti (Figure 13.8). Marsupial mammals arose when South America, Antarctica, and Australia were all joined; Australia separated before placental mammals evolved, so only marsupials diversified in Australia. During the Tertiary period, South America was home to an amazing collection of marsupial mammals.

The geologic process of plate tectonics has played a significant role in the distribution of plant and animal species. This theory states the Earth's crust is composed of various plates (some with continents as part of the plate) that are moving at slow speeds (a few mm/year). During the latter part of the Paleozoic era, almost all of our planet's landmasses were joined in a supercontinent known as Pangaea (Figure 13.9). During the Mesozoic era Pangaea began to split into modern day continents.

Biogeographers recognize several regions known as biogeographical regions. These regions are separated from each by some sort of barrier. In the case of land plants and animals, oceans can serve as such a barrier. The boundary between the Australian province and the Oriental province is known as Wallace's line. This deep channel remained even during the lower sea levels of the past few million years of the Pleistocene ice ages. South of the line we find animals characteristic of Australia, north of it we find animals characteristic of Asia. In the New World, the Nearctic province in the north is separated from the Neotropical province in the south. This barrier existed until 5 million years ago when the Isthmus of Panama formed, allowing animals to

FIGURE 13.8 Cacti and euphorbs.

University of Wisconsin

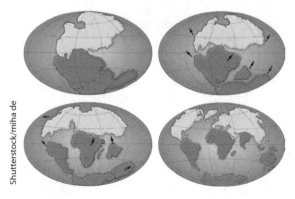

FIGURE 13.9 The breakup of Pangaea began during the Mesozoic era.

Shutterstock/miha de

migrate north and south. The formation of the isthmus closed a migratory route for organisms between the Atlantic and Pacific marine provinces.

13.4.3 Comparative Anatomy: Similarities Due to Common Ancestry

Organisms have anatomical similarities when they are closely related because of common descent, as substantiated by comparative anatomy. Homologous structures in different organisms are inherited from a common ancestor. Vertebrate forelimbs (Figure 13.10) contain the same sets of

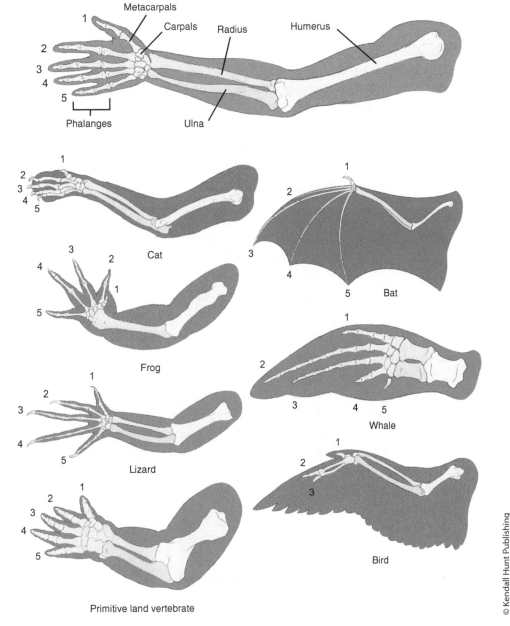

© Kendall Hunt Publishing

FIGURE 13.10 Homologous structures in selected vertebrate forelimbs.

bones organized in similar ways, despite their dissimilar functions. All of these animals belong to a subgroup of vertebrates known as tetrapods. Every tetrapod that retains its limbs has the same bones in the same order: one humerus connected to two lower limb bones, (the ulna and radius) followed by carpals, metacarpals, and phalanges. The forelimb of a human and a bird, for example, do not carry out the same function (carrying things as opposed to flight), yet they have the same basic bone structure sequence. The hypothesis that these bones are a shared feature reflecting a common ancestry explains the bone order.

13.4.4   Vestigial Structures

Vestigial structures are the remnants of a structure that was functional in some ancestor but is no longer functional in the organism in question. Most birds have well-developed wings, although some birds have reduced wings and do not fly (Figure 13.3E). Humans and chimpanzees have a tailbone (the coccyx) but no tail. The presence of vestigial structures is explained by the common descent hypothesis.

In the early 20th century, automobiles had to be started by a crank inserted in the front of the car. The driver would manually crank over the engine to get it to start. Does your car have such a crank that you use to start the engine? No, you turn a key that causes the starter motor to crank over the engine. The car designers removed the crank decades ago.

Evolution works by common ancestry, which means shared genes. The genes responsible for some bones have mutated to produce smaller bones, while other genes have undergone mutations to produce thicker bones, and so on. You and a bird share the genes to make your forelimbs. Since the common ancestry, hundreds of millions of years ago, mutations have changed those genes slightly as each lineage adapted to its mode of existence.

13.4.5   Embryology

Embryological development reveals a unity of body plan. During development, all vertebrates have a notochord and paired pharyngeal pouches (Figure 13.11). In fish and amphibian larvae, the pouches become gills. In humans, first pair of pouches becomes a cavity of middle ear and auditory tube; the second pair becomes tonsils, while third and fourth pairs become the thymus and parathyroid glands. This makes sense only if fish were ancestors of other vertebrate groups.

We often see similar embryological origins for diverse organs and structures. Again, this is consistent with shared ancestry and shared genes. Jaws were one of the great evolutionary novelties in vertebrate evolution. Development of jaws allowed early vertebrate groups to adapt to a predatory mode of nutrition as opposed to scavenging or filter feeding. The power of the jaw (and teeth embedded in the jaw) allowed the fish to crush through defensive shells.

13.4.6   Biochemistry: Differences and Similarities

Almost all living organisms use the same basic biochemical molecules, including DNA, ATP, and many identical or nearly identical enzymes. Organisms utilize the same DNA triplet base code

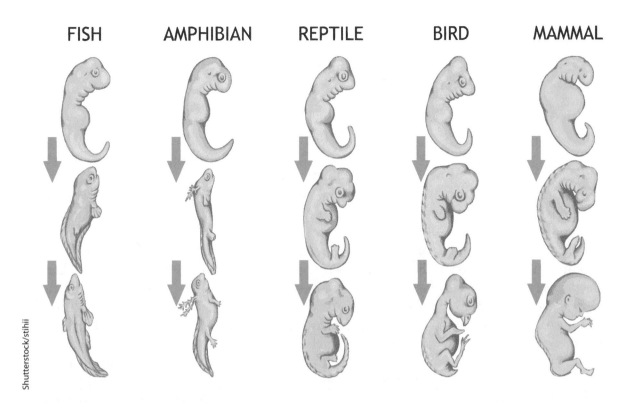

FIGURE 13.11 Embryological similarity between several different vertebrates.

and the same 20 amino acids to make their proteins. Many organisms share the same introns and types of repeat sequence DNA. We know of no obvious functional reason why these components need to be so similar unless they are inherited from a common ancestor. The process of glycolysis is common to all living things. Despite billions of years since common ancestry, many groups have nearly identical enzymes controlling glycolysis. The DNA polymerase from an organism in one domain works on the DNA of an organism from a different domain.

The biochemical similarity of life was not understood until the 20th century, long after Darwin made his case in *Origin of Species*. The mass of evidence supporting the common descent and ancestry of all life is compelling. There is no credible scientific idea in opposition.

13.5   The Modern Synthesis: Fusing Evolution and Genetics

Neither Darwin nor Wallace could explain how evolution occurred: how were these inheritable traits (variations) passed on to the next generation? Recall that Gregor Mendel had yet to publish his ideas about genetics. During the 20th century, genetics provided that answer and was linked to evolution in the Modern Synthesis. Scientists, such as German-born zoologist Ernst Mayr (1904–2005), in several fields of research began to seek a fusion of genetics and evolutionary biology.

13.5.1   Populations

Without variation (which arises from mutations of DNA molecules to produce new alleles) natural selection would have nothing on which to act. A population is a group of individuals living in the same geographical area and sharing a common gene pool. The gene pool is the sum of all genetic information carried by the members of a population.

All genetic variation in a population is generated by mutation. Mutation is any heritable change in an organism's DNA sequence. Mutations can be changes of a single nucleotide base or may involve changes in chromosome number. Whether a mutation is good, neutral, or harmful depends on how it affects survival and reproductive success.

There are several types of mutations, both at the gene-level and the chromosome-level. Gene mutations provide new alleles, making these mutations the ultimate source of variation. A gene mutation is an alteration in the DNA nucleotide sequence, producing an alternate sequence, termed an allele. Mutations occur at random, and can be beneficial, neutral, or harmful. Some chromosomal mutations are changes in the number of chromosomes inherited, while others are alterations in arrangement of alleles on chromosomes due to inversions and translocations.

In sexually reproducing organisms, genetic recombination is the reallocation of alleles and chromosomes. Recombination results from crossing-over during meiosis, the random segregation of chromosomes into gametes during meiotic division, and the random combination of gametes during fertilization. The entire genotype is subject to natural selection since new combinations of alleles may have improved the reproductive success of the organism. For polygenic traits, the most favorable combination may occur when the right alleles group by recombination.

Not only are new variations created by mutation, they are also preserved and passed on from one generation to the next. The gene pool is the total of all the alleles in a population, in the context of gene frequencies. Neither dominance nor sexual reproduction will change allele frequencies.

13.5.2   The Hardy–Weinberg Principle

Godfrey H, Hardy (1877–1947) was an English mathematician who developed a model to apply in the study of population genetics. Wilhelm Weinberg (1862–1937) was a German physician who independently developed the same model as Hardy. This principle states that an equilibrium of allele frequencies in a gene pool (using a formula $p^2 + 2pq + q^2 = 1$) remains in effect in each succeeding generation of a sexually reproducing population if five conditions are met (Table 13.1).

The conditions of the Hardy–Weinberg equilibrium are rarely met, so allele frequencies in the gene pool of a population more often than not do change from one generation to the next, resulting in evolution. We now consider that any change of allele frequencies in a gene pool indicates the occurrence of evolution within that population. The Hardy–Weinberg principle proposes those factors that violate the conditions listed in Table 13.1 cause evolution. Determination of allele frequencies provides a baseline by which to judge whether evolution has occurred. Hardy–Weinberg equilibrium is a constancy of gene pool frequencies that remains across generations, and might best be found among stable populations with no natural selection or where selection is stabilizing. Microevolution is the accumulation of small changes in a gene pool over a relatively short period.

TABLE 13.1 Conditions for a Hardy–Weinberg equilibrium

1	No mutation: no allelic changes occur.
2	No gene flow: migration of alleles into or out of the population does not occur.
3	Random mating: individuals pair by chance and not according to their genotypes or phenotypes.
4	No genetic drift: the population is large so changes in allele frequencies due to chance are insignificant.
5	No selection: no selective force favors one genotype over another.

13.5.3   Mutation Rate

Gene mutations result in the development of new alleles, and are the source of variation within populations. Mutations are ultimately behind the other mechanisms that provide variation. Due to DNA replication and DNA repair mechanisms, mutation rates of individual genes are low, but since each organism has many thousands of genes, and a population has many individuals, new mutations arise in populations all the time. Thus, mutations are relatively common, and the mutation rate is an adequate source of new alleles. High levels of molecular variation are common in natural populations, although many mutations (usually recessive) are hidden.

The mutation rate varies greatly among species and even among genes of an individual. Mutations are caused by errors in DNA replication, chemicals, or radiation. Large-scale effects of mutation result only when mutation is combined with other factors that reshuffle the gene pool.

Selection acts on individuals, not their individual genes. Sexual reproduction increases variation by reshuffling the genetic information from parents into new combinations in their offspring. Mutations produce new alleles.

13.5.4   Additional Sources of Variation

Gene flow moves alleles among populations through interbreeding as well as by migration of breeding individuals. This increases variation within a population by introducing new alleles produced in a different population. Continued gene flow tends to decrease the diversity between populations, causing gene pools of those populations to become increasingly similar. Reduction or restriction of gene flow between populations is essential for the development of new species, the process known as speciation.

The frequency of alleles can change from generation to generation as a result of chance alone in a small gene pool. This phenomenon is known as genetic drift.

Random mating involves individuals pairing by chance, not according to their genotypes or phenotypes. Nonrandom mating involves individuals inbreeding and assortative mating. Inbreeding is mating between relatives to a greater extent than by chance. This occurs if dispersal of offspring is so low that mates are likely to be related and does not change allele frequencies, but it does decrease the proportion of heterozygotes and increase the proportions of both homozygotes at all gene loci. Rare recessives (at least in the general population) will become more common in a population with continued inbreeding.

Assortative mating occurs when individuals tend to mate with those that have the same phenotype. An example of this is blonde people only mating with blond people. Assortative mating divides a population into two phenotypic classes with reduced gene exchange between each class.

Genetic drift is the changes in allele frequencies of a gene pool due to chance or random events. This can occur in large or small populations. Genetic drift causes gene pools of two isolated populations to become less similar as some alleles are lost and other are fixed within the population.

Genetic drift occurs when founders (or colonizers) establish a new population, or after a genetic bottleneck and resultant interbreeding. The founder effect is a case of genetic drift in which rare alleles, or combinations of alleles, occur in higher frequency in a smaller population isolated from the general population. Founding individuals contain a fraction of the total genetic diversity of original gene pool. The alleles carried by founders are determined by chance alone. Consider the Pilgrim colonists in New England. By no means did they represent all the genetic variation of the human species or even genetic variations among Europeans.

When a population descends from one or a few individuals randomly separated from a larger population, chance may dictate that allele frequencies in the new population may be very different from those of the original population. Many species on islands (such as Darwin's finches on the Galápagos, Figure 13.12) display founder effects. The Galápagos Islands are volcanic islands off the coast of South America. The island species vary from the mainland species, and from island-to-island. Each island had a variation of tortoise that correlated with different vegetation and environmental conditions on that island. Many of the animals and plants occurring here occur nowhere else in the world.

Finches on the Galápagos Islands resembled a mainland finch. However, more types of finches occurred on the islands (Figure 13.12). Darwin noted the Galápagos finches in his journals, and made a small collection of them. He also prepared specimens collected by other crewmembers. The significance of these finches became more apparent to him after his return to England. Darwin noted that species varied by nesting site, beak size, and eating habits. One unusual finch used a twig or thorn to pry out insects, a job normally done by a woodpecker. The finches posed questions to Darwin: did they descend from one mainland ancestor, did islands allow isolated populations to evolve independently, and could present-day species have resulted from changes occurring in each isolated population?

Modern genetic studies confirm that all Galápagos finches descended from a recent common ancestor. This supports the hypothesis of a group of ancestral finches blown off the mainland by a storm had managed to reach the islands. The Galápagos Islands were too far from the South American mainland for the birds to manage a flight back. The lack of predators on the islands (cats are not found, save those that have escaped domestication) and the open roles in the environment allowed the finch descendants to undergo an adaptive radiation as some adapted the eating large seeds on the ground while others occupied different roles.

FIGURE 13.12 Examples of finches from the Galápagos Islands. A. A finch from one of the islands; B. Cactus finch; C. Large Ground-Finch (*Geospiza magnirostris*), male on Santa Cruz Island; D. Male of Small Ground-Finch (*Geospiza fuliginosa*) on Floreana Island.

Drastic short-term reductions of population size caused by natural disasters, disease, or predators may result in (by chance) the survivors representing only a small portion of the original gene pool. Even when the population increases to its original size, a portion of its original genetic diversity remains lost. This situation, termed a bottleneck, is a problem with many endangered species. The bottleneck effect prevents most genotypes from participating in production of next generation.

A bottleneck is genetic drift in which a severe reduction in population size results from natural disaster, predation, or habitat reduction. This results in a severe reduction of the total genetic diversity of the original gene pool.

Imagine that you have a bowl full of different colored beads. These beads represent genes, and the bowl represents the population. We start with a population that is 40% red and 60% yellow beads. If we have an extreme selection where red beads are removed preferentially from the population, the allele frequency of red in succeeding populations declines. Over multiple generations of this selection against the red beads, their frequency in the

Shutterstock/Joe West

FIGURE 13.13 The Hawaiian silversword, a plant recently passing through a genetic bottleneck. Sunset on top of the Haleakalā Crater on the island of Maui, Hawaii.

population continues to decline. Descendant populations become increasingly dominated by yellow. When selection against the red beads declines, the populations will continue to be yellow-dominated for many generations.

The Haleakalā silversword, *Argyroxiphium sandwicense* subsp. *macrocephalum*, is a plant that (Figure 13.13) has recently passed through its own bottleneck. The plant is endemic to Maui, one of the Hawaiian Islands where it grows on the slopes of an extinct volcanic crater, Haleakalā. People used to pick up and take the plants as a souvenir. When goats were introduced to the area the population of silverswords plummeted since the goats ate the tough leaves of the plant. When goats were removed from the park, the silversword population rebounded. However, while their numbers increased, the genetic diversity among silversword populations has not. That will take time and future mutations to reestablish genetic diversity.

The bottleneck in the cheetah causes relative infertility due to intense inbreeding. Cheetahs passed through a genetic bottleneck event perhaps as recently as 10,000 years ago. The small numbers of survivors interbred, further reducing the population's genetic variation.

Recent studies on humans suggest that there may have been victims of a severe genetic bottleneck while modern humans were confined to Africa. The eruption of the Indonesian super-volcano Toba around 70,000 years ago is proposed as the cause of environmental degradation and human population decline in Africa. Other African animals species were also affected by the crisis, including cheetahs, chimpanzees, and gorillas. Studies suggest the human population fell as low as 10,000. Geneticists have long known that despite the outward obvious differences between groups of humans that our genetic variation is not terribly great. A bottleneck accounts for this lack of variation.

Migration into or out of a population can break down genetic differences between populations be introducing new genes into that population's gene pool. Mutations developing in one population may be spread to other populations by migration. This serves, like mutation, to introduce new alleles into populations. How common these genes become in the new population depends on a number of factors such as mating success, adaptation, and in some cases chance.

13.6   Natural Selection

Not all members of a population get an equal chance of surviving and reproducing due to competition for resources and mates. By virtue of small phenotypic variations, some individuals are just better adapted to their environment. The better adapted individuals are more "fit" and tend to survive and reproduce, passing on their adaptations to the next generation in greater frequency than those adaptations of the less "fit" members of the population.

Fitness is a measure of an individual's ability to survive and reproduce. Those with the highest fitness are more likely to survive and reproduce. Thus, they make a greater contribution to the gene pool, of the next generation than do those less "fit."

Natural selection is the process of differential survival and reproduction that inevitably leads to changes in allele frequencies over time. Those individuals who most fit survive and pass their genes to more offspring than less fit individuals. There are three patterns, or types, of natural selection. If we look at variation for a specific trait within a population, we can often represent this as a bell-shaped curve, with an average value and extremes.

13.6.1   Stabilizing Selection

Stabilizing selection (Figure 13.14A) favors the intermediate phenotype out of a range of phenotypes. The extremes in variation are selected against.

An example of stabilizing selection is seen in human birth weights. Infants who weigh significantly more or less than 7.5 pounds have higher rates of infant mortality than those closer to 7.5 pounds. Selection works against both extremes. The smaller infants are often premature and might therefore have a higher mortality rate. Larger babies have a different set of issues, but a higher mortality rate.

Living fossils (Figure 13.14B–F), like the coelacanth (*Latimeria*), ginkgo, and horseshoe crab, are examples of organisms that are relatively unchanged from their distant ancestors. Stabilizing selection, which selects for the average and against the extremes in variation, accounts for the millions of years of unchanging morphology.

13.6.2   Directional Selection

Directional selection (Figure 13.15A) tends to favor phenotypes at one extreme of the range of variation. Over time continued selection pushes the population in a direction, for example larger size, or change in color. Eventually the entire population may be shifted away from the range of variation expressed in the original population.

Insecticide resistance is an example of directional selection. The insecticide DDT was a widely used during the 1960s and 1970s. Within the population on insects were a few rare individuals possessing a gene that allowed them to resist the effects of DDT. When DDT was absent from the environment, this gene conferred to advantage. However, after a few years of extensive use, DDT began to lose its effectiveness on insects. The gene for resistance became favored and only those insects having the resistance gene survived to produce succeeding generations. Resistance to DDT is a genetic trait that the presence of DDT in the environment made into a favored trait. Only those insects resistant to DDT survived, leading over time to populations largely resistant to DDT.

The resistance of many bacterial species to antibiotics is another example of directional selection. Over 200 species show some degree of antibiotic resistance, necessitating the development

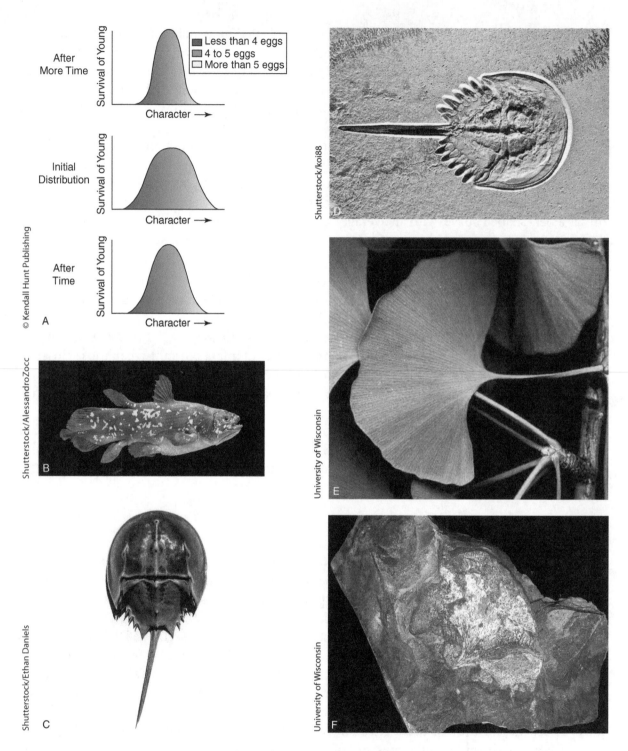

FIGURE 13.14 Stabilizing selection. A. Selection against the extremes in variation leads to maintaining the average value over time; B. Coelacanth, *Latimeria*; C. Living Atlantic horseshoe crab, *Limulus polyphemus*; D. Fossil horseshoe crab; E. Living *Ginkgo biloba* leaf; F. Paleocene fossil *Ginkgo* leaf.

and more prudent use of a new generation of antibiotic medicines. Antibiotic resistance genes occurred naturally among bacteria but were not common. During the 1950s and 1960s, the antibiotic penicillin was over-prescribed by doctors. This established the conditions favoring bacteria that happened to have the resistance genes.

The peppered moth, *Biston betularia*, is a small insect that inhabits forests in England (and elsewhere). Before the Industrial Revolution in the 19th and 20th centuries, light-colored moths (Figure 13.15B, C) were most commonly collected. There was a rare form of the moth, a dark-colored form (Figure 13.15D). The pollution associated with industrialization colored the light-colored woodland trees darker. The once rare dark-colored moths became more prevalent, while the once common light-colored moths became increasingly rare.

Between 1952 and 1972, the British scientist Bernard Kettlewell (1907–1979) conducted a series of experiments on the different forms of the moth. The agents of natural selection were the birds that preyed on the moths. The better the prey (moths) blended into the background the less likely they were to be eaten. Over several generations, the color of the moth population became increasing like the background of the trees in their environment. The case of the peppered moth is a classic example of natural selection in action.

13.6.3   Disruptive Selection

Disruptive selection (Figure 13.16) favors individuals at both extremes of variation: selection is against the middle of the curve. This causes a discontinuity of the variations, causing two or more morphs or distinct phenotypes. The African swallowtail butterfly (*Papilio dardanus*) produces two distinct morphs, both of which resemble brightly colored but distasteful butterflies of other species. Each morph gains protection from predation although it is in fact quite edible.

13.7   Speciation

As populations diverge, they form similar but related species. The process of forming a new species from an existing one is known as speciation. When do two populations become two separate species? The answer is when populations no longer interbreed, so we think of them as now belonging to separate species. As natural selection adapts populations occupying different environments, they will diverge into races, subspecies, and finally separate species.

A species can be defined as one or more populations of interbreeding organisms that are reproductively isolated in nature from all other organisms. Genetic divergence results when adaptation, drift, and mutation act on populations. Barriers to gene flow between populations isolate those populations, ultimately leading to the formation of new and separate species.

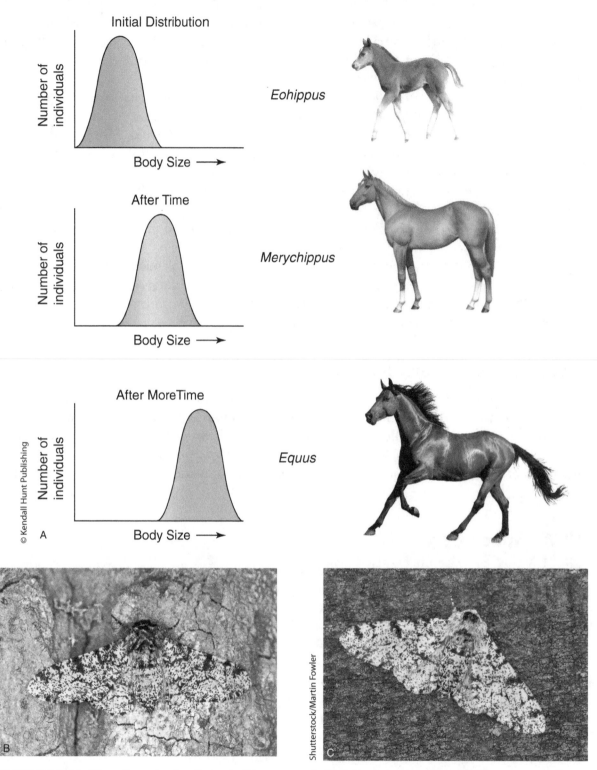

FIGURE 13.15 Directional selection. A. Diagram of directional selection altering populations over some passage of time; B. Light-colored-peppered moth (*Biston betularia*) on a light-colored background; C. Light-colored moth on a dark background; D. Dark-colored moth.

(Continued)

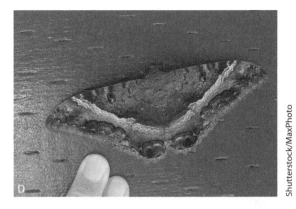

FIGURE 13.15 (*Continued*)

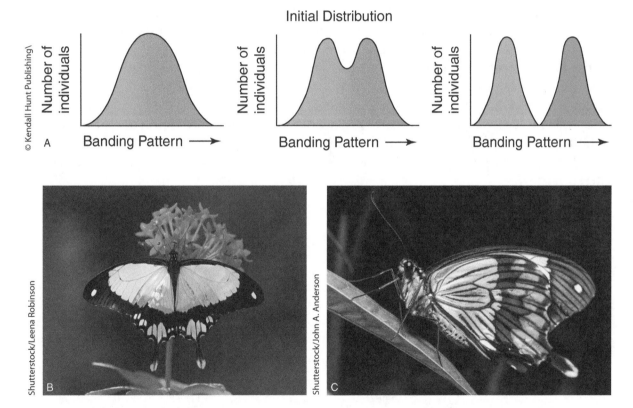

Initial Distribution

FIGURE 13.16 Disruptive selection. A. Graph illustrating disruptive selection; B. African swallowtail butterfly (*Papilio dardanus*); C. Different form of *P. dardanus* butterfly.

13.7.1 Allopatric Speciation

Populations begin to diverge when gene flow between them is restricted. Geographic isolation is often the first step in allopatric speciation (Figure 13.7). This method depends on some barrier restricting or cutting off gene flow between populations of the same species. Examples of barriers include rivers, deserts, mountain ranges, and oceans. Since the geographic barrier separates the two populations, new mutations will develop within each population. The lack of gene flow keeps these new genes within their own population. Eventually the barrier is removed and the populations can now interbreed. If enough time and genetic divergence has occurred that the individuals of the two populations cannot interbreed and produce viable, fertile, offspring, then two new species have formed.

An example of allopatric speciation is thought to have occurred in Africa between 1.5 and 1 million years ago. The formation of the Congo River is thought to have acted as a geographic barrier separating early chimpanzee populations. These animals are not reported to be strong swimmers, so the river eventually would have become a geographic barrier. Today, the bonobo (*Pan paniscus*) lives south of the river, and the related species known as the common chimpanzee (*Pan troglodytes*) lives on the other side.

Speciation can occasionally be viewed in action. Case in point is the speciation occurring among populations of mountain salamanders (*Ensatina eschscholtzii*) in California (Figure 13.18). This amphibian lives in the Coast Range and Sierra mountains of California. The species in California is divided into several subspecies populations. Adults do not typically migrate far from where they are born. On the edges of each population, some gene flow and hybridization occurs. While some gene flow occurs, it is quite a small amount. Consequently, neighboring populations can successfully interbreed, but populations further from each other produce infertile hybrids. These salamanders are today restricted to the mountain areas that are wetter. In the geologic past when climates were cooler and wetter in California's central valley, the valley did not act as a barrier to reproduction or migration.

Other mechanisms than geographic separation may develop that further restrict reproduction/gene flow between populations. These are the reproductive isolating mechanisms discussed later.

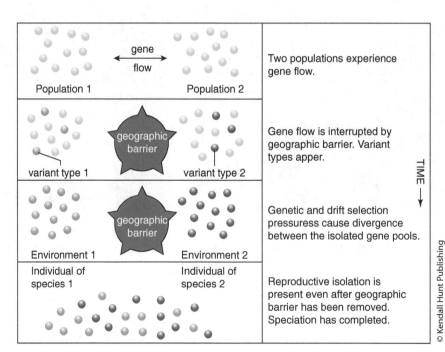

FIGURE 13.17 Allopatric speciation.

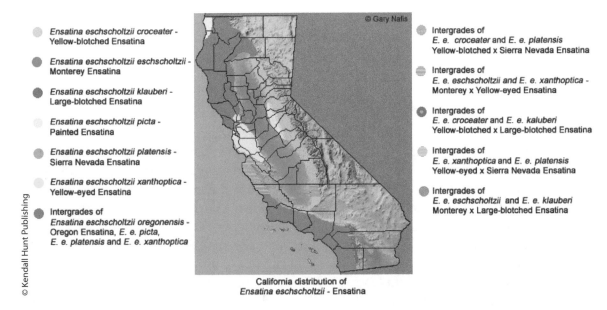

Ensatina eschscholtzii croceater -
Yellow-blotched Ensatina

Ensatina eschscholtzii eschscholtzii -
Monterey Ensatina

Ensatina eschscholtzii klauberi -
Large-blotched Ensatina

Ensatina eschscholtzii picta -
Painted Ensatina

Ensatina eschscholtzii platensis -
Sierra Nevada Ensatina

Ensatina eschscholtzii xanthoptica -
Yellow-eyed Ensatina

Intergrades of
Ensatina eschscholtzii oregonensis -
Oregon Ensatina, E. e. picta,
E. e. platensis and E. e. xanthoptica

Intergrades of
E. e. croceater and E. e. platensis
Yellow-blotched x Sierra Nevada Ensatina

Intergrades of
E. e. eschscholtzii and E. e. xanthoptica -
Monterey x Yellow-eyed Ensatina

Intergrades of
E. e. croceater and E. e. kaluberi
Yellow-blotched x Large-blotched Ensatina

Intergrades of
E. e. xanthoptica and E. e. platensis
Yellow-eyed x Sierra Nevada Ensatina

Intergrades of
E. e. eschscholtzii and E. e. klauberi
Monterey x Large-blotched Ensatina

© Kendall Hunt Publishing

California distribution of
Ensatina eschscholtzii - Ensatina

FIGURE 13.18 Distribution of populations of the salamander *Ensatina eschscholtzii* in California mountain chains.

13.7.2   Sympatric Speciation

Sympatric speciation (Figure 13.19) occurs when members of a population develop some genetic difference that prevents them from reproducing with the parent type. This mechanism is best understood in plants, where failure to reduce chromosome number results in polyploid plants that reproduce successfully only with other polyploid plants. Reproduction with their parent population (the diploids) produces sterile offspring.

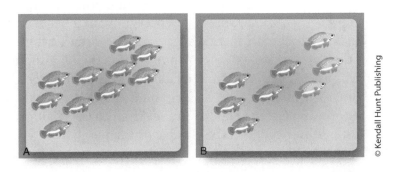

© Kendall Hunt Publishing

FIGURE 13.19 Sympatric speciation. A. Before isolating mechanism. B. After new species has developed.

13.8   Reproductive Isolating Mechanisms

A key feature of speciation is the establishment of reproductive isolation between the two populations. There are numerous ways this can be accomplished. Some of them are among the most interesting aspects of biology. A reproductive isolating mechanism is a structural, functional, or behavioral characteristic that prevents successful reproduction from occurring. These mechanisms divide into premating and postmating types.

13.8.1   Premating Mechanisms

Premating isolating mechanisms are anatomical or behavioral differences between two populations that prevent the possibility of mating. This lack of mating means there is no gene flow between the populations. New mutations will develop within each population and be unique to each population.

Geographic isolation occurs when two populations occupy different areas. Individuals of these two populations are less likely to meet and attempt to reproduce. An example of this is the isolation of tree squirrels in the Grand Canyon National Park. Geologists estimate that 5 million years ago the canyon did not exist. The Colorado River would eventually carve out the canyon. The north rim of the canyon is over 1,000 feet higher than the south rim due to movement of the north rim along faults. Before the canyon formed there were two populations of Abert's squirrels (*Sciurus aberti*), one on each side of the river. Occasionally squirrels could cross the river and mate, maintain the gene flow needed to keep the two populations part of the same species. The Kaibab squirrel is a subspecies (*S. a. kaibabensis*) of Abert's squirrel. Today it occurs only among Ponderosa pines on the Kaibab Plateau on the north rim of the canyon. Scientists suspect that during cooler climates of the geologic past the populations were closer together. Gene flow was occasionally possible. With the warming of the planet, the Ponderosa pines could only grow on higher elevations further from the river. This effectively separated the two populations in space (Figure 13.20).

Temporal isolation occurs when two species live in the same location, but each reproduces at a different time of the year, preventing a successful mating. Examples include the American toad (*Anaxyrus americanus*) and Fowler's toad (*Anaxyrus fowleri*) shown in Figure 13.21. The American toad reproduces during the early summer months. Fowler's toad has a reproductive season later in the summer. Both toad species occur in similar environments in the eastern United States, but do not hybridize in nature due to different mating seasons.

Behavioral isolation occurs when there are differences in mating behavior between two species. Many animal species have elaborate mating behaviors. These can serve as very effective isolating mechanisms as they involve sexual selection of mates. The blue-footed boobies (Figure 13.22A) of the Galápagos Islands perform a mating dance. If the male succeeds in his dance, the female will mate with him. The male displays his large blue feet for the female. The mating dance is a complex set of behaviors. Blue-footed boobies range from coastal California to Peru and the Galápagos Islands. Most nesting occurs on the Galápagos Islands.

The bowerbirds (Figure 13.22B, C) are a group of birds ranging from Australia to New Guinea. These birds display a complex series of mating behaviors that involve the nest built by males to attract a female. Not all bowerbirds build bower nests, but among those that do, male bowerbirds build one of two type of nests. One style of nests is a series of objects piled around a central sapling. The other is the building of two walls that form a bower. Males decorate the nest with objects of species-specific colors. The satin bowerbird decorates his nest with blue objects. The MacGregor's bowerbird builds a different nest style and decorates with pieces of charcoal. The female inspects multiple nests before wandering into the nest of her chosen male. The male then copulates with her.

FIGURE 13.20 Grand Canyon squirrels. A. Abert's squirrel (*Sciurus aberti*) occurs in many areas including the warmer south rim.

FIGURE 13.21 American and Fowler's toads overlap geographically but are isolated from each other by differing mating seasons. A. American toad (*Anaxyrus americanus*) B. Fowler's toad (*Anaxyrus fowleri*).

Mechanical isolation is the result of differences between two species in reproductive structures or other body parts, so that mating is prevented. Flowering plants utilize the process of pollination in their sexual reproduction. A pollinating agent such as insects, birds, or wind transfers pollen from one flower to the surface of the stigma of another flower. Pollen germinates and produces a pollen tube through which sperm cells travel to reach the egg cell. In many flower species, the length of a pollen tube is genetically determined. Species with a shot pollen tube will be reproductively isolated from species with a long style in their flowers even though both types of pollen are on the stigmatic surface of the same flower. In many animal species, the reproductive organs do not match, preventing successful copulation.

13.8.2 Postmating Mechanisms

Individuals of two species relatively recently diverged from a common ancestor may still mate with each other. If the reproductive isolating mechanisms are strong enough, there will be no

FIGURE 13.22 Reproductive isolation due to behavior. A. Two Blue-footed boobies in the Galápagos Islands performing a mating dance; B. Male satin bowerbird at his nest; C. Bower of the satin bowerbird surrounded with blue objects, Australia.

gene exchange even with successful mating activity. Postmating isolating mechanisms are the result of developmental or physiological differences between the members of two species after mating.

Gamete isolation is the physical or chemical incompatibility of gametes of two different species. If the gametes lack receptors to facilitate fusion, they cannot form a zygote. An egg may have receptors only for the sperm of its own species. Coral of different species often release their gametes at the same time. Some hybridization between species does occur, but not as much as would be expected.

Zygote mortality is a mechanism that works when hybrids (offspring of parents of two different species) do not live to reproduce. In many flowering plant species, hybrid embryos lose their nutritive endosperm and do not have the stored energy to develop.

Hybrid sterility occurs when the hybrid offspring (Figure 13.23) is sterile (e.g., mules). The hybrid itself is viable, but chromosomal or other problems reduce or eliminate the fertility of the hybrid. Plant hybrids are quite common. Reduced fertility does not seem to affect plant hybrids since many plants can reproduce sexually with themselves or through vegetative propagation. An example of this hybridization that is becoming important in many states is the blending of *Cannabis sativa* and *Cannabis indica* to produce a shorter plant that could be grown (illegally in most states) indoors.

FIGURE 13.23 Hybrid sterility. A. Mules climbing up with goods in Grand Canyon National Park in Arizona, USA; B. Full body view of a zonkey which is a cross between a donkey and a zebra, seen in Colombia; C. Large leopard jaguar hybrid.

13.8.3   Polyploidy and Hybridization

Polyploidy and hybridization are important speciation mechanisms in plants. Whereas animals tend to be unisexual, plants often have both sexes functional in the same individual. Consequently, plants can (if they lack a self-incompatibility mechanism) reproduce with themselves (both sexually and asexually), establishing a reproductively isolated species very rapidly.

Wheat has undergone millennia of modification from the diploid wild wheat. Some types of wheat are tetraploid and have four sets of chromosomes. This form of wheat is known as durum or macaroni wheat. Bread wheat (*Triticum aestivum*, Figure 13.24A) is hexaploid with six sets of chromosomes derived from three parental species of wheat. Polyploid plants often produce larger fruits.

Many agriculturally important plants of the genus *Brassica* are also tetraploids. Polyploidy is a mechanism of sympatric speciation because polyploids are usually unable to interbreed with their diploid ancestors. Strawberry plants (Figure 13.24B) are octaploid. The larger strawberries are not as flavorful as smaller wild ones, but who doesn't like a really big chocolate dipped strawberry? Watermelons (Figure 13.24C) are a triploid plant whose ancestors originated in Africa.

FIGURE 13.24 Some polyploid plants. A. Bread wheat (*Triticum aestivum*); B. Strawberry (*Fragaria*) is a hybrid octoploid plant; C. Watermelon (*Citrullus lanatus* var. *lanatus*) is a triploid plant having three sets of chromosomes.

13.9   The Pace of Evolution

We are an impatient species. Things have to happen right now! Our sense of time is very short. Processes that might take hundreds or thousands of years are almost unfathomable to most people. Science tells us the Earth is unfathomably old, 4.5 billion years. Processes that seem slow by human scale terms are relatively quick when viewed on a geological or deep time scale. Some bacteria can divide up to five times in an hour. That would be 48,300 bacterial generations in a single year. Life has been on Earth at least 3.45 billion years, or 166,635,000,000,000 bacterial generations!

13.9.1   Phyletic Gradualism

The pace of evolution is often slow, so slow that all of the stages in species formation are difficult to observe in a human timeframe. The traditional Darwinian view of evolution was that it was a very slow process, resulting from the gradual accumulation of small differences (Figure 13.25A). We call this process phyletic gradualism. In cases of gradualism, the fossil record shows a gradual change of one species into its descendant species. The sudden appearance of new species can be explained by the incomplete fossil record.

13.9.2   Punctuated Equilibrium

In 1972, American paleontologists Niles Eldredge (b. 1943) and Stephen Jay Gould (1941–2002) proposed a different mode of evolution. According to the fossil record punctuated equilibrium (Figure 13.25B) occurs rapidly over a short time in a peripherally isolated population (punctuation), followed by a long period of little or no change (equilibrium). "Short" means thousands or hundreds of thousands of years. This differs greatly from Darwin's original view of slow and gradual change continuing over very long periods of time. Because the speciation involves a small, isolated population the chance of finding missing link common ancestors is quite small.

Punctuated equilibrium model of evolution explains one of the great problems with the theory: the apparent lack of interconnecting fossil forms Darwin believed a complete fossil record would reveal. This model explains the apparent gaps in the fossil record.

13.10   Biological Diversity and Classification

Taxonomy is that branch of biology dealing with the identification and naming of organisms. The ancient Greek philosopher Aristotle (364-322 BCE) began the discussion on taxonomy with his *Scala Naturae* (Ladder of Life). Aristotle also began the classification of living things. British naturalist and clergyman John Ray (1627–1705) revised the concept of naming and describing organisms and classified plants based on similarities and differences based on observation. During the 1700s, Swedish botanist Carolus Linnaeus classified all then-known organisms into two large groups: the kingdoms Plantae and Animalia. American plant ecologist Robert Whittaker (1920–1980) first proposed in 1969 the five kingdoms classification: Plantae, Animalia, Fungi, Protista, and Monera. American microbiologist Carl Woese (1928–2012) in 1990 proposed three domains be employed: Archaea, Bacteria, and Eukarya. Most biologists today employ the three-domain system (Figure 13.26).

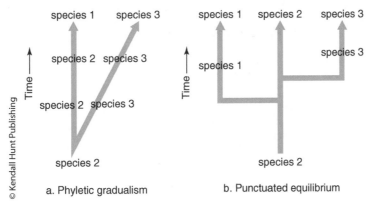

FIGURE 13.25 Modes of evolution. A. Phyletic gradualism; B. Punctuated equilibrium.

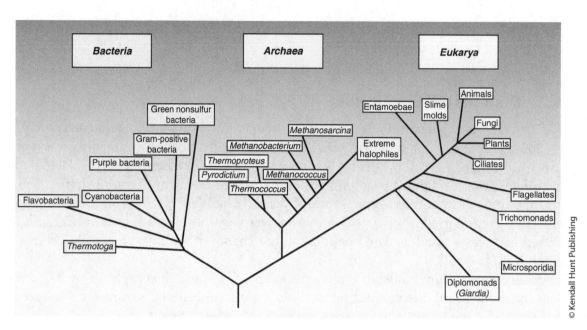

FIGURE 13.26 The three-domain classification system.

Linnaeus attempted to pigeonhole (or classify) all known species of his time (1753). Linnaean hierarchical classification was based on the premise that the species was the smallest unit, and that each species (or taxon) nested within a higher category (Table 13.2).

Linnaeus also developed the concept of binomial nomenclature, allowing scientists speaking and writing different languages to communicate in a clear and unambiguous manner. For example, Man in English is *Hombre* in Spanish, *Herr* in German, *Ren* in Chinese, and *Homo* in Latin. He settled on Latin, which was the language of learned men at that time. If a scientist refers today to the genus *Homo*, all scientists know what organism/taxon he or she means.

TABLE 13.2 Classification of some organisms.

Category	Humans	Bonobo chimpanzee	Corn	E. coli
Domain	Eukarya	Eukarya	Eukarya	Bacteria
Kingdom	Animalia	Animalia	Plantae	Eubacteria
Phylum	Chordata	Chordata	Magnoliophyta	Proteobacteria
Class	Mammalia	Mammalia	Liliopsida	Gammaproteobacteria
Order	Primates	Primates	Poales	Enterobacteriales
Family	Hominidae	Pongidae	Poaceae	Enterobacteriaceae
Genus	Homo	Pan	Zea	Escherichia
Species	Sapiens	paniscus	Mays	Coli

13.10.1   Construction of Phylogenetic Trees

Taxonomy is part of a larger division of biology known as systematics. Determination of phylogeny is the goal of systematics. Scientists construct phylogenetic trees that represent evolutionary hypotheses and attempts to define monophyletic groups. Sometimes taxa are polyphyletic, a situation where not all organisms in a taxon share a common ancestor. To build these trees, we must have data, which comes from the characteristics used in classification. There are several methods of classification: traditional and cladistic. They differ in how they value certain characters. Consider how traditional classification treats reptiles, birds, and mammals, as shown in Figure 13.27. The group of organisms is known as the amniota, after structures in their eggs. All amniotes possess these features. Traditionally systematists separated reptiles into one group characterized by scaly skin, birds by feathers, and mammals by hair. Dinosaurs are classified with reptiles. Recent discoveries of feathered, nonflying dinosaurs raise doubt about this classification.

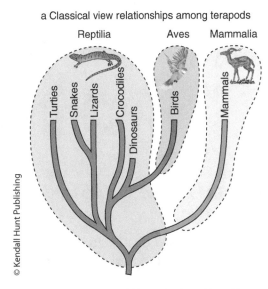

FIGURE 13.27 Traditional classification of reptiles, birds, and mammals.

13.10.2   Traditional Classification

Data used in traditional systematics stresses both common ancestry (monophylesis) and the amount of divergence among groups. The traditional view, dating to Linnaeus, is that birds have feathers, reptiles have scales, and mammals have hair. Using this as a major character, a classification like that in Figure 13.27 has been constructed. Fossils are not included in this classification. Since all of these groups have the amniotic egg, or a modification of it, they would be united in a larger taxon. Linnaeus placed each of these groups in a separate taxonomic class within the Phylum Chordata. A primitive (or ancestral) character is one present in the common ancestor and all members of the group, such as the amniotic egg for all amniotes. A derived character is one found only in a particular lineage within the larger group. In the amniotes, hair and feathers may be viewed as derived characters. A traditional view of our example group is that birds and mammals evolved from reptiles due to their unique derived characters.

13.10.3   Cladistics and Cladograms

Cladistics is a type of systematics developed by German biologist Willi Hennig (1913–1976), who attempted to formulate a more objective method of classifying organisms. Cladists group organisms based on the presence of shared derived characters, not the overall similarity of potential group members. In the example cited above, the amniotic egg would be used to unite a group sharing common ancestry, since it would NOT be present in a group that was not in the lineage. The use of feathers and hair to separate birds and mammals from reptiles would NOT factor into a cladistic hypothesis, or cladogram, since these are characters unique to only one taxon in our group. Such an approach is shown in Figure 13.28.

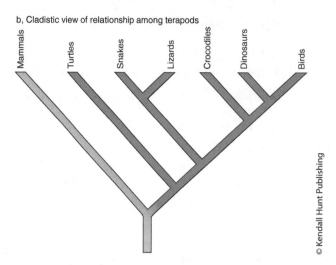

b, Cladistic view of relationship among terapods

Mammals Turtles Snakes Lizards Crocodiles Dinosaurs Birds

© Kendall Hunt Publishing

FIGURE 13.28 Cladogram of reptiles, birds, and mammals.

The value of cladistics to the study of systematics lies in its capacity to generate (and provide a set of criteria for the evaluation) of multiple hypotheses (alternate cladograms) that can be evaluated with additional data. Almost always the "correct" cladogram employs the principle of parsimony, which proposes that the shortest number of steps or character state changes is most likely correct. An important question: is evolution always parsimonious? However the ultimate answer to that question unfolds, the rigor cladistics introduces to systematics is useful in getting traditional systematists to look at their subjective classifications in a new light.

On the diagram shown in Figure 13.29, shared derived characters are indicated across the lines of descent. The mammal clade (in this case represented by mouse and chimpanzee) is united by fur, the lizard, pigeon, mouse-chimp clade is united by claws or nails, and so on. The presence of hair is a shared derived characteristic.

If the group in Figure 13.27 is treated cladistically, we see a very different classification! Note that crocodiles have more in common (in a cladistic sense) with birds than they do with other traditional reptiles. Remember that the traditional classification had anything with scales and an amniotic egg grouped with the reptiles. Birds and crocodiles form a clade, or monophyletic group united by shared derived characters not present in the other groups. If we construct a Linnaean group from this cladogram, we have a class of birds and crocodiles, a second class of lizards, snakes, and turtles, and a third class of mammals.

One of the more interesting applications of cladistics is to the question of the pandas. The giant panda was once thought to be a bear, but later its raccoon-like characters caused it to be placed closer to raccoons. The red (lesser) panda lives in the same areas of China as the giant panda, but has a far greater similarity with raccoons. DNA hybridization studies indicate the giant panda is in the bear clade, while the red panda is in the raccoon clade. Both share a common ancestry, as indicated by shared derived characters, followed by convergent evolution of other characters. Cladistic analysis makes a wonderful tool to spot convergence of characters. Traditional classifications are plagued by convergence and parallelism.

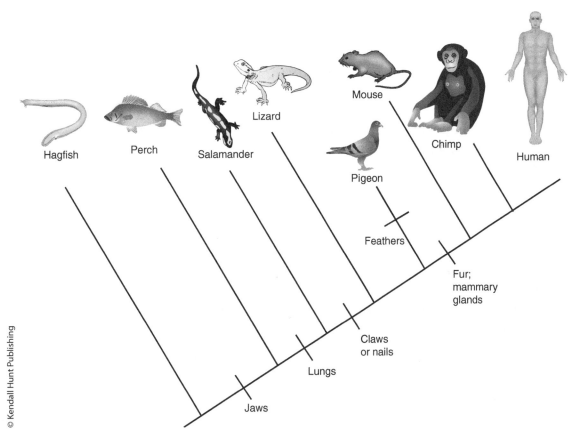

FIGURE 13.29 Cladogram of the vertebrate chordates.

13.10.4   Nomenclature

The naming of species and other taxa follows a set of rules, the International Code of Botanical Nomenclature (ICBN) for plants or the International Code of Zoological Nomenclature (ICZN) for animals. Some general rules for nomenclature:

1. All taxa must belong to a higher taxonomic group. Often a newly discovered organism is the sole species in a single genus, within a single family ... and so on.
2. The first name to be validly and effectively published has priority. This rule has caused numerous name changes, especially with fossil organisms: *Brontosaurus* is invalid, and the correct name for the big sauropod dinosaur is *Apatosaurus*. *Eohippus* (the tiny "dawn horse") was for many years considered to be an invalid name, with *Hyracotherium* having priority. Sometime, however, names can be conserved if a group of systematists agrees.
3. All taxa must have an author. When you see a scientific name such as *Homo sapiens* L, the L stands for Linnaeus, who first described and named that organism. Most scientists must have their names spelled out, for example, *Libopollis* Farabee et al. (an interesting fossil pollen type I stumbled across during my Master's degree work).

The case of *Eohippus* is an interesting one that illustrates how the rules of nomenclature are applied. The name *Eohippus* was applied to a small animal thought to be the ancestor of all horses. A similar animal, *Hyracotherium*, had been validly published earlier. Paleontologists incorrectly placed *Eohippus* as a junior synonym of *Hyracotherium*. Cladistic analysis of the species of *Hyracotherium* revealed that not all species were ancestral to horses (some are ancestral to both horse and rhinos, some to extinct mammal groups). The name *Eohippus* was revalidated for the single species that is ancestral to horses alone. Welcome back to *Eohippus*, the horse of the dawn, one of the coolest names ever bestowed upon a fossil.

Summary

It has been said that nothing makes sense in biology if not viewed through the lens of how does this help an organism survive and reproduce. Evolution by natural selection has adapted living things to their mode of existence. Understanding evolution is not just an academic exercise. Antibiotic and insecticide resistance are explainable from an evolutionary perspective. The unity and diversity of life makes sense when viewed from an evolutionary perspective. Dangers of genetically modified organisms can be seen evolutionarily. The mass extinction of organisms … well you get it. Evolution is at the root of biology.

Terms

absolute time
adaptation
adaptive radiation
alleles
allopatric speciation
alpha decay
amino acids
amniotic egg
archean eon
beta decay
biogeography
binomial nomenclature
bottleneck
catastrophism
convergent evolution
coprolites
directional selection
disruptive selection
endemic
endosperm
enzymes

eons
eras
evolution
extinct
fertilization
fossil record
fossils
founder effect
genetics
genetic drift
gene flow
gene pool
genotype
geographic isolation
glycolysis
half-life
homologous structures
inheritance of acquired
    characteristics
introns
inversions

larvae
marsupial mammals
meiosis
microevolution
monophyletic groups
mutation
natural selection
notochord
nucleotide
nucleotide sequence
pangaea
parsimony
periods
placental mammals
plate tectonics
phenotype
phyletic gradualism
phylogeny
photosynthesis
pollen tube
polygenic

polyploid
polyphyletic
population
proterozoic eon
punctuated equilibrium
radioisotope
radioactive isotopes
relative time

reproductive isolating
  mechanisms
sexual reproduction
sexual selection
speciation
species
stabilizing selection
stigma

style
sympatric speciation
systematics
taxon
taxonomy
translocations
Uniformitarianism
Vestigial structures

Review Questions

1. The codevelopers of the theory of evolution were ___.
   a. Darwin and Lamarck;
   b. Wallace and Ladmo;
   c. Darwin and Gould;
   d. Wallace and Darwin
2. Which of these is NOT part of the theory of evolution?
   a. over reproduction;
   b. adaptation;
   c. design;
   d. differential survival and reproduction
3. Evolution may be defined as ___.
   a. the change in life over time;
   b. descent with modification;
   c. change in allele frequency over time;
   d. all of these
4. The islands where Darwin observed the finch species and their adaptive radiation were the ___ Islands.
   a. Galapagos;
   b. Hawaiian;
   c. Sicilian;
   d. Indonesian
5. Selection against the extremes of variation for a trait is ___.
   a. directional;
   b. disruptive;
   c. stabilizing;
6. Selection against the average variation for a trait is ___.
   a. directional;
   b. disruptive;
   c. stabilizing;
7. Selection against one extreme of variation for a trait is ___.
   a. directional;
   b. disruptive;
   c. stabilizing;
8. Allopatric speciation usually relies on which of these isolating mechanisms?
   a. temporal;
   b. geographic;
   c. behavioral;
   d. mechanical
9. Sympatric speciation usually relies on all but one of these isolating mechanisms. Which one is not involved in sympatric speciation?
   a. temporal;
   b. geographic;
   c. behavioral;
   d. mechanical
10. The movement of alleles between populations is known as ___.
    a. speciation;
    b. gene flow;
    c. founder effect;
    d. mutation

11. The main source of variation in a population is ___.
    a. migration;
    b. mutation;
    c. emigration;
    d. asexual reproduction
12. Darwin's explanation of the giraffe neck was that ___.
    a. giraffe's had been specially created;
    b. giraffe ancestors had stretched their necks and acquired longer necks;
    c. variable neck lengths had existed between giraffe ancestors and those with longer necks were able to get food higher in the trees so they survived and passed their long neck genes to their progeny
13. Any evidence of past life is known as a/an ___.
    a. mutation;
    b. adaptation;
    c. fossil;
    d. enzyme
14. A group that includes the ancestor plus all descendants is a ___ group.
    a. polyphyletic;
    b. paraphyletic;
    c. monophyletic
    d. diphyletic
15. Which of these taxonomic categories is the most inclusive?
    a. species;
    b. genus;
    c. class;
    d. domain
16. Which of these taxonomic categories is the least inclusive?
    a. species;
    b. genus;
    c. class;
    d. domain
17. The scientific name for humans is ___.
    a. *Homo erectus*;
    b. *Homo sapiens*;
    c. *Zea mays*;
    d. *Pan sapiens*
18. Which of these domains do humans belong to?
    a. Archaea;
    b. Bacteria;
    c. Eukarya;
    d. Animalia
19. The ancestor if all horses was ___.
    a. *Homo*
    b. *Libopollis*;
    c. *Hyracotherium*;
    d. *Eohippus*
20. The sequence of bones in vertebrate forelimbs represents which of these evidences for evolution?
    a. comparative anatomy;
    b. fossils;
    c. biochemistry;
    d. vestigial structures
21. Cladistics recognizes groups or clades based on the presence of ___.
    a. unique features;
    b. convergent features;
    c. shared derived characters;
    d. ancestral characters
22. The Earth is ___ years old.
    a. 6,000;
    b. 35 million;
    c. 4.5 billion;
    d. 14 billion

23. The first flowering plants appeared on Earth during the ___ period.
    a. Paleocene;
    b. Triassic;
    c. Cretaceous;
    d. Cambrian
24. Life originated during the ___ time.
    a. Cambrian;
    b. precambrian;
    c. Paleozoic;
    d. Pleistocene
25. Structures inherited from a common ancestor are said to be ___, although they may now perform a different function in descendants.
    a. fossil;
    b. homologous;
    c. heterozygous;
    d. homozygous

Links

International Code of Botanical Nomenclature (Vienna): The nomenclature rules for plants, algae, and fungi. [http://www.bgbm.org/iapt/nomenclature/code/default.htm]

The Phylogeny of Life and Journey into Phylogenetic Systematics (UCMP, Berkeley): Both explain the relationships and theory behind such evolutionary hypotheses. The latter gives a brief introduction into cladistics. [http://www.ucmp.berkeley.edu/exhibit/phylogeny.html]

The International Willi Hennig Society: A society for cladists, with links to other sites as well as software. [http://www.cladistics.org]

Linnean Herbarium: (English Version) Swedish Museum of Natural History link provides links to over 3,000 herbarium sheets of collected and identified plants. [http://linnaeus.nrm.se/botany/fbo/welcome.html.en]

Science and Creationism: A View from the National Academy of Sciences: The National Academy of Science weighs in on the still raging debate between scientists and creationists. Nothing is more needed that scientific literacy, or at least the ability to distinguish between science and nonscience. [http://www.nap.edu/openbook.php?record_id=11876&page=37]

Enter Evolution: UCMP Berkeley presents a site detaining the basics of Darwin and Wallace's idea. [http://www.ucmp.berkeley.edu/history/evolution.html]

Darwin's Origin of Species: Available to cure all insomniacs! The text of Darwin's seminal work on evolution. Free. [http://www.literature.org/authors/darwin-charles/the-origin-of-species/]

The Darwin-Wallace 1858 Evolution Paper: Prepared by James L. Reveal, Paul J. Bottino and Charles F. Delwiche (U. of Maryland). An excellent site to discover the origins of one of biology's major theories. [http://www.plantsystematics.org/reveal/pbio/darwin/darwindex.html]

CHAPTER 14

Biodiversity: Viruses, Bacteria, and Archaeans

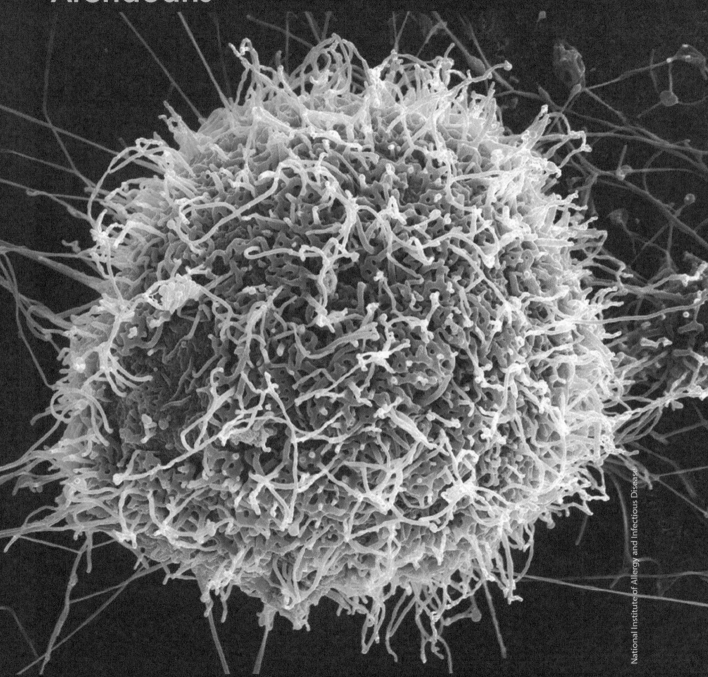

Chapter Opener

Colorized scanning electron micrograph of filamentous Ebola virus particles (blue) budding from a chronically infected VERO E6 cell (yellow-green). Image from the National Institute of Allergy and Infectious Diseases (NIAID).

Objectives

- Describe how viruses do or do not display the characteristics of life.
- Summarize the structural features of a bacteriophage virus.
- Describe the differences between a retrovirus and a bacteriophage virus.
- Discuss the consequences of a viral DNA becoming incorporated into a human egg or sperm cell.
- Describe what the enzyme reverse transcriptase does for a virus and the type of bacteria that has this chemical.
- Use your campus library or the Internet to locate information about a virally caused human disease and how it may be treated.
- Review the characteristics of life from the first chapter. Be able to discuss which of these is/are present in bacteria.
- Describe how prokaryotic cell structure differs from that of the eukaryotes.
- Discuss how prokaryotic and eukaryotic cell division processes differ.
- Describe the significance of bacteria to humans and other living things.
- List the main steps in the nitrogen-fixing process commonly used by bacteria.
- Use the Internet to locate information about a bacterially caused human disease.
- Compare and contrast between Bacteria and Archaeans.
- Describe the three-domain tree of life at the domain level.

Introduction

Bacteria and viruses have impacted humans from time immemorial. Although most of us know these pests only from the death and disease they cause, there is more to the story. We use bacteria and viruses in biotechnology applications such as making human insulin and Kosher cheese. Bacteria play roles in the production of a number of foods such as cheese, yogurt, sushi, and sauerkraut. Beneficial uses of viruses are harder to pin down outside of biotech. Vaccinations have long been the best or in some cases only way to deal with viral infections. Polio, smallpox, and other viral plagues of past generations have been in some cases eliminated by scientists and medical personnel. Although unseen, bacteria and archaeans exhibit all the characteristics of living things. They adapt to every environment on earth. Some have survived years in the harsh conditions on the Moon. This chapter deals with a group that we ought to collectively title the adaptive survivors.

14.1   Viruses and Viral Diseases

The French microbiologist Louis Pasteur (1822–1895) suspected something smaller than bacteria caused rabies. For this small infectious substance he used the Latin term for "poison." Russian botanist Dmitri Ivanovsky (1864–1920) (1822–1895) worked with tobacco mosaic virus. In 1892, he confirmed Pasteur's hypothesis of an infectious agent smaller than bacteria. The invention of the electron microscope in the 20th Century allowed scientists to visualize these infectious agents we know as viruses. Viruses cause a host of infectious diseases, from the 1918 to 1919 Spanish Flu pandemic, to the ongoing HIV crisis, Ebola outbreak in Africa in 2014, to your annual cold and flu seasons. We can use viruses in biotechnology as vectors and in medicine as immunizing agents. Scientists have studied several thousand viruses in detail. Figure 14.1 illustrates several different types of virus. So what then is a virus?

14.1.1   Virus Structure

A virus is a submicroscopic infectious particle composed of a protein coat and a nucleic acid core, as shown in Figure 14.2. Viruses are similar in size to a large protein macromolecule, generally smaller than 200 nm in diameter. Viruses, like cells, carry genetic information encoded in

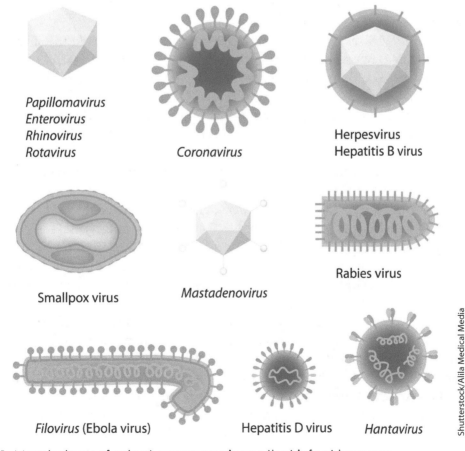

FIGURE 14.1 Morphology of select common viruses that infect humans.

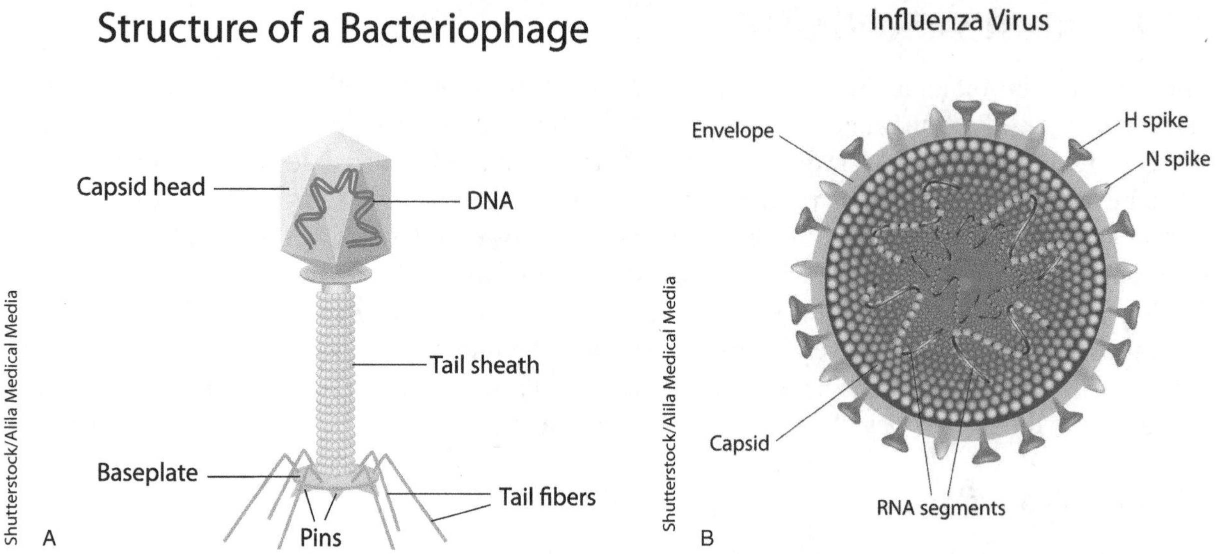

Structure of a Bacteriophage

Influenza Virus

FIGURE 14.2 Structure of several types of viruses. A. Bacteriophage virus; B. Influenza virus structure, bird flu and swine flu type.

their nucleic acid and can undergo mutations and reproduce; however, they cannot carry out metabolism and thus are not considered alive.

Biologists classify viruses by the type of nucleic acid they contain and the shape of their protein capsule. Examples of several viruses are shown in Figures 14.1. All viruses have at least two parts. An outer capsid composed of protein subunits and an inner core of either DNA or RNA, but *not* both. The viral genome has at most several hundred genes. In contrast, a human cell contains over thirty thousand genes. A viral particle may also contain various proteins, especially enzymes (such as polymerases and proteases), needed to produce viral DNA or RNA.

Several different replication cycle types are known for viruses (Figure 14.3). Some viruses, such as bacteriophages, attach to the outside of the host cell. Animal viruses pass through the cell membrane of their host cell (Figure 14.4).

Viruses are obligate intracellular parasites that can be maintained only inside living cells. When scientists refer to something as "obligate" indicates that the virus (in this case) must do or behave in the specified manner. Since viruses are obligate intracellular parasites, the term conveys the idea that viruses must carry out their reproduction by parasitizing a host cell. A virus cannot multiply outside a living cell, it can only replicate inside a specific host. Animal viruses in laboratories are raised in live chick embryos or propagated in cell tissue culture.

Viruses infect a variety of host cells, from bacteria to humans. Most viruses tend to be host specific. For example, the tobacco mosaic virus infects certain plants, the rabies virus infects only mammals, and HIV infects only certain human blood cells. The various viruses that cause hepatitis invade only liver tissues, whereas the poliovirus only reproduces in spinal nerve cells.

Viruses gain entry and are specific to a particular host cell because certain parts of the capsid (or spikes of the envelope) adhere to specific receptor sites on host cell plasma membrane. The viral nucleic acid gains entry to the cell, where the viral genome codes for the production of protein units in the capsid. Bacteriophages attach to the host bacterium, inject their DNA into the host, and take over the

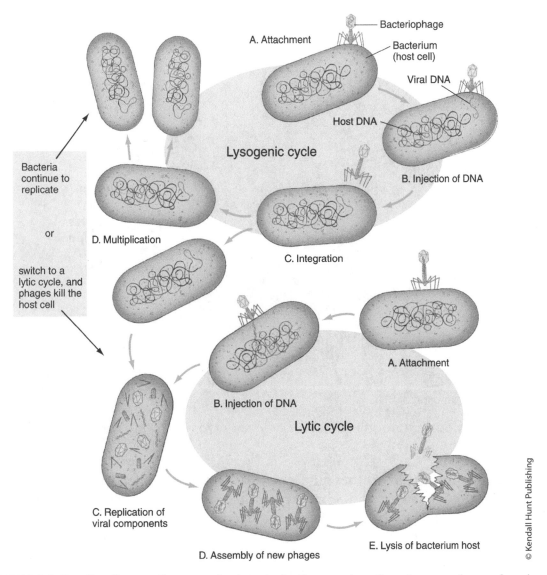

FIGURE 14.3 Replication pathways of a bacteriophage virus. Top: Lysogenic **cycle** where viral DNA integrates into host DNA; Bottom: Lytic cycle where the viral DNA takes over the host cell and directs production of the next generation of bacteriophage viruses.

cell. The viral DNA directs replication of the new viruses. When enough of these new viruses form, the bacterial host lyses or bursts, releasing the new viruses to go out and infect additional cells. Figure 14.3 illustrates several of these viruses being assembled in a host.

Under certain conditions the viral DNA inside the cell integrates into the host DNA, becoming a prophage. There it can lay dormant for many host cell generations, being copied, and passed to new bacteria. This pathway is the lysogenic pattern shown in Figure 14.3. Certain environmental factors, such as ultraviolet radiation, induce the prophage to enter the biosynthesis stage of the lytic cycle, followed by maturation and release. Some factor causes the viral DNA to become active and it enters the lytic pathway, directing the production of

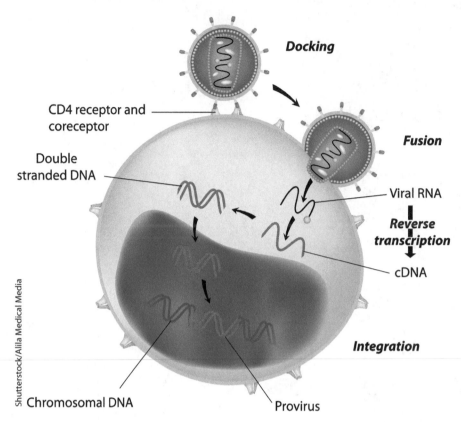

FIGURE 14.4 Human mmunodeficiency irus (HIV) entry to a human T cell.

new viruses. A virus may have genes for a few special enzymes needed for the virus to reproduce and exit from the host cell. The virus relies on host enzymes, ribosomes, transfer RNA (tRNA), and ATP for its own replication. A virus in essence takes over the metabolic machinery of the host cell when it reproduces.

Many animal viruses invade cells and replicate without killing the host cell immediately. New viruses are released by budding off the host cell's plasma membrane, turning the host cell for a time into a viral factory. The human immunodeficiency virus (HIV), the retrovirus that causes AIDS, replicates in this way.

Animal viruses replicate very much like bacteriophages do, although with modifications. If the virus has an envelope, glycoprotein spikes first adhere to plasma membrane receptors. The entire virus (not just the viral nucleic acid) is then taken into the host cell by endocytosis. Once inside the host cell, the virus loses its envelope and capsid. The freed viral nucleic acid proceeds with biosynthesis. Newly assembled viral particles are released not via cell lysis, but rather by budding. During this process, the viral particles pick up their envelopes from the host cell membrane. Components of viral envelopes are obtained from the plasma membrane as the viruses leave the cell. Budding does not necessarily result in the death of the host cell. This process is shown in Figure 14.5.

Active infection

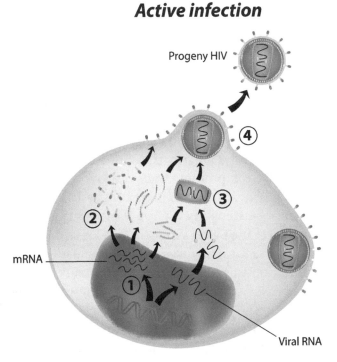

Progeny HIV

mRNA

Viral RNA

1. Transcription of proviral DNA
2. Synthesis of viral components
3. Assembly of viruses
4. Budding of viruses from the host cell

Shutterstock/Alila Medical Media

FIGURE 14.5 Budding of an animal virus from its host cell.

14.1.2   Viruses and Diseases

Viruses cause a variety of diseases among all groups of living things. Burning the infected plants can control viral plant diseases. Viral diseases in humans are controlled by preventing transmission, administering vaccines, and only recently by the administration of antiviral drugs. Virally caused human diseases include the flu, common cold, herpes, measles, chicken pox, smallpox, polio, and encephalitis. Antibiotics typically do not work against viruses. Vaccination, if a vaccine is available, offers protection for uninfected individuals. For airborne viruses like the flu and cold, covering your mouth when sneezing or coughing and frequent handwashing is quite effective at controlling transmission of the virus. For sexually transmitted viruses, some studies suggest condom use may help prevent transmission of HIV to an uninfected partner. Vaccines are substances that stimulate an immune system response without causing the illness. Commonly used virus vaccines include polio, measles, and mumps.

Antibiotics do not cure viral infections because viruses use enzymes produced by the host cell, rather than produce their own. Most antibiotics work by interfering with an infectious organism's enzymes that will not affect the host's enzymes. This does not happen in the case of viruses. A few antiviral drugs are available that interfere with viral replication without interfering with host metabolism in cells free of the virus. Antiviral medicines include acyclovir (for herpes) and AZT (for HIV). Despite recent successes with antiviral drugs, vaccination and the prevention of exposure remain the most effective ways to deal with viral infections.

Smallpox was effectively eliminated as a scourge on humanity by worldwide vaccination programs. The chances of getting smallpox from a bad vaccine were greater than those of ever encountering the virus in nature. The last U.S. case of smallpox occurred in 1949, with the last naturally occurring case in the rest of the world came from Somalia in 1977. In 1972 routine U.S. smallpox vaccinations were discontinued.

Hepatitis A, B, and C are all viral diseases that can cause liver damage. Like any viral disease, the major treatment efforts focus on treatment of symptoms, not removal of the viral cause.

Hepatitis A is usually a mild illness indicated by a sudden fever, malaise, nausea, anorexia, and abdominal discomfort. The virus causing Hepatitis A is primarily transmitted by fecal contamination, although contaminated food and water also can promote transmission.

A rare disease in the United States, Hepatitis B is endemic in parts of Asia where hundreds of millions of individuals are possibly infected. The Hepatitis B virus (HBV) is transmitted by blood and blood products as well as sexual contact. The blood supply in developed countries has been screened for the virus that causes this disease for many years, and transmission by blood transfusion is rare today. The risk of HBV infection was high among promiscuous homosexual men although it is also transmitted heterosexually. Correct use of condoms can reduce the risk of transmission. Effective vaccines are available for the prevention of Hepatitis B infection. Some individuals with chronic Hepatitis B may develop cirrhosis of the liver. Individuals with chronic hepatitis B are at an increased risk of developing primary liver cancer. Although this type of cancer is relatively rare in the United States, it is the leading cause of cancer death in the world, primarily because the virus causing it is endemic in eastern Asia.

Hepatitis C affects approximately 170 million people worldwide and 4 million in the United States. The Hepatitis C virus passes to new individuals primarily by blood and blood products. Most infected individuals have either received blood transfusions prior to 1990 (when screening of the blood supply for the Hepatitis C virus began) or have used intravenous drugs. Sexual transmission can occur between monogamous couples (rare), but infection is far more common in those who are promiscuous. In rare cases, Hepatitis C causes acute disease and even liver failure. About 20% of individuals with Hepatitis C who develop cirrhosis of the liver will also develop severe liver disease. Cirrhosis caused by Hepatitis C is presently the leading cause of the need for liver transplants in the United States. Individuals with cirrhosis from Hepatitis C also bear increased chances of developing primary liver cancer. All current treatments for Hepatitis C employ various preparations of the potent antiviral interferon alpha. However, not all patients who have the disease are good candidates for treatment, so infected individuals are urged to regularly consult their physician.

Beginning in the 1980s a new retrovirus intruded on the public consciousness: HIV. The virus is spread by body fluids, such as blood and semen. The 2008 Nobel Prize for Physiology/Medicine was awarded to French virologist Luc Montagnier (b. 1932) and Françoise Barré-Sinoussi for their 1980s discovery of HIV. American virologist Robert Gallo (b. 1937) and his research team proved that HIV (then known by another acronym) was the cause of AIDS. A related virus occurs in monkeys, so scientists suspect HIV moved to a human host during the early 20th Century. The virus causes people to produce specific antibodies that can be detected by blood screening. There are several strains of HIV in the world population. Access to antiviral medicines demonstrably lowers the spread of the disease, as does education and awareness. The virus can be dormant yet transmissible for many years after infection.

The 1918–1919 Spanish Flu Pandemic

Although the world was waging the war to end all Wars, World War I, a more deadly killer emerged, what was known as the Spanish flu. Despite the name, the Spanish flu did not originate in Spain! An estimated 675,000 Americans died of the flu pandemic. Worldwide fatalities range between 30 to over 50 million people. Compare that to the estimated 18 million soldiers killed during World War I and you see the pandemic was more of a threat even than the Great War.

Unlike most flu infections that kill more elderly, sickly, and juvenile individuals, the Spanish flu proved especially deadly to otherwise healthy young people. The first reported case of this disease in the United States was in March, 1918 from Haskell County, Kansas. The disease spread to a nearby military base, and then to Europe. The mobility of soldiers during the Great War contributed greatly to the spread of the virus.

Symptoms of the Spanish flu included fevers as high as 105° Fahrenheit, severe joint and muscle pain. An estimated 5%–10% of the patients developed pneumonia that often proved fatal. So many people took sick that accurate public records in many areas were impossible.

The Public Health Service was authorized to hire more doctors and nurses to fight the pandemic, although the war effort made finding qualified individuals difficult. Public gatherings were banned. Quarantines were imposed in areas where many people gathered: pool halls, theaters, churches, and saloons. In Phoenix, Arizona dogs were eradicated in the mistaken belief that dogs spread the disease. Arizona had laws mandating gauze masks be worn in public. In 1919 hockey's Stanley Cup was not awarded due to the influenza pandemic. The series was tied, but the final game was not played because the coach and several players were hospitalized. One player later died and the series was never finalized.

The pandemic subsided in 1919 after three waves of infection. The reason for the cessation of the pandemic is not known. The development of better vaccines during the 1960s along with increased understanding of the biology of the flu

BOX-FIGURE 1 St Louis, MO Red Cross workers preparing for action during the 1918–1919 Spanish flu pandemic.

Courtesy of the Library of Congress

virus led to less severe outbreaks. During the early part of the 21st Century, scientists began to restudy the virus, recovering samples from victims buried in permafrost. They were able to identify the genes responsible for the dangerous symptoms of the disease.

Scientists now identify the Spanish flu virus as a variant of the H1N1 swine flu virus. The 2009 pandemic resulted from a different variant of the H1N1 virus. The vaccine developed against the 2009 outbreak was tested against recreated 1918 Spanish flu virus and found to be somewhat effective. Despite celebrity and media driven hysteria (based on one refuted scientific paper) about vaccinations they remain the best method of dealing with viral infections, provided people get vaccinated.

Resources:

The Great Pandemic, The United States in 1918–1919 [link is http://www.flu.gov/pandemic/history/1918/]

14.1.3   Vaccination

Vaccination is a term derived from the Latin word *vacca* (cow, after the cowpox material used by British physician Edward Jenner (1749–1823) in the first vaccination in 1796). A vaccine stimulates the antibody production and formation of memory cells without causing the disease. Vaccines are made from killed pathogens or weakened strains that cause antibody production but not the disease. Recombinant DNA techniques can now be used to develop even safer vaccines.

The immune system can develop long-term immunity to some diseases. Scientists use this immunity process to develop vaccines. Active immunity develops after an illness or vaccine. Vaccines are weakened (or killed) viruses or bacteria that prompt the development of antibodies. Application of biotechnology allows development of vaccines, which are proteins (antigen) that in no way can cause the disease. Passive immunity is the type of immunity when the individual is given antibodies to combat a specific disease. Passive immunity is short lived.

14.1.4   The Vaccine Controversy

Based on a now discredited and retracted study published in the medical journal *The Lancet*, celebrity and media have created a doubt in the American population about the safety of vaccines by a spurious link to childhood autism. In 1998, *The Lancet* published an article that claimed a link between vaccination and autism, a disease that remains poorly understood.

Later analysis of the original article concluded the results were, in words of the *British Medical Journal* (BMJ) study, fraudulent. There is no conclusive link between vaccination and autism. Benefits of vaccination outweigh any perceived (and mythological) risks.

14.1.5   Emergent Viruses

Viruses are usually quite specific as to their hosts and even to the types of cells they infect in a multicellular host. Recently, some viruses appear to have shifted their host: HIV, hantavirus, and Ebola appear to be either viruses shifting to a new (human) host or else viruses whose existence and effects are just now being realized by scientists and the general public.

The Ebola virus was much in the news during the summer of 2014. The virus spreads by contact with blood or body fluid from an infected animal. The World Health Organization (WHO) reports spread of the virus by contact with contaminated areas. Infected individuals can spread the disease to other people. The first reported incidence of the disease was during 1976 during outbreaks in Sudan and the Democratic Republic of the Congo. The disease is named for the Ebola River near the village where the first outbreak was studied. There are no specific medicines designed for this virus.

During June 2009 the WHO declared that a new version of the flu virus, H1N1, had spread and become a pandemic. The new variety of virus was identified in the United States in a

10-year-old California child in April 2009. The virus seems to have originated in Veracruz, Mexico, and killed 18,000 people between 2009 and 2010. An international effort detected the virus occurring worldwide (Figure 14.6). The virus seemed to affect younger people, perhaps because older individuals had already developed an antibody to a similar virus. A vaccine was developed and immunization programs begun. Unlike the 1918–1919 Spanish flu pandemic, medicines to combat the illness had been developed and proved effective combatting H1N1.

14.2   The Domain Bacteria

Traditional classifications combined archaeans and bacteria in a single taxonomic kingdom due to their morphological similarity. The two groups are extremely different, as different from each other biochemically as eukaryotes are from either group. Under the three-domain classification system, the Archaea and Bacteria are placed into two separate domains, with the third one containing all the eukaryotes. This system is shown in Figure 14.7.

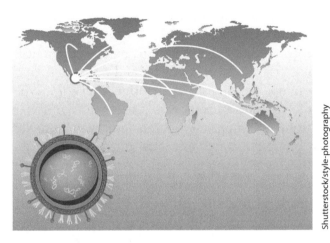

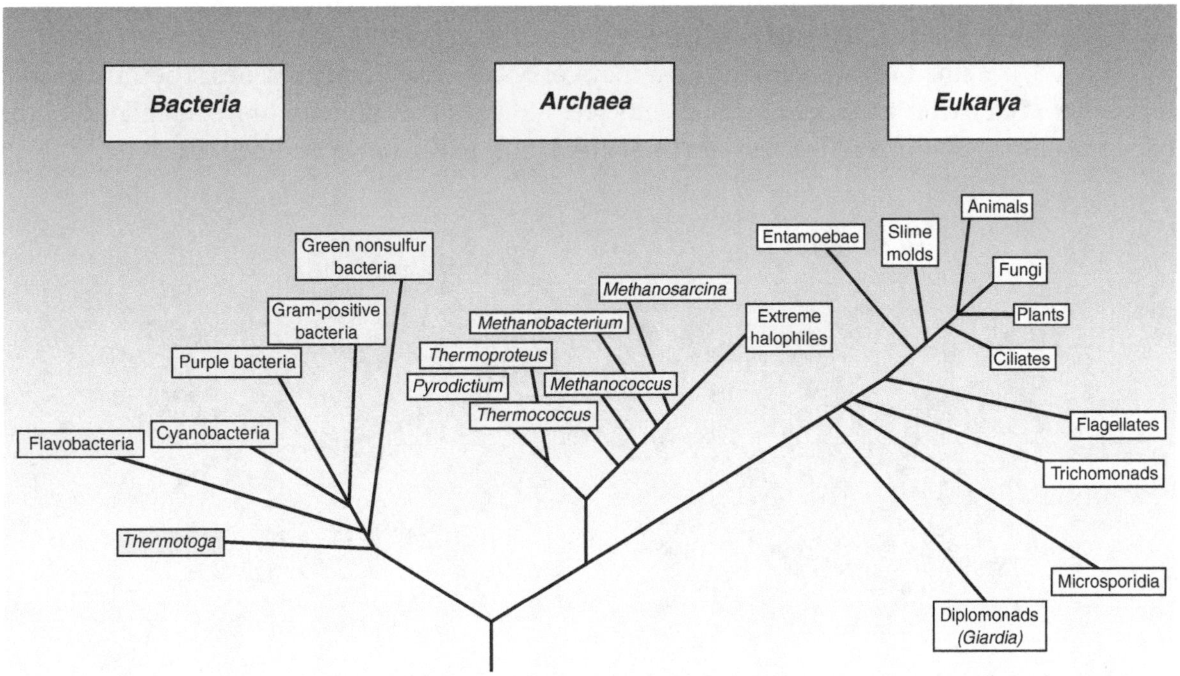

FIGURE 14.6 The spread of the 2009 H1N1 pandemic.

FIGURE 14.7 The three domains.

14.2.1   Bacterial Structure

The old taxonomic kingdom Monera consisted of the bacteria (meaning the heterotrophic bacteria and photosynthetic cyanobacteria) as well as the archaebacteria (now known as archaeans). The modern classification (Figure 14.8) separates each of these groups to separate domain status.

Organisms in the Domain Bacteria lack membrane-bound organelles such as the nucleus and endoplasmic reticulum that characterize and define the third domain, the Eukarya. All members of Domain Bacteria are prokaryotes. Heterotrophic bacteria and cyanobacteria are the major forms of life in this domain.

Their small size, ability to rapidly reproduce, and diverse habitats/modes of existence make bacteria the most abundant and diversified group of organisms on (and under!) the Earth. For example, the intestinal bacterium *Escherichia coli* can reproduce by binary fission every 15 minutes, 4 times an hour, or 48 times in a day! Bacteria occur in almost every environment on Earth, from the bottom of the ocean floor, deep inside solid rock, to the cooling jackets of nuclear reactors.

Bacteria are prokaryotes and lack a nuclear membrane and membrane-bound organelles. Biochemical processes that normally occur in a chloroplast or mitochondrion of eukaryotes occur in the cytoplasm of prokaryotes. Bacterial DNA is circular and arrayed in a region of the cell known as the nucleoid (Figure 14.8). Scattered within bacterial cytoplasm are numerous small loops of DNA known as plasmids. Bacterial genes are organized in gene systems known as operons. The cytoplasm also contains numerous ribosomes, the structures where proteins are assembled. Bacterial ribosomes are smaller than those in the other two domains. All bacteria also have a cell membrane, and most also produce a cell wall.

As a group, bacteria are nutritionally quite diverse. Some bacteria are photosynthetic autotrophs, whereas others are heterotrophs. Bacteria play important ecological roles as decomposers, as well as important elements of phytoplankton organisms at the base of many food chains.

Plasmids are small DNA fragments that may carry between 2 and 30 genes. They are known from almost all bacterial cells. Some plasmids seem to have the ability to move in and out of the bacterial chromosome. As such they are important tools to the biotechnology arsenal.

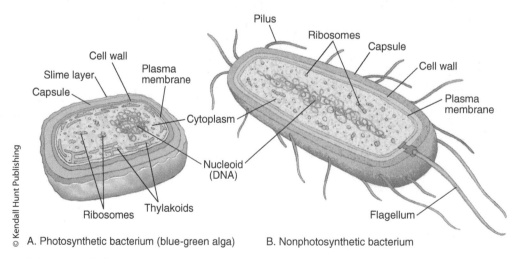

A. Photosynthetic bacterium (blue-green alga)   B. Nonphotosynthetic bacterium

© Kendall Hunt Publishing

FIGURE 14.8 Bacterial structure.

Bacteria have flagella, shown in Figure 14.8, although the bacterial flagellum has a different microtubule structure than the flagella of eukaryotes. Cell walls of bacteria contain peptidoglycan instead of the cellulose found in cell walls of plants and some algae. Ribosomes are the structures in cells where proteins are assembled. Bacterial ribosomes have smaller ribosomal subunits than do eukaryotes and archaeans.

The bacterial cell wall of some bacteria is surrounded by a capsule or sheath. Danish microbiologist Hans Christian Joachim Gram (1853–1938) developed a staining technique (that bears his name) to detect the presence of this capsule. If the purple stain is absorbed by the bacterium we say the cell is Grampositive. A Gram-negative bacterium does not absorb the stain and appears red. The capsule prevents the stain from reaching the wall, so Gram-negative bacteria *have* the capsule, whereas Gram-positive bacteria *lack* the capsule. The technique is outlined in Table 14.1.

Bacteria typically have one of three shapes (Figure 14.9): rods (bacilli), spheres (cocci), or spiral (spirilla). Unicellular, they often stick together forming clumps or filaments. Modifications of the basic shapes also occur. Two spherical cocci bacteria may occur as a diplococcus, or bacilli may be lightly modified.

14.2.2   Bacterial Reproduction

Prokaryotes are much simpler in their organization than are eukaryotes. There are a great many more organelles in eukaryotes, as well as more chromosomes to be moved around during cell division. The typical method of cell division is binary fission. The prokaryotic chromosome is a single DNA molecule that first replicates, then attaches each copy to a different part of the cell membrane. When the cell begins to pull apart, the two chromosomes thus are separated. Following cell splitting (cytokinesis), there are now two cells of identical genetic composition (except for the rare chance of a spontaneous mutation).

This asexual method of reproduction means that all cells in a bacterial colony are genetically the same. When treating a bacterial disease, a drug that kills one bacterium of a specific type will normally kill all other members of that colony it comes in contact with. Evolution requires genetic variation on which to operate. How then can bacteria increase their genetic variation if their typical mode of reproduction produces clones? Bacteria can accomplish genetic recombination in three ways:

1. Conjugation, shown in Figure 14.10, is the process where one bacterium passes DNA to another through a tube (the sex pilus) that temporarily joins the two conjugating cells. Conjugation occurs only between bacteria in same or closely related species.
2. Transformation involves a bacterium taking up free pieces of DNA secreted by live bacteria or released by dead bacteria into the surrounding environment. Recall that Griffith's experiment demonstrated this process.
3. Transduction happens when a bacteriophage transfers portions of bacterial DNA from one cell to another.

TABLE 14.1 Gram stain procedure

Reagents	Time Applied	Reactions	Appearance
Unstained smear			Cells are colorless and difficult to see.
Crystal violet	1 Minute, then rinse with water	Basic dye attaches to negatively charged groups in the cell wall, membrane, and cytoplasm.	Both gram-negative and gram-positive cells are deep violet.
Gram's iodine (mordant)	1 Minute, then rinse with water	Iodine strengthens the attachment of crystal violet to the negatively charged groups.	Both gram-negative and gram-positive cells remain deep violet.
Alcohol or acetone-alcohol mix (decolorizer)	10 to 15 seconds, then rinse with water	Decolorizer leaches the crystal violet and iodine from the cells. The color diffuses out of gram-positive cells more slowly than out of gram-negative cells because of the chemical composition and thickness of the gram-positive cell walls.	Gram-positive cells remain deep violet, but gram-negative cells become colorless and difficult to see.
Safranin (counterstain)	1 Minute; then rinse thoroughly, blot dry, and observe under oil immersion	Basic dye attaches to negatively charged groups in both cell types. Few negative groups are free of crystal violet in gram-positive cell, whereas most negative groups are free in gram-negative bacteria. Consequently, gram-positive bacteria remain deep violet, whereas gram- negative bacteria become pink or red.	Gram-positive cells remain deep violet, whereas gram-negative cells are stained pink or red.

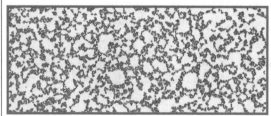

Gram stain of *Staphylococcus aureus*, a gram-positive coccus (×252). *Daniel Lim*.

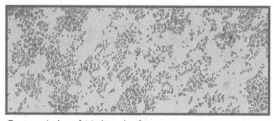

Gram stain of *Neisseria flavescens*, a gram-negative coccus (×252). *CDC*.

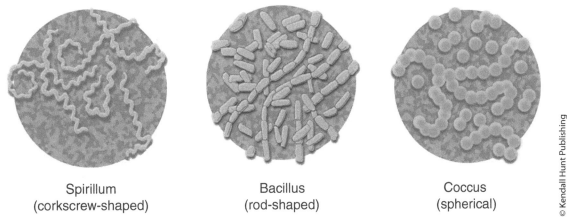

Spirillum
(corkscrew-shaped)

Bacillus
(rod-shaped)

Coccus
(spherical)

© Kendall Hunt Publishing

FIGURE 14.9 Shapes of bacteria.

Certain types of bacteria can "donate" a piece of their DNA to a recipient cell. The recombination is the bacterial equivalent of sexual reproduction in eukaryotes. Note that the entire DNA is not usually transferred, only a small piece.

Plasmids sometimes carry genes for resistance to antibiotics. Since they are also DNA, plasmids can be transferred between bacteria by any of the three processes mentioned above. Since genetic recombination in bacteria does not routinely occur (as it may in sexually reproducing eukaryotes), mutation is the most important source of genetic variation for evolutionary change. Normally bacteria have short generation times, and mutations are generated and distributed throughout bacterial populations more quickly than in eukaryotes. Prokaryotes have only a single chromosome, which makes them haploid. Consequently, mutations are not hidden by a dominant allele and will be expressed and evaluated by natural selection more rapidly than in diploid eukaryotes.

Endospores are a method of survival not one of reproduction. The formation of an endospore is shown in Figure 14.11. Certain bacteria will form an endospore inside their cell membrane that allows them to wait out deteriorating environmental conditions. Three heavy, protective spore coats surround a small portion of cytoplasm and a chromosome copy. The part of the bacterial cell outside the endospore deteriorates and the endospore is released. Endospores allow bacteria that produce them to survive in the harshest of environments. When conditions once again become suitable, the endospore absorbs water and grows out of its spore coat.

Certain disease-causing bacteria (such as *Bacillus anthracis*, the cause of the disease anthrax) remain capable of causing an infection for up to 1300 years after forming their endospore! Because of this, as well as other factors, the anthrax bacterium was used as a possible biological weapon. Following the September 11, 2001 terrorist attacks, several people died from anthrax exposure, and one postal facility was closed (as was the U.S. Senate building) for several weeks. No connection between these events has ever been established.

The Germans used anthrax bacteria as a weapon in World War I. During World War II, the British contaminated a Scottish island with a virulent strain of anthrax. The island was not cleared for human use until nearly 50 years had passed. The United States had anthrax in its biological arsenal until President Richard Nixon ordered the abandonment and destruction of American bioweapons stockpiles. Stockpiles amassed by the Soviet Union were not destroyed until 2002.

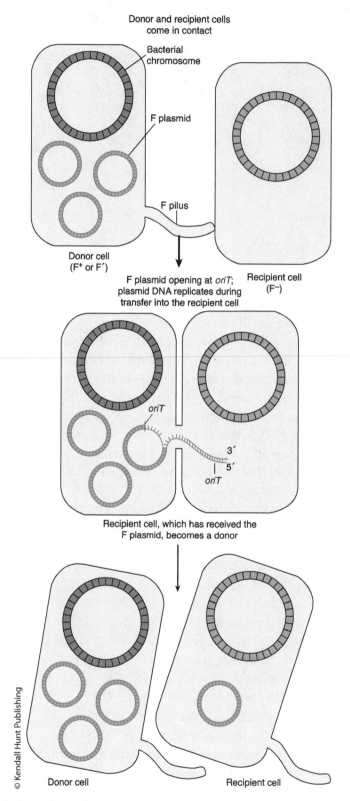

FIGURE 14.10 Bacterial conjugation.

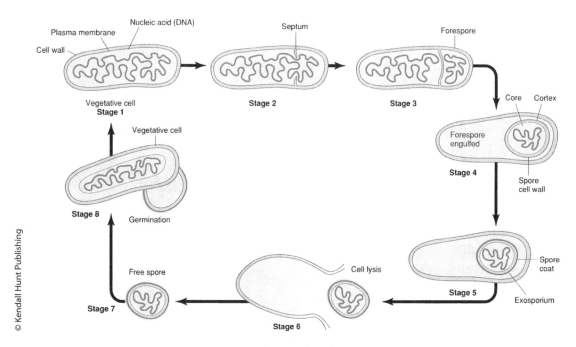

FIGURE 14.11 Endospore formation and germination.

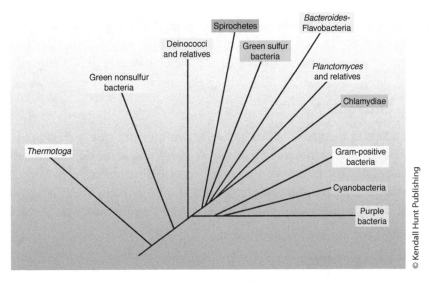

FIGURE 14.12 Detailed phylogeny of the Domain Bacteria.

14.2.3   Bacterial Diversity

Bacteria are classified into 11 clades based on molecular analysis. Traditional classifications relied on nutritional modes, wall staining, and other morphological features. Molecular and cladistic studies have reshaped these traditional groups into 11 clades used in this text (Figure 14.12). Below we examine select phyla.

14.2.3.1   Phylum Aquificae

This phylum, also known as the Green nonsulfur bacteria, also occurs at extremely high temperatures. One genus, *Aquifex*, can grow in water close to boiling. Bacteria in this phylum are chemoautotrophs and act as producers in these extreme environments.

14.2.3.2   Phylum Deinococcus-Thermus

Species in this phylum are highly resistant to radiation and heat. There are two major clades within this phylum. One group is capable of breaking down nuclear waste and survives even in the vacuum on the Moon. The other group includes *Thermus aquaticus*, an extremophile bacterium that factored into the development of polymerase chain reaction (PCR).

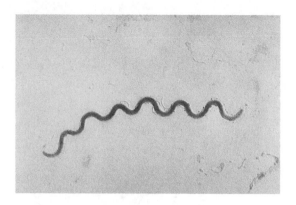

FIGURE 14.13 Light micrograph of a spirochete, *Treponema pallidum*, the causative agent of the sexually transmitted disease syphilis. Image courtesy of CDC/Susan Lindsley.

14.2.3.3   Phylum Spirochetes

The six genera of spiral-shaped, double-membrane bacteria in this phylum have impacted humanity in tremendous ways. Two of the most famous bacterially caused diseases, syphilis (Figure 14.13) and Lyme Disease, are caused by spirochetes. A unique set of axial filaments between the inner and outer membrane allow the spirochete to move by rotating the entire cell.

14.2.3.4   Phylum Chlorobi

This phylum, also known as the green sulfur bacteria, contains obligate anaerobic photosynthetic bacteria. Instead of using water as an electron donor as plants and algae do, these bacteria gain their electrons from sulfide ions. The photosystem complexes of chlorobi are also quite different from those of cyanobacteria and other common photosynthetic organisms. Some green sulfur bacteria have been found at the ocean floor, whereas others seem to thrive in lower light conditions at depth.

14.2.3.5   Phylum Bacteroidetes

The phylum consists of Gram-negative, rod-shaped, anaerobes. They occur in many places, and a few cause human illnesses. The genus *Bacteroides* is the most abundant bacterium in human feces. In the human gut these function to exclude opportunistic pathogens.

14.2.3.6   Phylum Firmicutes

This group stains mostly Gram-positive and included cocci as well as bacilli. Some members of this phylum are pathogens, like *Bacillus anthracis* and *Clostridium botulinum*. *Clostridium botulinum* produces the toxin botulinum that is heavily diluted to make the cosmetic treatment Botox (Figure 14.14). Botulinum is considered the most potent toxin known. Tetanus, also known as lockjaw, is caused by *C. tetanii*. Other members of this phylum can spoil beer and wine.

14.2.3.7 Phylum Actinobacteria

This phylum includes Gram-positive soil and aquatic bacteria. One group in this phylum includes the genus *Streptomyces*, a source of formerly important antibiotic streptomycin as well as several newer medicines. Species of the bacterial genus *Frankia* form symbiotic root nodules in which they fix atmospheric nitrogen. Many plants, from roses to alders can host *Frankia*.

14.2.3.8 Phylum Proteobacteria

Members of this phylum include many disease-causing Gram-negative bacteria as well as ecologically significant nitrogen-fixing bacteria. Notable disease causing Proteobacteria include *Yersinia*, the cause of bubonic plague. Stomach ulcers form because of the actions of *Helicobacter pylori*. The common food poisoning bacteria *Salmonella* has been in the news in recent years contaminating

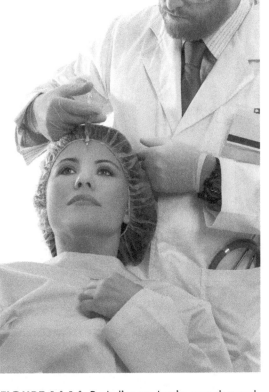

FIGURE 14.14 Botulinum toxin produced by the bacterium *Clostridium botulinum* reduces activity of muscles that cause frown lines between the brows to form.

Shutterstock/Leah-Anne Thompson

products from raw shellfish to peanut butter. The disease cholera results from *Vibrio cholerae* that often transmits by drinking contaminated water. The common intestinal bacterium *Escherichia coli* is a species of proteobacteria. Scientists recognize at least six clades within this group.

One group of proteobacteria of interest is the purple bacteria. These photosynthetic bacteria do not produce oxygen as a by-product. Some studies suggest purple bacteria were involved in endosymbiosis and the formation of the eukaryotic mitochondria.

The genus *Rhizobium* is noteworthy because it forms a major part of the nitrogen-fixing bacteria that convert dinitrogen (N_2) into organic nitrogen (ammonium, NH_4) in root nodules occurring in members of the pea family (Figure 14.15). All organic nitrogen used in nucleic acids, ATP, and amino acids derives from organically converted dinitrogen. Bacteria are the organisms that carryout this process.

The venereal disease gonorrhea is caused by the proteobacterium *Neisseria gonorrhoeae*. Bacterial meningitis is caused by *N. meningitides*. Antibiotic use greatly curtailed cases of both diseases. Antibiotic-resistant strains of both bacteria are becoming more commonplace.

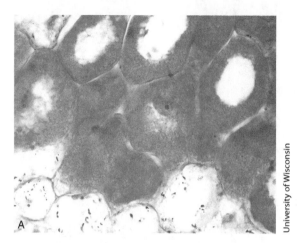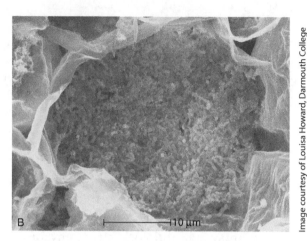

University of Wisconsin

Image courtesy of Louisa Howard, Darmouth College

⊢————10 µm

FIGURE 14.15 Root nodules in red clover harbor nitrogen-fixing bacteria. A. Light micrograph showing infected cells (Gram-stained red) in a root nodule; B. Scanning electron micrograph of a cross section though a soybean root nodule cell showing the symbiotic infestation of the root by nitrogen-fixing bacteria. Image courtesy of Louisa Howard, Dartmouth College.

14.2.3.9 Phylum Cyanobacteria

Cyanobacteria (Figure 14.16) are the major group of photosynthetic bacteria. Some early cyanobacteria may have formed the oxygen released into the early atmosphere, transforming our planet from one with an oxygen-free atmosphere to the modern one that has a significant amount of oxygen present. Stromatolites (Figure 14.16C) are fossil assemblages with a significant cyanobacterial component that greatly modified out planet's atmosphere over 2.5 billion years ago. In addition to chlorophyll *a*, cyanobacteria also have the blue pigment phycocyanin and the red pigment phycoerythrin.

Eukaryotic autotrophs all contain chloroplasts that localize the photosynthetic process. The typical chloroplast organization has thylakoids surrounded by a fluid-like stroma. The chloroplast is a membrane-bound organelle. Prokaryotes by definition lack such structures. How can bacteria carry out photosynthesis? By infolding their cell membrane to produce numerous thylakoids, prokaryotic autotrophs form thylakoids, in effect turning the bacterium into a single chloroplast.

14.2.4 Significance of Bacteria

Bacteria have been used beneficially for millennia. *Lactobacillus* is a bacterium used in the fermentation of milk to make yogurt. If you look at a tiny drop of yogurt with active cultures you will see a mass of rod-shaped bacteria. The Tillamook Cheese Company also uses biotechnologically engineered bacteria in the production of Kosher cheese. Bacteria also play role in the production of sauerkraut, soy sauce, wine, and cheese. Bacterial uses in biotechnology are numerous, from production of human insulin to alcohol and acetone production. Bacterial soups in which the plants are processed accomplish separation of fibers of hemp, and flax, among others. Current research into probiotics suggests some benefits from their use.

FIGURE 14.16 Examples of cyanobacteria. A. Light micrograph of the filamentous cyanobacterium *Oscillatoria*; B. Light micrograph of *Gleocapsa* showing the sheath around the clumps of cells, image photographed using differential image contrast filter; C. Stromatolites of cyanobacteria on the Shark Bay beach in Western Australia.

Many heterotrophic bacteria also cause diseases such as strep throat, rheumatic fever, cholera, gonorrhea, syphilis, bubonic plague, acne, dental caries, and toxic shock syndrome. Bacteria can cause disease by destroying cells, releasing toxins, contaminating food, or by the reaction of the body to the infecting bacteria.

Bacterial infections can be controlled by vaccinations and antibiotic treatments. Antibiotics interfere with some aspect of the replication of bacteria and are produced by microorganisms such as fungi that compete with bacteria for resources. Penicillin, the first antibiotic discovered, inhibits the synthesis of new cell walls in certain types of bacteria. However, the overuse of antibiotics during the past 50 years has led to natural selection favoring antibiotic resistance. The increasing prevalence of strains of antibioticresistant bacteria necessitates the development of new antibiotics and the frequent change of antibiotics in treatment. A new class of bacteria resistant to multiple antibiotics has arisen, the superbugs. We know them by acronyms like mRSA ethicillins resistant *Staphylococcus aureus*.

Peptic ulcers result when protective mechanisms for the stomach lining fail. Bleeding ulcers result when tissue damage is so severe that bleeding occurs into the stomach. Perforated ulcers are life-threatening situations, where a hole has formed in the stomach wall. At least 90% of all peptic ulcers are caused by the bacterium *Helicobacter pylori*. Other factors, including stress and aspirin, can also produce ulcers.

Gonorrhea and syphilis are among the most common bacterially caused sexually transmitted diseases. Both can be treated and cured with antibiotics, once diagnosed. These diseases were once considered likely to result in death. Both normally are curable with antibiotics, although overuse of antibiotics and the spread of antibiotic resistance can reduce antibiotic effectiveness.

Treponema pallidum (Figure 14.17A) is the bacterial species that causes syphilis. Syphilis is transmitted from an infected person to an uninfected one by direct contact with a syphilis sore (Figure 14.17B). Proper use of condoms has been demonstrated to reduce the incidence of syphilis. Syphilis sores occur mainly on the genitals, vagina, anus, or in the rectum, as well as on the lips and inside the mouth. Infected pregnant women can pass it to their unborn child. The urban myth about getting this disease from a toilet seat is untrue. Syphilis cannot be spread by toilet seats, door knobs, swimming pools, hot tubs, bath tubs, or sharing of clothing or eating utensils. There are three stages to the disease. The primary stage is the time between infection and the start of the first symptom, ranging from 10 to 90 days. The primary stage normally is indicated by the appearance of a single sore also known as a chancre (Figure 14.17B). The chancre is usually round, firm, small and painless, and appears where syphilis entered the body. If proper treatment is not utilized, the disease moves into the secondary stage. The secondary stage occurs when some area(s) of the skin develop a rash. These rashes can appear as the chancre is fading or can be delayed for weeks. The rash often appears as rough, red or reddish brown spots both on the palms of the hands and on the bottoms of the feet. The rash also may also appear on other parts of the body. Even without treatment rashes clear up spontaneously. In addition to rashes, second-stage symptoms can include fever, swollen lymph glands, sore throat, patchy hair loss, headaches, weight loss, muscle aches, and tiredness.

The disease can pass to sex partners when primary or secondary stage symptoms are showing. The latent, or hidden, stage of syphilis initiates when the symptoms of the second stage disappear. Without treatment, an infected individual still has syphilis, even though they do not

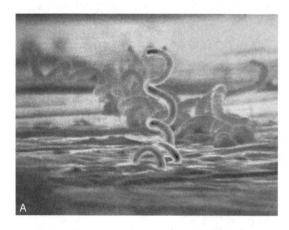 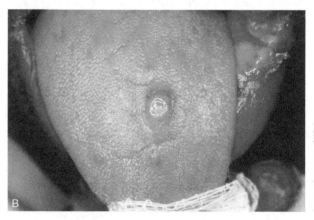

Image Courtesy of CDC

FIGURE 14.17 Syphilis, a bacterially caused sexually transmitted disease caused by *Treponema pallidum*. A. Scanning electron micrograph of *T. pallidum* illustrating the spiral shape; B. Chancre sore on a tongue is an indication of syphilis in the primary stage of infection.

display symptoms. *Treponema pallidum* remains in the body and so may begin to damage internal organs, such as the brain, nerves, eyes, heart, blood vessels, liver, bones, and joints. This internal damage may not show up until many years later when the person enters the late or tertiary stage of syphilis. Late stage symptoms include the inability to coordinate muscle movements, paralysis, numbness, gradual blindness, and dementia. This damage may be serious enough to cause death. Because of this progress of their disease, often resulting in death, the disease was one greatly feared before the advent of antibiotics. Early treatments included mercury, herbal remedies, and arsenic. These treatments had varying degrees of effectiveness, often with bad side effects. Penicillin's availability after World War II drastically reduced the dangers in treating syphilis.

Gonorrhea is another common sexually transmitted disease caused by the bacterium *Neisseria gonorrhoeae* (Figure 14.18). This organism can grow in the reproductive tract, including the cervix, uterus, and fallopian tubes in women, as well as in the urethra in both men and women. The bacteria can also grow in the mouth, throat, and anus. Gonorrhea is spread through vaginal, oral, or anal sexual contact. Ejaculation does not have to occur for gonorrhea to be transmitted or acquired. Gonorrhea can also be transmitted during birth. Symptoms include a burning sensation during urination and a yellowish white discharge from the penis. Some infected males may have painful or swollen testicles. Many women often do not show strong signs of the early symptoms of gonorrhea. The initial symptoms for women include a painful or burning sensation on urination, as well as a yellow or occasionally bloody vaginal discharge. Women with no or mild gonorrhea symptoms are still at risk of developing serious complications from the infection. Untreated gonorrhea in women can develop into pelvic inflammatory disease (PID). Rectal infection has symptoms such as discharge, anal itching, soreness, bleeding, and occasional painful bowel movements. Infections in the throat cause few symptoms. Penicillin is a common antibiotic no longer used to treat gonorrhea due to the development of penicillin-resistant strains of the gonorrhea bacterium.

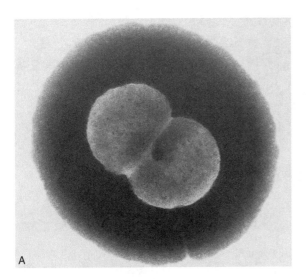
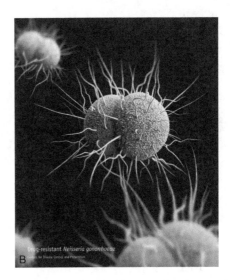

FIGURE 14.18 Gonorrhea is caused by *Neisseria gonorrhoeae*. A. Transmission electron micrograph (TEM) showing a diplococcal pair of *N. gonorrhoeae*, image from CDC/Dr. Wiesner; B. Computer-generated illustration of *N. gonorrhoeae*, image from CDC/Melissa Brower.

Salmonella is a genus of rod-shaped bacteria whose species cause typhoid fever and similar illnesses. The bacteria of this genus are widespread in animals, especially in poultry and pigs. Environmental sources of the organism include water, soil, insects, kitchen surfaces, feces, and raw meat, seafood, and poultry. The Centers for Disease Control (CDC) estimate over 450 deaths every year from the disease salmonella. Typhoid fever, caused by *Salmonella typhi* (Figure 14.19A), affects over 20 million people worldwide every year. Relatively rare in the United States, most cases are contracted while travelling abroad. A vaccination against this bacterium is available for those journeying to the nonindustrialized countries. Typhoid fever is spread through fecal contamination of the food and water supply (Figure 14.19B). The illness usually is cured by antibiotic treatments.

Some individuals recover from the disease but retain the bacteria in their blood. These people are known as carriers, such as the infamous Typhoid Mary (Mary Mallon, 1869–1938) a cook from the early 20th Century who may have infected 51 people with the illness. Mary was free from symptoms of the illness and was the first person identified as a carrier. She was quarantined several times by public health officials.

Staphylococcus (Figure 14.20) causes many diseases, perhaps the most famous being Methicillin-resistant *Staphylococcus aureus* (MRSA). *Staphylococcus aureus* occurs on the skin. It is a spherical bacterium that occurs in clusters of individual cells. Diseases caused by this bacterium include sinusitis, impetigo, acne, and pneumonia. Overuse of antibiotics set the stage for this bacterium to develop resistance.

Toxic shock syndrome was a problem during the 1980s when some brands of superabsorbent tampons were susceptible to the growth of *S. aureus* and *Streptococcus pyogenes*. The toxins produced led to several deaths as well as redesign and changes to tampons.

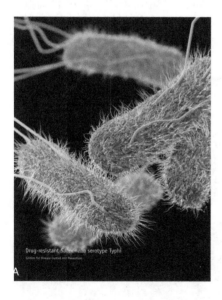

FIGURE 14.19 Typhoid fever. A. Computer-generated illustration of *Salmonella typhi*, the variant that causes typhoid fever; image from CDC/Melissa Brower; B. Historic photograph showing a leaking water pipe determined as the source from which sewage had the water supply for Benson, Minnesota. Considered as one of the causes of a typhoid fever outbreak in August, 1914. Image from CDC/Minnesota Department of Health, R.N. Barr Library; Librarians Melissa Rethlefsen and Marie Jones.

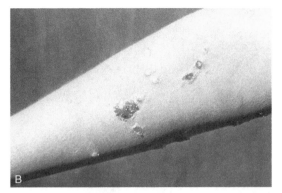

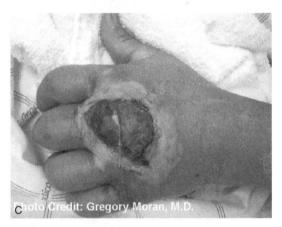

FIGURE 14.20 *Staphylococcus aureus* causes many diseases. A. Three-dimensional computer-generated illustration of an image of a cluster of vancomycin-resistant *S. aureus* (VRSA) bacteria; image from CDC/Melissa Brower; B. Lesions of this patient's forearm proved to be *Streptococcal* impetigo, a disease often also caused by *Staphylococcus aureus*; image from Washtenaw County Public Health, Michigan—Fact Sheet: Impetigo; C. Photograph of an abscess on the hand, resulting from MRSA; image from Gregory Moran, M.D.

The bacterial genus *Streptococcus* (Figure 14.21A, C) contains many diseases that plague humans: strep throat (Figure 14.21B), strep pneumonia, pink eye, and necrotizing fasciitis. Other species are an important part of our mouth's bacterial component and intestinal flora. *Streptococcus pneumoniae* causes strep pneumonia, but also occurs in the normal upper respiratory tract where it can cause sinusitis and ear infections. Other infections caused by *Streptococcus* are summarized in Table 14.2.

Bacteria seem to have participated in a vital **symbiosis** for hundreds of millions of years in their relationship with plants, both as soil nitrogen-fixing bacteria, chloroplasts, and as internal guests in the root nodules of plants of the pea family. Most organisms cannot use atmospheric dinitrogen (N_2) directly. Some bacteria have the metabolic pathways to convert inorganic N_2 into various forms of organic nitrogen. Mutualistic nitrogen-fixing bacteria, such as *Rhizobium*, live in nodules on the roots of soybean, clover, and alfalfa plants (all members of the pea family, Fabaceae), where they reduce N_2 to ammonium (NH_4) to the benefit of both themselves as well as their host. These bacteria also benefit by using some of the plant's photosynthetically produced organic molecules.

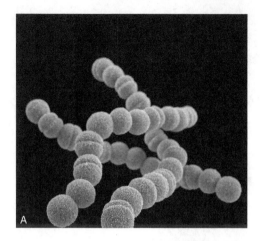

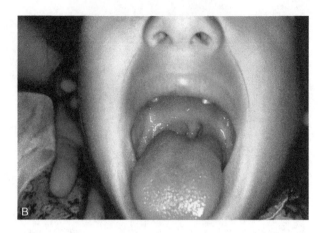

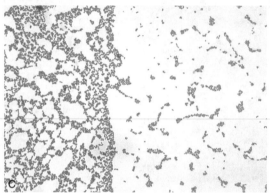

FIGURE 14.21 *Streptococcus* and its significance. A. Computer-generated image of a *Streptococcus pyogenes*, illustrating their arrangement in chains; image from CDC/ Melissa Brower; B. Strep throat, note the redder areas further back in the mouth; image from CDC; C. Light micrograph of *S. mutans*, the bacterium that causes dental caries, illustrating the Gram-negative nature of this species; image from CDC/Dr. Richard Facklam.

TABLE 14.2 Select species of *Streptococcus* and their significance

Species of *Streptococcus*	Disease
S. pneumoniae	Strep pneumonia; organisms transformed in Griffith's experiment (Chapter 10)
S. pyogenes	Bacterial sore throat, strep throat, necrotizing fasciitis
S. mutans	Dental caries
S. anginosus	Brain and liver abscesses

Bacteria also play vital roles in the decomposition of organic material in soil. This releases important nutrients back into the environment. Bacteria may also play roles in bioremediation of polluted soils as well as sewage processing.

14.3   The Domain Archaea

The members of the Domain Archaea are mostly restricted to marginal habitats such as hot springs or areas of low oxygen concentration. Archaea have significant differences in their cell walls and biochemistry when compared to the other prokaryotic domain, the bacteria. These differences are sufficient in most taxonomic schemes, to place the Archaea into a separate domain. Under the three-domain system, they are the taxonomic equivalents of the other bacteria and the eukaryotes (Domain Eukarya). It is thought that since bacteria and Archaea inhabit some of the modern environments thought by paleontologists to resemble what the early Earth was like, that both are descended from a common ancestor. The Eukarya later split from the Archaea.

The archaeans are for the most part life's extremists, often occupying environments that "normal" organisms find too harsh. Although they look like bacteria under a microscope, they are biochemically quite different. Cell membranes of members of this domain have significant variance with the other two domains. No archaeans form spores, and none carry out photosynthesis.

There are three major branches of archaeans: methanogens, halophiles, and thermacidophiles. It is an easy mistake to think of Domain Bacteria as occupying normal environments and Domain Archaea occurring in extreme environments. In fact, each domain has representatives in both the normal and extreme habitats. Archaeans even occur in the human intestine!

14.3.1   Archaean Diversity

Systematics of Domain Archaea is not yet finalized, although several phyla have been proposed. Two phyla are widely accepted by systematists, whereas one is gaining acceptance.

14.3.1.1   Phylum Crenarcheaota

Archaeans in this phylum may lack histone proteins that occur in other members of the domain. Although some members of this phylum are sulfur dependent, some others are abundant in the ocean. The phylum includes both thermophiles (growing in laboratory cultures at temperatures up to 113°C) as well as organisms that can grow in moderate temperatures. *Sulfolobus* is the best-studied member of this phylum. Some data suggest that this phylum might be closely related to eukaryotes.

14.3.1.2   Phylum Euryarcheota

Major clades in this phylum include the methanogens (methane-generating archaeans), halophiles (salt-loving archaeans), and some thermophiles (heat-loving archaeans). Like all archaeans these creatures lack the peptidoglycan cells walls characterizing Domain Bacteria.

Methanogens are obligate anaerobes with either rod or spherical shapes. The methanogens are not a monophyletic group. Unlike most organisms that need oxygen to generate ATP by chemiosmosis the methanogens reduce carbon dioxide (CO_2) into methane (CH_4) using hydrogen as the electron donor. In deep oceans these biologically produced methane molecules collect to form methane clathrates, an important sink for carbon.

Halophiles live in water containing a great deal of salt. Although there are some halophilic bacteria, the term halophile usually refers to halophilic archaeans (haloarchaeans). The haloarchaeans are facultative aerobes, some of which can absorb light to generate ATP. The purple pigment bacteriorhodopsin facilitates this and causes pools of these archaeans, such as *Halobacterium*, to look purplish.

14.3.2   Differences Between Bacteria and Archaea

In many ways archaeans are intermediates between bacteria and eukaryotes. Table 14.3 summarizes the characteristics of each of these domains. Genetic studies suggest that bacteria may have been the first cells to evolve on Earth.

Archaeans share a number of characters with bacteria, including the presence of a single, circular chromosome with genes organized in operons. Although both domains are unicellular and typically have cells with cell walls, the archaeans lack the peptidoglycan that characterizes bacterial walls. Shapes of the bacteria and archaeans are similar, although some archaeans have unique shapes. Both domains are unicellular, in contrast to the Domain Eukarya that includes many multicellular organisms. Bacteria and Archaea have similar-sized ribosomes.

Several microbiologists have suggested that archaeans evolved from Gram-positive bacteria due to antibiotic selection. These antibiotics target certain genes, and the hypothesis is that changes in those genes led to the divergence of archaeans from ancient bacteria. Due to the similar morphologies of both prokaryotic domains, the fossil record would be of no help, so genetic studies provide the evidence supporting this assertion.

The evolution of eukaryotes from some group of archaeans is well established. The question is which group of archaeans? One hypothesis suggests the divergence of eukaryotes from the archaean phylum Crenarchaeota occurred very late in the history of life. A more widely accepted hypothesis is that the divergence of the three domains occurred relatively early from a poorly defined common ancestor.

TABLE 14.3 Comparison of the three domains

Characteristic	Bacteria	Archaea	Eukarya
Membrane-bound nucleus	No	No	Yes
Cell wall with peptidoglycan	Yes, if wall is present	No	No
Histone proteins associated with DNA	No	Some have these, some do not	Yes
Chromosome shape	Circular	Circular	Linear
Introns	No	In general no; most are in RNA genes if present at all	Yes
Cells typically smaller than 20 μm	Yes	Yes	No
Unicellular	Yes	Yes	Yes
Multicellular	No	No	Yes
Spores	Some	None	Some
Ribosome size	70S	70S	80S

14.3.3   Significance of Archaeans

Archaeans are of significance in many ways. Ecologically they play roles in cycling of carbon, nitrogen, and sulfur. Some archaeans, such as *Sulfolobus*, produce sulfuric acid as a metabolic by-product. This can be a problem in many abandoned coal mines, where these archaeans grow on the sulfur often associated with the coal deposits. Methane-generating archaeans play important roles in sewage treatment plants as well as in swamps and bogs, where they convert organic carbon into methane. In some cases, this methane can be collected and used as fuel for electrical generation. Archaean enzymes that can function at higher temperatures play roles in the production of low-lactose milk, environmentally friendly synthesis of organic chemicals, biotechnology (DNA polymerase used in the PCR process), as well as in mining ores such as copper and gold.

Summary

The term prokaryote refers to organisms lacking a nucleus. The taxonomic domains Bacteria and Archaea both lack a nucleus but are as different from each other as they are different from the Domain Eukarya, the nucleated eukaryotes. Bacteria play important roles ecologically as decomposers and nitrogen-fixing bacteria, as well as cyanobacteria as photosynthetic components of the phytoplankton. Oxygen released as a waste product by ancient cyanobacteria transformed our planet. We make industrial use of bacteria, as well as suffer from infections of disease-causing strains like *Salmonella* and *Staphylococcus*. The archaeans do not cause human disease and are often difficult to culture in the laboratory. They play important roles in methane production, decomposition of organic matter, and nitrogen, carbon, and sulfur cycling. Some microbiologists suspect archaeans were involved in the endosymbiosis that led to the formation of eukaryotes. These creatures might be tiny, microscopic cells, but they impact our lives every day.

Viruses continue to lack the characteristics of living things, so they are not alive. However, they can kill us or make us ill, as in the case of the Ebola virus outbreak in Africa during 2014 and the Spanish flu outbreak of 1918–1919. Smallpox undoubtedly killed more Native Americans than General George Armstrong Custer did. Polio crippled many Americans, including President Franklin Delano Roosevelt (probably making him unelectable today). We use viruses as vectors in biotechnology to produce treatments and cures or once incurable diseases. Although not alive, viruses affect life in many ways.

Terms

anaerobic	binary fission	cocci
antibody	budding	conjugation
antigen	capsid	cyanobacteria
archaea	cellulose	cytokinesis
autotrophs	cell walls	endocytosis
asexual	cell membrane	endospores
bacilli	chemoautotrophs	endosymbiosis
bacteriochlorophyll	chloroplast	enzymes
bacteriophages	chlorophyll *a*	eukarya

facultative aerobes

food chains

genome

gonorrhea

halophiles

human immunodeficiency
  virus (HIV)

immune system

lysogenic cycle

lytic cycle

methanogens

metabolism

mitochondria

mutualism

mutation

natural selection

nitrogen-fixing bacteria

nucleic acid

nucleoid

organelles

operons

parasites

pathogen

peptic ulcers

peptidoglycan

phycocyanin

phycoerythrin

plasmids

polymerase chain reaction
  (PCR)

prokaryotes

prophage

protease

proviron

retrovirus

reverse transcriptase

ribosome

ribosomal subunits

stroma

stromatolites

salmonella

symbiosis

syphilis

thermoacidophiles

transformation

transduction

thylakoids

vaccination

vaccine

viroids

virus

Review Questions

1. Which of these characteristics of living things would a virus exhibit?
   a. heredity;
   b. metabolism;
   c. response to stimulus;
   d. interaction with the environment.

2. Of the following antibiotics, which is the most effective against most viral infections?
   a. penicillin;
   b. erythromycin;
   c. zanax;
   d. none of these, viruses do not respond to most antibiotics.

3. Transcription is the making of RNA off of a DNA template. Which of the following would be the best definition of reverse transcription?
   a. making a protein off of a DNA template;
   b. making a DNA using an RNA molecule as a template;
   c. making polysaccharides out of monosaccharides;
   d. none of these.

4. A capsid is ___.
   a. the lipid/protein membrane surrounding a virus;
   b. the nucleic acid core of a virus;
   c. the enzymes associated with a bacteriophage;
   d. the proteins that surround a typical virus

5. When a virus is in the lytic cycle, which of these will occur?
   a. viral DNA becomes incorporated into the host DNA;
   b. host cell produces many new viruses before it breaks apart;
   c. the viral DNA replicates and is separated by the cell's spindle apparatus;
   d. antiviral defenses of the cell expel the viral DNA.

6. When a virus is in the lysogenic cycle, which of these will occur?
   a. viral DNA becomes incorporated into the host DNA;
   b. host cell produces many new viruses before it breaks apart;
   c. the viral DNA replicates and is separated by the cell's spindle apparatus;
   d. antiviral defenses of the cell expel the viral DNA.

7. When animal viruses are produced, ___.
   a. the host cell lyses or ruptures;
   b. the new viruses bud off of the host cell membrane;
   c. the cell undergoes cytokinesis to produce a new virus and a new host cell.
   d. none of these occur.

8. Which body organ system is most directly concerned with vaccination?
   a. digestive;
   b. circulatory;
   c. respiratory;
   d. immune.

9. Which of these is not a typical shape for a bacterial cell?
   a. rod;
   b. spiral;
   c. spherical;
   d. all are typical bacterial shapes.

10. Bacteria divide to produce new cells using which of the following processes?
    a. mitosis;
    b. binary fission;
    c. meiosis;
    d. karyogamy.

11. Bacteria have which of these structures in common with eukaryotes?
    a. nucleus;
    b. mitochondria;
    c. ribosomes;
    d. endoplasmic reticulum.

12. The oldest known fossils on Earth are most similar to ___.
    a. animals;
    b. plants;
    c. fungi;
    d. bacteria.

13. Bacteria are important as ___.
    a. food;
    b. decomposers;
    c. producers of antibiotics and other medicines;
    d. all of these.

14. The form of nitrogen listed below that can be utilized by most of the living things is ___.
    a. N_2;
    b. H_2NO_3;
    c. NH_4;
    d. none of these can be used in their listed form by living things.

15. If two organisms are in a symbiotic relationship and one causes harm to the other, that relationship is described as ___.
    a. parasitism;
    b. communism;
    c. mutualism;
    d. capitalism.

16. Photosynthesis by bacteria produced ___ as a waste product.
    a. glucose;
    b. carbon dioxide;
    c. dioxygen (O_2);
    d. all of these are produced by photosynthesis.

17. Thylakoids are ___.
    a. infolding of the bacterial plasma membrane on which the enzymes of aerobic respiration are located;
    b. not found in photosynthetic bacteria;
    c. infolding of the bacterial plasma membrane on which the enzymes of photosynthesis are located;
    d. structures only found in eukaryotic chloroplasts.

18. Which of these is a bacterially caused disease?
    a. herpes;
    b. syphilis;
    c. AIDS;
    d. Huntington's disease.

19. Which of these bacterial diseases is spread by sexual contact?
    a. gonorrhea;
    b. salmonella;
    c. typhoid fever;
    d. food spoilage.

Links   20. peptidoglycan

The Nanoworld Image Gallery: Lots of interesting pictures and links for microscopes. [http://www.uq.edu.au/nanoworld/]

Edward Jenner and the Discovery of Vaccination: This online article summarizes the seminal work of British physician Edward Jenner and his development of the first vaccination in 1796. [http://library.sc.edu/spcoll/nathist/jenner.html]

Cells Alive!: Very interesting site with new features each month. Of note here are sections dealing with bacteria and diseases. [http://www.cellsalive.com]

The Microbe Zoo: What are they? Where are they? Why should I care? Answer these questions at this site. [http://commtechlab.msu.edu/sites/dlc-me/zoo/]

Introduction to the Bacteria: UCMP Berkeley series of pages about the Domain bacteria. [http://www.ucmp.berkeley.edu/bacteria/bacteria.html]

Introduction to the Cyanobacteria: UCMP Berkeley site covering many things about the blue-green bacteria [http://www.ucmp.berkeley.edu/bacteria/bacteria.html]

Introduction to the Archaea: These University of California, Berkeley sites offer some pertinent information about Domain Archaea. [http://www.ucmp.berkeley.edu/archaea/archaea.html]

Reference

Woese CR, Kandler O, Wheelis ML. 1990. "Towards a natural system of organisms: Proposal for the domains Archaea, Bacteria, and Eucarya." *Proceedings of the National Academy of Science*, 87(12):4576–4579.

Chapter Opener

A kelp forest, dominated by giant kelp (*Macrocystis pyrifera*), grows off the coast of northern California. This is an important habitat for a diverse array of eastern Pacific marine life.

Objectives

- The Protists, as they have been used traditionally, do not comprise a monophyletic group. Discuss the evidence supporting this statement.
- List the features that support the statement that plants are descended from some group of green algae.
- List the feature(s) or character(s) that define the apicomplexans as a monophyletic group.
- Prepare a list of the economic and environmental significance of several of the basal eukaryotes.
- Discuss the advantages as well as disadvantages that the presence of mitochondria might present to the host organism.
- The eukaryotic cell apparently developed by a series of endosymbiotic events. List and discuss the evidence supporting this idea.
- Discuss the significance of a red tide to fisheries and people living along affected coasts.
- Discuss the "Irish problem" as relates to the potato blight as well as its evolutionary connection.
- List the uses we make of algae, both in a positive and in a negative sense.
- List the evidence that links the chloroplast of red algae to cyanobacteria.

Introduction

The transition to eukaryotic cells appears to have occurred during the Proterozoic Era, about 2 billion years ago. The old Kingdom Protista, as I learned it long ago, thus contains some living groups that might serve as possible models for the early eukaryotes. This taxonomic kingdom has been broken into many new kingdoms, reflecting new studies and techniques that help elucidate the true phylogenetic sequence of life on Earth.

These basal eukaryotes, so named because they usually appear near the base of eukaryan phylogeny, have had profound effects on humans. A joke used to be made about "don't drink the water" when travelling to Mexico for a vacation. This was not an invitation to only drink *cervesa* and tequila, but was in fact rooted in biology. Many water supplies in Mexico are contaminated by a small eukaryan, *Entamoeba hystolytica* that produces a toxin that causes the disease amoebic dysentery, better known as Montezuma's Revenge. When I first met the chemicals produced by this organism, the 4-hour drive home from Mexico was a series of pit stops at Pemex gas stations and roadside rest stops. Locals adjust to the presence of this toxin, but over a weekend, us, Americans do not.

The 1960 election of U.S. President John Fitzgerald Kennedy was more than a change from Democrat to Republican in the White House. Kennedy was an Irish-American and his ascendance to the presidency marked the mainstreaming of a once despised immigrant group: the Irish! Every

U.S. president since Richard Nixon has been of Irish ancestry, including Barak Obama. In the 1974 movie <u>Blazing Saddles</u>, the town fathers grudgingly agree to grant land to the immigrant railroad workers who will help them, except for the Irish! Many movie goers thought this was just screenwrit-ers Mel Brooks and Richard Pryor being cute, but was in fact rooted in the discrimination and hatred directed to the wave of Irish immi-grants who arrived after the Irish Potato Blight of the 1840s. This crop failure was caused by *Phytophthora infestans*, a eukaryan that causes the late blight of the potato disease. When the potato crop, a staple of the Irish diet, failed, thousands of people died, while even more immigrated to America. The scene in the 2002 movie <u>Gangs of New York</u> that showed Irish immigrants getting off the boat and enlisting in the Union Army was historically accurate.

15.1   Review of Eukarya

The Domain Eukarya consists of nucleated, eukaryotic cells. Lynn Margulis' endosym-biosis theory suggests eukaryotes arose by serial endosymbiosis with prokaryotes. This occurred over 2 billion years ago. The pres-ence of membrane-bound organelles such as chloroplasts, mitochondria, and a nucleus surrounded by a nuclear envelope defines a **eukaryotic** cell. Compartmentalization of function within these organelles allows for division of labor. Those eukaryotes that have cell walls lack the peptidoglycan char-acteristic of bacterial walls. Cell membranes of eukaryotes are more like Gram-positive bacterial membranes rather than archaean membranes (Figure 15.1). Gram-negative bacteria have a second membrane outside the plasma membrane but inside their cell wall. Eukaryotic chromosomes are linear and their DNA is associated with histone proteins. The minimum number of chro-mosomes is four, and many eukaryotes have more than one set of chromosomes. Genes on these chromosomes contain intron sequences.

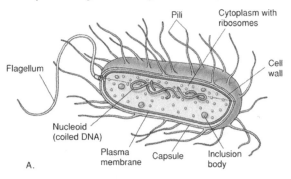

A.

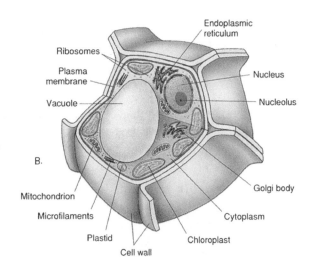

B.

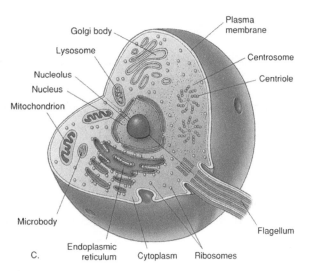

C.

FIGURE 15.1 Comparison of structures in prokaryotic and eukaryotic cells.

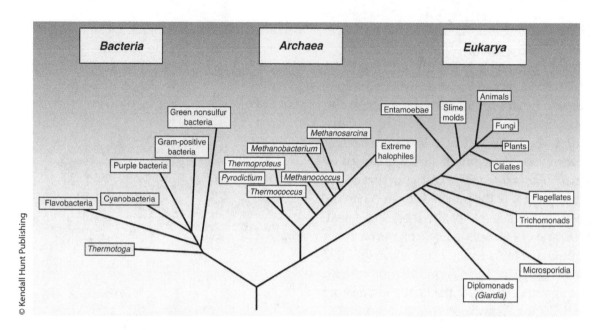

© Kendall Hunt Publishing

FIGURE 15.2 Phylogeny of Domain Eukarya.

Eukaryans exhibit a great deal of variation in their life histories (also referred to as life cycles). Many eukaryans exhibit an alternation between diploid and haploid phases similar to the alternation of generations found in plants. Eukaryan life cycles vary from diploid dominant, to haploid dominant.

The great diversity of form, habitat, mode of nutrition, and life history exhibited by eukaryotes suggest a diverse group with intense natural selection. Eukaryans may also have a unique method of cell division, meiosis, which occurs prior to sexual reproduction. The basal eukaryans are the group from which the other eukaryotic kingdoms evolved, as shown in Figure 15.2.

15.2   Endosymbiosis and the Origin of Domain Eukarya

Symbiosis is the interactive association of two or more species living together. There are several types of symbiosis. Parasitism is a symbiosis where one organism causes harm to the other, its host. An example of this is a disease-causing bacterium, such as *Treponema pallidum*, that causes the disease syphilis in humans. Tapeworms live inside the human intestine and take nutrients from the host (Figure 15.3A). Commensalism is a symbiosis where one creature benefits while the other is neither harmed nor helped. The symbiotic relationship between bacteria and human skin is an example of this. The bacteria live on our skin and we are not normally harmed by their presence. Another example of commensalism is, as is the remora, a small fish that attaches to a host animal and eats stray bits of food (Figure 15.3B). Mutualism is a symbiosis where both organisms benefit. Mutualism examples are abundant: zooxanthellae are dino-flagellates that live within the body of coral animals (Figure 15.3C); *E. coli* bacteria live in the human intestine; etc.

The endosymbiotic model proposed by American biologist Lynn Margulis suggests possible symbiosis of bacteria within early eukaryotic cells. Margulis proposed the mechanism of endosymbiosis, shown in Figure 15.4, to explain the origin of mitochondria and chloroplasts from permanent resident prokaryotes. According to this idea, a larger prokaryote (or perhaps early eukaryote) engulfed or surrounded a smaller prokaryote perhaps as long ago as 2 billion years.

Instead of digesting the smaller organisms the large one and the smaller one entered into a type of symbiosis known as mutualism, where both organisms benefit and neither is harmed. The larger organism gained excess adenosine triphosphate (ATP) provided by the "protomitochondrion" and excess sugar provided by the "protochloroplast," while providing a stable environment and the raw materials required by the endosymbionts. This has become so strong a symbiosis that eukaryotic cells cannot survive without their mitochondria (likewise photosynthetic eukaryotes cannot survive without their chloroplasts), and the endosymbionts cannot survive outside their hosts. Nearly all eukaryans have mitochondria. Mitochondrial division is remarkably similar to the prokaryotic methods that were studied in Chapter 8.

Chloroplasts and mitochondria still retain their own DNA, and have the diversity of structure and photosynthetic pigments that support the idea that the endosymbiosis events occurred independently several times. The photosynthetic pigments (see Table 15.1) in the red, brown, golden-brown, and green algae are very different, lending support for the hypothesis of several different, independent endosymbiotic events.

The DNA, ribosomes, biochemistry, and reproduction of chloroplasts and mitochondria are remarkably bacteria-like. Some living eukaryotes, such as the "amoeba" *Pelomyxa* (not to be confused with the unrelated genus *Chaos*), lack mitochondria, having instead endosymbiotic bacteria that perform mitochondrial duties of ATP generation.

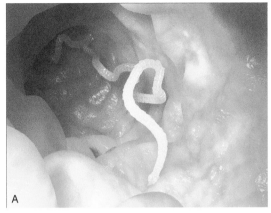

Shutterstock/Juan Gaertner

Shutterstock/Anna Segeren

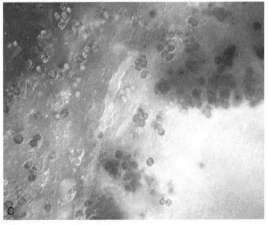

University of Wisconsin

FIGURE 15.3 Examples of symbiosis. A. Parasitism: tapeworm inside a human intestine; B. Commensalism: adult female green turtle (*Chelonia mydas*) swimming with striped remora's (*Echeneis naucrates*) attached; from Naama Bay, Sharm el Sheikh, Red Sea, Egypt; C. Mutualism: zooxanthellae living within a coral polyp.

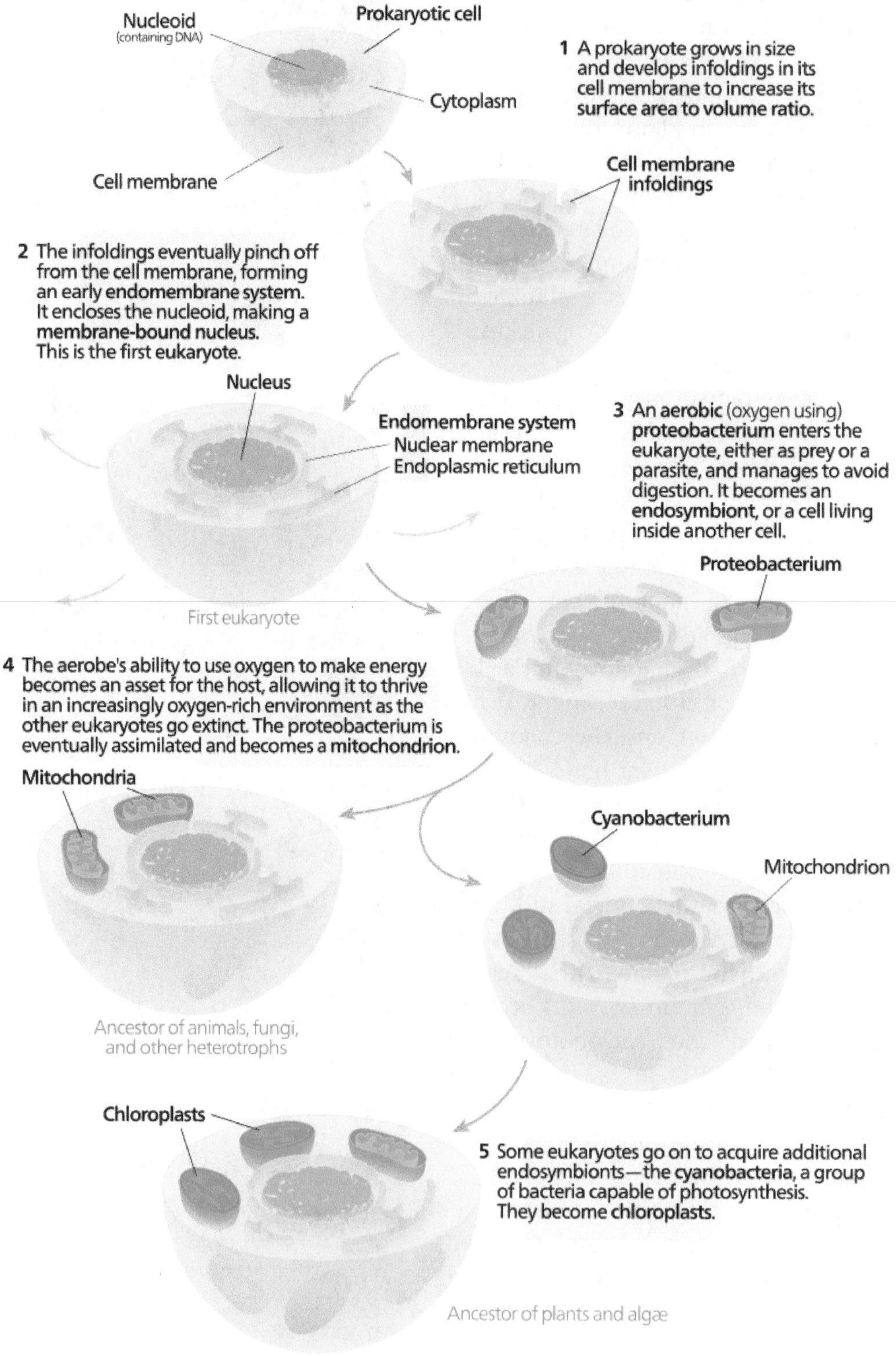

Nucleoid (containing DNA)

Prokaryotic cell

Cytoplasm

Cell membrane

1 A prokaryote grows in size and develops infoldings in its cell membrane to increase its surface area to volume ratio.

Cell membrane infoldings

2 The infoldings eventually pinch off from the cell membrane, forming an early endomembrane system. It encloses the nucleoid, making a membrane-bound nucleus. This is the first eukaryote.

Nucleus

Endomembrane system
Nuclear membrane
Endoplasmic reticulum

3 An **aerobic** (oxygen using) **proteobacterium** enters the eukaryote, either as prey or a parasite, and manages to avoid digestion. It becomes an **endosymbiont**, or a cell living inside another cell.

Proteobacterium

First eukaryote

4 The aerobe's ability to use oxygen to make energy becomes an asset for the host, allowing it to thrive in an increasingly oxygen-rich environment as the other eukaryotes go extinct. The proteobacterium is eventually assimilated and becomes a **mitochondrion.**

Mitochondria

Cyanobacterium

Mitochondrion

Ancestor of animals, fungi, and other heterotrophs

Chloroplasts

5 Some eukaryotes go on to acquire additional endosymbionts—the **cyanobacteria,** a group of bacteria capable of photosynthesis. They become **chloroplasts.**

Ancestor of plants and algæ

© Kendall Hunt Publishing

FIGURE 15.4 Endosymbiosis and the origin of eukaryotes.

TABLE 15.1 Photosynthetic pigments of photosynthetic prokaryotes, algae, and plants. Prokaryote groups are shown in red, protists in blue, and vascular plants in purple

Taxonomic Group	Photosynthetic Pigments
Cyanobacteria	chlorophyll *a*, chlorophyll *c*, phycocyanin, phycoerythrin
Chloroxybacteria	chlorophyll *a*, chlorophyll *b*
Red Algae (Rhodophyta)	chlorophyll *a*, phycocyanin, phycoerythrin, phycobilins
Brown Algae (Phaeophyta)	chlorophyll *a*, chlorophyll *c*, fucoxanthin and other carotenoids
Golden-brown Algae (Chrysophyta)	chlorophyll *a*, chlorophyll *c*, fucoxanthin and other carotenoids
Dinoflagellates (Dinoflagellata)	chlorophyll *a*, chlorophyll *c*, peridinin and other carotenoids
Green Algae (Chlorophyta) and Plants = Viridiplantae	chlorophyll *a*, chlorophyll *b*, carotenoids

15.3   The "Protistans": Stem Eukarya

The protists include all eukaryans that are not plants, animals, or fungi. The old Kingdom Protists (also known as the Protoctista) is abandoned in favor of several monophyletic kingdoms. The problem with the old Kingdom Protista, even as far back as the 1970s, was a lack of cohesion. Heterotrophs, autotrophs, and some organisms that can vary their nutritional mode depending on environmental conditions all were included. Protists occur in freshwater, saltwater, soil, and as symbionts within other organisms. Due to this tremendous diversity, classification of the Protista is difficult. The Protista never were monophyletic. Recall that the goal in systematics is the recognition of monophyletic groups.

Historically, the group has been subdivided based on the mode of nutrition, photosynthetic pigments, and the type of organelles used for locomotion. For example, the organisms using cilia to propel themselves were all placed in the Phylum Ciliata; those using pseudopodia were all in the Phylum Sarcodina. This is an example of form classification, and worked well enough until scientists began to more thoroughly examine the protists. They discovered that form classification did not support the existence of monophyletic groups, and thus should be abandoned. Several new kingdoms have been proposed for the old protista, although consensus among systematists working with these groups has yet to fully emerge. Several organisms once placed in the protists have been moved to other Kingdoms, while others have moved from the Kingdom Fungi to the protists.

15.4   Eukaryan Diversity

The Domain Eukarya divides into a number of Kingdoms: Viridiplantae, Animalia, Fungi, plus what was formerly classified in the abandoned Kingdom Protista. This latter group will be the focus of this section. Since the scientific community does not yet agree on the taxonomic ranks of these former protists, some categories will be unranked.

15.4.1   Kingdom Excavata

Organisms placed in this kingdom are often unicellular parasites, including some that affect humans. Some of the members of this kingdom lack mitochondria. Scientists interpret this as an indication of the divergence of this group from other "protists" prior to the endosymbiosis event that led to the development of the mitochondrion. However, some recent studies seem to indicate that some of the organisms placed in this group are secondarily lacking in mitochondria: their ancestors had mitochondria but lost them over time. Other excavates have mitochondria with different cristae structures than occur among other eukaryans.

15.4.1.1   Phylum Metamonada

Members of this subgroup of excavates have two flagella, two nuclei, and no mitochondria functioning in ATP generation. A few have mitosomes whose function is not yet well known. *Giardia lamblia*, an intestinal parasite that causes giardiasis, is a member of this group. A colorized scanning electron micrograph (SEM) of this organism is shown in Figure 15.5A and B. The parasite can occur free-living in freshwater and is transferred to its human host by ingestion of fecal contaminated food or water or by oral-anal contact by unwashed or poorly washed hands. The organism divides by binary fission (Figure 15.5A), and its spores can be passed out through the excretory system. Proper sanitation and a safe water supply help keep this disease rare in the United States.

15.4.1.2   Phylum Euglenozoa

This phylum includes eukaryans with one or two flagella emerging from an anterior pocket, and paramylum (a glucose polymer) as the storage product for sugars. Some members of this group are autotrophic, while others are heterotrophic.

15.4.1.3   Class Euglenoidea

Organisms in the euglenoids group have two flagella, a contractile vacuole, a photoreceptive eyespot, several chloroplasts, and no cell wall. Euglenoids can live as either autotrophs or heterotrophs. Some autotrophic species of *Euglena* (Figure 15.6) become heterotrophic when light levels

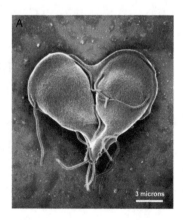
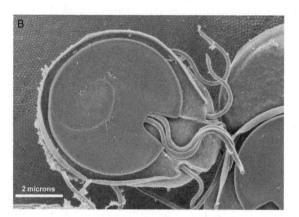

FIGURE 15.5 Colorized scanning electron micrographs of *Giardia*. A. *Giardia lamblia*, a human parasite of the gastrointestinal tract that causes the disease giardiasis. In this image, the organism is in the late stage of cell division; image courtesy of CDC/ Dr. Stan Erlandsen; B. *Giardia muris* trophozoite has four pairs of flagella that are responsible for the organism's motility; image courtesy of CDC/ Dr. Stan Erlandsen.

are low. Eugleniod chloroplasts are surrounded by three membranes instead of the more typical two membranes discussed in Chapter 3. Euglenoid chloroplasts resemble those of green algae in terms of pigments, and are probably derived from the green algae through endosymbiosis. However, the euglenoid pyrenoid produces an unusual type of carbohydrate polymer (paramylum) not seen in green algae.

Euglenoids lack cell walls. In its place, however, is a flexible pellicle composed of protein strips. Euglenoids also have a contractile vacuole like many other protists, for eliminating excess water and maintaining osmotic balance. Euglenoids reproduce by longitudinal cell division, and sexual reproduction is not known to occur.

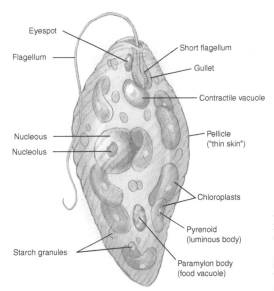

FIGURE 15.6 The structure of *Euglena*, a flagellated eukaryan.

15.4.1.4 Class Kinetoplastida

The kinetoplastids comprise the other group within phylum Euglenozoa. All kinetoplastids are symbiotic, with some being parasitic. *Trypanosoma brucei* (Figure 15.7) is a trypanosome transmitted by the bite of the tsetse fly that causes African sleeping sickness.

15.4.2 Kingdom Alveolata

Kingdom Alveolata was only recently recognized. The feature uniting this clade is the presence of small saccules (alveoli) below the cell membrane surface. Major groups in this kingdom are the ciliates, dinoflagellates, and apicomplexans (a group of parasites that cause malaria and other diseases).

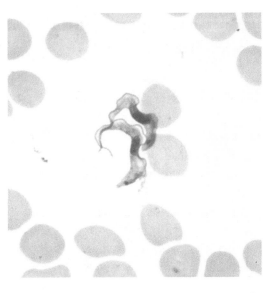

FIGURE 15.7 Two *Trypanosoma brucei* parasites in a human blood smear; image courtesy of CDC/ Blaine Mathison.

15.4.2.1 Phylum Ciliophora

Phylum Ciliophora contains about 8,000 species of eukaryans known as ciliates. These eukaryans move by coordinated strokes of hundreds of cilia projecting through tiny holes in a semirigid pellicle. Ciliates discharge long, barbed trichocysts for defense and for capturing prey, as well as toxicysts that release a poison.

Ciliates are complex, heterotrophic protozoans that lack cell walls and use multiple small cilia for locomotion. To increase strength of the cell boundary, ciliates have a pellicle, a sort of tougher membrane that still allows them to change shape. Most of the 8,000 species occur in fresh water, although some also occur in the oceans. The majority of ciliates have two nuclei: a macronucleus that contains hundreds of copies of the genome and controls metabolism. Ciliates also have a single small micronucleus that contains a single copy of the organism's genome and functions in sexual reproduction. *Paramecium* (Figure 15.8) is a common ciliate observed by students in introductory biology labs.

Since ciliates (and many freshwater protozoans) are hypotonic, removal of water crossing the cell membrane by osmosis is a significant problem. One commonly employed mechanism by unicellular eukaryans is a contractile vacuole, shown in Figure 15.8A, B. Water is collected in the central ring of the vacuole and actively transported from the cell.

Food is taken into the ciliate by an oral groove (or gullet, as shown in Figure 15.8A, D), where small particles of the food are phagocytized into food vacuoles. Often, this can be accomplished in the laboratory period by using yeast stained with Congo red dye, allowing students to see food vacuoles forming. The food vacuoles travel through the cytoplasm and are digested, with the molecules eventually passing into the cytoplasm, and wastes being expelled from the cell by exocytosis through the anal pore (also referred to as the cytoproct, Figure 15.8A).

Ciliates travel along a spiral path, as shown in video). The ciliate rotates along its long axis so that the direction of travel resembles a sine wave.

During asexual reproduction, ciliates divide by transverse binary fission, as shown in Figure 15.8F. You may recall that bacteria have a somewhat similar type of binary fission, although no nuclei occur in bacteria.

Ciliates possess two types of nuclei—a large macronucleus and one or more small micronuclei. The macronucleus controls the normal metabolism of the cell. The micronucleus is involved in sexual reproduction in a process known as conjugation that is shown in Figure 15.8D. The macronucleus disintegrates and the micronucleus undergoes meiosis. Two ciliates then exchange a haploid micronucleus. The micronuclei give rise to a new macronucleus containing certain housekeeping genes.

Paramecium is by no means the only ciliate, merely one of the most common one students will encounter during a laboratory session. Other ciliates (Figure 15.9) include

Vorticella, a stalked ciliate bearing a ring of cilia at its "mouth", and *Stentor*, a ciliate that resembles a giant blue vase with stripes.

15.4.2.2   Phylum Dinoflagellata

The phylum Dinoflagellata contains about 1,000 species of dinoflagellates, two members of which are shown in Figure 15.10. Members of this group have cell walls and store excess sugar as starch. Protective cellulose plates may surround dinoflagellates. Some dinoflagellates also are "armored," having numerous plates that cover the cell. Ornamentation on these plates can be quite beautiful.

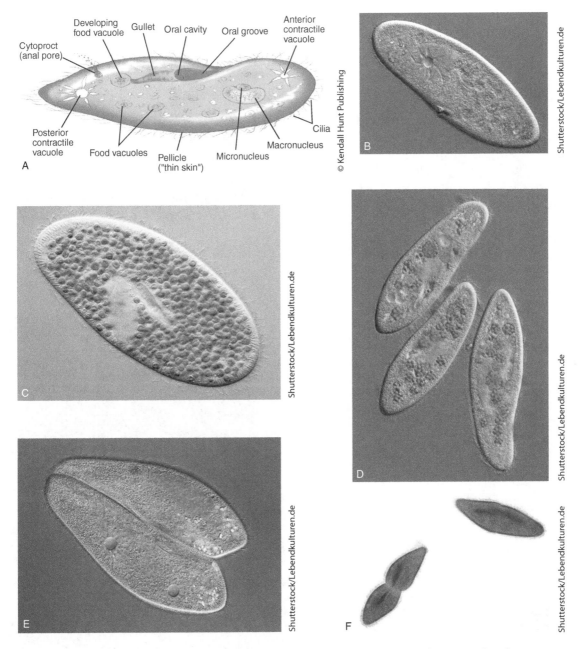

FIGURE 15.8 *Paramecium*. A. Structures of *Paramecium*; B. Light micrograph of *Paramecium caudatum* using differential interference contrast Differential Interference Contrast (DIC) focus showing contractile vacuoles, cilia, food vacuoles, and crystals; C. *Paramecium bursaria* with symbiotic algae, as seen using differential interference contrast DIC; D. *Paramecium caudatum* with colored yeast cells inside food vacuoles; E. *Paramecium caudatum* cells conjugating, light micrograph using differential interference contrast DIC focus on cilia; F. Two stages of binary fission in *Paramecium*.

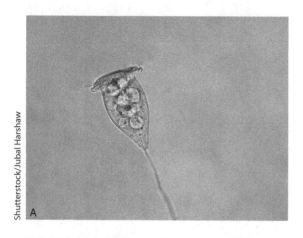

FIGURE 15.9 Ciliate diversity. A. Living *Vorticella* protozoan in fresh water; magnification 400×X; B. *Stentor polymorphus* colored green by symbiotic green algae against a blue dark field.

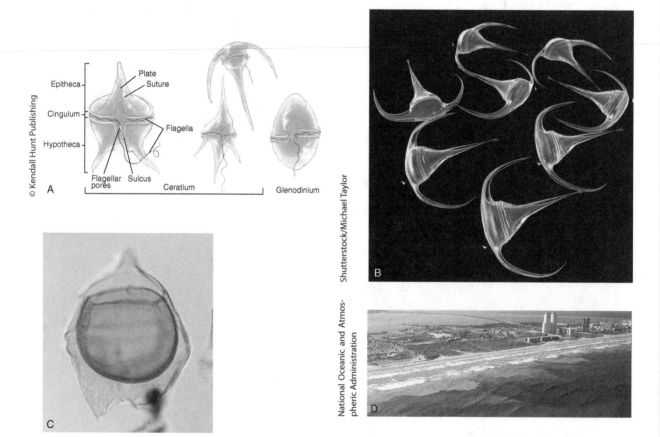

FIGURE 15.10 Dinoflagellates. A. Structure of a dinoflagellate; B. Dinoflagellate *Ceratium long-pipe*; C. Fossil dinoflagellate cyst *Deflandrea phosphoritica* from the Watkins School core in Virginia. Specimen is about 60 μm across. Image courtesy of Lucy E. Edwards, U.S. Geological Survey; D. A Red Tide is a population explosion of certain toxic dinoflagellate species.

Most dinoflagellates are autotrophic, having chlorophyll *a*, chlorophyll *c* in their chloroplasts, as well as a unique pigment peridinin, and some carotenoid pigments. Not all dinoflagellates are autotrophs; some are heterotrophs. Dinoflagellates can be extremely numerous, with concentrations being measured up to 30,000 individuals per cubic millimeter. Dinoflagellates are therefore an important source of food in certain ecosystems. Dinoflagellates have two flagella; one occurs in a longitudinal groove and acts as a rudder, the other occupies a transverse groove and its beating causes the cell to spin as it moves forward.

Coral and related animals may have dinoflagellates living inside their bodies. These dinoflagellates are known as zooxanthellae. The genus *Symbiodinium* contains the majority of these endosymbiotic dinoflagellates. The dinoflagellates provide color to the coral, as well as oxygen and food. When coral reefs bleach, the dinoflagellates have left the coral, producing the dying, bleached coral reef.

Red tides (Figure15.10D) are oceanic phenomena caused by population explosions of certain types of dinoflagellates that release a neurotoxin into the environment after they die. Shellfish concentrate this toxin into a high enough dose that it can kill people who eat the contaminated shellfish. The dinoflagellates are so numerous in the water that the red eyespot in each cell causes the water to appear red.

The fossil record of dinoflagellates is excellent, with most palynologists accepting fossils from the Triassic period as representing some stage of the dinoflagellate life history. The oldest fossil that might be a dinoflagellate cyst is *Arpylorus antiquus*, from Silurian-aged rocks. A group of microfossils that may in part be dinoflagellate cysts are the hystrichospherids, some of which date from the precambrian. Acritarchs, an abundant group of precambrian and Paleozoic microfossils, may also in part be dinoflagellates or might also represent some other group of algae.

15.4.2.3 Phylum Apicomplexa

This group consists of parasitic organisms united by their possession of a unique apical complex of microtubules. Many of the organisms now placed in this group were formerly classified in the old Phylum Sporozoa. Apicomplexans have complex life cycles with diverse forms at different stages.

Members of this group cause human diseases such as malaria and toxoplasmosis. The life history of each organism has it infecting a different host for part of its growth. Toxoplasmosis is transmitted from cats to humans, with between 7% and 72% of the population infected, depending on the geographic area.

Malaria is a disease that affects an estimated 300 million people worldwide. There are several organisms that cause malaria, most of which are spread by mosquitoes, transfusions, and shared hypodermic needles. Control of mosquito populations has led to a decline in malaria in many areas. Infected individuals can be treated with a variety of medicines. However, some of the organisms that cause malaria have developed immunity to some of the more commonly used medicines.

Plasmodium vivax, the cause of one type of malaria, is the most widespread human parasite. When a female *Anopheles* mosquito bites a person, the parasite eventually invades the person's red blood cells, as shown in Figure 15.11. Chills and fever appear when red blood cells burst and release toxin into the person's blood.

15.4.2.4   Kingdom Straminopila

This kingdom includes the diatoms, golden algae, brown algae, and water molds and many other phyla not covered in this book. All members of this kingdom have numerous hairlike projections from their flagellae. Molecular systematic methods established the monophyletic nature of this group. When they are photosynthetic, chlorophyll *c* is the main accessory pigment. This kingdom includes diatoms, giant kelps, and mildews, making it a very diverse group both in terms of lifestyle as well as the size of organisms.

15.4.2.5   Phylum Chrysophyta

This group of freshwater, marine, and terrestrial algae includes the golden algae. Although most members of this group are autotrophs, the vast majority of them can become heterotrophs under low light levels. Food is stored as oils, and photosynthetic pigments include chlorophyll *a* and *c* and yellow carotenoid pigments such as fucoxanthin. This phylum includes several distinct groups, some of which may be removed to other phyla in the future, such as the silicoflagellates and yellow-green algae.

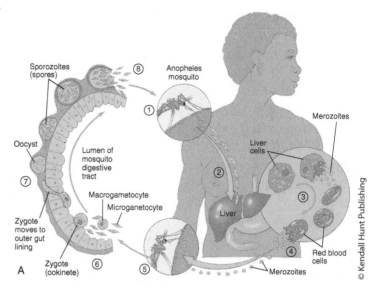

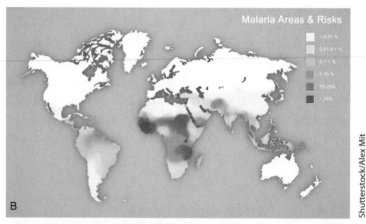

FIGURE 15.11 Malaria. A. Life cycle of *Plasmodium vivax*, the organism that causes the disease malaria; B. Malaria areas and risk; C. Female *Anopheles* mosquito feeding on a human host; image courtesy of CDC/ James Gathany.

15.4.2.6   Phylum Bacillarophyta: Diatoms that live in glass houses

Diatoms are the most numerous unicellular algae in the oceans. They are extremely numerous and an important source of food and O_2 for heterotrophs in aquatic systems, both marine and freshwater. They have the accessory pigment fucoxanthin in their chloroplasts. Examples of the various types of diatoms are shown in Figure

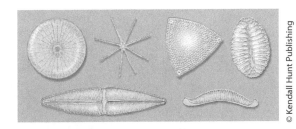

FIGURE 15.12 Diatom structure.

15.12. Diatoms have a cell wall comprising two halves that are technically referred to as valves (or frustules). These valves are mostly made of silica (SiO_2). The diatom cell wall is perforated by numerous small openings. When diatoms reproduce asexually, each received one old valve. The new valve fits inside the old one; therefore, the new diatom is smaller than the original one. Once the shells reach a certain size, the diatom reproduces sexually and restores its size, allowing the asexual reproduction cycle to begin anew.

Diatoms secrete a silicon dioxide shell (called a frustule) that forms the fossil deposits known as diatomaceous earth, which is used in filters and as abrasives in polishing compounds. Diatoms divide into two groups, the pennaleans with bilateral symmetry and elongated shape, and another, the centraleans, with radial symmetry and a rotund shape. Certain diatoms also are important indicators of water quality, while others are useful fossils for age-dating Quaternary deposits.

15.4.2.7   Phylum Phaeophyta: The brown algae

Phylum Phaeophyta, commonly referred to as the brown algae, form a group of exclusively multicellular algae. All of brown algae contain the accessory pigment fucoxanthin, the brown pigment that gives the group its name. Brown algae also store sugar as the carbohydrate laminarin. The chloroplasts contain both chlorophylls *a* and *c*. Members of the group include the giant kelp that can be over 100 m long. Brown algae are used in foods, animal feeds, fertilizers, and as a source for alginate, a chemical emulsifier added to ice cream, salad dressing, and candy. Brown algae also provide food and habitat for marine organisms, as witnessed by the great biodiversity found among the kelp "forests" off the California coast (Figure 15.13).

Fucus is a brown alga differentiated into a floating "blade," flotation bladder, stalk (or stipe), and basal holdfast. *Sargassum*, common in the Sargasso Sea region of the Atlantic Ocean, floats and maintains position by a flotation bladder filled with gas. *Laminaria* is kelp found in the intertidal zone. It is unique among protists because it has tissue differentiation.

15.4.2.8   Phylum Oomycota: The water molds

Phylum Oomycota includes about 580 species of the water molds. As indicated by the name, this group was once considered to belong to the Kingdom Fungi. Aquatic water molds parasitize fishes, forming furry growths on their gills. Some terrestrial water molds parasitize insects and plants; water mold was responsible for Irish potato famine. The body of water molds is vwalls).

FIGURE 15.13 Brown algae. A silhouetted Calico Bass in a kelp forest offshore of Catalina Island, California; B. *Fucus*; C. *Sargassum*; D. *Macrocystis*.

During asexual reproduction, they produce diploid motile spores ($2n$ zoospores; most fungi lack motile spores). Unlike fungi, the adult phase of the life cycle is diploid, producing gametes by meiosis. Eggs are produced in enlarged structures known as oogonia.

15.4.3 Kingdom Rhizaria

This group, here treated as a taxonomic kingdom, is mostly unicellular organisms moving by pseudopodia of varying morphologies. Some produce shells made of silica or other material extracted from water. The common amoeba seen in introductory science labs is not included in this group.

15.4.3.1 Phylum Foraminifera

Foraminifera (also known as forams) are eukaryans that live in the oceans and secrete a shell (also known as a test) composed of silica or calcium carbonate (Figure 15.14). The cytoplasm of forams extends out from under the shell as long, thin pseudopodia. When the organism dies its shell falls to the ocean floor, becoming part if a sedimentary rock. Thus, the fossil record of

The Irish Problem

The Irish potato famine of the mid-1800s was a terrible disaster caused by a water mold, *Phytophthora infestans* (Box Figure 1). This scourge is an example of the impact that a disease can have on the political, economic, and social structure of several countries. Potato is a crop imported to Europe from South America where the Inca people of Peru domesticated it (Box Figure 2). The Inca Empire encompassed a variety of environments from sea level to the heights of the Andes Mountains. When transplanted to Europe, the potato proved well adapted to colder climates like that of Ireland. The potato thrived in Ireland, and the Irish Ireland exploded from 4.5 million in 1800 to approximately 8 million in 1845. Most of the Irish depended on the potato as their food for ten months of the year. Then there was a cold and wet season, ideal growing conditions for *Phytophthora infestans* to proliferate. Some studies suggest the parasite originated in Mexico, but how it got to Ireland and other areas in Europe is a guess. Once there, it found large fields of one type of potato, the lumper. You might recall from your laboratory that potato cells are little more than sack for starch grains. The lumper is now only grown for educational or heirloom purposes.

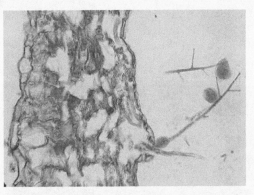

University of Wisconsin

BOX FIGURE 1 *Phytophthora infestans* causes the late blight of the potato.

Shutterstock/Tony Moran

Shutterstock/Mark Skainy

Shutterstock/SeDmi

BOX FIGURE 2 Potatoes. A. Ancient Inca terraces and circles once used as an agriculture laboratory at Moray, Peru; B. Looking down on sacks of potatoes in a Peru marketplace in the Urubamba Valley; C. Potato plant uprooted to show the underground potatoes we all love to eat.

The late blight of potato thus had a very serious consequence to the Irish: famine and starvation. Between 1845 and 1860, more than one million Irish died as a result of the famine brought about by the blight. During the same time, another 1.5 million left Ireland, mostly to the east coast of the United States. Among immigrants during this time were ancestors of Presidents Kennedy, Reagan, Obama, and others.

The effect of the potato blight was more severe in Ireland due to the dependence of the people on just one crop to sustain their population. Coupled with harsh laws against the importing of grain, starvation was a logical outcome. The blight subsided, but not before the population of Ireland had declined by an estimated 25%.

The disease still occurs today, affecting not just potatoes, but the related tomato plants as well. Modern methods have prevented the outbreak as bad as the mid-1840s.

FIGURE 15.14 Foraminifera from Long Island Sound. A. Scanning electron micrograph (SEM) of *Elphidium excavatum clavatum*; B. SEM of *Ammonia beccarii*; C. SEM of *Elphidium incertum*; D. SEM of *Eggerella advena*.

forams is quite good. Oxygen isotope data from foraminifera has been used to calculate ocean temperature fluctuations over the past several hundred thousand years, giving us important data regarding climate change.

15.4.4   Kingdom Rhodophyta, the Red Algae

The red algae are placed in their own kingdom, the Rhodophyta, consisting of about 4,000 species. They are chiefly marine, multicellular organisms that are, as a rule, smaller and more delicate that the brown algae. Some are filamentous, but most are branched, having a feathery, flat, or ribbon-like appearance. Sexual reproduction involves oogamy, although the sperm are not flagellated. The food reserve is floridean starch, a polysaccharide that resembles glycogen.

Red algae have large amounts of the red pigment phycoerythrin (Figure 15.15), and range from unicellular to multicellular in their body plans (sometimes attaining greater than 1 m in length). Red algae are thought to have originated by endosymbiosis of cyanobacteria (which also have phycoerythrin).

Some red algae, the coralline algae, are important contributors to tropical reefs. Mucilaginous material in cell walls is source of agar used to make drug capsules, dental impressions, and cosmetics. Agar is also a major microbiological growth media, and when purified, is a gel for electrophoresis in biotechnology. Agar is also used in food preparation to keep baked goods from drying and to set jellies, and desserts. Carrageenan is an additive to puddings and ice creams; dried sheets of red algae are used in some Japanese dishes.

The Unikonta

This group above the kingdom but below the domain level was proposed back in 1992 to include the taxonomic kingdoms amoebozoa, fungi, and animals. The latter two kingdoms will be considered separately in subsequent chapters. All unikonts possess a single flagellum, or, in the case of amoebas, have pseudopodia. A smaller clade within the unikonts is the opisthokonts: fungi and animals.

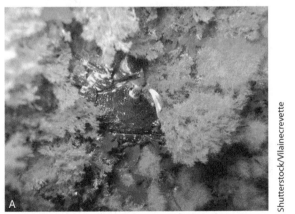

FIGURE 15.15 Examples of red algae. A. *Pachygrapsus* shore crab camouflaged in the red algae *Corallina elongata*, Argeles sur Mer, Roussillon, Pyrenees Orientales, Mediterranean sea, France; B. Unidentified red algae.

15.4.5   Kingdom Amoebozoa

The amoeboids and slime molds that comprise this group, which includes approximately 40,000 species. They both move and engulf their prey with pseudopodia, cytoplasmic extensions formed as cytoplasm streams in one direction. Traditionally this group has included the amoebas, foraminifera, and radiolaria; some of which have been removed to other groups due to recent studies.

Amoeba proteus (Figure 15.16A, B) is a commonly studied member of this phylum. When amoeboids feed, they phagocytize their food when their pseudopods surround and engulf a prey item. Digestion then occurs within a food vacuole. Freshwater amoeboids, including *Amoeba proteus*, have contractile vacuoles used to eliminate excess water.

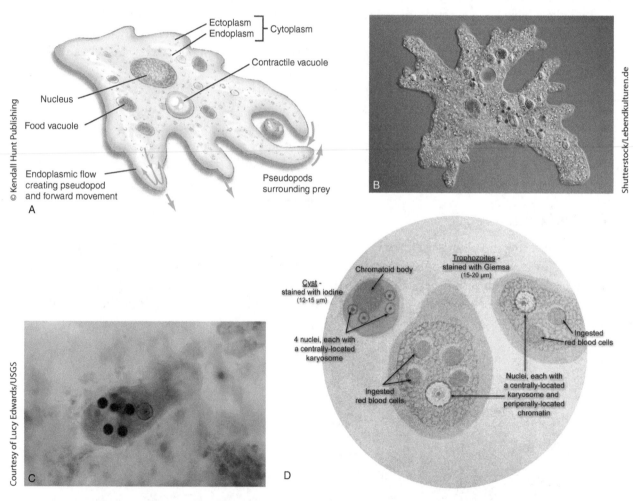

FIGURE 15.16 Representatives of the Amoebozoa. A. *Amoeba* structure; B. *Amoeba proteus* light micrograph (differential interference contrast) focus to show the single nucleus, pseudopodia, and food vacuoles with *Paramecium bursaria* and *Haematococcus pluvialis*; C. *Entamoeba histolytica* trophozoite containing several erythrocytes; image courtesy of CDC/Dr. Mae Melvin, Dr. Greene; D. Illustration of a composite photomicrograph showing details of two stages of the life cycle of *E. histolytica*, the cystic stage (left), and the vegetative, trophozoite stage (center and right).

Amoeba moves by extensions of their cytoplasm known as pseudopodia. Pseudopodia (Figure 15.16A, B) are used by many cells and are not fixed structures like flagella but rather are associated with **actin** near the moving edge of the cytoplasm.

Entamoeba hystolitica (Figure 15.16C, D) is an intestinal parasite in humans that causes amoebic dysentery (sometimes known as Montezuma's Revenge). The organism occurs in the water supply of many communities in Mexico (and other countries), and unless specifically filtered, toxins from this amoeba will cause a disease that can ruin a vacation. Over time, your body adjusts to the toxins, but since many of us only are exposed for short times, our bodies will not be able to cope. Drinking filtered water should prevent contacting this illness.

15.4.5.1   Slime molds

Slime molds are a distinct subset of the Amoebozoa known as the Mycetozoa. Slime molds reproduce by spores. Many slime molds were previously classified as fungi, although now most specialists consider them slime molds to mostly fit into this group. In fact, slime molds do not form a monophyletic group, and will have been split with most falling into Mycetozoa and others classifying into the Bikonta. Slime molds are not closely related to other groups of plants or animals. Slime molds, which spend part of their life as single-celled forms, can aggregate to form multicellular forms known as a plasmodium (not to be confused with the genus *Plasmodium*, some species of which cause malaria). They thus may represent a transition between unicellular and multicellular forms, the second major advancement after the evolution of eukaryotic cells. Figure 15.17 illustrates some of the stages of a plasmodial life history.

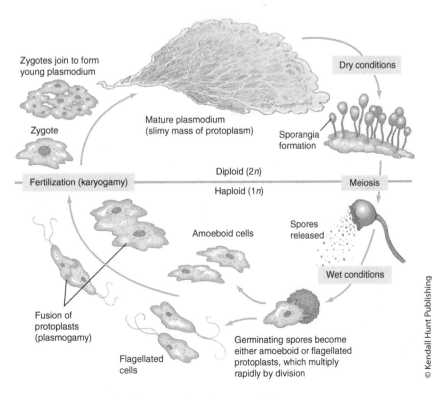

FIGURE 15.17 Life history of a slime mold.

Summary

Eukaryotes most likely arose by endosymbiosis where a large cell engulfed a smaller one. But instead of digesting it, the large cell provided space for the guest symbiont cell, in exchange for rent in the form of sugar, oxygen, or ATP. This once seemingly crazy idea has revolutionized our study of the basal eukaryans, the group informally known as the protistans. This group plays vital roles ecologically from their roles as primary producers, to decomposers. Protistans also produce products of economic importance, such as agar and carageenan. Several diseases, such as malaria, caused by protistans still plague us to this day.

Terms

actin
acritarchs
alternation of generations
binary fission
bilateral symmetry
brown algae
carrageenan
chloroplasts
commensalism
contractile vacuole
diatom
diatomaceous earth
dinoflagellates
diplomonads
endocytosis
endosymbiosis
exocytosis
floridean starch
foraminifera
fucoxanthin
fusulinids
frustules

gametophyte
genome
giardiasis
histone proteins
hypotonic
intron
laminarin
life cycles
life histories
macronucleus
malaria
meiosis
micronucleus
mitochondria
mitosomes
monophyletic groups
mutualism
neurotoxin
nucleus
nuclear envelope
oogamy
oogonia

organelles
osmosis
paramylum
parasitism
palynologists
pennaleans
pellicle
peptidoglycan
peridinin
phagocytized
phytoplankton
pyrenoid
pseudopodia
radiolaria
radial symmetry
red tides
red algae
ribosomes
symbiosis
toxin
zooxanthellae
zoospores

Review Questions

1. The oldest eukaryotic fossils are from the ___.
   a. pPrecambrian;
   b. Cambrian;
   c. Cretaceous;
   d. refrigerator in a science lab

2. The old Kingdom Protista has been subdivided into ___ new taxonomic kingdoms.
   a. two;
   b. three;
   c. five;
   d. sixty four

3. Which of these diseases is caused by the eukaryan *Giardia lamblia*?
   a. Montezuma's revenge;
   b. syphilis;
   c. giardiasis;
   d. valley fever

4. The euglenoids have ___ flagella.
   a. one;
   b. two;
   c. three;
   d. zero

5. The presence of cilia covering the organism's surface characterizes which of these groups?
   a. apicomplexans;
   b. diatoms;
   c. ciliates;
   d. dinoflagellates

6. Pseudopodia occur in which of these groups?
   a. dinoflagellates;
   b. diatoms;
   c. kelp;
   d. amoebozoa

7. Zooxanthellae are ___ that occur within the body of a coral animal.
   a. dinoflagellates;
   b. kelp;
   c. green algae;
   d. diatoms

8. The late blight of the Irish potato was caused by ___.
   a. *Giardia*;
   b. *Pfeisteria*;
   c. *Phytophthora infestans*;
   d. *Paramecium aurelia*

9. The red tide phenomenon is caused by a population increase in ___.
   a. red algae;
   b. dinoflagellates;
   c. water molds;
   d. cyanobacteria

10. Carageenan is an emulsifying agent added to commercial ice creams. It is a product of which of these groups of eukaryans?
    a. red algae;
    b. brown algae;
    c. green algae;
    d. euglenoids

11. The group listed here that contains silica in its surface covering is the ___.
    a. ciliates;
    b. green algae;
    c. diatoms;
    d. water molds

Links

- **Cells Alive!** Very interesting site with new features each month. Of note here are sections dealing with viral life cycles. [http://www.cellsalive.com]

- **The Nanoworld Image Gallery** Lots of interesting pics and links for microscopes. [http://www.uq.edu.au/nanoworld/]

- **The Microbe Zoo** What are they? Where are they? Why should I care? Answer these questions at this site. [http://commtechlab.msu.edu/sites/dlc-me/zoo/]

- **Endosymbiosis and The Origin of Eukaryotes** This clearly presented page gives the elements of the endosymbiosis concept. Page by Dr. John Kimball. [http://users.rcn.com/jkimball.ma.ultranet/BiologyPages/E/Endosymbiosis.html]

- **Endosymbiosis and Parasitism** This selection of images from the Protist Databank shows numerous examples of endosymbiosis. [http://protist.i.hosei.ac.jp/PDB/Images/Subjects/EndosymbiosisE.html]

- **Introduction to the Dinoflagellata** This page from the University of California Museum of Paleontology at Berkeley presents information about the ecology, systematics, fossil record, and morphology of dinoflagellates. [http://www.ucmp.berkeley.edu/protista/dinoflagellata.html]

- **Return of the Potato Blight** Why were Ronald Reagan and John F. Kennedy Presidents of the United States instead of Ireland? Look here for plenty of facts and links to answer THAT question. [http://whyfiles.org/128potato_blight/]

- **Introduction to the Eukaryota Fungi, Protists, Plants, Animals** This page from the University of California Museum of Paleontology at Berkeley presents information about the Domain Eukarya [http://www.ucmp.berkeley.edu/alllife/eukaryota.html]

CHAPTER 16

Biodiversity: The Viridiplantae: Green Algae and Plants

Chapter Opener

Rain forest showing the incredible plant diversity.

Objectives

- Discuss the phylogenetic reason that the green algae must be included in the same taxonomic kingdom as the plants.
- Describe the variation in body style and life cycles seen in the green algae.
- Discuss the evidence supporting the statement that red algae are the sister group to the Viridiplantae.
- Describe the role of endosymbiosis in the evolution of the green algae.
- Describe the differences in life cycle between vascular and nonvascular plants.
- Both bryophytes and vascular plants have leaf-like structures. Prepare a single sentence that can tell the reader what a leaf is, as well as what it is not.
- List some of the constraints heterospory and homospory imposes on the gametophyte generation.
- Compare and contrast the typical plant life cycle and a typical animal one.
- Discuss the chief differences between vascular and nonvascular plants.
- Detail the differences between a megaphyll and microphyll type of leaf.
- Describe the plant body organization of a typical living lycophyte.
- Compare and contrast the characteristics of seed, nonseed, and nonvascular plants.
- List the uses of some common gymnosperm plants, such as pines and ginkgoes, and their uses.
- List some of the uses of flowering plants.
- It has been stated that the ancestor of flowering plants most likely was a gnetalean plant (or at least a plant closely related to them). List the evidence supporting this assertion.

Introduction

This book is titled *Green Harvest* to emphasize the significance of plants, algae, and photosynthetic bacteria life on Earth. Oxygen generating photosynthesis by cyanobacteria over 2.5 billion years ago transformed our planet from an atmosphere lacking dioxygen (O_2) into one with increasing levels of that gas. Algae and other photosynthetic eukaryans form the base of many marine and freshwater food webs. Plants colonized the land during the Ordovician period and the first forests developed during the Devonian. Vertebrate animals followed plants onto the land during the Devonian.

Overstating the significance of plants to our daily lives is practically impossible. We wear plant products as part of cotton, denim, and hemp clothing. Even if we eat only meat, the animals that produced that meat grazed on plants, such as corn, silage, or hay. Fruits and vegetables form important components of the diets of almost every human society. Plants provide materials used to construct our dwellings: wood for beams, fabric for drapes and upholstery, flowers for decoration. For thousands of years, people preserved the harvest by fermenting apples, grapes, and grains. Many medicines derive from plants, as do illegal and harmful drugs like heroin and cocaine. We value flowers for their aesthetic quality. Any beginning art student knows the joy of drawing a still life with an apple and a pear!

Plants were originally one of the two taxonomic kingdoms Linnaeus classified life into in the 1700s. The current classification has three groups in the Kingdom Viridiplantae: Green Algae, nonvascular plants, and vascular plants. Recall from an earlier chapter that monophyletic groups include the ancestor plus all descendants. Biologists have compelling evidence from morphologic and genetic studies that some group of green algae gave rise to the vascular and nonvascular plant groups.

16.1   Characteristics of Plants

The Kingdom Viridiplantae includes unicellular to multicellular green algae and traditional plant groups. All members of this kingdom have chlorophyll *a* and *b* in their chloroplasts, along with carotenoid accessory pigments. Excess glucose is stored as starch. A pyrenoid is present in some but not all members of this kingdom. Cell walls are made of cellulose and other chemicals, although not all cells have a cell wall.

16.2   Systematics of Viridiplantae

The Kingdom Viridiplantae contains several phyla we will examine in greater detail.

16.2.1   Phylum Chlorophyta: Green Algae

What I grew up referring to as the green algae is not a real taxonomic group: it is a paraphyletic group in need to separation. Paraphyletic groups include the ancestor and not all of its descendants. There seem to be two main lineages within the traditional green algae, and these may turn out to make good monophyletic groups in future systematic revisions of the green algae.

Green algae have cellulose cell walls, both chlorophylls *a* and *b*, and store excess sugar as starch. Some members of this group have been considered the undoubted ancestors of plants. Not all members of this group are allied to the plants, however. Body types in the green algae include unicellular to colonial as well as simple multicellular. We will examine several of these representative groups.

Chlamydomonas, shown in Figure 16.1, and similar cells appear to be a starting point within this group. These autotrophic, unicellular forms have a single, cup-shaped chloroplast and two apically inserted flagella. *Chlamydomonas* cells also possess a contractile vacuole and pyrenoid. Excess sugars are stored as starch surrounding the pyrenoid.

Chlamydomonas reproduces sexually when growth conditions are unfavorable, a common process employed by many protists to withstand or outlast a deteriorating environment. Gametes from two different mating types (since this organism is typically have equally small gametes that fuse, we cannot use the terms male and female) come into contact and join to form a diploid

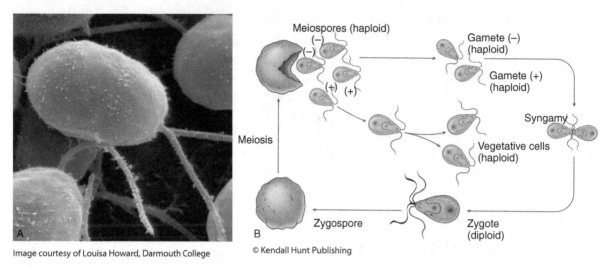

Image courtesy of Louisa Howard, Darmouth College

© Kendall Hunt Publishing

FIGURE 16.1 *Chlamydomonas*. A. Colorized scanning electron micrograph of *Chlamydomonas reinhardtii*; B. Life cycle of *Chlamydomonas*.

zygote (Figure 16.1B). A heavy wall forms around the zygote, in effect turning the diploid zygote into a resistant zygotic spore that can survive until conditions become favorable once again.

Multicellular green algae have some division of labor, producing various reproductive cells and structures. *Ulva*, the sea lettuce illustrated in Figure 16.2, exhibits alternation of generations, producing free-living gametophyte and sporophyte forms. The common sea lettuce is usually haploid (the gametophyte) and reproduces asexually. Gametes are produced by mitosis, fuse, and produce a diploid zygote. The 2*n* zygote germinates and grows to become the sporophyte. Meiosis occurs in certain of the cells in the sporophyte, producing haploid swimming spores that will settle to the ocean floor and produce the next generation haploid gametophyte stage.

Filamentous algae produce gametes by mitosis within one cell of the filament. These gametes are released and swim away until they meet, fuse, and form a diploid zygote. The zygote undergoes meiosis to produce haploid zoospores that swim, rest on the sea floor, and develop into the next generation gametophyte phase.

Filamentous algae are organized into long chains or filaments of cells. Usually, these cells are the same, except when reproduction or nitrogen fixation is occurring. *Ulothrix* has the long axis of its cells perpendicular to the long axis of its filament.

A *Volvox* colony (Figure 16.3) is an example of a colonial alga. Each *Volvox* is a hollow sphere with thousands of cells arranged in a single layer on its perimeter. Individual *Volvox* cells resemble a *Chlamydomonas* cell. A new colony arises as if daughter cells fail to separate.

16.2.2   Phylum Charophyta

The charophytes have long been recognized as the sister group to the organisms traditionally considered plants: the bryophytes and the vascular plants. Some charophytes, for example, *Spirogyra* (Figure 16.4A, B), reproduce by producing a conjugation tube. These charophytes

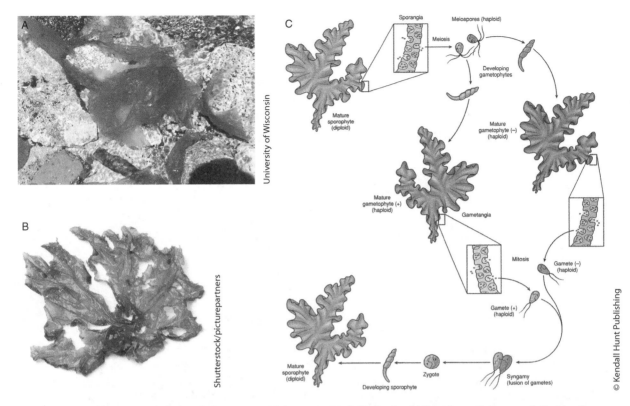

FIGURE 16.2 *Ulva*, a multicellular green alga. A. Habit shot of *Ulva* in a tide pool; B. Thallus of *Ulva*; C. Life cycle of *Ulva* showing the alternation of generations.

produce gametes lacking the flagella characteristic of most charophytes and primitive land plants. The desmids are a group of charophytes characterized by a semicell organization (Figure 16.4C). Charophytes and land plants have similarities in their cell division in their production of a phragmoplast during cytokinesis. The two living charophytes considered possible sister groups to land plants are *Chara* (Figure 16.4D) and *Coleochaete* (Figure 16.4E). However, a 2011 study suggests conjugating charophytes such as *Spirogyra* may be the closest relative to land plants.

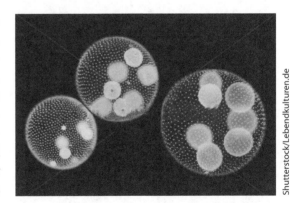

FIGURE 16.3 The colonial alga *Volvox aureus* showing asexually produced daughter colonies in side the mother colony.

16.2.3 Subkingdom Embryophyta

The land plants, the Subkingdom Embryophyta, include multicellular phototrophs that occur on land (although some of them have secondarily returned to water). The earliest embryophyte fossils come from terrestrial deposits. There are more than 300,000 living species of terrestrial plants known, as well as an extensive fossil record.

The plant life cycle (Figure 16.5) shows an alternation between haploid (the gametophyte) and diploid (the sporophyte) generations. When examining any life cycle diagram there are two major events to look for. First is meiosis, the cellular division process studied in an earlier chapter. Meiosis reduces the number of sets of chromosomes by half; in most eukaryans diploid ($2n$) cell produces up to four haploid (n) cells. These haploid cells grow by mitosis to become

FIGURE 16.4 Representative charophytes. A. *Spirogyra*; B. *Spirogyra* showing conjunction tubes and zygospores; C. The desmid *Micrasterias rotata*; D. *Chara*; E. *Choleochaete*.

the gametophyte phase of the plant life cycle. Some gametophytes are large, conspicuous plants, while others are microscopic. Gametophytes produce gametes by mitosis. Male gametes originate in an antheridium, while female gametes form in an archegonium. Gametes fuse during fertilization to produce a single-celled diploid zygote. In multicellular eukaryans, the zygote grows by mitosis to become the next generation sporophyte. Some single-celled eukaryans, such as dinoflagellates and *Chlamydomonas* (Figure 16.1), have their zygote divide by mitosis to produce haploid cells.

Within the plant kingdom, the dominance of phases varies. Nonvascular plants, the mosses and liverworts, have the gametophyte phase dominant. Vascular plants show a progression of increasing sporophyte dominance from the ferns and "fern allies" to angiosperms.

Plants have two further variations on their life cycles. Plants that produce bisexual gametophytes have those gametophytes germinate from isospores (*iso* = same) that are about all the same size. This state is referred to as homospory (sometimes also called isospory). Homosporous plants produce bisexual gametophytes. Ferns are a classic example of a homosporous plant.

Plants that produce separate male and female gametophytes have those gametophytes germinate from (or within the case of the more advanced plants) spores of different sizes (heterospores; *hetero* = different). The male gametophyte produces sperm, and is associated with smaller or

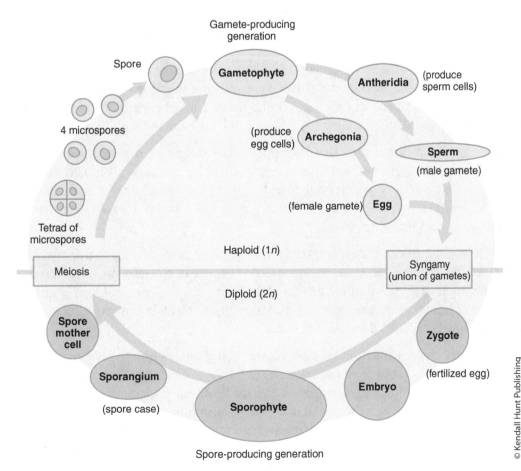

FIGURE 16.5 Generalized plant life cycle.

© Kendall Hunt Publishing

microspores. The female gametophyte is associated with the larger or megaspores. Botanists consider heterospory a significant step toward the development of the seed. Seeds enabled plats to withstand bad environmental conditions.

16.2.3.1   Plant Adaptations to Life on Land

Organisms in water do not face many of the challenges that terrestrial creatures do. Water supports the organism, the moist surface of the creature serves as a superb surface for gas exchange, and so forth. For organisms to exist on land, a variety of challenges must be met.

Drying out Once removed from water and exposed to air, organisms must deal with the need to conserve water. Living things have developed number of approaches, such as the development of waterproof skin (in animals), living in very moist environments (amphibians, bryophytes), and production of a waterproof surface (the cuticle in plants, cork layers, and bark in woody trees).

Gas exchange Organisms that live in water exchange carbon dioxide and oxygen gases across their surfaces, such as cell membranes. These exchange surfaces are moist, thin layers across which diffusion occurs. Organismal response to the challenge of drying out tends to make these surfaces thicker, and waterproof, although this interferes with gas exchange across those surfaces. Many fish already had gills and swim bladders, so when some of them began moving between ponds, the swim bladder (a gas retention structure helping buoyancy in the fish) began to act as a gas exchange surface, ultimately evolving into the terrestrial lung. Many arthropods had gills or other internal respiratory surfaces that were modified to facilitate gas exchange on land. Plants to share common ancestry with the charophycean algae. The plant solution to gas exchange is a new structure, the guard cells that flank openings (stomata) in the above ground parts of the plant. By opening these guard cells, the plant is able to allow gas exchange by diffusion through the open stomata.

Support The dense liquid they live in supports the weight of organisms living in water. The largest animals that ever lived were not the land-dwelling dinosaurs, but certain modern whale species. Once on land, organisms had to deal with the less dense air that could not support their weight. Adaptations to deal with support include animal skeletons and specialized plant cells/tissues that support the plant.

Conduction Single celled organisms only have to move materials in, out, and within their cells. A multicellular creature must do this at each cell in its body, plus move material in, out, and within the organism. Adaptations to this include the circulatory systems of animals, and the specialized conducting tissues xylem and phloem in plants. Some multicellular algae and bryophytes also have specialized conducting cells.

Reproduction Organisms in water can release their gametes into the water, where the gametes will swim by flagella until they encounter each other and fertilization happens. On land, such a scenario is not possible. Land animals have had to develop specialized reproductive systems involving fertilization when they return to water (amphibians), or internal fertilization and an amniotic egg (reptiles, birds, and mammals). Insects developed similar mechanisms. Plants have also had to deal with this, either by living in moist environments like the ferns and bryophytes do, or by developing specialized delivery systems like pollen tubes to get the sperm cells to the egg.

Embryophytes divide into two groups: plants lacking lignin-containing conducting cells (the nonvascular plants or bryophytes) and those containing lignin-impregnated conducting cells (the vascular plants, or Tracheophytes). Living groups of nonvascular plants include the liverworts, hornworts, and mosses. Vascular plants comprise the more familiar plants, such as pines, ferns, corn, and oaks. The phylogenetic relationships within the Viridiplantae are shown in Figure 16.6.

16.2.4   Bryophytes

Bryophytes are small, nonvascular plants that first evolved approximately 500 million years ago. The earliest land plants were most likely bryophytes. Bryophytes lack vascular tissue and have life cycles dominated by their gametophyte phase. Their lack of conducting cells limits the size of bryophytes, generally keeping them to less than 12 cm (5 in.) high. Bryophytes lack true roots, bit in their place have root-like structures known as rhizoids. Bryophytes include the hornworts, liverworts, and mosses. Recent phylogenetic studies suggest mosses are polyphyletic.

16.2.4.1   Phylum Marchantiophyta: The Liverworts

Liverworts are nonvascular plants with a lobed plant body known as a thallus. There are two groups of liverworts, the more well-known thallose liverworts (Figure 16.7) that resemble the lobes of the liver, and the leafy liverworts that look very much like mosses. Gemmae are vegetative reproductive structures in liverworts. Gametophyte cells in the gemma can be spread by rainfall. While there are gas exchange structures on liverworts, they are not the stomata that occur in all other plants. This has led systematists to consider liverworts as early offshoots in the pathway of plant evolution.

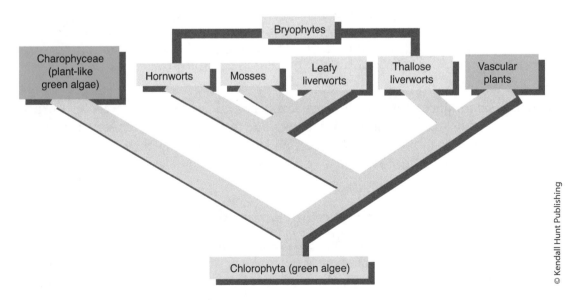

© Kendall Hunt Publishing

FIGURE 16.6 Phylogeny of the Kingdom Viridiplantae.

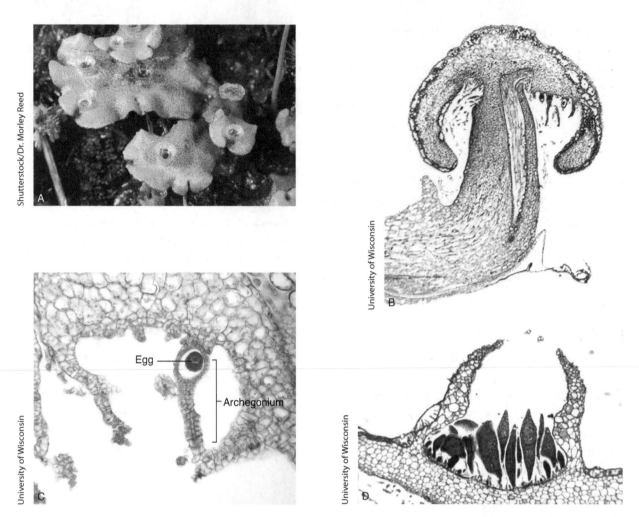

FIGURE 16.7 Liverworts. A. Thalloid liverwort with gemma cups, a type of vegetative reproduction mechanism; B. Light micrograph of a section through an archegoniophore; note the archegonia pointing downward; C. Light micrograph of a section through an archegonium; D. Light micrograph of a section through the gemma.

Economic significance of liverworts is practically negligible today. They were once considered important plants for treating diseases of the liver due to the thallose liverworts resemblance to the liver. This was due to the ancient medical philosophy known as the doctrine of signatures. According to this idea, the shape of a plant or plant part would indicate the diseases it could treat.

16.2.4.2   Phylum Anthocerotophyta: The Hornworts

This small phylum of relatively common but inconspicuous plants contains thallose forms that produce columellar sporophytes that have a horn-like appearance and give the group its common name of hornworts (Figure 16.8). The presence of cyanobacteria inside pockets left by dead cells can produce a distinctive blue-green color for the hornwort gametophyte.

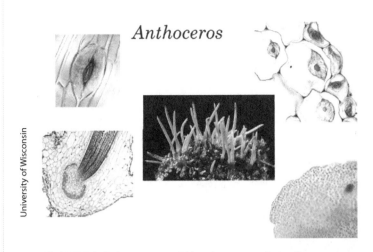

Anthoceros

University of Wisconsin

FIGURE 16.8 Images of the hornwort *Anthoceros*.

16.2.4.3 Phylum Bryophyta: The Mosses

The 12,000 moss species make this the most diverse and largest phylum of the nonvascular plants. This phylum includes the sister group for the tracheophytes. Mosses (technically, the true mosses as there are other plants and even animals that bear the name moss) have numerous leaf-like structures projecting form their stems, but since these "leaves" lack vascular tissue they are not true leaves. In contrast to the liverwort thallus that is not very tall, gametophytes of mosses can typically tower to 10 cm heights (Figure 16.9A). One moss has gametophytes that reach up to 50 cm tall. There may be several leafy shoots arising from an underground rhizome.

Sphagnum, peat moss (Figure 16.9B), is a common moss in peat bogs. These bogs accumulate the dead peat moss, which becomes compressed into the fossil fuel known as peat. In many areas of northern Europe peat was a cheap fuel to heat dwellings. In one region of Scotland, charcoal made from dried peat (Figure 16.9C) is used to smoke the barley as part of making the local form of Scotch whisky. Peat moss is commonly added to garden soils as the dead plants will absorb water as well as fertilize the soils as they decompose.

The gametophytes dominate the life cycle while the sporophyte depends on the gametophyte for nutrition. The moss gametophytes are either male or female. Male gametangia (antheridia; Figure 16.9D) are produced on the tops of a male gametophyte shoot, while female gametangia (archegonia; Figure 16.9D) occur on top of a female shoot. When there is enough water, the flagellated, swimming sperm are released and swim from the antheridium to a nearby archegonium. Once the haploid sperm and haploid egg fuse during fertilization, the zygote cell divides by mitosis to become the next generation sporophyte. The moss sporophyte produces spores in a sporangium that is borne on a stalk that raises it even higher above the gametophyte. Meiosis occurs in the moss sporophyte to make huge numbers of spores that are released when the operculum covering the sporangium opens (Figure 16.9E). The spores eventually settle to the ground some distance from their source. A few of the spores will germinate to produce the next generation gametophyte, referred to as a protonema.

16.2.5 Tracheophytes: The Vascular Plants

The vascular plants (also known as tracheophytes) have specialized transporting cells xylem (for transporting water and mineral nutrients) and phloem (for transporting sugars from leaves to the rest of the plant). When most people think of plants they invariably picture vascular plants. Tracheophytes tend to be larger and more complex than bryophytes, and have a life cycle where the sporophyte is more prominent than the gametophyte. Vascular plants also demonstrate increased levels of organization by having organs and organ systems. The novel features of the vascular plants are summarized in Table 16.1.

Shutterstock/Anita Huszti

Shutterstock/Kuttelvaserova Stuchelova

Shutterstock/Paul van den Berg

© Kendall Hunt Publishing

Gametangia clusters
(either male or female)

Male gametangia
(antheridia containing
sperm cells)

Mature
gametophytes

Female gametangia
(archegonia containing eggs)

FIGURE 16.9 Examples of moss. A. Habit shot of *Polytrichum*, a moss commonly examined in introductory biology classes; note the sporophytes emerging from the lower gameto-phytes in the image; B. *Sphagnum*, peat moss, showing the sporophytes emerging from the leafy gametophytes; C. Drying peat in the highlands of cape Rua Reidh, Scotland; D. The moss gamete producing organs; E. The life cycle.   (*Continued*)

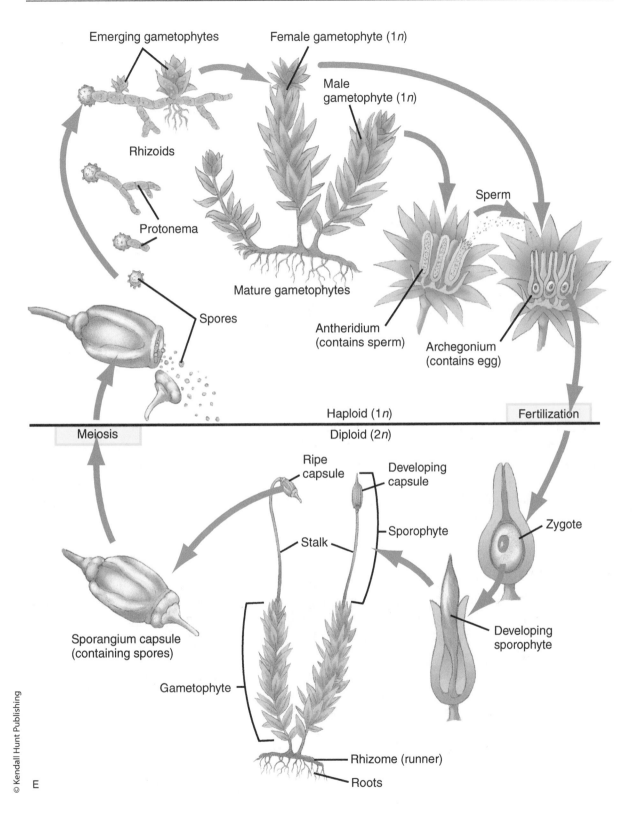

Emerging gametophytes

Female gametophyte (1n)

Male gametophyte (1n)

Rhizoids

Sperm

Protonema

Mature gametophytes

Spores

Antheridium (contains sperm)

Archegonium (contains egg)

Fertilization

Haploid (1n)

Meiosis

Diploid (2n)

Ripe capsule

Developing capsule

Sporophyte

Zygote

Stalk

Sporangium capsule (containing spores)

Gametophyte

Developing sporophyte

Rhizome (runner)

Roots

E

FIGURE 16.9 (*continued*)

TABLE 16.1 Major evolutionary advances of the vascular plants

Advance	Green Algae	Bryophytes	Tracheophytes
Development of the root-stem-leaf vascular system	Nonvascularized body (thallus) that may be variously shaped, no leaves, shoots, or roots	No vascular system Leaf-like structures on vertical stems; no vascular tissue	Vascularized leaves, stems, roots
Reduction in the prominence of the gametophyte	Wide range of life cycles, some have gametophyte dominant, others have sporophyte dominant	Sporophyte generation dependent on gametophyte generation for food; gametophyte is free-living and photosynthetic	Progressive reduction in gametophyte, leading to its dependence on sporophyte for food in seed plants; three-celled male gametophyte and a (usually) eight-celled female gametophyte
Development of seeds	No seeds	No seeds	Some but not all have seeds
Spores/Pollen	Spores for resisting environmental degradation	Spores germinate to form gametophyte	Spores germinate to form gametophyte generation

Vascular plants first developed during the Silurian period, about 400 million years ago. The earliest vascular plants had no roots, leaves, fruits, or flowers, and reproduced by spores. *Cooksonia* was a typical early vascular plant. It was less than 15 cm tall, with stems that branched dichotomously. Dichotomous branching (where the stem divides into two equal branches) appears primitive or ancestral in vascular plants. Some branches on *Cooksonia* terminated in sporangia that produced a single size of spore.

16.2.5.1   Phylum Lycophyta

Members of the Phylum Lycophyta bear sporangia at the tips of some of their shoots in what botanists term strobili (singular: strobilus). A strobilus is a series of sporangia and modified leaves closely grouped on a stem tip. The leaves in strobili are soft and fleshy as opposed to the hard, modified leaves in cones.

Leaves containing vascular tissue (a leaf vein) are major advance for lycophytes. This increases the surface area of the stem for photosynthesis. Lycophyte leaves are microphylls that do not form a leaf gap in the vascular supply of the stem. Ferns and other plants produce megaphylls that produce a leaf gap.

Today, there are fewer genera of lycophytes than during the group's heyday, the Paleozoic era. Major living lycophytes include *Lycopodium* (Figure 16.10A), commonly called the club moss although it is not a moss, *Selaginella* (the so-called resurrection plant, Figure 16.10B, C), and *Isoetes*.

Lycopodium is a homosporous plant (Figure 16.10F). Spores of *Lycopodium* germinate in the soil and produce a bisexual gametophyte (Figure 16.10D). These spores are all approximately the same size. *Selaginella* and *Isoetes* are heterosporous, and thus produce two sizes of spores: small microspores (Figure 16.10G) that produce the male gametophyte and larger megaspores (Figure 16.10G, H) that produce the female gametophyte. The production of two sizes of spores leads to separate unisexual gametophytes, and marks an important step toward the evolution of seeds. Modern lycophytes are small, herbaceous plants. Many of the prominent fossil members of this group produced large amounts of wood and were significant trees in the Carboniferous-aged coal swamps.

Selaginella is a heterosporous lycophyte. Some species of this genus can withstand drying out by going dormant until they are rehydrated. For this reason, these forms of the genus are commonly called resurrection plants (Figure 16.10B).

FIGURE 16.10 Representative lycophytes. A. Stiff club moss (*Lycopodium annotinum*) in summer, Carpathian Mountains, Ukraine; B. Rose of Jericho (*Selaginella lepidophylla*), also known as the resurrection plant; C. *Selaginella argentea* showing the small, closely spaced leaves; D. Life cycle of *Lycopodium*; E. Micrograph of strobili of *Lycopodium* and *Selaginella* allowing comparison of homosporous versus heterosporous nature of the plants; F. Light micrograph of *Lycopodium* sporangium on a sporophyll; G. Light micrograph of megaspores and microspores of *Selaginella*; H. Light micrograph of megaspores in a megasporangium of *Selaginella*; note the thick exine of the spores and cross-sectional view of ornamentation of the exine; I. Light micrograph of microspores in a microsporangium of *Selaginella*. *(Continued)*

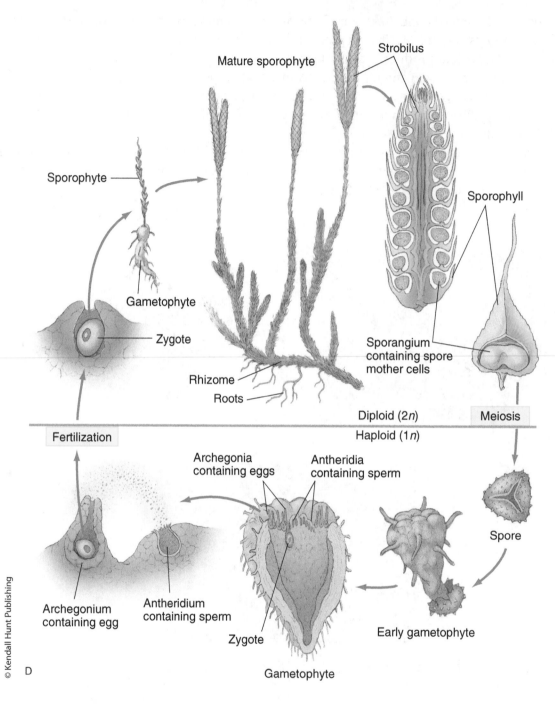

D

FIGURE 16.10 (*Continued*)

Strobili

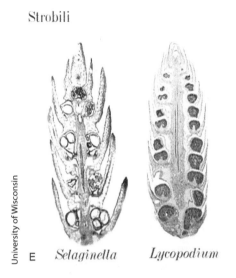

University of Wisconsin

E   *Selaginella*   *Lycopodium*

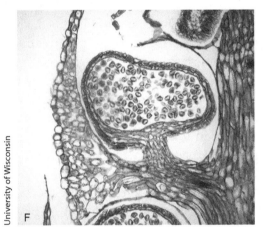

University of Wisconsin

F

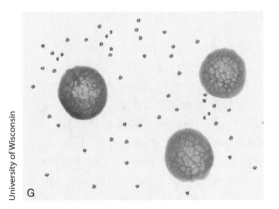

University of Wisconsin

G

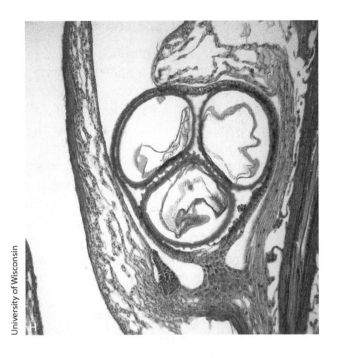

University of Wisconsin

H

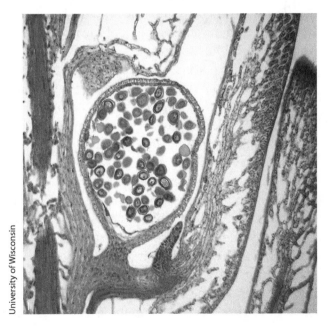

University of Wisconsin

FIGURE 16.10 *(Continued)*

16.2.5.2   Phylum Polypodiophyta

Ferns reproduce by spores from which the free-living bisexual gametophyte generation germinates. There are 12,000 species of ferns today, placed in the Phylum Polypodiophyta. The fossil history of ferns shows them to have been a dominant plant group during the Paleozoic Era. Most ferns have pinnate leaves, exhibiting small leaflets on a frond, as shown in Figure 16.11. Ferns have megaphyll leaves, which cause a leaf gap in the vascular cylinder of the stem/rhizome. Most fern fronds are subdivided into a number of leaflets (Figure 16.11A). A few ferns are trees (Figure 16.11A), but the vast majority of ferns we commonly encounter are smallish, shrubby plants. A few ferns, like the staghorn fern shown in Figure 16.11B grow as epiphytes on other plants. Fern fronds develop from a fiddlehead (Figure 16.11E).

The fern gametophyte, referred to as a prothallium, produces both male and female gametes. Spores shed from the underside of the sporophyte leaves (Figure 16.11F) germinate to produce the gametophyte. Once fertilization occurs, the next generation sporophyte develops from the egg located in the gametophyte (Figure 16.11F). After growing and maturing, sporophytes produce collections of sporangia known as sori (singular sorus) on the underside of the leaflets (Figure 16.11F). Many fern sporangia have a row of cells on the outside known as an annulus. Meiosis occurs inside the sporangia to produce spores. The drying of the annulus opens up the sporangium, releasing the spores. Some ferns have their sori covered by a structure known as an indusium.

Ferns are used in some medicines, as landscaping and floral components, and as food in some societies. Fern fiddleheads are eaten raw in salads or cooked in certain dishes. The aquatic fern *Azolla* is used as a fertilizer in rice paddies in Southeast Asia (Figure 16.12). The cyanobacterium *Anabaena* grows in a symbiotic relationship with *Azolla*. Nitrogen fixed by the cyanobacterium is released into the environment of the rice paddy, eliminating the need for petrochemical fertilizers. Arctic populations of *Azolla* are also thought to have broken the extreme greenhouse conditions of the Paleocene–Eocene Thermal Maximum during the Paleogene period by drastically reducing atmospheric carbon dioxide levels. Further back in time ferns were some of the first plants to begin growing after the Cretaceous–Paleogene mass extinction event 65 million years ago. In some areas today, ferns are important pioneer species that repopulate areas following vegetation disruption by fires or logging activity.

Class Equisetophyta The plants in the class Equisetophyta once dominated forests during the Paleozoic era. Today, the equisetophytes are relegated to minor roles as herbaceous plants. The class contains the single surviving genus, *Equisetum* (Figure 16.13A). The group is defined by their green, jointed, hollow stems, with many small megaphylls produced at a node (Figure 16.13A), production of spores in strobili produced at the tips of stems (Figure 16.13B), and spores bearing elaters (Figure 16.13C) that aid in spore dispersal. The gametophyte is small, bisexual, photosynthetic, and free-living. Silica concentrated in the stems gives this group one of their common names: scouring rushes. American pioneers to scour their pots and pans out on the trail reportedly used *Equisetum*. The fossil members of this group are often encountered in coal deposits of Carboniferous age in North America and Europe.

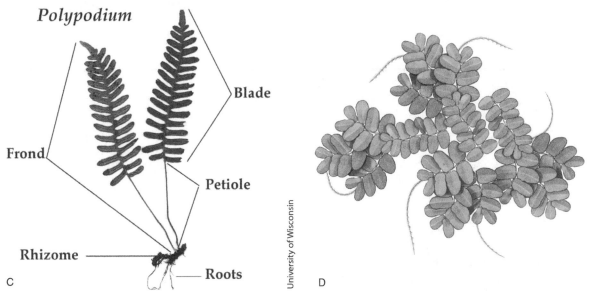

FIGURE 16.11 Ferns. A. Aerial view of a group of tree ferns; B. Staghorn fern growing as an epiphyte on a tree; C. Labeled sporophyte of *Polypodium*; D. *Azolla*, an aquatic fern; E. Christmas Fern Fiddleheads (*Polystichum acrostichoides*) on the forest floor; F. Life cycle of a fern. *(Continued)*

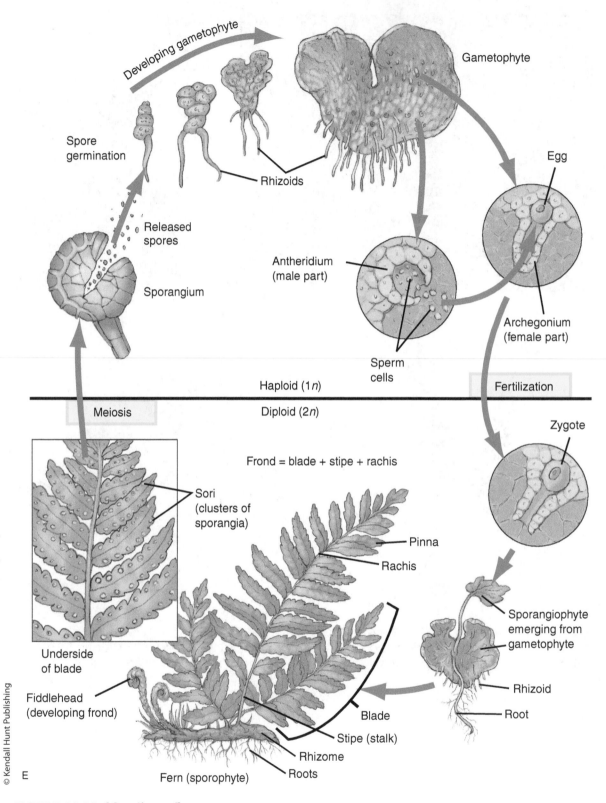

© Kendall Hunt Publishing

E

FIGURE 16.11 (Continued)

Class Psilotopsida *Psilotum* (Figure 16.14A) has three fused sporangia, termed a synangium (Figure 16.14B), located on the sides of the stems that produce homospores. *Psilotum* lacks leaves and roots. Small, nonvascularized ennations project from the plant stem.

Ophioglossum (Figure 16.14C) is a genus of fern that has significant differences from the traditional ferns. Species in the genus *Ophioglossum* have a complete leaf, as opposed to the pinnate leaf produced by most ferns. The plant also has the highest number of chromosomes, with over 1000.

The Seed Plants

Gymnosperms have seeds but not fruits or flowers. *Gymnos* means naked, *sperm* means seed: thus, the term gymnosperm literally means

FIGURE 16.12 Rice plants and mosquito fern (*Azolla*, the red color in the image) growing in a rice paddy. Cyanobacteria growing symbiotically with the *Azolla* provide organic nitrogen to the rice and produce the red color.

naked seeds. Gymnosperms developed during the Paleozoic era and became the dominant seed plant group during the early Mesozoic era. The ancestors of gymnosperms were some now-extinct type of heterosporous fern or related group. There are 700 living species of gymnosperms placed into four phyla: conifers (such as pines and spruce), cycads (such as the sago palm, *Cycas revoluta*), ginkgoes (the maidenhair tree, *Ginkgo biloba*), and gnetophytes (such as Mormon tea, *Ephedra*).

Gymnosperms are undoubtedly the group from which the angiosperms developed. As Charles Darwin noted in *Origin of Species*, which group "remains an abominable mystery." Numerous gymnosperm groups have been proposed as flowering plant ancestors over the past century.

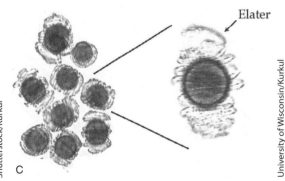

FIGURE 16.13 *Equisetum*, the scouring rush, or horsetail. A. *Equisetum giganteum* sporophyte; B. *Equisetum* strobilus showing the sporophylls and sporangia; C. *Equisetum* spores showing the elaters.

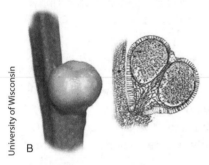

FIGURE 16.14 Psilotopsida. A. Habit shot of *Psilotum*; B. *Psilotum* synangium; C. *Ophioglossum*, a small fern with a nonfernlike leaf.

16.2.5.3   Phylum Cycadophyta

Phylum Cycadophyta contains gymnosperm plants known as Cycads (Figure 16.15). These plants retain several fern-like features, notably pinnate leaves and circinate vernation (Figure 16.15B). Because of their fern-like leaves, cycads are often mistaken for ferns or palm trees. However, cycads usually produce cones of nonphotosynthetic sporophylls, unlike ferns that produced numerous sori on the undersides of their leaves. Palms are flowering plants, although their flowers are quite small and have reduced, nonshowy petals. Cycads (like all seed plants) are heterosporous, unlike the ferns that are mostly homosporous. Cycad cones (Figure 16.15C, D) are either pollen producing (male) or ovule-producing (female); in fact, the plants producing them are dioecious, having separate male and female plants. Cycads also produce free-swimming sperm (a feature also found only in ginkgoes among living seed plant groups).

Cycads were much more prominent in the forests during the Mesozoic era than they are today. Presently, they are restricted to the tropics. *Zamia floridana* is the only cycad occurring natively in the continental United States. Several species of *Cycas*, notably *C. revoluta* (Figure 16.15), are commonly encountered cultivated plants in warm, moist areas. *C. revoluta* leaves are often used in Palm Sunday services in some churches, both for their feathery appearance and availability from local greenhouses. Cycads today are restricted to tropical or subtropical areas where they range from arid to wet regions.

16.2.5.4   Phylum Ginkgophyta

The ginkgoes also were a much more prominent group in the past than they are today. The sole survivor of this once widespread group is *Ginkgo biloba*, the maidenhair tree shown in Figure 16.16. Extensively cultivated as an ornamental plant, *Ginkgo* was thought extinct in the wild until it was discovered growing natively in a remote area of China. Ginkgoes are dioecious, with separate male and female plants. The males are more commonly planted since the females produce seeds that have a nasty odor. Pollination is by wind. *Ginkgo* has become known as an herbal supplement that improves memory. Scientific studies refuted that claim.

FIGURE 16.15 Cycads. A. Habit shot of cultivated cycads in Vietnam; B. New whorl of leaves emerging; C. Butterfly on male *Cycas cairnsiana* pollen cone. *Cycas cairnsiana* is native to northern Australia; D. Close-up on cone in C, showing pollen sporangia on the underside of the cone sporophylls; E. Female cone of *Cycas revoluta*.

FIGURE 16.16 *Ginkgo biloba*. A. *Ginkgo biloba* green leaves on a tree. The *Ginkgo* leaf is the symbol of the Japanese tea ceremony. *Ginkgo* is used to improve memory in alternative medicine; B. Ginkgoes have a unique long-shoot short-shoot growth pattern where leaves grow only from the short shoots; C. Seeds and leaves of *Ginkgo* tree; D. Paleocene-age leaf fossil of *Ginkgo*.

Precise systematic placement of the ginkgoes has yet to be determined. Ginkgoes have motile (swimming) sperm, a rarity among living seed plants (only ginkgoes and cycads have this feature today), although the vegetative anatomy of ginkgoes is more conifer-like (long-shoot and short-shoot morphology; structure of their wood). Ginkgoes, like the cycads, are dioecious, and also have similar seed features to cycads. Several phylogenetic studies suggest ginkgoes and cycads are among the more primitive seed plants.

16.2.5.5   Phylum Pinophyta

The **conifers** remain a major group of gymnosperms that include the pines (Figure 16.17A–C), spruce, fir, bald cypress, and the Norfolk Island pine (*Araucaria*; Figure 16.17D, E). The Phylum Pinophyta contains approximately 550 species of conifers. Conifers are cone-producing trees and

FIGURE 16.17 Conifers. A. Bristlecone pine tree (*Pinus longaeva*) in the White Mountains of California; B. Ponderosa Pine (*Pinus ponderosa*) on the eastern slope of the Sierra Nevada Mountains; C. Pine cones and long needles of the Ponderosa pine tree in the Okanagan area of British Columbia; D. *Araucaria araucana*, the monkey puzzle tree; E. Female cones of *A. araucana*; F. Little toddler girl hugging the giant, several thousand year-old *Sequoia*; G. View up a mature *Sequoia*. *(Continued)*

FIGURE 16.17 (*Continued*)

shrubs that usually have evergreen, needle-like leaves with a thick cuticle, sunken stomates, and a reduced surface area. The conifers, as a group, are well adapted to withstand extremes in climate and occur in nearly all habitats from the equator to the subpolar regions. The **taiga biome** consists largely of various conifer plants. Pines can even grow as cultivated plants in the Arizona desert (the Goldwater pine).

Araucarias (Figure 16.17D, E) have numerous small, scale-like leaves spiraling around their stems. *Araucaria*, a major genus that gives its name to the group, is a common ornamental plant because of the symmetry and beauty of its growth form. The fossil record of Araucarias and similar plants is quite good. The fossil genus *Araucarioxylon* that grew during the Triassic period in Arizona comprises the largest group of petrified wood in the Petrified Forest National Park of Arizona.

Sequoias include some of the tallest trees. Sequoias have been significant members of the world's forests since the Mesozoic. *Sequoia* (Figure 16.17F, G) and *Sequoiadendron* are major genera in this group.

The Pine Life Cycle

Pines have a life cycle (Figure 16.18) that takes two years to complete. Not all seed plants have such a long time span to complete their life history: some flowering plants manage to do it in as little as a few weeks.

The sporophyte, as in all other vascular plant groups, is the dominant, photosynthetic part of the life cycle: when you are holding pine needles in your hand you are holding sporophyte parts. Pines have specialized reproductive structures in which meiosis occurs: pine cones. **Pollen grains** are produced in the male cones, and contain the male gametophyte (which consists of only a very few

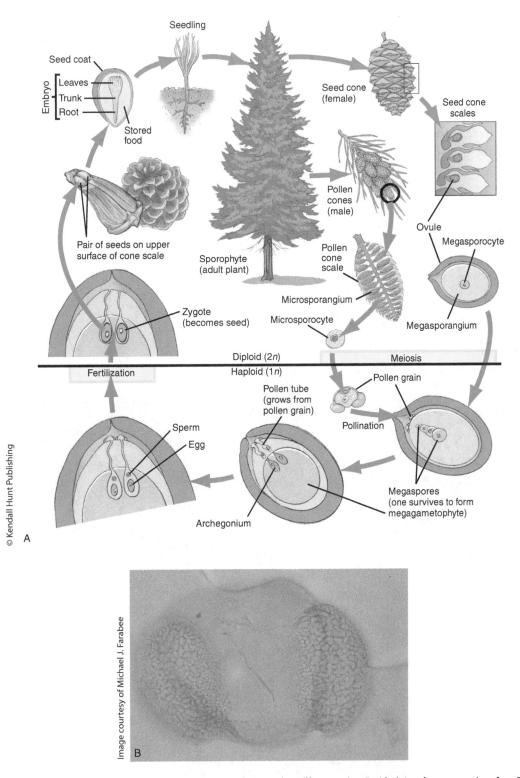

FIGURE 16.18 Pine life cycle. A. Diagram of the pine life cycle; B. Light micrograph of a 59.1-million-year-old pine pollen grain from near Almont, ND, photograph by Michael J. Farabee.

cells). Pollen released from the male cones is carried by wind to the female cones, where it lands. The cones close and the next year the pollen grain germinates to produce a pollen tube that grows into the female gametophyte. The sperm cell (from the pollen grain) and egg cell fuse, forming the next generation sporophyte that develops into an embryo encased within a seed. The seed is eventually transported by the wind to where it lands and germinates. If you have seen a large pine tree you realize there are hundreds of female cones on such a tree. Pine pollen has been noted to travel several hundred miles from the plant that produced it, if the wind is strong enough. To aid this transport, pine pollen has two air sacs, and thus is quite distinctive, as shown in Figure 16.18B–D.

16.2.5.6   Phylum Gnetophyta

The gnetophytes, shown in Figure 16.19, are an odd group: they have some angiosperm-like features but are not themselves angiosperms. Cladistic analyses support the hypothesis that the gnetales (or

FIGURE 16.19 Gnetophytes. A. *Ephedra*; B. *Welwitschia*; C. Leaves of *Gnetum gnemon* tree, Melinjo.

some portion of them) are outgroups for the angiosperms (flowering plants). Three distinctive genera comprise this group: *Welwitschia*, *Gnetum*, and *Ephedra*. *Ephedra* (Figure 16.19A) occurs in the western United States where it has the common name "Mormon tea." It is a natural source for the chemical ephedrine, although there is no evidence the Mormons in Utah (where the plant is extremely common) ever used it other than as an herbal medicine. *Welwitschia* (Figure 16.19B) is limited to coastal deserts in South Africa, although fossil leaf, cuticle, and pollen evidence indicates plants of this type were widespread during the Mesozoic Era. *Welwitschia* is noted for its two long, prominent leaves. *Gnetum* (Figure 16.19C) has leaves that look remarkably like those in angiosperms, as well as vessels in the xylem, generally considered an angiosperm characteristic.

16.2.5.7   Phylum Magnoliophyta

The angiosperms (Figure 16.20) were the last of the seed plant groups to evolve, appearing during the later part of the Cretaceous period over 140 million years ago. Genetic studies suggest a divergence of early angiosperms, the flowering plants, from some gymnosperm group more than 200 million years ago. As yet no undisputed fossil angiosperms of this age have been recovered. Imagine the world before flowering plants: no brightly colored flowers or delicious fruits to eat, terrestrial floras dominated by ferns and gymnosperms, such as cycads, ginkgoes, and conifers.

All flowering plants produce flowers. Within the female parts of the flower angiosperms produce a diploid zygote and triploid endosperm. Fertilization is accomplished by a variety of pollinators, including wind, animals, and water (Figure 16.21). Two sperm are released into the female gametophyte: one fuses with the egg to produce the zygote, the other helps form the nutritive tissue known as endosperm.

The angiosperms (*angios* = hidden; *sperm* = seed) produce modified leaves grouped into flowers that in turn develop fruits and seeds. There are presently more than 240,000 known living species. Most angiosperms also have larger xylem cells known as vessels that improve the efficiency of their vascular systems.

Flowers (Figure 16.22A) are collections of reproductive and sterile tissue arranged in a tight whorled array having very short internodes. Sterile parts of flowers are the sepals and petals. Reproductive parts of the flower are the stamen (collectively termed the androecium) and carpel (often the carpel is referred to as the pistil, collectively termed the gynoecium).

Flowers may be complete, where all parts of the flower are present and functional, or incomplete, where one or more parts of the flower are absent. A number of angiosperms produce a single flower on the tip of a shoot. Other plants produce a stalk bearing numerous flowers, termed an inflorescence, such as in orchids and snapdragons. Many flowers exhibit adaptations for insect pollination, bearing numerous white or yellow petals. Others, like the grasses, oaks, and elms, are wind pollinated and have their petals reduced and often inconspicuous.

Angiosperm Life Cycle

Flowering plants also exhibit the typical plant alternation of generations, shown in Figure 16.22B. The dominant phase is the sporophyte, with the gametophyte being much reduced in size and wholly dependent on the sporophyte for nutrition. This not a unique angiosperm condition, but

FIGURE 16.20 Angiosperms, the flowering and fruiting plants. A. *Victoria regia* (water lily) in a botanical garden; B. A southern magnolia tree (*Magnolia grandiflora*) covered with large white blossoms in the spring; C. Cactus in flower; D. Summer wildflowers.

occurs in all seed plants as well. What makes the angiosperms unique is their flowers and the "double fertilization" that occurs. Technically this is not double fertilization, but rather a single egg-sperm fusion (fertilization proper) plus a fusion of the second of two sperm cells with two haploid cells in the female gametophyte to produce triploid (3n) endosperm, a nutritive tissue for the developing embryo.

Angiosperm Systematics

The flowering plants, the division Magnoliophyta, contain more than 235,000 species, six times the number of species of all other plants combined. The flowering plants historically divided into two large groups, informally named the monocots and the dicots (Figure 16.23).

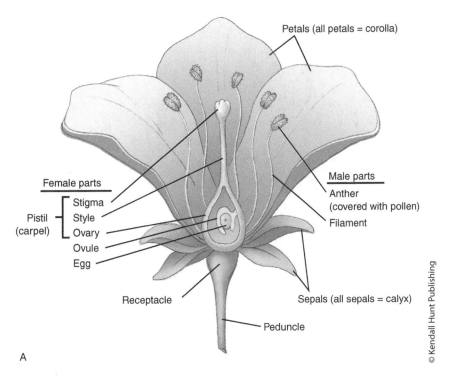

FIGURE 16.21 Flowers and pollination. A. Bee pollinating a flower and gaining a reward of nectar from the flower; B. Female Ruby-Throated Hummingbird feeding at red salvia; C. Hummingbird Hawk-moth, *Macroglossum stellatarum*.

FIGURE 16.22 Flowering plant life history. A. Diagram of a flower; B. Angiosperm life cycle.

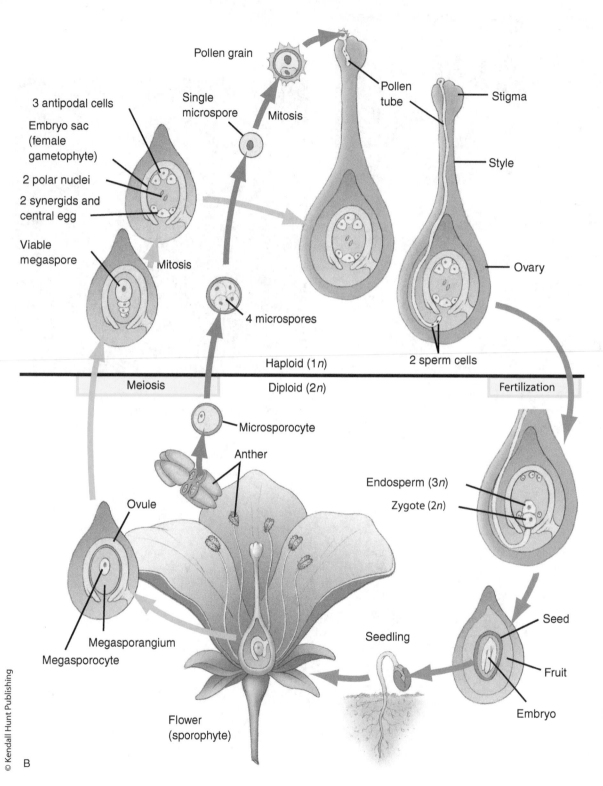

B

FIGURE 16.22 (*Continued*)

Eudicot (two cotyledons)

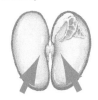

| Pollen grains have three pores or furrows | Seeds have two cotyledons | Flowers have four or five floral parts (or multiples thereof) | Leaves are oval or palmate, with net-like veins | Vascular bundles arranged in a ring around stem | Tap roots |

Monocot (one cotyledon)

| Pollen grains have one pore or furrow | Seeds have one cotyledon | Flowers have three floral parts (or multiples thereof) | Leaves are narrow, with parallel veins | Vascular bundles small, and spread throughout stem | Fibrous roots |

FIGURE 16.23 Comparison of monocots and eudicots.

The technical names for these groups are the class Magnoliopsida for dicots and the class Liliopsida for monocots. As you might expect from reading of other chapters in this section, revisions to this classification have occurred, first in 2009 and then again in 2010. Monocots remain a well-defined clade, while the dicots have been subdivided into the eudicots and the group loosely called the basal magnolids. The taxon that is basal is *Amborella*, with the water lilies next to diverge.

The eudicots have these features: either woody or herbaceous growth habit (habit for short); flower parts usually in fours, fives, or multiples; leaves usually net-veined; vascular bundles arranged in a circle within the stem; and production of two cotyledons in their seed. Prominent eudicot families include the mustards, maples, cacti, peas, and roses. Several eudicot families are noteworthy because of the illegal drugs (shown in Figure 16.24) derived from them: the Cannabinaceae (marijuana), Papaveraceae (poppies from which opium and heroin are derived), and *Erythroxylum coca* (family Erythroxylaceae), the plant from which the illegal drug cocaine is extracted.

Not all plants can be misused to produce illegal drugs. Notable eudicot families with legitimate uses include the pea family, which includes the crop plants beans, lentils, and peas (Figure 16.25A) as well as many ornamental landscape plants such as acacias. Beans are an excellent source of nonanimal protein as well as fiber. Another eudicot of enormous importance is cotton, *Gossypium* (Figure 16.25B). Chocolate and cola are products of the plant family Sterculiaceae

(Figure 16.25C, D). Coffee (Figure 16.25E) is produced from *Coffea arabica*, while tea comes from *Camelia sinensis* (Figure 16.25F), a plant native to China.

The class Liliopsida has plants that are herbaceous (palms and bamboo stand out as rare monocot trees), flower parts are in threes, leaves are usually parallel-veined, vascular bundles are scattered within the stem, and produce one cotyledon (seed leaf) at germination. Monocot families include lilies, palms, orchids, irises, and grasses (Table 16.2).

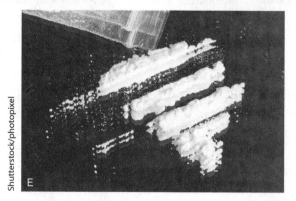

FIGURE 16.24 Drug plants. A. *Cannabis* plant with young leaves; B. A coffee shop in Amsterdam legally selling cannabis; C. Opium poppy field where raw opium is collected from the poppy fruits; D. Coca plant, *E. coca*, growing in a tub showing a close-up of the leaves from which cocaine is derived and which are chewed dried as a stimulant; E. Cocaine powder in lines and packet on mirror.

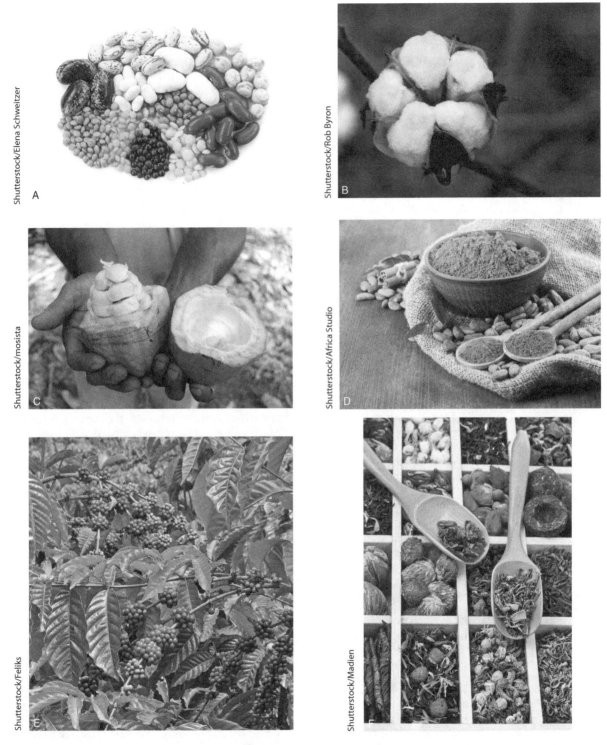

FIGURE 16.25 Economic eudicots. A. Beans, lentils, and peas; B. Cotton boll; C. Ripe cacao ready to pick; D. Cocoa powder and cocoa beans after processing; E. Coffee plants with fruit ready to pick, Java, Indonesia; F. Different tea types: green, black, china, floral, herbal in a wooden box with bamboo spoons.

TABLE 16.2 Plant classification

Phylum	Characteristics	Examples and Uses
Chlorophyta (Green algae)	Unicellular-multicellular, freshwater to marine habitats; cellulose cell walls, chlorophyll *a* and *b*, store excess sugar as starch.	*Chlamydomonas* and *Volvox*, often examined in college laboratory exercises; important parts of phytoplankton and food webs, Charophytes are thought to be the group ancestral to other plants.
Marchantiophyta, Anthoceratophyta, and Bryophyta; the nonvascular land plants	Nonvascular plants, gametophyte-dominant life cycles; no lignified conducting cells.	Mosses, liverworts, hornworts generally lack economic significance; peat moss an important carbon sink, landscaping material, fuel for heating; source for charcoal for making some Scotch whisky.
Lycophyta (Club mosses)	Microphyll leaves, sporangia in strobili; more significant in the Paleozoic; part of coal age forests that generated coal deposits.	*Lycopodium*, a homosporous plant, *Selaginella*, a heterosporous plant; no commercial uses except as ground cover in some areas; *Lepidodendron* and *Sigillaria* were dominant elements of Carboniferous coal swamp forests.
Polypodiophyta (ferns, horsetails, and psilophytes)	Pinnately compound megaphyll leaves, sporangia clumped in sori on underside of leaves, leaves arise by circinate vernation.	Ornamental plants like the Boston fern; tree ferns; commercial applications as ornamentals; ecologically important plants in some areas; fern fiddleheads sometimes eaten in salads; *Equisetum*, the horsetail; *Psilotum*, the whisk fern.
Cycadophyta (cycads)	Long, pinnately compound megaphyll leaves with a leathery feel arising from soft wooded stems by circinate vernation; new leaves arise as a crown or whorl; reproduction by seeds produced in female cones, pollen produced in male cones.	*Cycas revoluta*, a common ornamental known as the Sago palm; *Zamia floridana*, only cycad native to the 48 contiguous United States; commercial uses as ornamental plants, eaten as food some cultures.
Ginkgophyta (the ginkgoes)	Fan-shaped, bi-lobed leaves on tree with long and short shoots; seeds produce a foul odor when mature.	*Ginkgo biloba*, the maidenhair tree; a living fossil plant; commercial uses as ornamental plants and allegedly as a memory aid herbal supplement.
Pinophyta (the conifers)	Needle-like or scale-like leaves with thick cuticles and sunken stomata; soft wooded plants; seeds lacking fruit, dispersed from hardened cones.	*Pinus* (wood, resin, pine straw, pine nuts, paper); *Taxus* (yew) a natural source for the anticancer drug taxol; Douglas fir (wood); ornamental plants; Sequoia, the world's tallest trees also a source of redwood.
Gnetophyta	Plant group most closely related to flowering plants; vessels in some members of group; reproductive structures similar to flowers.	*Ephedra* (Mormon tea) source of ephedrine; *Gnetum* sometimes used in Asian cuisines; *Welwitschia* has no commercial uses.
Magnoliophyta flowering plants (angiosperms)	Encase seeds within a ripened ovary wall known as a fruit; fruits dry or fleshy, single or multiple; two major classes the monocots and eudicots; xylem may include vessels as well as tracheids; range from herbaceous annuals to perennial trees	Monocots: cereal grains form staple of economy and diet; palms are used in many places as building material; ecological impact as pioneer species in disturbed habitats; Eudicots: food crops such as beans, peas; fibers from cotton used to make clothing and paper; illegal drugs such as marijuana, cocaine, heroin; legal products such as chocolate, tea, and coffee; *Nicotiana* leaves make tobacco; ornamental plants; grains and fruits can be fermented to produce alcohol for biofuels or human consumption.

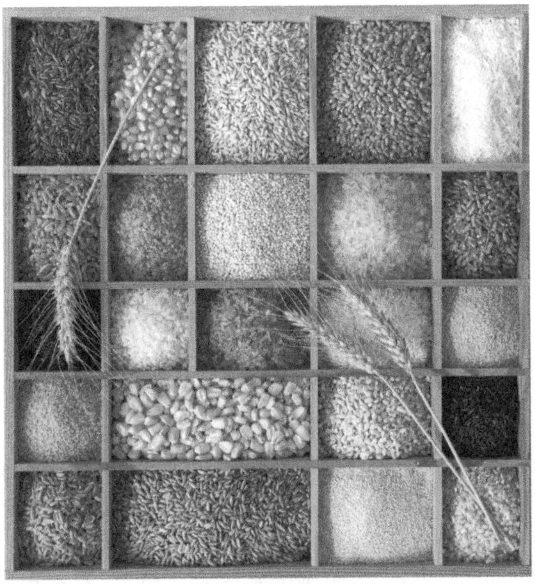

The monocot family Poaceae includes the grasses, such as corn, oats, wheat, rye, and rice that are staple food products as well as ornamental plants, such as crabgrass and tiff grass. The importance of this plant family to modern civilization cannot be overstated, as the first six plants mentioned in the previous sentence provide 75% of our food, either directly as food we eat or indirectly as food for animals we eat (Figure 16.26).

FIGURE 16.26 Economic monocots: cereal grains in a wooden box.

Trends in Plant Evolution

Several evolutionary trends occur within the plant kingdom, summarized in Table 16.1. The monophyletic nature of this kingdom is not in dispute, with the first major division being between vascular and nonvascular plants. Within the vascular plants, we see increasing changes in the relationship between sporophyte and gametophyte, culminating in flowering plants.

Developing from green algal ancestors, plants show a trend for reduction of the complexity, size, and dominance of the gametophyte generation. In nonvascular plants, the gametophyte is the conspicuous, photosynthetic, free-living phase of the life cycle. Conversely, the angiosperm gametophyte is reduced to between three and eight cells (hence it is very inconspicuous) and is dependent on the free-living, photosynthetic sporophyte for its nutrition.

Plants also developed and refined the root-shoot-leaf axis with its specialized conducting cells of the xylem and phloem. The earliest vascular plants, such as *Cooksonia* and *Rhynia*, were little more than naked photosynthetic stems lacking leaves. Some plants later developed secondary growth that produced wood. Numerous leaf modifications are known, including "carnivorous" plants such as the Venus flytrap, as well as plants that have reduced or lost leaves, such as *Psilotum* and the members of the cactus family.

A third trend is the development of the seed to promote the dormancy of the embryo. The seed allows the plant to wait out harsh environmental conditions. With the development of the seed during the Paleozoic era plants became less prone to mass extinctions.

The fourth trend in plant evolution is the encasing of a seed within a fruit. The only plant group that produces true fruit is the flowering plants, the angiosperms. Fruits serve to protect the seed, as well as aid in seed dispersal.

16.3   Significance of Plants

The importance of plants to life on Earth would be very difficult to overstate. We eat plants or animals that eat plants themselves. Our dwellings are often constructed using plant materials such as timbers for beams and roofing materials and fabrics made from plant fibers for use and decoration. The oxygen in the air we breathe is in large part produced by the photosynthesis of plants. Fossil fuels burned to power modern civilization are generally derived from plants that lived and died in ancient swamps. Biofuels are a modern use of plant material fermented to make alcohols that can be burned in an engine as fuel or in a power plant to generate electricity. For millennia societies have been keeping records, recipes, myths, and religious instructions on paper and papyrus derived from plant fibers. The diploma you plan to receive upon completion of your degree is printed on plant material! We know of the thoughts and words of long dead scholars and teachers like Aristotle, Newton, Confucius, Shakespeare, and Darwin because their ideas were recorded on paper, a plant product.

16.3.1   Plants as Food

Most of the food we eat is plant material produced by angiosperms. Fruits are the product of a flower and may or may not contain seeds. Many fruits, such as apples and grapes, satisfy our desire for sweetness and provide a great source of natural fruit sugar as well as dietary fiber. Nuts are normally a type of fruit that provide a great deal of energy as well as dietary fiber. Many berries provide a great deal of antioxidant chemicals important to our general health.

The six cereal grains: corn, oats, wheat, rye, barley, and rice form the basis of almost every culture on the planet. Development of farming assured a more constant food supply and transformed the landscape as more and more wild spaces were cleared and cultivated.

Not every plant food that we eat if a fruit or a seed. Vegetables are the nonreproductive parts of a plant. Broccoli, potatoes, cabbage, leafy salads, rhubarb, kale, and jicama are but a few vegetative parts of a plant we eat as our vegetables.

Fermentation of plant material has many applications. Preserving grain harvests may have been an impetus to the fermentation of ancient grains. The fermentation process also purified the water, making it safer to drink. Add to that the intoxicating effects of the alcohol, and we get the wonder drink of early America: beers and ales. Apples were fermented as hard ciders as well. Modern uses of fermentation include the production of biofuels like E95 that can be used alone as a fuel for engines or mixed with gasoline.

16.3.2   Plants as Medicines and Drugs

Plants have long been used a remedies or treatments for various ailments. Plants produce secondary chemicals that are not involved in the metabolism of the plant. Many of these secondary chemicals have medicinal properties.

Pain-killing properties have led to the cultivation and trade of a number of plants. *Papaver somniferum*, the opium poppy, produces opioid chemicals that interfere with pain nerve signal transmission. The fruit of the poppy is sliced in the field, causing a latex material containing these chemicals to ooze from the cut. The latex is collected and refined. The legal medicine morphine is derived from this material, as are the illegal drugs heroin and opium. About half of the world production of heroin makes it way to the United States.

Cannabis has long been recognized for its effect, or high. The chemical that produces this effect is tetrahydrocannabinol (THC). The chemical structure was deciphered during the 1960s by Israeli biochemist Raphael Mechoulam (b. 1930) and coworkers. Ancient cultures long ago

FIGURE 16.27 Uses of wood. A. Bamboo scaffolding used in Hong Kong; B. Pile of wood logs; C. Turned wood vase; D. Waste paper recycling.

recognized cannabis as an important medicinal herb. In the United States, the drug was legal until the 1930s, when it was criminalized. Most countries have criminalized growing, possession, and use of cannabis. Over 20 states have allowed medical marijuana programs, and two have legalized the drug for recreational uses.

Cocaine, and its derivative drug crack, can be extracted from the coca plant. The ancient Inca people used the leaves as a mild stimulant. European scientists developed processing techniques for the coca leaves during the 19th century. Medicinal uses of cocaine are few. The drug remains illegal in almost every country.

Ginkgo has been touted as an herbal remedy for memory. This claim has no merit and no controlled scientific studies backing the assertion. However, as an herbal supplement, ginkgo and similar herbs fall outside the stricter rules governing medicines administered by the US Food and Drug Administration.

Caffeine is considered the number one psychoactive drug on Earth. Nine out of ten people in North America drink caffeinated beverages daily. Caffeine alters the metal state of those who consume it. Don't believe me? Ask me after my morning coffee, or suffer the consequences! Caffeine occurs in a number of plants, most commonly from the beans of the coffee plant and leaves of the tea plant. Doses are usually low enough that toxicity is not a problem.

Digitalis and similar drugs are extracted from the foxglove plant (*Digitalis* sp.). This medicine is used to deal with heart failure. Its first use was in the mid 1750s, with several plants in the genus *Digitalis* producing chemicals humans have repurposed for medicinal use.

16.3.3   Plants as Materials

Wood is perhaps the single most important building material in human history. Wood comes from the secondary xylem of tree stems. Throughout China, bamboo is still used as scaffolding on high-rise buildings (Figure 16.27A). Trees have been cut and stacked for use as fuel or in construction (Figure 16.27B). Wood can be turned on a lathe to make candlesticks, table and chair legs, as well as functions and artistic bowls and vases (Figure 16.27C). In some cases, turned wood bowls by an establish artisan can sell for over US$1200!

The majority of modern paper is made from pulped wood fibers, although other materials can be used, such as cotton fibers, hemp, and rags. The pulped fibers are spread out to dry on a grid and water is pressed from the paper. Many schools and cities now recycle items, such as paper (Figure 16.27D) and metal. Some textbooks are now printed on recycled paper.

Summary

Plants are vitally important to human beings. We depend on these creatures for food, shelter, medicines, and a host of other uses. The most important plant group is the flowering plants. Plants evolved during the Ordovician period from some group of green algae, most like the charophytes. Plants made the transition to land by the late Ordovician. There are two major groups of land plants, the vascular plants and the nonvascular plants.

The world's first forests appeared during the Devonian period, but spread and became more widespread during the Carboniferous. These coal swamp forests left behind an impressive fossil record. They also contributed to the formation of much of the coal burned in Europe and eastern North America.

Flowering plants evolved from some unknown group of gymnosperms, possibly gnetophytes, during the Mesozoic era. Despite being relative late occurring in the history of life on Earth, the flowering plants have many more times the number of species as any of the other groups.

Terms

alternation of generations	bark	complete flower
amniotic egg	bryophytes	cones
androecium	carpel	conifers
angiosperms	cellulose	cork
antheridium	charophytes	cuticle
archegonium	circulatory systems	cycads

cytokinesis	homosporous	reproductive systems
diffusion	incomplete flower	rhizoids
diploid	indusium	sepals
dioecious	internodes	Silurian
endosperm	leaf gap	sori
epiphytes	lignin	sporangium
Ephedra	megaphylls	spores
fertilization	megaspores	sporophyll
flagella	microphylls	sporophyte
flowers	microspores	stamen
gametophyte	mitosis	stomata
gemmae	node	strobilus
ginkgoes	nonvascular plants	taiga biome
gnetales	petals	thallus
gnetophytes	phloem	tracheophytes
guard cells	phototrophs	vascular plants
gymnosperms	phragmoplast	xylem
gynoecium	pistil	zygote
haploid	pollen	
heterosporous	pollen tubes	

Review Questions

1. Which of these plant groups may include the ancestors of plants?
   a. red algae;
   b. green algae;
   c. brown algae;
   d. fungi

2. Plants and their ancestral group share which of the following features?
   a. chlorophylls *a* and *b*;
   b. starch as a storage product;
   c. cellulose cell walls;
   d. all of these

3. Vascular plants have ___, specialized cells that help support the plant as well as transport water and nutrients upward from their roots.
   a. phloem;
   b. trumpet hyphae;
   c. xylem;
   d. arteries

4. The ___ generation of a moss is the dominant phase of its life history.
   a. sporophyte;
   b. adult;
   c. embryo;
   d. gametophyte

5. The lack of conducting cells in bryophytes limits their maximum size to ___.
   a. 100 m;
   b. 5 cm;
   c. 1 m;
   d. no limit is set by the lack of these cells

6. Which of these plants is known only from fossils?
   a. *Cooksonia*;
   b. *Lycopodium*;
   c. *Equisetum*;
   d. *Tmesipteris*

7. The ___ generation of a fern is the dominant phase of its life history.
   a. sporophyte;
   b. adult;
   c. embryo;
   d. gametophyte

8. Endosperm tissue is unique to which of these groups?
   a. cycads;
   b. conifers;
   c. flowering plants;
   d. ferns

9. Seed plants have ___.
   a. pollen grains with male gametophytes developing inside;
   b. female gametophytes developing inside an ovule retained on the sporophyte;
   c. roots;
   d. all of these

10. Which of these plants is not a gymnosperm?
    a. corn;
    b. pine;
    c. redwood;
    d. ginkgo

11. Which of these plants is not a flowering plant?
    a. corn;
    b. wheat;
    c. lily;
    d. fir

12. Cycads and ginkgoes were important plants to the world's terrestrial ecosystems during the ___.
    a. Paleozoic era;
    b. Cenozoic era;
    c. Mesozoic era;
    d. precambrian

13. The presence of long-shoot/short-shoot anatomy characterizes which of these plants?
    a. *Ginkgo*;
    b. *Cycas*;
    c. *Zamia*;
    d. ferns

14. Angiosperms are most closely related to which of these plant groups?
    a. gnetophyta;
    b. pinophyta;
    c. cycadophyta;
    d. charophyta;
    e. chlorophyta

15. The most primitive living angiosperm is ___.
    a. *Helianthus*;
    b. *Amborella*;
    c. *Nymphaea*;
    d. *Quercus*;
    e. *Carnegia*

16. Which of these plants is not used as an illegal drug?
    a. *Cannabis*;
    b. *Erythoxylon*;
    c. *Zamia*;
    d. *Papaver*

17. Which of these characteristics is not a monocot feature?
    a. flower parts in threes or multiples of three;
    b. ringed vascular bundles in the stem;
    c. leaves with parallel veins;
    d. pollen with at most one aperture

18. Presence of scattered vascular bundles in the stem is characteristic of plants in which of these groups?
    a. eudicots;
    b. ferns;
    c. cycads;
    d. monocots;
    e. mosses

19. Large lignified cells in vascular plants are known as _____.
    a. tracheids;
    b. phloem;
    c. vessels;
    d. meristems

Links

- **Non-flowering Plant Family Access Page**: Sorted by family on the nonflowering plants. Thumbnail photos are linked to larger versions. This site is a great educational resource maintained by Gerald D. Carr. [http://www.botany.hawaii.edu/faculty/carr/nfpfamilies.htm]

- **Introduction to the Bryophyta: The Mosses**: This University of California Museum of Paleontology site offers a systematic perspective to the mosses by providing succinct information as well as links to a number of pertinent sites. [http://www.ucmp.berkeley.edu/plants/bryophyta/bryophyta.html]

- **Introduction to the Anthocerotophyta: The Hornworts**: This University of California Museum of Paleontology site offers a systematic perspective to the hornworts by providing succinct information as well as links to a number of pertinent sites. [http://www.ucmp.berkeley.edu/plants/anthocerotophyta.html]

- **Garden Web Glossary**: A nice contrast to the above site, this glossary has over 4000 terms, and is also from a commercial site. [http://glossary.gardenweb.com/glossary/]

- **Introduction to the Lycophyta: Club Mosses and Scale Trees**: This University of California Museum of Paleontology site offers a systematic perspective to the lycophytes, their ecology, systematics, and fossil record. [http://www.ucmp.berkeley.edu/plants/lycophyta/lycophyta.html]

- **Introduction to the Sphenophyta: Yesterday's Trees, Today's Horsetails**: This University of California Museum of Paleontology site offers a systematic perspective to the sphenophytes (*Equisetum* and its extinct relatives), their ecology, systematics, and fossil record. [http://www.ucmp.berkeley.edu/plants/sphenophyta/sphenophyta.html]

- **Mazon Creek Fossils**: The Illinois State Museum maintains this site that details and illustrates some of the exquisite plant and animal fossils from the Mazon Creek deposits in that state. [http://www.museum.state.il.us/exhibits/mazon_creek/index.html]

- **Die Rhynie Chert Flora**: This site offers pictures illustrating the vascular nature, trilete spores, and stomata that characterize *Rhynia* as a vascular plant. [http://www.uni-muenster.de/GeoPalaeontologie/Palaeo/Palbot/rhynie.html]

- **The Botanical Society of America:** The official website of the plant biologists, oh well, call them botanists! [http://www.botany.org]

- *Ginkgo biloba*: History, uses, and other information about this living "fossil tree" whose leaves are essentially unchanged since the tertiary period. [http://kwanten.home.xs4all.nl]

Reference

The Angiosperm Phylogeny Group. An update of the Angiosperm Phylogeny Group classification for the orders and families of flowering plants: APG III. *Botanical Journal of the Linnaean Society.* 2009;161(1):105–121.

CHAPTER 17
Biodiversity: Fungi

Chapter Opener

Several rows of brown bracket fungi grow vertically on a bright tree stump in the forest. This picture illustrates the role of fungi as decomposers, breaking down dead organic matter and recycling nutrients.

Objectives

- Describe how fungi obtain their nutrition and compare that to plants and animals.
- Discuss the evidence indicating the phylogenetic relationship of fungi to some group of protists.
- List the features that support the claim that the chytrids are the most primitive group of living fungi.
- List of the advantages and harmful effects of fungi.
- List the types of sexual spores and structures that distinguish the different phyla of fungi.
- Lichens are a symbiosis of an alga and a fungus. Discuss the advantages and disadvantages each partner gains in this association.
- Consider a pizza (let us make it a vegetarian pizza for good measure; sigh). Yummy! Discuss how fungi are involved in the production of that pizza pie.
- List one or two examples of fungi making documented impact on human history.

Introduction

Fungi are almost entirely multicellular (with yeast, *Saccharomyces cerviseae*, being a prominent unicellular fungus), heterotrophic (deriving their energy from another organism, whether alive or dead), and usually having some cells with more than one nucleus (multinucleate, as opposed to the more common one, or uninucleate, condition) per cell. Ecologically this kingdom is important (along with certain bacteria) as decomposers and recyclers of nutrients. Economically, fungi provide us with food (mushrooms; Bleu cheese/Roquefort cheese; yeast for baking and brewing), antibiotics (the first of the wonder drugs, penicillin, was isolated from the fungus *Penicillium*), and crop parasites (doing several billion dollars per year of damage worldwide). Fungi are also important aiders of plant root function, as mycorrhizae. Examples of this diverse group are shown in Figure 17.1.

The evolution of multicellular eukaryotes increased the size and complexity of organisms, allowing them to exploit the terrestrial habitat. Fungi first evolved in water but made the transition to land through the development of specialized structures that prevented their drying out. First classified as plants, fungi are now considered different enough from plants to be placed in a separate kingdom, and in fact are more like animals than plants.

Fungi are often referred to as the middle kingdom of the eukaryans. The fungi exhibit several plant-like characters that caused Linnaeus to classify them as plants in his original system. During the 1960s scientists discovered that although fungi look superficially like plants, metabolically they are more similar to animals. This led to fungi being placed into a separate taxonomic kingdom, the Fungi in 1969.

FIGURE 17.1 Examples of Fungi. A. Yeast; B. Assorted mushrooms for use in cooking; C. The death cap mushroom; D. Corn smut, *Ustilago maydis*; E. *Penicillium* fungi on an agar plate and tubes with antibiotics.

Fungi impact humans in a variety of ways, both positive as well as negative. Beneficial uses of fungi include as additives in the brewing and baking process (Figure 17.1A). The single-celled brewer's yeast, *Saccharomyces cerevisae*, serves a vital role in the rising of bread. The carbon dioxide produced as yeast ferments sugars in bread dough causes the bread to rise and give off that awesome aroma that draws us to bakeries. The same yeast can also serve as a primary fermenter in alcohol fermentation. According to some historians the Pilgrim colonists of New England landed at Plymouth Rock not to settle but because they were running out of beer and did not trust drinking water. We now make an important biofuel, E95, by using yeast to ferment plant material not to get us drunk, but to run cars and buses.

Mushrooms form an important ingredient in a number of cuisines. The mushroom is a reproductive structure of a type of fungus known as a club fungus (Figure 17.1B, C).

Fungi are important both as a source of food and in the preparation of food. Edible fungi include mushrooms, truffles, and morels. Gorgonzola, Roquefort, Stilton, and Bleu Cheeses have fungal colonies that give theses cheeses their distinctive flavors. Beer and wine are produced through the action of yeasts, such as *Saccharomyces cerevisae*.

Some fungi are important as crop parasites. These include the rusts and smuts (Figure 17.1D) that infect a wide range of plants. The 1972 US corn crop was almost completely eradicated by a fungus. Fungal parasites annually cause many billions of dollars in crop damage and food spoilage.

Fungi are important as producers of antibiotics, like the penicillin produced by the *Penicillium* fungus (Figure 17.1E). The fungus competes with bacteria for food and produces a number of chemicals that inhibit bacterial growth. If these chemicals are not too toxic for humans we can use these molecules as antibacterial or antibiotic treatments.

Fungi are important decomposers involved in nutrient cycling in the environment. This generates the organic material in soil, humus, which is an important part of soil fertility. Mycorrhizae are soil fungi in a mutualistic relationship with plants. This relationship is vital to plant growth.

17.1   Characteristics of Fungi

Fungi contain unicellular, multinucleate, and multicellular forms. They are classified on the basis of their reproductive spores and the nature of their multinucleate or multicellular filaments known as hyphae (Figure 17.2). Fungal cells have cell walls containing the carbohydrate chitin. Chitin also occurs in the exoskeletons of the animal phylum Arthropoda.

Fungi are absorptive heterotrophs: they break food macromolecules down by secreting digestive enzymes onto a substrate and then absorb the resulting small food molecules. Fungal hyphae have a small volume but large surface area, enhancing the fungal absorptive capacity. Excess sugar is stored as the polysaccharide glycogen, the storage product for sugars in animals.

Fungal hyphae are collectively termed a mycelium (Figure 17.3). Some fungi are saprophytes that obtain their food from the decaying bodies/body parts of other creatures. Other fungi are

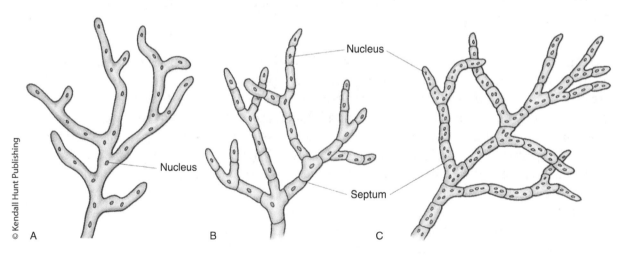

© Kendall Hunt Publishing

Nucleus

Nucleus

Septum

A   B   C

FIGURE 17.2 Types of fungal hyphae. A. Coenocytic hyphae lacking cross walls between nuclei; B. Septate hyphae with each nucleus in the hypha separated by a cross wall; C. Multinucleate hyphae with multiple nuclei per cell.

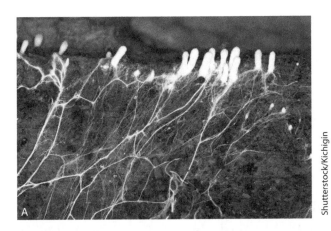
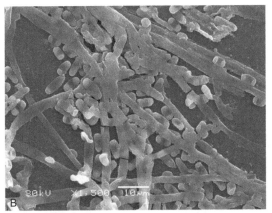

FIGURE 17.3 The fungal body. A. The mycelium of a fungus growing through a soil profile. Note the small hyphae dispersed through the soil. Reproductive structures are just beginning to develop on the top of the soil; B. Scanning electron microscope image of fungal mycelium and spores.

parasites that cause harm to their hosts. All fungi, except the chytrids, lack flagella. Fungal reproduction occurs when the meeting of opposite strains of hyphae brings gametes together.

17.2   Systematics of Fungi

The Opisthokont clade includes fungi as well as amoeboids and animals. Over 60,000 species of fungi have been described. Mycologists, the scientists who study fungi, classify these organisms by their method of sexual reproduction and associated structures. Historically fungi have been divided into four taxonomic phyla: Zygomycota, Ascomycota, Basidiomycota, and Deuteromycota. The Deuteromycota are not a monophyletic group and so lack validity in a modern classification scheme. Molecular studies are creating a great deal of flux within the fungi. In this text, we focus on a few of the major groups of fungi.

Fungi and the nucleariids form one clade within the Opisthokonta, with animals and choanoflagellates forming another. The nucleariids and choanoflagellates were previously classified as protists. Nucleariids form the sister group to the fungi. The nucleariids are unicellular eukaryans. They have mitochondria with discoid cristae in their mitochondria. Pseudopodia extend outward from the cell.

17.2.1   Phylum Chytridiomycota

The Phylum Chytridiomycota (Figure 17.4) includes some of the oldest known fungal fossils (from the latest precambrian of Russia). There are over 700 species of chytrids. All chytrids differ from other fungi by their possession of flagellated gametes. Most chytrids have chitin comprising their cell walls. Chytrids are aquatic, not terrestrial as are almost all other fungi. They thus may provide us with a glimpse of the earliest fungi, both in habit as well as structure. This phylum also has quite a diverse array of body plans and habitats. *Allomyces* is a chytrid used

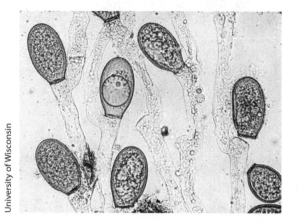

University of Wisconsin

FIGURE 17.4 The chytrid *Allomyces*.

University of Wisconsin

FIGURE 17.5 Mycorrhizae (white colored) growing into a pine root (amber colored).

in some experiments. Recent systematic studies suggest the phylum could be subdivided into several monophyletic groups. For now, we will retain them all in the chytrids. Many frog and toad species worldwide are declining due to chytridiomycosis, a disease caused by a chytrid fungus.

17.2.2   Phylum Glomeromycota

This phylum contains over 250 species of fungi most of which form mutualistic symbiotic relationships with the roots of plants. These are the arbuscular mycorrhizae (Figure 17.5). This association benefits both the plant and the fungus. However, not all members of this phylum must grow in association with plant roots. Glomeromycetes produce glomerospores from the tips of their hyphae.

17.2.3   Phylum Zygomycota

Phylum Zygomycota consists of fewer than 1000 species. Zygomycete hyphae do not have one nucleus per cell, but rather have long multinucleate, haploid hyphae that comprise their mycelia. Cell walls in zygomycetes include a unique form of chitin. Asexual reproduction in zygomycetes occurs by spores produced in stalked sporangia, such as shown in Figure 17.6. Most zygomycetes are terrestrial and function ecologically as decomposers. Most of us have seen old, moldy bread. The black blotches are the sporangia that have emerged from the bread. The zygomycete mycelium, most likely *Rhizopus*, permeates the bread. Sexual reproduction in zygomycetes involves the fusion of haploid mating hyphae to produce a diploid zygospore, a process shown in Figure 17.7.

There are less than 1000 species of zygomycetes. Common bread molds are in this group, as are a few species that parasitize plants and animals. Most zygomycetes feed on dead or decaying plant and animal material. Expose some bread to air for a few hours and it very likely will become infected with spores of a zygomycete.

The life cycle of *Rhizopus* (Figure 17.7) has two components: an asexual reproductive phase, and a sexually cycle that involves meiosis producing a zygospore (Figure 17.6D). Normally the multinucleate hyphae grow through their substrate, in this case bread. Nuclear division is by mitosis. Occasionally, the bread mold fungus will produce sporangiophores that erupt through

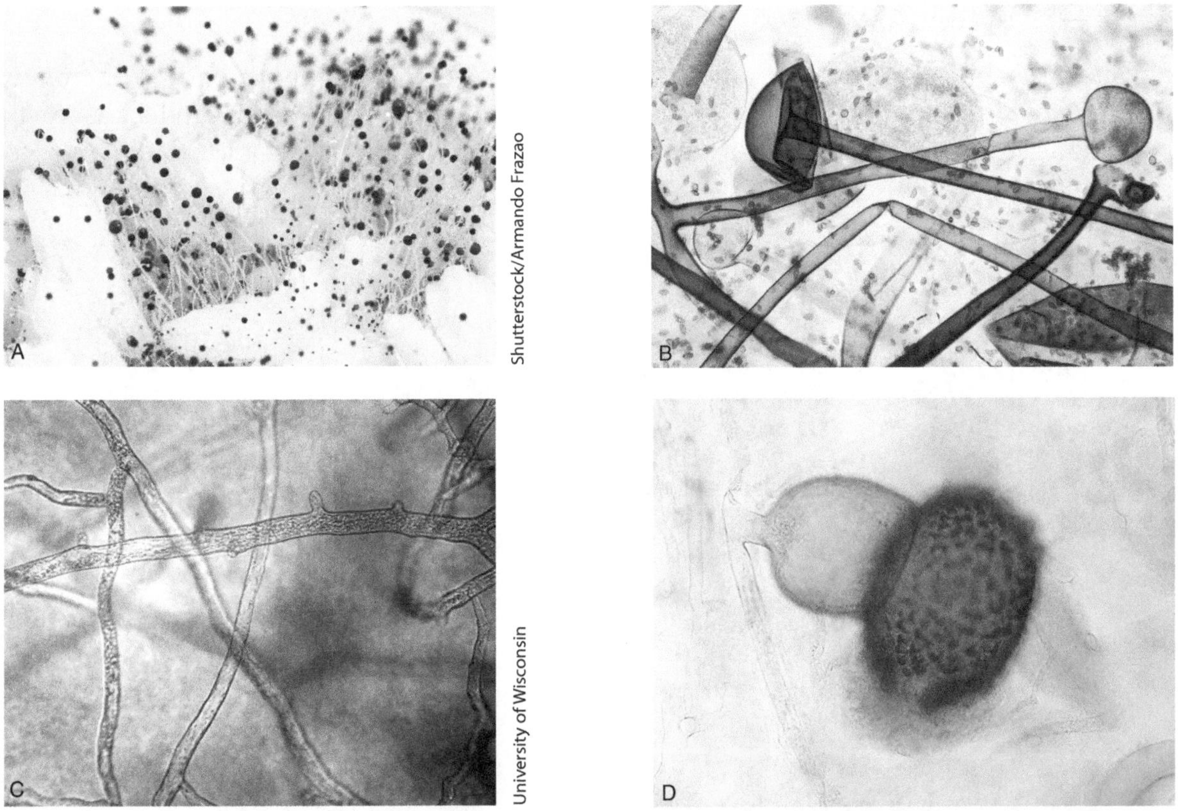

FIGURE 17.6 *Rhizopus*, the black bread mold. A. Habit shot of black bread mold growing on rice; B. *Rhizopus* sporangia on sporangiophores, bright field microscopy; magnification 400X; C. Coenocytic, multinucleate hyphae of *Rhizopus*; D. Zygosporangium of *Rhizopus*.

the surface. Fungal spores will be produced by mitosis in the sporangium that caps the sporangiophore. These spores will be released and carried by wind to settle on another slice of bread and germinate to produce new hyphae. The sexual phase begins when haploid hyphae of two opposite strains (indicated as **– mating type** and **+ mating type** in Figure 17.7) meet and fuse. Eventually, the nuclei fuse to produce a diploid zygote, a process known as karyogamy. The zygote is encased inside a thick-walled zygospore. Meiosis reduces the ploidy of the zygote and a haploid stalked sporangium grows and sheds spores that germinate into hyphae if and when they fall onto a suitable substrate for growth.

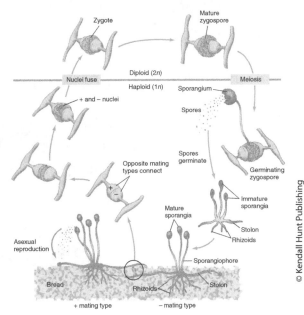

FIGURE 17.7 Life cycle of *Rhizopus*.

17.2.4   Phylum Ascomycota

Phylum Ascomycota contains more than 30,000 species of fungi ranging in body style from of unicellular yeasts to multicellular fungi such as morels (Figure 17.8). Yeasts reproduce asexually by budding and sexually by forming a sac (or ascus). One particular type of yeast, *Saccharomyces*

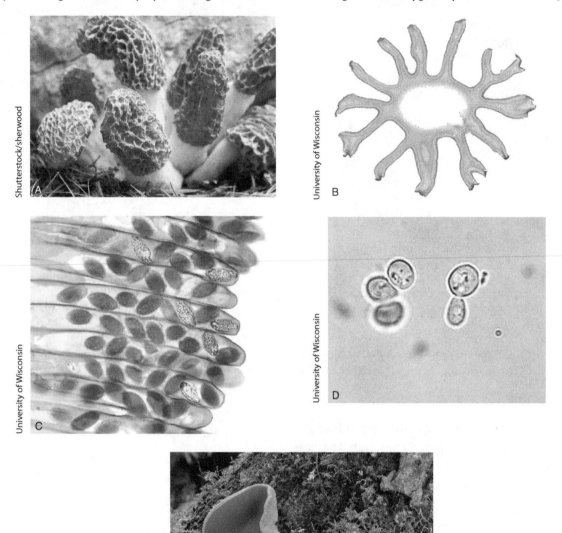

FIGURE 17.8 Examples of ascomycete fungi. A. A group of black morels (*Morchella*) in southwest Ontario, Canada; B. Light micrograph of a stained prepared slide of a morel; C. Light micrograph of a higher magnification view of several asci, each containing eight ascospores; D. Light micrograph of budding yeast cells of *Saccharomyces cerevisiae*; E. Scarlet Elf Cup Fungi, *Sarcoscypha coccinea*.

cerevisiae, is important for genetic research as well as its commercial applications in baking and brewing. Yeasts are part of the Human Genome Project and serve as easily studied models for eukaryotic gene systems. Yeast chromosomes have also been modified to serve as vectors for transporting human DNA fragments for use in gene mapping. Other notable ascomycetes include *Morchella esculentum* (Figure 17.8A), the morel, and *Neurospora crassa*, the organism used by George Beadle and Edward Tatum to develop the "one-gene-one-enzyme" hypothesis during the 20th century.

Some ascomycetes also cause disease or can make chemicals associated with diseases. In this group is *Aspergillus flavus*, which produces a contaminant of nuts and stored grain that acts both as a toxin and the most deadly known natural carcinogen. *Candida albicans* is another sac fungus that causes diaper rash and vaginal infections. Clearly this group, which may include nearly three-fourths of the fungal species, offers humans both blessings as well as curses.

Sac fungi are also important in decomposing and recycling organic matter. Some ascomycetes are parasites responsible for Dutch elm disease and Chestnut blight. Other sac fungi are used in commercial baking and brewing, wine making, and in the production of antibiotics, including some species of *Penicillium*, the fungus that produced penicillin, the first commercial antibiotic.

The term yeast is widely applied to single-celled ascomycetes such as *Candida albicans* and *Saccharomyces cerevisiae* (sold as brewer's yeast or baker's yeast). The latter fungus is useful to humans as a leavening agent in bread as well as brewing of beer and similar alcoholic beverages. These fungi typically are unicellular and reproduce by asexual budding as well as the sexual process involving the formation of asci.

Some ascomycetes are (along with basidiomycetes) the symbiotic mycorrhizae fungi that are important to plant root function. Plants with mycorrhizae grow better: the plant gets nutrients from the fungus in exchange for carbohydrates.

The ascomycete life cycle differs from the zygomycete life cycle in several ways. Perhaps, the most profound is the presence of a two-nucleate phase between fusion of the gametes and fusion of the nuclei. This phase can in occasionally persist for some time.

There is an asexual cycle as well as a sexual cycle. The sexual cycle begins with the fusion of haploid mating hyphae (plasmogamy shown in Figure 17.9 as step 2). This produces the dikaryon phase (n + n to differentiate it from the diploid 2n phase that occurs after karyogamy). A fruiting body, known as an ascocarp (step 5) develops from proliferation of the dikaryotic hyphae. Once this structure has formed (it does not form in all ascomycetes though) the haploid nuclei at the tip of numerous hyphae in the ascocarp fuse to produce a diploid zygote cell. The zygote divides by first meiosis then mitosis to produce an ascus containing eight cells (step 4). These spores are released and if they find a suitable substrate will germinate into new haploid hyphae.

17.2.5 Phylum Basidiomycota

Mushrooms, toadstools, and puffballs are commonly encountered basidiomycetes. These conspicuous fungal features are the reproductive structures known as fruiting bodies (although they do NOT produce fruit, but rather, characteristic basidiospores). Sexual reproduction involves the formation of basidiospores on club-shaped cells known as basidia, as shown in Figure 17.10.

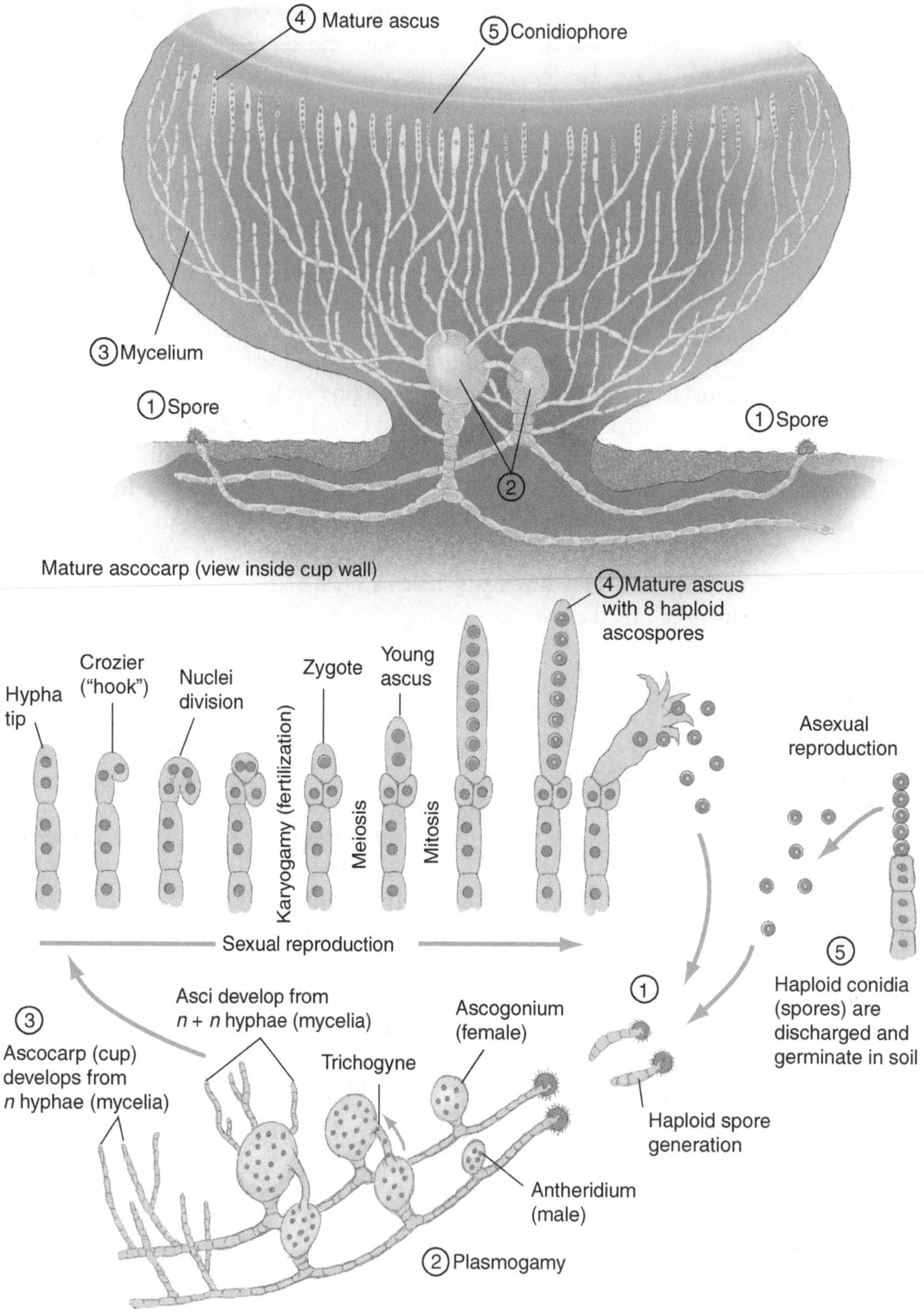

FIGURE 17.9 Life cycle of an ascomycete.

FIGURE 17.10 Examples of basidiomycetes. A. Commercial mushrooms, *Agaricus bisporis*; B. Portobello mushrooms (a different variety of *Agaricus bisporis*); C. Shiitake mushrooms (*Lentinus edodes*) growing on tree; D. *Dictyophora indusiata* illustrating the skirt characteristic of this type of basidiomycete; E. Common stinkhorn (*Phallus impudicus*); F. *Amanita muscaria*, commonly known as the fly agaric, is a highly poisonous basidiomycete fungus; G. *Psilocybe* mushrooms in a beech tree trunk at Irati Navarra Pyrenees of Spain; some species of this genus are known as magic mushrooms; H. *Amanita phalloides*, the death cap mushroom.

Club fungi are important as commercial crops. They also cause many diseases that result in loss or reduction of grain yields. *Agaricus bisporis* is the common commercial mushroom found in grocery stores as the white button mushroom, crimini mushroom, and the fabulous portabella mushroom (Figure 17.10A, B). *Lentinus edodes* (Figure 17.10C) is the less commonly bought shitake mushroom (to my inner hobbit mushroom-loving mind a tasty addition to food)! More than $14 billion per year of these products are sold worldwide.

Amanita is a fungal genus that contains some of the most poisonous of all mushrooms: *Amanita bisporigera*, *A. virosa*, and *A. verna*, collectively known as the death angel. These fungi produce a small protein that affects the liver and kidney functions, producing death within 5 days unless transplantation can happen to replace the damaged organs. *Amanita phalloides*, shown in Figure 17.10H, is also a deadly fungus. Not all species of this genus are deadly. *Amanita muscaria*, the fly agaric (Figure 17.10F), will make you sick and have hallucinations if you eat it. That species has been associated with religious ceremonies in several cultures as well as the famous Viking ferocity in battle.

Certain mushrooms also have hallucinogenic properties, such as the drug psilocybin, found in certain species of the basidiomycete *Psilocybe* (Figure 17.10G) as well as other basidiomycetes. Often these mushrooms are important in native religious rituals in Central and South America as well as other parts of the world.

The basidiomycete life cycle is shown in Figure 17.11. Haploid hyphae generate from spores. When these hyphae fuse they produce the dikaryotic (n + n) phase of the life cycle. This phase, when certain environmental stimuli occur will begin producing a basidiocarp. The mature basidiocarp consists of a cap atop a stalk (Figure 17.12A). On the underside of the cap these are hundreds of gills (Figure 17.12B, C), each covered in thousands of basidia. The haploid nuclei fuse in each basidium to produce the diploid zygote cell. This cell undergoes meiosis to produce four basidiospores on each basidium (Figure 17.12D, E). These spores are released and then transported by the wind until they settle upon a suitable substrate and germinate hyphae to form the new mycelium.

17.3   Significance of Fungi

Fungi play important roles as ecological decomposers, nutrient cyclers, parasites, and pathogens. They also have a surprising number of uses in ancient and modern human societies.

17.3.1   Uses of Fungi

Brewing and baking may be among the mist ancient if human applications of fungi. Brewer's yeast, *Saccharomyces cerevisae*, is available from most grocery stores in the baking section. During the baking of bread yeast produce carbon dioxide as they ferment sugars in the bread dough. The dough is thick enough to keep the gas from escaping. This trapped gas causes the bread to rise.

Brewing is another ancient human technology. Among the oldest preserved writing is a beer recipe. Fermenting the grain harvest was one way to cut down on spoilage. It also produced, in the days before water purification, a safe beverage to drink. As cities grew so did the pollutants

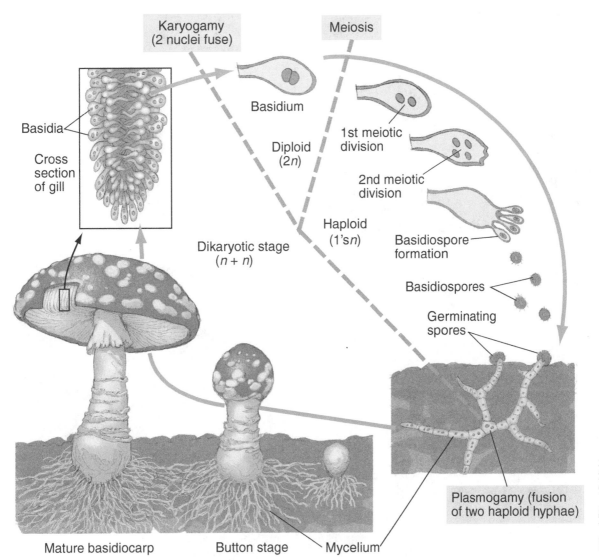

FIGURE 17.11 Life cycle of a basidiomycete.

produced by people. This pollution led to unsafe, unsanitary water for drinking. Fermentation solved both grain spoilage as well as safe liquid for drinking. It also produced an intoxicating effect.

During the brewing process yeast is added to the grain and water mixture termed the mash (Figure 17.13C). Fermentation is accomplished commercially in large vats (Figure 17.13D). Various species of yeast will be used, depending on the style of beer desired. The type of yeast used is but one of many factors determining the color, taste, and style of beer being brewed. A lambic style beer uses only yeasts that fall from the air.

Fermentation is also employed in wine making (Figure 17.13E). Most modern wineries have well equipped microbiology laboratories as the specific strain of yeast added to the grapes plays a large role in the nature of the wine produced.

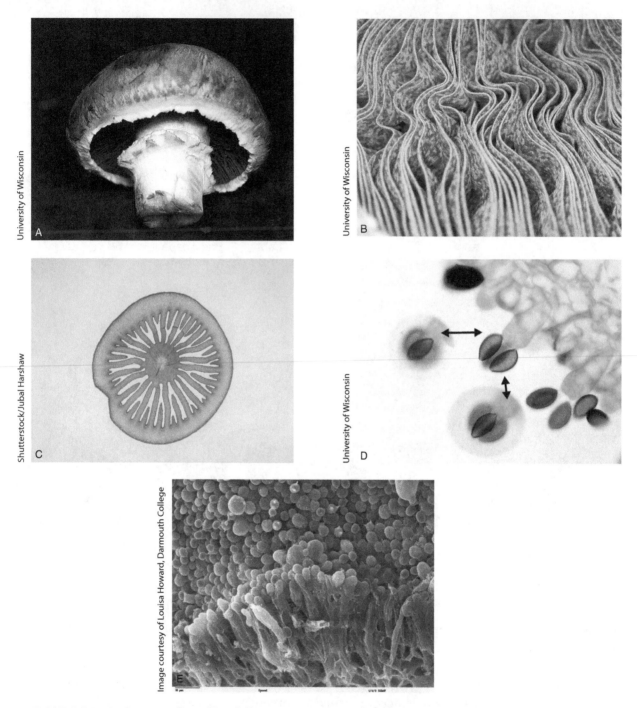

FIGURE 17.12 Composite of basidiomycete structure. A. *Agaricus* mushroom; B. Close-up of *Agaricus* gills; C. Light micrograph of a prepared slide of a cross-section through a mushroom; D. Several different focal levels of a basidium; E. Scanning electron micrograph of gills, basidia, and basidiospores of *Agaricus bisporus*; courtesy of Louisa Howard and Charles P. Daghlian, Dartmouth College Electron Microscopy Facility.

FIGURE 17.13 Uses of fungi. A. Bread rising in pans in a traditional bakery; B. Brewer's yeast; each grain is a single celled ascomycete; C. The fermentation of beer; D. Mash vats in a brewery; E. Cabernet sauvignon winemaking with grapes and fermentation stainless steel tank vessels; F. *Penicillium* fungi on agar plate; G. Bleu Basque variety of Bleu cheese; note the blue color is caused by the *Penicillium roqueforti* fungus.

Penicillin was the first of the so-called wonder drugs. This antibiotic is naturally produced by the *Penicillium* fungus (Figure 17.13F) and kills a wide variety of bacteria. In 1928 British scientist Sir Alexander Fleming (1881–1955) discovered *Penicillium* mold (Figure 17.13F) growing in a Petri dish of bacteria had a clear zone around the fungus in which no bacteria grew. Further investigations led him to conclude the mold secreted a substance that killed the bacteria. He later identified the mold as *Penicillium* and named the substance penicillin. Other scientists developed the techniques to produce the antibiotic in quantity and its use continues to save millions of lives per year. Other fungi produce a variety of antibiotics effective against a range of diseases. Several fungi produce statins used to inhibit cholesterol production.

The fungus *Penicillium roqueforti* is used in the production of Bleu (Figure 17.13G), Gorgonzola, and Roquefort cheeses. There are a number of bleu cheeses besides the ones just mentioned. Roquefort cheese is made from the milk of certain breeds of sheep. Gorgonzola and Stilton (an English Bleu cheese) use cow's milk.

17.3.2   Animal and Human Diseases

Fungi cause a variety of human diseases, including athlete's foot (sometime also known as jock itch), valley fever, ringworm, tineas, and fungal pneumonia. Medical treatments often use antifungal medicines derived from bacteria other fungi. Let us examine a few of the numerous animal and human diseases caused by fungal infections.

The deserts of the southwestern United States and northern Mexico (as well as areas in South America) are home to an endemic fungus, *Coccidioides immitis* (Figure 17.14A, B), which causes a disease in humans and animals (Figure 17.14A) known as valley fever. The disease, formally known as coccidioidomycosis, usually begins as a respiratory infection. Soon after moving where the fungus occurs most people develop what they think of as a cold. While most people recover, the organism remains encysted in their lungs. In the most severe cases death results, although most sufferers survive and are thought relatively immune for the remainder of their lives. Medical treatments are available if diagnosed properly. Rumors of the use of this organism as a bioweapon are thought to be just that, due to the extreme care needed to grow and work with this organism. Those at higher risk from *Coccidioides* include people with compromised immune systems (AIDS patients, transplant recipients, diabetics), certain ethnicities, and those whose work exposes them to desert soils at certain times of the year. This fungus, whose sexual stage is unknown at present, is of uncertain taxonomic placement: some structures look like zygomycetes, but the ribosomal RNA data suggest this fungus is an ascomycete.

Pneumocystis jirovecii (formerly *P. carnii*) is an ascomycete that typically lives inside human lungs. This organism normally does not bother people with healthy immune systems. Those with compromised immune systems develop infections, like the one shown in Figure 17.14C. This organism was important during the 1980s in the recognition of HIV/AIDS infections. It can often be one of the first signs that a patient has progressed to AIDS stage of the HIV infection.

Ringworm (Figure 17.4D) is formally known as dermatophytosis. Despite the implication of an animal causing this disease, it results from a fungus. The fungus feeds on the keratin, a chemical in our skin. Ringworm is caused by *Trichophyton verrucosum*. These fungi cause jock itch, athlete's foot, and other diseases.

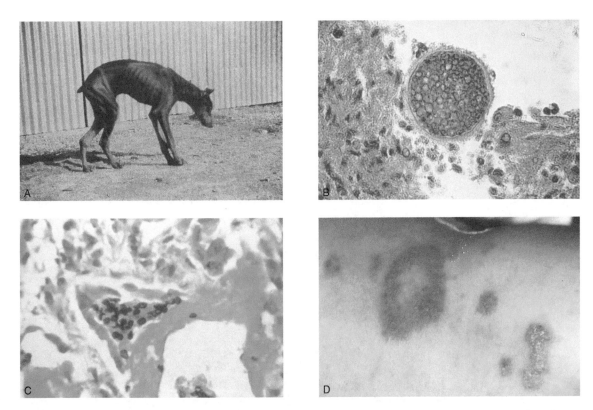

FIGURE 17.14 Disease-causing ascomycetes. A. Valley fever is a human (and animal) disease epidemic throughout the southwestern United States. This Arizona Doberman Pinscher displayed the wasting, lethargy, and disorientation resulting from to a fungal infection known as coccidioidomycosis, which is caused by a fungus from the genus *Coccidioides*. Note the head-down posture, and trembling gait, as well as the dog's loss of mass, so much so that its ribs and other skeletal elements were clearly visible. (Image courtesy of CDC/Dr. Maddy and Dr. Lucille K. Georg); B. Lymph node tissue showing the presence of a spherule of a *Coccidioides* sp. fungal organism, magnification of 480×. (Image courtesy of the CDC); C. *Pneumocystis jirovecii* (formerly *P. carnii*) in alveolar lung tissue of a patient suffering from pulmonary pneumocystosis. (Image courtesy of CDC/Dr. Francis Chandler); D. Close view of ringworm lesions caused by the fungal organism *Trichophyton verrucosum* on the torso of a patient. (Image courtesy of CDC/Dr. Lucille K. Georg).

17.3.3   Plant Diseases

Claviceps purpurea (Figure 17.15A), cause of the crop disease known as wild ergot (or Jack-in-the-Rye), is a natural source of a hallucinogen chemically similar to the artificial drug LSD. Some scholars speculate that an outbreak of wild ergot may have been responsible for the hallucinations associated with the Great Awakening in 17th century America. The parasite causes the production of a long, dark purple spur (Figure 17.15A; hence the species name "purpurea") that contains the dormant fungus. During this dormant phase the fungus produces several defense chemicals known as alkaloids, as well as lysergic acid and related compounds. These compounds

FIGURE 17.15 Plant fungal diseases. A. *Claviceps purpurea* growing on a fruiting sheaf of a rye plant; B. Cedar apple rust; C. Corn smut, *Ustilago maydis*.

can cause the reported psychotropic effects. Some studies suggested that the hysteria that led to the Salem witchcraft trials in colonial Massachusetts resulted in part from an outbreak of ergotism. Other studies dispute this assertion.

Some ascomycetes are parasites responsible for Dutch elm disease and Chestnut blight.

Rusts and smuts (Figure 17.15B, C) can be significant crop parasites: corn smut (Figure 17.15C) almost destroyed the entire US corn crop in the 1970s. During the late 1990s wheat fields in central Arizona (yes, we did grow wheat in the desert before all of the urban sprawl) had to be destroyed due to the presence of karnal bunt fungus. Billions of dollars of food crops worldwide are annually destroyed by these basidiomycetes.

17.3.4   Ecological Significance

Fungi are important in many ecological roles. Together with bacteria they form what we collectively term the decomposers. These organisms breakdown organic matter in soil and sediment, recycling nutrients locked up in leaves, bodies, shells, wood, and feces so it can re-enter the various nutrient cycles discussed in a later chapter. Two other important ecological roles of fungi are as components in lichens and as fungal partners with plants, the mycorrhizae.

17.3.4.1   Mycorrhizae

Mycorrhizae are fungi (usually a zygomycete or basidiomycete) symbiotic with the roots of plants. This relationship is mutualistic: both parties benefit. Fungi provide water and nutrients from the soil while the plant provides food to the fungus. This association of fungus and plant benefits both. Fungi grow into the cells of a plant root and gain sugars produced by the plant leaves transported to the root by the plant's phloem. The fungi in turn greatly enhance the surface area of the plant's roots for absorbing water and mineral nutrients from soil.

17.3.4.2   Lichens

Lichens are a symbiosis between a photosynthetic organism (an alga or cyanobacterium) and a fungus (either an ascomycete or a basidiomycete). Lichens often live in marginal environments and may grow only 1 or 2 cm per year. Historically, this symbiosis has been considered a classic example of mutualism, where both organisms benefit from the association. Organization of a typical lichen is shown in Figure 17.16. Some lichens do not grow on soil, but rather on rock (Figure 17.16). The fungus secretes acids that break down minerals in the rock. These minerals are passed then to the plant. Three basic body styles of lichens occur: fruticose (Figure 17.16A), crustose (Figure 17.16B), and foliose (Figure 17.16C).

FIGURE 17.16 Lichens. A. Cup lichens; B. Heart shaped *Xanthoria parietina* lichen (Common Orange Lichen) growing on stone with unidentified gray lichens; C. Two types of foliose lichens growing on a tree branch.

Lichens have long been recognized as useful organisms for humans. Certain species of lichen serve as indicators of environmental pollution; indigenous people to make natural dyes, or even to make poison-tipped arrowheads have used other types of lichen. Because they often live in marginal habitats, lichens have had to develop chemical defenses, making them prime targets for natural antibiotic research. One estimate places half of lichen species as possessing some sort of antibiotic chemicals. Some lichens are even edible, although many others are harmful if eaten, so extreme caution should be used if investigating edible fungi.

Terms

antibiotics	chytrids	parasitism
absorptive heterotrophs	flagella	*penicillium*
Agaricus bisporis	fungi	parasites
Amantia	glomerospores	penicillin
ascocarp	glycogen	phloem
ascomycete	heterotrophic	rusts and smuts
ascospore	hypha/hyphae	*Saccharomyces Cerevisiae*
ascus	immune systems	saprophytes
basidiocarp	keratin	sporangia
basidiomycete	karyogamy	spores
basidiospore	lichens	symbiosis
basidium	multicellular	unicellular
bread molds	multinucleate	uninucleate
Claviceps purpurea	mutualism	valley fever
Coccidioides immitis	mycelium	zygomycete
chitin	mycorrizhae	zygospore

Review Questions

1. When we see a toadstool we are seeing the _____ of the fungus.
   a. vegetative mycelia;
   b. asexual reproductive structure;
   c. sexual reproductive structure;
   d. lichen

2. Which of these fungi would you likely encounter at a typical dinner table serving mushroom pizza and a salad with bleu cheese dressing?
   a. *Agaricus bisporis;*
   b. *Amanita;*
   c. *Penicillium roqueforti;*
   d. a and b at the very least

3. The first great antibiotic was _____.
   a. AZT;
   b. penicillin;
   c. zoltran;
   d. Keflex

4. Brewer's/baker's yeast is responsible for _____.
   a. commercial alcohol brewing;
   b. leavening bread;
   c. a model organism for the Human Genome Project;
   d. all of these

5. Individual strands of the fungal body are known as _____.
   a. mycelium;
   b. hyphae;
   c. ascocarp;
   d. zygospore

6. The collective term for the fungal body is _____.
   a. mycelium;
   b. hyphae;
   c. ascocarp;
   d. zygospore

7. Fungi that have not been observed in their sexual stages used to be placed in the _____.
   a. Basidiomycetes;
   b. Deuteromycetes;
   c. Ascomycetes;
   d. Zygomycetes

8. Valley Fever is caused by _____.
   a. *Penicillium roqueforti*;
   b. *Amanita*;
   c. *Agaricus bisporis*;
   d. *Coccidioides immitis*

9. Hyphae with more than one nucleus per cell are termed _____ hyphae.
   a. septate;
   b. uniseriate;
   c. coenocytic;
   d. mycelia

10. The presence of a _____ phase suggests that ascomycetes and basidiomycetes are part of a monophyletic group within the Kingdom Fungi.
    a. mycelium;
    b. spores;
    c. zygote;
    d. dikaryotic

11. The most primitive group of fungi is the _____.
    a. Glomeromycota;
    b. Ascomycota;
    c. Chytridiomycota;
    d. Basidiomycota;
    e. Zygomycota

12. The presence of flagellated spores characterizes which of these fungal groups?
    a. Glomeromycota;
    b. Ascomycota;
    c. Chytridiomycota;
    d. Basidiomycota;
    e. Zygomycota

13. The presence of a sac in which spores are produced by meiosis characterizes which of these fungal groups?
    a. Glomeromycota;
    b. Ascomycota;
    c. Chytridiomycota;
    d. Basidiomycota;
    e. Zygomycota

14. You are eating a pizza topped with mushrooms. To which of these groups do your mushrooms belong?
    a. ~~Glomeromycota;~~
    b. ~~Ascomycota;~~
    c. ~~Chytridiomycota;~~
    d. Basidiomycota;
    e. Zygomycota

15. You are eating a salad topped with Bleu cheese dressing. To which of these groups does the fungus that produced the bleu cheese flavor belong?
    a. Deuteromycota;
    b. Ascomycota;
    c. ~~Chytridiomycota;~~
    d. Basidiomycota;
    e. Zygomycota

16. The term for a fruiting body of a sac fungus is _____.
    a. ascocarp;
    b. basidiocarp;
    c. basidium;
    d. ascus

17. The term for a fruiting body of a club fungus is _____.
    a. ~~ascocarp;~~
    b. basidiocarp;
    c. basidium;
    d. ascus

18. The polysaccharide carbohydrate storage product fungi share with animals is _____.
    a. amylose;
    b. glucose;
    c. glycogen;
    d. chitin;
    e. cellulose

19. Which of these fungal genera includes magic mushrooms?
    a. *Saccharomyces*;
    b. ~~*Agaricus*;~~
    c. *Psilocybe*;
    d. *Coccidioides*;
    e. *Morchella*

20. You are in a restaurant and order fried mushrooms as an appetizer. More than likely they will belong to which of these genera?
    a. ~~*Sacchzaromyces*;~~
    b. *Agaricus*;
    c. ~~*Psilocybe*;~~
    d. *Coccidioides*;
    e. *Morchella*

Links

- **The Nanoworld Image Gallery:** Lots of interesting pics and links for microscopes. [http://www.uq.edu.au/nanoworld/]

- **The Microbe Zoo:** What are they? Where are they? Why should I care? Answer these questions at this site. [http://commtechlab.msu.edu/sites/dlc-me/zoo/]

- **Introduction to the Fungi:** UCMP Berkeley site details systematics, morphology, and more! [http://www.ucmp.berkeley.edu/fungi/fungi.html]

- **Tom Volk's Fungi:** Want a well-illustrated site for fungi? This is the place. Loads of images and even some lecture materials provided by Tom Volk. [http://botit.botany.wisc.edu/toms_fungi/]

- **North American Lichen Project:** Lichen or not, these symbiotic organisms are very interesting. This site offers a great wealth of links and images. [http://www.lichen.com]

- **Coccidioides immitis:** The causative organism of Valley Fever was Tom Volk's Fungus of the Month in January 2002. This well-illustrated page gives some useful details of the life history and impact of this fungus. [http://botit.botany.wisc.edu/toms_fungi/jan2002.html]

- **Ascomycota Sac Fungi:** This page from the Tree of Life project is written by John W. Taylor, Joey Spatafora, and Mary Berbee. It looks in detail at the sac fungi and their characteristics and phylogenetic implications. [http://tolweb.org/tree?group=Ascomycota&contgroup=Fungi#TOC1]

CHAPTER 18
Biodiversity: Invertebrate Animals

Shutterstock/Rich Carey

Chapter Opener

Nudibranch Sea Slug (*Hypselodoris apolegma*) against some soft hydroid corals.

Objectives

- List the characteristics that distinguish animals from the other members of domain Eukarya.
- Describe and name the three cell types that make up the sponge body.
- Describe the criteria used for subdivision of phylum Porifera into taxonomic classes.
- Detail the advantages radial symmetry presents when compared with bilateral symmetry. Contrast that with the advantages bilateral symmetry presents when compared with radial symmetry.
- List some of the economic and environmental importance of members of Phylum Cnidaria.
- List some of the various diseases caused by organisms discussed in this chapter.
- There are several types of animal body: prepare a list of the advantages that each type would present to the animal.

Introduction

Kingdom Animalia (Figure 18.1) is the group of organisms most of us would name as alive on our first day in a general biology class. Plants and fungi do not move, and we only know bacteria from headlines about MRSA and Salmonella infections. Seaweed? Heck we wrap it around our sushi, was it once alive? We have domesticated many animals as companions, beasts of burden, food, materials we wear. Wild animals also serve a purpose as we admire the power of a great white shark, the ferocity of a lion, or the majestic flight of a bald eagle. This chapter examines animals and gives us a small taste of the great diversity of animal life on our planet.

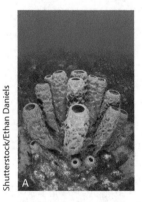
Shutterstock/Ethan Daniels

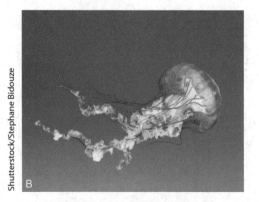
Shutterstock/Stephane Bidouze

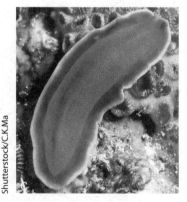
Shutterstock/C.K.Ma

FIGURE 18.1 Examples of invertebrate animals. A. Sponges growing on reef in the Caribbean Sea; B. Orange bell jellyfish in aquarium, Osaka, Japan; C. Sea slug on corals; D. Octopus on a coral outcrop; E. Green haired red King Crab holding a clam; F. Two sharks offshore of Bimini, Bahamas; G. Frog in a Peruvian rainforest; H. Emerald tree boa snake; I. Hummingbird; J. Mountain lion.   (*Continued*)

Shutterstock/Nicram Sabod

Shutterstock/Kari Kolehmainen

Shutterstock/Matt9122

Shutterstock/Dirk Ercken

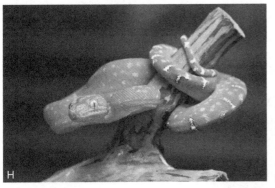

Shutterstock/bluedogroom

Shutterstock/Tmore Campbell

Shutterstock/pixelparticle

FIGURE 18.1 (*Continued*)

18.1   Characteristics of Animals

Animals form a clade of multicellular, ingestive heterotrophs that lack cell walls. At some point during their lives, animals move about. In the most commonly encountered animals, this stage is the adult, although some animals such as coral have sessile nonmobile adult phases and mobile juvenile forms. Animal and plant evolutionary history both show the development of multicellularity and the move from water to land (as well as secondary adaptation back to water).

Animals developed skeletons to provide support. Support in water is not a tremendous problem, but when animals moved to land these skeletons proved their value. The evolution of increasingly waterproof skin to prevent or lessen water loss also reflected the move onto land. Muscles allowed animals to crawl, walk, swim, and even fly in search of food, mates, or to escape a predator. Brains and nervous systems allowed animals to integrate stimuli and control responses. Internal digestive systems allowed animals to ingest their food and move on as opposed to having to stay in one place and digest their food the way their close relatives the fungi do.

Most animals have a life cycle with a preadult stage. This stage of development oftentimes does not compete with the adult stage for food. For example, many insects have their larval stages develop in water while the adult lives on land. Some other animals lay their eggs on one plant where the young feed, while the adult eats elsewhere. Animal life cycles lack an alternation of generations like we see in plants. In contrast to fungi where the haploid phase dominates the life cycle, animal life cycles are dominated by the diploid phase.

18.1.1   Animal Body Plans

Animal body plans fall into one of two categories: sac body or tube-within-a-tube body (Figure 18.2). The sac body has on opening through which material enters the body and leaves it. We only see this body plan in the more primitive types of animals like corals and sponges. The tube-within-a-tube body plan is much more common. Studies show that this body plan is 10% more effective at obtaining nutrients through digestion. The separation of food intake through a moth from waste elimination though an anus characterizes this body plan.

18.1.2   Animal Embryonic Development

All animals, except sponges, have cells organized into tissues. These tissues arise from various embryonic tissues summarized in Table 18.1.

The ectoderm forms the outer covering of the animal, and any sensory outgrowth of that outer covering. It also forms elements of the nervous system such as the neural crest and neural tube. In vertebrate chordates, the neural crest develops into the dentin of teeth, the peripheral nervous system, cartilage of the face region, and the adrenal medulla of the kidneys. The neural tube develops into the retinal of the eyes, the brain and spinal cord (the central nervous system), the front part of the pituitary gland (the so-called master gland of our bodies), and motor neurons that carry nerve messages from the brain and spinal cord to muscles and glands.

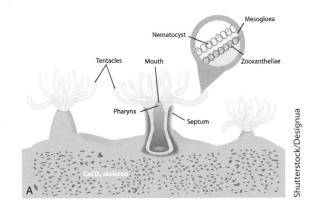

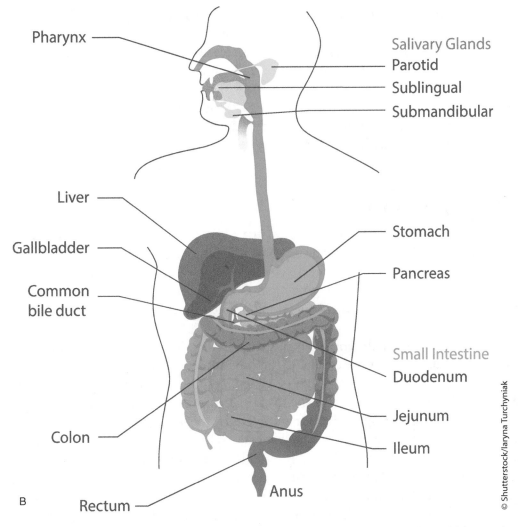

FIGURE 18.2 Animal body plans. A. Sac body plan of a coral; B. Tube-within-a-tube body plan.

TABLE 18.1 Embryonic Tissue Layers

Embryonic Tissue Layer	Adult Tissues Derived from This Layer	Animal Clade Having This Layer
Ectoderm	Tissues of the epidermal (skin) layer; neural crest, neural tube	Diploblasts, Triploblasts
Endoderm	Digestive system, lung epithelium, urinary tract	Diploblasts, Triploblasts
Mesoderm	Muscles, kidneys, bone, cartilage, lymphatic and circulatory system (notochord in chordates)	Triploblasts

The endoderm develops into the cells lining most of the organs inside the body, such as the lining of the esophagus, stomach, liver, pancreas, and parts of the trachea and lungs.

The mesoderm develops into the adult tissues of the kidneys (except the adrenal medulla) and gonads, cartilage, skeletal muscle, and the dermis layer of the skin, the circulatory and lymphatic systems, and a few other internal structures that are not part of the gut lining. The mesoderm only develops in a group of animals known as triploblasts because they develop all three embryonic tissue layers. The other clade of animals with tissues is the diploblasts, who only develop the endoderm and ectoderm germ tissue layers.

18.1.3   Animal Reproduction

All animals reproduce sexually by producing a large egg as well as smaller swimming sperm gametes. While asexual reproduction does occur in some animals, it is limited as a rule. Animals often have mating rituals during which prospective mates check each other out and select the most desirable mate. Some animals, like penguins and swans (Figure 18.3A, B), are monogamous in that they mate for life. Other animals, such as lions and horses may have a top male that gets to mate with all of the females.

Mating also involves various rituals, combats, and such that act as excellent behavioral isolating mechanisms. One classic example of this is the blue-footed boobies (Figure 18.3C) on the Galapagos Islands and other areas around the Pacific Ocean. The male booby engages the female by posturing and calling. If he performs the ritual successfully she mates with him. Other animals, such as the elephant seal (Figure 18.3D) and bighorn sheep engage in male combat to determine which male gets to mate with a particular female.

Many animals lay eggs that are fertilized outside the mother's body. Fish, frogs (Figure 18.4A), corals, and many types of worms reproduce in this manner. Other animals, such as sharks (Figure 18.4B), rays, octopi, reptiles (Figure 18.4C), and birds have fertilization inside the mother's body before she deposits her eggs. Animals, such as some sharks and mammals, fertilization is internal and the egg is retained inside the mother's body until the development of the embryo has finished and the mother gives birth to live young (Figure 18.4D, E).

FIGURE 18.3 Animal mating. A. Emperor Penguin family in the Antarctic Weddel Sea. Atka Bay; B. Swans with nestlings; C. Blue-footed boobies performing their species mating ritual; D. Elephant seals fight during mating season near San Simeon, California.

FIGURE 18.4 Animal reproduction. A. Red-eyed tree frogs mating and depositing their eggs on a tree branch; B. Cocoons of a shark showing the embryos within; C. Green turtle (*Chelonia mydas*) laying her eggs and covering her nest on the beach in the daytime; D. Eastern grey kangaroo with her Joey peering out from her pouch; E. Belgian shepherd taking care of her newborn puppy.

FIGURE 18.5 Animal coverings. A. Shells; B. Fish scales; C. Skin of a zebra shark; D. Alligator skin; E. Harlequin Macaw feathers; F. Nose of a Chihuahua.

18.1.4 Animal Organ Systems

Sponges lack tissues, organs, and organ systems. All other animals have tissues organized into organs, and organs in turn organized into organ systems. Many animals lack some of the organ systems we see in humans. The major organ systems are summarized in Table 18.2.

Mammals also use their skin for thermoregulation. Amphibians carry out a significant portion of their gas exchange through their skin. Many animals communicate through their skin, like the cuttlefish and octopus.

TABLE 18.2 Major organ systems of animals

Organ System	Description
Integumentary	Outer covering of body; contains protective layers, such as bone, shell, and hair. Also in this covering are sensory structures for temperature, touch, pain, etc.
Muscular	Three types of muscle: Skeletal muscle also known as voluntary muscle. Cardiac muscle occurs only in the heart. Smooth muscle also known as involuntary muscle; it is not under conscious control. When you breathe, sneeze, shiver, or digest food, smooth muscle is involved.
Skeletal	Worms use a hydrostatic skeleton using fluid pressure to produce a strong surface. Arthropods use an exoskeleton produced outside their bodies. Vertebrates have an endoskeleton located under the animal's muscles.
Circulatory	Functions in delivery of fluid plasma containing dissolved nutrients, hormones, immune system elements, and cells. This fluid is collectively termed blood. Blood travels from a heart through arteries. In an open circulatory system blood flows from the artery and diffuses through the body tissues back to the heart. A closed circulatory system has the blood confined, usually inside blood vessels such as veins, arteries, and capillaries. Material diffuses from the blood out to the tissues and vice versa. Blood cells usually remain inside vessels.
Digestive	Occur only in animals with a tube-within-a-tube body plan. Food is broken down into monomers in organs such as the mouth, stomach, and intestine. Monomers are absorbed in the small intestine, and nondigestible material is packaged into stool in the large intestine. Many animals, such as corals and free-living flatworms combine the function of the digestive and circulatory systems into a gastrovascular cavity.
Nervous	Integrate and control response to stimuli. Sponges lack a nervous system. Corals and jellyfish have a nerve net. All other animals have a brain and nerve cord system. Nerve cells transmit signals to the brain, which integrates and controls a response.
Endocrine	Coordinates all responses with nervous system by the animal. Whereas the nervous system responses tend to be rapid, reflexive responses, the effects of the endocrine system can be longer term in their effect. Endocrine glands and organs secrete hormones that effect response on one or more targets within the body. Insulin, glucagon, testosterone, and estrogen are examples of hormones.
Immune	System functions in recognition of self. Lymphocyte blood cells produce specific antibodies that counter a specific antigen. The immune response is an important factor in defending an animal body from pathogens like viruses, bacteria, and fungi.
Excretory	System not present in all animals. Those that have it, however, use this system to remove metabolic wastes from the body, as well as for osmoregulation of water balance. Wastes are filtered from the blood, typically in the kidneys, and passed out from the body as urine.
Reproductive	System involved in the production of gametes by meiosis. Animals have a diploid dominated life cycle. Gametogenesis occurs in sex organs known as gonads. Fertilization in animals is followed by growth of the zygote by mitosis.

Sensory organs and structures are scattered throughout the skin. Touch and tempera-ture receptors occur all over the animal's body. These send signals to the nerves and from there to the brain. Receptors may be clustered in a sense organ, such as an eye, ear, tongue, and so on.

18.1.5   Symmetry

Animals exhibit a variety of symmetries of body form. Sponges are considered asymmetrical as a group since there is no plane on most sponges where you can cut the animal in two and pro-duce mirror images. Bilateral symmetry (Figure 18.6A) has only one plane of symmetry. Coral, jellyfish, and starfish are examples of radially symmetrical organisms. Fish, worms, birds, and mammals are examples of bilaterally symmetrical organisms. Radial symmetry (Figure 18.6B) has an almost infinite number of planes of symmetry.

18.1.6   Body Cavities

Animals have three types of body cavities, termed coeloms between their gut and the body wall. These coeloms allow internal organs to be suspended into the cavity and move independently of the body wall. Acoelomate animals like flatworms (Figure 18.7A), have a solid body with no cavity. Pseudocoelomates have a body cavity incompletely lined by mesoderm (Figure 18.7B). Coelomates have a body cavity completely lined by mesoderm. Humans are coelomates.

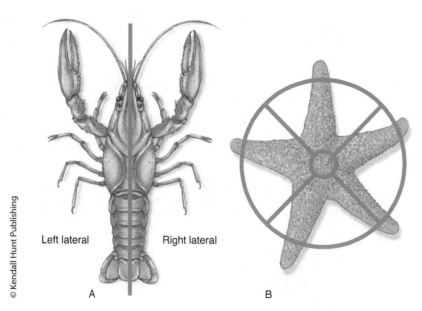

FIGURE 18.6 Symmetry in animals. A. Bilateral symmetry as exemplified by a cray fish; B. Radial symmetry as exemplified by a starfish.

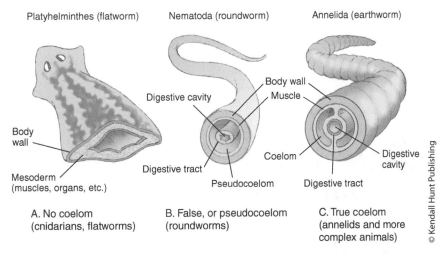

Platyhelminthes (flatworm)   Nematoda (roundworm)   Annelida (earthworm)

Body wall

Digestive cavity

Body wall

Muscle

Coelom

Digestive cavity

Mesoderm (muscles, organs, etc.)

Digestive tract

Digestive tract

Pseudocoelom

© Kendall Hunt Publishing

A. No coelom (cnidarians, flatworms)

B. False, or pseudocoelom (roundworms)

C. True coelom (annelids and more complex animals)

FIGURE 18.7 Body cavities in animals. A. Acoelomate; B. Pseudocoelomate; C. Coelomate.

The types of body cavities also vary. Humans have three body cavities: cranial, thoracic, and abdominal. The cranial cavity holds the brain and part of the spinal cord. The thoracic cavity contains the heart and lungs in land vertebrates. It is separated from the abdominal cavity by a sheet of muscle known as the diaphragm. The organs contained within the abdominal cavity are collectively termed the viscera. This includes the organs of the reproductive, excretory, and digestive systems.

18.1.7   Protostome versus Deuterostome

Coelomates, animals with a true mesoderm-lined body cavity, fall into either protostomes or deuterostomes, depending on how their embryos develop. Protostomes (from the Greek meaning *proto* first and *stome* mouth, literally "first mouth") are coelomates whose embryonic development makes a blastopore (the first opening in the blastula) that later develops into a mouth. Deuterostomes ("second mouth") are coelomates whose embryonic development produces a blastopore that later on forms an anus, with a second opening forming the mouth (hence the designation of "second mouth"). Vertebrates and echinoderms are deuterostomes. Arthropods, molluscs, and annelids are protostomes.

18.1.8   Segmentation

Some animals have their bodies divided into segments, as shown in Figure 18.8. Segmentation allows them to specialize certain segments, such as for antennae, eyes, claws, and so on. Humans, insects, and earthworms are examples of segmented animals. The systematic value of segmentation has been downplayed, with most specialists favoring segmentation arising from convergent

FIGURE 18.8 Segmentation in animals. A. The marine polychaete worm *Nereis* illustrating segmentation in annelids; B. Green with yellow spots Metallic Beetle illustrating the segmentation of the body and the presence of paired appendages.

evolution. However, the genes controlling segmentation in each of these groups are the same, leading to a rethinking of the taxonomic value of segmentation.

18.2 Systematics of Animals

Animals probably evolved from marine protists, although no group of protists has been identified from an at-best sketchy fossil record for early animals. Cells in primitive animals (sponges in particular) show similarities to collared choanoflagellates as well as pseudopod-producing amoeboid cells.

Multicellular animal fossils and burrows (presumably made by multicellular animals) first appear nearly 700 million years ago, during the late precambrian time (the part of the Proterozoic eon termed the Ediacaran). All known Ediacaran animal fossils had soft body parts: no shells or hard (and hence preservable as fossils) parts. Animals in numerous phyla appear at (or in many cases before) the beginning of the Cambrian Period.

Beginning 540 million years ago, during the early Cambrian time, animals with external skeletons appeared in great abundance. This sudden appearance of fossils was used to define the beginning of the Cambrian. External skeletons were hard enough to be more readily preserved, leading to the apparent explosion of animals early in the Cambrian.

Modern animals are classified into between 30 and 35 phyla. All major modern phyla had evolved by the beginning of the Cambrian, along with a great variety of now-extinct phyla recorded in the Burgess Shale (Cambrian) in Canada. Of the animal phyla, scientists consider nine major invertebrate phyla and the chordates to be of major importance in terms of biological diversity. Evolutionary relationships have been established for the most part on studies of living (referred to as extant) animal anatomy.

Several monophyletic clades exist within the animal kingdom. All animals are thought to have descended from a colonial protistan, a choanoflagellate. Sponges, which lack tissues and symmetry, diverged followed by the branch of radially symmetrical animals known as the Radiata (Figure 18.9). All Radiata are diploblastic, have tissues, and radial symmetry. All other animals belong to the Bilatera (Figure 18.9), a clade of triploblastic, bilaterally symmetrical animals. The next split within the bilaterally symmetrical animals was that of protostome and deuterostome.

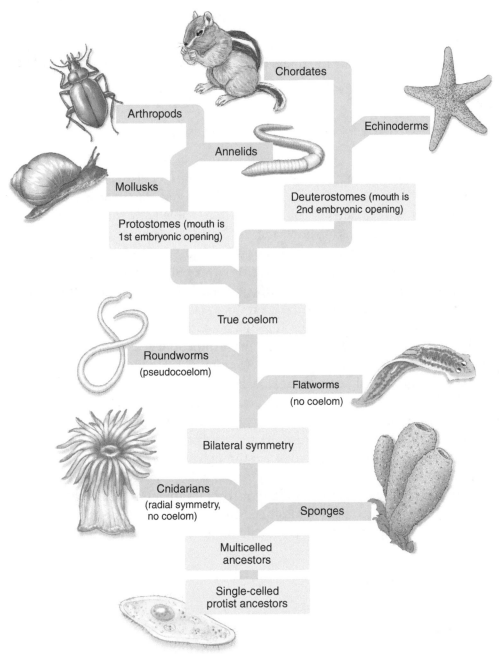

FIGURE 18.9 Phylogeny of the animal kingdom.

The phyla Echinodermata and Chordata are deuterostomes. The protostomes divided into the Lophotrochozoa and the Ecdysozoa. The phyla Arthropoda and Nematoda (the roundworms) are the ecdysozoan phyla. These animals shed their outer covering, a process known as ecdysis (Figure 18.10). The lophotrochs all have a characteristic horseshoe-shaped feeding appendage at some point during their life cycle. Annelids, rotifers, molluscs, and flatworms are members of this clade.

FIGURE 18.10 Ecdysis of the exoskeleton of a cicada.

18.2.1   Phylum Porifera

Phylum Porifera ("pore-bearing"; Figure 18.11) consists of approximately 5,000 species of sponges. These asymmetrical animals have sac-like bodies that lack tissues, and are usually interpreted as representing the cellular level of evolution. Cells from fragmented sponges can reorganize/regenerate the sponge organism, something not possible with animals that have tissues. Most zoologists consider sponges as offshoots that represent an evolutionary dead-end, although others consider some groups of sponges as being related to other animal groups. Sponges are aquatic, largely marine, animals with a great diversity in size, shape, and color.

Epidermal cells in sponges line the outer surface. Flagellated collar cells (known as choanocytes) line the inner cavity. Beating collar cells produce water currents that flow through pores in sponge wall into a central cavity and out through an osculum, the upper opening. A 10-cm tall sponge will filter as much as 100 L of water a day. Amoeboid cells occupy the "inner" layer, along with hardened structures known as spicules (Figure 18.11C). Living sponges fall into three groups: the calcareous, glass, and demosponges, based on the chemical composition of spicules.

Sponges feed by drawing water into the body through a network of pores (hence the name *porifera*, pore-bearer). This incoming water contains oxygen as well as small food particles. The flagellated choanocyte cells that line the inner cavity trap food. Food is then passed to the amoebocyte cells and then to the epidermal cells. Wastes pass out through the large opening (osculum) at the top end of the body. The current to move this water comes from the beating of the choanocyte flagella.

Sponges can reproduce asexually (by budding or from fragments) or sexually. These animals produce eggs and sperm that are released into a central cavity of the sponge, in which the zygote develops into a ciliated larva. The larval stage is able to move about while the adult is sessile.

18.2.2   Phylum Cnidaria

Phylum Cnidaria includes 10,000 species characterized by adults displaying radial symmetry. Cnidarians are aquatic, mostly all marine. The cnidarian body has only the ectoderm and endoderm tissue layers, making this group diploblastic. Members of this phylum all have stinging cells that eject a barbed thread and possibly a toxin. Only cnidaria have these cnidocytes (shown in Figure 18.12A, B), a specialized cell that contains a nematocyst, a fluid-filled capsule

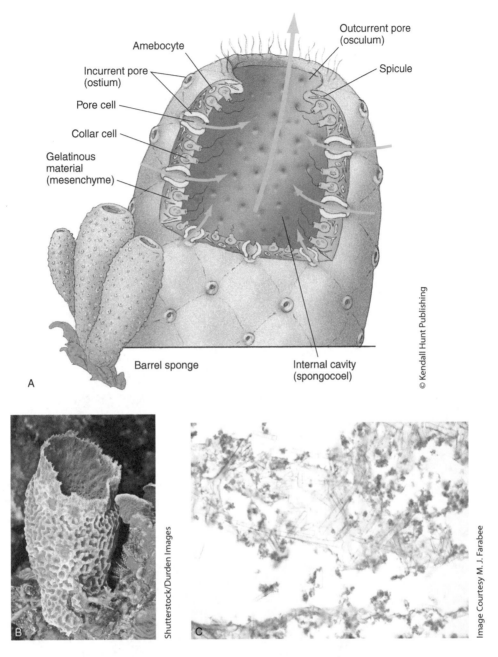

Amebocyte

Incurrent pore
(ostium)

Pore cell

Collar cell

Gelatinous
material
(mesenchyme)

Outcurrent pore
(osculum)

Spicule

Barrel sponge

Internal cavity
(spongocoel)

A

© Kendall Hunt Publishing

B

Shutterstock/Durden Images

C

Image Courtesy M. J. Farabee

FIGURE 18.11 Sponges, the Phylum Porifera. A. Anatomy of a typical sponge; B. Azure vase sponge (*Callyspongia plicifera*), a pink/purple vase-like sponge that is fluorescing light blue on its edges. The exterior is highly textured with convoluted ridges and valleys; C. Sponge spicules.

containing a long, spirally coiled hollow thread. When the trigger of the cnidocyte is touched, the nematocyst is discharged. Some threads merely trap a prey or predator, while others have spines that penetrate and inject paralyzing toxins. These toxins make some jellyfish (and a related group the box jellies) among the most poisonous of animals.

Cnidarians may have two body forms: a mobile medusa and a sessile (fancy term for not mobile) polyp, both of which are shown in Figure 18.12. Both body forms have tentacles arranged around an opening into the two-layered sac-like body. The inner tissue layer (derived from embryonic endoderm) secretes digestive juices into the gastrovascular cavity that digests food and circulates nutrients (doing the jobs of our circulatory *and* digestive systems). Muscle fibers occur at the base of the epidermal and gastrodermal cells, making this the first group of

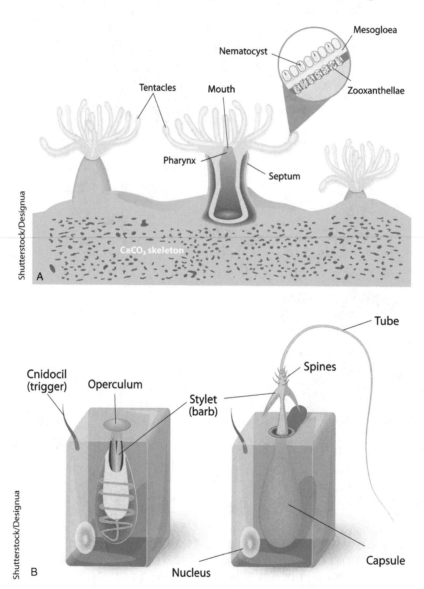

FIGURE 18.12 Phylum Cnidaria. A. Structure of a coral polyp. The coral polyps tend to live in colonies and form the building blocks of a coral reef; B. Structure of cnidocyte; C. Tropical fish on a coral reef; D. Sea fan coral branch showing individual polyps; E. The Great Barrier Reef in Queensland, Australia; F. Dangerous jellyfish *Pelagia noctiluca* near surface, Mediterranean Sea, Corsica, France; G. *Physalia*, the Portuguese Man of War, a colony of polyps suspended under a gas-filled bag.   *(Continued)*

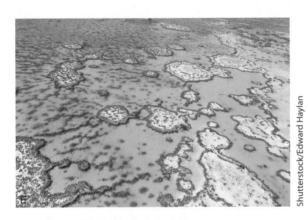

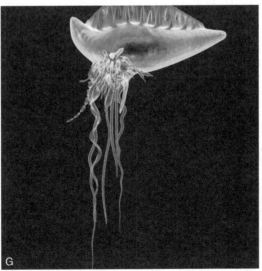

FIGURE 18.12 (*Continued*)

muscled animals. Nerve cells located below the epidermis near the mesoglea interconnect and form a nerve net throughout the body. Cnidarians have both muscle fibers and nerve fibers, making these animals capable of directional movement. The nerve net allows transmission of messages in more than one direction, possibly an advantage in a radially symmetrical animal, while contraction of muscle fibers (under control of the nerve fibers) allows for movement. One group, the box jellies have simple eyes and a rudimentary brain.

Cells are organized into tissues. The adult in most species of cnidarian is radially symmetrical. The typical cnidarian life cycle involves both sexual and asexual reproduction. A bilaterally symmetrical larva known as a planula, develops from a zygote. The planula moves around and eventually settles down in an appropriate location and grows into the adult polyp. The polyp grows and may eventually reproduce asexually to form one or more medusae. Each medusa develops gonads and uses meiosis to form gametes.

The phylum Cnidaria is usually subdivided into four taxonomic classes: class Anthozoa, class Hydrozoa, class Scyphozoa, and class Cubozoa (Table 18.3).

TABLE 18.3 Classes of Cnidaria

Class	Description	Example
Anthozoa	Solitary polyps often brightly colored, resemble flowers; thick, heavy body rests on a pedal disk and supports an upward-turned mouth surrounded by hollow tentacles. Sea anemones eat invertebrates and fish. Most coral occur in warm shallow water and build reefs	© Shutterstock
Hydrozoa	Polyp stage dominant; Portuguese man-of-war is a colony of polyps, with the original polyp becoming a gas-filled float; *Hydra* is solitary, freshwater hydrozoan polyp.	© Shutterstock
Scyphozoa	Medusa stage dominant; all marine; this class contains true jellyfish; polyp of scyphozoans small. Jellyfish serve as food for larger marine animals. Large populations of jellyfish have disrupted fisheries as well as caused closing of beaches and swimming areas due to the toxins in their cnidocyte cells.	© Shutterstock
Cubozoa	Medusa is cube shaped as opposed to the round medusa in the true jellyfish. Three box jellies are among the most poisonous animals in the world. Box jellies are the only cnidarians that have true eyes. They are active swimmers as opposed to the more or less floating behavior seen in most true jellyfish.	© Shutterstock

18.2.3   Phylum Platyhelminthes

Phylum Platyhelminthes (Figure 18.13) contains about 13,000 species of flatworms subdivided into four taxonomic classes: three parasitic and one free-living. The planaria and relatives are free-living aquatic (mostly) animals placed in the class Turbellaria (Figure 18.13A–C). Tapeworms are internal parasites and form the class Cestoda (Figure 18.13D, E). Flukes are external or internal parasites belonging to the class Trematoda (Figure 18.13F). The class Monogenea

FIGURE 18.13 Phylum Platyhelminthes. A. Freshwater flatworm as seen under a microscope from a whole mount prepared slide; B. Gold-dotted marine flatworm (*Thysanozoon*); C. Colorful flatworm in the ocean off Indonesia; D. The tapeworm *Taenia solium*; E. The tapeworm head; F. *Dicrocoelium dendriticum*, a liver fluke; G. The monogenean *Diplozoon paradoxum*.   *(Continued)*

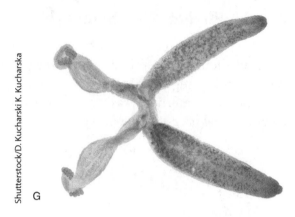

FIGURE 18.13 *(Continued)*

(Figure 18.13G) is a small class of parasitic flatworms found in the gills of fish. The phylum as a whole has adult bilateral symmetry and cephalization (the development of a head with sensory organs, in most members).

Flatworms have three tissue layers: ectoderm, mesoderm, and endoderm, and a body plan that is acoelomate and sac-like with a single opening. The mesoderm layer gives rise to muscles and reproductive organs. Free-living forms have muscles, a nerve cord, and digestive organs, but lack both the respiratory and circulatory systems common to the so-called "higher" animals (in other words like ourselves). Flatworms, as shown in Figure 18.14, have a branched gastrovascular cavity that is the site of extracellular digestion and which distributes nutrients throughout the body. Gas exchange occurs by diffusion through the animal's skin. Platyhelminthes have an excretory system that also functions as an osmotic-regulating system. Flatworms have a ladder-style nervous system composed of paired ganglia that form a brain connected via nerve cells to sensory cells in the body wall.

Parasitic members of this phylum, such as flukes and tapeworms, are characterized by these modifications:

1. Loss of cephalization producing a head bearing hooks and suckers to attach to the host as opposed to the sensory organs of free-living forms.
2. Extensive development of the reproductive system coinciding with the loss of other systems.
3. Lack of a well-developed nervous and gastrovascular system.
4. Development of a tegument that protects them from host digestive juices.

Both flukes and tapeworms use secondary or intermediate hosts to transport the species from primary host to primary host. The primary host is infected with the sexually mature adult while the secondary host contains the larval stage(s). The four classes of this phylum are summarized in Table 18.4.

The blood fluke causes schistosomiasis, a disease found predominantly in tropical Africa and in South America. Unlike most flukes, blood flukes have separate male or female animals. Flukes deposit eggs in blood vessels around the host's intestine. Eggs migrate to the

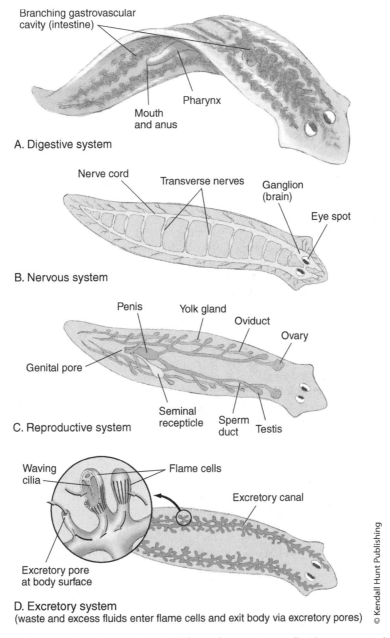

A. Digestive system

B. Nervous system

C. Reproductive system

D. Excretory system
(waste and excess fluids enter flame cells and exit body via excretory pores)

© Kendall Hunt Publishing

FIGURE 18.14 Anatomy of a flatworm. A. Digestive system; B. Nervous system; C Reproductive system; D. Excretory system.

intestine and are passed out of the body with feces. Larvae hatch in water and swim about until they detect and enter a particular species of snail. The larvae reproduce asexually and eventually leave the snail. Once larvae penetrate human skin they begin to mature in the liver, and implant in blood vessels of the small intestine. A weakened person is then more likely to die from secondary diseases.

TABLE 18.4 Classes of Platyhelminthes

Class	Description	Example
Turbellaria	Free-living freshwater or marine flatworms; head often arrow-shaped, with side extensions for sensory organs; two light-sensitive eyespots; gland cells secrete a mucous material upon which the animal slides or glides; can reproduce both sexually and asexually; hermaphroditic, possessing both male and female sex organs, and can cross-fertilize each other.	© Shutterstock
Trematoda	Flukes, such as blood, liver, and lung flukes are named after the organs they inhabit; bodies tend to be oval and elongate and lack a definite head, although an oral sucker surrounded by sensory papillae occurs; reduced digestive, nervous, and excretory systems; usually hermaphroditic; many cause diseases.	© Shutterstock
Cestoda	The tapeworm scolex (head/neck region) has hooks and suckers (Figure 18.13E) allowing it to attach to host's intestinal wall; proglottid segments contain male and female genitalia; no digestive system needed; only rudiments of nerves occur.	© Shutterstock
Monogenea	Small animals (Figure 18.13G), usually around 2 cm long; all parasitize animals; Monogeneans lack an intermediate host like in flukes and tapeworms have.	© Shutterstock

The liver fluke (Figure 18.15A) requires two intermediate hosts. Humans become infected when they eat uncooked fish. Adults migrate to the liver and deposit eggs in the bile duct, which carries the eggs to the intestine. The larval flukes must then pass through two intermediate hosts, a snail and a fish.

Following fertilization (Figure 18.15B), tapeworm proglottids become a bag of eggs that when mature, breaks off and passes out of the host body with the host's feces. If pigs or cattle ingest the eggs of tapeworms the larvae become encysted in the muscle of the host animal. The covering of ingested eggs is digested away and the larvae burrow through the intestinal wall and travel by bloodstream to lodge and encyst in muscle; a cyst is a hard-walled structure sheltering a larval worm. If humans eat the meat of infected pigs or cattle and fail to cook it properly, they also become infected.

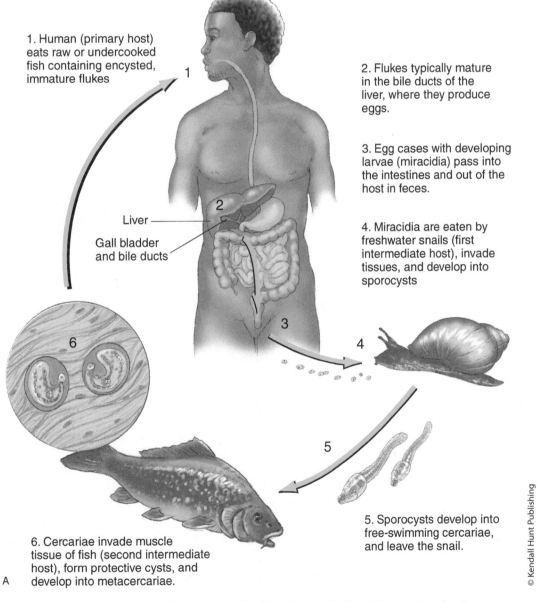

1. Human (primary host) eats raw or undercooked fish containing encysted, immature flukes

2. Flukes typically mature in the bile ducts of the liver, where they produce eggs.

3. Egg cases with developing larvae (miracidia) pass into the intestines and out of the host in feces.

4. Miracidia are eaten by freshwater snails (first intermediate host), invade tissues, and develop into sporocysts

Liver

Gall bladder and bile ducts

5. Sporocysts develop into free-swimming cercariae, and leave the snail.

6. Cercariae invade muscle tissue of fish (second intermediate host), form protective cysts, and develop into metacercariae.

A

© Kendall Hunt Publishing

FIGURE 18.15 Life cycles. A. The life cycle of a liver fluke. B. The life cycle of a tapeworm. (*Continued*)

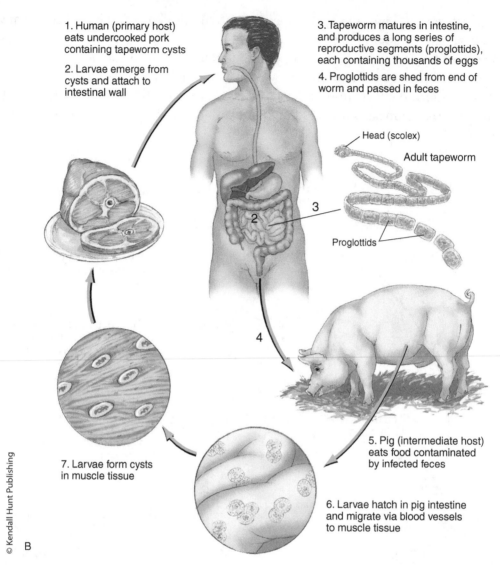

1. Human (primary host) eats undercooked pork containing tapeworm cysts

2. Larvae emerge from cysts and attach to intestinal wall

3. Tapeworm matures in intestine, and produces a long series of reproductive segments (proglottids), each containing thousands of eggs

4. Proglottids are shed from end of worm and passed in feces

Head (scolex)

Adult tapeworm

Proglottids

5. Pig (intermediate host) eats food contaminated by infected feces

6. Larvae hatch in pig intestine and migrate via blood vessels to muscle tissue

7. Larvae form cysts in muscle tissue

© Kendall Hunt Publishing

B

FIGURE 18.15 (*Continued*)

18.2.4   Phylum Nematoda

Phylum Nematoda contains more than 20,000 described species of roundworms (Figure 18.16). Most nematodes are free-living, although some are parasitic (pinworms are thought to infect 30% of all US children). Adult nematodes have a pseudocoelom (tube-within-a-tube; Figure 18.16D), a closed fluid-filled space that acts as a hydrostatic skeleton, aids in circulation and dispersal of nutrients. Nematodes lack a circulatory system, but do have a well-developed digestive system.

One nematode, *Caenorhabditis elegans*, has only one thousand genes in its genome and its developmental pathways are well known. *Caenorhabditis elegans* served as a model for eukaryote gene systems and has been extensively studied as part of the Human Genome Project.

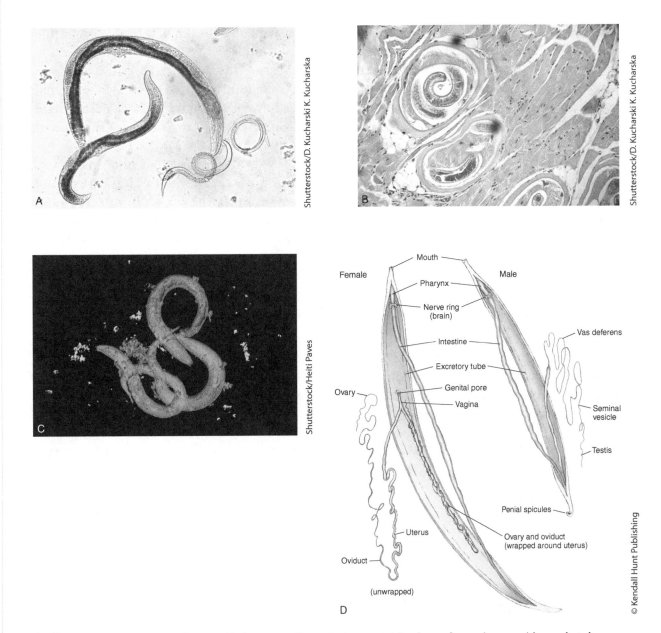

FIGURE 18.16 Nematodes. A. Entomopathogenic nematodes—females and invasive juvenile; B. *Trichinella spiralis* is a parasitic roundworm in muscle; C. *Caenorhabditis elegans*, a free-living, transparent nematode (roundworm), about 1 mm in length. Green: neurons; red: digestive tract; yellow: bacteria; D Anatomy of a nematode.

Ascaris is a parasitic roundworm. These worms are not segmented and have a smooth outside wall. They move by whip-like motions. Mating produces eggs that mature in the soil, limiting most roundworms to warmer climates. When eggs are swallowed, larvae burrow through the intestinal wall, moving to the liver, heart and/or lungs. Once within the lungs, larvae molt and, after ten days, migrate up the windpipe to throat where they are swallowed. Inside the intestine, the mature worms mate and the female deposits eggs that are passed out of the body with feces.

This mix of eggs and feces must reach the mouth of the next host to complete the life cycle, thus, proper sanitation is an important aspect to prevent infection.

Humans contract *Trichinella* (the roundworm that causes the disease trichinosis, illustrated in Figure 18.16B) by eating raw or undercooked pork containing encysted larvae. Mature female adults burrow into the wall of the host's small intestine. Live offspring travel through the bloodstream to the skeletal muscles where they encyst. Religious dietary injunctions against eating pork may in part be a reflection of the prevalence of this disease in the Middle East.

Filarial worms cause various diseases. *Dirofilaria* causes heartworm in dogs, and is a common filarial worm in temperate zones. Elephantiasis is a disease associated with tropical Africa that is also caused by a filarial worm that utilizes mosquitos as secondary hosts. Adult worms reside in and block lymphatic vessels of the host. This results in limbs of an infected individual swelling to monstrous size. Elephantiasis is treatable in its early stages but not after scar tissue has blocked lymphatic vessels.

18.2.5   Coelomates: Animals with Internal Body Cavities

Coelomates are animals that have internal body cavities, or coeloms. Humans are coelomates; we have an abdominal cavity (digestive organs, some of the excretory and reproductive organs), a thoracic cavity (heart and lungs), and a cranial cavity (brain). Coelomates also form a variety of internal and external skeletons. External skeletons and coeloms appeared during the Cambrian-Ordovician time. These skeletons offered several advantages to their producers:

- Secretion of a mineral shell that allowed the animal to use the shell as a mineral repository.
- Protection from drying out in the intertidal zone during low tides.
- Protection from predators.
- Sites for anchoring muscle attachments, offering new patterns of locomotion and increased strength.

18.2.6   Phylum Arthropoda

Phylum Arthropoda (Figure 18.17) contains animals with paired segmented appendages on their body segments. Arthropods occupy every habitat, and are in many respects the most successful animal group on Earth. There are conservatively over 1 million species of living arthropods. American biologist E.O. Wilson (b. 1929) estimates there are 10 million living species of life on our planet, 9 million of which are arthropods. Certain groups of arthropods have extremely complete fossil records.

Arthropod features that have contributed to their success include:

- A hard exoskeleton, a strong but flexible outer covering composed primarily of the carbohydrate chitin. The arthropod exoskeleton functions in protection, as attachment for muscles, aids in locomotion, and prevents the animal drying out (if it happens not to live in water).

FIGURE 18.17 Arthropod diversity. A. Trilobite fossil from the Devonian of Morocco; B. Rhinoceros beetle; C. Red cliff crab; D. Centipede; E. Giant peacock moth; F. Fresh lobster on ice.

- Presence of jointed appendages. Trilobites (Figure 18.17A), which flourished during Cambrian period and were important animals in marine ecosystems for the remainder of the Paleozoic era, had paired appendages on each body segment. Modern arthropod appendages are specialized for walking, swimming, reproduction, and so on. These modifications account for much of the diversity and success of arthropods.

- A complex nervous system with a brain connected to a ventral solid nerve cord. The head bears various sensory organs. Compound eyes have many complete visual units, each of which collects light independently. The lens of each visual unit focuses the image on light sensitive membranes of a small number of photoreceptors within that unit. In simple eyes (like our own), a single lens brings the image to focus into many receptors, each of which receives only a portion of the image.

- A unique respiratory system that employs a variety of respiratory organs. Marine arthropods utilize gills composed of a vascularized, thin-walled tissue specialized for gas exchange. Terrestrial forms have book lungs (e.g., spiders) or tracheae (e.g., insects). Book lungs are invaginations to serve in gas exchange between air and blood. Trachea are air tubes that serve as ways to deliver oxygen directly to cells.

- A complex, yet adaptable, life cycle. Metamorphosis is a drastic change in form and physiology that happens when an immature stage becomes an adult. Metamorphosis contributes to the success of arthropods because the larval stage eats food and lives in environments different from the adult; reducing competition between immature and adults of a species. Reduction in competition thus allows more members of the species to exist at one time.

The arthropod body (Figure 18.18) consists of three major collections or zones of body segments: head, thorax, and abdomen. Due to their great diversity of appendages, lifestyles, and other features, arthropods are usually separated into several subphyla.

18.2.6.1   Subphylum Chelicerata

Subphylum Chelicerata includes spiders, scorpions, ticks, mites, and horseshoe crabs (Figure 18.19). The first pair of appendages on these arthropods is the chelicerae, the second pair is the pedipalps, and the next four pairs are walking legs. Chelicerae are appendages that function as feeding organs. Pedipalps are feeding or sensory in function; although in scorpions, they are large pincers. All appendages attach to a cephalothorax, a fusion of the head and thoracic regions. The head lacks antennae, mandibles, or maxillae appendages.

Class Merostomata contains the extinct "sea scorpions" (or eurypterids; Figure 18.19A) and the extant (living) horseshoe crabs (Figure 18.19B). Eurypterids were important marine animals 500–250 million years ago during the Paleozoic Era. Some were huge, reaching a length of over 10 feet. Horseshoe crabs are an ancient group consisting today of only four living species in the genera *Tachypleus* and *Limulus*. All horseshoe crabs have a large shield that covers the cephalothorax. The compound eyes are reduced. The second pair of appendages, the pedipalps, that resemble walking legs. Horseshoe crabs have a long, spike-like telson projecting from the rear of their bodies. Respiration is accomplished by book gills, precursors to book lungs.

Class Arachnida

The class Arachnida includes over 60,000 described species of spiders (around 35,000), mites and ticks (25,000), scorpions (1,200), and other forms. Nearly all of the modern arachnids live on land.

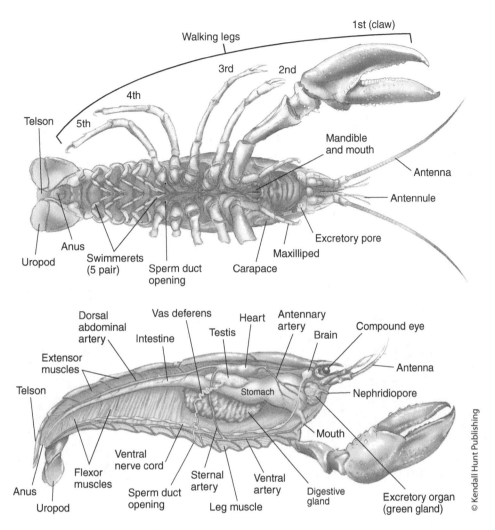

FIGURE 18.18 Crayfish anatomy.

Arachnids have a cephalothorax covered with a carapace-like shield. The abdomen may be segmented or unsegmented. Appendages on the abdomen are absent or modified, for example forming the spinnerets of spiders. Respiration is via tracheae or book lungs.

Spiders (Figure 18.19C, D) have a narrow waist separating the cephalothorax from the abdomen. Spiders have numerous simple eyes rather than compound eyes. The chelicerae are modified as fangs with ducts from poison glands. The abdomen has silk glands used to spin a web to trap prey. Invaginations of the body wall form lamellae (pages) of the book lungs. Air flows across the lamellae in the opposite direction from blood flow to exchange gases more efficiently.

Ticks (Figure 18.18E) are parasites that suck blood and often transmit diseases. Chiggers are larvae of certain mites and feed on the skin of vertebrates.

Scorpions (Figure 18.18F) are the oldest known group of terrestrial arthropods. All scorpions are nocturnal and spend most of the day hidden under a log or rock. Their pedipalps are large pincer-like appendages, and their abdomen ends in a stinger containing venom.

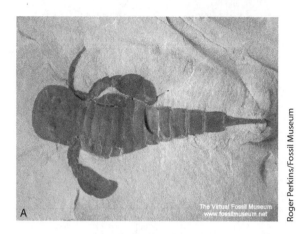

Roger Perkins/Fossil Museum

Shutterstock/Ilya D. Gridnev

Shutterstock/AppStock

Shutterstock/Tomatito

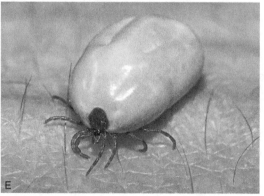

Shutterstock/Bildagentur Zoonar GmbH

Shutterstock/Mauro Rodrigues

FIGURE 18.19 Chelicerates. A. *Eurypterus remipes*, an extinct sea scorpion; B. Horseshoe crab; C. Mexican red knee tarantula (*Euathlus smithi)*; D. Mediterranean jumping spider close up; E. Tick; note the distended abdomen; F. Close view detail of a buthus scorpion (*Scorpio occitanus*).

18.2.6.2   Subphylum Crustacea

The subphylum Crustacea (Figure 18.20) contains 30,000 mostly marine species. A few crustaceans, such as crayfish, live in freshwater. Lobsters, crabs, crayfish, shrimp, copepods, barnacles, and several other groups of organisms belong to this subphylum. All crustaceans possess two pairs of antennae, a pair of mandibles, a pair of compound eyes (usually on stalks), and two pair of maxillae on their heads, followed by a pair of appendages on each body segment. Crustacean bodies usually have a head, thorax, and abdomen. Crustaceans utilize gills for gas exchange.

Most crustaceans are free-living, but some are sessile and a few are even parasitic. Some crustaceans filter tiny plankton or bacteria from the water, while others are active predators. A few crustaceans scavenge nutrients from detritus.

Many species, including lobsters, crayfish, barnacles, and crabs are economically important (yum, yum). Krill and a few other species form the base of extremely important marine food chains. Still others are crucial in recycling nutrients trapped in the bodies of dead organisms.

The subphylum contains several taxonomic classes. We will focus on one, the class Malacostraca, which includes the shrimp, lobsters, and so on.

FiGURE 18.20 Crustaceans. A. Crayfish; B. Antarctic krill floating in the water near the Antarctic Peninsula; C. Peacock mantis shrimp at Palong divesite on Phi Phi, Thailand; D. King crab showing the abdomen wrapped under the cephalothorax; E. Three lobsters with their claws banded.

Class Malacostraca

The class Malacostraca is the largest taxonomic class of Crustaceans, having over 20,000 primarily marine species. Some malacostracans occur in freshwater, while others occupy diverse terrestrial habitats. Typical malacostracans include sow bugs, krill, and a very large order, the Decapoda, which contains many kinds of shrimp, crabs, lobsters, and crayfish. Malacostracans typically possess a body with eight thoracic and six abdominal body segments, each bearing a pair of appendages. Class Malacostraca contains a number of economically significant species, such as edible lobsters, shrimp, crayfish and crabs (Figure 18.20). Many malacostracans are a significant portion of the plankton and as such are at the base of an immensely important marine food chain.

18.2.6.3   Subphylum Uniramia

This subphylum contains arthropods that have unbranched appendages. The uniramian body has two or three tagmata, and an abdomen that has many segments. Appendages in the head region include paired antennae and mandibles, and also two pairs of maxillae. Gas exchange is by means of tracheae and spiracles. This subphylum includes millipedes, centipedes, and insects. The insects are the largest and most successful class, so we will focus on them.

Class Insecta

Insects (Figure 18.21) comprise the largest group of animals. There are in excess of one million identified and named species (and undoubtedly a greater number as yet unknown to us). Insects live in almost all terrestrial and freshwater habitats, with a few species living in the oceans.

Many insects have some thoracic appendages modified for flight. Insects are important as pollinators for flowering plants, as well as for the damage they do annually to crops, and the diseases they transmit, for example, malaria, some forms of encephalitis, Dengue Fever, and the West Nile virus.

Insects display a wide huge variation in body styles, although there seems to be a size limit on the insect-style of body organization. Common features shared by most living insects are shown in Table 18.5.

Insects have a complete, complex digestive system. They exchange gases through a tracheal system, with external openings called spiracles dividing into finely branched tubules that carry gases directly to metabolizing tissues. Aquatic forms may exchange gases through the body wall or may have various kinds of gills. Excretion of nitrogenous waste takes place via Malpighian tubules. The nervous system of insects is complex, including a number of ganglia and a ventral, double nerve cord. Sense organs are complex and acute. In addition to ocelli and compound eyes, some insects are quite sensitive to sounds, and their chemoreceptive abilities are excellent.

Growth patterns of insects are quite variable. Some insects hatch from eggs as miniature adults, which in turn shed their exoskeleton. Most insect species have newly hatched young that are completely different in appearance from adults. These larval forms usually live in different habitats, eat different foods, and look completely different from their adult stages. When larval growth is completed, the larva stops feeding and builds a case or cocoon around itself. In this condition (pupa or chrysalis) the larva undergoes a complete transformation or "metamorphosis" of its body form, eventually emerging as a fully formed adult.

Insects are very valuable to humans. While insects eat our food, feed on our blood and skin, contaminate our dwellings, and transmit diseases, we could not exist if they were not here. Insects are a vital part of our ecosystem, functioning in: (1) pollination of many flowering plants; (2) decomposition of organic materials; (3) recycling of carbon, nitrogen, and other essential nutrients; (4) control of populations of harmful invertebrate species (including other insects); (5) direct production of certain foods like honey; and (6) manufacture of useful products such as silk and shellac. So, have you hugged a bug today?

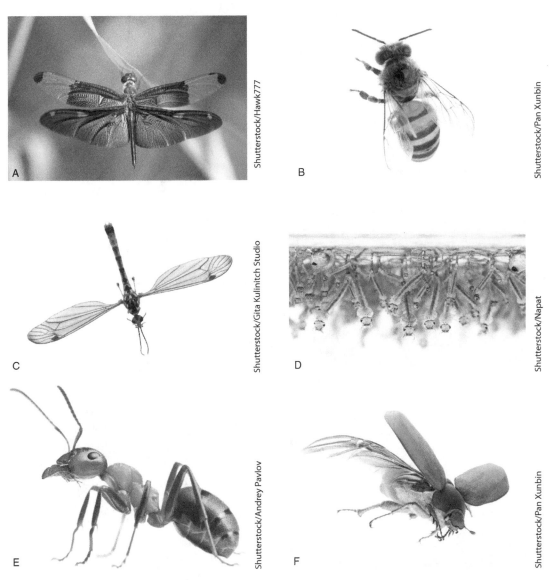

FIGURE 18.21 Insecta. A. Dragonfly; B. Bee; C. Mosquito, illustrating the wing arrangement; D. Mosquito larvae in water; E. Red ant *Formica rufa*; F. Scarab May Beetle showing the hardened first pair of wings and the flying second pair of wings in action; G. Beautiful Luna Moth (*Actias luna*) on purple clematis flowers; H. Anatomy of a grasshopper.

(Continued)

Shutterstock/StevenRussellSmithPhotos

G

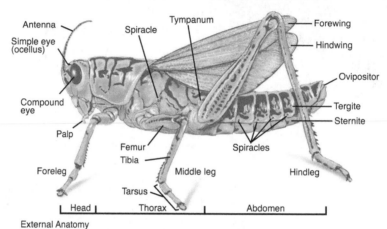

External Anatomy

Antenna
Simple eye (ocellus)
Compound eye
Palp
Foreleg
Spiracle
Tympanum
Femur
Tibia
Tarsus
Middle leg
Spiracles
Forewing
Hindwing
Ovipositor
Tergite
Sternite
Hindleg

Head | Thorax | Abdomen

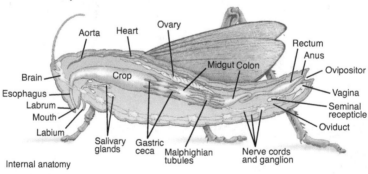

Internal anatomy

Aorta
Heart
Ovary
Brain
Crop
Esophagus
Labrum
Mouth
Labium
Salivary glands
Gastric ceca
Malphighian tubules
Midgut Colon
Rectum
Anus
Ovipositor
Vagina
Seminal recepticle
Oviduct
Nerve cords and ganglion

© Kendall Hunt Publishing

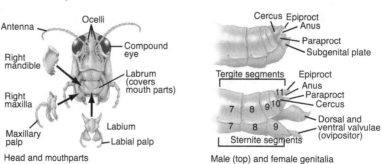

Antenna
Ocelli
Compound eye
Right mandible
Labrum (covers mouth parts)
Right maxilla
Maxillary palp
Labium
Labial palp

H   Head and mouthparts

Cercus Epiproct
Anus
Paraproct
Subgenital plate

Tergite segments   Epiproct
Anus
11   Paraproct
7   8   9 10   Cercus
Dorsal and ventral valvulae (ovipositor)
7   8   9
Sternite segments

Male (top) and female genitalia

FIGURE 18.21 (*Continued*)

TABLE 18.5 Common features of insects

Characteristic	Dragonfly	Bee	Mosquito	Ant
Body composed of three tag-mata: head, thorax, and abdomen	Yes	Yes	Yes	Yes
One pair of rela-tively large com-pound eyes	Yes	Yes	Yes	Yes
Usually three ocelli located on the head	Yes	Yes	Yes	Yes
One pair of anten-nae on the head	Yes	Yes	Yes	Yes
Mouthparts consisting of a labrum, a pair of mandibles, a pair of maxillae, a labium, and a tongue-like hypopharynx	Yes	Yes	Yes	Yes
Two pairs of wings derived from outgrowths of the body wall	Yes	Yes, although there appear to be only one set of wings as the back set of wings are smaller	No, only one functional pair of wings one pair modified to act as a gyroscope	No, only in certain forms, wings absent in most ants
Three pairs of walking legs	Yes	Yes	Yes	Yes

18.2.7   Phylum Mollusca

Phylum Mollusca (Figure 18.22) contains over 100,000 species with a variety of body forms and lifestyles. In mollusks, the coelom is reduced and limited to the region around the heart. The mollusk body first appeared during the Cambrian period.

All mollusks have several common features (Figure 18.23). A visceral mass contains the mollusk internal organs, including the digestive tract, paired kidneys, and reproductive organs. All mollusks have a mantle that surrounds but does not cover entirely the visceral mass and secretes a shell (if one is present). The mantle also contributes to formation of gills or lungs. Mollusks have a head/foot region containing sensory organs and a muscular structure, the foot. Mollusks use the foot for locomotion, attachment to a substrate, food capture, or a combination of functions. A radula is an organ that bears many rows of teeth and is used for grazing on food. The mollusk nervous system consists of several ganglia connected by nerve cords.

FIGURE 18.22 Mollusca. A. Chiton on a rock in a tide pool at low tide; B. Scaly Giant Clam, Kakaban, Indonesia; C. A common octopus, *Octopus vulgaris*, resting on a reef. This mollusk can be found in the Mediterranean Sea and in the Atlantic Ocean; D. *Nautilus* swimming; E. Horse Conch or Crown Conch eating other shells; F. Close-up of a Yellow and Black banded snail carrying a tiny snail on her back; G. Opalescent nudibranch (*Hermissenda crassicornis*).

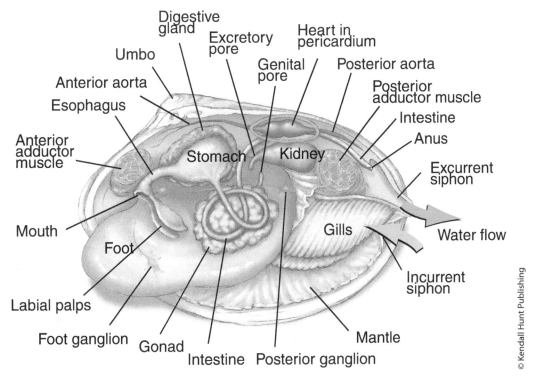

FIGURE 18.23 Anatomy of a clam.

Most mollusks have an open circulatory system with a heart that pumps hemolymph through vessels into a hemocoel. Blood diffuses back into the heart and is pumped out to the body again. Some mollusks are slow moving, and have with no head, while others are active predators that have a head and sense organs.

Classification of the mollusks is undergoing some degree of revision. Table 18.6 summarizes some of the better-defined taxonomic classes of this phylum.

18.2.7.1 Gastropods

In aquatic gastropods, gills form in the mantle cavity. The mantle of terrestrial gastropods is richly supplied with blood vessels and functions as a lung when air is moved in and out through respiratory pores. Terrestrial gastropod embryonic development skips the swimming larval stage, as is the case in aquatic gastropods. For terrestrial snails, their shell not only offers protection but also prevents drying out. The muscular foot contracts in peristaltic waves from anterior to posterior causing the secretion of mucus.

Terrestrial gastropods are hermaphroditic. In premating behavior, they meet and shoot calcareous darts into each other's body wall. Each inserts a penis into the vagina of the other, providing sperm for future fertilization of eggs. Eggs are deposited in the soil and development proceeds without formation of a larval stage, a common theme in some terrestrial invertebrates. Hermaphroditism assures that any two animals that meet can mate, which is especially useful in slow-moving animals.

TABLE 18.6 Classes of Mollusca

Class	Description	Example
Polyplacophora	Chitons have a shell of eight plates; a ventral muscular foot allows the chiton to creep along the substrate, and to cling to rocks; chiton feeds by scraping algae and plants from rocks with its well-developed radula	© Shutterstock
Gastropoda	Snails, terrestrial slugs, whelks, conchs, periwinkles, sea hares, and sea slugs; most are marine, some freshwater and terrestrial forms occur; many are herbivores using their radula to scrape food from surfaces; carnivores use their radula to bore through a surface, such as a shell, to obtain food; most have a head with eyes and tentacles projecting from a coiled shell that protects the visceral mass; coiled shells often fossilize; nudibranchs and terrestrial slugs lack shells	© Shutterstock
Bivalvia	Organisms have two-part hinged shells closed by powerful muscles; bivalves have no head, no radula, and little cephalization; clams use their hatchet-shaped foot for burrowing; mussels use it to produce threads to attach to objects; scallops can both burrow or swim; rapid closing and opening of their two valves releases water in spurts	© Shutterstock
Cephalopoda	Includes squids, cuttlefish, octopuses, and nautiluses; presence of a shell yielded an impressive fossil record, like the ammonoids	© Shutterstock

18.2.7.2   Bivalves

The mantle secretes the bivalve shell composed of protein and calcium carbonate with an inner layer of pearl. Pearls form as layers of shell-forming material deposited about a foreign particle lodged between the mantle and the shell. A compressed muscular foot projects down from shell. By expanding the tip, the foot pulls the body after it. Beating cilia of the gills cause water to enter the mantle cavity by way of the incurrent siphon and to exit by way of the excurrent siphon. While cilia of gills move water through the mantle cavity, gills also capture particles in water and move them toward the mouth. From the mouth food goes to the stomach, then to the intestine, which passes through the heart and ends at the anus.

Bivalves, like other mollusks, have an open circulatory system. Their nervous system consists of three pairs of ganglia. Two excretory kidneys below the heart remove ammonia waste from the pericardial cavity into the mantle cavity, from which it leaves the body.

Bivalve sexes in class are separate. The gonad is located around the coils of the intestine. Many bivalves alternate reproducing once as a female, then next time as a male. Certain clams and annelids have the same type of larva, hinting at a possible evolutionary relationship between the two groups.

Since they have hard shells, the fossil record of this mollusk class is remarkably good. Hard shells (or hard parts) are one of the features that make an organism more likely to fossilize.

18.2.7.3 Cephalopods

Class Cephalopoda (literally "head-footed") includes squids, cuttlefish, octopuses, and nautiluses (and extinct relatives, the goniatites, ammonoids, and ammonites). The presence of a shell in many representatives of this class has yielded an impressive fossil record, like the ammonoids.

Squids and octopuses can squeeze water from their mantle cavity out through a funnel (shown in Figure 18.24), thus propelling them with a form of jet propulsion. Surrounding their head are tentacles with suckers that can grasp prey and deliver it to a powerful beak/mouth. Cephalopods in general have well-developed sense organs, including focusing camera-type eyes. Most cephalopods, especially octopuses, have well-developed brains and show a capacity for learning. Nautiluses are enclosed in shells; squids have a shell that is reduced and internal, while octopuses lack a shell.

Squids and octopuses possess ink sacs from which they squirt a cloud of ink, as a means of escaping predators. Squids possess a vestigial skeleton under the mantle, called the pen, which surrounds the visceral mass. A squid has three hearts, one pumps blood to internal organs; two pump blood to the gills in the mantle cavity. Gonads make up a large portion of the visceral mass. Cephalopods have separate sexes. Spermatophores contain sperm, which the male passes to the female mantle cavity by way of one of his tentacles. After fertilization, strings of up to 100 eggs are attached to the substratum.

During much of their evolutionary history cephalopods possessed a hard shell. Their abundance, the presence of a shell, and the environments they lived in led to an excellent fossil record for the group.

The ammonoids underwent three separate diversifications from a nautiloid-like stock. In each case, the fold pattern of sutures became more complex. These suture patterns are fantastic characters for identifying species, making ammonoids excellent index fossils. The first of these occurrences was the goniatites, a group that ranged from the Devonian to the Permian. The ceratites are a Triassic group, while the last group, the ammonites ranged from the Triassic to the Cretaceous. Ammonoids finally went extinct in the great end-of-the-Cretaceous extinction. The living genus *Nautilus* is the sole survivor of this once diverse group.

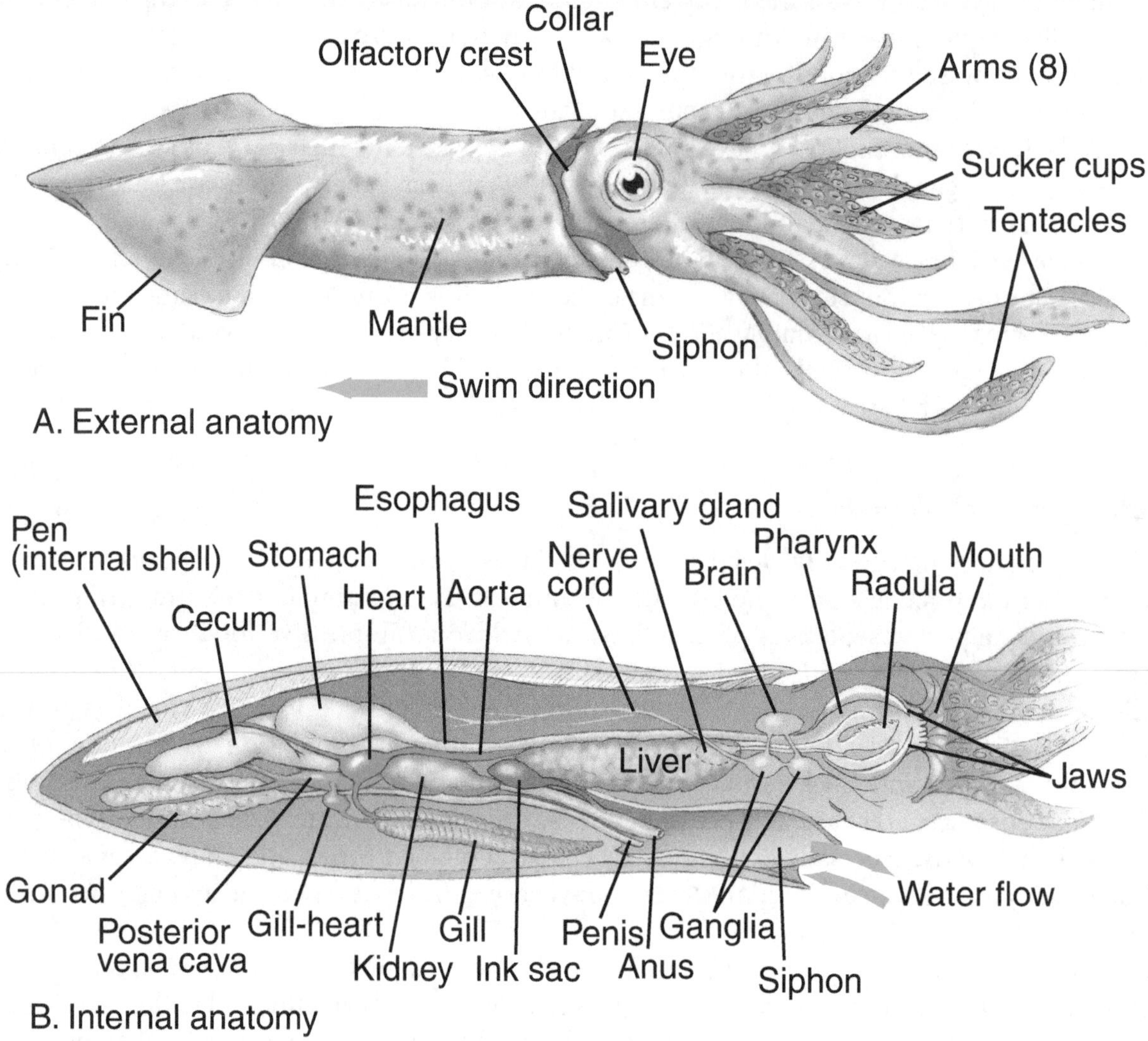

Collar
Olfactory crest   Eye
Arms (8)
Sucker cups
Tentacles
Fin   Mantle   Siphon
Swim direction
A. External anatomy

Pen
(internal shell)   Stomach
Cecum
Esophagus   Salivary gland
Heart Aorta   Nerve   Pharynx   Mouth
cord   Brain   Radula
Liver
Jaws
Gonad
Posterior Gill-heart   Gill   Penis Ganglia   Water flow
vena cava   Kidney Ink sac   Anus   Siphon
B. Internal anatomy

FIGURE 18.24 Anatomy of a squid.

© Kendall Hunt Publishing

18.2.8 Phylum Annelida

Phylum Annelida contains segmented worms, such as the common earthworm (Figures 18.25C and 18.26). Segmented bodies allow specialization in different segments. Annelids have an enlarged coelom to accommodate more complex internal organs. The well-developed, fluid-filled coelom and the tough integument act as a hydrostatic skeleton. There are about 12,000 marine, freshwater, and terrestrial species usually divided into three taxonomic classes. Similarities of larval forms to mollusks suggest annelids share a common ancestral group.

Annelids have a closed circulatory system with blood vessels running the length of the body and branching into every segment. Closed circulatory systems are more efficient than open ones for moving materials within a body. The annelid nervous system consists of a brain connected to a ventral solid nerve cord, with a ganglion in each segment. Annelids have a complete digestive

FIGURE 18.25 Annelids. A. Nereis, a polychaete marine annelid; B. Feather duster worms are marine annelids; C. A group of earthworms; D. Medical leech illustrating the mouth and segmented body.

system that includes a pharynx, stomach, intestine, and accessory glands. Excretory nephridia in each segment collect waste material from coelom and excrete it through the body wall. Classes of annelids are summarized in Table 18.7.

Earthworms reside in moist soil where a moist body wall facilitates gas exchange. Earthworms are scavengers that extract organic remains from the soil they eat. A muscular pharynx draws food into the mouth. Ingested food is stored in a crop and ground up in a muscular gizzard. The dorsal surface of the intestine is expanded into a typhlosole that allows more surface area for digestion. External segments correspond to internal septa (walls) separating each body segment.

The earthworm excretory system has coiled nephridia tubules in each segment with two openings: one is a ciliated funnel that collects coelomic fluid, and the other is an exit in the body wall. Between the two openings, the coiled nephridia tubule allows removal of waste materials from blood vessels.

Red blood is moved anteriorly by a dorsal blood vessel and pumped by five pairs of hearts (sometimes referred to as aortic arches) to a ventral vessel. Earthworms are hermaphroditic, having both testes with seminal vesicles, and ovaries with seminal receptacles. Mating involves the worms lying parallel to each other facing opposite directions and exchanging sperm. Each

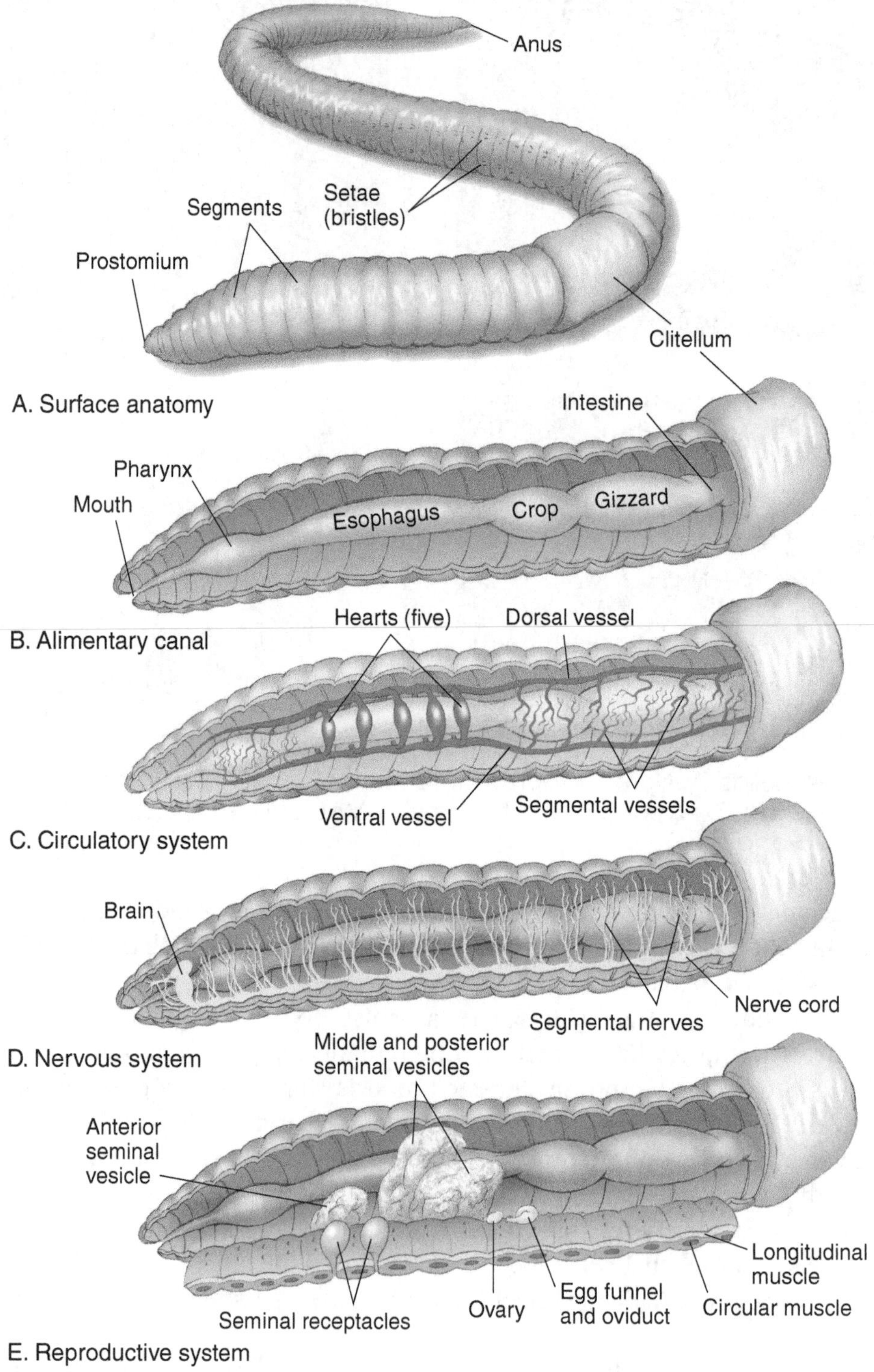

FIGURE 18.26 Anatomy of an earthworm. A. Surface anatomy; B. Alimentary canal; C. Circulatory system; D. Nervous system; E. Reproductive system; F. Cross section of an earthworm; G. Dorsal view of worm structure. *(Continued)*

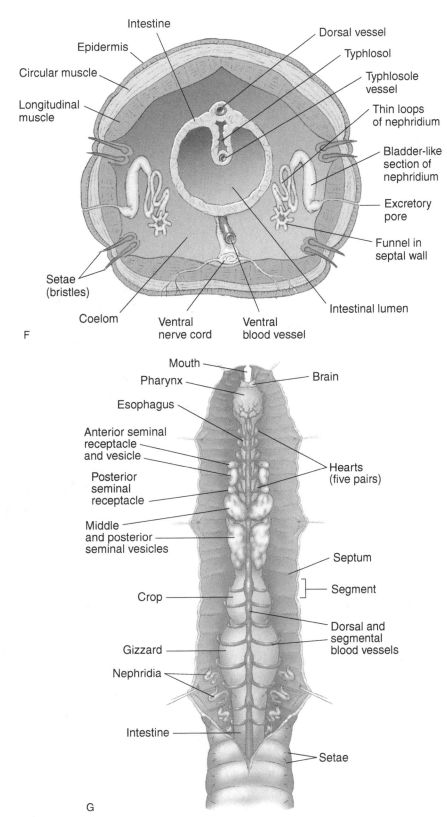

FIGURE 18.26 (*Continued*)

TABLE 18.7 Classes of annelids

Class	Description	Example
Polychaeta	Marine worms possessing parapodia and setae; parapodia are paddle-like appendages used in swimming and respiratory organs; setae are bristles, attached to parapodia that help anchor polychaetes to their substratum and also help them to move; many polychaetes have head with well-developed jaws, eyes, and other sense organs; filter feeders, such as the Christmas Tree worms and feather dusters, possess tentacles with cilia to create water currents and to select food particles. Most annelids are polychaetes	© Shutterstock
Oligochaeta	Earthworms have their setae protruding in clusters directly from their body; poorly developed heads or parapodia; locomotion coordinated by movement of the body muscles and assistance of setae; longitudinal muscles contract, segments bulge and setae protrude and anchor into the soil; circular muscles contract, causing the worm to lengthen, setae are withdrawn and the segment moves forward like a Slinky toy.	© Shutterstock
Hirudinea	Most leeches live in freshwater, but a few occur in marine and terrestrial environments; each body ring has several transverse grooves; leeches possess a small anterior sucker around the mouth and a larger posterior sucker; some are free-living predators, most are fluid feeders; leeches that suck blood keep that blood from coagulating by hirudin, an anticoagulant in their saliva; leeches were commonly used in early medicine to "bleed" the patient	© Shutterstock

worm possesses a clitellum that then secretes mucus, protecting sperm and eggs from drying out. Embryonic development lacks a larval stage.

18.3   Significance of Invertebrate Animals

Animals have played significant roles in human history. People recognized the significance of animals, even in ancient cave paintings. Invertebrate animals cause a variety of diseases, as well as serve roles in the production of food as well as human artifacts.

18.3.1   Uses

Animals serve as food for many people. In China fried silk worms are eaten at banquets, along with shrimp, crabs, and lobsters. Chinese street markets sell deep fried starfish, squid, cuttlefish, octopus, and scorpions. Some southwestern US native tribes roast cicadas, a type of local insect as a seasonal treat. Cable television's *Deadliest Catch* program detailed the quest for crab from the Bering Sea for over 10 years. Oysters produce pearls that people for millennia have used for decorations. The later Roman emperors in Byzantium used an extract from a sea snail to produce Tyrian purple dye used to color imperial garments.

18.3.2   Diseases and in Medicine

Many animals cause human illness and disease. Jellyfish stings can kill humans, or at the least ruin a vacation. Tapeworms and flukes infect human hosts. The biblical injunction against eating pork has a biological cause—the prevalence of the roundworm *Trichinella* in pork throughout the Middle East.

18.3.3   Ecological

Animals are important consumers ecologically. Bees and other insect pollinators play vital roles in the outcrossing of many flowering plant species. Fruit set in many plants require the actions of pollinators. Many animals are symbionts. Ants are in a mutualistic association with the Acacia tree. Corals are important builders of the reef where other animals live.

Summary

Members of the animal kingdom share certain characteristics. They can move at some point during their lives and are ingestive, multicellular heterotrophs. Animals are capable of complex behaviors such as mating and courtship rituals, learning, and flight.

Terms

acoelomate
antibodies
antigen
anus
arteries
archaeocyathids
bilateral symmetry
bivalves
blastula
book lungs
compound eyes
cardiac muscle
capillaries
cell walls
central nervous system

cephalization
cephalothorax
chitin
chidocytes
choanocytes
circulatory system
closed circulatory
  system
coelomates
coelom
connective tissue
coral
craniates
cranium
deuterostomes

digestive system
diploblastic
echinoderm
ectoderm
endoderm
endoskeleton
epidermis
epithelial tissue
excretory system
exoskeleton
extracellular digestion
flame cell
food chains
ganglia
gastrovascular cavity

gills	nervous system	sac-like body
gnathostome	nephridia	schistosomiasis
gonads	neural crest	scolex
hemocoel	neural tube	segmentation
hemolymph	ocelli	setae
herbivores	open circulatory system	sessile
hormones	osmoregulation	skeletons
hydrostatic skeleton	Paleozoic era	skeletal muscle
ingestive heterotrophs	parapodia	small intestine
large intestine	pharynx	smooth muscle
lymphocyte	pituitary gland	spicules
mantle	plankton	spiracles
medusae	planula	stomach
mesoderm	polyp	telson
mesoglea	pollinators	tracheae
metamorphosis	protostomes	trichinosis
motor neurons	pseudocoelomate	triploblastic
muscle fibers	radial symmetry	"tube-within-a-tube"
nematocyst	radiata	body
nerve cells	radula	vein
nerve cords	respiratory system	vertebrates
nerve net	reproductive system	zooxanthellae

Review Questions

1. Which of these features would you not find in an animal cell?
   a. mitochondrion;   c. cell wall;
   b. nucleus;   d. rough endoplasmic reticulum

2. Which of these is a feature unique to animals?
   a. multicellular;   c. ingestive heterotrophs;
   b. eukaryotic;   d. store excess sugar as glycogen

3. The ancestral protist for the animal kingdom is most likely a _____.
   a. choanoflagellates;   c. bacteria;
   b. amoeba;   d. yeast

4. The oldest animal fossils date to the _____.
   a. Archean;   d. Cretaceous;
   b. Proterozoic;   e. Pleistocene
   c. Cambrian;

5. Bees belong to which of these phyla?
   a. Cnidaria;
   b. Arthropoda;
   c. Chordata;
   d. Echinodermata

6. Coral and jellyfish belong to which of these phyla?
   a. Cnidaria;
   b. Arthropoda;
   c. Chordata;
   d. Echinodermata

7. Cnidocyte stinging cells would be found in which of these animals?
   a. sponges;
   b. jellyfish;
   c. rotifers;
   d. earthworms;
   e. snakes

8. Zooxanthellae are protists living inside the body of which of these animals?
   a. sponges;
   b. jellyfish;
   c. rotifers;
   d. earthworms;
   e. snakes

9. Spicules would be found in which of these animals?
   a. sponges;
   b. jellyfish;
   c. rotifers;
   d. earthworms;
   e. snakes

10. Flying arthropods belong to which of these classes?
    a. Insecta;
    b. Trilobitomorpha;
    c. Decapoda;
    d. Gastropoda

11. The first land animals belonged to which of these phyla?
    a. Mollusca;
    b. Amphibia;
    c. Arthropoda;
    d. Chondrichthyes

12. The first flying animals belonged to which of these phyla?
    a. Chordata;
    b. Amphibia;
    c. Arthropoda;
    d. Sarcopterygii

13. The shell of a mollusk is secreted from the _____.
    a. foot;
    b. mantle;
    c. head;
    d. gills

14. Nudibranchs are a group of marine _____.
    a. flatworms;
    b. mollusks;
    c. vertebrates;
    d. coral

15. _____ are a group of arthropods with six walking legs.
    a. Insecta;
    b. Amphibia;
    c. Arachnida;
    d. Cycadeoidea

16. _____ are a group of arthropods with eight walking legs.
    a. Insecta;
    b. Amphibia;
    c. Arachnida;
    d. Cycadeoidea

17. Which of these phyla is a diploblast?
    a. Cnidaria;
    b. Choedata;
    c. Arthropoda;
    d. Platyhelminthes

18. Triploblasts have which of these embryonic tissue layers that is absent in diploblasts?
    a. Endoderm;
    b. Ectoderm;
    c. Mesoderm

19. _____ are a group of arthropods with eight walking legs.
    a. Insecta;
    b. Amphibia;
    c. Arachnida;
    d. Cycadeoidea

20. _____ are a group of arthropods with four fixed wings.
    a. fruit flies;
    b. honey bees;
    c. dragon flies;
    d. house flies

Links

- **The Radiation of the First Animals:** Dr. Jere Lipps presents a well-illustrated look at early animal evolution. [http://www.accessexcellence.org/BF/bf02/lipps/]

- **Introduction to the Metazoa: Animals, Animals, Animals!** This University of California Berkeley Museum of Paleontology site offers excellent information about the evolution and diversity of various animal groups. [http://www.ucmp.berkeley.edu/phyla/phyla.html]

CHAPTER 19
Biodiversity: Deuterostomes

Chapter Opener

Leafy sea dragon photographed in Indonesia. These animals resemble the kelp they live in.

Objectives

- Describe the characteristics of deuterostomes and contrast them to protostomes.
- List the features that unite the phylum Echinodermata.
- Compare and contrast characteristics of any two of the echinoderm classes.
- List the four uniting features of the phylum Chordata.
- Describe the structure of a tunicate.
- Discuss the evolutionary significance of an endoskeleton.
- Describe the jawless chordate groups.
- Compare and contrast three chordate classes.
- Differentiate between the three groups of mammals.

19.1   Phylum Echinodermata

There are 6,000 species of echinoderms all of which live in the oceans. Phylum Echinodermata includes the crinoids sea urchins, sea stars, sea cucumbers, and starfish (Figure 19.1). Most adult echinoderms have a modified five-parted radial symmetry, while their larvae are bilaterally symmetrical. Embryos of echinoderms follow the deuterostome developmental pathway. Echinoderms have an endoskeleton consisting of calcareous plates bearing spines. Radial symmetry appears to be an advantage to the mostly bottom-dwelling echinoderms that can feed in every direction. Adult echinoderms have no brain. Members of this phylum have a water vascular system that powers their multitude of tube feet.

19.1.1   Class Crinoidea

Class Crinoidea (Figure 19.1A, B) includes about 600 species of crinoids, the stalked sea "lilies" and the motile feather stars. Their branched arms are used for filter feeding and give the animals a flowerlike or plantlike appearance that gives them their common name of sea lilies. Crinoid stalks and blastoid heads are common fossils in certain parts of North America. Crinoid fossils can commonly be found in many Paleozoic marine rock formations.

19.1.2   Class Holothuroidea

The class Holothuroidea has 1,500 species of sea cucumbers (Figure 19.1C, D). Holothuroideans have a long leathery body between 10 and 30 cm long, and feed by tentacles located around their mouth. Some sea cucumbers are filter feeders while others extract organic matter from the sea

FIGURE 19.1 Echinoderms. A. Crinoid shrimp (*Periclemenes ambionensis*) on its host crinoid, Lembeh Straits, Indonesia; B. Death assemblage of a fossil crinoid population;
normally crinoids are broken apart after death; C. Sea cucumber that has eviscerated
respiratory tubules as a defense measure; D. Sea cucumber in an aquarium illustrating the
rows of tube feet and feeding appendages; E. Sand dollar; F. Tropic sea urchin;
G. Sea urchin stings (*Paracentrotus lividus*); H. Brittle star (*Ophionereis schayeri*); I. Starfish;
J. A Crown-of-thorns sea star (*Acanthaster planci*) clings to a rocky reef near Cocos
Island, Costa Rica. Crown-of-thorns sea stars feed on coral and can destroy entire reefs
under the right conditions.

floor. There are five rows of tube feet running along the sea cucumber body. Some sea cucumbers can eviscerate respiratory tubules through their anus as a defense mechanism. Others will emit a poisonous chemical. Sea cucumbers are used in certain Asian cuisines and are being researched to verify folkloric claims of medicinal value.

19.1.3   Class Echinoidea

Scientists generally place about 950 species of sand dollars (Figure 19.1E) and sea urchins (Figure 19.1F, G) in the class Echinoidea. The fossil record of this class dates from the Ordovician period. Both sea urchins and sand dollars use their spines for locomotion, defense, and burrowing. Larvae are bilaterally symmetrical and develop the five-parted symmetry of this phylum later during development. Sea urchins often have long, blunt spines, although some have extremely sharp and painful spines. Careless scuba divers, like your author, have acquired a series of painful sea urchin spines known locally as a Hawaiian tattoo. Sea urchins usually eat algae and are in turn food for other animals. Sand dollars are flattened with a five-part flowerlike pattern of pores for skin projections. Sea urchin roe is often available at a Sushi bar. Many Mediterranean and Asian cuisines employ sea urchin in their dishes. Sand dollars are an example of irregular sea urchins.

19.1.4   Class Ophiuroidea

The class Ophiuroidea consists of approximately 2,000 species of brittle stars and basket stars (Figures 19.1H and 19.2). Most brittle stars live in shallow marine environments. Brittle stars have a central disk from which long, flexible arms radiate. These long arms allow them to move rapidly. Basket stars usually are encountered in deeper parts of the ocean.

Shutterstock/Vilainecrevette

Shutterstock/LauraD

FIGURE 19.2 Brittle stars. A. Close-up view of a sponge brittle star (*Ophiothrix suensonii*) over yellow tube sponges; B. Basket star deployed at night.

19.1.5   Class Asteroidea

The class Asteroidea contains about 1,500 species of sea stars (commonly known as starfish; Figures 19.1I, and 19.3). Most starfish have a dorsoventrally flattened body. Starfish have a central disk to which five, or a multiple of five, sturdy arms are attached. Sea stars are common along rocky coasts where they eat clams, oysters, and other bivalves.

The five-rayed body has an oral (mouth) and aboral (upper) side (Figure 19.3). Spines project from the endoskeletal plate through the thin dermis. Pincer-like pedicellariae keep the surface free from particles. Gas exchange occurs through skin gills. On the oral surface, each arm has a groove lined with tube feet.

A sea star feeds by everting its stomach. It positions itself over a bivalve and attaches tube feet to each side of the shell. By working tube feet in an alternating fashion, it opens the shell open. Only a small crack is needed to insert its cardiac stomach into the prey. Stomach enzymes begin digesting the bivalve as it is trying to close its shell. Partially digested food is then taken into the pyloric stomach for complete digestion. A short intestine opens at the anus on the aboral side.

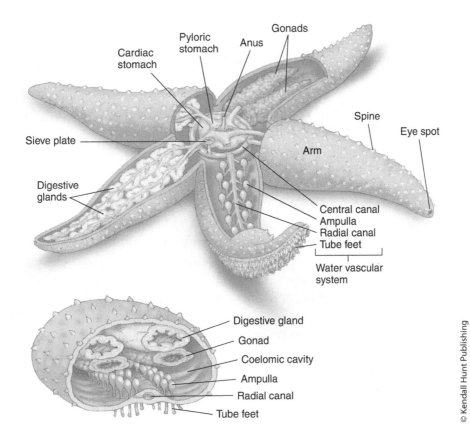

© Kendall Hunt Publishing

FIGURE 19.3 Anatomy of a starfish.

Each arm has a well-developed coelom containing a pair of digestive glands and male or female gonads. The nervous system is a central ring with radial nerves in each arm. A light-sensitive eyespot is at the end of each arm, facilitating coordinated but slow responses.

Locomotion depends upon the water vascular system. Water enters on the aboral side through the sieve plate, which is also known as the madreporite. Water passes through a stone canal to a ring canal and into the radial canals in each arm. The radial canals feed into lateral canals extending into tube feet, each of which has an ampulla. Contraction of the ampulla forces water into the tube foot, expanding it; when the foot touches a surface, the center withdraws forming suction and adhering to surfaces.

Echinoderms lack complex respiratory, excretory, and circulatory systems. Fluids within the coelomic cavity carry out the function of diffusing substances and gases. Gas exchange occurs across the skin gills and tube feet. Nitrogenous wastes diffuse through coelomic fluid and across the body wall. Cilia on the peritoneum lining the coelom keep the coelomic fluid moving.

Sea stars reproduce both sexually and asexually. If the body is fragmented, each fragment can regenerate a whole animal. Sea stars spawn and release either eggs or sperm at the same time. The bilateral larvae undergo a metamorphosis to become radially symmetrical adults.

19.2 Phylum Chordata

Phylum Chordata includes about 45,000 species that occupy nearly all environments. All chordates at sometime during their life history have:

1. a notochord: a dorsal supporting rod located dorsally just below the nerve cord; it provides support and is replaced by the vertebral column in vertebrates
2. a dorsal hollow nerve cord: a fluid-filled canal; spinal cord is protected by vertebrae
3. pharyngeal gill pouches: openings that function in feeding, gas exchange, or both
4. a postanal tail: a tail that extends past the anus

These features are seen only during embryonic development in most vertebrates. Not all chordates are vertebrates. In the invertebrate chordates, fish, and amphibian larvae, pharyngeal gill pouches become functioning gills. Terrestrial vertebrates have their pouches modified for various purposes; in humans, the first pouches become the auditory tubes, the second become tonsils, and the third and fourth pairs become the thymus and parathyroid glands (Figure 19.4).

Most chordates have an internal skeleton against which muscles work. Most have a postanal tail that extends beyond the anus. In humans, this may only appear in embryos.

The evolutionary origin of chordates remains unclear, although biochemistry and comparative embryology suggest echinoderms and chordates share a common ancestry. Although scanty, fossil finds from Cambrian-aged rocks suggest chordates were present in the Burgess Shale deposits.

FIGURE 19.4 *(Continued)*

FIGURE 19.4 Chordates. A. Blue tunicates in Anilao, Philippines; B. Lancelet *Branchiostoma*; C. Two lampreys, jawless vertebrates; D. Tiger shark in Tiger Beach, Bahamas; E. The brown trout (*Salmo trutta*) in a mountain lake; F. *Latimeria*, the coelacanth; G. Blue strawberry poison DART frog (*Dendrobates pumilio*) from the tropical rain forest of Panama; H. The Komodo dragon (*Varanus komodoensis*) from Indonesia is the largest living lizard in the world; I. Frontal view of flying Blue Tit; J. Jaguar, a member of the cat family.

Invertebrate Chordates

Not all chordates are vertebrates (Figure 19.5). Some chordates are invertebrates, lacking a vertebral column. In these invertebrate chordates, the notochord persists and is never replaced by the vertebral column.

19.2.1   Subphylum Tunicata

The subphylum Tunicata contains 1,250 species of tunicates that have gill slits (Figure 19.6). Adults have a body composed of an outer tunic with an incurrent and excurrent siphon. When disturbed, tunicates tend to squirt out water. This has given them their common name of sea squirts. Water passes into a pharynx and out numerous gill slits, the only chordate characteristic that remains in adults. Microscopic particles adhere to a mucous secretion in the pharynx and are eaten. The larvae are bilaterally symmetrical and have all four of the chordate characteristics. Tunicate larvae metamorphose into the sessile adult. Beating of numerous cilia lining the inside of the pharynx creates a current to move water through a tunicate. Some studies suggest larvae became sexually mature without developing tunicate characteristics; thus, the tunicate larva was ancestor to vertebrates.

19.2.2   Subphylum Cephalochordata

The lancelets have three chordate characteristics. The 23 species of lancelets are in the genus *Branchiostoma* in the subphylum Cephalochordata. Their elongated, lance-shaped body resembles the lancelet, a two-edged surgical knife (Figure 19.7). They inhabit shallow coastal waters; they lie partly buried in sandy substrates and filter feed. Lancelets feed on microscopic particles

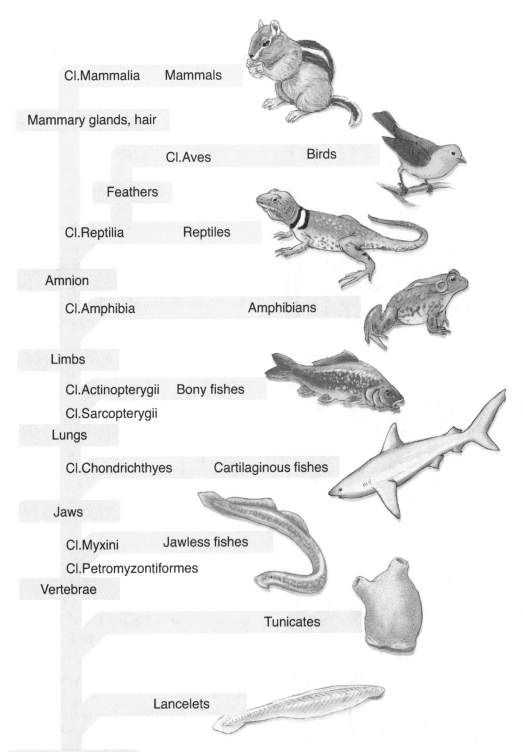

Cl.Mammalia   Mammals

Mammary glands, hair

Cl.Aves   Birds

Feathers

Cl.Reptilia   Reptiles

Amnion

Cl.Amphibia   Amphibians

Limbs

Cl.Actinopterygii   Bony fishes

Cl.Sarcopterygii

Lungs

Cl.Chondrichthyes   Cartilaginous fishes

Jaws

Cl.Myxini   Jawless fishes

Cl.Petromyzontiformes

Vertebrae

Tunicates

Lancelets

Ancestral chordates

FIGURE 19.5 Chordate phylogeny.

filtered from the constant stream of water that enters the mouth and exits through the gill slits into an atrium that opens at the atriopore. Lancelets retain all four of the chordate characteristics as an adult. The notochord extends from head to tail, accounting for the name "Cephalochordata." Lancelets have segmented muscles and their dorsal hollow nerve cord has periodic branches.

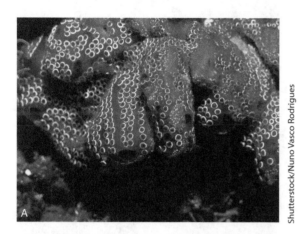

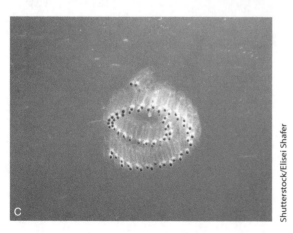

FIGURE 19.6 Tunicates. A. Colonial tunicate; B. Sea squirt seen from the side; C. Salp floating in the ocean.

19.2.3   Subphylum Vertebrata

Subphylum Vertebrata consists of about 43,700 species of animals with backbones. Vertebrates exhibit all three of the chordate characteristics at some point during their lives. The embryonic notochord is replaced by a vertebral column in the adult. The vertebral column is made of individual hard segments (vertebrae) surrounding the dorsal hollow nerve cord. The dorsal hollow nerve cord is the only chordate feature present in the adult phase of **all** vertebrates. The vertebral column, part of a flexible but strong endoskeleton, is evidence that vertebrates are segmented. Living tissue (either cartilage or bone) that grows as the animal grows comprises the vertebrate skeleton (Figure 19.8).

The endoskeleton and muscles form the musculoskeletal system that permits rapid and efficient movement. Pectoral and pelvic fins of one group of fish evolved into jointed appendages that allowed vertebrates to move onto land. The most anterior component of the main axis of the vertebrate endoskeleton, the skull, encases the brain in the craniates. This clade of vertebrates has some degree of a cranium covering the brain. The high degree of cephalization in vertebrates is accompanied by complex sense organs concentrated in the head region. Eyes developed as outgrowths of the brain. Ears were equilibrium devices in aquatic vertebrates that function as sound-wave receivers in land vertebrates. Vertebrates have a complete digestive system and a large coelom. Their circulatory system is closed, with respiratory pigments contained within blood vessels. Gas exchange is efficiently

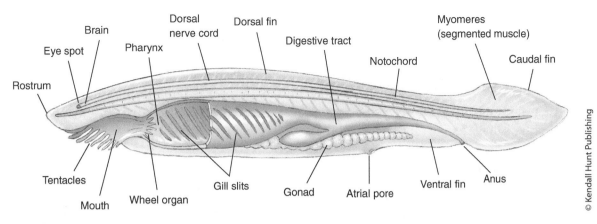

FIGURE 19.7 Anatomy of a lancelet.

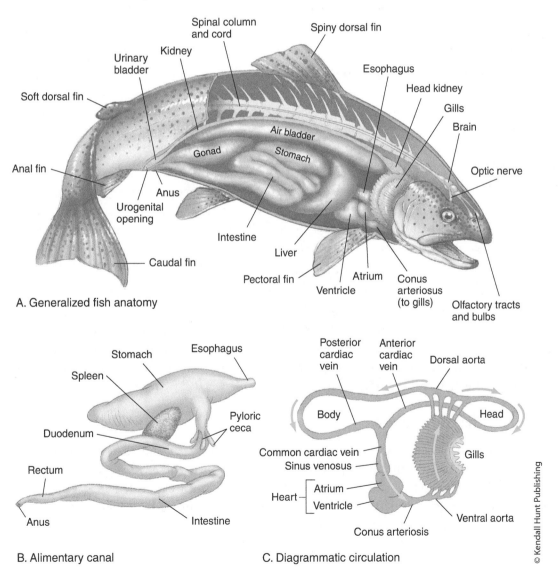

A. Generalized fish anatomy

B. Alimentary canal

C. Diagrammatic circulation

FIGURE 19.8 Anatomy of a fish, exemplifying a vertebrate animal.

accomplished by gills, lungs, and in a few cases, moist skin. Kidneys are efficient in excretion of nitrogenous waste and regulation of water. Reproduction is usually sexual with separate sexes.

The first vertebrates were fishlike. Fishes are aquatic, gill-breathing vertebrates that usually have fins and skin covered with scales. The larval form of a modern-day lamprey, looks very much like a lancelet, and may resemble the first vertebrates: it has the three chordate characteristics (like the tunicate larva), as well as a two-chambered heart, a three-part brain, and other internal organs that are like those of vertebrates.

19.2.3.1   Class Myxini

Members of the class Myxini have a partial cranium (skull), but no vertebrae. Their skeleton is made of cartilage, as is that of sharks. Members of this class have a skull but lack vertebrae. Hagfish lack jaws, and for this reason used to be classified with the lampreys in a group called the Agnatha ("no jaws") or the Cyclostomata ("round mouth").

19.2.3.2   Class Petromyzontiformes

These long, eel-like, jawless fishes are free-swimming predators on other fishes (Figure 19.4C). Lampreys hatch in freshwater and many live their lives entirely in freshwater. Some lampreys migrate to the sea, but must return to freshwater to reproduce. Lampreys have a sucker-like mouth that lacks a jaw.

Gnathostomes

Vertebrates with jaws   The fish first appeared during the Cambrian period. Jawless fishes are the most primitive group, although they were a very important group during the Silurian and Devonian periods. Hagfish and lampreys are the only living members of this class today. They have long, cylindrical bodies with cartilage skeletons and no paired fins.

The first jawed fish group was the Placoderms, an extinct group of Devonian-aged jawed fishes. Placoderms were armored with heavy plates and had strong jaws and paired pectoral and pelvic fins. Paired fins allow fish to balance and to maneuver well in water, which facilitate both predation and escape. The evolution of jaws is an example of evolutionary modification of existing structures to perform new functions. Jaws are modified gill arches, and allowed the exploitation of new roles in the habitats: predators with powerful jaws. There are two classes of jawed fish: the cartilaginous fish and the bony fish.

19.2.3.3   Class Chondrichthyes

The class Chondrichthyes contains approximately 850 species of skates, rays, and sharks (Figures 19.9 and 19.10). They have jaws, lots of teeth, paired fins, and a cartilage endoskeleton. Cartilaginous fish first appeared during the Devonian period and expanded in diversity during the Carboniferous and Permian before nearly disappearing during the great extinction that occurred near the end of the Permian. A large group of cartilaginous fish still survives today and is an important part of the marine fauna.

FIGURE 19.9 Chondrichthyes. A. Great white shark (*Carcharodon carcharias*); B. Great hammerhead shark (*Sphyrna mokarran*) offshore of Bimini, Bahamas; C. Leopard shark (*Triakis semifasciata*); D. Giant manta ray (*Manta birostris*) gliding in the Maldives sea; E. Darkspotted stingray (*Himantura uarnak*).

These fishes have five to seven gill slits on both sides of the pharynx, and lack the gill covers found in bony fish. The chondrichthyan body is covered epidermal placoid (or tooth-like) scales. Developmental studies show the teeth of sharks are enlarged scales.

The largest sharks are filter feeders, not the predators of Hollywood movies. Basking and whale sharks eat tons of crustaceans (small krill, etc.) filtered from the water. Most sharks are fast swimming, open-sea predators. The great white shark feeds on dolphins, sea lions and seals (and people sometimes). In other words, anything it wants to!

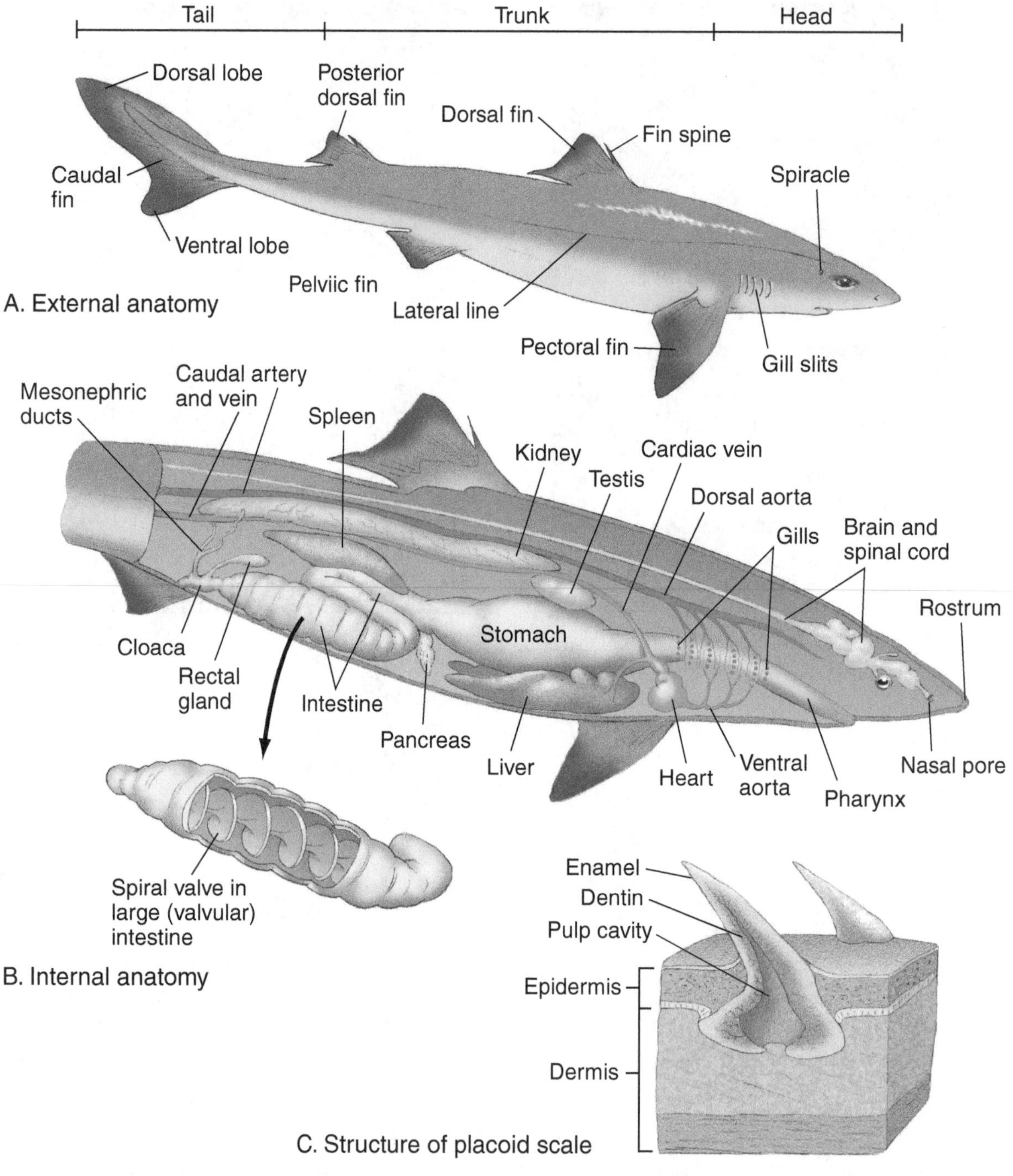

FIGURE 19.10 Anatomy of a dogfish shark.

Rays and skates live on the ocean floor; their pectoral fins are enlarged into wing-like fins; they swim slowly. Stingrays have a venomous spine. The electric ray family can feed on fish that have been stunned with electric shock of over 300 volts. Sawfish rays have a large anterior "saw" that they use to slash through schools of fish.

19.2.3.4   Class Actinopterygii

There are about 20,000 species of bony fish, found both in marine and freshwater, comprising the super class Osteichthyes. This group is divided into two classes: the lobe-finned (Sarcopterygii) and ray-finned fish (Actinopterygii). The bony fish has a bony skeleton. Most species in this class are ray-finned with thin, bony rays supporting the fins. A few fishes are lobe-finned and might represent the ancestors of amphibians.

The ray-finned fish include familiar species such as tuna, bass, perch, and trout (Figure 19.11). Ray-finned fishes are the most successful and diverse of the vertebrates (more than half of all vertebrate species belong to this group). Thin, bony supports with radiating bones (hence the term ray-finned) hold the fins away from the body. Ray-finned fishes obtain their food by filter feeding and by preying on insects and other animals. The skin of these fishes consists of scales formed from bone. These scales are homologous to our own hair (and the feathers of birds), being derived from the same embryonic tissues. The gills in this group of fish do not open separately and are covered by an operculum. Ray-finned fishes have a swim bladder, a gas-filled sac that regulates buoyancy and depth. Sharks lack this feature, which enables fish to "sleep" without sinking. The swim bladder acts much the way a ballast tank does on a submarine to control buoyancy.

Salmon, trout, and eels can migrate from fresh water to salt water, but must adjust kidney and gill function to the tonicity of their environments. In freshwater, the fish is **hypotonic** relative to its aqueous (watery) environment. Water is constantly flooding into the fish, and must be removed by the fish's **excretory system**. In seawater, the fish is **hypertonic** or **isotonic** relative to the seawater, requiring conservation of body water.

FIGURE 19.11 Actinopterygii.
A. Bluefin tuna (*Thunnus thynnus*) in the Mediterranean Sea; B. Copper rockfish (*Sebastes caurinus*); C. Giant moray eel (*Gymnothorax javanicus*) with cleaner fish.

Bony fishes depend on color vision to detect both rivals and mates. Sperm and eggs are released into the water, with not much parental care for the newborn. Most fishes have fertilization and embryonic development taking place outside the female's body.

19.2.3.5   Class Sarcopterygii

This group (Figure 19.12) includes six species of lungfishes and one species of coelacanth that has muscular fins with large, jointed bones attaching the fins to the body. Lobe-finned fishes have fleshy fins supported by central bones, homologous to the bones in your arms and legs. These fins underwent modification, becoming the limbs of amphibians and their evolutionary descendants such as lizards, canaries, dinosaurs, and humans.

The lungfish is a small group found mostly in freshwater stagnant water or ponds that dry up in Africa, South America, and Australia.

Coelacanths live in deep oceans. They were once considered extinct, although more than 200 have been captured since 1938. Mitochondrial DNA analysis supports the hypothesis that lungfishes are probably the closest living relatives of amphibians. Crossopterygian fishes (represented by the marine extant deep-living coelacanth and extinct freshwater forms) are regarded as ancestors of early amphibians. Extinct crossopterygians had strong fins, lungs, and a streamlined body capable of swimming as well as traveling short distances out of water.

The Tetrapods

The term "tetrapod" (meaning four-limbed or four-footed) has historically been applied to the land vertebrates (amphibians, reptiles, dinosaurs, birds, and mammals). Recent proposals call for the restriction of this term to a more cladistically sound definition. All other animals from this point have four limbs and are called tetrapods. I use the term here not in the strict cladistic sense, but in a more inclusive sense to include the living forms as well as fossil vertebrates that had free digits.

Most zoologists accept Devonian lobe-finned fishes as ancestors to amphibians. Animals (both vertebrate as well as many invertebrates such as insects) that live on land use limbs to support the

FIGURE 19.12 Sarcopterygii. A. The coelacanth, *Latimeria* was believed to be extinct but was discovered in 1938 to still be living; B. *Protopterus* fish in the aquarium, a lungfish.

body, especially since air is less buoyant than water. Lobe-finned fishes and early amphibians also had lungs and internal nares to respire air.

Two hypotheses have been proposed to explain the evolution of amphibians from lobe-finned fishes.

- Lobe-finned fishes capable of moving from pond-to-pond had an advantage over those that could not.
- The supply of food on land, and the absence of predators, promoted adaptation to land.

The first amphibians diversified during the Carboniferous period (commonly known as the Age of Amphibians).

19.2.3.6 Class Amphibia

This class includes 4,000 species of animals that spend their larval/juvenile stages in water, and their adult life on land. Amphibians (Figure 19.13) must return to water to mate and lay eggs. Most adults have moist skin functioning to assist their small, inefficient lungs with gas exchange.

FIGURE 19.13 Amphibia. A. Poison arrow frog (*Ranitomeya amazonica*) in the tropical Amazon rain forest in Peru; B. Texas horned lizard (*Phyrnosoma cornutum*); C. American Axoloto salamander newt showing the external gills; D. Fish caecilian.

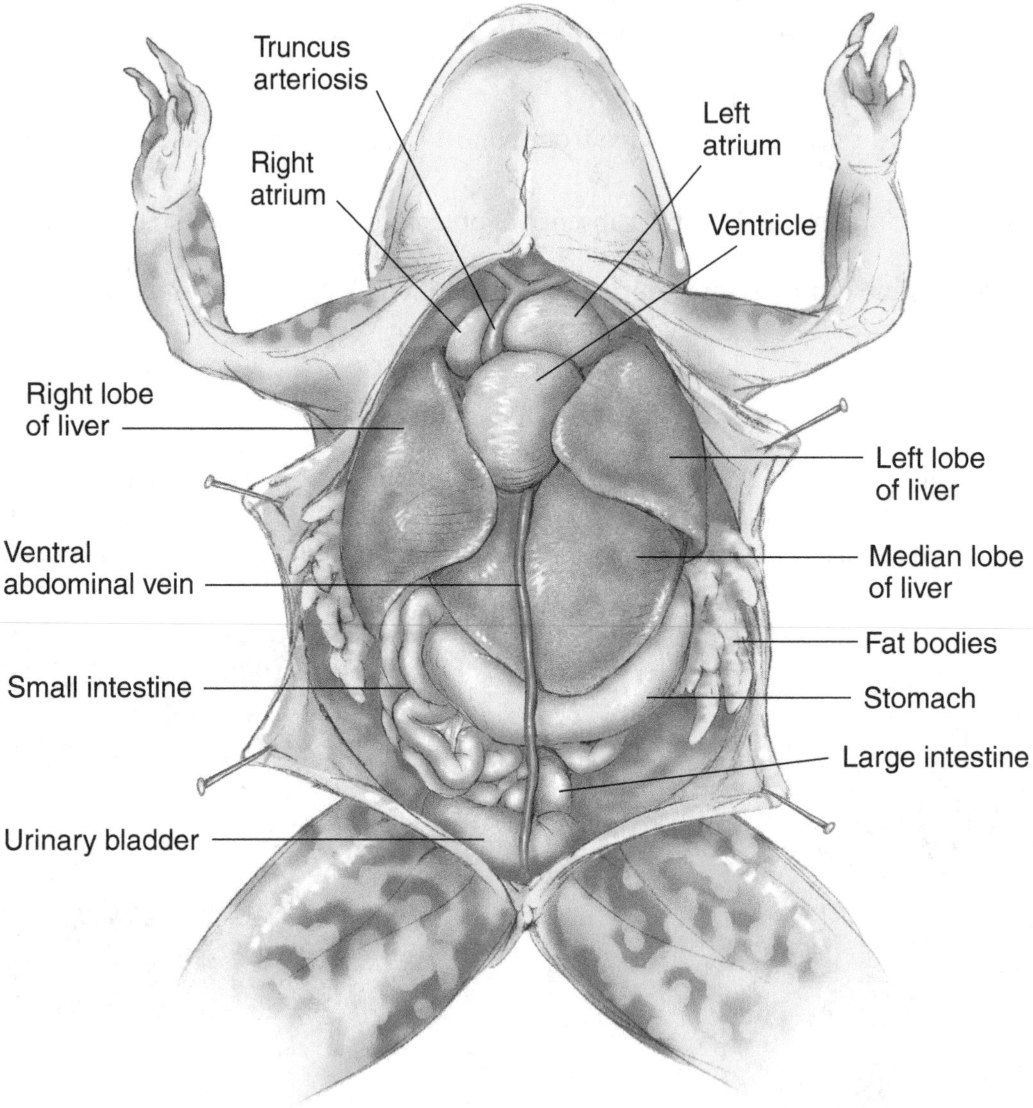

FIGURE 19.14 Anatomy of a frog.

Frogs, toads, newts, salamanders, and mud puppies are in this transitional group between water and land.

Amphibian features not also seen in bony fish include limbs with girdles of bone (pelvic and scapular) adapted for walking on land. A tongue that can be used for catching prey as well as sensory input is an amphibian adaptation. Eyelids that help keep the eyes moist. Ears adapted for detecting sound waves moving through the thin (as compared with water) medium of the air is first seen in amphibians. A larynx adapted for vocalization as sound travels differently in air than in water. Amphibians needed a larger brain than that of fish, and a more developed cerebral cortex to deal with a more dynamic terrestrial environment. Skin that is thin, smooth, nonscaly, and contains numerous mucous glands; the skin plays an active role in osmotic balance and respiration. Amphibians had to deal with gas exchange and their solution was to develop a lung that is permanently used for gas exchange in the adult form. Some amphibians supplement lung function by exchange of gases across a porous (moist) skin. Amphibians evolved a closed double-loop circulatory system that replaces the single-loop circulatory path of fish. To complement this, circulatory change amphibians developed a three-chambered heart that pumps mixed blood before and after it has gone to the lungs.

Reproduction in amphibians usually involves a return to the water. The term "amphibian" refers to two life styles, one in water the other on land. Amphibians normally shed eggs into the water where external fertilization occurs, as it does in fish. Generally, amphibian eggs are protected by a coat of jelly but not by a shell like we see in reptiles, birds, and some mammals. The young hatch into aquatic larvae with gills (tadpoles). Aquatic larvae usually undergo metamorphosis to develop into a terrestrial adult. Amphibians have a number of modifications to the in-the-water reproduction. Frogs in many tropical areas skip the water based tadpole phase and hatch a miniature adult frog from their egg. Most salamanders and caecilians have internal fertilization.

Amphibians, like fish, are ectothermic they depend upon external heat to regulate body temperatures. If the environmental temperature becomes too low, ectotherms become inactive.

19.2.3.7 Class Reptilia

This class of 6,000 species includes the snakes, lizards, turtles, alligators, and crocodiles (Figure 19.15). This large and diverse group formerly included the dinosaurs and should include the mammals and birds to be a true monophyletic group. Reptiles lay an egg surrounded by a thick protective shell and a series of internal membranes. Reptiles have internal fertilization: their gametes do not need to be released into water for fertilization to occur. These in a sense made reptiles the first truly terrestrial tetrapods. In this chapter, we will use reptile in the broad sense, excluding birds, mammals, and dinosaurs.

The amniotic egg (Figure 19.16) is a superb adaptation to life on land. While amphibians need to lay their eggs in water, their descendants (reptiles) were not as strongly tied to moist environments and could truly expand into more arid areas. Reptiles were the first land vertebrates to practice internal fertilization through copulation and to lay eggs that are protected by a leathery shell with food and other support for the growing embryo.

The amniote egg contains extraembryonic membranes that are not part of the embryo and are disposed of after the embryo has developed and hatched. These membranes protect the embryo, remove nitrogenous wastes, and provide the embryo with oxygen, food, and water. The amnion, one of these extraembryonic membranes, creates a sac that fills with fluid and provides a watery environment in which the embryo develops. The embryo develops in a "pond within the shell."

Reptiles first evolved during the Carboniferous period and partly displaced amphibians in many environments. The first reptiles (often referred to as stem reptiles) gave rise to several lineages, each of which adapted to a different way of life. Reptilian success was due to their terrestrial

FIGURE 19.15 Reptilia. A. Sea turtle; B. Tuatara (*Sphenodon punctatus*) in New Zealand; C. The endangered Gila monster (*Heloderma suspectum*) is the only venomous lizard found in the United States; D. Frilled lizard (*Chlamydosaurus kingii*) exhibiting defensive display; E. Gecko lizard showing adhesive fingers; F. Gavial (*Gavialis gangeticus*).

amniotic egg and internal fertilization, as well as their tough leathery skin, more efficient teeth and jaws, and in some, bipedalism (traveling on their hind legs, allowing the forelimbs to grasp prey or food, or become wings).

Dinosaurs and mammal-like reptiles had their limbs beneath the body providing increased agility and facilitating gigantic size. Lizards have their elbows out like you do when you do a traditional push-up. By having their elbows in, dinosaurs and mammals place more of the weight of the body on the long bones instead of the elbows, ankles, and knees.

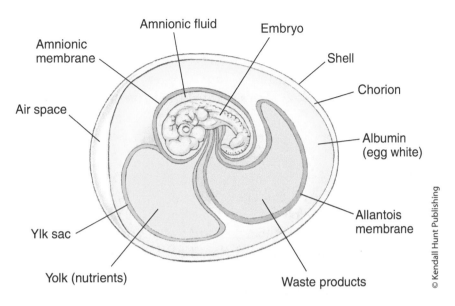

Amnionic fluid

Embryo

Amnionic membrane

Shell

Chorion

Air space

Albumin (egg white)

Allantois membrane

Ylk sac

Yolk (nutrients)

Waste products

FIGURE 19.16 Amniotic egg.

Reptiles dominated the Earth for about 170 million years during the Mesozoic era. The mass extinction of many reptile groups at the close of the Mesozoic era (the Cretaceous/Paleogene extinction) has been well documented and the subject of many hypotheses. The survivors of this mass extinction, birds and mammals, reaped the spoils and diversified during the ensuing Cenozoic era. Three groups of reptiles remain: turtles, snakes/lizards, and crocodiles/alligators.

Lizards and snakes live on land, while turtles and alligators live in water for much of their lives. Reptiles have a thick, scaly skin that has significant amounts of keratin that makes it impermeable to water. This same keratin is a protein found in hair, fingernails, and feathers. Protective skin prevents water loss but requires several molts a year.

Reptilian lungs are more developed than those of amphibians. Air moves in and out of the lungs due to the presence of an expandable rib cage in all reptiles except turtles. Most reptiles have a nearly four-chambered heart. The crocodile has a completely four-chambered heart that fully separates oxygen-rich blood from oxygen-poor blood.

Lizards (Figure 19.15C–E) have four clawed legs and are carnivorous. The marine iguanas on the Galapagos Islands spend time in the sea; frilled lizards display a collar to scare predators, and blind worm lizards live underground. Snakes evolved from lizards and lost their legs as an adaptation to burrowing. Their jaws can readily dislocate to engulf large food. The snake's tongue collects airborne molecules and transfers them to the Jacobson's organ for tasting. Some poisonous snakes have special fangs for injecting their venom.

Turtles (Figure 19.15A) have a heavy shell fused to the ribs and thoracic vertebrae; they lack teeth but use a sharp beak; sea turtles must leave the ocean to lay eggs onshore.

Crocodiles and alligators are largely aquatic, feeding on fishes and other animals. They both have a muscular tail that acts as a paddle to swim and a weapon. The male crocodile bellows to attract mates. In some species, the male also protects the eggs and young.

Cladistic analyses place the birds, alligators, and dinosaurs in the same clade, the Archosauria (or "ruling reptiles"). This group is a major clade of diapsids (vertebrates that have two openings in their skulls) that have single openings in each side of the skull, in front of the eyes (antorbital fenestrae), among other characteristics. These openings serve to lighten the skull, as well as provide more room for muscles and other tissues. Skull flexibility when eating also increases. Other typical archosaurian characteristics include another opening in the lower jaw (the mandibular fenestra), a high narrow skull with a pointed snout, teeth set in sockets, and a modified ankle joint.

19.2.3.8 Class Aves

Class Aves (birds; Figure 19.17) contains about 9,000 species. Birds evolved from a dinosaurian group during the Jurassic (or possibly earlier). The earliest bird fossils, such as the Jurassic-aged *Archaeopteryx*, display a mosaic of reptilian and bird features (teeth in the bill, a jointed tail, and claws on the wing are reptilian; feathers and hollow bones are bird-like). The distinguishing feature of birds is feathers: which provide insulation as well as aid in flight.

Remember that not all flying animals have feathers. Almost every endothermic animal (warm-blooded) has a covering of hair or feathers for insulation. The discovery of "feathered" dinosaurs adds credence to this speculation. The dinosaurs could not fly, so they must have used feathers for insulation (or possibly mating behavior).

Modern birds appeared during the early Paleogene period. Birds have adapted to all modes of life: flying (condors, eagles, hummingbirds), flightless-running (ostriches, emus), and swimming (penguins). Birds exhibit complex mating rituals as well as social structure.

19.2.3.9 Class Mammalia

Class Mammalia (Figure 19.18) contains around 5,000 species usually placed in 26 orders. The three unifying mammalian characteristics are: (1) hair; (2) the presence of three middle ear bones; and (3) the production of milk by mammary glands.

Milk is a substance rich in fats and proteins. Mammary glands usually occur on the ventral surface of females in rows (when there are more than two glands). Humans and apes have two mammary glands (one right, one left), while other animals can have a dozen or more. All mammals have hair at some point during their life. Mammalian hair is composed of the protein keratin. Hair has several functions: (1) insulation; (2) sensory function (whiskers of a cat); (3) camouflage, a warning system to predators, communication of social information, gender, or threats; and (4) protection as an additional layer or by forming dangerous spines that deter predators.

Modifications of the malleus and incus (bones from the jaw in reptiles) work with the stapes to allow mammals to hear sounds after they are transmitted from the outside world to their inner ears by a chain of these three bones. The fossil record provides an excellent series of fossils detailing this transition.

Mammals first evolved from the mammal-like reptiles during the Triassic period, about the same time as the first dinosaurs. However, mammals were minor players in the faunas of the Mesozoic era, and only diversified and became prominent after the extinction of dinosaurs at the close of the Cretaceous period.

FIGURE 19.17 Aves. A. Great blue heron (*Ardea herodias*) in profile; B. Female African ostrich (*Struthio camelus*) with young chicks in the Negev desert, Hai Bar National Reservation, near Eilat, Israel; C. Wild turkey (*Meleagris gallopavo*); D. Lesser bird of paradise (*Paradisaea minor*), one of the most exotic birds in Papua New Guinea; E. Andean condor (*Vultur gryphus*) in wildness area.

Mammals have since occupied all roles once held by dinosaurs and their relatives (flying: bats; swimming: whales, dolphins; large predators: tigers, lions; large herbivores: elephants, rhinos), as well as a new one (thinkers and tool makers: humans). There are 4,500 species of living mammals.

FIGURE 19.18 Mammalia. A. Platypus (*Ornithorhynchus anatinus*) in rainforest creek at Eungella National Park, Queensland, Australia; this mammal lays eggs like a reptile; B. Echidna (*Tachyglossus aculeatus*), another egg-laying mammal; C. Kangaroos are pouched, marsupial mammals; D. Tasmanian devil (*Sarcophilus harrisii*); E. Zebras in Namibia National Park; F. American bison (*Bison bison*); G. Atlantic bottlenose dolphin (*Tursiops truncatus*); H. Bust portrait of a gorilla male (*Gorilla gorilla*), severe silverback.

Mammals developed several adaptations that help explain their success. Teeth are specialized for cutting, shearing or grinding; thick enamel helps to prevent teeth from wearing out. Mammals are capable of rapid locomotion. Brain sizes are larger per pound of body weight than most other animals. Mammals have more efficient control over their body temperatures than do birds. Hair provides insulation. Mammary glands provide milk to nourish the young.

Subclass Prototheria Order Monotremata: Monotremes (typified by the platypus and echinda) lay eggs that have similar membranes and structure to reptilian eggs. Female monotremes burrow in ground and incubate their eggs. Both males and females produce milk to nourish the young. Platypuses lack nipples instead they have milk run down hairs to reach the mouth of their young. There are two families living today and quite a few known from the fossil record of Gondwana. Monotremes are today restricted to Australia and New Guinea. The earliest fossil monotreme is from the early Cretaceous, and younger fossils hint at a formerly more widespread distribution for the group. While their fossil record is scarce, zoologists believe that monotremes probably diverged from other mammals during the Mesozoic era. Monotremes have many differences with other mammals and are often placed in a separate group, the subclass Prototheria. They retain many characters of their mammal-like reptile ancestors, such as laying eggs, limbs oriented with humerus and femur held lateral to body (more lizard-like), a cloaca, skulls with an almost birdlike appearance, and a lack of teeth in adults. This suggests that monotremes are the sister group to all other mammals. However, monotremes do have all of the mammalian defining features of the group (Figure 19.18A, B).

Subclass Metatheria Marsupials (such as the koala, opossum, and kangaroo Figure 19.18C, D) are born while in an embryonic stage and finish development outside the mother's body, often in a pouch. Marsupial young leave the uterus, crawl to the pouch, and attach to the nipple of a mammary gland and continue their development. Marsupials were once widespread, but today are dominant only in Australia, where they underwent adaptive radiation in the absence of placental mammals. The Metatheria contains 272 species classified in several orders. Metatheres diverged from the lineage leading to the eutherian (placental) mammals by the middle of the Cretaceous period in North America. The earliest marsupial fossils resemble North American opossums. Marsupial fossils are found on other northern hemisphere continents, although they seem not to have been prominent elements of those faunas. On the other hand, in South America and Australia, marsupials continued to be dominant faunal elements. The marsupials of South America began to go extinct in the late Miocene and Early Pliocene (Cenozoic era) when volcanic islands grew together and formed the Isthmus of Panama, allowing North American placental mammals to cross into South America. Australian marsupials remain diverse and dominant native mammals of the fauna. During the Cenozoic Era many marsupials in South America and Australia underwent parallel (or convergent) evolution with placental mammals elsewhere, producing marsupial "wolves," "lions," and saber-toothed marsupial "cats".

Subclass Eutheria There are 4,000 described species of placental mammals, a group that includes dogs, cats, and people. The subclass is defined by the presence of a true placenta nourishing and protecting the embryos. These embryos stay within their mother's body for an extended gestation period (nearly 2 years for an elephant, and 9 **very** long months for a human). The eutherian placenta has extra-embryonic membranes modified for internal development within the uterus. The chorion is the fetal portion of placenta, while the uterine wall grows the maternal portion. The mother's placenta exchanges nutrients, oxygen, and waste between fetal blood and maternal blood (Figure 19.18E–H).

There are 12 orders of placental mammals. Classification is based on the mode of locomotion and methods of obtaining food. Prominent orders include the bats (order Chiroptera), horses (order Perissodactyla), whales (order Cetacea), mice (order Rodentia), dogs (order Carnivora), and monkeys/apes/humans (order Primates).

19.3   Significance of Animals

Animals have played significant roles in human history. People recognized the significance of animals, even in ancient cave paintings (Figure 19.19). Domestication of dogs gained us a partner and watcher; domestication of herd animals gained us an assured supply of meat providing the protein our brains require; domestication of horses, donkeys, and oxen gained us beasts of burden for transport and tilling our fields. Leather and furs from the hides of animals clothed us and protected us from harsh environments.

19.3.1   Uses

Animals serve as food for many people. Each year in the United States more than 50 billion chicken eggs are produced, and 8 billion chickens are eaten. Forty-five million turkeys are eaten each year for Thanksgiving. In 2012, the beef industry was estimated to be worth $88 billion (US).

19.3.2   Diseases and in Medicine

Animals have been used in folkloric medicine for centuries. In some Asian medicines parts of tigers are used to treat various ailments such as toothaches and to prevent curses. Poaching has led to a decline in many tiger species. More than $50,000 can be gained from the part of just one

Shutterstock/Pichugin Dmitry

Shutterstock/wcpmedia

FIGURE 19.19 Animal images from cave paintings. A. Paleolithic cave painting from Europe; B. Bushman rock paintings in Kamberg, South Africa.

tiger. Rhinoceros horn was used to treat high blood pressure in China, although science refuted that claim. The Chinese alligator has almost been hunted to extinction related to it being thought to cure the common cold. The gall bladder of the sun bear has been used to treat a wide range of ailments, none of them backed by scientific study.

19.3.3   Ecological

Animals are important consumers ecologically. Herd animals help keep grasses in check on grasslands. Bees and other pollinators pay vital roles in outcrossing of many flowering plant species. Fruit set in many plants require the actions of pollinators. Many animals are symbionts. Ants are in a mutualistic association with the Acacia tree. Coral are important builders of the reef where other animals live.

Summary

Members of the animal kingdom share certain characteristics. They can move at some point during their lives and are ingestive, multicellular heterotrophs. Animals are capable of complex behaviors such as mating and courtship rituals, learning, and flight.

Terms

amniotic egg
amphibian
anus
bilateral symmetry
blastula
cephalization
chordates
coelom
craniates
cranium
deuterostomes
nerve cord
echinoderm
ectothermic
embryos
endoskeleton
excretory system
fossil record
gestation
gnathostome

gondwana
hypertonic
hypotonic
incus
isotonic
invertebrate chordates
jaws
keratin
malleus
mammal
mammary glands
mammal-like reptiles
marsupial
monotreme
notochord
parallel (or convergent)
  evolution
pharyngeal gill pouches
placenta
placental mammal

postanal tail
protostomes
radial symmetry
reptile
skeletons
stapes
uterus
ventral
vertebrae
vertebrate chordates
vertebrates

Review Questions

1. The phylum to which humans belong is the ___.
   a. Cnidaria;
   b. Arthropoda;
   c. Chordata;
   d. Echinodermata

2. Which of these materials would you expect the skeleton of a shark to contain?
   a. bone;
   b. cellulose;
   c. chitin;
   d. cartilage

3. Tube feet occur in which of these phyla?
   a. Echinodermata;
   b. Chordata;
   c. Cnidaria;
   d. Mollusca;
   e. Annelida

4. The ___ is linked to coral reef destruction.
   a. crown-of-thorns starfish;
   b. brittle star;
   c. sand dollar;
   d. red sea urchin;
   e. purple sea urchin

5. The presence of similar bones in the flipper of a coelacanth and the arm of a human is an example of which of these?
   a. heterozygous features;
   b. analogous structures;
   c. homologous structures;
   d. homozygous structures

6. Which of these fish groups is directly ancestral to the tetrapods?
   a. Chondrichthyes;
   b. Mixini;
   c. Actinopterygii;
   d. Sarcopterygii

7. The ___ are a group of mammals that lay eggs.
   a. placentals;
   b. monotremes;
   c. marsupials;
   d. trilobites

8. The pouched mammals belong to which of these groups?
   a. placentals;
   b. monotremes;
   c. marsupials;
   d. trilobites

9. Tetrapods colonized the land during which of these geologic periods?
   a. Permian;
   b. Paleogene;
   c. Devonian;
   d. Cambrian;
   e. Silurian

10. The first land animals belonged to which of these phyla?
    a. Mollusca;
    b. Amphibia;
    c. Arthropoda;
    d. Chondrichthyes

11. The first flying animals belonged to which of these phyla?
    a. Chordata;
    b. Amphibia;
    c. Arthropoda;
    d. Sarcopterygii

12. Amphibians use their ____ in addition to their lungs for gas exchange.
    a. gills;
    b. skin;
    c. stomach;
    d. cloaca

13. The first land vertebrates belonged to which of these phyla?
    a. mammals;
    b. reptiles;
    c. ray-finned fish;
    d. amphibians

14. The ____ is a living fossil with bones in its fins homologous to bones in our own arms.
    a. coelomate;
    b. coelacanth;
    c. lungfish;
    d. ginkgo;
    e. horseshoe crab

15. Mammals have which of these as a common unique character?
    a. hair;
    b. mammary glands;
    c. a bony endoskeleton;
    d. a bony tail

16. Mammals have a jaw composed of how many bones on each side of the jaw?
    a. 1;
    b. 2;
    c. 3;
    d. 4

17. Reptiles have a jaw composed of how many bones on each side of the jaw?
    a. 1;
    b. 2;
    c. 3;
    d. 4

18. The early bird fossil ____ has claws on its wing, scales on its neck, teeth in its mouth, and bones in its tail.
    a. *Archaeocyathea*;
    b. *Archaeopteris*;
    c. *Archaeopteryx*;
    d. Archmage

Links

Introduction to the Metazoa: Animals, Animals, Animals! This University of California Berkeley Museum of Paleontology site offers excellent information about the evolution and diversity of various animal groups. [http://www.ucmp.berkeley.edu/phyla/phyla.html]

The Great White Shark: Learn the truth about the great white shark (no, not golfer Greg Norman). How do they live, reproduce, and feed? [http://www.ucmp.berkeley.edu/vertebrates/Doug/shark.html]

References

Stromberg J, Zielinski S (2011). Ten Threatened and Endangered Species Used in Traditional Medicine. http://www.smithsonianmag.com/science-nature/ten-threatened-and-endangered-species-used-in-traditional-medicine-112814487/#VEp1GHdy3Z3UDRX1.99

USDA. Statistics and information. Cattle and Beef. http://www.ers.usda.gov/topics/animal-products/cattle-beef/statistics-information.aspx#.VCNArUuMnyB

Glossary

A

Abiogenesis: Early theory that held that some organisms originated from nonliving material.

Abnormal hemoglobin: Hemoglobin molecule with a different shape due to an altered sequence of **amino acids** (ultimately caused by an altered DNA base sequence), such as in the inherited disease **sickle-cell anemia**.

Abscisic acid: A plant **hormone** that promotes dormancy in **perennial** plants and causes rapid closure of leaf **stomata** when a leaf begins to wilt.

Abscission: The process by which plants prepare for leaves and fruits to be removed from the plant.

Absolute time: One of the two types of geologic time (**relative time** being the other), with a definite age date established mostly by the decay of radioactive elements, although ages may also be obtained by counting tree rings, decay of a specific type of atom, or annual sedimentary layers (such as varves in lakes or layers in a glacier). The term is in some disfavor because it suggests an exactness that may not be possible to obtain.

Absorption: The process by which the products of **digestion** are transferred into the body's internal environment, enabling them to reach the cells.

Absorptive feeders: Animals such as tapeworms that ingest food through the body wall.

Accessory pigments: Pigment molecules associated with **photosystems** embedded in thylakoid membranes. Accessory pigments absorb some of the energy that **chlorophyll a** does not.

Acetylcholine: A chemical released at neuromuscular junctions that binds to receptors on the surface of the plasma membrane of muscle cells, causing an electrical impulse to be transmitted. The impulse ultimately leads to muscle contraction.

Acetyl CoA: An intermediate compound formed during the breakdown of **glucose** by adding a two-carbon fragment to a carrier molecule (Coenzyme A or CoA).

Acid: A substance that increases the number of hydrogen ions in a solution.

Acid rain: The precipitation of sulfuric acid and other acids as rain. The acids form when sulfur dioxide and nitrogen oxides released during the combustion of fossil fuels combine with water and oxygen in the atmosphere. The term acid rain is a part of acid precipitation.

Acoelomate: Type of animal body plan lacking a body cavity (**coelom**).

Acquired immunodeficiency syndrome (AIDS): A collection of disorders that develop as a result of infection by the **human immunodeficiency virus (HIV)**, which attacks **helper T cells**, crippling the immune system and greatly reducing the body's ability to fight infection; results in premature death brought about by various diseases that overwhelm the compromised immune system.

Actin: The **protein** composing **microfilaments**; forms the contractile filaments of **sarcomeres** in muscle cells.

Action potential: A reversal of the electrical potential in the plasma membrane of a **neuron** that occurs when a nerve cell is stimulated; caused by rapid changes in membrane permeability to sodium and potassium.

Active site: the region of the enzyme where the substrate molecules fit.

Active transport: Transport of molecules against a concentration gradient (from regions of low concentration to regions of high concentration) with the aid of proteins in the cell membrane and energy from **ATP**.

Adaptation: Tendency of an organism to suit its environment; one of the major points of Darwin's theory of evolution by **natural selection**: organisms adapt to their environment. Those organisms best adapted will have a greater chance of surviving and passing their **genes** on to the next generation.

Adaptive radiation: The development of a variety of species from a single ancestral form; occurs when a new habitat becomes available to a **population**. Evolutionary pattern indicated by the **divergence** of many species from a common ancestral species as a result of novel adaptations or a recent **mass extinction**. Examples: mammals during the **Cenozoic era** after the extinction of dinosaurs at the close of the **Mesozoic era**, flowering plants during the Cretaceous period diversified because of their reproductive advantages over **gymnosperm** and nonseed plants that dominated the floras of the world at that time.

Adenine: One of the four nitrogen-containing bases occurring in **nucleotides**, the building blocks of the organic macromolecule group known as **nucleic acids** (DNA and RNA). Adenine is also the base in the energy-carrying molecule **ATP (adenosine triphosphate)** that is the energy currency of the cell.

Adenosine diphosphate (ADP): Lower energy form of ATP, having two (instead of the three in ATP) phosphate groups attached to the adenine base and ribose sugar.

Adenosine triphosphate (ATP): n

Adhesion: The ability of molecules of one substance to adhere to a different substance.

Adipose: Specialized animal cells that store fats in large central **vacuoles**.

Adrenocorticotropic hormone (ACTH): A hormone produced by the anterior pituitary that stimulates the adrenal cortex to release several hormones including cortisol.

Adventitious roots: Roots that develop from the stem following the death of the primary root. Branches from the adventitious roots form a **fibrous root** system in which all roots are about the same size; usually found in **monocots**.

Aerobic: Referring to the presence of dioxygen (O_2).

Age structure: The relative proportion of individuals in each age group within a population.

Aggregates: Fairly random associations of animals with little or no internal organization; form in response to a single stimulus and disperse when the stimulus is removed; one of the three broad classes of social organization.

Albinism: Genetic condition caused by the body's inability to manufacture pigments; a **recessive trait** found on **autosomes**.

Aldosterone: A **hormone** secreted by the adrenal glands that controls the reabsorption of sodium in the **renal tubule** of the **nephron**.

Alleles: Alternate forms of a **gene**.

Allergens: **Antigens** that provoke an allergic reaction.

Alpha decay: Type of **radioactive decay** occurring when a **radioisotope** emits a large but slow-moving particle consisting of two protons and two neutrons.

Alternation of generations: A life cycle in which a multicellular **diploid** stage is followed by a **haploid** stage and so on; found in land plants, many algae, and certain eukaryans.

Altitudinal gradient: As altitude increases, a gradient of cooler, drier conditions occurs.

Alveoli: Tiny, thin-walled, inflatable sacs in the **lungs** where oxygen and carbon dioxide are exchanged.

Amino acids: The **monomer** subunits from which **polymers** known as **proteins** are assembled. Each amino acid consists of an amino functional group, and a carboxyl acid group, and differs from other amino acids by the composition of an R group.

Amino acid sequence: Also known as the **primary structure** of a protein/polypeptide; the sequence of amino acids in a protein/polypeptide controlled by the sequence of DNA bases.

Amniocentesis: A method of prenatal testing in which amniotic fluid is withdrawn from the uterus through a needle. The fluid and the fetal cells it contains are analyzed to detect biochemical or chromosomal disorders.

Amniotic egg: An egg with compartmentalized sacs (a liquid-filled sac in which the **embryo** develops, a food sac, and a waste sac) that allowed certain groups of **vertebrates** to reproduce on land.

Amoebocytes: Amoeboid cells in sponges that occur in the matrix between the epidermal and collar cells. They transport nutrients.

Amphibians: Class of terrestrial **vertebrates** that lay eggs (and also mate) in water but live on land as adults following a juvenile stage where they live in water and breathe through gills. Amphibians were the first group of land vertebrates; today they are mostly restricted to moist habitats.

Anabolic reactions: Reactions in cells in which new chemical bonds form during which new molecules develop; generally require energy that involve **reduction**.

Anaerobic: Refers to organisms that are not dependent on oxygen for **respiration**.

Analogous structures: Body parts that serve the same function in different organisms, but differ in structure and embryological development; for example, the wings of insects and birds.

Anaphase: Phase of **mitosis** in which the **chromosomes** begin to separate.

Anaphylaxis: A severe allergic reaction in which **histamine** is released into the circulatory system; occurs upon subsequent exposure to a particular **antigen**; also called anaphylactic shock.

Androecium: Collective term applied to all of the male (**stamen**) parts of the flower.

Aneuploidy: Variation in **chromosome** number involving one or a small number of chromosomes; commonly involves the gain or loss of a single chromosome.

Angina: Chest pain, especially during physical exertion or emotional stress, which is caused by gradual blockage of the **coronary arteries**.

Angiosperms: Flowering plants. First appearing at least 142 million years ago from an unknown **gymnosperm** ancestor, flowering plants have risen to dominance in most of the world's floras. The male **gametophyte** is two to three cells contained within a **pollen** grain; the female gametophyte is usually eight cells contained within an **ovule** retained on the **sporophyte** phase of the plant's life cycle.

Animalia: Animal Kingdom. Multicellular **eukaryotic** group characterized by **heterotrophic** nutritional mode, usually organ and tissue development, and motility sometime during the organism's life history.

Annelids: Animal **phylum** containing the segmented worms.

Annuals: Plants that grow and reproduce sexually during one year.

Antagonistic muscles: A pair of muscles that work to produce opposite effects where one contracts as the other relaxes: for example, the bicep and tricep muscles on opposite sides of your upper arm.

Anther: The top of a stamen's filament; divided into **pollen** sacs in which the pollen grains form.

Antheridium: Type of **gamete** producing organ in plants that makes sperm by **mitosis**.

Antibiotics: Substances produced by some microorganisms, plants, and vertebrates that kill or inhibit the growth of bacteria.

Antibiotic resistance: Tendency of certain bacteria to develop a resistance to commonly overused antibiotics, such as penicillin.

Antibodies: **Proteins** produced by **immune system** cells that bind to foreign molecules and microorganisms and inactivate them.

Antibody-mediated immunity: Immune reaction protecting primarily against invading viruses and bacteria through **antibodies** produced by **plasma cells**; also known as humoral immunity.

Anticodon: A sequence of three **nucleotides** on the **transfer RNA** molecule that recognizes and pairs with a specific **codon** on a **messenger RNA** molecule; helps control the sequence of amino acids in a growing polypeptide chain.

Antidiuretic hormone (ADH): A **hormone** produced by the **hypothalamus** and released by the **pituitary gland** that increases the permeability of the **renal tubule** of the **nephron** and thereby increases water reabsorption; also known as **vasopressin**.

Antigenic determinant: The site on an **antigen** to which an **antibody** binds, forming an antigen–antibody complex.

Antigens: Molecules carried or produced by microorganisms that initiate antibody production; mostly **proteins** or proteins combined with **polysaccharides**.

Antinutrients: Chemicals produced by plants as a defense mechanism; inhibit the action of digestive **enzymes** in insects that attack and attempt to eat the plants.

Anus: The posterior opening of the digestive tract through which wastes are expelled from the body.

Aorta: The **artery** carrying blood from the left **ventricle** for distribution throughout the tissues of the body. The aorta has the largest diameter and thickest walls of any artery in the body.

Apical meristem: A **meristem** (embryonic tissue) at the tip of a shoot or root that is responsible for increasing the plant's length.

Apnea: A disorder in which breathing stops for periods longer than 10 seconds during sleep; can be caused by failure of the automatic respiratory center to respond to elevated blood levels of carbon dioxide.

Apocrine glands: Sweat glands that are located primarily in the armpits and groin area; larger than the more widely distributed **eccrine** glands.

Apoptosis: term applied to programmed cell death where the cell destroys itself.

Appendicular skeleton: The bones of the appendages (wings, legs, and arms or fins) and of the pelvic and pectoral girdles that join the appendages to the rest of the skeleton; one of the two components of the skeleton of **vertebrates**.

Appendix: Blind sac at the end of the large intestine that usually ruptures during final exams; a **vestigial** organ in humans.

Archaea: Taxonomic domain of prokaryotic organisms with a mix of eukaryotic and bacterial features.

Archaeocyathids: An extinct group of animals that were part of Cambrian-aged reef environments, but which were extinct by the close of the Cambrian period.

Archean/Proterozoic Eon: The span of geologic time beginning 4.6 billion years ago with the formation of the Earth and ending 542 million years ago.

Archegonium: Type of gamete producing organ in plants that makes an egg cell by mitosis.

Aridity: The condition of receiving sparse rainfall; associated with cooler climates because cool air can hold less water vapor than warm air. Many deserts occur in relatively warm climates, however, because of local or global influences that block rainfall.

Arrector pili: A muscle running from a hair follicle to the dermis of the skin. Contraction of this muscle causes the hair to rise perpendicular to the skin surface, forming "goose pimples."

Arteries: Thick-walled vessels that carry blood away from the heart. Singular = artery.

Arterioles: The smallest arteries; usually branch into a **capillary bed**.

Artificial selection: The process in which breeders choose the variants to be used to produce succeeding generations.

Ascocarp: A sexual reproductive structure, sometimes known as a fruiting body, that forms in some **ascomycetes**.

Ascomycetes: Phylum of **fungi** that contains the yeasts and morels; ascomycetes produce an **ascus** (or sac) in which **ascospores** form.

Ascospore: A haploid spore produced in an **ascus** by an **ascomycete** fungus.

Ascus: Structure produced by sac fungi in which sexual **ascospores** develop.

Asexual reproduction: A method of reproduction in which genetically identical offspring are produced from a single parent; occurs by many mechanisms, including fission, budding, and fragmentation.

Assortment: One way in which **meiosis** produces new combinations of genetic information. Paternal and maternal chromosomes line up randomly during **synapsis**, so each daughter cell is likely to receive an assortment of maternal and paternal chromosomes rather than a complete set from either.

Aster: Short fibers produced by cells during **mitosis** and **meiosis**. These fibers radiate from the **centriole** (if it is present).

Asteroid impacts: Hypothesis that links some **mass extinction** events with the impact of a comet or asteroid, most notably the mass extinction 65 million years that caused the disappearance of nonavian dinosaurs and many other animal groups. Asteroid impacts early in Earth history may have contributed to the formation of the atmosphere and oceans.

Asthma: A respiratory disorder caused by allergies that constrict the **bronchioles** by inducing spasms in the muscles surrounding the lungs, by causing the bronchioles to swell, or by clogging the bronchioles with **mucus.**

Asymmetrical: In animals, a term referring to organisms that lack a general body plan or axis of symmetry that divides the body into mirror-image halves.

Atmosphere: The envelope of gases that surrounds the Earth; consists largely of dinitrogen (78%, N_2) and dioxygen (21%, O_2).

Atom: The smallest indivisible particle of an chemical **element** of **matter** that can have an independent existence.

Atomic mass: The sum of the masses of an atom's **protons** and **neutrons**, the atomic mass differs between **isotopes** of the same **element**.

Atomic number: The number of **protons** in the **nucleus** of an atom.

Atrioventricular (AV) node: Tissue in the right **ventricle** of the heart that receives the impulse from the **atria** and transmits it through the **ventricles** by way of the bundles of His and the Purkinje fibers.

Atrioventricular (AV) valve: The valve between each auricle and **ventricle** of the heart.

Atrium: Term for the upper chamber(s) of the heart.

Auricle: The chamber of the heart that receives blood from the body returned to the heart by the **veins**. Also referred to as atrium.

Autonomic system: The portion of the **peripheral nervous system** that stimulates smooth muscle, cardiac muscle, and glands; consists of the **parasympathetic** and **sympathetic** systems.

Autosomes: The chromosomes other than the **sex chromosomes**. Each member of an autosome pair (in **diploid** organisms) is of similar length and in the **genes** it carries.

Autotrophic: Refers to organisms that synthesize their nutrients and obtain their energy from inorganic raw materials.

Autotrophs: Organisms that synthesize their own nutrients; include some bacteria that are able to synthesize organic molecules from simpler inorganic compounds, as well as photosynthetic creatures. Self-feeders.

Auxins: A group of **hormones** involved in controlling plant growth and other functions; once thought responsible for **phototropism** by causing the cells on the shaded side of a plant to elongate, thereby causing the plant to bend toward the light.

Axial skeleton: The skull, vertebral column, and rib cage; one of the two components of the skeleton in **vertebrates.**

Axillary buds: Buds borne in the axil (where the leaf meets the stem) of a stem.

Axons: Long fibers that carry signals away from the cell body of a **neuron.**

B

Bacillus: Rod shaped prokaryotes. Plural: bacilli.

Bacteria: Prokaryotic domain that contains unicellular forms with peptidoglycan in their cell walls.

Bacteriochlorophyll: **Chlorophyll** molecule occurring in photosynthetic bacteria.

Bacteriophages: **Viruses** that attack and kill bacterial cells; composed only of DNA and protein.

Bark: The outer layer of the stems of woody plants; composed of an outer layer of dead cells (**cork**) and an inner layer of **phloem**.

Barr body: Inactivated **X-chromosome** in mammalian females. Although inactivated, the Barr body is replicated prior to cell division and thus is passed on to all descendant cells of the embryonic cell that had one of its X-chromosomes inactivated.

Barriers to gene flow: Factors, such as geographic, mechanical, and behavioral isolating mechanisms that restrict gene flow between **populations**, leading to populations with differing allele frequencies.

Basal body: A structure at the base of a **cilium** or **flagellum**; consists of nine triplet **microtubules** arranged in a circle with no central microtubule.

Base: A substance that lowers the hydrogen ion concentration in a solution; bases increase the pH number of the solution.

Basidia: Specialized club-shaped structures on the underside of club fungi (**Basidiomycetes**) within which spores form (singular = basidium).

Basidiocarp: Reproductive structure produced by club fungi. The basidiocarp grows to become what we commonly call a mushroom or toadstool.

Basidiomycetes: The club fungi, a phylum of **fungi** that all produce a structure (**basidium**) on which **basidiospores** form. Includes mushrooms and toadstools.

Basidiospores: The spores formed on the **basidia** of club fungi (**Basidiomycetes**).

B cells: Type of **lymphocyte** responsible for **antibody-mediated immunity**; mature in the bone marrow and circulate in the circulatory and lymph systems where they transform into antibody-producing **plasma cells** when exposed to **antigens**.

Benthic zone: One of the two basic subdivisions of the marine **biome**; includes the sea floor and bottom-dwelling organisms.

Beta decay: Type of **radioactive decay** in which a **radioisotope** emits a small, negatively charged, and fast-moving particle from its nucleus. The beta particle is similar in size, charge, and speed to an electron and forms when a neutron in the radioisotope's nucleus converts to a proton.

Bicarbonate ions: A weak base present in saliva that helps to neutralize acids in food.

Big bang theory: A model for the evolution of the Universe that holds that all matter and energy in the Universe were concentrated in one point, which suddenly exploded. Subsequently, matter condensed to form atoms, elements, and eventually galaxies and stars.

Bilateral symmetry: In animals, refers to those that have a single axis of symmetry producing mirror sides to the body.

Biliary system: The bile-producing system consisting of the liver, gallbladder, and associated ducts.

Binary fission: The method by which bacteria reproduce. The circular DNA molecule is replicated; then the cell splits into two identical cells, each containing an exact copy of the original cell's DNA.

Binding sites: Areas on the **ribosome** within which **tRNA**-amino acid complexes fit during **protein synthesis**.

Binomial nomenclature: A system of **taxonomy** developed by Linnaeus in the 18th century. Each **species** of plant and animal receives a two-term name; the first term is the **genus**, and the second is the **species**.

Biochemical cycle: The flow of an element through the living tissue and physical environment of an **ecosystem**; for example, the carbon, hydrogen, oxygen, nitrogen, sulfur, and phosphorus cycles.

Biochemical reactions: Specific chemical processes that occur in living things.

Biochemistry: Chemical processes associated with living things.

Biodiversity: Biological diversity; can be measured in terms of genetic, species, or **ecosystem** diversity.

Biogeography: The study of the distribution of plants and animals across the Earth.

Bioluminescent: Refers to organisms that emit light under certain conditions.

Biomass: The total weight of living tissue in a **community**.

Biome: A large-scale grouping that includes many communities of a similar nature.

Biosphere: All **ecosystems** on Earth as well as the Earth's crust, waters, and atmosphere on and in which organisms exist; also, the sum of all living matter on Earth.

Biotechnology: Use of living organisms to produce novel gene-based products.

Birds: Taxonomic class of terrestrial **vertebrates** characterized by **endothermy** and feathers; descended from one group of dinosaurs. Since merged with dinosaurs and crocodiles in the Class Archosauria.

Birth rate: The ratio between births and individuals in a specified **population** at a particular time.

Bivalves: Group of animals in phylum Mollusca that have two hinged shells.

Bladder: A hollow, distensible organ with muscular walls that stores **urine** and expels it through the **urethra**.

Blastocoel: The fluid-filled cavity at the center of a **blastula**.

Blastocyst: The developmental stage of the fertilized ovum by the time it is ready to implant; formed from the **morula** and consists of an inner cell mass, an internal cavity, and an outer layer of cells (the **trophoblast**).

Blastula: A ball of cells surrounding a fluid-filled cavity (the **blastocoel**) that is produced by the repeated cleavage of a **zygote**.

Blending: Term applied to 19th century belief that parental traits "blended" in offspring; disproven by Mendel's work.

Blood group or type: One of the classes into which blood can be separated on the basis of the presence or absence of certain **antigens**; notably, the ABO types and the Rh blood group.

B memory cells: Long-lived B cells that are produced after an initial exposure to an **antigen** and play an important role in **secondary immunity**. They remain in the body and facilitate a more rapid response if the antigen is encountered again.

Body fossil: The actual remains (however mineralized, compressed or otherwise postmortem altered) of an organism; includes bones, shells, and teeth.

Bolus: A mass of chewed food mixed with salivary secretions propelled into the **esophagus** during the swallowing phase of digestion.

Bony fish: Term applied collectively to all groups of fish with bony (as opposed to cartilaginous) skeletons.

Book lungs: Type of gas exchange structure in certain **arthropods**.

Bottlenecks: Drastic short-term reductions in population size caused by natural disasters, disease, or predators; can lead to random changes in the population's **gene pool**.

Brachiopods: A phylum of hinge-shelled animals that have left an excellent **fossil record**; brachiopods live on or in the ocean floor.

Brachydactly: Human genetic disorder that causes production of an shorter than normal digits, normally inherited as a dominant allele.

Brain: The most anterior, most highly developed portion of the **central nervous system**.

Brain stem: The portion of the brain that is continuous with the **spinal cord** and consists of the **medulla oblongata** and **pons** of the hindbrain and the midbrain.

Bronchi: Tubes that carry air from the trachea to the lungs (singular: bronchus).

Bronchioles: Small tubes in the lungs that are formed by the branching of the **bronchi**; terminate in the **alveoli**.

Bronchitis: A respiratory disorder characterized by excess **mucus** production and swelling of the bronchioles; caused by long-term exposure to irritants such as cigarette smoke and air pollutants.

Brown algae: Multicellular protistans placed in the Phylum Phaeophyta, includes kelp.

Brush border: The collection of **microvilli** forming a border on the intestinal side of the **epithelial cells** of the **small intestine**.

Bryophytes: The nonvascular plants, characterized by life cycles dominated by the **gametophyte** phase. This group includes the mosses, liverworts, and hornworts, all of which lack lignified conducting tissues.

Budding: (1) **Asexual** production of new organisms; usually found in yeast; (2) The process by which **HIV** and similar **viruses** leave the cell (other than by lysing).

Buffers: Chemicals that maintain **pH** values within narrow limits by absorbing or releasing hydrogen ions.

Bulbourethral glands: Glands that secrete a mucus-like substance that is added to **sperm** and provides lubrication during intercourse.

Bursae: Small sacs lined with **synovial** membrane and filled with synovial fluid; act as cushions to reduce friction between **tendons** and bones.

C

Calcitonin: A **hormone** produced by the thyroid that plays a role in regulating calcium levels.

Calcium carbonate: Chemical that also occurs in limestone and marble.

Calvin cycle: Series of biochemical, **enzyme**-mediated reactions during which atmospheric carbon dioxide is chemically **reduced** and incorporated into organic molecules, eventually some of this forms sugars. In **eukaryotes**, this occurs in the **stroma** of the **chloroplast**.

Calyx: Term collectively applied when referring to all of the **sepals** of a flower.

Cambium: A lateral **meristem** in plants. Types of cambiums include **vascular**, **cork**, and intercalary.

Cambrian: Geologic period that begins the **Paleozoic era** 542 million years ago. Marked in its beginning by a proliferation of animals with hard, preservable parts, such as **brachiopods**, **trilobites**, and **archaeocyathids**.

Campodactyly: A dominant trait in which a muscle improperly attaches to bones in the little finger, causing the finger to be permanently bent.

Capillaries: Small, thin-walled blood vessels that allow dioxygen to diffuse from the blood into the cells and carbon dioxide to diffuse from the cells into the blood.

Capillary bed: A branching network of capillaries supplied by **arterioles** and drained by **venules**.

Capsid: The protein covering surrounding a viral nucleic acid core.

Capsule: (1) Structure produced around certain bacteria; (2) Structure produced by the **bryophyte sporophyte** that contains **spores** produced by **meiosis**.

Carbohydrates: Organic molecules composed of carbon, hydrogen, and oxygen that serve as energy sources and structural materials for cells of all living things.

Cardiac cycle: One heartbeat; consists of atrial contraction and relaxation, ventricular contraction and relaxation, and a short pause.

Cardiac muscle: The type of muscle that is found in the walls of the heart. Cardiac muscle is striated but branched, unlike the straight-shaped striated **skeletal muscle** cells.

Cardiovascular system: The human circulatory system consisting of the heart and the vessels that transport blood to and from the heart.

Carnivores: Term applied to a **heterotroph**, usually an animal that eats other animals. Carnivores function as secondary, tertiary, or top consumers in **food chains** and **food webs**.

Carotenoids: Major group of **accessory pigments** in plants; includes beta carotene.

Carpals: The bones that make up the wrist joint in **vertebrate** animals.

Carpels: The female reproductive structures of a **flower**; consisting of the **ovary**, **style**, and **stigma**.

Carrageenan: Chemical extracted from **red algae** that is added to commercial ice creams as an emulsifying agent.

Carrying capacity: The maximum population size that can be regularly sustained by an environment; the point where the population size levels off in the logistic growth model.

Casparian strip: In plants, an impermeable waxy layer between the cells of the **endodermis** that stops water and solutes from entering the **xylem**, except by passing through the cytoplasm of adjacent cells.

Cast: A type of **fossil** preservation where the original material of the fossil has decayed and been replaced later by another material, much the way a plaster cast is made in a mold.

Catabolic reactions: Reactions in cells in which existing chemical bonds are broken and molecules are broken down; generally produce **energy**, involve **oxidation**, and lead to a decrease in atomic order.

Catastrophism: Once-popular belief that events in Earth history had occurred in the past as sudden events and by processes unlike those operating today. Periods of catastrophic change were followed by long periods of little change.

Cell body: In a **neuron**, the part that contains the **nucleus** and most of the **cytoplasm** and the **organelles**.

Cell cycle: The sequence of events from one division of a cell to the next; consists of **mitosis** (or division) and **interphase**.

Cell-mediated immunity: Immune reaction directed against body cells that have been infected by **viruses** and bacteria; controlled by **T cells**.

Cell plate: In plants, a membrane-bound space produced during cytokinesis by the vesicles of the **Golgi apparatus**. The cell plate fuses with the plasma membrane, dividing the cell into two compartments.

Cells: The smallest structural units of living **matter** capable of functioning independently.

Cell theory: One of the unifying concepts in biology. The cell theory states that all living things are composed of at least one cell and that the cell is the fundamental unit of function in all organisms. Corollaries: the chemical composition of all cells is fundamentally alike; all cells arise from preexisting cells through cell division.

Cellular respiration: The transfer of **energy** from various **molecules** to produce **ATP**; occurs in the **mitochondria** of **eukaryotes**, the cytoplasm of **prokaryotes**. In the process, oxygen is consumed and carbon dioxide is generated.

Cellulose: A **polysaccharide** composed of unbranched chains of **glucose**; the major structural **carbohydrate** of plants; cellulose does not dissolve in water, and does not digest in the human intestine.

Cell wall: Structure produced by some cells outside their cell membrane; variously composed of **chitin**, **peptidoglycan**, or **cellulose**.

Cenozoic era: The period of geologic time beginning after the end of the **Mesozoic era** 65 million years ago and encompassing the present. Commonly referred to as the age of mammals.

Central nervous system (CNS): The division of the **nervous system** that includes the **brain** and **spinal cord**.

Centralean: The group of **radially symmetrical diatoms**.

Centriole: Paired cellular **organelle** that functions in the organization of the **spindle** during **mitosis**.

Centromere: Specialized region on each **chromatid** to which **kinetochores** and sister chromatids attach.

Cephalization: The concentration of sensory tissues in the anterior part of the body (head).

Cephalothorax: Structure in certain **arthropods** where the head and thorax regions fused together.

Cerebellum: That part of the **brain** controlling fine motor coordination and body movement, posture, and balance; part of the hindbrain and attaches to the rear portion of the **brain stem**.

Cerebral cortex: The outer layer of gray matter in the cerebrum; consists mainly of neuronal **cell bodies** and **dendrites** in humans; associated with higher functions, including language and abstract thought.

Cerebrum: The part of the **forebrain** that includes the **cerebral cortex**; the largest part of the human brain.

Cervix: The lower neck of the **uterus** that opens into the **vagina**.

Channels: Transport proteins that act as gates to control the movement of sodium and potassium ions across the plasma membrane of a nerve cell.

Charophytes: Group of green algae from which the land plants evolved.

Chemical equilibrium: The condition when the forward and reverse reactions occur at equal speed and the concentrations of the products remain constant.

Chemiosmosis: The process by which **ATP** is produced in the inner membrane of a **mitochondrion**. The **electron transport system** transfers **protons** from the inner compartment to the outer; as the protons flow back to the inner compartment, the energy of their movement is used to add phosphate to **ADP**, forming **ATP**.

Chemosynthesis: Process by which certain deep ocean bacteria use energy and chemicals from the Earth's internal heat engine to produce their own carbohydrates.

Chemotrophs: Organisms (usually bacteria) that derive **energy** from inorganic reactions; also known as chemosynthesis.

Chiasma: The site where the exchange of **chromosome** segments between **homologous chromosomes** takes place (**crossing-over**) (plural: chiasmata).

Chitin: A **polysaccharide** contained in **fungi**; also forms part of the hard outer covering of insects, shrimp, crabs, and lobsters.

Chlamydia: A sexually transmitted disease caused by a **parasitic** bacterium that lives inside cells of the reproductive tract.

Chlorofluorocarbons (CFCs): Chemical substances used in refrigerators, air conditioners, and solvents that drift to the upper stratosphere and dissociate. Chlorine released by CFCs reacts with **ozone**, eroding the ozone layer.

Chlorophyll: The pigment in green plants that absorbs solar energy.

Chlorophyll *a*: The green pigment common to all **photosynthetic** organisms.

Chlorophyll *b*: An accessory chlorophyll found in green algae and plants.

Chlorophyll *c*: An accessory chlorophyll found in some **protistans**.

Chlorophyta: The plant phylum that contains what are commonly called the green algae; ancestral group to the land plants.

Chloroplasts: Disk-like **organelles** with a double membrane found in **eukaryotic** cells; contain **thylakoids** and are the site of **photosynthesis**.

Cholecystokinin: A **hormone** secreted in the **duodenum** that causes the gallbladder to release bile and the **pancreas** to secrete **lipase**.

Cholesterol: A **steroid** molecule occurring in many cell membranes.

Chorion: The two-layered structure formed from the **trophoblast** after implantation; secretes **human chorionic gonadotropin**.

Chorionic villi sampling (CVS): A method of prenatal testing in which fetal cells from the fetal side of the **placenta** (chorionic villi) are extracted and analyzed for **Chromosomal** and **biochemical** defects.

Chromatid: Generally refers to a strand of a replicated **chromosome**; consists of **DNA** and **protein**.

Chromatin: A complex of **DNA** and **protein** in **eukaryotic** cells that is dispersed throughout the **nucleus** during **interphase** and condensed into **chromosomes** during **meiosis** and **mitosis**.

Chromoplasts: plastids specialized for storing colored pigments, such as in the skin of ripe fruit or petals of a flower.

Chromosomes: Structures in the **nucleus** of a **eukaryotic** cell that consist of DNA molecules that contain the **genes**.

Chromosome theory of inheritance: Theory that states that chromosomes are the cellular components that physically contain **genes**; proposed in 1903 by Walter Sutton and Theodore Boveri.

Chrysophytes: **Protistan** phylum that is referred to as the golden brown algae.

Chytrids: Group of basal fungi that have flagella as well as some cellulose on their cell walls.

Cilia: Hair-like organelles extending from the membrane of many **eukaryotic** cells; often function in locomotion (singular: cilium).

Circadian rhythms: Biorhythms that occur on a daily cycle.

Circinate vernation: the uncoiling pattern of new leaf opening in ferns and cycads. The leaf uncoils as it grows, looking like a shepherd's crook.

Circulatory system: One of eleven major body organ systems in animals; transports oxygen, carbon dioxide, nutrients, and waste products between cells and the **respiratory system** and carries chemical signals from the **endocrine system**; consists of the blood, heart, and blood vessels.

Circulatory system, closed: A system that uses a continuous series of vessels of different sizes to deliver blood to body cells and return it to the heart; found in **echinoderms** and **vertebrates**.

Circulatory system, open: A system in which the circulating fluid is not enclosed in vessels at all times; found in insects, crayfish, some mollusks, and other invertebrates.

Citric acid cycle: Biochemical cycle in cellular aerobic metabolism where **acetyl CoA** is combined with oxaloacetate to form citric acid; the resulting citric acid is converted into a number of other chemicals, eventually reforming oxaloacetate; **NADH**, some **ATP**, and $FADH_2$ are produced and carbon dioxide is released.

Chondrocyte: Cell type that forms cartilage.

Classes: **Taxonomic** subcategories of **phyla**.

Clavicle: The collarbone.

Cleavage furrow: A constriction of the cell membrane at the equator of the cell that marks the beginning of **cytokinesis** in animal cells. The cell divides as the furrow deepens.

Climax community: The stage in **community** succession where the community has become relatively stable through successful adjustment to its environment.

Clitoris: A short shaft with a sensitive tip located where the **labia minora** meet; consists of erectile tissue and is important in female sexual arousal.

Clone: An exact copy of a **DNA** segment; produced by recombinant DNA technology.

Closed community: A **community** in which **populations** have similar range boundaries and density peaks; forms a discrete unit with sharp boundaries.

Coccus: Spherical shaped bacteria. Plural: cocci.

Codominance: A type of inheritance in which **heterozygotes** fully express both **alleles**.

Codon: A sequence of three **nucleotides** in **messenger RNA** that codes for a single **amino acid**.

Coelom: In animals, a body cavity between the body wall and the **digestive system** that forms during development.

Coelomates: Animals that have a coelom or body cavity lined with **mesoderm**.

Coenzymes: Chemicals required by a number of **enzymes** for proper functioning; also known as enzyme cofactors.

Cohesion: The force that holds molecules of the same substance together.

Cohesion-adhesion theory: Describes the properties of water that help move it through a plant. Cohesion is the ability of water molecules to stick together (held by **hydrogen bonds**), forming a column of water extending from the roots to the leaves; **adhesion** is the ability of water molecules to stick to the **cellulose** in plant cell walls, counteracting the force of gravity and helping to lift the column of water.

Collenchyma: One of the three major cell types in plants; are elongated and have thicker walls than **parenchyma** cells and are usually arranged in strands; provide support and are generally in a region that is growing.

Colonial: (1) Level of organization intermediate between **unicellular** and **multicellular** organisms are composed of multiple cells but fail to exhibit specialization of those cells. Example: *Volvox*, a colonial alga. (2) Term applied to organisms that occur in a fixed location, with one generation growing atop previous generations, as in coral reefs.

Commensalism: **Symbiotic** relationship in which one organism benefits and the other is not affected.

Community: All **species** or **populations** living in the same area.

Community age: One of the factors that helps cause the latitudinal diversity gradient.

Community simplification: The reduction of overall species diversity in a community; generally caused by human activity.

Community succession: The sequential replacement of species in a community by immigration of new species and by local **extinction** of old ones.

Compact bone: The outer dense layer that forms the shaft of the long bones; made up of concentric layers of mineral deposits surrounding a central opening.

Companion cells: Specialized cells in the **phloem** that load sugars into the **sieve elements** and help maintain a functional **plasma membrane** in the sieve elements.

Competition: One of the biological interactions that can limit population growth; occurs when two species vie with each other for the same resource.

Competitive exclusion: Competition between species that is so intense that one species completely eliminates the second species from the area.

Competitive release: Occurs when one of two competing species is removed from an area, thereby releasing the remaining species from one of the factors that limited its population size.

Complementary nucleotides: The bonding preferences of nucleotides, **Adenine** with **Thymine**, and **Cytosine** with **Guanine**. Also referred to as complementary base pairing.

Complement system: A chemical defense system that kills microorganisms directly, supplements the **inflammatory response**, and works with, or complements, the **immune system**.

Complete dominance: The type of inheritance in which both **heterozygotes** and dominant **homozygotes** have the same **phenotype**.

Complete flower: Condition in which all flower parts are present. Example: lily.

Compound: A substance formed by two or more chemical **elements** combined in a fixed ratio.

Compound leaf: A leaf in which the blade forms small leaflets. Compound leaves that have several small leaflets originating from a central axis are termed pinnately compound; example: rose. Compound leaves that have their leaflets originating from a common point are termed palmately compound; example: palm.

Compression: Type of fossilization in which the fossil is flattened (compressed) by the weight of overlying sediment.

Condensation reaction: Type of reaction where a covalent bond forms between two monomers by the removal of a hydroxyl (OH) from one monomer and removal of one hydrogen (H) from the other.

Conditioned response: The response to a stimulus that occurs when an animal has learned to associate the **stimulus** with a certain positive or negative effect.

Cones: (1) Light receptors in primates' eyes that operate in bright light; provide color vision and visual acuity; (2) In seed plants, a hardened **strobilus** containing many **sporophylls**.

Conifers: Group of **gymnosperms** that reproduce by cones and have needle-like leaves (in general); includes the pines.

Conjugation: (1) The connection through a sex pilus of two bacteria to exchange all or part of their DNA; (2) Process by which certain eukaryotes exchange genetic material, such as when two *Spirogyra* filaments form a conjugation tube between every cell in each filament and the cytoplasm from one cell passes through the tube onto the corresponding cell in the other filament.

Connective tissue: Animal tissue composed of cells embedded in a matrix (gel, elastic fibers, liquid, or inorganic minerals). Includes loose, dense, and fibrous connective tissues that provide strength (bone, cartilage), storage (bone, adipose), and flexibility (tendons, ligaments).

Consumers: The higher levels in a **food pyramid**; consist of primary consumers, which feed on the **producers**, and secondary consumers, which feed on the primary consumers.

Continuous variation: Occurs when the **phenotypes** of traits controlled by a single **gene** cannot be sorted into two distinct phenotypic classes, but rather fall into a series of overlapping classes.

Contractile vacuole: Organelle in many eukaryotes that acts as a pump that carries out **active transport** of excess water from the cell.

Contrast: In relation to microscopes, the ability to distinguish different densities of structures.

Convergent evolution: The development of similar structures in distantly related organisms as a result of **adapting** to similar environments and/or strategies of life. Example: wings of birds and insects, the body shape of dolphins, sharks, and the extinct marine reptiles known as ichthyosaurs.

Convergent plate boundary: The boundary between two tectonic crustal plates moving toward one another.

Coprolites: Fossilized feces.

Coral: Group of reef-building cnidarians that extract calcium carbonate from seawater and use it to build the animal body.

Cork: The outer layer of the bark in woody plants; composed of dead cells.

Cork cambium: A layer of lateral **meristematic tissue** between the **cork** and the **phloem** in the bark of woody plants.

Corolla: Term applied when referring to all of the **petals** of a flower.

Coronary arteries: **Arteries** that supply the heart's muscle fibers with nutrients and oxygen.

Corpus callosum: Tightly bundled nerve fibers that connect the right and left hemispheres of the **cerebrum**.

Corpus luteum: A structure formed from the ovulated **follicle** in the **ovary**; secretes **progesterone** and **estrogen**.

Cortex: (1) The outer part of an organ, for example, the adrenal cortex, which produces several **steroid hormones**; (2) in plants, the region of the stem or root between the **epidermis** and the **vascular bundle(s)**.

Cortisol: The primary **glucocorticoid hormone**; released by the adrenal cortex.

Cotyledon: A leaf-like structure that is present in the seeds of **flowering plants**; appears during seed germination and sometimes is referred to as a seed leaf.

Countercurrent flow: An arrangement by which fish obtain oxygen from the water that flows through their gills. Water flows across the **respiratory surface** of the gill in one direction while blood flows in the other direction through the blood vessels on the other side of the surface.

Courtship behavior: Behavioral sequences that precede mating.

Covalent bond: A chemical bond created by the sharing of **electrons** between atoms.

Craniates: Group of bilateral animals that have a definite head and brain.

Cranium: The braincase; composed of several bones fitted together at immovable joints.

Crenation: Condition where and animal cell loses so much water that it assumes a spiky appearance.

Cretaceous period: The geologic period between the Jurassic Period (140 million years ago) and the Tertiary/Paleogene period (beginning 65 million years ago).

Cristae: Structures formed by the folding of the inner membrane of a **mitochondrion** (singular: crista).

Critical wavelength: Wavelength of energy necessary to cause a metal to emit a stream of electrons.

Crossing-over: During the first meiotic **prophase**, the process in which part of a **chromatid** is physically exchanged with another chromatid to form **chromosomes** with new **allele** combinations.

Crossopterygians: A type of lobe-finned fish with lungs (as well as gills) that was ancestral to **amphibians**.

Crustaceans: A large **taxonomic** class of **arthropods** that includes lobsters, shrimps, and crabs.

Cuticle: A layer composed of wax and **cutin** that occurs on the external surface of plant stems and leaves that helps to prevent water loss.

Cyanobacteria: Blue-green bacteria; **unicellular** or filamentous chains of cells that carry out **photosynthesis**.

Cycadeoids: A group of **gymnosperm** seed plants not closely related to, but superficially resembling, the cycads.

Cycads: Group of **gymnosperm** seed plants that have large fern-like leaves and reproduce by cones but not flowers.

Cycle: A recurring sequence of events; for example, the secretion of certain **hormones** at regular intervals.

Cyclin: A **protein** found in the dividing cells of many organisms that acts as a control during cell division.

Cystic fibrosis: An **autosomal recessive** human genetic disorder that causes the production of **mucus** that clogs the airways of the lungs and the ducts of the **pancreas** and other secretory glands.

Cytokinesis: The division of the **cytoplasm** during cell division.

Cytokinins: A group of **hormones** that promote cell division and inhibit aging of green tissues in plants.

Cytology: Branch of biology dealing with cell structure.

Cytoplasm: The viscous semiliquid inside the plasma membrane of a cell; contains various **macromolecules** and **organelles** in solution and suspension.

Cytoplasmic streaming: movement of organelles within a cell along paths determined by the cell's **cytoskeleton**. Examples include chloroplast movement in Elodea and organelle movement in *Amoeba* and *Paramecium*.

Cytosine: One of the **pyrimidine** nitrogenous bases occurring in both **DNA** and **RNA**.

Cytoskeleton: A three-dimensional network of **microtubules** and **filaments** that provides internal support for the cells, anchors internal cell structures, and functions in cell movement and division.

Cytoxic T cells: **T cells** that destroy body cells infected by **viruses** or bacteria; also attack bacteria, fungi, **parasites**, and cancer cells and will kill cells of transplanted organs if they are recognized as foreign; also known as killer T cells.

D

Dark reactions: The **photosynthetic** process in which food (sugar) molecules form from carbon dioxide from the environment with the use of ATP; can occur in the dark as long as ATP is present.

Death rate: The ratio between deaths and individuals in a specified population at a particular time.

Decay series: Most **radioisotopes** do not decay into a stable daughter element in one single decay, but rather through a series of radioactive intermediaries.

Deciduous: Term applied to plants that lose the leaves and have a dormancy period at least once per year.

Decomposers: Term applied to fungi and bacteria that recycle nutrients in the ecosystems.

Deletion: The loss of a **chromosome** segment without altering the number of chromosomes.

Dendrite: Short, highly branched fibers that carry signals toward the **cell body** of a **neuron.**

Dendrochronology: The process of determining the age of a tree or wood used in structures by counting the number of annual **growth rings.**

Deoxyribonucleic acid (DNA): A **nucleic acid** composed of two **polynucleotide** strands wound around a central axis to form a double helix; the repository of genetic information.

Deoxyribose: Five-carbon sugar found in **nucleotides** of **DNA.**

Depth diversity gradient: The increase in species richness with increasing water depth until about 2,000 meters below the surface, where species richness begins to decline.

Depth of field: A measure of the amount of a specimen that can be in focus.

Dermal system: Tissue system that provides covering for the plant.

Dermis: One of the two layers of skin; a **connective tissue** layer under the **epidermis** containing elastic and collagen fibers, capillary networks, and nerve endings.

Desert biome: Characterized by dry conditions and plants and animals that have **adapted** to those conditions; found in areas where local or global influences drastically lower rainfall.

Desmosome: A circular region of membrane cemented to an adjacent membrane by a molecular glue made of **polysaccharides**; found in tissues that undergo stretching.

Deuterostomes: Animals in which the first opening that appears in the **embryo** becomes the **anus** while the mouth appears at the other end of the **digestive system.** Main groups include chordates and echinoderms.

Devonian period: Unit of geologic time between 419 and 359 million years before the present. Life on land diversified, with the amphibians appearing late in this period. Plants underwent major changes, including the development of forests and seeds. In the water, fish diversified into all modern groups as well as numerous now-extinct forms.

Diabetes mellitus, Types I and II: Disorder associated with defects in insulin action. Type I diabetes is characterized by inadequate insulin secretion; Type II diabetes is characterized by impaired insulin secretion in response to elevated blood **glucose** levels or by loss of sensitivity to insulin by **target cells.**

Diaphragm: A dome-shaped muscle that separates the **thoracic** and abdominal cavities.

Diastole: The filling of the **ventricle** of the heart with blood.

Diatom: Unicellular, autotrophic eukaryans that secrete a silicon dioxide (SiO_2) **frustule** around their cells.

Diatomaceous earth: Fossilized deposits of **diatoms**; used for abrasives, polishes, and as a filtering agent.

Dictyosomes: **Organelles** in plant cells composed of a series of flattened membrane sacs that sort, chemically modify, and package **proteins** produced on the **rough endoplasmic reticulum**. Also known as the **Golgi Apparatus**.

Diencephalon: Part of the **forebrain**; consists of the **thalamus** and **hypothalamus**.

Diffusion: The movement of material from an area of higher concentration to an area of lower concentration.

Digestion: The process of breaking down food into its molecular and chemical components so that these nutrient molecules can cross **plasma membranes**.

Digestive system: One of eleven major body organ systems in animals; converts food from the external environment into nutrient molecules that can be used and stored by the body and eliminates solid wastes; involves five functions: movement, secretion, digestion, absorption, and elimination.

Dihybrid cross: In genetics, a cross that tracks two sets of characteristics.

Dinoflagellates: Single-celled to colonial basal eukaryans characterized by two **flagella**, one girdling the cell and the other trailing the cell. Some dinoflagellates occur in such high numbers that the water is colored red, a phenomenon known as a **red tide**.

Dinosaurs: Any of the **Mesozoic** diapsids (once considered to be reptiles) belonging to the groups designated as ornithischians and saurischians.

Dioecious: Term applied to plants having separate male and female plants.

Diploid: Cells that contain homologous chromosomes. The number of chromosomes in the cells is the diploid number ($2n$).

Diploblasts: Clade of animals with tissues that only develop the two embryonic tissue layers the **endoderm** and the **ectoderm**.

Diplomonads: Flagellated eukaryans that can sometimes cause human diseases.

Directional selection: A form of **natural selection** that tends to favor **phenotypes** at one extreme of the character range.

Disaccharides: Sugars made up of two **monosaccharides** held together by a **covalent bond**; such as sucrose and lactose.

Discontinuous variation: Occurs when the **phenotypes** of traits controlled by a single gene can be sorted into two distinct phenotypic classes.

Disruptive selection: A form of **natural selection** that favors individuals at both extremes of a phenotypic range.

Dissociate: The tendency of larger molecules to break apart into smaller molecules.

Distal tubule: The section of the **renal tubule** where **tubular secretion** occurs.

Divergent evolution: The divergence of a single interbreeding **population** or **species** into two or more descendant species.

Divergent plate boundary: The boundary between two tectonic plates that are moving in opposite directions.

Diversity: The different types of **organisms** that occur in a **community**.

DNA hybridization: The formation of hybrid DNA molecules that contain a strand of DNA from two different species. The number of complementary sequences in common in the two strands is an indication of the degree of relatedness of the species.

DNA ligase: In recombinant DNA technology, an **enzyme** that seals together two DNA fragments from different sources to form a recombinant DNA molecule.

DNA polymerase: In DNA replication, the **enzyme** that links the complementary nucleotides together to form the newly synthesized strand.

Dominance: The property of one of a pair of **alleles** that suppresses the expression of the other member of the pair in **heterozygotes**.

Dominance hierarchy: A social structure among a group of animals in which one is dominant and the others have subordinate nonbreeding positions.

Dominant: Refers to an **allele** expressed in **heterozygotes**.

Double fertilization: A characteristic of **angiosperms** in which a **pollen tube** carries two sperm cells to the female **gametophyte** in the **ovule**. One sperm cell fuses with the egg cell and gives rise to a **diploid embryo**. The other sperm cell fuses with the two polar cells to form a triploid cell that develops into the **endosperm**.

Duodenum: The upper part of the **small intestine**.

Duplication: An extra copy of a **chromosome** segment or gene.

Dystrophin: **Protein** making up only 0.002% of all protein in **skeletal muscle** but which appears vital for proper functioning of the muscle. Sufferers of muscular dystrophy appear to lack dystrophin.

E

Eccrine glands: Sweat glands that are linked to the **sympathetic nervous system** and are widely distributed over the body surface.

Echinoderm: Phylum of **deuterostomes** characterized by five-parted (pentamerous) symmetry. Includes starfish, sea urchins, and sand dollars.

Ecological niche: The role an organism occupies and the function it performs in an **ecosystem**; closely associated with feeding.

Ecological time: A timescale that focuses on **community** events that occur on the order of tens to hundreds of years.

Ecology: The study of how **organisms** interact with each other and their physical environment.

Ecosystem: The **community** living in an area and its physical environment.

Ecotones: Well-defined boundaries often seen in **closed communities**.

Ecotype: A subdivision of a **species**; a stage in the formation of a species such that **reproductive isolation** has occurred.

Ectoderm: The outer layer of cells in embryonic development; gives rise to the skin, brain, and **nervous system**.

Ectotherms: Animals with a variable body temperature that is determined by the environment. Examples: fish, frogs, and reptiles.

Effector: In a closed system, the initiator of an action in response to a signal from a **sensor**. In human systems, a muscle or gland often serves as an effector.

Ejaculatory duct: In males, a short duct that connects the **vas deferens** from each **testis** to the **urethra**.

Electron: A subatomic particle with a negative charge. Electrons circle the atom's **nucleus** in regions of space known as **orbitals**.

Electron acceptor: A molecule that forms part of the electron transport system that transfers electrons ejected by **chlorophyll** during **photosynthesis**. Part of the energy carried by the electrons is transferred to **ATP**, part is transferred to NADPH, and part is lost in the transfer system.

Electron transport: A series of coupled **oxidation/reduction** reactions where electrons pass from one membrane-bound protein/enzyme to another before being finally attached to a terminal electron acceptor (usually oxygen or NADPH). **ATP** forms by this process.

Electrostatic attraction: The force between atoms of opposite charge that holds the atoms together in **ionic bonds**.

Element: A substance composed of atoms with the same **atomic number**; cannot be broken down in ordinary chemical reactions.

Elongation: During **protein synthesis**, the growth of the polypeptide chain through the addition of **amino acids**; the second step in **translation**.

Embryo: Term applied to the **zygote** after the beginning of **mitosis** that produces a multicellular structure.

Embryo sac: Alternate term applied to the **angiosperm** female **gametophyte** contained within a **megaspore**.

Emphysema: Lung disease characterized by shortness of breath, often associated with smoking.

Endemic: Term applied to an organism that occurs only in one island or small geographic area.

Endergonic: Chemical reactions that require energy input to begin.

Endochondral ossification: The process by which human bones form from cartilage.

Endocrine system: One of eleven major body organ systems in animals; a system of glands that works with the **nervous system** in controlling the activity of internal organs, especially the **kidneys**, and in coordinating the long-term response to external stimuli.

Endocytosis: The incorporation of materials from outside the cell by the formation of vesicles in the **plasma membrane**. The vesicles surround the material so the cell can engulf it.

Endoderm: The inner layer of cells in embryonic development that gives rise to organs and tissues associated with digestion and respiration.

Endodermis: A layer of cells surrounding the vascular cylinder of plants.

Endometrium: The inner lining of the **uterus**.

Endoplasmic reticulum (ER): A network of membranous tubules in the cytoplasm of a cell; involved in the production of a number of molecules. Rough ER is studded with ribosomes; smooth ER is not.

Endoskeleton: An internal supporting skeleton with muscles on the outside; in vertebrates, consists of the skull, spinal column, ribs, and appendages.

Endosperm: A food storage tissue that provides nutrients to the developing **embryo** in **angiosperms**; formed from the triploid cell produced when a sperm cell fertilizes the central cell.

Endospores: Spores produced within the cytoplasm of certain spore-forming bacteria.

Endosymbiosis: Theory that attempts to explain the origin of the DNA-containing **mitochondria** and **chloroplasts** in early **eukaryotes** by the engulfing of various types of bacteria that were not digested but became permanent additions to the ancestral "eukaryote."

Endothermic: A reaction that gives off energy. The product is in a lower energy state than the reactants.

Endotherms: Animals that have the ability to maintain a constant body temperature over a wide range of environmental conditions.

Endothermy: The internal control of body temperature; the ability to generate and maintain internal body heat; often termed warm-blooded.

Energy: The ability to bring about change or to do work.

Energy flow: The movement of energy through a **community** via feeding relationships.

Energy of activation: The minimum amount of **energy** required for a given reaction to occur; varies from reaction to reaction.

Entropy: The degree of disorder in a system. As energy is transferred from one form to another, some is lost as heat; as the energy decreases, the disorder in the system, and thus the entropy, increases.

Enzymes: Protein molecules that act as catalysts in biochemical reactions.

Eon: The longest duration unit of geological time.

Epidermis: (1) The outermost layer of skin consisting of several layers of **epithelial** cells; notably **keratinocytes** and, in the inner layer of the epidermis, basal cells and **melanocytes**; (2) The outer layer of cells in the plant body, often covered by a waxy **cuticle**.

Epididymis: A long, convoluted duct on the **testis** where sperm are stored prior to ejaculation or reabsorption.

Epiglottis: A flap of tissue that closes off the **trachea** during swallowing.

Epinephrine: A **hormone** produced by the adrenal medulla and secreted under stress; contributes to the "fight or flight" response.

Epiphyte: Term applied to a plant that grows on another plant, like the staghorn fern that grows on trees.

Epistasis: The masking of the effects of one gene by the action of another, example: widow's peak masked by the baldness gene.

Epithelial tissue: Cells in animals that are closely packed in either single or multiple layers, and which cover both internal and external surfaces of the animal body. Also referred to as epithelium.

Epoch: Subdivision of a geological period.

Eras: One of the major divisions of the geologic time scale.

Erythrocytes: Red blood cells; doubly concave, enucleated cells that transport oxygen in the blood.

Esophagus: The muscular tube extending between and connecting the **pharynx** to the stomach.

Estrogen: A female sex **hormone** that performs many important functions in reproduction.

Ethylene: A gaseous plant **hormone** that stimulates fruit ripening and the dropping of leaves.

Eudicots: One of the two main types of flowering plants; characterized by having two **cotyledons**, floral organs arranged in cycles of four or five, and leaves with reticulate veins; include trees (except conifers) and most ornamental and some crop plants.

Euglenoids: Phylum of **protozoans** that have one long **flagellum** and a short one, no cell wall, and which may have **chloroplasts**.

Eukarya: Taxonomic domain containing all eukaryotic organisms.

Eukaryote: A type of cell found in many organisms including single-celled protists and multicellular fungi, plants, and animals; characterized by a membrane-bounded **nucleus** and other membranous organelles; an organism composed of such cells.

Euphotic zone: The upper part of the marine **biome** where light penetrates and **photosynthesis** occurs; usually extends to about 200 meters below the water surface.

Eutrophication: "Runaway" growth of aquatic plants that occurs when agricultural fertilizers containing phosphorus and nitrogen run off into lakes and ponds; also ultimately increases the plant death rate with the result that the bacterial decomposition of the dead plants uses up oxygen, causing fish and other organisms to suffocate.

Evaporation: The part of the hydrologic cycle in which liquid water is converted to vapor and enters the atmosphere.

Evolution: (1) The change in life over time by **adaptation**, variation, over-reproduction, and differential survival/reproduction, a process referred to by Charles Darwin and Alfred Wallace as **natural selection**. (2) Descent with modification.

Evolutionary tree: A diagram showing the evolutionary history of organisms based on differences in amino acid sequences. Organisms with fewer differences are placed closer together while those with more differences are further apart.

Excretion: The process of removing the waste products of cellular **metabolism** from the body.

Excretory system: One of eleven major body systems in animals; regulates the volume and molecular and ionic constitution of internal body fluids and eliminates metabolic waste products from the internal environment.

Exergonic reaction: Chemical reaction that releases energy stored in the reactants.

Exine: Outer covering of **pollen grains**, often containing **sporopollenin**, an acid-resistant **polysaccharide** that allows pollen grains to become **fossils**.

Exocytosis: The process in which a membrane-enclosed **vesicle** first fuses with the **plasma membrane** and then releases its contents to the outside of the cell.

Exon: The **DNA** bases that code for an **amino acid sequence**. Exons are separated by **introns** that code for no amino acid sequences.

Exoskeleton: A hard, jointed, external covering that encloses the muscles and organs of an organism; typical of many **arthropods** including insects.

Exothermic: A reaction where the product is at a higher energy level than the reactants.

Exponential rate: An extremely rapid increase, for example, in the rate of population growth.

Expression: The **phenotypic** manifestation of a trait. Expression may be age-dependent (e.g., Huntington disease) or affected by environmental factors (e.g., dark fur on Siamese cats).

Extinction: The elimination of all individuals in a group, both by natural (dinosaurs, trilobites) or human-induced (dodo, passenger pigeon) means.

Extracellular digestion: A form of **digestion** found in annelids, crustaceans, and chordates including **vertebrates**; takes place within the lumen of the **digestive system**, and the resulting nutrient molecules are transferred into the blood or body fluid.

Extracellular route: Path taken by water through the root in which water moves through the spaces between cell walls of the **parenchyma** in the **cortex**.

Eyespot: (1) A pigmented photoreceptor in euglenoids and other basal eukaryans. The eyespot senses light and orients the cell for maximum rates of **photosynthesis**; (2) Term applied to a photosensitive area in starfish.

F

Facilitated diffusion: Process by which large molecule such as glucose passes the cell membrane via a channel protein through the membrane.

Facultative anaerobes: Anaerobic organisms that can tolerate the presence of oxygen.

Families: (1) In **taxonomy**, term applied to subcategories within orders. (2) Term applied to a group of similar things, such as languages, **chromosomes**, and so on.

Fats: Solid **triglycerides** at room temperature.

Fauna: Term referring collectively to all animals in an area.

Feces: Semisolid material containing undigested foods, bacteria, bilirubin, and water that is produced in the large intestine and eliminated from the body.

Fsemur: The upper leg bone in **tetrapods**.

Fermentation: The breakdown of **glucose** into either alcohol or lactic acid in the absence of oxygen following **glycolysis**.

Fertilization: The fusion of two **gametes** to produce a **zygote** that develops into a new individual. Strictly speaking, fertilization can be divided into the fusion of the cells (**plasmogamy**) and the fusion of **nuclei (karyogamy)**.

Fibroblast: A term applied to a cell of animals **connective tissue** separated from similar cells by some degree of matrix material; fibroblasts secrete elastin and collagen protein fibers.

Fibrous root: A root system found in **monocots** where branches develop from the **adventitious roots**, forming a system in which all roots are about the same size and length.

Filaments: Slender, thread-like stalks that make up the **stamens** of a flower; filaments are topped by the **anthers**.

Filter feeders: Organisms such as sponges that feed by removing food from water that filters through their body.

Filtration: The removal of water and solutes from blood; occurs in the **glomerulus** of the **nephron**.

First law of thermodynamics (conservation): **Energy** is neither created nor destroyed, but rather changes from one form to another.

Fitness: A measure of an individual's ability to survive and reproduce.

Flagella: long, whip-like locomotion organelles found in both **prokaryotic** and **eukaryotic** cells; singular: flagellum.

Flame cell: A specialized cell at the blind end of a **nephridium** that filters fluids.

Flora: Term collectively applied to all of the plants in an area.

Floridean starch: **Carbohydrate** storage product in the **red algae**, a **polysaccharide** resembling **glycogen** in structure.

Flowers: The reproductive structures in **angiosperm sporophytes** where **spores** that will produce the **gametophytes** form.

Fluid feeders: Animals such as aphids, ticks, and mosquitoes that pierce the body of a host plant or animal and obtain food from ingesting fluids produced by that organism.

Fluid-mosaic: Widely accepted model of the **plasma membrane** in which proteins are embedded in **lipids**.

Fluorescence: the phenomenon where a pigment that has absorbed energy emits light, for example **chlorophyll**.

Follicles (ovary): Structures in the **ovary** consisting of a developing egg surrounded by a layer of follicle cells.

Follicles (thyroid): Spherical structures that make up the **thyroid gland**.

Follicle-stimulating hormone (FSH): A **hormone** secreted by the anterior **pituitary** that promotes **gamete** formation in both males and females.

Fontanels: Membranous areas in the human cranial bones that do not form bony structures until the child is between 14 and 18 months old; know as "soft spots."

Food chain: The simplest representation of energy flow within a **community**.

Food pyramid: A way of depicting energy flow within an **ecosystem**; shows **producers** on the first level and **consumers** on the higher levels of the pyramid.

Food web: A complex network of feeding interrelations among species in a natural **ecosystem**; a more accurate and more complex depiction of energy flow than in a food chain.

Foraminifera: Single-celled **eukaryans** that secrete a shell or test. Accumulations of the shells of dead foraminifera and other microscopic sea-creatures form chalk deposits.

Forebrain: The part of the brain that consists of the diencephalon and **cerebrum**.

Fossil: (1) The remains or traces of prehistoric life preserved in rocks of the Earth's crust. (2) Any evidence of past life.

Fossil fuels: Deposits formed in the Earth from plant or animal remains, extracted and burned to generate energy; for example, coal, petroleum, and natural gas.

Fossil record: The observed remains of once-living organisms taken as a whole.

Founder effect: The difference in **gene pools** between an original **population** and a new population founded by one or a few individuals randomly separated from the original population, as when an island population is founded by one or a few individuals; often accentuates **genetic drift**.

Fovea: The area of the eye in which the **cones** are concentrated.

Freshwater biome: The aquatic **biome** consisting of water containing fewer salts than the waters in the **marine biome**; divided into two zones: running waters (rivers, streams) and standing waters (lakes, ponds).

Frontal lobe: The lobe of the **cerebral cortex** responsible for motor activity, speech, and thought processes.

Fruit: A ripened **ovary** wall produced from a flower.

Frustule: The silicon dioxide (glass) covering secreted by a **diatom**.

Fucoxanthin: Brown **accessory pigment** found in and characteristic of the **brown algae**.

Fungi: Nonmobile, absorptive **heterotrophic**, mostly multicellular **eukaryotes**, including yeasts and mushrooms. Fungi form the middle kingdom of the advanced eukaryan taxa.

Fusulinids: Group of extremely large single-celled **foraminifera** that went extinct by the close of the **Permian period**.

G

Gaia: A hypothesized superorganism composed of the Earth's four spheres: the **biosphere**, **hydrosphere**, **lithosphere**, and **atmosphere**.

Gametes: **Haploid** reproductive cells that recombine during **fertilization**.

Gametophyte: The **haploid** stage of an organism exhibiting **alternation of generations**, produces gametes by the process of **mitosis**.

Ganglia: Clusters of **neurons** that receive and process signals.

Gap junctions: Junctions between the **plasma membranes** of animal cells that allow communication and chemical transfer between the **cytoplasm** of adjacent cells.

Gastric pits: The folds and grooves into which the stomach lining is arranged.

Gastrin: **Hormone** produced by the pyloric area of the stomach that stimulates stomach acid secretion.

Gastroesophageal sphincter: Ring of muscle at the junction of the **esophagus** and the stomach that remains closed except during swallowing to prevent the stomach contents from entering the esophagus.

Gastrovascular cavity: The common cavity inside a cnidarian where the functions of digestion and circulation simultaneously occur.

Gene pool: The sum of all the genetic information carried by members of a **population**.

Gel electrophoresis: Technique used to separate a variety of organic **macromolecules** by passing an electrical charge through a gel.

Gemma: Vegetative reproduction structure found in **liverworts**; plural: gemmae.

Genes: Specific segments of **DNA** that control cell structure and function; the functional units of inheritance. Sequence of DNA bases usually code for a **polypeptide** sequence of **amino acids**.

Gene therapy: The insertion of normal or genetically altered **genes** into cells through the use of **recombinant DNA technology**; usually done as part of the treatment of genetic disorders.

Genetically modified organisms (GMOs): Organisms in which **biotechnology** has been employed to add genes from a different **species**. Example, the BT Potato.

Genera: Taxonomic subcategories within families (singular: genus), composed of one or more **species**.

Genetic code: The series of DNA **nucleotides**, read as triplets, that dictates the sequence of **amino acids** in **proteins**. Each triplet specifies a certain amino acid, and the same codons are used for the same amino acids in most life-forms, an indication of the universal nature of the code.

Genetic divergence: The separation of a **gene pool** from the gene pools of other **populations** due to **mutation**, **genetic drift**, and natural selection. Continued divergence may lead to **speciation**.

Genetic drift: Random changes in the frequency of **alleles** from generation to generation; especially in small **populations**, can lead to the elimination of a particular allele by chance alone.

Genetic maps: Diagrams showing the order of and distance between **genes**.

Genetics: The study of the structure and function of genes and the transmission of **genes** from parents to offspring.

Genital herpes: A sexually transmitted disease caused by the herpes **virus**; results in sores on the mucus membranes of the mouth or genitals.

Genome: **Genes** shared by individuals of a **population** or **species**.

Genotype: The **alleles** of an organism with regard to a given trait.

Geographic isolation: Separation of populations by geographic means (distance, mountains, rivers, oceans, etc.) leading to reproductive isolation of those populations.

Geographic range: The total area occupied by a **population**.

Geologic time: The span of time that has passed since the formation of the Earth and its physical structures; a timescale that focuses on events on the order of thousands of years or more.

Geotropism/gravitropism: A plant's response to gravity: roots grow downward, showing positive geotropism, while shoots grow upward in a negative response.

Germ cells: Collective term for cells in the reproductive organs of multicellular organisms that divide by **meiosis** to produce **gametes**.

Gestation: Period of time between **fertilization** and birth of an animal. Commonly called pregnancy.

Giardiasis: Disease caused by the **diplomonad *Giardia lamblia***.

Gibberellins: A group of plant hormones that stimulate cell division and elongation. Gibberellic acid (GA), the first of this class to be discovered, causes bolting (extreme elongation) of stems. GA is also applied to certain plants to promote larger fruits and seedless fruit varieties.

Gills: Gas exchange structures found in many aquatic animals such as fish, and **arthropods**.

Gill slits: Opening or clefts between the gill arches in fish. Water taken in by the mouth passes through the gill slits and bathes the gills.

Ginkgoes: Group of seed plants today restricted to a single genus and species (*Ginkgo biloba*); ginkgoes were more diverse during the **Mesozoic era**.

Glial cells: Nonconducting cells that serve as support cells in the **nervous system** and help to protect **neurons**.

Glomeromycete: Member of the phylum Glomeromycota, a type of **fungus** often in a **mutualistic** association with plant roots.

Glomerospore: Type of reproductive spore produced by a **glomeromycete fungus**.

Glomerulus: A tangle of **capillaries** that makes up part of the **nephron**; the site of **filtration**.

Glucagon: A **hormone** released by the **pancreas** that stimulates the breakdown of **glycogen** and the release of **glucose**, thereby increasing blood levels of glucose. Glucagon and **insulin** work together to maintain blood sugar levels.

Glucocorticoids: A group of **steroid hormones** produced by the adrenal cortex that are important in regulating the metabolism of **carbohydrates**, fats, and **proteins**.

Glucose: A six-carbon sugar; the most common **energy** source.

Glycogen: **Polysaccharide** consisting of numerous **glucose** molecules linked together. The animal equivalent of starch.

Glycolipids: **Polysaccharides** formed by sugars linked to **lipids**, a part of the **plasma membrane**.

Glycolysis: The universal cellular metabolic process in the cell's **cytoplasm** where 6-carbon **glucose** is split into two 3-carbon **pyruvate** molecules, and some **ATP** and **NADH** are produced.

Glycoproteins: **Polysaccharides** formed from sugars linked to **proteins**. On the outer surface of a membrane, they act as receptors for molecular signals originating outside the cell.

Gnathostome: Term for all animals with jaws.

Gnetales: Group of seed plants restricted to three genera today (*Gnetum*, *Ephedra*, and *Welwitschia*); the possible sister group for flowering plants.

Golden brown algae: Common name applied to the phylum **Chrysophyta**.

Golgi complex: Organelles in animal cells composed of a series of flattened sacs that sort, chemically modify, and package proteins produced on the rough **endoplasmic reticulum**.

Gonadotropin-releasing hormone (GnRH): A **hormone** produced by the **hypothalamus** that controls the secretion of **luteinizing hormone**.

Gonadotropins: **Hormones** produced by the anterior **pituitary** that affect the **testis** and **ovary**; include **follicle-stimulating hormone** and **luteinizing hormone**.

Gonads: The male and female sex organs.

Gondwana: Name of the ancient (Paleozoic-early Mesozoic) southern hemisphere supercontinent that rifted apart to form present-day Antarctica, India, Africa, Australia, and South America. The southern part of **Pangaea**.

Gonorrhea: A sexually transmitted disease that is caused by a bacterium that inflames and damages **epithelial cells** of the **reproductive system**.

Grana: A series of stacked **thylakoid** disks containing **chlorophyll**; found in the inner membrane of **chloroplasts**.

Grassland biome: Occurs in temperate and tropical regions with reduced rainfall or prolonged dry seasons; characterized by deep, rich soil, an absence of trees, and large herds of grazing animals.

Green algae: Common name for algae placed in the phylum **Chlorophyta**.

Greenhouse effect: The heating that occurs when gases such as carbon dioxide trap heat escaping from the Earth and radiate it back to the surface; so-called because the gases are transparent to sunlight but not to heat and thus act like the glass in a greenhouse.

Ground system: Plant tissue system, composed mainly of **parenchyma** cells with some **collenchyma** and **sclerenchyma** cells, that occupies the space between the **epidermis** and the **vascular system**; is involved in **photosynthesis**, water and food storage, and support; one of the four main tissue systems in plants.

Growth hormone (GH): A peptide **hormone** produced by the anterior **pituitary** that is essential for growth.

Growth rings: Features of woody stems produced by plants growing in areas with seasonal (as opposed to year-long) growth. The growth ring marks the position of the **vascular cambium** at the cessation of the previous year's growth.

Guanine: One of the nitrogenous bases in **nucleic acids**, guanine is one of the two **purine** bases.

Guard cells: Specialized **epidermal** cells that flank **stomates** and whose opening and closing regulates gas exchange and water loss for plants.

Gymnosperms: Flowerless, seed plants; extant groups include the pines, ginkgoes, gnetales, and cycads.

Gynoecium: Collective term for all of the **carpels** (or **pistils**) in a flower. Some flowers have many pistils that are partially or wholly fused.

H

Habitat disruption: A disturbance of the physical environment in which a population lives.

Hair bulb: The base of a hair; contains cells that divide mitotically to produce columns of hair cells.

Hair root: The portion of a hair that extends from the skin's surface to the hair bulb.

Hair shaft: The portion of a hair that extends above the skin's surface.

Half-life: The time required for one-half of an original unstable radioactive element to be converted to a more stable daughter element.

Halophiles: A group of archaeans capable of tolerating high salt concentrations.

Haploid: Cells that contain only one member of each **homologous** pair of **chromosomes** (haploid number = n). At **fertilization**, two haploid **gametes** fuse to form a single cell with a **diploid** number of **chromosomes**.

Hardwoods: Term applied to eudicot trees, as opposed to softwoods, a term applied to gymnosperms.

Haversian canal: The central opening of **compact bone**; contains nerves and blood vessels.

Heart: The multicellular, chambered, muscular structure that pumps blood through the **circulatory system** by alternately contracting and relaxing.

Heartwood: Inner rings of **xylem** that have become clogged with metabolic by-products and no longer transport water; visible as the inner darker areas in the cross section of a tree trunk.

Helper T cells: A type of **lymphocyte** that stimulates the production of **antibodies** by activating **B cells** when an **antigen** is present.

Hemizygous: Having one or more genes that have no **allele** counterparts. Usually applied to genes on the male's **X-chromosome** (in humans).

Hemocoel: Term for the body cavity in animals with open circulatory systems in which hemolymph surrounds the animal's cells in this system.

Hemoglobin: A red pigment in red blood cells that can bind with oxygen and is largely responsible for the blood's oxygen-carrying capacity. Hemoglobin is composed of four **polypeptide** chains, two alpha and two beta chains.

Hemolymph: The circulatory fluid in **arthropods** and **molluscs** with **open circulatory systems**, analogous to blood in a **closed circulatory system**.

Hemophilia: A human **sex-linked recessive** genetic disorder resulting in the absence of certain blood-clotting factors, usually Factor VIII. Hemophiliacs suffer from an inability to clot their blood.

Hepatitis B: A potentially serious **viral** disease that affects the liver; can be transmitted through sexual contact or through contact with infected blood.

Herbaceous: Term applied to a nonwoody stem/plant with minimal **secondary growth**.

Herbivores: Term pertaining to a **heterotroph**, usually an animal, that eats plants or algae. Herbivores function in **food chains** and **food webs** as primary **consumers**.

Hermaphrodite: Term applied to an animal with both sets of sex organs functioning.

Heterogametic sex: The gender with two different **sex chromosomes**, such as males in humans and *Drosophila*.

Heterospory: Term applied to a plant that produces two sizes of spores: large **megaspores** that germinate to produce the female **gametophyte**; small **microspores** that germinate to produce the male **gametophyte**.

Heterotrophic: Refers to organisms, such as animals, that depend on preformed organic molecules from the environment (or another organism) as a source of nutrients/energy.

Heterotrophs: Organisms that obtain their nutrition by breaking down organic molecules in foods; include animals and fungi.

Heterozygous: Having two different **alleles** of a gene.

Histamine: A chemical released during the **inflammatory response** that increases **capillary** blood flow in the affected area, causing heat and redness.

Histone proteins: **Proteins** associated with **DNA** in **eukaryote chromosomes**.

Homeobox genes: Pattern **genes** that establish the body plan and position of organs in response to gradients of regulatory molecules.

Homeostasis: The ability to maintain a relatively constant internal environment.

Hominid: Primate group that includes humans and all fossil forms leading to man only.

Hominoid: Primate group that includes common ancestors of humans and apes.

Homogametic sex: The gender with two of the same size sex chromosomes, such as females in humans and *Drosophila*.

Homologous structures: Body parts in different organisms that have similar bones and similar arrangements of muscles, blood vessels, and nerves and undergo similar embryological development, but do not necessarily serve the same function; e.g., the flipper of a whale, a human arm, a bird wing, and the forelimb of a horse.

Homologues: A pair of **chromosomes** in which one member of the pair is obtained from the organism's maternal parent and the other from the paternal parent; found in **diploid** cells. Also commonly referred to as homologous chromosomes.

Homospory: Term applied to a plant that produces only one size of spore that germinates to produce a bisexual **gametophyte**.

Homozygous: Having identical **alleles** for a given gene.

Hormones: Chemical substances that are produced in the **endocrine** glands and travel in the blood to target organs where they elicit a response.

Human chorionic gonadotropin (hCG): A peptide **hormone** secreted by the **chorion** that prolongs the life of the **corpus luteum** and prevents the breakdown of the uterine lining.

Human Genome Project: Federally and privately funded project to determine the **DNA** base sequence of every **gene** in the human genome.

Human immunodeficiency virus (HIV): The **retrovirus** that attacks **T-cells** in the human **immune system**, destroying the body's defenses and allowing the development of **AIDS**.

Huntington disease: A progressive and fatal disorder of the **nervous system** that develops between the ages of 30 and 50 years; inherited as a **dominant** trait.

Hydrocarbon: A molecule of carbon atoms covalently linked to form a carbon backbone.

Hydrogen bond: A weak bond between two atoms with partial but opposite electrical charges.

Hydrolysis reaction: Type of reaction where a covalent bond between two monomers is broken by water, with the addition of a hydroxyl (OH) to one monomer and addition of a hydrogen (H) to the other.

Hydrophilic: Water-loving. Term applied to polar molecules that can form a hydrogen bond with water.

Hydrophobic: Water-fearing. Term applied to nonpolar molecules that cannot bond with water.

Hydrophytic leaves: The leaves of plants that grow in water or under conditions of abundant moisture.

Hydrosphere: The part of the physical environment that consists of all the liquid and solid water at or near the Earth's surface.

Hydrostatic skeleton: Fluid-filled closed chambers that give support and shape to the body in organisms such as jellyfish and earthworms.

Hypertension: High blood pressure; blood pressure consistently above 140/90.

Hypertonic: A solution having a high concentration of solute.

Hyphae: The multinucleate or multicellular filaments that make up the **mycelium** (body) of a **fungus** (singular: hypha).

Hypothesis: An idea that can be experimentally tested; an idea with the lowest level of confidence.

Hypothalamus: A region in the brain beneath the **thalamus**; consists of many aggregations of nerve cells and controls a variety of **autonomic** functions aimed at maintaining **homeostasis**.

Hypotonic: A solution having a low concentration of solute.

I

Ice age: Interval of **geologic time** between 2 million and 10,000 years ago during which the northern hemisphere experienced several episodes of continental glacial advance and retreat along with a climatic cooling.

Ileum: The third and last section of the **small intestine**.

Immovable joint: A joint in which the bones interlock and are held together by fibers or bony processes that prevent the joint from moving, for example, the bones of the skull.

Immune system: One of the eleven major body organ systems in **vertebrates**; defends the internal environment against invading microorganisms and **viruses** and provides defense against the growth of cancer cells.

Immunoglobulins: The five classes of protein to which antibodies belong (IgD, IgM, IgG, IgA, IgE).

Implantation: The process in which the **blastocyst** embeds in the **endometrium**.

Incomplete dominance: A type of inheritance in which the **heterozygote** expresses a **phenotype** intermediate to those of its **homozygous** parents.

Incomplete flower: Condition in which one or more "typical" flower parts are absent. Example: grass flowers such as corn tassels that are male and lack **pistils**.

Incus: One of three bones comprising the middle ear of mammals.

Index fossil: Term applied to a **fossil** that is useful in identifying the age of the rock in which it occurs.

Indusium: An umbrella-like cover over a **sorus** consisting of multiple **sporangia** in ferns.

Inflammation: A reaction to the invasion of microorganisms through the skin or through the **epithelial** layers of the **respiratory**, **digestive**, or **urinary system**; characterized by four signs: redness, swelling, heat, and pain.

Inflammatory response: The body's reaction to invading infectious microorganisms; includes an increase in blood flow to the affected area, the release of chemicals that draw **white blood cells**, an increased flow of plasma, and the arrival of **monocytes** to clean up the debris.

Ingestive feeders: Animals that ingest food through a mouth.

Inheritance of acquired characteristics: Lamarck's view that features acquired during an organism's lifetime would be passed on to succeeding generations, leading to inheritable change in life over time.

Initiation: The first step in **translation**; occurs when a **messenger RNA** molecule, a **ribosomal** subunit, and a **transfer RNA** molecule carrying the first **amino acid** bind together to form a complex; begins at the start **codon** on mRNA.

Initiation codon (AUG): Three-base sequence on the **messenger RNA** coding for the **amino acid** methionine; the start command for **protein synthesis**.

Insertion: A type of **mutation** in which a new DNA base inserts into an existing sequence of DNA bases. This shifts the reference frame in **protein synthesis**, possibly resulting in an altered amino acid sequence.

Insulin: Animal **hormone** secreted by the **pancreas** that stimulates the uptake of **glucose** by body cells. Insulin works antagonistically with **glucagon** to control blood sugar levels.

Integration: The process of combining incoming information; one of the functions of the **nervous system**.

Integument: Something that covers or encloses, for example, the skin.

Integumentary system: The skin and its derivatives (hair, nails, feathers, horns, antlers, and glands), which in multicellular animals protect against invading foreign microorganisms and prevent the loss or exchange of internal fluids.

Interferons: Proteins released by cells in response to viral infection; activate the synthesis and secretion of antiviral proteins in neighboring cells.

Internal environment: In multicellular organisms, the aqueous environment that is outside the cells but inside the body.

Interneurons: **Neurons** that process signals from one or more **sensory neurons** and relay signals to **motor neurons**.

Internodes: The stem regions between **nodes** in plants.

Interphase: The period between cell divisions when growth and replacement occur in preparation for the next division; consists of gap 1 (G1), synthesis (S), and gap 2 (G2).

Interstitial: Being situated within a particular organ or tissue.

Interstitial fluid: Fluid surrounding the cells in body tissues of animals; provides a path through which nutrients, gases, and wastes can travel between **capillaries** and cells.

Intracellular digestion: A form of **digestion** in which food is taken into cells by **phagocytosis**.

Intracellular parasites: **Viruses** that enter a host cell and take over the host's cellular machinery to produce new viruses.

Intracellular route: Path taken by water through the cells of the root between the **epidermis** and the **xylem**, moving through **plasmodesmata**.

Intron: In **eukaryotes**, bases of a **gene transcribed** but later excised from the **mRNA** molecule prior to exporting from the **nucleus** and subsequent translation of the message into a polypeptide.

Inversion: A reversal in the order of **genes** on a **chromosome** segment.

Ion: An atom that has lost or gained **electrons** from its outer shell and therefore has a positive or negative charge, respectively; symbolized by a superscript plus or minus sign and sometimes a number, for example, H^+, Na^{+1}, Cl^{-2}.

Ionic bond: A chemical bond in which atoms of opposite charge are held together by electrostatic attraction.

Isomer: Molecules having the same chemical formula but different arrangements of atoms.

Isotonic: Term applied to two solutions with equal solute concentrations.

Isotopes: Atoms with the same **atomic number** but different numbers of **neutrons**; indicated by adding the mass number to the element's name, for example, carbon 12 or ^{12}C.

J

Jaws: Occurring in **gnathostomes**, movable feeding appendages that bear teeth or baleen.

Jejunum: The second portion of the **small intestine**.

Jurassic period: Middle period of the **Mesozoic era**, between 185 and 140 million years ago.

K

Karyogamy: The fusion of two nuclei to produce a diploid zygote nucleus.

Karyotype: The **chromosomal** characteristics of a cell; also, a representation of the chromosomes aligned in pairs.

Keratin: Fibrous protein that occurs in mature **keratinocytes** near the skin's surface.

Keratinocytes: The basic cell type of the **vertebrate epidermis**; produced by basal cells in the inner layer of the **epidermis**.

Kidney stones: Crystallized deposits of excess wastes such as uric acid, calcium, and magnesium that may form in the **kidney**.

Killer T cells: See **cytoxic T cells**.

Kilocalorie: The energy needed to heat 1,000 grams of water from 14.5°C to 15.5°C.

Kinetic energy: The form of **energy** is use or motion.

Kinetochores: Structures at the **centromeres** of the **chromosomes** to which the mitotic **spindle** fibers connect.

Kingdoms: Broad taxonomic categories into which organisms are grouped, based on common characteristics; subdivisions of **domains**.

Klinefelter syndrome: In humans, a genetically determined condition in which an individual has two X- and one Y-chromosome. Affected individuals are male and typically tall and infertile.

L

Labia majora: The outer folds of skin that cover and protect the genital region in women.

Labia minora: Thin membranous folds of skin outside the **vaginal** opening.

Lactose intolerance: A genetic trait characterized by the absence of the enzyme lactase that breaks down lactose, the main sugar in milk and other dairy products.

Laminarin: Carbohydrate storage produces unique to brown algae.

Langerhans' cells: **Epidermal** cells that participate in the inflammatory response by engulfing microorganisms and releasing chemicals that mobilize **immune system** cells.

Large intestine: Consists of the cecum, **appendix**, colon, and rectum; absorbs some nutrients, but mainly prepares **feces** for elimination.

Larva: A stage in the development of many insects and other organisms including sea urchins and sponges.

Larynx: A hollow structure at the beginning of the **trachea**. The vocal cords extend across the opening of the larynx.

Lateral roots: Plant roots extending away from the main root.

Latitudinal diversity gradient: Decrease in **species** richness that occurs as we move away from the equator.

Latitudinal gradient: As latitude increases, a gradient of cooler, drier conditions occurs.

Laurasia: The northern part of the Paleozoic supercontinent **Pangaea**, composed of the present-day North America, Europe, and Asia.

Laurentia: Name applied to the "core" of North America in the times from the breakup of the precambrian-aged supercontinent Rodinia to the formation of **Pangaea**.

Law of the minimum: Scientific concept that holds that **population** growth is limited by the resource in shortest supply.

Laws of thermodynamics: The rules that govern energy transformations.

L-dopa: A chemical related to dopamine that is used in the treatment of Parkinson's disease.

Leaf gap: Term applied to an interruption of the vascular supply of a stem caused by the departure of the **leaf vein**.

Leaf primordia: Embryonic leaves recently formed by the shoot **apical meristem**, located at the tip of a plant stem.

Leaf veins: **Vascular tissue** in leaves, arranged in a net-like network (reticulate venation) in **eudicots**, and running parallel (parallel venation) to each other in **monocots**.

Leaves: The site of **photosynthesis**; one of the three major organs in plants.

Leukocytes: White blood cells; primarily function in fighting infection.

Leucoplasts: Specialized starch storage structures in photosynthetic eukaryotes.

Lichens: **Autotrophic** organisms composed of a **fungus** (sac or club fungus) and a **photosynthetic unicellular** organism (a **cyanobacterium** or alga) in a **symbiotic** relationship; are resistant to extremes of cold and drought and can grow in marginal areas such as Arctic **tundra**.

Life cycle: Diagram representing the major events and **ploidy** of an organism's **life history**.

Life history: The age at sexual maturity, age at death, and age at other events in an individual's lifetime influencing reproductive traits.

Ligaments: Dense parallel bundles of **connective tissue** that strengthen joints and hold the bones in place.

Light reactions: The **photosynthesis** process where solar energy is harvested and transferred into the chemical bonds of **ATP** and possibly **NADPH**.

Lignin: A **polymer** in secondary **cell walls** of woody plants that strengthen and stiffen the wall; related term lignified.

Linkage: The condition in which the inheritance of a specific group of **genes** on their **chromosome**.

Lipids: One of the four classes of organic **macromolecules**. Lipids function in the long-term storage of biochemical **energy**, insulation, structure, and control. Examples of lipids include the fats, waxes, oils, and **steroids** (such as testosterone and cholesterol).

Lipases: **Enzymes** secreted by the **pancreas** that are active in the digestion of fats.

Lithosphere: The solid outer layer of the Earth; includes both the land area and the land beneath the oceans and other water bodies.

Lobe-finned: Term applied to a group of fish with muscular fins containing large jointed bones that attach to the body; one of the two main types of bony fish.

Logistic growth model: A model of **population** growth in which the population initially grows at an exponential rate until it is limited by some factors; then, the population enters a slower growth phase and eventually stabilizes.

Long-day plants: Plants that flower in the summer when nights are short and days are long; examples include spinach and wheat.

Loop of Henle: A U-shaped loop between the proximal and distal tubules in the kidney.

Lungfish: A type of **lobe-finned** fish that breathe by a modified swim bladder (or lung) as well as by gills.

Lungs: Sac-like structures of varying complexity where blood and air exchange dioxygen and carbon dioxide; connected to the outside by a series of tubes and a small opening. In humans, the lungs are situated in the **thoracic cavity** and consist of the internal airways, the **alveoli**, the pulmonary circulatory vessels, and elastic **connective tissues**.

Luteal phase: The second half of the ovarian cycle when the **corpus luteum** is formed; occurs after **ovulation**.

Luteinizing hormone (LH): Animal **hormone** secreted by the anterior **pituitary gland** that stimulates the secretion of **testosterone** in men and **estrogen** in women.

Lymph: The fluid in the **lymphatic system**.

Lymphatic circulation: A secondary **circulatory system** that collects fluids from between the cells and returns it to the main circulatory system; the circulation of the **lymphatic system**, which is part of the **immune system**.

Lymphatic system: A network of glands and vessels that drain **interstitial fluid** from body tissues and return it to the **circulatory system**.

Lymph hearts: Contractile enlargements of vessels that pump lymph back into the **veins**; found in fish, amphibians, and reptiles.

Lymphocytes: White blood cells that arise in the bone marrow and mediate the immune response; include **T cells** and **B cells**.

Lyon hypothesis: Idea proposed by Mary Lyon that mammalian females inactivate one or the other **X-chromosome** during early embryonic development. This deactivated **chromosome** forms the **Barr body**.

Lysis: Condition where a cell gains so much water that its **plasma membrane** fails and the cell bursts.

Lysogenic cycle: Viral reproductive cycle where viral DNA gets incorporated into host DNA and passed along as the host cell reproduces.

Lytic cycle: Viral reproductive cycle where virus hijacks host cell and begins replicating the next group of viruses.

Lysosomes: Membranous **organelles** containing digestive **enzymes**. Lysosomes fuse with food vacuoles and enzymes contained within the lysosome chemically breakdown and/or digest the food vacuole's contents.

M

Macroevolution: The combination of events associated with the origin, diversification, **extinction**, and interactions of **organisms** that produced the **species** currently inhabiting Earth.

Macromolecules: Large molecules made up of many small organic molecules that are often referred to as **monomers**, for example, **carbohydrates**, **lipids**, **proteins**, and **nucleic acids**. Macromolecules are **polymers** of many individual **monomers**.

Macronucleus: In ciliates, the large **nucleus** that carries up to several hundred copies of the **genome** and controls metabolism and **asexual reproduction**.

Macronutrients: (1) Elements needed by plants in relatively large (primary) or smaller (secondary) quantities. (2) Foods needed by animals daily or on a fairly regular basis.

Macrophages: A type of **white blood cell** derived from **monocytes** that engulf invading **antigenic** molecules, **viruses**, and microorganisms and then display fragments of the antigen to activate **helper T cells**; ultimately stimulating the production of **antibodies** against that specific antigen.

Magnification: Ratio of enlargement or reduction of an image or object seen through a microscope.

Malaria: Mosquito-borne disease caused by the **eukaryan** *Plasmodium vivax*.

Malleus: One of the bones comprising the middle ear of mammals.

Malpighian tubules: The excretory organs of insects; a set of long tubules that open into the gut.

Mammal: Group of **deuterostomes** that produce milk in **mammary glands** to nourish their young.

Mammal-like reptiles: Group of Permian-Triassic reptiles having some possible mammalian features, notably a more prominent dentary (tooth-bearing) bone and reduction of the **incus** and **malleus** (that are part of the reptilian jaw along with the dentary). Mammal-like reptiles are thought to have been the reptile group from which mammals evolved.

Mammary glands: Paired structures that when activated will produce nourishing milk for the young.

Mantle: In mollusks, a membranous or muscular structure that surrounds the visceral mass and secretes a shell if one is present.

Marine biome: The aquatic **biome** consisting of saltwater; includes the oceans and covers more than 70% of the Earth; divided into **benthic** and **pelagic zones**.

Marsupials: Pouched mammals. The young develop internally, but are born while in an embryonic state and remain in a pouch on the mother's abdomen until development is complete; this group includes kangaroos, koalas, and opossums.

Mass extinction: A time during which **extinction** rates accelerate so that more than 50% of all species then living become extinct; results in a marked decrease in the diversity of organisms.

Mast cells: Cells that synthesize and release **histamine**, as during an allergic response; found most often in **connective tissue** surrounding blood vessels.

Matrix: The inner compartment of the **mitochondrion** where the **preparatory reaction** and **Citric Acid Cycle** occur.

Matter: Anything that has mass and occupies space.

Matter cycling: The flow of matter through organisms and the physical environment.

Maximum sustainable yield (MSY): The maximum number of a food or game **population** that can be harvested without harming the population's ability to grow back.

Medulla: (1) A term referring to the central portion of certain organs, such as the **medulla oblongata** of the **brain** and the adrenal medulla, which synthesizes **epinephrine** and **norepinephrine**. (2) In more common usage, the area in the brain that regulates breathing, heartbeat, blood pressure and similar activities.

Medulla oblongata: The region of the **brain** that, with the **pons**, makes up the hindbrain; controls heart rate, constriction and dilation of blood vessels, respiration, and digestion.

Medusa: The motile bell-shaped form of body plan in cnidarians, such as jellyfish.

Megakaryocytes: Cells found in the bone marrow that produce **platelets**.

Megaphyll: Type of leaf where the vascular supply of the leaf produces a **leaf gap** in the vascular supply of the plant stem. Megaphyll leaves are the type of leaves in all plant groups except lycophytes.

Megaspores: Four **haploid** cells produced by **meiosis** in an **ovule**. Usually three of these cells degenerate, with the remaining cell becoming the female gametophyte phase of the plant's **life cycle**.

Megaspore mother cell: Cells that undergo **meiosis** to produce **megaspores**.

Meiosis: Type of **eukaryotic** cell division in which the **chromosomes** replicate, followed by two nuclear divisions. Each of the resulting **gametes** (in animals, **spores** in plants) receives a **haploid** set of chromosomes.

Meissner's corpuscles: Sensory receptors concentrated in the **epidermis** of the fingers and lips that make these areas very sensitive to touch.

Melanin: A pigment that gives the skin color and protects the underlying layers against damage by ultraviolet light; produced by **melanocytes** in the inner layer of the **epidermis**.

Melanocytes: The cells in the inner layer of the **epidermis** that produce **melanin**.

Membrane-attack complex (MAC): A large cylindrical multi-protein complex formed by the **complement system**; kills invading microorganisms by embedding in their plasma membrane, creating a pore through which fluid flows, ultimately causing the cell to burst.

Menstrual cycle: The recurring secretion of **hormones** and associated **uterine** tissue changes; typically 28 days in length.

Menstruation: The process in which the **endometrium** of the **uterus** breaks down and sheds cells, resulting in bleeding; occurs approximately once a month. The first day marks the beginning of the menstrual and ovarian cycles.

Meristematic tissue: Embryonic tissue located at the tips of plant stems and roots and occasionally along their entire length; can divide to produce new cells; one of the four main tissue systems.

Mesentery: **Epithelial cells** supporting the digestive organs.

Mesoderm: The middle layer of cells in embryonic development; gives rise to muscles, bones, and structures associated with reproduction.

Mesoglea: A gel-like matrix that occurs between the outer and inner **epithelial** layers in cnidarians.

Mesophyll: Layer of leaf tissue between the **epidermis** layers; literally meaning "middle of the leaf."

Mesophytic leaves: The leaves of plants that grow under moderately humid conditions with abundant soil and water.

Mesozoic era: The period of **geologic time** beginning 251 million years ago and ending 65 million years ago.

Messenger RNA (mRNA): "Blueprint" for protein synthesis that is **transcribed** from one strand of the **DNA (gene)** and which is **translated** at the ribosome into a polypeptide sequence.

Metabolic pathway: A series of individual chemical reactions in a living system that combine to perform one or more important functions. The product of one reaction in a pathway serves as the substrate for the following reaction. Examples include **glycolysis** and the **Citric Acid Cycle**.

Metabolism: The sum of all chemical reactions (energy exchanges) in cells.

Metamorphosis: The process of changing from one form to another, for example, in insects, from the larval stage to the pupa stage to the reproductive adult stage.

Metaphase: The stage of eukaryotic cell division (**mitosis** or **meiosis**) in which the **chromosomes** line up at the equator of the cell.

Metastasis: The process in which cancer cells break away from the original tumor mass and establish new tumor sites somewhere else in the body.

Methanogens: A group of **archaeans** that produce methane as a byproduct of their **metabolism**.

Methionine: The **amino acid** coded for by the **initiation codon**; all **polypeptides** begin with methionine, although post-translational reactions may remove it.

Micelles: Structures formed when bile salts surround digested fats in order to enable the water-insoluble fats to be absorbed by the **epithelial cells** lining the **small intestine**.

Microevolution: A small-scale evolutionary event such as the formation of a **species** from a preexisting one or the divergence of reproductively isolated **populations** into new species.

Microfilaments: Rods composed of **actin** occurring as part of the cytoskeleton and are involved in **cell division** and movement.

Microgametophyte: Stage of the plant **life cycle** that develops from or within a **Microspore**. The microgametophyte produces sperm in specialized structures known as **antheridia**.

Micronucleus: In the ciliates, the small nucleus containing a single copy of the **genome** that is used for sexual reproduction.

Micronutrients: Elements that are required by plants in very small quantities, but are toxic in large quantities: iron, manganese, molybdenum, copper, boron, zinc, and chloride.

Microphyll: Type of leaf found in **lycophytes** where the vascular supply of the leaf does not produce a **leaf gap** in the vascular supply of the stem.

Micropyle: The end of the **embryo sac** where the egg cell and **synergids** are located.

Microsporangia: Structures of the **sporophyte** in which **microspores** are produced by **meiosis**. In flowering plants, the microsporangia are known as **anther sacs**.

Microspore mother cell: Cells in the microsporangium that undergo **meiosis** to produce **microspores**. In flowering plants, the microspore is known as the **pollen grain**, and contains a three-celled male.

Microspores: Four **haploid** cells produced by the meiotic division in the pollen sacs of flowers or **microsporangia** of **gymnosperms**. Microspores undergo **mitosis** and become encased in a thick protective wall to form **pollen grains**.

Microtubules: Filaments about 25 nanometers in diameter found in **cilia**, **flagella**, and the **cytoskeleton**.

Microvilli: Hair-like projections on the surface of the **epithelial** cells of the **villi** in the small intestine; increase the surface area of the intestine to improve absorption of digested nutrients.

Midbrain: A network of **neurons** that connects with the **forebrain** and relays sensory signals to other integrating centers.

Middle lamella: A layer composed of pectin that cements two adjoining plant cells together.

Migration: Movement of organisms either permanently (as in the migration of humans to the Americas) or temporarily (migratory birds such as Canadian geese).

Mineralocorticoids: A group of **steroid hormones** produced by the adrenal cortex that are important in maintaining electrolyte balance.

Minerals: Trace elements required for normal **metabolism**, as components of cells and tissues, and in nerve conduction and muscle contraction.

Minimum viable population (MVP): The smallest **population** size that can avoid **extinction** due to breeding problems or random environmental fluctuations.

Mitochondria: Self-replicating membrane-bound cytoplasmic **organelles** in most **eukaryotic** cells that complete the breakdown of **glucose**, producing **NADH** and **ATP** (singular term: mitochondrion). The powerhouse of the cell. Organelles within eukaryotes that generate (by **chemiosmosis**) most of the ATP the cell needs to function and stay alive.

Mitosis: The division of the cell's **nucleus** and nuclear material of a cell; consists of four stages: **prophase**, **metaphase**, **anaphase**, and **telophase**.

Mitosome: A plastid in some unicellular eukaryans such as *Giardia* and *Entamoeba* whose function is not known other than that it does not function in oxidative production of **ATP**.

Mitotic spindle: A network of **microtubules** formed during **prophase**. Some microtubules attach to the **centromeres** of the **chromosomes** and help draw the chromosomes apart during **anaphase**.

Mold: Type of **fossil** preservation where the original material of the fossil has decayed but has left an impression in the surrounding sediments. Molds are often filled with a different material, producing strikingly beautiful fossils.

Mole: Avogadro's number (6.02 × 10²³ atoms) of a substance. A measure of a set number of atoms.

Molecules: Units of two or more **atoms** held together by chemical bonds. The product of atoms attached by chemical bonds with other component atoms in definite ratios, such as water (two H to one O; H_2O).

Molecular biology: Field of biology that studies the molecular level of organization.

Monocots: One of the two major types of flowering plants; characterized by having a single **cotyledon**, flower parts arranged in threes or multiples of three, and parallel-veined leaves; include grasses, cattails, lilies, and palm trees.

Monoculture: The growth of only one **species** in a given area; such as a cornfield or other agricultural field.

Monocytes: **White blood cells** that clean up dead **viruses**, bacteria, and fungi and dispose of dead cells and debris at the end of the **inflammatory response**.

Monohybrid cross: In genetics, a cross that involves only one characteristic.

Monomer: An organic chemical unit linked to other units (usually by a **covalent bond** formed by the removal of water) to produce a larger molecule (**macromolecule**) known as a **polymer**.

Monophyletic group: A group of organisms descended from (and including) a common ancestor.

Monosaccharides: Simple **carbohydrates**, usually with a five- or six-carbon skeleton, for example, **glucose** and fructose. A carbohydrate composed of a single sugar unit, such as **glucose**, ribose, deoxyribose.

Monosomy: Condition where an individual is missing one **chromosome**, making them 2n-1 as opposed to the typical **diploid**, or 2n, state.

Monotremes: Egg-laying mammals; the echidna and platypus are the only living members of this mammal clade.

Morph: A distinct **phenotypic** variant within a **population**.

Morphological convergence: The evolution of basically dissimilar structures to serve a similar function. For example: the wings of birds and insects.

Morula: The solid-ball stage of the animal **embryo** before it implants in the **uterus**.

Mosaic evolution: A pattern of **evolution** where all features of an **organism** do not evolve at the same rate. Some characteristics are retained from the ancestral condition while others are more recently evolved.

Motor neurons: **Neurons** that receive signals from **interneurons** and transfer the signals to **effector** cells that produce a response. Nerve cells connected to a muscle or gland.

Motor output: A response to the stimuli received by the **nervous system**. A signal is transmitted to organs that can convert the signals into action, such as movement or a change in heart rate.

Motor (efferent) pathways: The portion of the **peripheral nervous system** that carries signals from the **central nervous system** to the muscles and glands.

Motor units: Consist of a motor neuron with a group of muscle fibers; form the units into which **skeletal muscles** are organized; enable muscles to contract on a graded basis.

Mouth: The oral cavity; the entrance to the **digestive system** where food is broken into pieces by the teeth and saliva begins the digestion process.

Mucus: A thick, lubricating fluid produced by the mucous membranes that line the respiratory, digestive, urinary, and reproductive tracts; serves as a barrier against infection and, in the digestive tract, moistens food, making it easier to swallow.

Multicellular: **Organisms** composed of multiple cells and exhibiting some division of labor and specialization of cell structure and function.

Multinucleate: Cells having more than one nucleus per cell.

Muscle fibers: Long, multinucleated cells found in skeletal muscles.

Muscular system: One of eleven major body organ systems in animals; allows movement and locomotion, powers the **circulatory**, **digestive**, and **respiratory** systems, and plays a role in regulating temperature.

Mutagen: Chemical or radiation that causes a change in the **DNA** base sequence, a **mutation**.

Mutation: Any heritable change in the **nucleotide** sequence of **DNA**; can involve substitutions, insertions, or deletions of one or more nucleotides.

Mutation rate: The average occurrence of **mutations** in a **species** per a given unit of time.

Mutualism: A form of **symbiosis** in which both species benefit; type of symbiosis where both organisms benefit from the interaction.

Mycelium: The mass of interwoven filaments of **hyphae** in a **fungus**.

Mycorrhiza: Term applied to a fungus that grows around or into a plant's roots and forms a symbiotic relationship. Fungal hyphae absorb minerals from the soil and pass them on to the plant roots while the fungus obtains carbohydrates from the plant (plural: mycorrhizae).

Myelin sheath: Layers of specialized **glial cells**, called **Schwann cells**, that coat the **axons** of many **neurons**.

Myofibrils: Striated contractile microfilaments in **skeletal muscle** cells. One of the four major groups of vertebrate cell/tissue types, muscle cells contract/relax, allowing movement of and/or within the animal.

Myosin: Thick protein filaments in the center sections of **sarcomeres**.

N

Nares: Nostrils; the openings in the nose through which air enters.

Nastic movement: A plant's response to a stimulus in which the direction of the response is independent of the direction of the stimulus.

Natural selection: The process of differential survival and reproduction of better adapted **genotypes**; can be **stabilizing**, **directional**, or **disruptive**. Better-adapted individuals are more likely to survive to reproductive age and thus leave more offspring and make a larger contribution to the **gene pool** than do less fit individuals.

Nectaries: Nectar-secreting organs in flowering plants that serve as insect feeding stations and thus attract insects, which then assist in the transfer of **pollen**.

Negative feedback: The stopping of the synthesis of an **enzyme** by the accumulation of the products of the enzyme-mediated reaction.

Negative feedback control: Occurs when information produced by the feedback reverses the direction of the response; regulates the secretion of most hormones.

Negative feedback loop: A biochemical pathway where the products of the reaction inhibit production of the **enzyme** that controlled their formation.

Nektonic organisms: "Swimmers"; one of the two main types of organisms in the pelagic zone of the **marine biome**.

Nematocyst: Stinging cells produced in the tentacles of cnidarians.

Nephridium: The excretory organ in flatworms and other invertebrates; a blind-ended tubule that expels waste through an excretory pore.

Nephron: A tubular structure that is the filtering unit of the kidney; consists of a **glomerulus** and **renal tubule**.

Nerve cord: A **dorsal** tubular cord of **nervous tissue** above the **notochord** of a **chordate**.

Nerve net: An interconnected mesh of **neurons** that send signals in all directions; found in **radially symmetrical** cnidarians, such as jellyfish and sea anemones, that have no head region or brain.

Nerves: Bundles of neuronal processes enclosed in **connective tissue** that carry signals to and from the **central nervous system**.

Nervous system: One of eleven major body **organ systems** in animals; coordinates and controls actions of internal organs and body systems, receives and processes sensory information from the external environment, and coordinates short-term reactions to these stimuli.

Net primary productivity (NPP): The rate at which **producer** (usually plants or algae) **biomass** is created in a **community**.

Net secondary productivity (NSP): The rate at which **consumer** and **decomposer biomass** is produced in a **community**.

Neural crest: Part of the **ectoderm** germ layer that develops into the dentin of teeth, the **peripheral nervous system**, cartilage of the face region, and the **adrenal medulla** of the kidneys.

Neural tube: A tube of **ectoderm** in the **embryo** that will form the spinal cord.

Neuromuscular junction: The point where a **motor neuron** attaches to a muscle cell.

Neurons: Highly specialized cells that generate and transmit bioelectric impulses from one part of the body to another; the functional unit of the **nervous system**.

Neurotoxin: Chemical that paralyzes nerves. Neurotoxins are produced by a variety of **organisms**.

Neurotransmitters: Chemicals released from the tip of an **axon** into the **synaptic cleft** when a nerve impulse arrives; may stimulate or inhibit the next **neuron**.

Neutron: An uncharged subatomic particle in the **nucleus** of an atom; the large electrically neutral particle that may occur in the atomic nucleus.

Niche: The biological role played by a **species**.

Niche overlap: The extent to which two **species** require similar resources; specifies the strength of the competition between the two species.

Nicotinamide adenine dinucleotide (NAD): A **coenzyme** that carries **electrons** (when chemically reduced to form NADH) to the **electron transport system**, where the energy in each NADH ultimately produces the energy to make 3 **ATP** molecules.

Nicotine adenine dinucleotide phosphate (NADP⁺): A substance to which **electrons** are transferred from **photosystem I** during **photosynthesis**; the addition of the electrons reduces NADP, which acquires a hydrogen ion to form NADPH, which is a storage form of energy that can be transferred to the **Calvin Cycle** for the production of **carbohydrate**.

Nitrogen-fixing bacteria: Bacteria that convert atmospheric N_2 into organic nitrogen.

Node: The stem region of a plant where one or more leaves attach.

Node of Ranvier: A gap between two of the Schwann cells that make up an **axon's myelin sheath**; serves as a point for generating a nerve impulse.

Nondisjunction: The failure of **chromosomes** to separate properly during cell division.

Nonvascular plants: Group of plants lacking lignified **vascular tissue (xylem)**, vascularized leaves, and having a free-living, photosynthetic **gametophyte** stage that dominates the **life cycle**. Common examples are the mosses and liverworts.

Norepinephrine: A **hormone** produced in the **adrenal medulla** and secreted under stress; contributes to the "fight or flight" response.

Notochord: In **chordates**, a cellular rod that runs the length of the body and provides dorsal support; a structure of **mesoderm** in the **embryo** that will become the **vertebrae** of the spinal column.

Nuclear area: In **prokaryotic** cells, a region containing the cell's genetic information; also known as the nucleoid.

Nuclear envelope: The double membrane that surrounds the cell's **nucleus**.

Nuclear pores: Openings in the membrane of a cell's **nuclear envelope** that allow the exchange of materials between the **nucleus** and the **cytoplasm**.

Nucleic acids: **Polymers** composed of **nucleotides**; for example, **DNA** and **RNA**.

Nucleoid: The area of the **prokaryotic cytoplasm** where the **chromatin** occurs.

Nucleolus: A round or oval body in the **nucleus** of a **eukaryotic** cell; consists of **DNA** and **RNA** and produces **ribosomal RNA** (plural: nucleoli).

Nucleosomes: Spherical bodies formed by coils of **chromatin**. The nucleosomes in turn are coiled to form the **chromosomes**.

Nucleotide sequences: The **genetic code** encrypted in the sequence of bases along a **nucleic acid**.

Nucleotides: The subunits of **nucleic acids**; composed of a phosphate, a sugar, and a nitrogen-containing base.

Nucleus (atom): An atom's core; contains **protons** and one or more **neutrons** (except hydrogen, which has no neutrons).

Nucleus (cell): The largest, most prominent **organelle** in **eukaryotic** cells; a round or oval body that is surrounded by the **nuclear envelope** and contains the genetic information necessary for control of cell structure and function.

Nyctinasty: A nastic movement in a plant that is caused by light and dark.

O

Occipital lobe: The lobe of the **cerebral cortex**, located at the rear of the head, is responsible for receiving and processing visual information.

Ocelli: Sensory organs on the head of insects.

Oils: Triglycerides that are liquid at room temperature.

Oncogenes: **Genes** that can activate cell division in cells that normally do not divide or do so only slowly.

"One gene, one enzyme hypothesis": Holds that a single **gene** controls the production, specificity, and activity of each **enzyme** in a **metabolic pathway**.

"One gene one polypeptide hypothesis": A revision of the **one gene, one enzyme hypothesis**. Some **proteins** are composed of different **polypeptide** chains encoded by separate **genes**, so the **hypothesis** now holds that **mutation** in a gene encoding a specific polypeptide can alter the ability of the encoded protein to function and thus produce an altered **phenotype**.

Oocyte: A cell that will undergo development into a female **gamete**.

Oogamy: Type of sexual reproduction with a large egg cell gamete and smaller sperm.

Oogenesis: The production of **ova**.

Oogonium: Term for a structure containing egg cells; (plural: oogonia).

Open community: A **community** in which the **populations** have different density peaks and range boundaries and are distributed more or less randomly.

Operon: Organizational gene unit in **prokaryotes** (rare in **eukaryotes**) consisting of an operator gene, promoter gene, regulator gene, and structural genes.

Opposable: The capability of being placed against the remaining digits of a hand or foot; the ability of the thumb to touch the tips of the fingers on that hand.

Opsins: Molecules in cones that bind to pigments, creating a complex that is sensitive to light of a given wavelength.

Optic nerve: The nerve that transmits the visual nerve messages from the eye to the brain.

Orbital: Area of space surrounding an atomic **nucleus** in which there is a 90% chance of finding an electron.

Orders: Taxonomic subcategories of **classes**.

Ordovician extinction: Paleozoic-aged **mass extinction** possibly related to glaciation in the southern-hemisphere supercontinent **Gondwana**.

Ordovician period: Geologic period of the **Paleozoic era** following the end of the **Cambrian period** between 500 and 435 million years ago. Major advances during this period include the bony fish and land plants.

Organelles: Cell components that carry out individual functions, for example, the cell **nucleus** and the **endoplasmic reticulum**.

Organism: An individual, composed of **organ systems** (if **multicellular**).

Organs: Differentiated structures consisting of **tissues** and performing some specific function in an organism. Structures made of two or more tissues that function as an integrated unit, for example, the heart, kidneys, liver, and stomach.

Organ systems: Groups of organs that perform related functions.

Orgasm: Rhythmic muscular contractions of the **genitals** (sex organs) combined with waves of intense pleasurable sensations; in males, results in the ejaculation of **semen**.

Osmoconformers: Marine organisms that have no system of **osmoregulation** and must change the composition of their body fluids as the composition of the water changes; include animals such as jellyfish, scallops, and crabs.

Osmoregulation: The regulation of the movement of water by **osmosis** into and out of cells; the maintenance of water balance within the body.

Osmoregulators: Marine animals whose body fluids have about one-third of the solute concentration of seawater; must therefore undergo **osmoregulation**.

Osmosis: **Diffusion** of water molecules across a membrane in response to differences in solute concentration. Water moves from areas of high-water/low-solute concentration to areas of low-water/high-solute concentration.

Osmotic pressure: The pressure generated by water moving by **osmosis** into or out of a cell.

Ossicles: Collective term for the three middle ear bones (incus, malleus, and stapes) in mammals.

Ossification: The process by which **embryonic cartilage** is replaced with bone.

Osteoarthritis: A degenerative condition associated with the wearing away of the protective cap of **cartilage** at the ends of bones. Bone growths or spurs develop, restricting movement and causing pain.

Osteoblasts: Bone-forming cells.

Osteoclasts: Cells that remove material to form the central cavity in a long bone.

Osteocytes: Bone cells that lay down new bone; found in the concentric layers of compact bone. Bone cell, a type of **connective tissue**.

Osteoporosis: A disorder in which the mineral portion of bone is lost, making the bone weak and brittle; occurs most commonly in postmenopausal women.

Ostracoderms: Extinct group of **Ordovician** jawless fish.

Out of Africa hypothesis: Holds that modern human populations (*Homo sapiens*) are all derived from a single speciation event that took place in a restricted region in Africa.

Ovaries: (1) In animals, the female **gonads**, which produce eggs (**ova**) and female **sex hormones**. (2) In flowers, part of the female reproductive structure in the **carpel**; contain the **ovules**, where egg development occurs.

Overkill: The shooting, trapping, or poisoning of certain **populations**, usually for sport or economic reasons.

Oviducts: Tubes that connect the **ovaries** and the **uterus**; transport sperm to the **ova**, transport the fertilized ova to the uterus, and serve as the site of **fertilization**; also called the fallopian tubes or uterine tubes.

Ovulation: The release of the **oocyte** onto the surface of the **ovary**; occurs at the midpoint of the ovarian cycle. The release of the ovum (egg) from the ovary after the peaking of **luteinizing hormone** concentration in the blood during the **menstrual cycle**.

Ovule: In seed plants, a protective structure in which the female **gametophyte** develops, fertilization occurs, and seeds develop; contained within the ovary.

Ovum: The female **gamete**, egg.

Oxidation: The loss of **electrons** from the outer shell of an **atom**; often accompanied by the transfer of a **proton** and thus involves the loss of a hydrogen ion; the loss of electrons or hydrogen ions in a chemical reaction.

Oxytocin: A peptide **hormone** secreted by the posterior **pituitary** that stimulates the contraction of the **uterus** during childbirth.

Ozone: A triatomic (O_3) form of oxygen formed in the stratosphere when sunlight strikes oxygen atoms. Stratospheric ozone helps filter radiation from the Sun.

P

Pacemaker: See **sinoatrial node**.

Pacinian corpuscles: Sensory receptors located deep in the **epidermis** that detect pressure and vibration.

Paleontology: The study of ancient life by collection and analysis of **fossils**.

Paleozoic era: The period of **geologic time** beginning 540 million years ago ending 251 million years ago; falls between the Proterozoic and Mesozoic eras and is divided into the Cambrian, Ordovician, Silurian, Devonian, Carboniferous, and Permian periods.

Palindrome: A sequence that reads the same in either direction; in **genetics**, refers to an **enzyme** recognition sequence that reads the same on both strands of **DNA**.

Palisade: Layer of **mesophyll cells** in leaves that are closely placed together under the **epidermal** layer of the leaf. Palisade parenchyma is columnar cells located just below the upper epidermis in leaves the cells where most of the light absorption in **photosynthesis** occurs.

Palynology: The study of **palynomorphs** and other acid-resistant microfossils usually produced by plants, protists, and fungi.

Palynomorph: Generic term for any object a palynologist studies.

Pancreas: A gland in the abdominal cavity that secretes digestive **enzymes** into the small intestine and also secretes the **hormones insulin** and **glucagon** that regulate blood glucose levels. A digestive organ that produces trypsin, chymotrypsin, and other enzymes as a pancreatic juice, but which also has **endocrine** functions in the production of the hormones **somatostatin**, insulin, and glucagon.

Pancreatic islets: Clusters of **endocrine** cells in the **pancreas** that secrete **insulin** and **glucagon**; also known as Islets of Langerhans.

Pangaea: Name proposed by the German meteorologist Alfred Wegener for a supercontinent that existed at the end of the **Paleozoic era** and consisted of all the Earth's landmasses joined together.

Parallel evolution: The development of similar characteristics in **organisms** that are not closely related (not part of a **monophyletic group**) due to **adaptation** to similar environments and/or strategies of life.

Paramylum: A **glucose polymer** for carbohydrate storage in euglenoids.

Parapodia: The term applied to paired lateral protrusions from the segments that bear the **setae** in **annelids**.

Parasites: **Organisms** that live in, with, or on another organism. The parasites benefit from their association and usually cause harm to the host.

Parasitism: A form of **symbiosis** in which the **population** of one **species** benefits at the expense of the population of another species; similar to **predation**, but differs in that parasites act more slowly than predators and do not always kill their host.

Parasympathetic system: The subdivision of the **autonomic nervous system** that reverses the effects of the **sympathetic nervous system**; part of the **autonomic nervous system** that controls heartbeat, respiration and other vital functions.

Parenchyma: One of the major cell types in plants, having thin, usually multisided walls, unspecialized but carry on **photosynthesis** and cellular **respiration** and can store food; form the bulk of the plant body; found in the fleshy tissue of fruits and seeds, photosynthetic cells of leaves, and the **vascular system**.

Parietal lobe: The lobe of the **cerebral cortex** that lies at the top of the brain; processes information about touch, taste, pressure, pain, and heat and cold.

Parsimony: Principle applied to **systematics** that the evolutionary hypothesis with the fewest changes is most likely the correct one.

Passive transport: **Diffusion** in which the cell expends no cellular energy.

Pathogen: A virus or organism that cause a disease in a host.

Pectin: A substance in the middle lamella that cements adjoining plant cells together.

Pectoral girdle: In humans, the bony arch by which the arms are attached to the rest of the skeleton; composed of the clavicle and scapula.

Pedigree analysis: A type of genetic study where inheritance of a trait is traced through several generations of a family. The information is displayed in a pedigree chart using standardized symbols.

Pelagic zone: One of the two basic subdivisions of the marine **biome**; consists of the water above the sea floor and its **organisms**.

Pellicle: Flexible covering in euglenoids.

Pelvic girdle: In humans, the bony arch by which the legs are attached to the rest of the skeleton; composed of the two hipbones.

Pelvis: The hollow cavity formed by the two hipbones.

Penicillin: The first of the so-called wonder drugs; discovered by Sir Alexander Fleming in 1928.

Pennalean: The group of **bilaterally symmetrical** diatoms.

Pepsin: An **enzyme** produced from pepsinogen that initiates **protein** digestion by breaking down protein into large peptide fragments.

Pepsinogen: An inactive form of **pepsin**; synthesized and stored in cells lining the **gastric pits** of the stomach.

Peptic ulcer: Damage to the **epithelial layer** of the stomach lining; generally caused by bacterial infection.

Peptide bond: A covalent bond that links two **amino acids** together to form a **polypeptide** chain.

Peptides: Short chains of **amino acids**.

Peptidoglycan: A polymer of sugars and **amino acids** found in cell walls of bacteria.

Perianth: Collective term for the **sepals** and **petals** of the flower.

Pericardium: Sac surrounding the heart.

Perichondrium: A layer of **connective tissue** that forms around the **cartilage** during bone formation. Cells in the perichondrium lay down a peripheral layer that develops into **compact bone**.

Peridinin: Photosynthetic pigment occurring in dinoflagellate **chloroplasts**.

Perennials: Plants that persist in the environment for more than one year (the opposite of plants known as **annuals**).

Period: A unit of the **geologic time** scale, subdivisions of eras.

Periosteum: A fibrous membrane that covers bones and serves as the site of attachment for **skeletal muscles**; contains nerves, blood vessels, and **lymphatic vessels**.

Peripheral nervous system: The subdivision of the nervous system that connects the **central nervous system** to other parts of the body; transmit messages to the central nervous system.

Peristalsis: Involuntary contractions of the **smooth muscles** in the walls of the **esophagus**, stomach, and intestines that propel food along the digestive tract.

Permian period: The last period of the **Paleozoic era**, noted for the greatest **mass extinction** in Earth history, when nearly 96% of species died out.

Peroxisomes: Membrane-bound **vesicles** in **eukaryotic** cells that contain oxidative **enzymes**.

Pesticides: Chemicals those are applied to agricultural crops or domesticated plants and which kill or inhibit growth of insects.

Petals: Usually brightly colored elements of a flower that may produce fragrant oils; nonreproductive structures that attract pollinators.

Petiole: The stalk of the leaf that attaches the leaf blade to the stem; celery and rhubarb are examples of a leaf petiole that we use as food.

Petrifaction: Mode of fossilization where f organic matter is replaced with silica.

PGA (phosphoglycerate): A 3-carbon molecule formed when carbon dioxide is added to ribulose biphosphate (RuBP) during the **Calvin Cycle** of **photosynthesis**.

PGAL (phosphoglyceraldehyde): A substance formed from **PGA** during the **Calvin Cycle** of **photosynthesis**.

pH: The negative logarithm of the H^+ ion concentration. The pH measures the acidity of a solution. Since it measures a fraction, the larger the pH number, the less H^+ ions are present in a solution.

pH scale: A logarithm-based scale expressing the concentration of H^+ ions as a whole number between 0 and 14. Strong acids, like stomach acid, have a higher concentration of these ions than do strong bases like oven cleaner.

Phagocytes: **White blood cells** that engulf (by **phagocytosis**) and destroy microorganisms including **viruses** and bacteria; cells in this category include **neutrophils** and **monocytes**.

Phagocytosis: A form of **endocytosis** in which cells surround and engulf invading bacteria or **viruses**.

Pharyngeal gill pouches: One of the four chordate characters.

Pharynx: The passageway between the mouth and the **esophagus** and **trachea**. Food passes from the pharynx to the esophagus, and air passes from the pharynx to the trachea.

Phenotype: The physical manifestation of the **alleles** possessed by an **organism**.

Pheromones: Chemical signals that travel between **organisms** rather than between cells within an organism; serve as a form of communication between animals.

Phloem: Tissue in the **vascular system** of plants that moves dissolved sugars and other products of **photosynthesis** from the leaves to other regions of the plant. Phloem tissue consists of cells called **sieve tubes** and **companion cells**.

Phosphate group: A chemical group composed of a central phosphorous bonded to three or four oxygen atoms. The overall electrical charge on the group is negative.

Phospholipids: **Lipid** molecules with a **hydrophilic** head and two **hydrophobic** tails. Lipids with a phosphate group in place of one of the three fatty acid chains. Phospholipids are the building blocks of cellular membranes.

Phosphorylation: The chemical attachment of phosphorous to a molecule, usually associated with the storage of energy in the **covalent bond** that forms. Example: attachment of the third **phosphate group** to **ADP** in the formation of the higher energy form, **ATP**.

Photic zone: The layer of the ocean penetrated by sunlight; extends to a depth of about 200 meters.

Photoelectric effect: Property of certain metals to emit a stream of electrons when subjected to energy of a critical wavelength.

Photoperiodism: The ability of certain plants to sense the relative amounts of light and dark in a 24-hour period; controls the onset of flowering in many plants.

Photosynthesis: The process by which plant cells use solar energy to produce **ATP**. The conversion of unusable sunlight energy into usable chemical energy, associated with the actions of **chlorophyll**.

Photosystems: Clusters of several hundred molecules of **chlorophyll** in a **thylakoid** in which **photosynthesis** occurs.

Phototrophs: **Organisms** that use sunlight to synthesize organic nutrients as their energy source, for example, **cyanobacteria**, algae, and plants.

Phototropism: The reaction of plants to light during which the plants bend toward the light.

Phragmoplast: A structure unique to plants and the **charophytes** that helps organize the formation of a **cell plate** during **cytokinesis**.

Phycocyanin: An accessory pigment found in **cyanobacteria** and the chloroplasts of **red algae**.

Phycoerythrin: An accessory pigment found in **cyanobacteria** and the chloroplasts of **red algae**.

Phyletic gradualism: Mode of **evolution** where an entire species slowly evolves into a new species. In this mode the **fossil record** would be filled with intermediate forms recording the evolution of the new species from a parental species.

Phylogeny: (1) the study of evolutionary relationships within a **monophyletic group**. (2) evolutionary **hypothesis** represented as a tree-like branching diagram.

Phylogenetic: Pertaining to a **phylogeny**.

Phylum: The broadest taxonomic category within kingdoms (pl.: phyla).

Phytochrome: A pigment in plant leaves that detects day length and generates a response; partly responsible for **photoperiodism**.

Phytoplankton: A floating layer of **photosynthetic** creatures, including algae, that are an important source of atmospheric oxygen and form the base of the aquatic **food chain**.

Pilus: Projection from surface of a bacterial cell (F⁺) that can donate genetic material to another (F⁻).

Pineal gland: A small gland located between the cerebral hemispheres of the brain that secretes melatonin.

Pinnate leaves: Leaves that have a feather-like appearance, typically fern and cycad leaves.

Pinocytosis: The process of forming vesicles to import **solutes** into the cell.

Pioneer community: The initial **community** of colonizing **species**.

Pistil: Female reproductive structures in flowers, consisting of the **stigma**, **style**, and **ovary**. Also known as a **carpel** in some books.

Pith: Central area in plant stems, largely composed of **parenchyma** tissue modified for storage.

Pituitary gland: A small gland located at the base of the brain; consists of an anterior and a posterior lobe and produces numerous **hormones**; the master gland of the **endocrine system**; pituitary hormones target specific areas as well as those that stimulate other glands to secrete their own hormones. Part of the pituitary is nervous tissue, the rest is glandular **epithelium**.

Placenta: An organ produced from interlocking maternal and embryonic tissue in **placental mammals**; supplies nutrients to the embryo and fetus as well as removes wastes.

Placental mammals: One of three groups of mammals; placental mammals carry their young in the mother's body for long periods during which the fetus is nourished by the **placenta** prior to birth. Humans are placental mammals.

Planaria: Small free-living flatworms (phylum Platyhelminthes) and parasitic tapeworms/flukes with **bilateral symmetry** and **cephalization**.

Placoderm: An extinct group of armored jawed fish.

Planktonic organisms: "Floaters"; one of the two main types of organisms in the **pelagic zone** of the marine **biome**.

Plasma: The liquid portion of the blood. Along with the extracellular fluid, it makes up the internal environment of **multicellular** creatures.

Plasma cells: Cells produced from **B cells** that synthesize and release **antibodies**.

Plasmids: Self-replicating, extra-chromosomal circular **DNA** molecules found in bacterial cells; often used as vectors in **recombinant DNA technology**. Small circles of double-stranded DNA found in some bacteria. Plasmids can carry from four to twenty genes.

Plasmodesmata: Junctions in plants that penetrate cell walls and **plasma membranes**, allowing direct communication between the **cytoplasm** of adjacent cells (singular: plasmodesma).

Plasmogamy: The fusion of the **cytoplasm** of two **haploid gamete** cells or mating **hyphae**.

Plasmolysis: **Osmotic** condition in which a cell loses water to its outside environment.

Plastids: Membrane-bound **organelles** in plant cells that function in storage (of food or pigments) or food production; term applied to any double membrane-bound organelle.

Platelets: In **vertebrate** animals, cell fragments that bud off from the **megakaryocytes** in the bone marrow; carry chemicals needed for blood clotting.

Plate tectonics: The movement of the Earth's crustal plates that make up the surface of our planet, and their interactions. The revolutionary paradigm in geology that the Earth's crust is composed of rigid segments (plates) in constant (although considered slow in a human-scale timeframe) motion (tectonics) relative to each other.

Pleiotropic: A term describing a **genotype** with multiple **phenotype** effects. For example: **sickle-cell anemia** produces a multitude of consequences in those it affects, such as heart disease, kidney problems, nervous system issues.

Pleistocene: The first geologic **epoch** of the **Quaternary period** of the **Cenozoic era** that ended 10,000 years ago with the current and ongoing retreat of the continental glaciers.

Pleura: A thin sheet of **epithelium** that covers the inside of the **thoracic cavity** and the outer surface of the lungs.

Pleural cavity: The space between the sheets of **pleura** (one covering the inside of the **thoracic cavity**, the other covering the outside of the lungs).

Polar covalent bond: A **covalent bond** in which atoms share **electrons** in an unequal fashion. The resulting molecule has regions with slightly positive and slightly negative charges. The presence of polar covalent bonds allows other polar molecules to surround a molecule: example: **glucose** in water.

Pollen grains: The containers for male **gametophytes** of seed plants produced inside a **microsporangium** by **meiosis**.

Pollen tube: Structure produced by the tube nucleus in the **pollen grain** through which the sperm nucleus (or nuclei in **angiosperms**) proceed to travel through to reach the egg.

Pollination: The transfer of pollen from the **anthers** to the **stigma** by a pollinating agent such as wind, insects, birds, bats, or the opening of the flower itself.

Polydactyly: **Autosomal** dominant trait where a sixth digit is produced on at least one hand or foot.

Polygenic inheritance: Occurs when a trait is controlled by several **gene** pairs; usually results in continuous variation.

Polymer: Organic macromolecule composed of smaller units known as **monomers**, for example starch is a polymer of **glucose; proteins** are polymers of **amino acids**.

Polymerase chain reaction (PCR): A method of amplifying or copying **DNA** fragments that is faster than cloning. The fragments are combined with **DNA polymerase**, **nucleotides**, and other components to form a mixture in which the DNA is cyclically amplified.

Polynucleotides: Long chains of **nucleotides** formed by chemical links between the sugar and **phosphate groups**.

Polyp: The sessile form of life history in **cnidarians**; for example, the freshwater hydra.

Polyphyletic: Term applied when a taxon contains members that do not all share the same common ancestor.

Polyploidy: Abnormal variation in the number of **chromosome** sets. The condition when a cell or organism has more than the customary two sets of chromosomes. This is an especially effective speciation mechanism in plants since the extra chromosomes will establish **reproductive isolation** with the parental **population(s)**, an essential for **speciation**.

Polysaccharides: Long chains of **monosaccharides covalently bonded** together; for example, **glycogen**, starch, and **cellulose**.

Pons: The region that, with the **medulla oblongata**, makes up the hindbrain, which controls heart rate, constriction, and dilation of blood vessels, respiration, and digestion.

Population: A group of individuals of the same **species** living in the same area at the same time and sharing a common **gene pool**. A population is group of potentially interbreeding creatures living in a geographic area.

Population dynamics: The study of the factors that affect the growth, stability, and decline of **populations**, as well as the interactions of those factors.

Portal system: An arrangement in which **capillaries** drain into a **vein** that opens into another capillary network.

Positive feedback: Biochemical control where the accumulation of the product stimulates production of an **enzyme** responsible for that product's production.

Positive feedback control: Occurs when information produced by the feedback increases and accelerates the response.

Potential energy: The form of **energy** stored or at rest, not in use. Examples: charged cell phone battery, stored energy in gasoline or food.

Precambrian: Informal term describing 7/8 of **geologic time** from the formation of the Earth to the beginning of the **Cambrian period** of the **Paleozoic era**.

Precipitation: The part of the hydrologic cycle in which the water vapor in the atmosphere falls to Earth as rain or snow.

Predation: One of the biological interactions that can limit **population** growth; occurs when creatures kill and consume other creatures.

Predatory release: Occurs when a predator species is removed from a prey species such as by great reduction in the predator's population size or by the migration of the prey species to an area without major predators. Removal of the predator releases the prey from one of the factors limiting its population size.

Prehensile movement: The ability to seize or grasp.

Prenatal testing: Testing to detect the presence of a genetic disorder in an embryo or fetus; commonly done by **amniocentesis** or **chorionic villi sampling**.

Presymptomatic screening: Testing to detect genetic disorders that only become apparent later in life. The tests are done before the condition actually appears, such as with **Huntington disease**.

Prey switching: The tendency of predators to switch to a more readily available prey when one prey **species** becomes rare; allows the first prey **population** to rebound and helps prevent its **extinction**.

Primary body: Those parts of a plant produced by the shoot and root **apical meristems**.

Primary cell wall: The cell wall outside the **plasma membrane** that surrounds plant cells; composed of the **polysaccharide cellulose**.

Primary compounds: Chemicals made by plants and needed for the plant's own **metabolism**.

Primary consumers: In a food chain, the term applied to creatures that feed upon the **producers**. Primary consumers are eaten by **secondary consumers**.

Primary growth: Cells produced by an **apical meristem**. The growth a plant by the actions of apical meristems on the shoot and root apex in producing plant primary tissues.

Primary macronutrients: Elements that plants require in relatively large quantities: nitrogen, phosphorus, and potassium.

Primary meristems: The **apical meristems** on the shoot and root apices in plants that produce plant primary tissues.

Primary phloem: Those **phloem** cells produced by the **procambium** as part of the plant primary body.

Primary producers: Organisms at the base of the **food chain**, typically some form of **autotrophic** creatures like **cyanobacteria**, algae, or plants.

Primary root: The first root formed by a plant after it germinates.

Primary structure: The sequence of **amino acids** in a **protein**.

Primary xylem: The **xylem** cells produced by the **procambium** as part of the plant **primary body**.

Primates: The **taxonomic order** of mammals that includes prosimians (lemurs and tarsiers), monkeys, apes, and humans; characteristics include a large brain, stereoscopic vision, and a grasping hand.

Principle of independent assortment: Mendel's second great discovery; holds that during **gamete** formation, **alleles** in one gene pair segregate into gametes independently of the alleles of other gene pairs. As a result, if enough gametes are produced, the collective group of gametes will contain all combinations of alleles possible for that **organism**.

Principle of segregation: Mendel's first great discovery; holds that each pair of factors of heredity separate during **gamete** formation so that each gamete receives one member of a pair.

Prions: Infectious agents composed only of one or more **protein** molecules without any accompanying genetic information.

Procambium: The lateral **meristem** located between the **primary xylem** and **primary phloem** in the **vascular bundle** of the **primary plant body**.

Producers: The first level in a **food pyramid**; consist of **organisms** that generate the food used by all other organisms in the **ecosystem**; usually consist of creatures that make food by **photosynthesis**.

Progesterone: One of the two female animal reproductive **hormones** secreted by the **ovaries**.

Prokaryote: Type of cell that lacks a membrane-bound **nucleus** and has no membrane-bound organelles; a bacterium or archaean. Prokaryotes are more primitive than **eukaryotes**.

Prolactin: A **hormone** produced by the **anterior pituitary**; secreted at the end of pregnancy when it activates milk production by the mammary glands.

Promoter: The specific **nucleotide sequence** in **DNA** that marks the beginning of a **gene**.

Prophage: Term applied to **viral DNA** that has integrated into the host DNA.

Prophase: (1) The first stage of **mitosis** during which **chromosomes** condense, the **nuclear envelope** disappears, and the **centrioles** divide and migrate to opposite ends of the cell. (2) The first stage of **mitosis** and **meiosis** (although in meiosis this phase is denoted with either a roman numeral I or II) where the **chromatin** condenses to form chromosomes, **nucleolus** dissolves, nuclear envelope dissolves, and the **spindle** begins to form.

Prostaglandins: A class of **fatty acids** that has many of the properties of **hormones**; synthesized and secreted by many body tissues and have a variety of effects on nearby cells.

Prostate gland: A gland that is located near and empties into the **urethra**; produces a secretion that enhances sperm viability. Gland involved in the **reproductive system** in males, the prostate secretes a sperm-activating chemical into the **semen** during the arousal/ejaculation response.

Protease: Retroviral enzyme that helps to make proteins for the next generation of viruses inside an infected host cell.

Proteinoids: **Polymers** of **amino acids** formed spontaneously from inorganic molecules; have enzyme-like properties and can catalyze chemical reactions.

Proteins: **Polymers** made up of **amino acids** that perform a wide variety of cellular functions such as structure and control.

Prothallus: In ferns, a small heart-shaped bisexual **gametophyte**.

Protista: The **taxonomic Kingdom** from which the other three **eukaryotic** kingdoms evolved.

Protists: Single-celled to multicellular **organisms**; a type of **eukaryote**.

Proton: A subatomic particle in the **nucleus** of an **atom** that carries a positive charge and a mass of one atomic mass unit.

Protostomes: Animals in which the first opening that appears in the **embryo** becomes the mouth, for example, mollusks, annelids, and arthropods.

Protozoa: Single-celled **protists** grouped by their method of locomotion. This group includes *Paramecium*, *Amoeba*, and many other commonly observed protists.

Proviron: A more general term applied to any viral **DNA** incorporated into the host DNA.

Proximal tubule: The winding section of the **renal tubule** where most reabsorption of water, sodium, **amino acids**, and sugar takes place.

Pseudocoelom: In round worms, a closed fluid-containing cavity that acts as a **hydrostatic skeleton** to maintain body shape, circulate nutrients, and hold the major body organs.

Pseudocoelomates: Animals that have a body cavity that is in direct contact with the outer muscular layer of the body and does not arise by splitting of the **mesoderm**; roundworms for example.

Pseudopodia: Temporary cytoplasmic extensions from a cell that enables it to move (singular: pseudopodium).

Pulmonary artery: The **artery** that carries blood from the right **ventricle** of the vertebrate heart to the lungs.

Pulmonary circuit: The loop of the **circulatory system** that carries blood to and from the lungs.

Pulmonary vein: The **vein** that carries oxygenated blood from the lungs to the left atrium of the heart. Veins carrying oxygenated blood from the lungs to the heart.

Punctuated equilibrium: A model that holds that the evolutionary process is character-ized by long periods with little or no change interspersed with short periods of rapid speciation.

Purine: One of the groups of nitrogenous bases that are part of a **nucleotide**. Purines are **ade-nine** and **guanine**, and are double-ring structures.

Pyloric sphincter: The ring of muscle at the junction of the stomach and small intestine that regulates the movement of food into the small intestine.

Pyrenoid: A structure in the **chloroplasts** of some algae and hornworts associated with carbon dioxide concentration.

Pyrimidine: One of the groups of nitrogenous bases that are part of a **nucleotide**. Pyrimidines are single ringed, and consist of the bases **thymine** (in DNA), **uracil** (replacing thymine in **RNA**), and **cytosine**.

Q

Quantum models of speciation: Models of **evolution** that hold that **speciation** sometimes occurs rapidly as well as over long periods, as the classical theory proposed.

Quaternary period: The most recent geologic **period** of the **Cenozoic era**, the Quaternary began 2 million years ago with the growth of northern hemisphere continental glaciers and the **ice age**.

Quaternary structure: In some **proteins**, a fourth structural level created by interactions with other proteins.

R

Race: Subdivision of a **species** that is capable of interbreeding with other members of that same species.

Rachis: Term applied to the central branch in a pinnately compound leaf.

Radially symmetrical: In animals, refers to creatures with their body parts arranged around a central axis. Such animals tend to be circular or cylindrical in shape.

Radiata: Animal clade of cnidarians and ctenophorans that are all **radially symmetrical**.

Radiation: **Energy** emitted from the unstable nuclei of radioactive **isotopes**.

Radioactive decay: The spontaneous breakdown of the **nucleus** of an **atom** that forms an atom of a different **element**.

Radioisotope: Term applied to a radioactive **isotope**, such as carbon-14 or uranium 238. Radioisotope nuclei are unstable and spontaneously breakdown and emit one of a number of types of radiation.

Radiolaria: A group of silica-secreting **heterotrophic eukaryans**.

Radiometric time: Type of **absolute time** determined by the relative proportions of **radioisotopes** to stable daughter **isotopes**.

Radula: The scraping tongue characteristic of mollusks.

Ray-finned: **Taxonomic** group of fish, such as trout, tuna, salmon, and bass, that have thin, bony supports holding the fins away from the body and an internal swim bladder that changes the buoyancy of the body; one of the two main types of bony fishes.

Reabsorption: The return to the blood of most of the water, sodium, **amino acids**, and sugar that were removed during filtration; occurs mainly in the **proximal tubule** of the **nephron**.

Receptacle: The base that attaches a flower to the stem.

Receptor: Protein on or protruding from the cell surface to which select chemicals can bind. The opiate receptor in brain cells allows both the natural chemical as well as foreign (opiate) chemicals to attach.

Receptor-mediated endocytosis: Process by which **solutes** outside the cell bind to specific receptor on the **plasma membrane**, causing the formation of a **vesicle** containing the receptor specified chemical.

Recessive: Refers to an **allele** of a **gene** that is expressed when the **dominant** allele is not present. An allele expressed only in **homozygous** state, when the dominant allele is not present.

Recombinant DNA molecules: New combinations of **DNA** fragments formed by cutting DNA segments from two sources with the same **restriction enzyme** and then joining of the fragments together by **DNA ligase**. Interspecies transfer of genes usually through a **vector** such as a **virus** or **plasmid**.

Recombinant DNA technology: A series of techniques in which **DNA** fragments are linked to self-replicating forms of DNA to create recombinant DNA molecules. These molecules in turn are replicated in a host cell to create copies (or clones) of the inserted segments.

Recombination: A way in which **meiosis** produces new combinations of genetic information. During **synapsis**, **chromatids** may exchange segments with other chromatids, leading to a physical exchange of **chromosome** parts; thus, **genes** from both parents may be combined on the same chromosome, creating a new combination.

Red algae: Common name for algae in the phylum Rhodophyta.

Red blood cell: Component of the blood that transports oxygen with the **hemoglobin** molecule. See also **erythrocyte**.

Red tides: Phenomenon associated with population explosions (blooms) of certain types of **dinoflagellates**; red-colored structures inside the dinoflagellate cells cause the water to take on a reddish color.

Reduction: The gain of an **electron** or a hydrogen by another molecule; that molecule is then said to be reduced.

Reductional division: The first division in **meiosis**; results in each daughter cell receiving one member of each pair of **chromosomes**.

Reflex: A response to a stimulus that occurs without conscious effort; one of the simplest forms of behavior.

Reflex arc: Pathway of **neurons**, effector(s) and sensory receptors that participate in a **reflex**.

Region of division: The area of **cell division** in the tip of a plant root.

Region of elongation: The area in the tip of a plant root where cells grow by elongating, thereby increasing the length of the root.

Region of maturation (differentiation): The area where primary tissues and **root hairs** develop in the tip of a plant root.

Relative time: Type of **geologic time** that places events in a sequence relative to each other.

Renal tubule: That portion of the **nephron** where **urine** is produced.

Renin: An enzyme secreted by the kidneys that converts angiotensinogen into angiotensin II.

Replication: Process by which **DNA** replicates prior to **cell division**.

Reproductive isolating mechanism: Biological or behavioral characteristics that reduce or prevent interbreeding with other **populations**, for example, the production of sterile hybrids. Establishment of reproductive isolation is considered essential for development of a new **species**.

Reproductive system: One of eleven major body **organ systems** in animals; is responsible for reproduction and thus the survival of the **species**.

Reptiles: Taxonomic class of **vertebrates** characterized by scales and **amniotic eggs**; the first truly terrestrial vertebrate group.

Resolution: The ability to distinguish between two points, increases to a degree as magnification increases.

Resource partitioning: The division of resources such that a few dominant **species** exploit most of the available resources while other species divide the remainder; helps explain why a few species are abundant in a **community** while others are represented by only a few individuals.

Respiration: (1) breathing as part of gas exchange; or (2) cellular metabolism.

Respiratory surface: A thin, moist, **epithelial** surface that oxygen can cross to move into the body and carbon dioxide can cross to move out of the body.

Respiratory system: One of eleven major body **organ systems** in animals; moves oxygen from the external environment into the internal environment and removes carbon dioxide from the body.

Resting potential: The difference in electrical charge across the **plasma membrane** of a **neuron**.

Restriction enzymes: **Enzymes** that attach to **DNA** molecules at specific **nucleotide sequences** and cut both strands of DNA at those sites.

Restriction fragment length polymorphism (RFLP): A heritable difference in **DNA** fragment length and number; passed from generation to generation in a codominant way.

Retina: The inner, light-sensitive layer of the eye; includes the **rods** and **cones**.

Retroviruses: **Viruses** that contain a single strand of **RNA** as their genetic material and reproduce by copying the RNA into a complementary **DNA** strand using the **enzyme reverse transcriptase**. The single-stranded DNA is then copied, and the resulting double-stranded DNA is inserted into a **chromosome** of the host cell.

Reverse transcriptase: An **enzyme** used in the **replication** of **retroviruses**; aids in copying the retrovirus's **RNA** into a **complementary** strand of **DNA** once inside the host cell.

Reverse transcription: Process of **transcribing** a single-stranded **DNA** from a single-stranded **RNA** (the reverse of transcription); used by **retroviruses** as well as in **biotechnology**.

Rheumatoid arthritis: A crippling form of arthritis that begins with inflammation and thickening of the synovial membrane, followed by bone degeneration and disfigurement.

Rhizoids: Filamentous structures in the plants group known as **bryophytes** that attach to a substrate and absorb moisture. The term is also applied to similar structures found outside the bryophytes.

Rhizome: In ferns, a horizontal stem with upright leaves containing **vascular tissue**.

Rhodopsin: A visual pigment contained in the **rods** of the **retina** in the eye.

Ribonucleic acid (RNA): **Nucleic acid** containing **ribose** sugar and the base **Uracil**; RNA functions in **protein synthesis**. The single stranded molecule **transcribed** from one strand of the **DNA**.

Ribose: Sugar found in **nucleotides** of **RNA** and in **ATP**.

Ribosomal RNA (rRNA): One of the three types of RNA; rRNA is a structural component in **ribosomes**.

Ribosomal subunits: Two units that combine with **mRNA** to form the ribosomal-mRNA complex where **protein synthesis** occurs.

Ribosomes: Small **organelles** made of **rRNA** and **protein** in the **cytoplasm** of **prokaryotic** and **eukaryotic** cells; aid in the production of proteins on the **rough endoplasmic reticulum** and ribosome complexes.

Ribozyme: Small RNA molecule that has both informational and enzymatic properties.

Ribulose biphosphate (RuBP): The 5-carbon chemical that combines with carbon dioxide at the beginning of the **Calvin Cycle**.

RNA polymerase: During **transcription**, an **enzyme** that attaches to the promoter region of the **DNA** template, joins **nucleotides** to form the synthesized strand of **RNA** and detaches from the template when it reaches the terminator region.

RNA transcript: Term applied to **RNA transcribed** in the **nucleus**.

Rodinia: Name applied to the **precambrian** supercontinent.

Rods: Light receptors in **primates'** eyes that provide vision in dim light.

Root cap: Structure that covers and protects the **apical meristem** in plant roots.

Root hairs: Extensions of the root **epidermis** that increase the root's ability to absorb water.

Root-leaf-vascular system axis: Refers to the arrangement in **vascular plants** in which the roots anchor the plant and absorb water and nutrients, the leaves carry out **photosynthesis**, and the **vascular system** connects roots and leaves, carrying water and nutrients to the leaves and carrying sugars and other products of photosynthesis from the leaves to other regions of the plant.

Roots: Organs, usually occurring underground, that absorb nutrients and water and anchor the plant; one of the three major plant **organ systems**.

Root system: Plant **organ system** that anchors the plant in place, stores excess sugars, and absorbs water and mineral nutrients. That part of the plant below ground level.

Rough endoplasmic reticulum: The type of endoplasmic reticulum where numerous ribosomes attach to the edge of the reticulum membrane and synthesize proteins.

S

S phase: That part of **interphase** when new **DNA** is synthesized as part of **replication** of **chromatin**.

Sac-like body: Animal body type characterized by a common mouth/anus.

Salivary amylase: Animal **enzyme** secreted by the **salivary glands** that begins the breakdown of complex sugars and starches in the mouth.

Salivary glands: Glands that secrete saliva into the mouth.

Saprophytes: Organisms that obtain their nutrients from decaying plants and animals. Saprophytes are important in recycling organic material.

Sapwood: Layers of **secondary xylem** that remain functional in older woody plants; visible as the outer lighter areas in the cross section of a tree trunk.

Sarcomeres: The functional units of **skeletal muscle**; consist of filaments of **myosin** and **actin**.

Saturated fat: A fat with single **covalent bonds** between the carbons of its **fatty acids**. Because of the bonding, the fat is saturated with as much hydrogen as possible.

Schistosomiasis: Human disease caused by the blood fluke; common in tropical Africa and South America.

Schwann cells: Specialized **glial cells** that form the **myelin sheath** that coats many **axons**.

Scientific method: Systematic approach of observation, **hypothesis** formation, hypothesis testing, and hypothesis evaluation that forms the basis for modern science.

Sclereids: Plant cells with thick secondary walls that provide the gritty textures in pears.

Sclerenchyma: One of the three major cell types in plants; have thickened, rigid, secondary walls that are hardened with **lignin**; provide support for the plant. Sclerenchyma cells include fibers and **sclereids**.

Scolex: The term for the head of a tapeworm.

Scrotum: In mammals, a pouch of skin located outside the body cavity into which the **testes** descend; provides proper temperature for the testes.

Secondary cell wall: In woody plants, a second wall inside the primary cell wall; contains alternating layers of **cellulose** and **lignin**.

Secondary compounds: Plant products that are not important in **metabolism** but serve other purposes, such as attracting animals to act as **pollination** or killing **parasites**.

Secondary consumers: In a **food chain**, the term applied to creatures that feed upon the **primary consumers**. Secondary consumers are eaten by tertiary consumers, and so on. This level is **heterotrophic**.

Secondary extinction: The death of one **population** due to the **extinction** of another, often a food species.

Secondary growth: Cells in a plant that are produced by a **cambium**. Increase in girth of a plant due to the action of lateral **meristems** such as the **vascular cambium**. The main cell produced in **secondary growth** is **secondary xylem**, better known as **wood**.

Secondary immunity: Resistance to an **antigen** the second time it appears. Because of the presence of **B** and **T** memory cells produced during the first exposure to the antigen, the second response is faster and more massive and lasts longer than the primary immune response.

Secondary macronutrients: Elements that plants require in relatively small quantities: calcium, magnesium, and sulfur.

Secondary (lateral) meristems: Plant **meristems** that produce **Secondary growth** from a **cambium**.

Secondary phloem: **Phloem** produced by the **vascular cambium** in a woody plant stem or root.

Secondary structure: The structure of a **protein** created by the formation of **hydrogen bonds** between different **amino acids**; can be a pleated sheet, alpha helix, or random coil. Shape of a protein caused by attraction between R-groups of the amino acids.

Secondary xylem: **Xylem** produced by the **vascular cambium** in a woody plant stem or root; **wood**.

Second law of thermodynamics (entropy): The **energy** available after a chemical reaction is less than that at the beginning of a reaction; energy conversions are not 100% efficient.

Second messenger: The mechanism by which non-steroid **hormones** work on target cells. A hormone binds to receptors on the cell's **plasma membrane** activating a molecule–the second messenger–that activates other intracellular molecules that elicit a response. The second messenger can be cyclic AMP, cyclic GMP, inositol triphosphate, diacrylglycerol, or calcium.

Secretin: A **hormone** produced in the **duodenum** that stimulates alkaline secretions by the **pancreas** and inhibits gastric emptying.

Secretion: The release of a substance in response to the presence of food or specific neural or hormonal stimulation.

Sediment: Loose aggregate of solids derived from preexisting rocks, or solids precipitated from solution by inorganic chemical processes or extracted from solution by **organisms**.

Sedimentary rock: Any rock composed of sediment, such as solid particles and dissolved minerals. Examples include rocks that form from sand or mud in riverbeds or on the sea bottom.

Seed: Structure produced by some plants in which the next generation **sporophyte** is surrounded by **gametophyte** nutritive tissues.

Seed coat: The tough outer layer of the **seed**, derived from the outer layers of the **ovule**.

Segments: Repeating units in the body parts of some animals.

Segregation: Separation of replicated **chromosomes** to opposite sides of the cell; the distribution of **alleles** on chromosomes into cells formed during **meiosis**.

Selective breeding: The selection of individuals with desirable traits for use in breeding. Over many generations, the practice leads to the development of strains with the desired characteristics.

Selectively permeable: Term describing a barrier that allows some chemicals to pass but not others. The **plasma membrane** is such a barrier.

Semen: A mixture of **sperm** and various glandular secretions.

Semiconservative replication: Process of **DNA replication** in which the DNA helix is unwound and each strand serves as a template for the synthesis of a new complementary strand, which is linked to the old strand. Thus, one old strand is retained in each new molecule.

Semilunar valve: A valve between each **ventricle** of the heart and the **artery** connected to that ventricle.

Seminal vesicles: Glands that contribute fructose to **sperm**. The fructose serves as an energy source.

Seminiferous tubules: Tubules on the interior of the **testes** where **sperm** form and mature.

Sensor: In a closed system, the element that detects change and signals the **effector** to initiate a response.

Sensory cortex: A region of the brain associated with the **parietal lobe**.

Sensory input: Stimuli that the **nervous system** receives from the external or internal environment; includes pressure, taste, sound, light, and blood pH.

Sensory neurons: **Neurons** that carry signals from receptors and transmit information about the environment to processing centers in the brain and spinal cord.

Sensory (afferent) pathways: The portion of the **peripheral nervous system** that carries information from the organs and tissues of the body to the **central nervous system**.

Sepals: Modified leaves that protect a flower's inner petals and reproductive structures.

Separation: Splitting of the **cytoplasm** by **cytokinesis**.

Setae: Term applied to the small bristles on the **parapodia** of annelid worms.

Severe combined immunodeficiency (SCID): A genetic disorder in which afflicted individuals have no functional **immune system** and are prone to infections. Both the **cell-mediated immune response** and the **antibody-mediated response** do not function properly.

Sex chromosomes: The **chromosomes** that determine the sex of an organism. In humans, females have two **X-chromosomes**, and males have one X-chromosome and one **Y-chromosome**.

Sex hormones: A group of steroid **hormones** produced by the adrenal cortex. Hormones that are produced in the **gonads** and promote development and maintenance of the secondary sex characteristics and structures, prepare the female for pregnancy, and aid in development of **gametes**. Males produce **testosterone**, while females produce **estrogen** and **progesterone**.

Sex linkage: The condition in which the inheritance of a **sex chromosome** is coupled with that of a given **gene** carried on that chromosome, for example, red-green color blindness and hemophilia in humans.

Sexual reproduction: A system of reproduction in which two **haploid** cells (**gametes**) fuse to produce a **diploid zygote**.

Sexual selection: A form of **natural selection** where some individuals are more successful at mating and therefore leave a greater number of offspring. This often involves males competing for mates.

Shoot: The plant stem; provides support for the leaves and flowers; one of the three major plant organs; also referred to as the shoot system.

Short-day plants: Plants that flower during early spring or fall when nights are relatively long and days are short, for example, poinsettia and dandelions.

Sickle cell anemia: Human **autosomal recessive** disease that causes production of abnormal **red blood cells** that collapse (or sickle) and cause circulatory problems.

Sieve cells: Conducting cells in the phloem of vascular plants. See also **sieve elements**.

Sieve elements: Tubular, thin-walled cells that form a system of connected cells extending from the roots to the leaves in the **phloem** of plants; lose their nuclei and organelles at maturity, but retain a functional **plasma membrane**.

Sieve plates: Pores in the end walls of **sieve elements** that connect the sieve elements together.

Sieve tube members: **Phloem** cells that form long sieve tubes.

Silica: Silicon dioxide, SiO_2.

Silurian period: The **geological time** unit of the **Paleozoic era** following the **Ordovician**, between 435 and 395 million years ago, when plants colonized the land.

Simple leaf: A leaf in which the blade does not form leaflets.

Sink: (1) A body or process that acts as a storage device or disposal mechanism, for example, plants and the oceans act as sinks absorbing atmospheric carbon dioxide; (2) A location in a plant where sugar is being consumed, either in **metabolism** or by conversion to starch.

Sinoatrial (SA) node: Area of modified muscle cells in the right **atrium** that sends timed impulses to the heart's other muscle cells, causing them to contract; the heart's pacemaker.

Sister chromatids: **Chromatids** joined by a **centromere** and carrying identical genetic information (unless **crossing-over** has occurred).

Skeletons: Support structures in animal bodies.

Skeletal muscle: Muscle that is generally attached to the **skeleton** that causes body parts to move; consists of **muscle fibers**. Voluntary muscle cells that have a striated appearance. These muscles control skeletal movements and are normally under conscious control.

Skeletal system: One of eleven major **organ systems** in animals; supports the body, protects internal organs, and, with the **muscular system**, allows movement and locomotion.

Skin: One of eleven major **organ systems** in animals; the outermost layer protecting animals from the loss or exchange of internal fluids and from invasion by microorganisms; composed of two layers: the **epidermis** and **dermis**. Also known as the integumentary system.

Sleep movement: In legumes, the movement of the leaves in response to daily rhythms of dark and light. The leaves are horizontal in daylight and folded vertically at night.

Sliding filament model: Model of muscular contraction in which the **actin** filaments in the **sarcomere** slide past the **myosin** filaments, shortening the sarcomere and therefore the muscle.

Slime molds: Eukaryan group that may represent a transition to **fungi**.

Small intestine: A coiled tube in the abdominal cavity that is the major site of chemical digestion and absorption of nutrients; composed of the **duodenum**, **jejunum**, and **ileum**.

Smog: A local alteration in the atmosphere caused by human activity; mainly an urban problem that is often due to pollutants produced by fuel combustion.

Smooth endoplasmic reticulum: Type of **endoplasmic reticulum** lacking **ribosomes**; where **lipids** synthesis and toxin neutralization occurs.

Smooth muscle: Muscle that lacks striations; found around **circulatory system** vessels and in the walls of such organs as the stomach, intestines, and bladder. Involuntary muscle composed of nonstriated cells that control **autonomic** functions such as digestion and artery contraction.

Sodium-potassium pump: The mechanism that uses **energy** from **ATP** to reset the sodium and potassium ions after transmission of a nerve impulse.

Soil: Weathered rock and mineral fragments combined with air, water, and organic matter that can support plant growth.

Solute: A solid dissolved in a liquid, for example, the sugar added to a cup of coffee.

Solvent: A liquid that dissolves a chemical added to it, for example, sugar in coffee, the coffee is the solvent.

Somatic: Relating to the nongonadal tissues and organs of an organism's body.

Somatic cell: A cell that is not or will not become a **gamete**; the cells of the body.

Somatic senses: All senses except vision, hearing, taste, and smell; include pain, temperature, and pressure.

Somatic nervous system: The portion of the **peripheral nervous system** consisting of the **motor neuron** pathways that innervate **skeletal muscles**.

Somatostatin: Pancreatic **hormone** controlling the rate of nutrient absorption into the bloodstream.

Somites: Mesodermal structures formed during embryonic development that give rise to segmented body parts such as the muscles of the body wall.

Sorus: Collection of **sporangia** in ferns (plural: sori).

Special senses: Vision, hearing, taste, and smell.

Species: One or more **populations** of interbreeding or potentially interbreeding **organisms** reproductively isolated from all other organisms; populations of individuals capable of interbreeding and producing viable, fertile offspring; the least inclusive **taxonomic** category commonly used.

Species diversity: The number of living species on Earth.

Species packing: The phenomenon in which present-day **communities** generally contain more **species** than earlier communities because organisms have evolved more **adaptations** over time.

Species richness: The number of species present in a **community**.

Sperm: The male **gamete**.

Spermatogenesis: The development of sperm cells from spermatocytes to mature sperm, including **meiosis**.

Spicules: Needle-shaped skeletal elements in sponges that occur in the matrix between the **epidermal** and collar cells.

Spinal cord: A cylinder of nerve tissue extending from the brain stem; receives sensory information and sends output motor signals; with the brain, forms the **central nervous system**.

Spindle apparatus: **Microtubule** structure that aligns and segregates **chromosomes** during **eukaryotic cell division**.

Spiracles: The external openings of the **trachea** on the abdomen of terrestrial **arthropods**.

Spleen: An organ that produces **lymphocytes** and stores **erythrocytes**.

Spongy bone: The inner layer of bone; found at the ends of long bones; less dense than **compact bone**. Some spongy bone contains red marrow.

Spongy mesophyll: Parenchyma cells found in plant leaves that are irregularly shaped and have large intracellular spaces.

Sporangia: The structures in which **spores** are produced (singular: sporangium).

Spores: Impervious structures formed by some cells that encapsulate the cells and protect them from the environment; **haploid** cells that can survive unfavorable conditions and germinate into new haploid individuals or act as **gametes** in **fertilization**.

Sporophyll: Term applied to a leaf bearing a **sporangium**.

Sporophyte: The **diploid** stage of a plant or alga exhibiting **alternation of generations**. The term applied to the diploid, spore-producing phase of the plant life cycle.

Sporopollenin: Complex **polysaccharide** normally occurring in **spore** and **pollen** walls.

Sporozoans: Eukaryans that are referred to as slime molds; may include **organisms** resembling the ancestors of **fungi**.

Stability: One of the phases of a **population's life history**. The population's size remains roughly constant, fluctuating around an average density.

Stabilizing selection: A form of **natural selection** with selection against the extremes in variation.

Stalk: A leaf's **petiole**; the part of a leaf that attaches to a stem

Stamens: The male reproductive structures of a flower; usually consist of slender, thread-like **filaments** topped by **anthers**.

Stapes: One of the three bones that function in hearing in mammals.

Start codon: The AUG **codon** on a **messenger RNA** molecule that begins **protein synthesis**.

Steinkerns: Internal **casts** of a **fossil**. Steinkerns may reveal internal anatomy of an organism, such as muscle attachment, and other details of soft tissue structure.

Stem cells: Cells in bone marrow that produce lymphocytes.

Sternum: The breastbone.

Steroids: Lipids with a skeleton of four rings of carbon to which various side groups attach; one of the main classes of **hormones**.

Sticky ends: Term applied to DNA sequences cut with **restriction enzymes** where the cuts will bond with each other or with another sequence cut with the same enzyme.

Stigma: Part of the female reproductive structure of the **carpel** of a flower; the sticky surface at the tip of the **style** to which **pollen grains** attach.

Stimulus: A physical or chemical change in the environment that leads to a response controlled by the **nervous** and/or **endocrine systems**.

Stolons: Stems that grow along the surface of the ground; a method of plant vegetative propagation.

Stomach: The muscular organ between the **esophagus** and **small intestine** that stores, mixes, and digests food and controls the passage of food into the small intestine.

Stomata: Openings on the underside of leaves (and some stems) that can be opened or closed to control gas exchange and water loss.

Stomatal apparatus: The stomata and **guard cells** that control the size of the **stoma**.

Stop codon: The **codon** on a **messenger RNA** molecule that stops **protein synthesis**.

Stratification: The division of water in lakes and ponds into layers with different temperatures and oxygen content. Oxygen content declines with depth, while the uppermost layer is warmest in summer and coolest in winter.

Stressed community: A **community** that is disturbed by human activity, such as road building or pollution, and is inadvertently simplified. Some species become superabundant while others disappear.

Strobilus: Term applied to a collection of spore-bearing leaves (**sporophylls**) located at the tips of stems with a very small gap between sporophylls. As opposed to cones, strobili are soft (plural: strobili).

Stroma: The fluid surrounding the **grana** in the inner membrane of **chloroplasts**.

Stromatolite: A sedimentologic and biologic "fossil" representing colonies of bacteria/cyanobacteria alternating with layers of sediments. Becoming more common during the **Proterozoic**, stromatolites persist today in marine environments where grazing by herbivorous organisms is limited.

Style: Part of the female reproductive structure in the **carpel** of a flower; formed from the **ovary** wall.

Subatomic particles: The three kinds of particles that make up atoms: protons, neutrons, and electrons.

Suberin: Waxy, waterproof chemical in some plant cells, notably cork in stems and **endodermis** cells in roots.

Subspecies: A **taxonomic** subdivision of a **species**; a population of a particular region genetically distinguishable from other such populations and capable of interbreeding with them.

Substitution: A type of **mutation** where one base substitutes for another.

Substrate feeders: Animals such as earthworms or termites that eat the soil or wood through which they burrow.

Substrate-level phosphorylation: Process of forming **ATP** from **ADP** by **enzymes** in the **cytoplasm**, as opposed to **chemiosmosis**.

Sudden infant death syndrome (SIDS): A disorder resulting in the unexpected death during sleep of infants, usually between the ages of two weeks and one year.

Superior vena cava: Blood from the head returns to the heart through this main vein.

Suppressor T cells: **T cells** that slow down and stop the immune response of **B cells** and other T cells. Immune system cells that shut off **antibody** production when an infection is under control.

Suprachiasmic nucleus (SCN): A region of the **hypothalamus** that controls internal cycles of **endocrine** secretion.

Symbiosis: An interactive association between individuals of two **species** living together; may be **parasitic**, **commensalistic**, or **mutualistic**.

Sympathetic system: The subdivision of the **autonomic nervous system** that dominates in stressful or emergency situations and prepares the body for strenuous physical activity, for example, causing the heart to beat faster.

Sympatric speciation: Formation of a new **species** where **reproductive isolation** results from a nongeographic mechanism, such as timing of reproductive season, mating behavior. In this type of speciation, the two **populations** share the same geographic area.

Synapse: The junction between an **axon** and an adjacent **neuron**.

Synapsis: The alignment of **chromosomes** during **meiosis** so that each **chromosome** is beside its **homologue**.

Synaptic cleft: The space between the end of a **neuron** and an adjacent cell.

Synaptic vesicles: **Vesicles** at the **synapse** end of an **axon** that contain the **neurotransmitters**.

Synergid: Cells in the **embryo sac** of **angiosperms** that flank the egg cell. The **pollen tube** grows through one (usually the smaller) of the synergids.

Synovial joint: The most movable type of joint. The bones are covered by connective tissue, the interior of which is filled with synovial fluid, and the ends of the bones are covered with cartilage.

Syphilis: A sexually transmitted disease caused by a bacterial infection that produces an ulcer on the genitals and can have potentially serious effects if untreated.

Systematics: The classification of **organisms** based on information from observations and experiments; includes the reconstruction of evolutionary relatedness among living organisms.

Systemic circuit: The loop of the **circulatory system** that carries blood through the body and back to the heart.

Systole: The contraction of the **ventricles** that opens the **semilunar valve** and forces blood into the **arteries**.

Systolic pressure: The peak blood pressure when ventricles contract.

T

Taiga biome: The region of coniferous forest extending across much of northern Europe, Asia, and North America; characterized by long, cold winters and short, cool summers and by acidic, thin soils.

Tap root: A primary root that grows vertically downward and gives off small lateral roots. Root system in plants characterized by one root longer than the other roots. Example: carrot.

Target cell: A cell that a particular **hormone** effects by its direct action (either passing through the membrane or binding to a surface receptor).

Tarsals: The bones that make up the ankle joint.

Taxis: The behavior when an animal turns and moves toward or away from an external stimulus (plural: taxes).

Taxon: Term applied group of **organisms** comprising a given taxonomic category.

Taxonomy: A systematic method of classifying living things. Classification of organisms based on degrees of similarity purportedly representing evolutionary (**phylogenetic**) relatedness.

T cells: The type of **lymphocyte** responsible for **cell-mediated immunity**; also protects against infection by parasites, fungi, and protozoans and can kill cancerous cells; circulate in the blood and become associated with **lymph nodes** and the **spleen**.

Tectonic plates: Segments of the **lithosphere** that comprise the surface of the Earth much the way a turtle shell is composed of its plates.

Telophase: The final stage of **mitosis** when **chromosomes** migrate to opposite poles, a new **nuclear envelope** forms, and the chromosomes uncoil.

Temperate forest biome: Extends across regions of the northern hemisphere with abundant rainfall and long growing seasons. Deciduous, broad-leaved trees are the dominant plants.

Template strand: The strand of **DNA transcribed** to make **RNA**.

Temporal lobe: The lobe of the **cerebral cortex** that is responsible for processing auditory signals.

Tendons: Bundles of **connective tissue** that link muscle to bone.

Tepals: Term applied to the **sepals** and **petals** of a flower that resemble each other in shape, color, and pattern, as in the case of lily and tulip.

Terminal buds: Buds located at the end of a plant shoot.

Termination: The end of **translation**; occurs when the **ribosome** reaches the **stop codon** on the **messenger RNA** molecule and the **polypeptide**, the **messenger RNA**, and the **transfer RNA** release from the ribosome.

Termination codon: One of the three three-base sequences that initiate **termination** of the **protein synthesis** process. See **stop codon**.

Tertiary structure: The folding of a **protein's secondary structure** into a functional three-dimensional configuration. Shape assumed by protein due to interactions between **amino acids** far apart on the chain.

Test cross: Genetic crossing of an **organism** with known **genotype** (one that exhibits the **recessive phenotype**) with an individual expressing the **dominant** phenotype but of unknown heritage.

Testes: The male **gonads** that produce spermatozoa and male **sex hormones** (singular: testis).

Testosterone: Male **sex hormone** that stimulates **sperm** formation, promotes the development of the male duct system in the fetus, and is responsible for secondary sex characteristics such as facial hair growth and muscle mass.

Tetrad: The four **chromatids** in each cluster during **synapsis**; formed by the two sister **chromatids** in each of the two **homologous chromosomes**.

Tetrapod: Clade of **vertebrates** that all have four legs: amphibians, reptiles, and mammals.

Thalamus: The brain region that serves as a switching center for sensory signals passing from the brain stem to other brain regions; part of the **diencephalon**.

Thallus: Term applied to a flattened body of a variety of eukaryans, such as liverworts, **fungi**, and certain algae.

Thecodonts: Informal term for a variety of **Permian** and Triassic reptiles that had teeth set in individual sockets. Small, bipedal thecodonts were the probable ancestors of dinosaurs.

Theory: A **hypothesis** that has withstood extensive testing by a variety of methods, and in which a higher degree of certainty may be placed. A theory is NEVER a fact, but instead is an attempt to explain one or more facts.

Thermoacidophiles: Group of **Archaea** able to tolerate high temperatures and acidic **pH**.

Thermogenesis: The generation of heat by raising the body's metabolic rate; controlled by the **hypothalamus**.

Thermoregulation: The regulation of body temperature.

Thigmotropism: Plant response to contact with a solid object, for example, tendrils' twining around a pole.

Thoracic cavity: The chest cavity in which the heart and lungs occur.

Thorax: In many **arthropods**, one of three regions formed by the fusion of the segments (others are the head and abdomen).

Thorns: Stems modified to protect the plant.

Thoroughfare channels: Shortcuts within the **capillary** network that allow blood to bypass a **capillary bed**.

Thylakoids: The specialized membrane structures in which the first stages of photosynthesis occur. Internal membranes in the **chloroplast** where the **light reaction** chemicals are embedded. Collections of thylakoids are referred to as **grana**.

Thymine: One of the **pyrimidine** bases in **DNA**, thymine is replaced by **uracil** in **RNA**.

Thyroid: Endocrine gland that produces **thyroxin**.

Thyroid-stimulating hormone: A **hormone** produced by the anterior **pituitary** that stimulates the production and release of thyroid hormones.

Thyroxin: A hormone produced by the **thyroid** gland that regulates the body's metabolism.

Tight junctions: Junctions between the **plasma membranes** of adjacent cells in animals that form a barrier, preventing materials from passing between the cells.

Tissues: Groups of similar cells organized to carry out one or more specific functions.

Toxins: Term applied to poisons in living systems.

Trace fossil: Any indication of prehistoric organic activity, such as tracks, trails, burrows, wastes, or nests.

Trachea: In insects and spiders, a series of tubes that carry air directly to cells for gas exchange; in humans, the air-conducting duct that leads from the **pharynx** to the lungs.

Tracheids: Long, tapered cells with pitted walls that form a system of tubes in the **xylem** and carry water and solutes from the roots to the rest of the plant; one type of xylem cell. Tracheids are dead at maturity and have **lignin** in their secondary walls.

Tracheophytes: Clade of embryophytes that contains the vascular plants.

Transcription: The synthesis of **RNA** from a **DNA** template.

Transduction: Process where a **bacteriophage** transfers portions of bacterial **DNA** from one cell to another.

Transfer RNAs (tRNAs): Small, single-stranded **RNA** molecules that bind to specific **amino acids** and deliver them to the proper **codon** dictated by the **messenger RNA**. Abbreviated tRNA.

Transformation: In Griffith's experiments with strains of pneumonia bacterium, the process by which hereditary information passed from dead cells of one strain into cells of another strain, causing them to take on the characteristic virulence of the first strain.

Transforming factor: Griffith's name for the unknown material leading to transformation; later found to be **DNA**.

Transition/preparatory reaction: Biochemical process of converting 3-carbon pyruvate into 2-carbon acetyl and attaching it to **coenzyme A (CoA)** so it can enter the **Citric Acid Cycle**. Carbon dioxide is also released and **NADH** forms (from NAD and H) in this process.

Translation: The synthesis of **protein** on a template of **messenger RNA**; consists of three steps: **initiation**, **elongation**, and **termination**. Making of a polypeptide sequence by translating the **genetic code** of an mRNA molecule associated with a **ribosome**.

Translocation: (1) The movement of a segment from one **chromosome** to another without altering the number of chromosomes. (2) movement of fluids through the **phloem** from one part of a plant to another, with the direction of movement depending on the pressure gradients between source and sink regions.

Transpiration: The loss of water molecules from the leaves of a plant; creates an osmotic gradient; producing tension that pulls water upward from the roots.

Triassic period: The first geologic period of the **Mesozoic era** between 250 and 185 million years ago. Pangaea began to breakup during this time. The ancestors of dinosaurs were present, as were early mammals and mammal-like reptiles.

Trichinosis: Human disease caused by the roundworm *Trichinella*; transmitted by eating raw or undercooked contaminated pork.

Trichomes: Extensions from the **epidermis** of the plant that provide shade and protection for the plant.

Trichocysts: Barbed, thread-like organelles of ciliated protozoans that can be discharged for defense or to capture prey.

Trilobites: A group of **benthonic**, detritus-feeding, extinct marine **invertebrate** animals (phylum **Arthropoda**), having skeletons of an organic compound called **chitin**.

Triplet: Three-base sequence of **mRNA** that codes for a specific **amino acid** or **termination codon**.

Triploblasts: Clade of animals with **tissues** that develop all three embryonic tissue layers: **endoderm**, **mesoderm**, and **ectoderm**.

Trisomy: A condition where a cell has an extra **chromosome**, indicated as $2n + 1$.

Trophic levels: In the basic structure of a **food chain** or **food web**, the levels that relate to how an **organism** obtains its **energy**.

Trophoblast: The outer layer of cells of a **blastocyst** that adhere to the **endometrium** during implantation.

Tropical rain forest biome: The most complex and diverse **biome**; found near the equator in South America and Africa; characterized by thin soils, heavy rainfall, and little fluctuation in temperature.

Tropic hormone: **Hormone** made by one gland that causes another gland to secrete a different hormone.

Tropism: The movement of plant parts toward or away from a stimulus in the plant's environment.

True-breeding: Occurs when self-fertilization gives rise to the same traits in all offspring, generation after generation. Now interpreted as equivalent to **homozygous**.

Trypanosomes: A type of roundworm, responsible for human disease associated with eating raw or undercooked pork.

Tubal ligation: A contraceptive procedure in women in which the **oviducts** are cut, preventing the egg from reaching the **uterus**.

Tubal pregnancy: Occurs when the **morula** remains in the **oviduct** and does not descend into the **uterus**.

Tube-within-a-tube system: A type of body plan in animals. The organism has two openings—one for food and one for the elimination of waste; and a specialized **digestive system**.

Tube feet: Feature occurring in all **echinoderms** that allow them to adhere to their substrate and move.

Tube nucleus: One of the cells in the male **gametophyte** in seed plants. In flowering plants, the tube nucleus grows through the **stigma**, **style**, and into the **ovule**, allowing the sperm nuclei to enter the **embryo sac**.

Tubers: Swollen underground stems in plants that store food, such as the Irish potato.

Tubular secretion: The process in which ions and other waste products are transported into the **distal tubules** of the **nephron**.

Tubulins: The **protein** subunits from which **microtubules** are assembled.

Tumor suppressor genes: Genes that normally keep **cell division** under control, preventing the cell from responding to internal and external commands to divide.

Tundra biome: Extensive treeless plain across northern Europe, Asia, and North American between the **taiga** to the south and the permanent ice to the north. Much of the soil remains frozen in permafrost, and grasses and other vegetation support herds of large grazing mammals.

Turgor pressure: The pressure caused by the **cytoplasm** pressing against the **cell wall**.

Turner syndrome: In humans, a genetically determined condition in which an individual has only one **sex chromosome** (a single **X-chromosome**). Affected individuals are always female and are typically short and infertile.

U

Umbilical cord: The structure that connects the **placenta** and the embryo; contains the umbilical arteries and the umbilical vein.

Unicellular: Single-celled creatures.

Uniformitarianism: The idea that geological processes have remained uniform over time and that slight changes over long periods can have large-scale consequences; proposed by James Hutton in 1795 and refined by Charles Lyell during the 1800s. The principle on which modern geology was founded: processes operating today on the earth operated in much the same way in the geologic past.

Uninucleate: Term applied to cells having only a single **nucleus**.

Unsaturated fat: A triglyceride with double **covalent bonds** between some carbon atoms.

Uracil: The **pyrimidine** that replaces **thymine** in RNA.

Urea: Ammonia excretion product produced by animals; a major component of **urine**.

Ureter: A muscular tube that transports urine by peristaltic contractions from the kidney to the **bladder**.

Urethra: A narrow tube that transports urine from the **bladder** to the outside of the body. In males, it also conducts sperm and semen outside the body.

Urine: Fluid containing various wastes that is produced in the kidney and excreted from the **bladder**.

Uterus: The organ that houses and nourishes the developing embryo and fetus. The womb.

V

Vaccination: The process of protecting against infectious disease by introducing into the body a **vaccine** that stimulates a **primary immune response** and the production of memory cells against the disease-causing agent.

Vaccine: A preparation containing dead or weakened **pathogens** that when injected into the body elicit an **immune response**.

Vacuoles: Membrane-bound fluid-filled spaces in plant and animal cells that remove waste products and store ingested food.

Vagina: The tubular organ that is the site of sperm deposition and also serves as the birth canal.

Vascular bundle: Groups of **xylem**, **phloem**, and **cambium** cells in stems of plants descended from the **procambium** embryonic tissue layer.

Vascular cambium: A layer of lateral **meristematic** tissue between the **xylem** and **phloem** in the stems of woody plants. Lateral meristem tissue in plants that produce **secondary growth**.

Vascular cylinder: A central column formed by the vascular tissue of a plant root; surrounded by **parenchyma ground tissue**.

Vascular parenchyma: Specialized **parenchyma** cells in the **phloem** of plants.

Vascular plants: Group of plants having lignified conducting tissue (**vessels** or **tracheids**).

Vascular system: Specialized tissues for transporting fluids and nutrients in plants; also plays a role in supporting the plant; one of the four main tissue systems in plants.

Vas deferens: The duct that carries sperm from the **epididymis** to the ejaculatory duct and **urethra**.

Vasectomy: A contraceptive procedure in men in which the **vas deferens** is cut and the cut ends are sealed to prevent the transportation of sperm.

Vasopressin: See **antidiuretic hormone**.

Vectors: Self-replicating **DNA** molecules that can be joined with DNA fragments to form **recombinant DNA** molecules.

Veins: Thin-walled vessels that carry blood to the heart.

Ventilation: The mechanics of breathing in and out through the use of the diaphragm and muscles in the wall of the **thoracic cavity**.

Ventral: Term applied to the lower side of a fish, or to the chest of a land vertebrate.

Ventricle: The lower chambers of the heart that pump the blood into the blood vessels that carry it away from the heart.

Venules: The smallest veins; blood flows into them from the **capillary beds**.

Vernalization: Artificial exposure of seeds or seedlings to cold to enable the plant to flower.

Vertebrae: The segments of the spinal column; separated by disks made of **connective tissue** (singular: vertebra).

Vertebrate: Any animal having a segmented vertebral column; members of the subphylum Vertebrata; include reptiles, fish, mammals, and birds.

Vesicles: Small membrane-bound spaces in most plant and animal cells that transport **macro-molecules** into and out of the cell and carry materials between organelles in the cell.

Vessel elements: Short, wide cells arranged end to end, forming a system of tubes in the **xylem** that moves water and solutes from the roots to the rest of the plant. Large diameter cells of the xylem that are extremely specialized and efficient at conduction.

Vestigial structures: Nonfunctional remains of organs that were functional in ancestral **species** and may still be functional in related species, for example, the dewclaws of dogs.

Villi: Finger-like projections of the lining of the small intestine that increase the surface area available for absorption. Also, projections of the **chorion** that extend into cavities filled with maternal blood and allow the exchange of nutrients between the maternal and embryonic circulations.

Viridiplantae: Eukaryan kingdom composed of the green algae and plants.

Viroids: Infective forms of nucleic acid without a protective coat of **protein**; naked single-stranded **RNA** molecules that infect plants.

Virus: Infectious chemical agent composed of a nucleic acid (either **DNA** or **RNA** but never both) inside a **protein** coat.

Vitamins: A diverse group of organic molecules that are required for metabolic reactions and generally cannot be synthesized in the body.

Vulva: A collective term for the external genitals in women.

W

White blood cell: Component of the blood that functions in the **immune system**. Also known as a **leukocyte**.

Wood: The inner layer of the stems of woody plants; composed of **secondary xylem**.

X

X-chromosome: One of the **sex chromosomes**.

Xerophytic leaves: The leaves of plants that grow under arid conditions with low levels of soil and water. Usually characterized by water-conserving features such as thick **cuticle** and sunken **stomata**.

X-ray diffraction: Technique utilized to study atomic structure of crystalline substances by noting the patterns produced by x-rays shot through the crystal.

Xylem: Tissue in the **vascular system** of plants that moves water and dissolved nutrients from the roots to the leaves; composed of various cell types including **tracheids** and **vessel elements**.

Y

Y-chromosome: The smaller **sex chromosome** that determines the male gender in mammals.

Z

Zebroid: A hybrid animal that results from breeding zebras and horses.

Z lines: Dense areas in **myofibrils** that mark the beginning of the **sarcomeres**. The **actin filaments** of the sarcomeres are anchored in the Z lines.

Zone of differentiation: Area in plant roots where recently produced cells develop into different cell types.

Zone of elongation: Area in plant roots where recently produced cells grow and elongate prior to differentiation.

Zone of intolerance: The area outside the geographic range where a population is absent; grades into the zone of physiological stress.

Zone of physiological stress: The area in a population's geographic range where members of population are rare due to physical and biological limiting factors.

Zoospore: Term applies to any motile, flagellated spore produced by a eukaryan.

Zooxanthellae: Dinoflagellates living symbiotically inside the bodies of corals and other **cnidarians**.

Zygomycetes: A phylum of fungi characterized by the production of **zygospores**; includes the black bread molds.

Zygospore: In fungi, a structure that forms from the **diploid zygote** created by the fusion of **haploid hyphae** of different mating types. After a period of dormancy, the zygospore forms **sporangia**, where **meiosis** occurs and spores form.

Zygote: A **diploid** fertilized egg.